CAPTAIN AMERICA

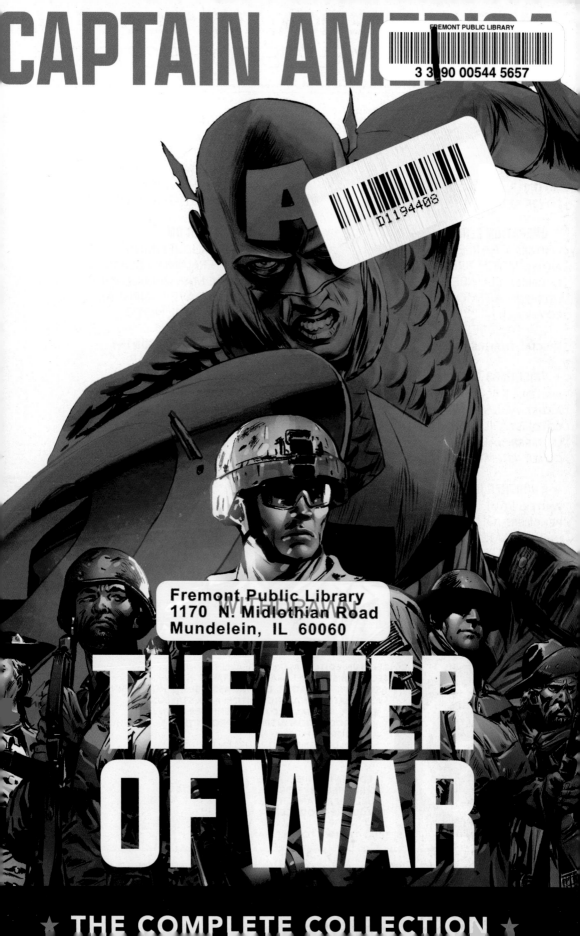

FREMONT PUBLIC LIBRARY

3 3090 00544 5657

D1194408

Fremont Public Library
1170 N. Midlothian Road
Mundelein, IL 60060

WITHDRAWN

THEATER OF WAR

★ THE COMPLETE COLLECTION ★

CAPTAIN AMERICA: THEATER OF WAR
★ THE COMPLETE COLLECTION ★

★ AMERICA THE BEAUTIFUL
WRITER: PAUL JENKINS
ARTIST: GARY ERSKINE
COLORIST: CHRIS SOTOMAYOR
LETTERER: DAVE LANPHEAR
COVER ART: STEVE EPTING

★ OPERATION ZERO-POINT
WRITERS: CHARLES & DANIEL KNAUF
ARTIST: MITCH BREITWEISER
COLORIST: ELIZABETH BREITWEISER
LETTERER: ARTMONKEYS STUDIOS
COVER ART: MITCH & ELIZABETH
　　　　　　　BREITWEISER
SPECIAL THANKS TO SEBASTIAN GIRNER

★ PRISONERS OF DUTY
WRITERS: KYLE HIGGINS & ALEC SIEGEL
ARTIST: AGUSTIN PADILLA
COLORIST: GIULIA BRUSCO
LETTERER: JARED K. FLETCHER
COVER ART: MIRCO PIERFEDERICI

★ A BROTHER IN ARMS
WRITER: PAUL JENKINS
PENCILER: JOHN McCREA
INKERS: JAMES HODGKINS, ALLEN
　　　　　MARTINEZ & VICTOR OLAZABA
COLORISTS: ANDREW ELDER &
　　　　　　SOTOCOLOR'S LARRY MOLINAR &
　　　　　　CHRIS GARCIA
LETTERER: DAVE LANPHEAR
COVER ART: MITCH BREITWEISER

★ AMERICA FIRST!
WRITER & ARTIST: HOWARD CHAYKIN
COLORIST: EDGAR DELGADO
LETTERER: DAVE LANPHEAR
COVER ART: HOWARD CHAYKIN &
　　　　　　EDGAR DELGADO

★ TO SOLDIER ON
WRITER: PAUL JENKINS
ARTIST: FERNANDO BLANCO
COLORIST: MARTA MARTINEZ
LETTERER: DAVE LANPHEAR
COVER ART: PHIL NOTO

★ GHOSTS OF MY COUNTRY
WRITER: PAUL JENKINS
ARTIST: ELIA BONETTI
COLORIST: JORGE MAESE
LETTERER: JARED K. FLETCHER
COVER ART: BUTCH GUICE &
　　　　　　FRANK D'ARMATA

EDITORS: JEANINE SCHAEFER &
　　　　　LAUREN SANKOVITCH WITH
　　　　　AUBREY SITTERSON
EXECUTIVE EDITOR: TOM BREVOORT

★ CAPTAIN AMERICA CREATED BY ★
JOE SIMON & JACK KIRBY

COLLECTION EDITOR: MARK D. BEAZLEY
ASSOCIATE EDITOR: SARAH BRUNSTAD
ASSOCIATE MANAGER, DIGITAL ASSETS: JOE HOCHSTEIN
ASSOCIATE MANAGING EDITOR: ALEX STARBUCK
EDITOR, SPECIAL PROJECTS: JENNIFER GRÜNWALD
VP, PRODUCTION & SPECIAL PROJECTS: JEFF YOUNGQUIST
LAYOUT: JEPH YORK
BOOK DESIGNER: RODOLFO MURAGUCHI
SVP PRINT, SALES & MARKETING: DAVID GABRIEL

EDITOR IN CHIEF: AXEL ALONSO
CHIEF CREATIVE OFFICER: JOE QUESADA
PUBLISHER: DAN BUCKLEY
EXECUTIVE PRODUCER: ALAN FINE

SPECIAL THANKS TO MIKE HANSEN

CAPTAIN AMERICA: THEATER OF WAR — THE COMPLETE COLLECTION. Contains material originally published in magazine form as CAPTAIN AMERICA THEATER OF WAR: AMERICA THE BEAUTIFUL, A BROTHER IN ARMS, TO SOLDIER ON, GHOSTS OF MY COUNTRY, AMERICA FIRST!, OPERATION ZERO POINT, and PRISONERS OF DUTY. First printing 2016. ISBN# 978-0-7851-9601-3. Published by MARVEL WORLDWIDE, INC., a subsidiary of MARVEL ENTERTAINMENT, LLC. OFFICE OF PUBLICATION: 135 West 50th Street, New York, NY 10020. Copyright © 2016 MARVEL No similarity between any of the names, characters, persons, and/or institutions in this magazine with those of any living or dead person or institution is intended, and any such similarity which may exist is purely coincidental. **Printed in the U.S.A.** ALAN FINE, President, Marvel Entertainment; DAN BUCKLEY, President, TV, Publishing & Brand Management; JOE QUESADA, Chief Creative Officer; TOM BREVOORT, SVP of Publishing; DAVID BOGART, SVP of Business Affairs & Operations, Publishing & Partnership; C.B. CEBULSKI, VP of Brand Management & Development, Asia; DAVID GABRIEL, SVP of Sales & Marketing, Publishing; JEFF YOUNGQUIST, VP of Production & Special Projects; DAN CARR, Executive Director of Publishing Technology; ALEX MORALES, Director of Publishing Operations; SUSAN CRESPI, Production Manager; STAN LEE, Chairman Emeritus. For information regarding advertising in Marvel Comics or on Marvel.com, please contact Vit DeBellis, Integrated Sales Manager, at vdebellis@marvel.com. For Marvel subscription inquiries, please call 888-511-5480. **Manufactured between** 2/26/2016 and 4/4/2016 by R.R. DONNELLEY, INC., SALEM, VA, USA.

10 9 8 7 6 5 4 3 2 1

NUMBER	RECEIVED BY	CHECK

In the dark days of the early 1940s, Steve Rogers, a struggling young artist from the Lower East Side of Manhattan, found himself horrified by the war raging overseas. Desperate to help, he was rejected by the US Army as unfit for service when he tried to enlist.

Undeterred, convinced this was where he needed to be, he was selected to participate in a covert military project called Operation: Rebirth. There, he was chosen by scientist Abraham Erskine as the first human test subject, and overnight was transformed into America's first Super-Soldier.

Enhanced to the peak of human perfection with superior strength, reflexes and speed, Steve Rogers now fights to protect the people and the country he loves from the forces that would destroy them as CAPTAIN AMERICA.

VALOR
UNITED STATES OF AMERICA

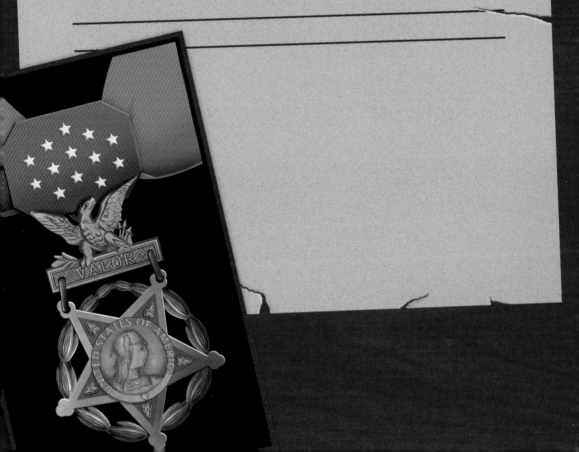

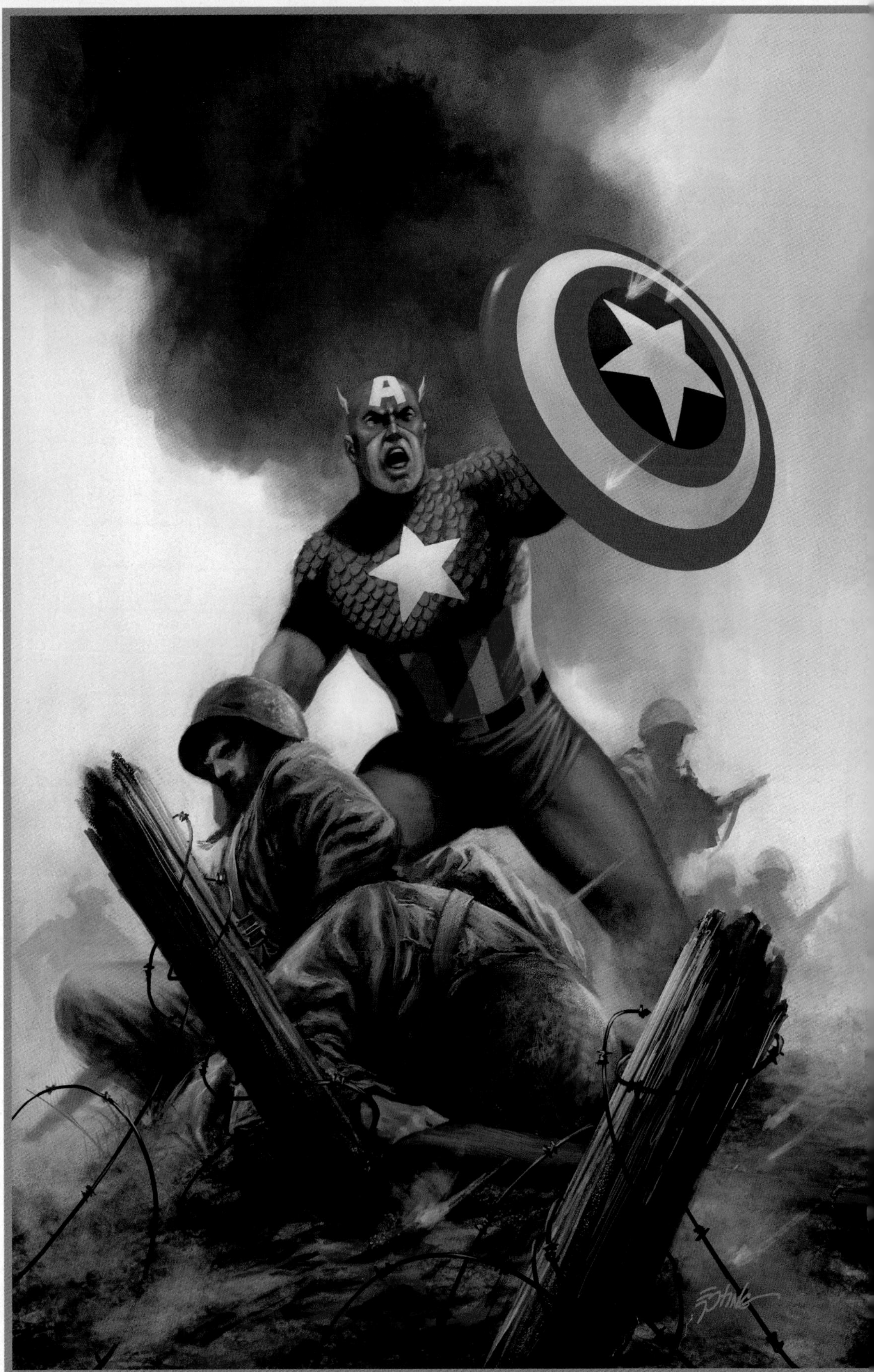

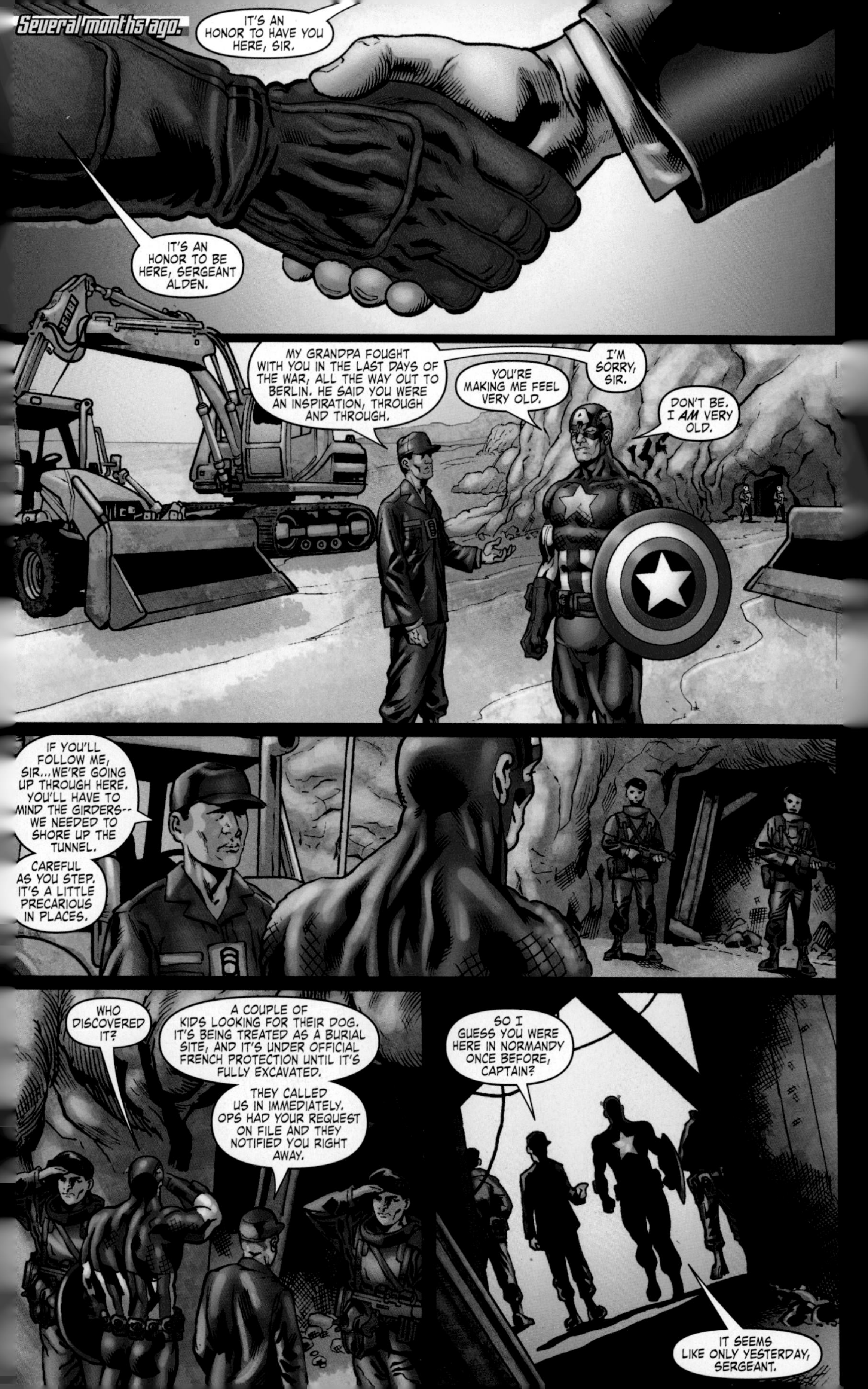

Several months ago.
IT'S AN HONOR TO HAVE YOU HERE, SIR.
IT'S AN HONOR TO BE HERE, SERGEANT ALDEN.
MY GRANDPA FOUGHT WITH YOU IN THE LAST DAYS OF THE WAR, ALL THE WAY OUT TO BERLIN. HE SAID YOU WERE AN INSPIRATION, THROUGH AND THROUGH.
YOU'RE MAKING ME FEEL VERY OLD.
I'M SORRY, SIR.
DON'T BE. I AM VERY OLD.
IF YOU'LL FOLLOW ME, SIR...WE'RE GOING UP THROUGH HERE. YOU'LL HAVE TO MIND THE GIRDERS-- WE NEEDED TO SHORE UP THE TUNNEL.
CAREFUL AS YOU STEP. IT'S A LITTLE PRECARIOUS IN PLACES.
WHO DISCOVERED IT?
A COUPLE OF KIDS LOOKING FOR THEIR DOG. IT'S BEING TREATED AS A BURIAL SITE, AND IT'S UNDER OFFICIAL FRENCH PROTECTION UNTIL IT'S FULLY EXCAVATED.
THEY CALLED US IN IMMEDIATELY. OPS HAD YOUR REQUEST ON FILE AND THEY NOTIFIED YOU RIGHT AWAY.
SO I GUESS YOU WERE HERE IN NORMANDY ONCE BEFORE, CAPTAIN?
IT SEEMS LIKE ONLY YESTERDAY, SERGEANT.

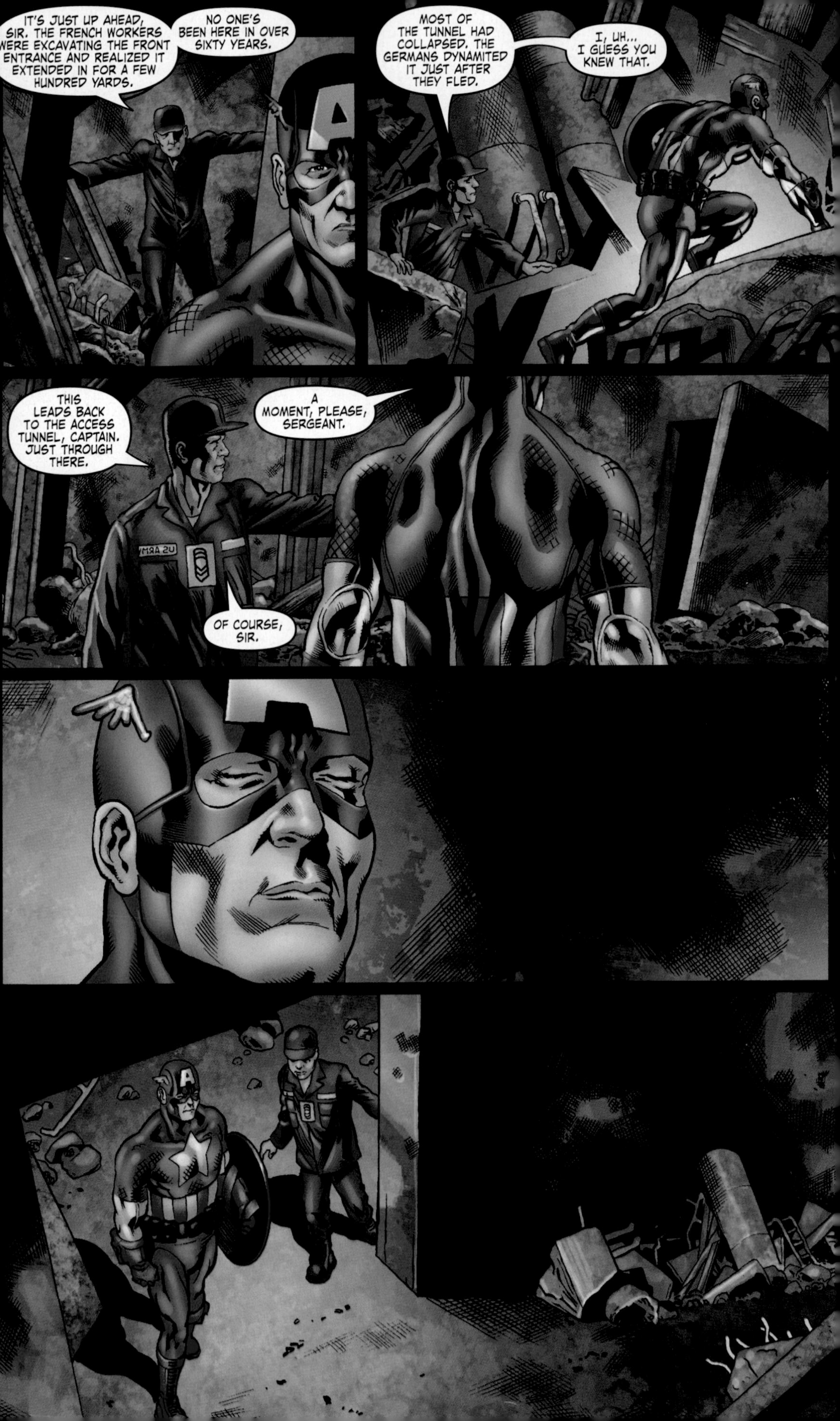
IT'S JUST UP AHEAD, SIR. THE FRENCH WORKERS WERE EXCAVATING THE FRONT ENTRANCE AND REALIZED IT EXTENDED IN FOR A FEW HUNDRED YARDS.
NO ONE'S BEEN HERE IN OVER SIXTY YEARS.
MOST OF THE TUNNEL HAD COLLAPSED. THE GERMANS DYNAMITED IT JUST AFTER THEY FLED.
I, UH... I GUESS YOU KNEW THAT.
THIS LEADS BACK TO THE ACCESS TUNNEL, CAPTAIN. JUST THROUGH THERE.
A MOMENT, PLEASE, SERGEANT.
OF COURSE, SIR.

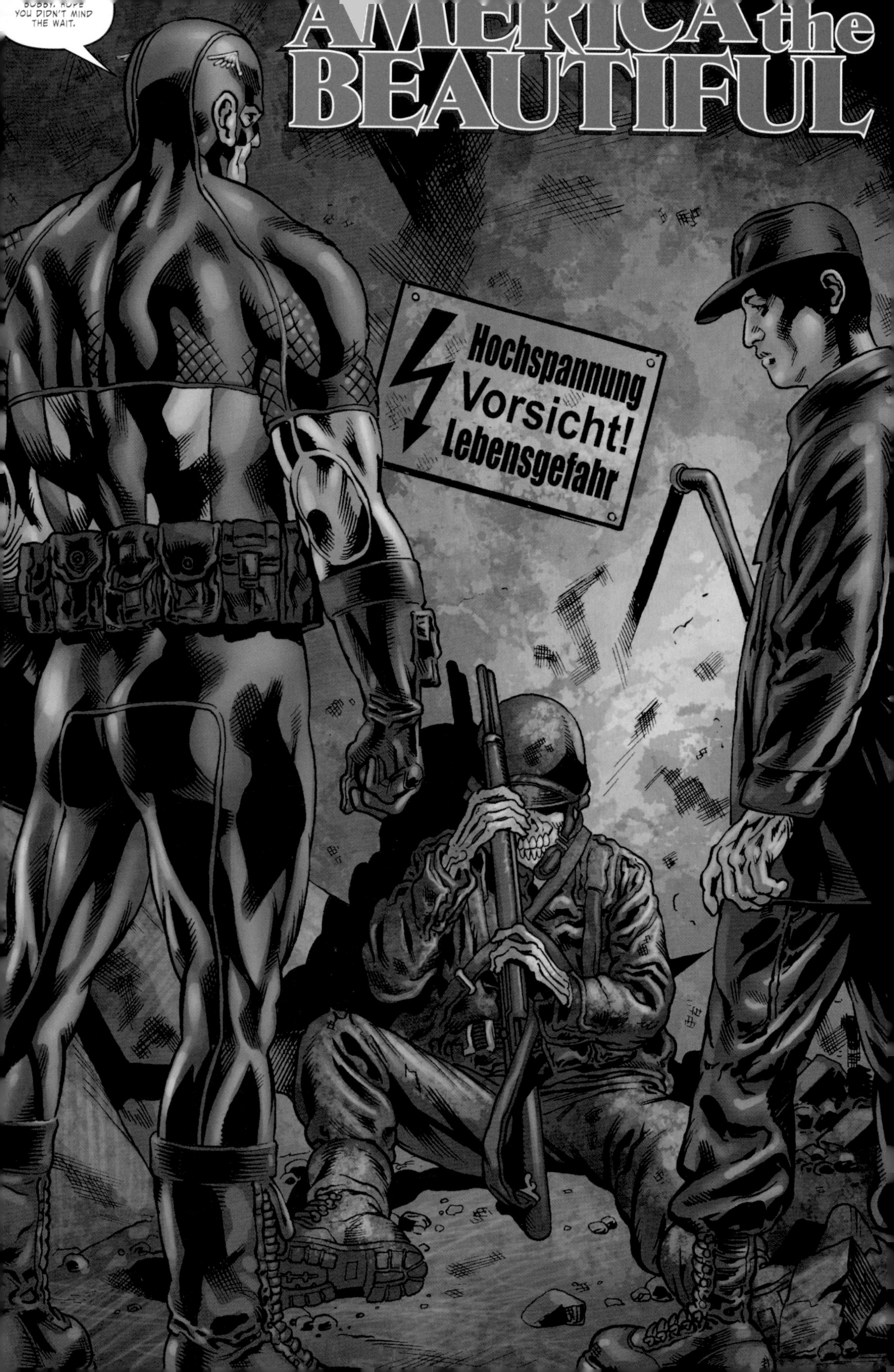
YOU DIDN'T MIND
THE WAIT.
AMERICA the
BEAUTIFUL
Hochspannung
Vorsicht!
Lebensgefahr

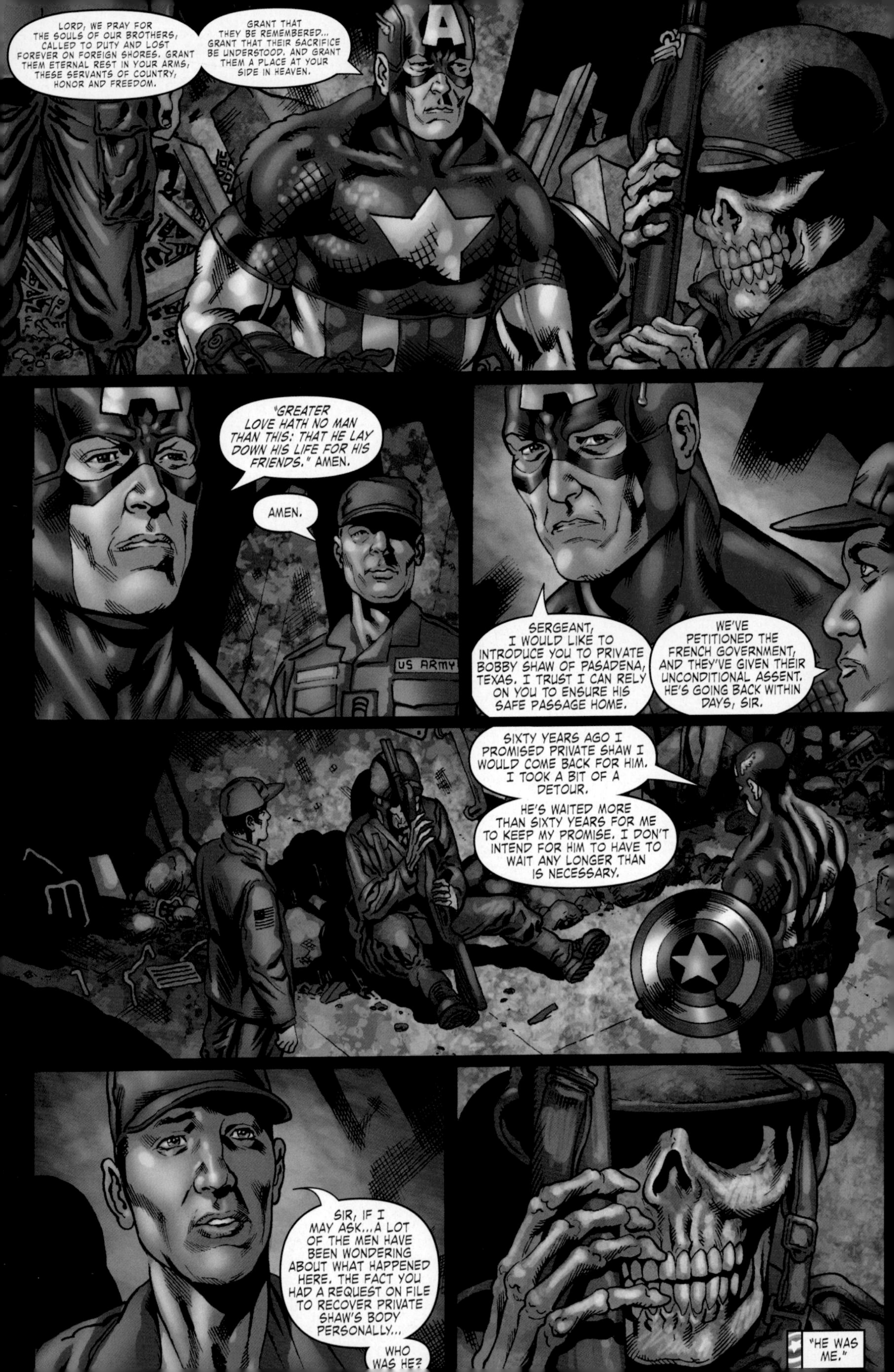
LORD, WE PRAY FOR THE SOULS OF OUR BROTHERS, CALLED TO DUTY AND LOST FOREVER ON FOREIGN SHORES. GRANT THEM ETERNAL REST IN YOUR ARMS, THESE SERVANTS OF COUNTRY, HONOR AND FREEDOM.
GRANT THAT THEY BE REMEMBERED... GRANT THAT THEIR SACRIFICE BE UNDERSTOOD, AND GRANT THEM A PLACE AT YOUR SIDE IN HEAVEN.
"GREATER LOVE HATH NO MAN THAN THIS: THAT HE LAY DOWN HIS LIFE FOR HIS FRIENDS." AMEN.
AMEN.
US ARMY
SERGEANT, I WOULD LIKE TO INTRODUCE YOU TO PRIVATE BOBBY SHAW OF PASADENA, TEXAS. I TRUST I CAN RELY ON YOU TO ENSURE HIS SAFE PASSAGE HOME.
WE'VE PETITIONED THE FRENCH GOVERNMENT, AND THEY'VE GIVEN THEIR UNCONDITIONAL ASSENT. HE'S GOING BACK WITHIN DAYS, SIR.
SIXTY YEARS AGO I PROMISED PRIVATE SHAW I WOULD COME BACK FOR HIM. I TOOK A BIT OF A DETOUR.
HE'S WAITED MORE THAN SIXTY YEARS FOR ME TO KEEP MY PROMISE. I DON'T INTEND FOR HIM TO HAVE TO WAIT ANY LONGER THAN IS NECESSARY.
SIR, IF I MAY ASK...A LOT OF THE MEN HAVE BEEN WONDERING ABOUT WHAT HAPPENED HERE. THE FACT YOU HAD A REQUEST ON FILE TO RECOVER PRIVATE SHAW'S BODY PERSONALLY...
WHO WAS HE?
"HE WAS ME."

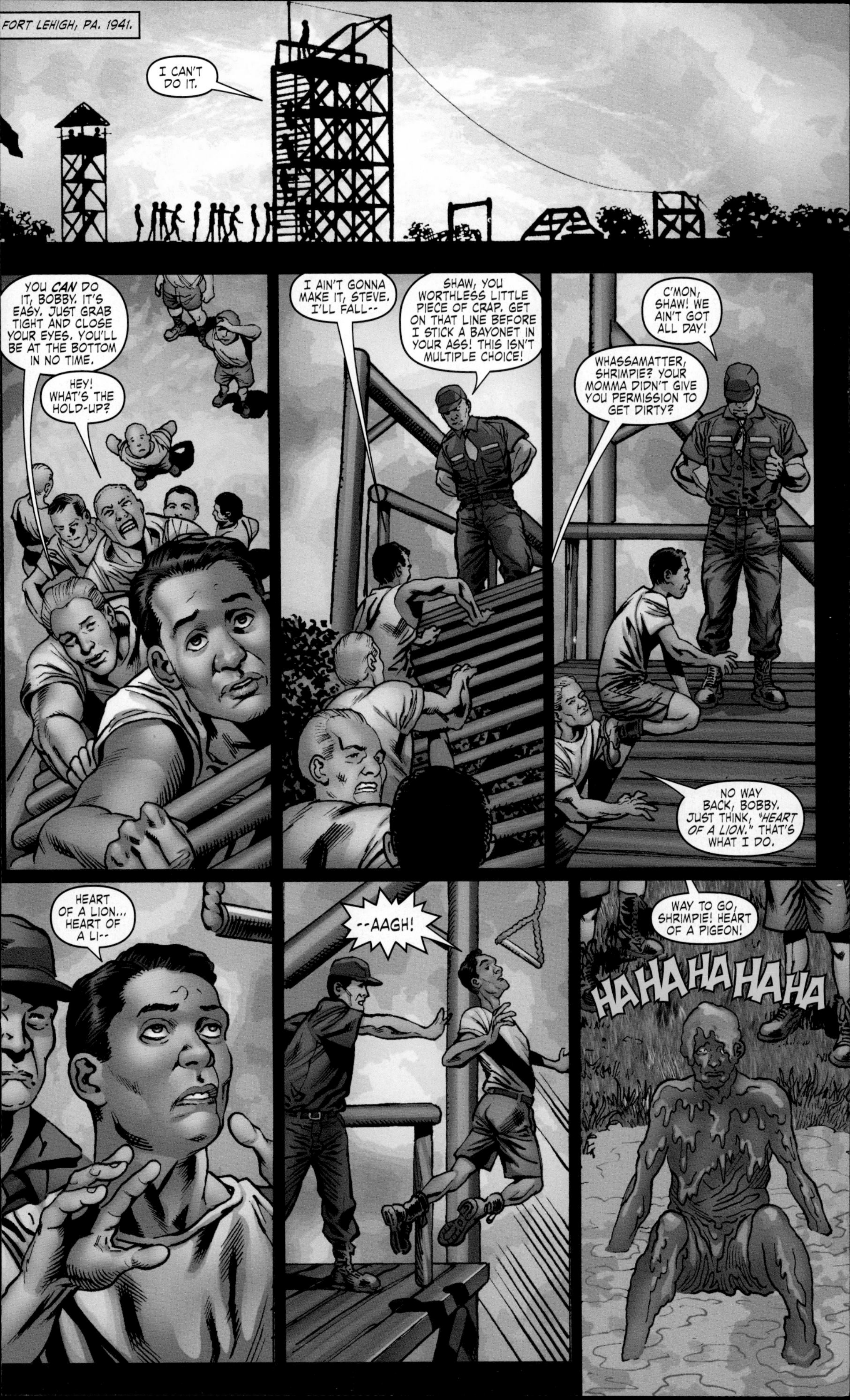
FORT LEHIGH, PA. 1941.
I CAN'T DO IT.
YOU CAN DO IT, BOBBY. IT'S EASY. JUST GRAB TIGHT AND CLOSE YOUR EYES. YOU'LL BE AT THE BOTTOM IN NO TIME.
HEY! WHAT'S THE HOLD-UP?
I AIN'T GONNA MAKE IT, STEVE. I'LL FALL--
SHAW, YOU WORTHLESS LITTLE PIECE OF CRAP. GET ON THAT LINE BEFORE I STICK A BAYONET IN YOUR ASS! THIS ISN'T MULTIPLE CHOICE!
C'MON, SHAW! WE AIN'T GOT ALL DAY!
WHASSAMATTER, SHRIMPIE? YOUR MOMMA DIDN'T GIVE YOU PERMISSION TO GET DIRTY?
NO WAY BACK, BOBBY. JUST THINK, "HEART OF A LION." THAT'S WHAT I DO.
HEART OF A LION... HEART OF A LI--
--AAGH!
WAY TO GO, SHRIMPIE! HEART OF A PIGEON!
HAHAHAHAHA

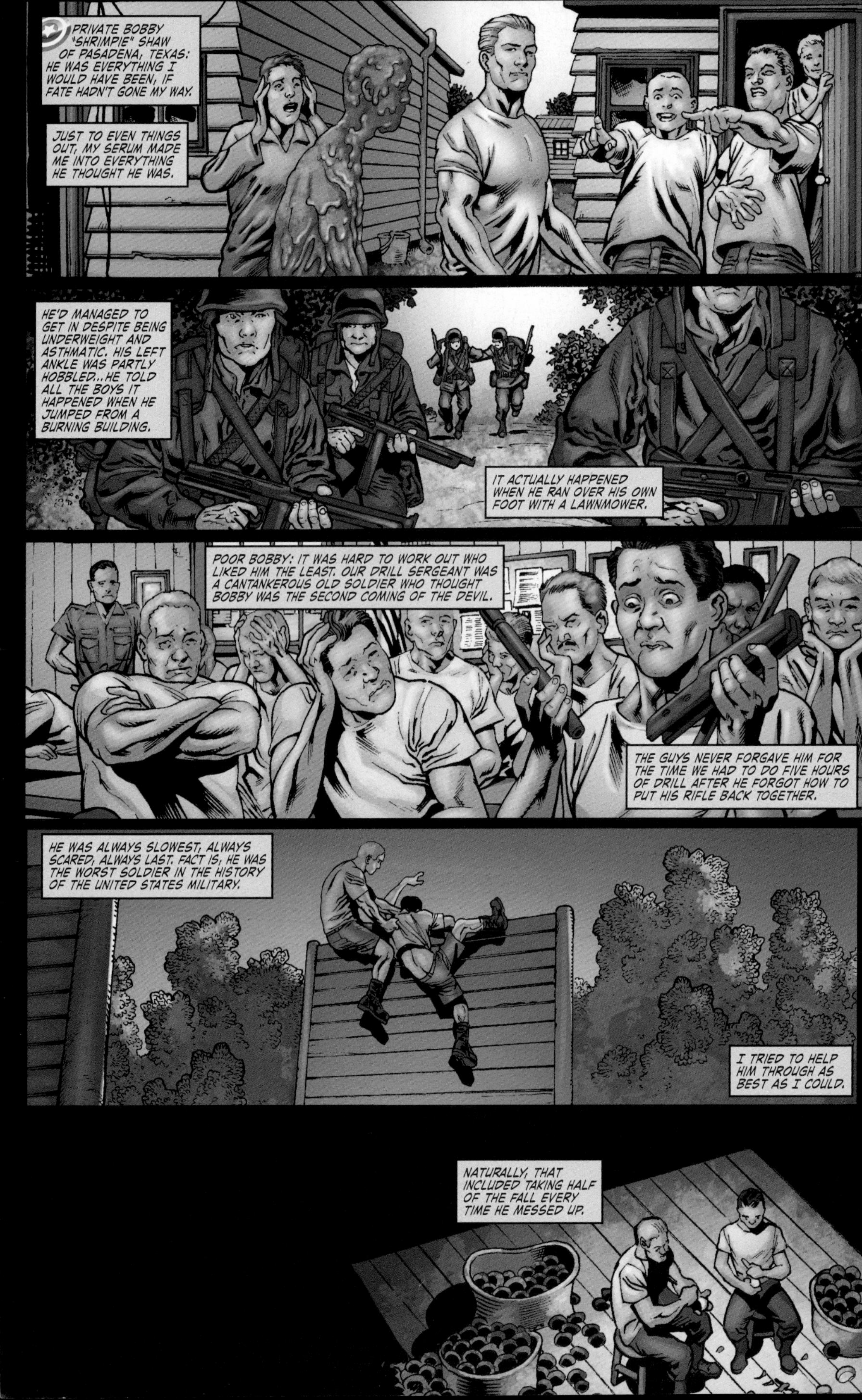
PRIVATE BOBBY "SHRIMPIE" SHAW OF PASADENA, TEXAS: HE WAS EVERYTHING I WOULD HAVE BEEN, IF FATE HADN'T GONE MY WAY.
JUST TO EVEN THINGS OUT, MY SERUM MADE ME INTO EVERYTHING HE THOUGHT HE WAS.
HE'D MANAGED TO GET IN DESPITE BEING UNDERWEIGHT AND ASTHMATIC. HIS LEFT ANKLE WAS PARTLY HOBBLED...HE TOLD ALL THE BOYS IT HAPPENED WHEN HE JUMPED FROM A BURNING BUILDING.
IT ACTUALLY HAPPENED WHEN HE RAN OVER HIS OWN FOOT WITH A LAWNMOWER.
POOR BOBBY: IT WAS HARD TO WORK OUT WHO LIKED HIM THE LEAST. OUR DRILL SERGEANT WAS A CANTANKEROUS OLD SOLDIER WHO THOUGHT BOBBY WAS THE SECOND COMING OF THE DEVIL.
THE GUYS NEVER FORGAVE HIM FOR THE TIME WE HAD TO DO FIVE HOURS OF DRILL AFTER HE FORGOT HOW TO PUT HIS RIFLE BACK TOGETHER.
HE WAS ALWAYS SLOWEST, ALWAYS SCARED, ALWAYS LAST. FACT IS, HE WAS THE WORST SOLDIER IN THE HISTORY OF THE UNITED STATES MILITARY.
I TRIED TO HELP HIM THROUGH AS BEST AS I COULD.
NATURALLY, THAT INCLUDED TAKING HALF OF THE FALL EVERY TIME HE MESSED UP.

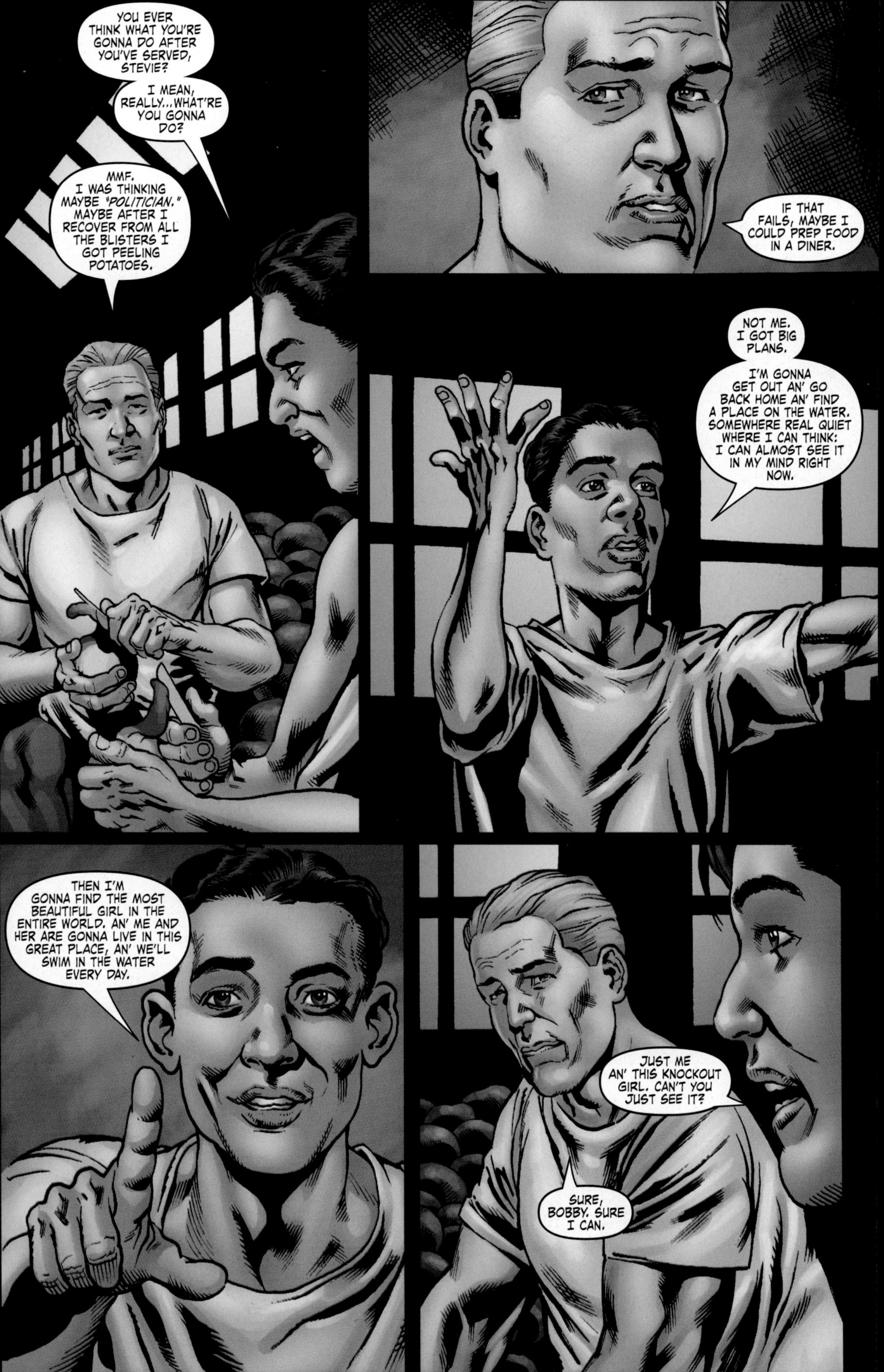
YOU EVER THINK WHAT YOU'RE GONNA DO AFTER YOU'VE SERVED, STEVIE?
I MEAN, REALLY...WHAT'RE YOU GONNA DO?
MMF. I WAS THINKING MAYBE "POLITICIAN." MAYBE AFTER I RECOVER FROM ALL THE BLISTERS I GOT PEELING POTATOES.
IF THAT FAILS, MAYBE I COULD PREP FOOD IN A DINER.
NOT ME. I GOT BIG PLANS.
I'M GONNA GET OUT AN' GO BACK HOME AN' FIND A PLACE ON THE WATER. SOMEWHERE REAL QUIET WHERE I CAN THINK: I CAN ALMOST SEE IT IN MY MIND RIGHT NOW.
THEN I'M GONNA FIND THE MOST BEAUTIFUL GIRL IN THE ENTIRE WORLD. AN' ME AND HER ARE GONNA LIVE IN THIS GREAT PLACE, AN' WE'LL SWIM IN THE WATER EVERY DAY.
JUST ME AN' THIS KNOCKOUT GIRL. CAN'T YOU JUST SEE IT?
SURE, BOBBY. SURE I CAN.

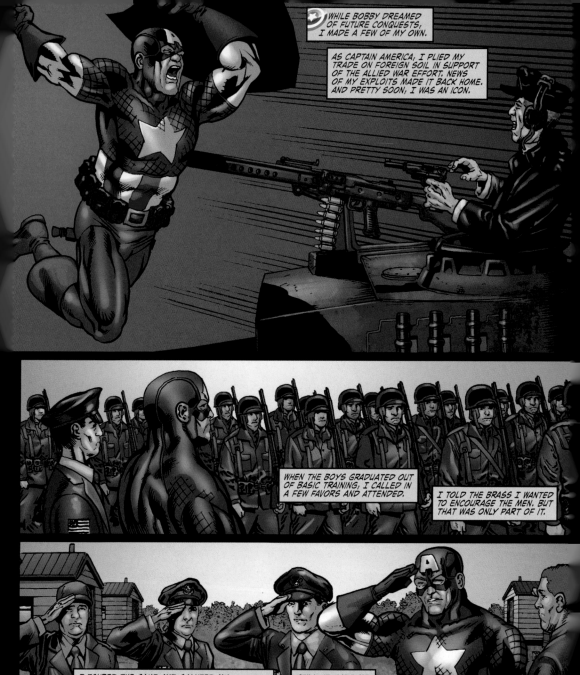

WHILE BOBBY DREAMED OF FUTURE CONQUESTS, I MADE A FEW OF MY OWN.

AS CAPTAIN AMERICA, I PLIED MY TRADE ON FOREIGN SOIL IN SUPPORT OF THE ALLIED WAR EFFORT. NEWS OF MY EXPLOITS MADE IT BACK HOME. AND PRETTY SOON, I WAS AN ICON.

WHEN THE BOYS GRADUATED OUT OF BASIC TRAINING, I CALLED IN A FEW FAVORS AND ATTENDED.

I TOLD THE BRASS I WANTED TO ENCOURAGE THE MEN. BUT THAT WAS ONLY PART OF IT.

I TOURED THE CAMP AND SALUTED MY UNSUSPECTING CAMP MATES EVERY CHANCE I GOT. PART OF ME WISHED I COULD BE WITH THEM INSTEAD, BUT THAT WAS A PRICE I ALWAYS PAID.

STILL, IT MADE ME PROUD ENOUGH TO SEE THESE BOYS BECOMING MEN.

THERE WAS ALWAYS ONE PARTICULAR SOLDIER I WANTED TO KEEP TABS ON.

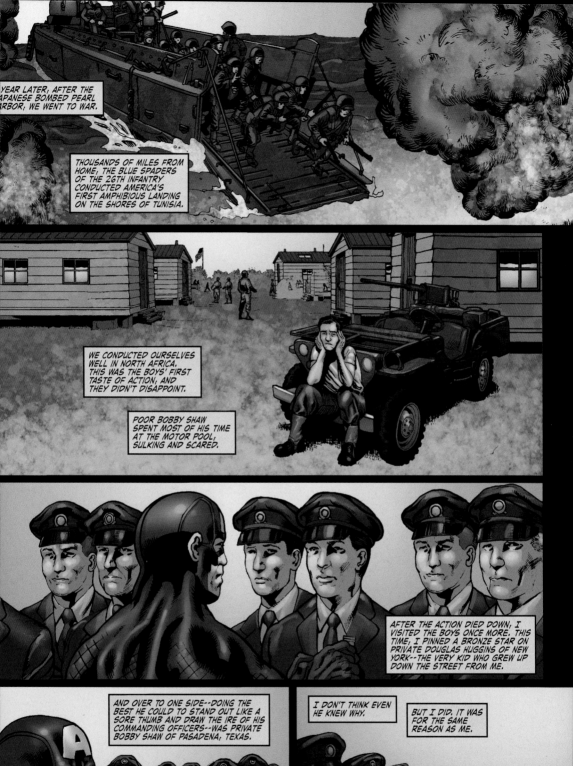

YEAR LATER, AFTER THE [JA]PANESE BOMBED PEARL [H]ARBOR, WE WENT TO WAR.

THOUSANDS OF MILES FROM HOME, THE BLUE SPADERS OF THE 26TH INFANTRY CONDUCTED AMERICA'S FIRST AMPHIBIOUS LANDING ON THE SHORES OF TUNISIA.

WE CONDUCTED OURSELVES WELL IN NORTH AFRICA. THIS WAS THE BOYS' FIRST TASTE OF ACTION, AND THEY DIDN'T DISAPPOINT.

POOR BOBBY SHAW SPENT MOST OF HIS TIME AT THE MOTOR POOL, SULKING AND SCARED.

AFTER THE ACTION DIED DOWN, I VISITED THE BOYS ONCE MORE. THIS TIME, I PINNED A BRONZE STAR ON PRIVATE DOUGLAS HUGGINS OF NEW YORK--THE VERY KID WHO GREW UP DOWN THE STREET FROM ME.

AND OVER TO ONE SIDE--DOING THE BEST HE COULD TO STAND OUT LIKE A SORE THUMB AND DRAW THE IRE OF HIS COMMANDING OFFICERS--WAS PRIVATE BOBBY SHAW OF PASADENA, TEXAS.

I DON'T THINK EVEN HE KNEW WHY.

BUT I DID. IT WAS FOR THE SAME REASON AS ME.

I COULD ALMOST READ HIS MIND AT THAT MOMENT. WHAT HAD HE GOTTEN HIMSELF INTO? WHY HAD HE EVEN JOINED UP?

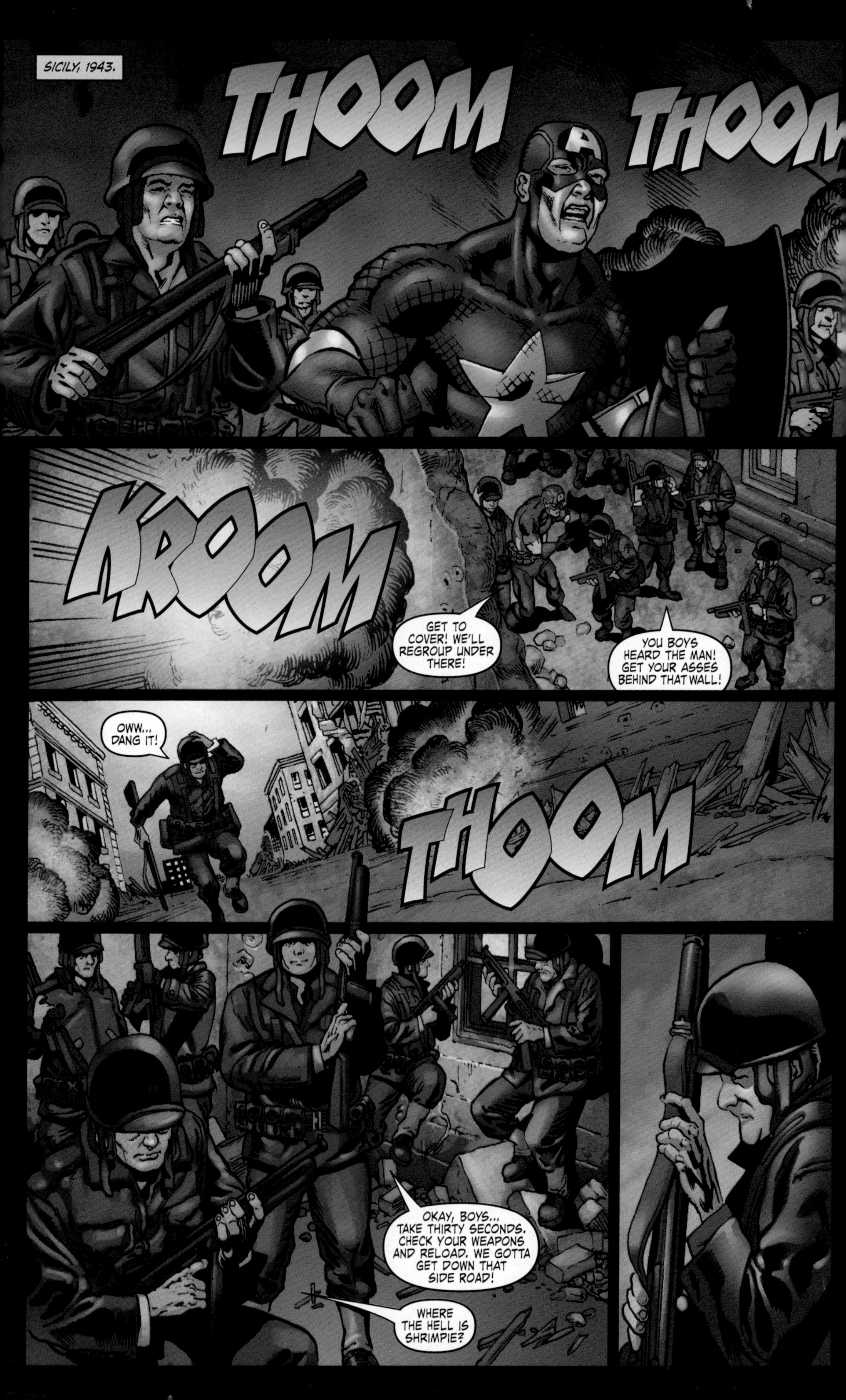
SICILY, 1943.
THOOM
THOOM
KROOM
GET TO COVER! WE'LL REGROUP UNDER THERE!
YOU BOYS HEARD THE MAN! GET YOUR ASSES BEHIND THAT WALL!
OWW... DANG IT!
THOOM
OKAY, BOYS... TAKE THIRTY SECONDS. CHECK YOUR WEAPONS AND RELOAD. WE GOTTA GET DOWN THAT SIDE ROAD!
WHERE THE HELL IS SHRIMPIE?

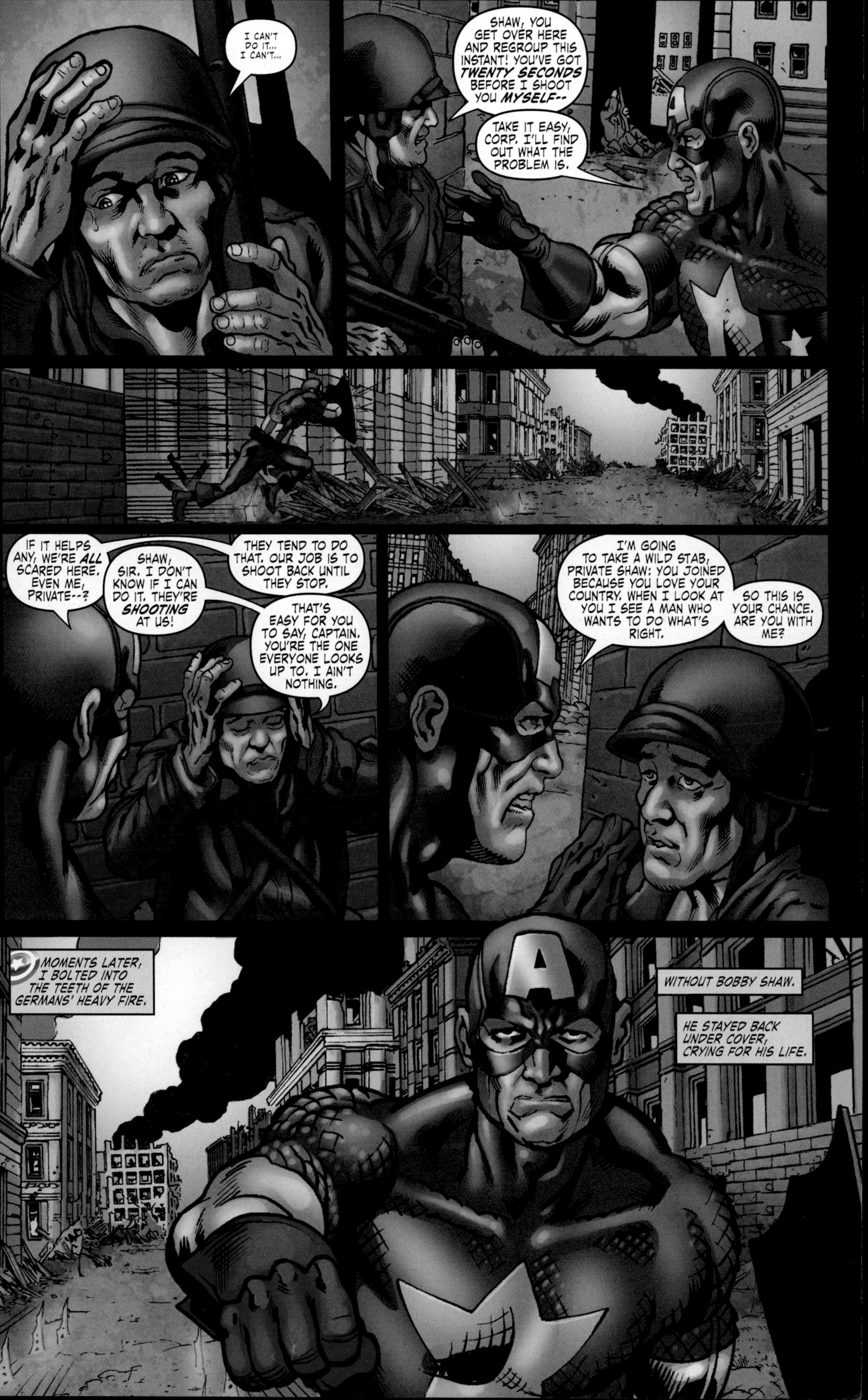
I CAN'T DO IT... I CAN'T...
SHAW, YOU GET OVER HERE AND REGROUP THIS INSTANT! YOU'VE GOT TWENTY SECONDS BEFORE I SHOOT YOU MYSELF--
TAKE IT EASY, CORP. I'LL FIND OUT WHAT THE PROBLEM IS.
IF IT HELPS ANY, WE'RE ALL SCARED HERE. EVEN ME, PRIVATE--?
SHAW, SIR. I DON'T KNOW IF I CAN DO IT. THEY'RE SHOOTING AT US!
THEY TEND TO DO THAT. OUR JOB IS TO SHOOT BACK UNTIL THEY STOP.
THAT'S EASY FOR YOU TO SAY, CAPTAIN. YOU'RE THE ONE EVERYONE LOOKS UP TO. I AIN'T NOTHING.
I'M GOING TO TAKE A WILD STAB, PRIVATE SHAW: YOU JOINED BECAUSE YOU LOVE YOUR COUNTRY. WHEN I LOOK AT YOU I SEE A MAN WHO WANTS TO DO WHAT'S RIGHT.
SO THIS IS YOUR CHANCE. ARE YOU WITH ME?
MOMENTS LATER, I BOLTED INTO THE TEETH OF THE GERMANS' HEAVY FIRE.
WITHOUT BOBBY SHAW.
HE STAYED BACK UNDER COVER, CRYING FOR HIS LIFE.

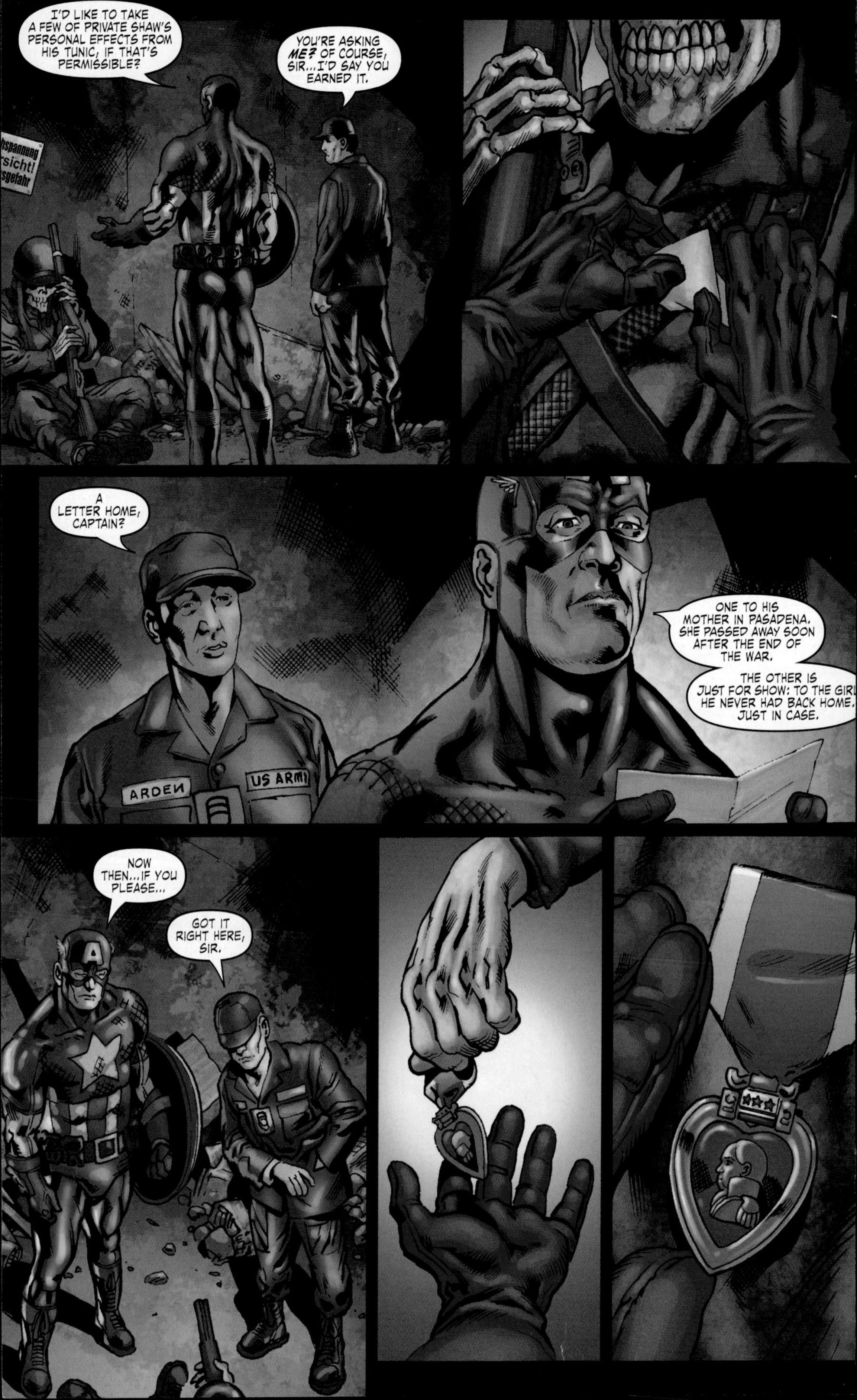
I'D LIKE TO TAKE A FEW OF PRIVATE SHAW'S PERSONAL EFFECTS FROM HIS TUNIC, IF THAT'S PERMISSIBLE?
YOU'RE ASKING ***ME?*** OF COURSE, SIR...I'D SAY YOU EARNED IT.
A LETTER HOME, CAPTAIN?
ARDEN
ONE TO HIS MOTHER IN PASADENA. SHE PASSED AWAY SOON AFTER THE END OF THE WAR.
THE OTHER IS JUST FOR SHOW: TO THE GIRL HE NEVER HAD BACK HOME. JUST IN CASE.
NOW THEN...IF YOU PLEASE...
GOT IT RIGHT HERE, SIR.

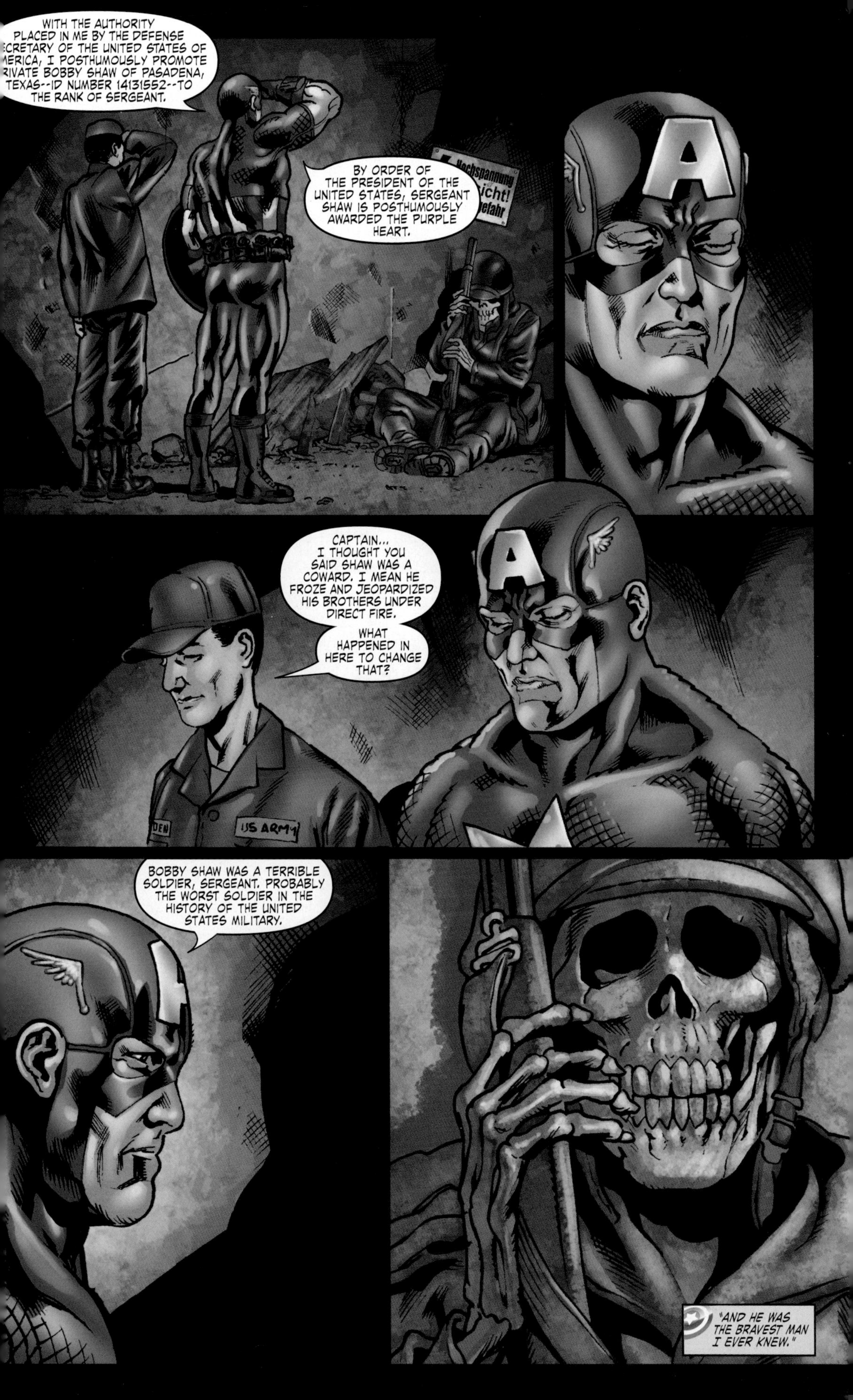
WITH THE AUTHORITY PLACED IN ME BY THE DEFENSE ECRETARY OF THE UNITED STATES OF MERICA, I POSTHUMOUSLY PROMOTE RIVATE BOBBY SHAW OF PASADENA, TEXAS--ID NUMBER 14131552--TO THE RANK OF SERGEANT.
BY ORDER OF THE PRESIDENT OF THE UNITED STATES, SERGEANT SHAW IS POSTHUMOUSLY AWARDED THE PURPLE HEART.
CAPTAIN... I THOUGHT YOU SAID SHAW WAS A COWARD. I MEAN HE FROZE AND JEOPARDIZED HIS BROTHERS UNDER DIRECT FIRE.
WHAT HAPPENED IN HERE TO CHANGE THAT?
US ARMY
BOBBY SHAW WAS A TERRIBLE SOLDIER, SERGEANT. PROBABLY THE WORST SOLDIER IN THE HISTORY OF THE UNITED STATES MILITARY.
"AND HE WAS THE BRAVEST MAN I EVER KNEW."

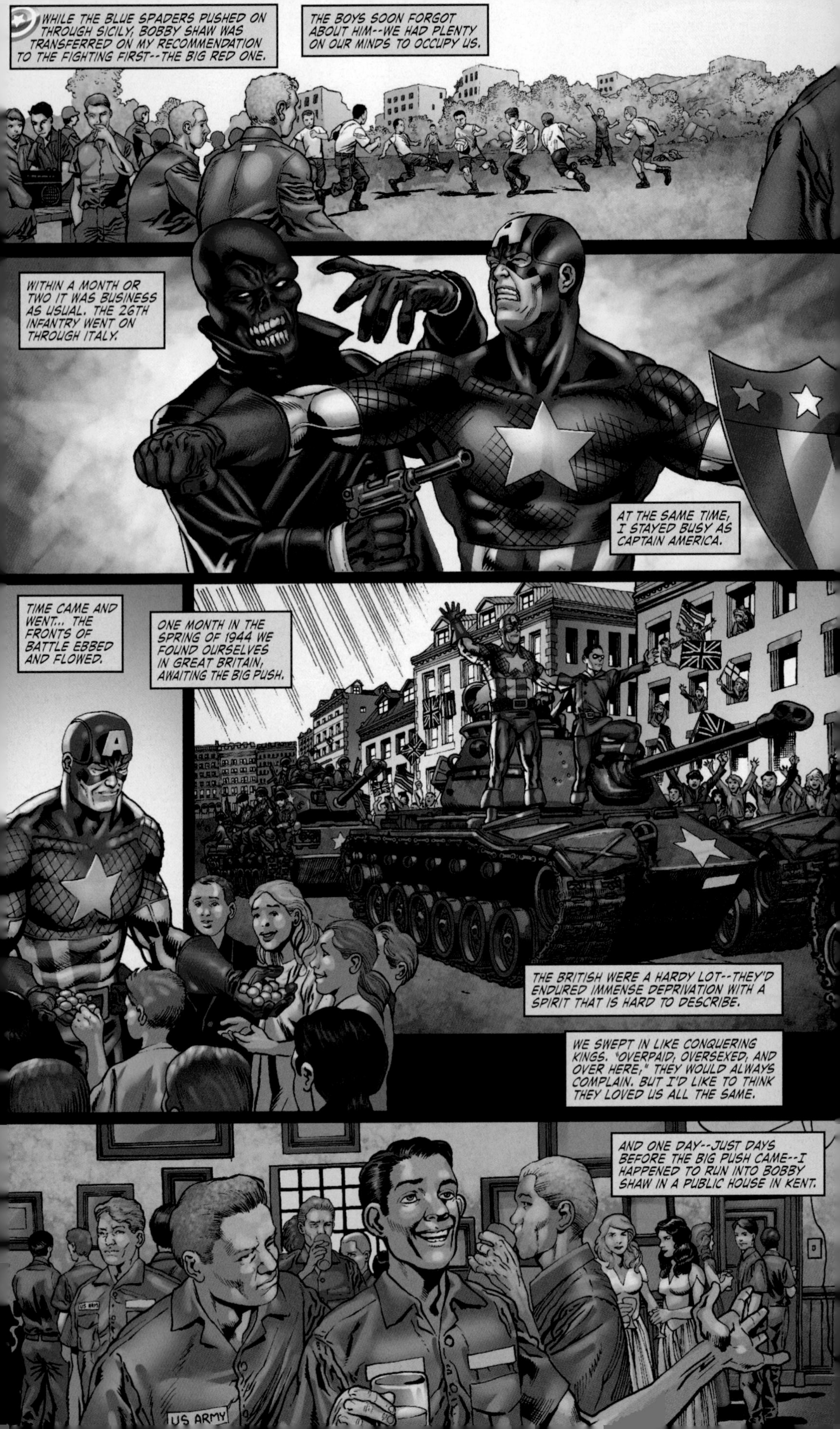
WHILE THE BLUE SPADERS PUSHED ON THROUGH SICILY, BOBBY SHAW WAS TRANSFERRED ON MY RECOMMENDATION TO THE FIGHTING FIRST--THE BIG RED ONE.
THE BOYS SOON FORGOT ABOUT HIM--WE HAD PLENTY ON OUR MINDS TO OCCUPY US.
WITHIN A MONTH OR TWO IT WAS BUSINESS AS USUAL. THE 26TH INFANTRY WENT ON THROUGH ITALY.
AT THE SAME TIME, I STAYED BUSY AS CAPTAIN AMERICA.
TIME CAME AND WENT... THE FRONTS OF BATTLE EBBED AND FLOWED.
ONE MONTH IN THE SPRING OF 1944 WE FOUND OURSELVES IN GREAT BRITAIN, AWAITING THE BIG PUSH.
THE BRITISH WERE A HARDY LOT--THEY'D ENDURED IMMENSE DEPRIVATION WITH A SPIRIT THAT IS HARD TO DESCRIBE.
WE SWEPT IN LIKE CONQUERING KINGS. "OVERPAID, OVERSEXED, AND OVER HERE," THEY WOULD ALWAYS COMPLAIN. BUT I'D LIKE TO THINK THEY LOVED US ALL THE SAME.
AND ONE DAY--JUST DAYS BEFORE THE BIG PUSH CAME--I HAPPENED TO RUN INTO BOBBY SHAW IN A PUBLIC HOUSE IN KENT.
US ARMY

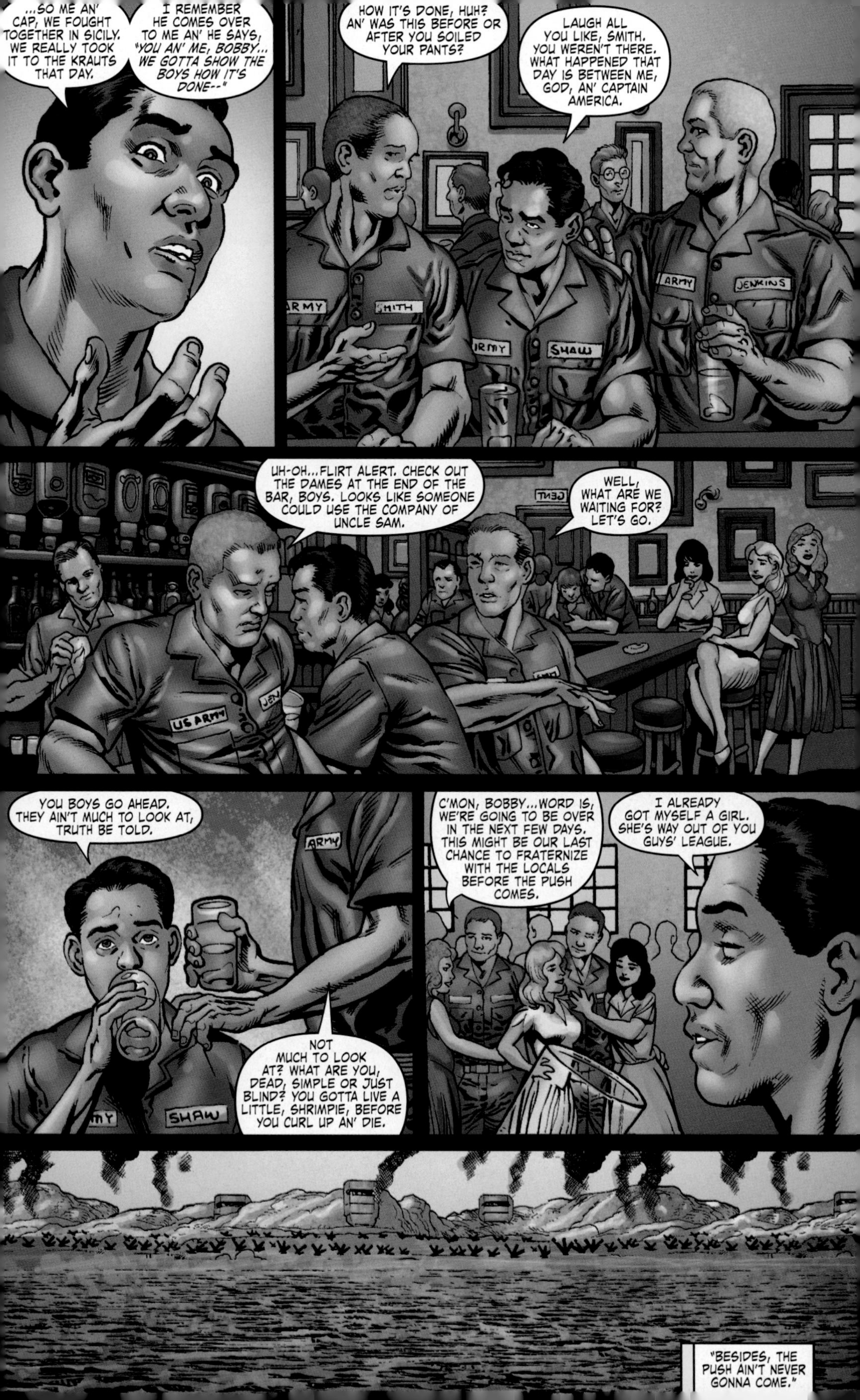
...SO ME AN' CAP, WE FOUGHT TOGETHER IN SICILY. WE REALLY TOOK IT TO THE KRAUTS THAT DAY.
I REMEMBER HE COMES OVER TO ME AN' HE SAYS, "YOU AN' ME, BOBBY... WE GOTTA SHOW THE BOYS HOW IT'S DONE--"
HOW IT'S DONE, HUH? AN' WAS THIS BEFORE OR AFTER YOU SOILED YOUR PANTS?
LAUGH ALL YOU LIKE, SMITH. YOU WEREN'T THERE. WHAT HAPPENED THAT DAY IS BETWEEN ME, GOD, AN' CAPTAIN AMERICA.
ARMY
SMITH
ARMY
SHAW
ARMY
JENKINS
UH-OH...FLIRT ALERT. CHECK OUT THE DAMES AT THE END OF THE BAR, BOYS. LOOKS LIKE SOMEONE COULD USE THE COMPANY OF UNCLE SAM.
WELL, WHAT ARE WE WAITING FOR? LET'S GO.
US ARMY
YOU BOYS GO AHEAD. THEY AIN'T MUCH TO LOOK AT, TRUTH BE TOLD.
ARMY
NOT MUCH TO LOOK AT? WHAT ARE YOU, DEAD, SIMPLE OR JUST BLIND? YOU GOTTA LIVE A LITTLE, SHRIMPIE, BEFORE YOU CURL UP AN' DIE.
SHAW
C'MON, BOBBY...WORD IS, WE'RE GOING TO BE OVER IN THE NEXT FEW DAYS. THIS MIGHT BE OUR LAST CHANCE TO FRATERNIZE WITH THE LOCALS BEFORE THE PUSH COMES.
I ALREADY GOT MYSELF A GIRL. SHE'S WAY OUT OF YOU GUYS' LEAGUE.
"BESIDES, THE PUSH AIN'T NEVER GONNA COME."

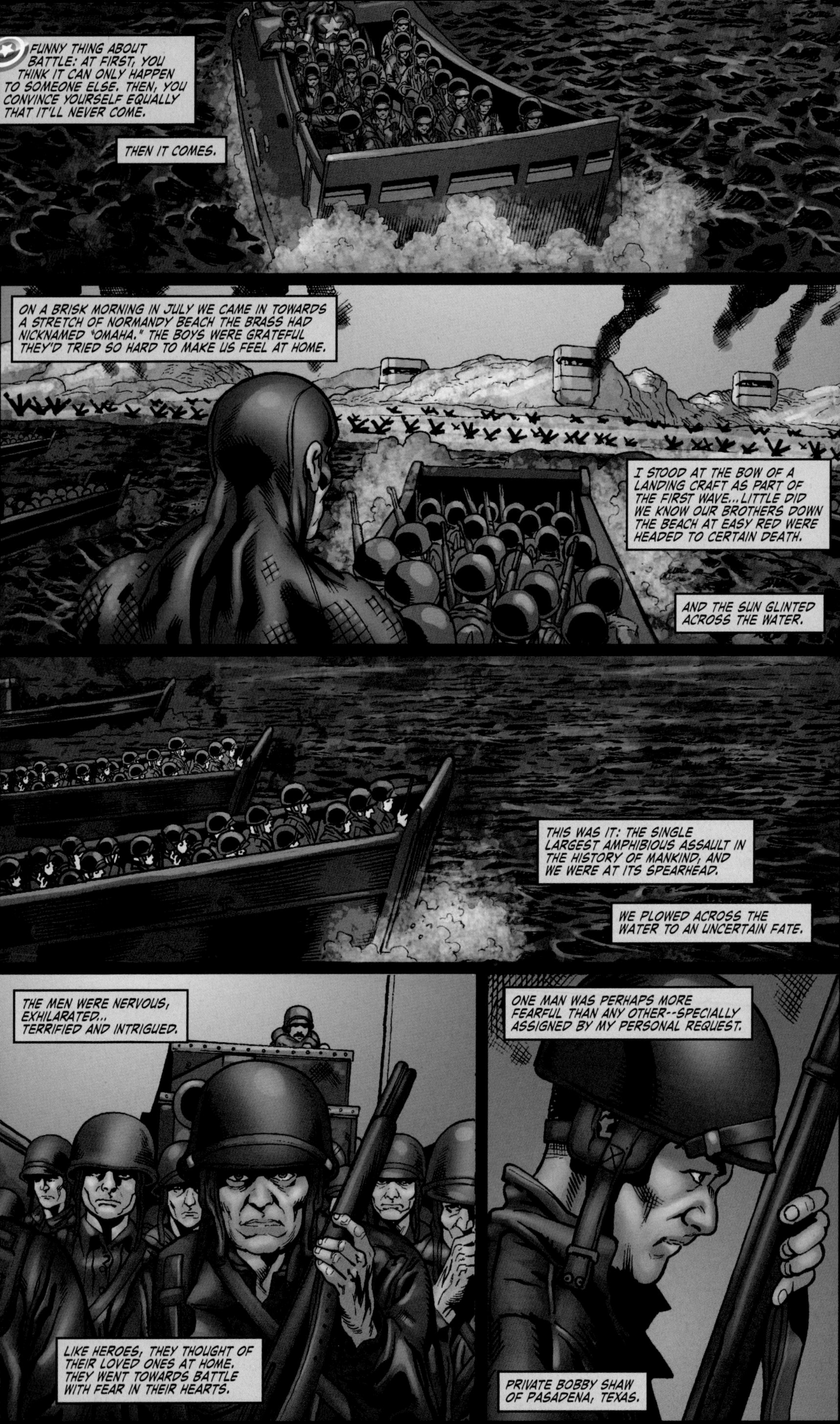
FUNNY THING ABOUT BATTLE: AT FIRST, YOU THINK IT CAN ONLY HAPPEN TO SOMEONE ELSE. THEN, YOU CONVINCE YOURSELF EQUALLY THAT IT'LL NEVER COME.
THEN IT COMES.
ON A BRISK MORNING IN JULY WE CAME IN TOWARDS A STRETCH OF NORMANDY BEACH THE BRASS HAD NICKNAMED "OMAHA." THE BOYS WERE GRATEFUL THEY'D TRIED SO HARD TO MAKE US FEEL AT HOME.
I STOOD AT THE BOW OF A LANDING CRAFT AS PART OF THE FIRST WAVE...LITTLE DID WE KNOW OUR BROTHERS DOWN THE BEACH AT EASY RED WERE HEADED TO CERTAIN DEATH.
AND THE SUN GLINTED ACROSS THE WATER.
THIS WAS IT: THE SINGLE LARGEST AMPHIBIOUS ASSAULT IN THE HISTORY OF MANKIND, AND WE WERE AT ITS SPEARHEAD.
WE PLOWED ACROSS THE WATER TO AN UNCERTAIN FATE.
THE MEN WERE NERVOUS, EXHILARATED... TERRIFIED AND INTRIGUED.
LIKE HEROES, THEY THOUGHT OF THEIR LOVED ONES AT HOME. THEY WENT TOWARDS BATTLE WITH FEAR IN THEIR HEARTS.
ONE MAN WAS PERHAPS MORE FEARFUL THAN ANY OTHER--SPECIALLY ASSIGNED BY MY PERSONAL REQUEST.
PRIVATE BOBBY SHAW OF PASADENA, TEXAS.

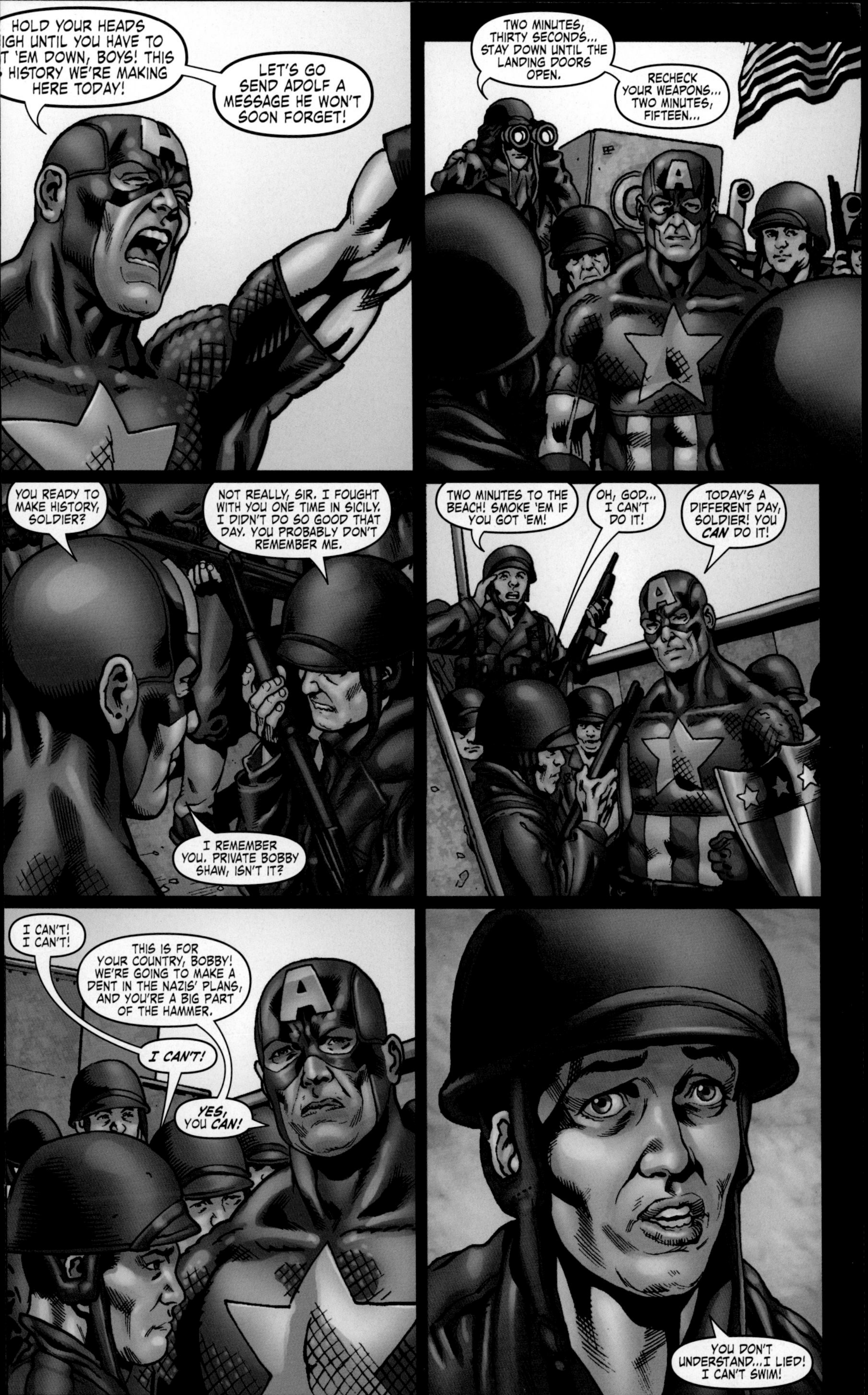
HOLD YOUR HEADS
IGH UNTIL YOU HAVE TO
T 'EM DOWN, BOYS! THIS
HISTORY WE'RE MAKING
HERE TODAY!
LET'S GO SEND ADOLF A MESSAGE HE WON'T SOON FORGET!
TWO MINUTES, THIRTY SECONDS... STAY DOWN UNTIL THE LANDING DOORS OPEN.
RECHECK YOUR WEAPONS... TWO MINUTES, FIFTEEN...
YOU READY TO MAKE HISTORY, SOLDIER?
NOT REALLY, SIR. I FOUGHT WITH YOU ONE TIME IN SICILY. I DIDN'T DO SO GOOD THAT DAY. YOU PROBABLY DON'T REMEMBER ME.
I REMEMBER YOU. PRIVATE BOBBY SHAW, ISN'T IT?
TWO MINUTES TO THE BEACH! SMOKE 'EM IF YOU GOT 'EM!
OH, GOD... I CAN'T DO IT!
TODAY'S A DIFFERENT DAY, SOLDIER! YOU *CAN* DO IT!
I CAN'T! I CAN'T!
THIS IS FOR YOUR COUNTRY, BOBBY! WE'RE GOING TO MAKE A DENT IN THE NAZIS' PLANS, AND YOU'RE A BIG PART OF THE HAMMER.
I CAN'T!
YES, YOU *CAN!*
YOU DON'T UNDERSTAND... I LIED! I CAN'T SWIM!

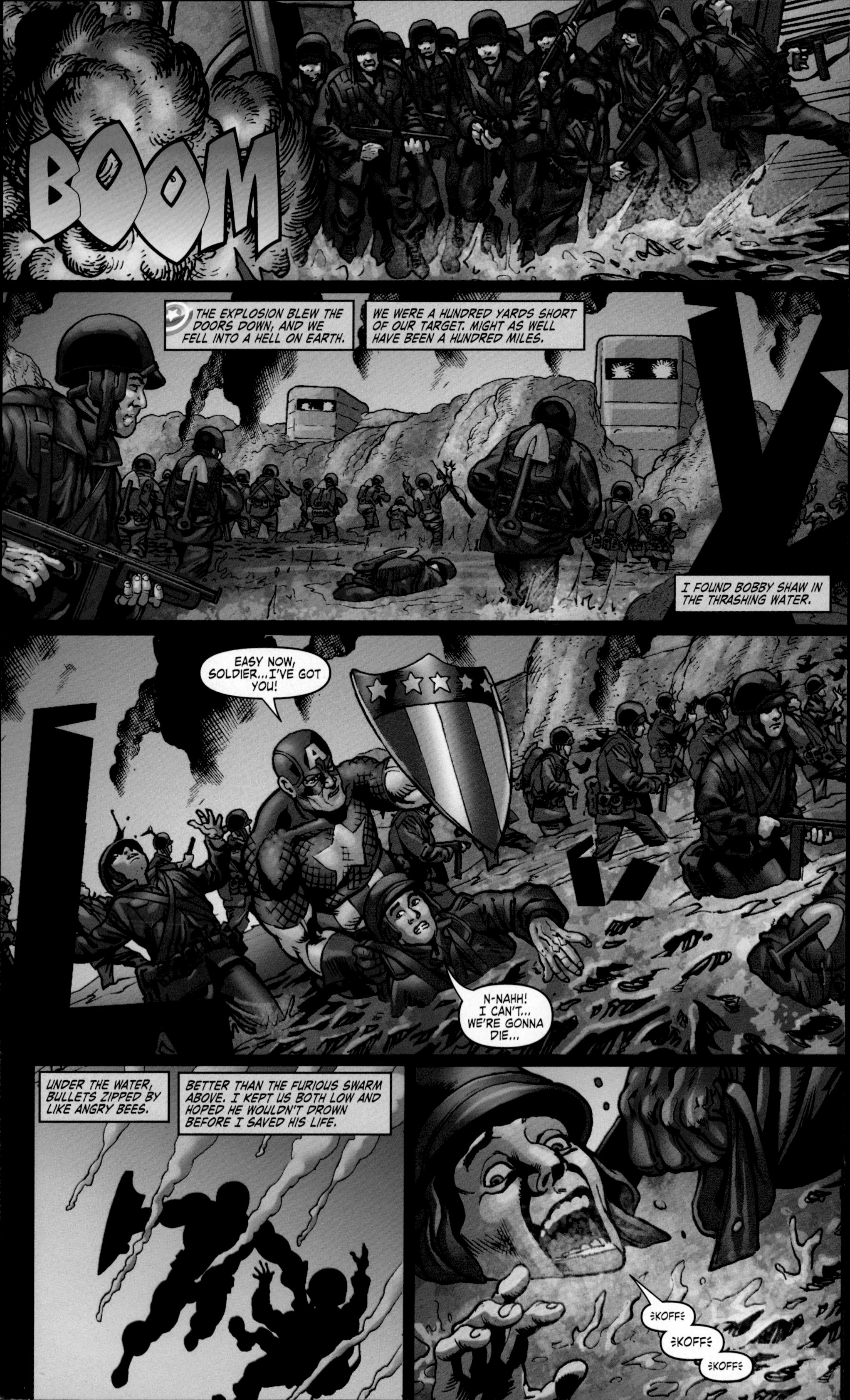
BOOM
THE EXPLOSION BLEW THE DOORS DOWN, AND WE FELL INTO A HELL ON EARTH.
WE WERE A HUNDRED YARDS SHORT OF OUR TARGET. MIGHT AS WELL HAVE BEEN A HUNDRED MILES.
I FOUND BOBBY SHAW IN THE THRASHING WATER.
EASY NOW, SOLDIER...I'VE GOT YOU!
N-NAHH! I CAN'T... WE'RE GONNA DIE...
UNDER THE WATER, BULLETS ZIPPED BY LIKE ANGRY BEES.
BETTER THAN THE FURIOUS SWARM ABOVE. I KEPT US BOTH LOW AND HOPED HE WOULDN'T DROWN BEFORE I SAVED HIS LIFE.
KOFF
KOFF
KOFF

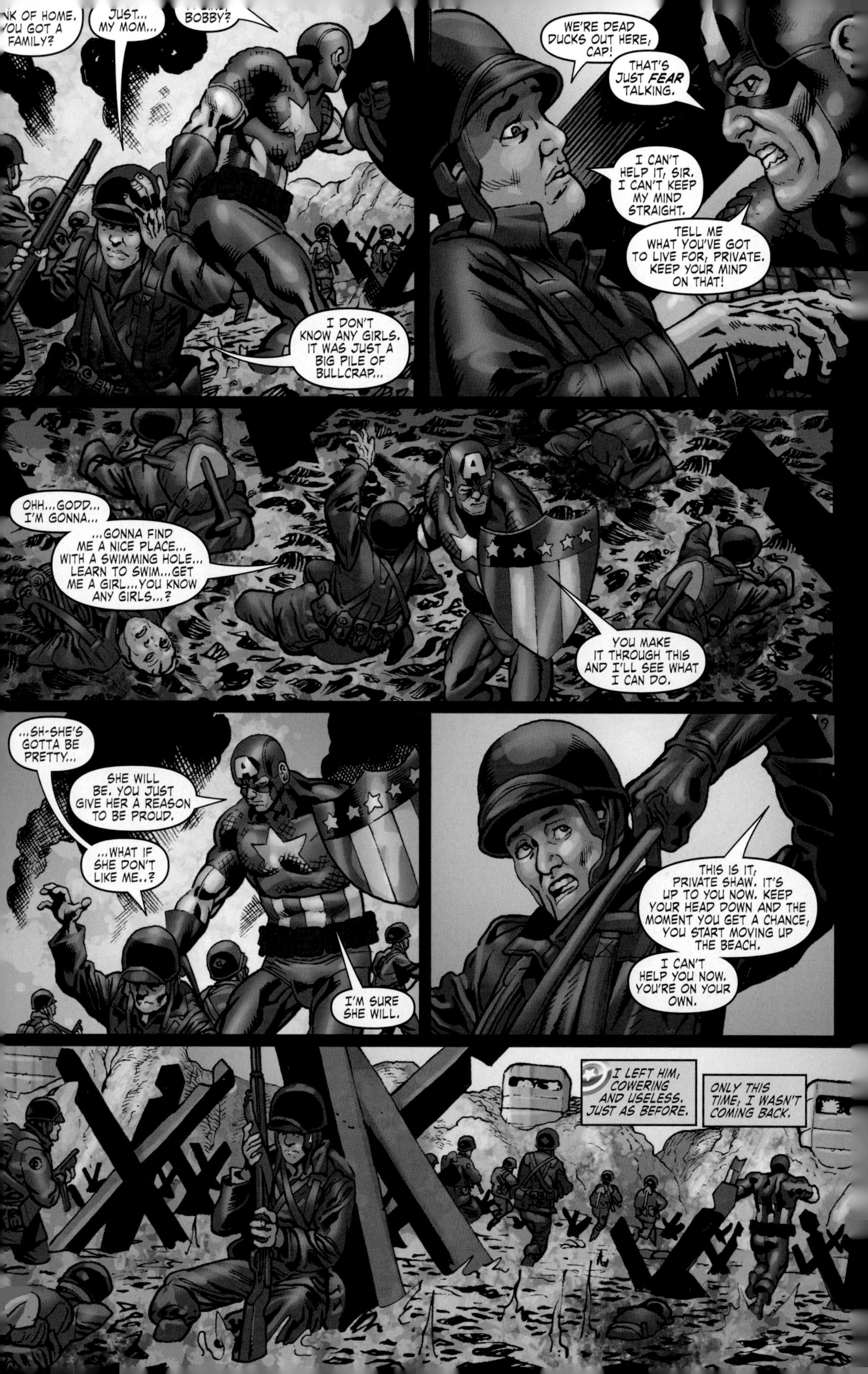
NK OF HOME. YOU GOT A FAMILY?
JUST... MY MOM...
BOBBY?
I DON'T KNOW ANY GIRLS. IT WAS JUST A BIG PILE OF BULLCRAP...
WE'RE DEAD DUCKS OUT HERE, CAP!
THAT'S JUST FEAR TALKING.
I CAN'T HELP IT, SIR. I CAN'T KEEP MY MIND STRAIGHT.
TELL ME WHAT YOU'VE GOT TO LIVE FOR, PRIVATE. KEEP YOUR MIND ON THAT!
OHH...GODD... I'M GONNA...
...GONNA FIND ME A NICE PLACE... WITH A SWIMMING HOLE... LEARN TO SWIM...GET ME A GIRL...YOU KNOW ANY GIRLS...?
YOU MAKE IT THROUGH THIS AND I'LL SEE WHAT I CAN DO.
...SH-SHE'S GOTTA BE PRETTY...
SHE WILL BE. YOU JUST GIVE HER A REASON TO BE PROUD.
...WHAT IF SHE DON'T LIKE ME..?
I'M SURE SHE WILL.
THIS IS IT, PRIVATE SHAW. IT'S UP TO YOU NOW. KEEP YOUR HEAD DOWN AND THE MOMENT YOU GET A CHANCE, YOU START MOVING UP THE BEACH.
I CAN'T HELP YOU NOW. YOU'RE ON YOUR OWN.
I LEFT HIM, COWERING AND USELESS. JUST AS BEFORE.
ONLY THIS TIME, I WASN'T COMING BACK.

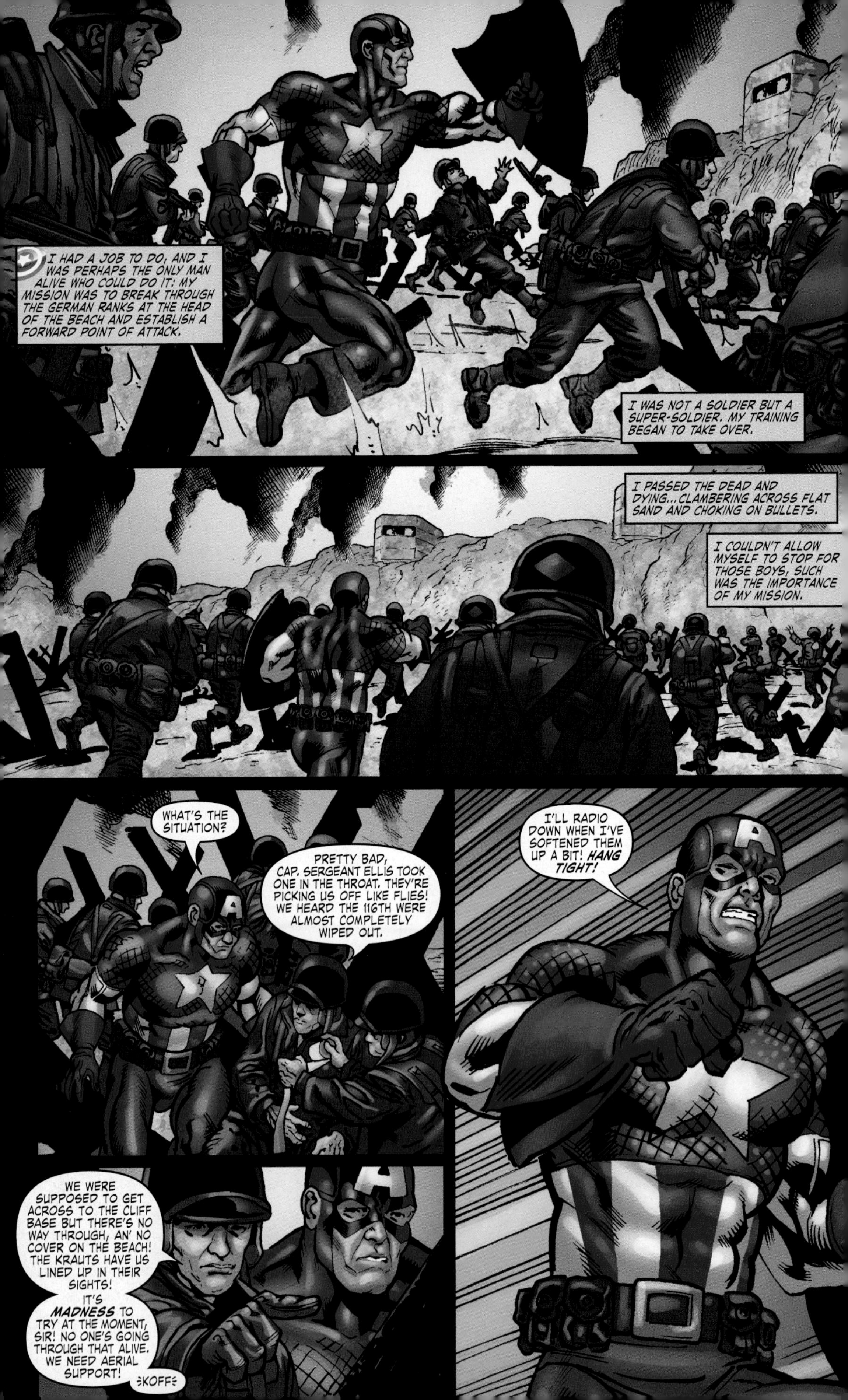
I HAD A JOB TO DO, AND I WAS PERHAPS THE ONLY MAN ALIVE WHO COULD DO IT: MY MISSION WAS TO BREAK THROUGH THE GERMAN RANKS AT THE HEAD OF THE BEACH AND ESTABLISH A FORWARD POINT OF ATTACK.
I WAS NOT A SOLDIER BUT A SUPER-SOLDIER. MY TRAINING BEGAN TO TAKE OVER.
I PASSED THE DEAD AND DYING...CLAMBERING ACROSS FLAT SAND AND CHOKING ON BULLETS.
I COULDN'T ALLOW MYSELF TO STOP FOR THOSE BOYS, SUCH WAS THE IMPORTANCE OF MY MISSION.
WHAT'S THE SITUATION?
PRETTY BAD, CAP. SERGEANT ELLIS TOOK ONE IN THE THROAT. THEY'RE PICKING US OFF LIKE FLIES! WE HEARD THE 116TH WERE ALMOST COMPLETELY WIPED OUT.
WE WERE SUPPOSED TO GET ACROSS TO THE CLIFF BASE BUT THERE'S NO WAY THROUGH, AN' NO COVER ON THE BEACH! THE KRAUTS HAVE US LINED UP IN THEIR SIGHTS!
IT'S MADNESS TO TRY AT THE MOMENT, SIR! NO ONE'S GOING THROUGH THAT ALIVE. WE NEED AERIAL SUPPORT!
KOFF
I'LL RADIO DOWN WHEN I'VE SOFTENED THEM UP A BIT! HANG TIGHT!

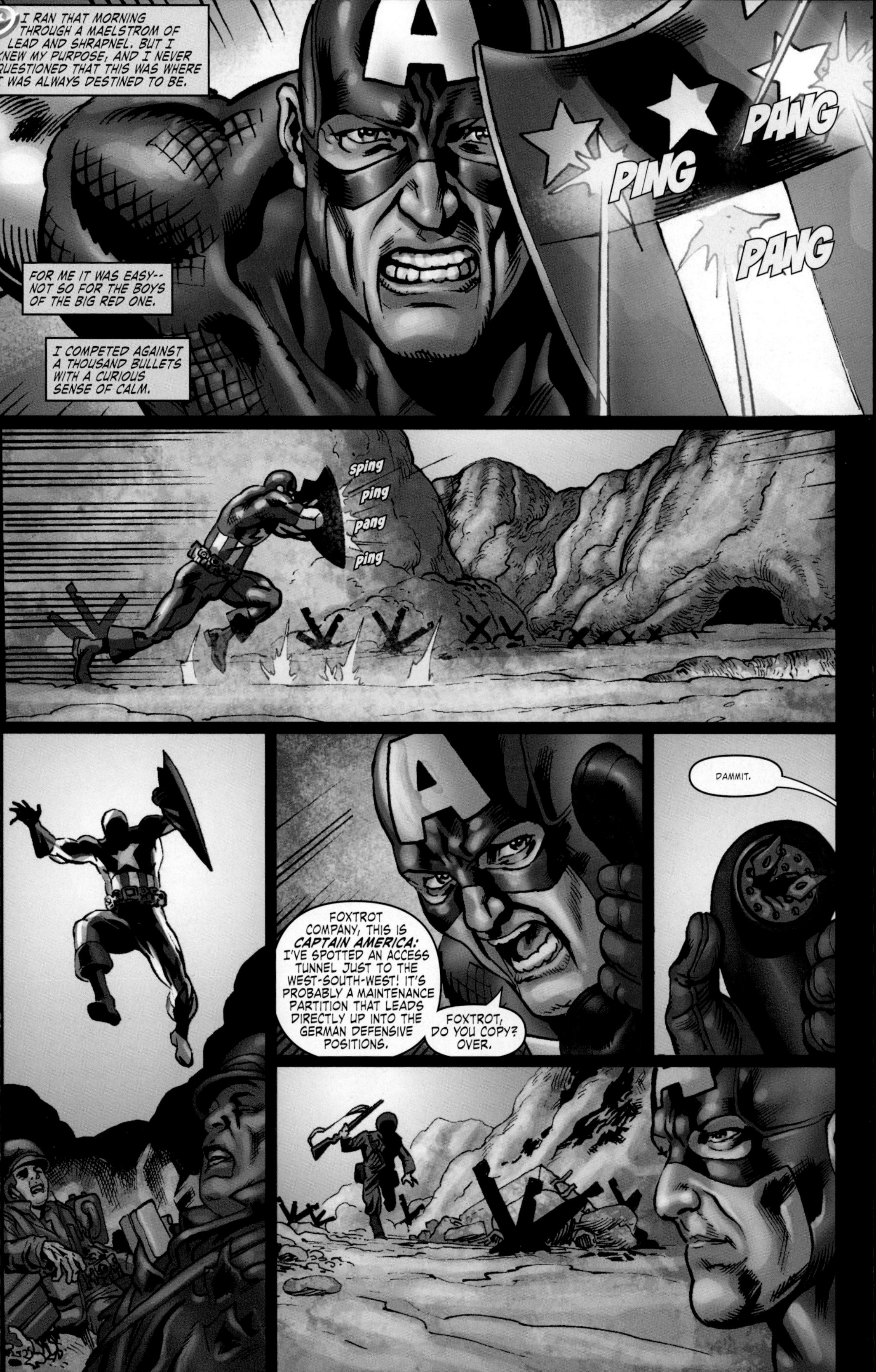
I RAN THAT MORNING THROUGH A MAELSTROM OF LEAD AND SHRAPNEL. BUT I KNEW MY PURPOSE, AND I NEVER QUESTIONED THAT THIS WAS WHERE I WAS ALWAYS DESTINED TO BE.
PANG
PING
PANG
FOR ME IT WAS EASY--NOT SO FOR THE BOYS OF THE BIG RED ONE.
I COMPETED AGAINST A THOUSAND BULLETS WITH A CURIOUS SENSE OF CALM.
sping
ping
pang
ping
FOXTROT COMPANY, THIS IS CAPTAIN AMERICA: I'VE SPOTTED AN ACCESS TUNNEL JUST TO THE WEST-SOUTH-WEST! IT'S PROBABLY A MAINTENANCE PARTITION THAT LEADS DIRECTLY UP INTO THE GERMAN DEFENSIVE POSITIONS.
FOXTROT, DO YOU COPY? OVER.
DAMMIT.

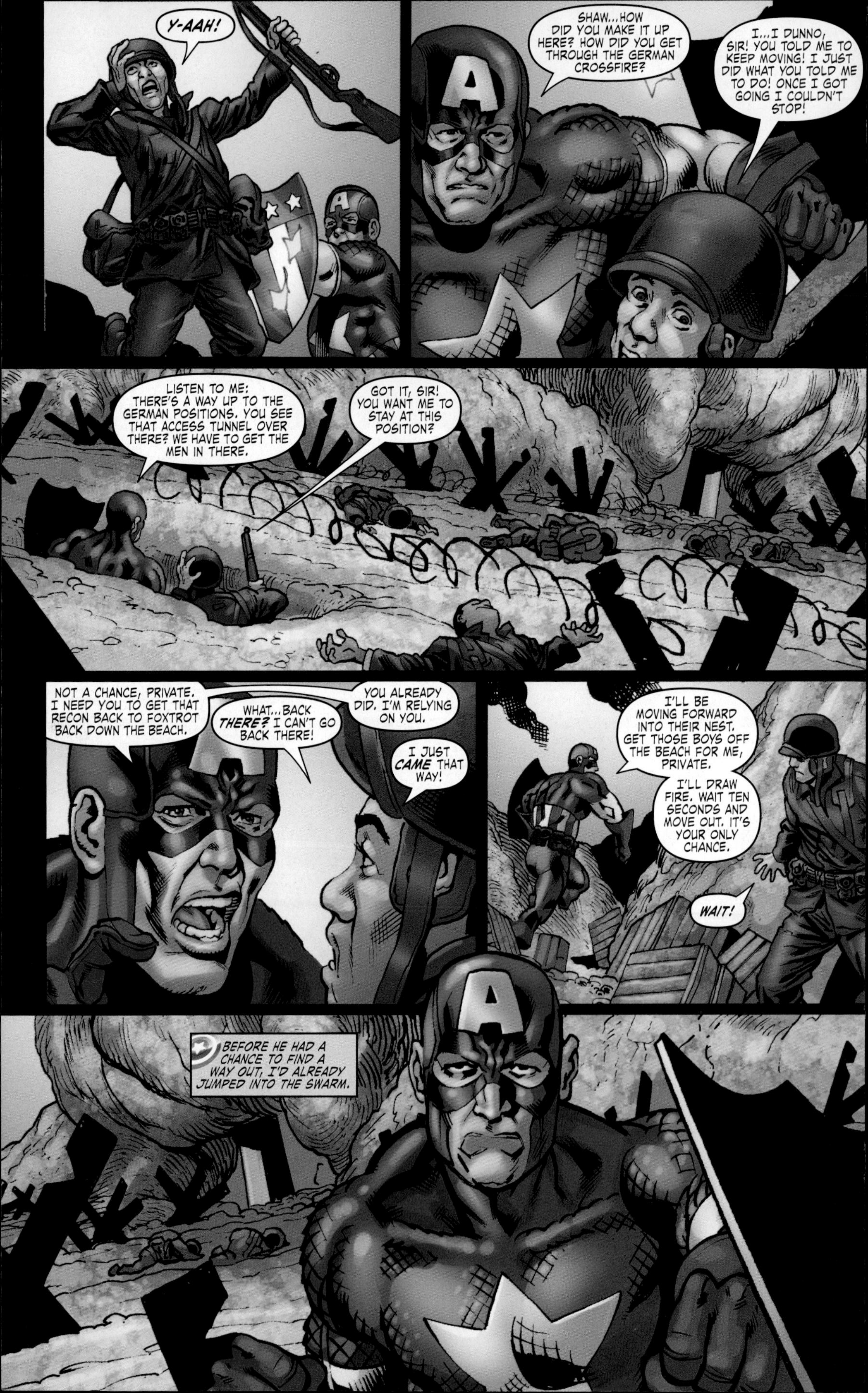
Y-AAH!
SHAW...HOW DID YOU MAKE IT UP HERE? HOW DID YOU GET THROUGH THE GERMAN CROSSFIRE?
I...I DUNNO, SIR! YOU TOLD ME TO KEEP MOVING! I JUST DID WHAT YOU TOLD ME TO DO! ONCE I GOT GOING I COULDN'T STOP!
LISTEN TO ME: THERE'S A WAY UP TO THE GERMAN POSITIONS. YOU SEE THAT ACCESS TUNNEL OVER THERE? WE HAVE TO GET THE MEN IN THERE.
GOT IT, SIR! YOU WANT ME TO STAY AT THIS POSITION?
NOT A CHANCE, PRIVATE. I NEED YOU TO GET THAT RECON BACK TO FOXTROT BACK DOWN THE BEACH.
WHAT...BACK THERE? I CAN'T GO BACK THERE!
YOU ALREADY DID. I'M RELYING ON YOU.
I JUST CAME THAT WAY!
I'LL BE MOVING FORWARD INTO THEIR NEST. GET THOSE BOYS OFF THE BEACH FOR ME, PRIVATE.
I'LL DRAW FIRE. WAIT TEN SECONDS AND MOVE OUT. IT'S YOUR ONLY CHANCE.
WAIT!
BEFORE HE HAD A CHANCE TO FIND A WAY OUT, I'D ALREADY JUMPED INTO THE SWARM.

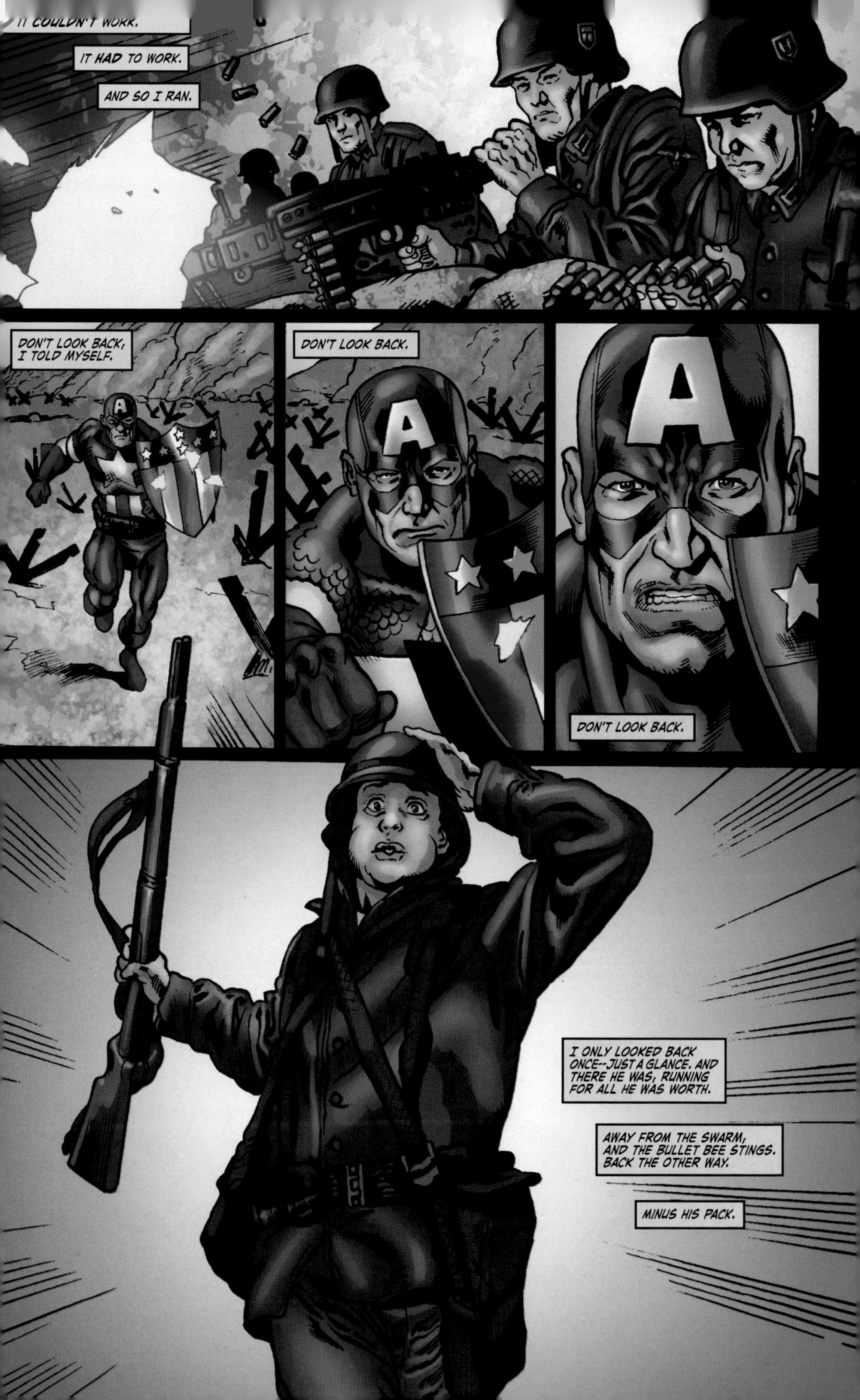
IT COULDN'T WORK.
IT HAD TO WORK.
AND SO I RAN.
DON'T LOOK BACK, I TOLD MYSELF.
DON'T LOOK BACK.
DON'T LOOK BACK.
I ONLY LOOKED BACK ONCE--JUST A GLANCE. AND THERE HE WAS, RUNNING FOR ALL HE WAS WORTH.
AWAY FROM THE SWARM, AND THE BULLET BEE STINGS. BACK THE OTHER WAY.
MINUS HIS PACK.

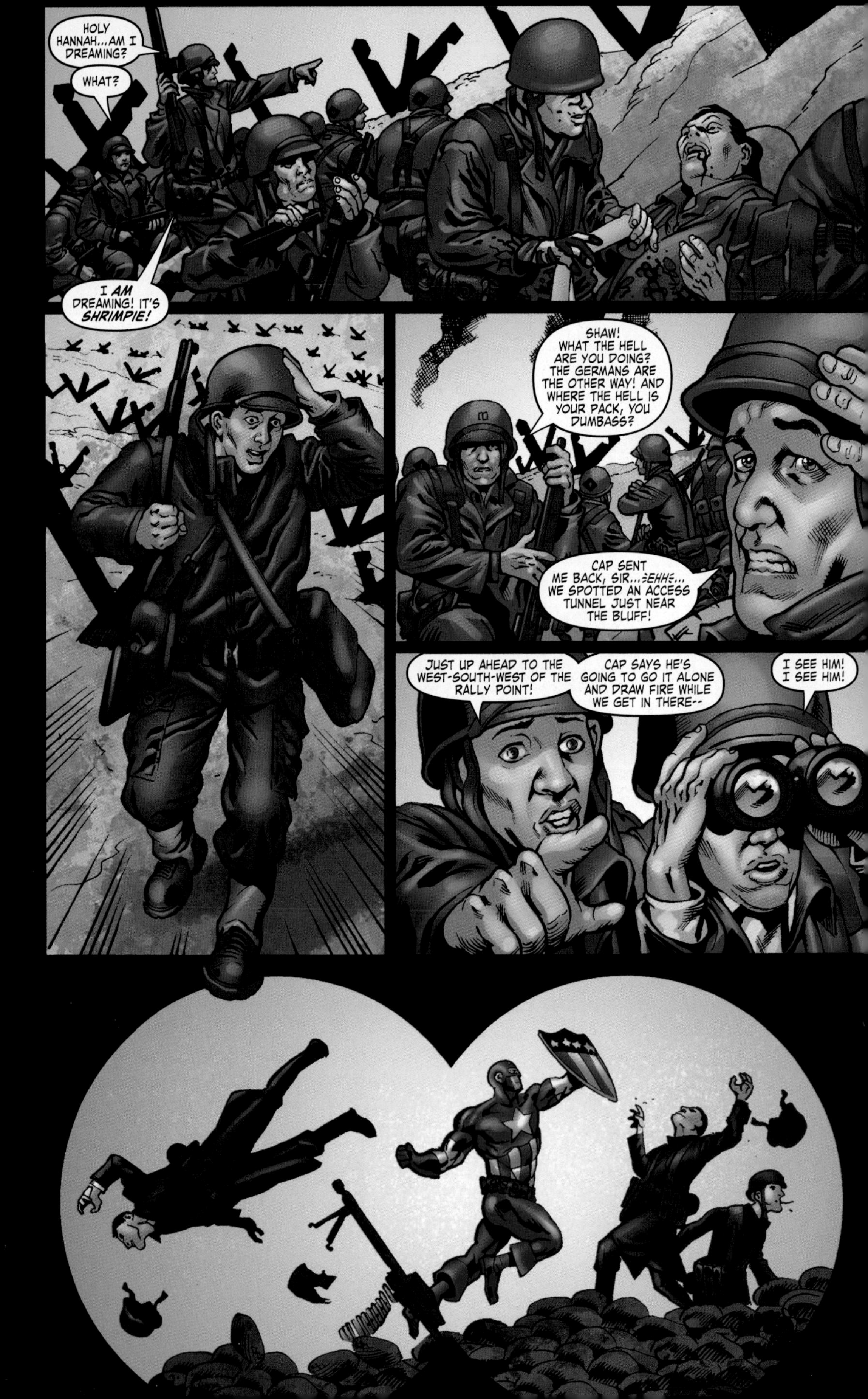
HOLY HANNAH...AM I DREAMING?
WHAT?
I AM DREAMING! IT'S SHRIMPIE!
SHAW! WHAT THE HELL ARE YOU DOING? THE GERMANS ARE THE OTHER WAY! AND WHERE THE HELL IS YOUR PACK, YOU DUMBASS?
CAP SENT ME BACK, SIR...HEHH... WE SPOTTED AN ACCESS TUNNEL JUST NEAR THE BLUFF!
JUST UP AHEAD TO THE WEST-SOUTH-WEST OF THE RALLY POINT!
CAP SAYS HE'S GOING TO GO IT ALONE AND DRAW FIRE WHILE WE GET IN THERE--
I SEE HIM! I SEE HIM!

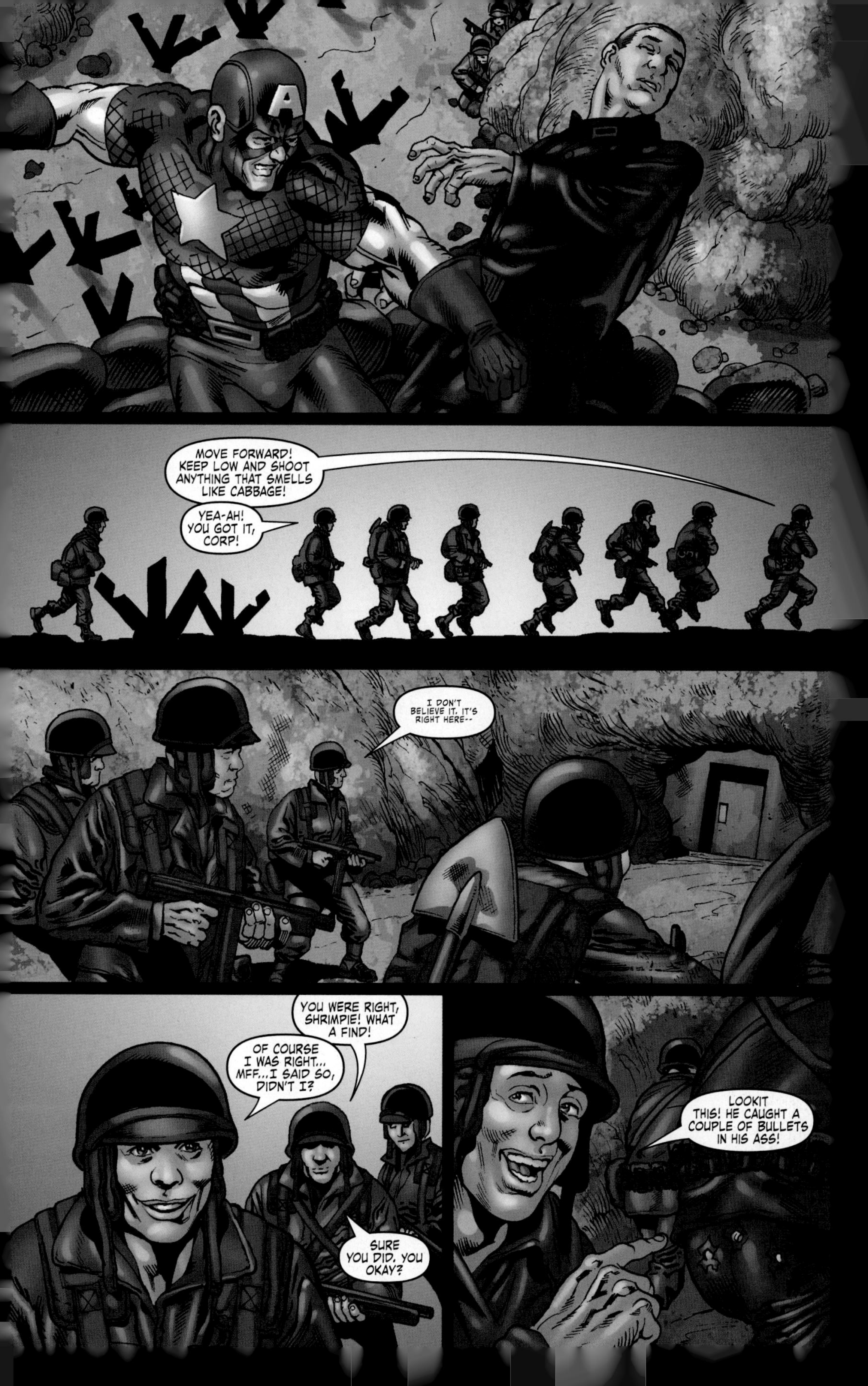
MOVE FORWARD! KEEP LOW AND SHOOT ANYTHING THAT SMELLS LIKE CABBAGE!
YEA-AH! YOU GOT IT, CORP!
I DON'T BELIEVE IT. IT'S RIGHT HERE--
YOU WERE RIGHT, SHRIMPIE! WHAT A FIND!
OF COURSE I WAS RIGHT... MFF...I SAID SO, DIDN'T I?
SURE YOU DID. YOU OKAY?
LOOKIT THIS! HE CAUGHT A COUPLE OF BULLETS IN HIS ASS!

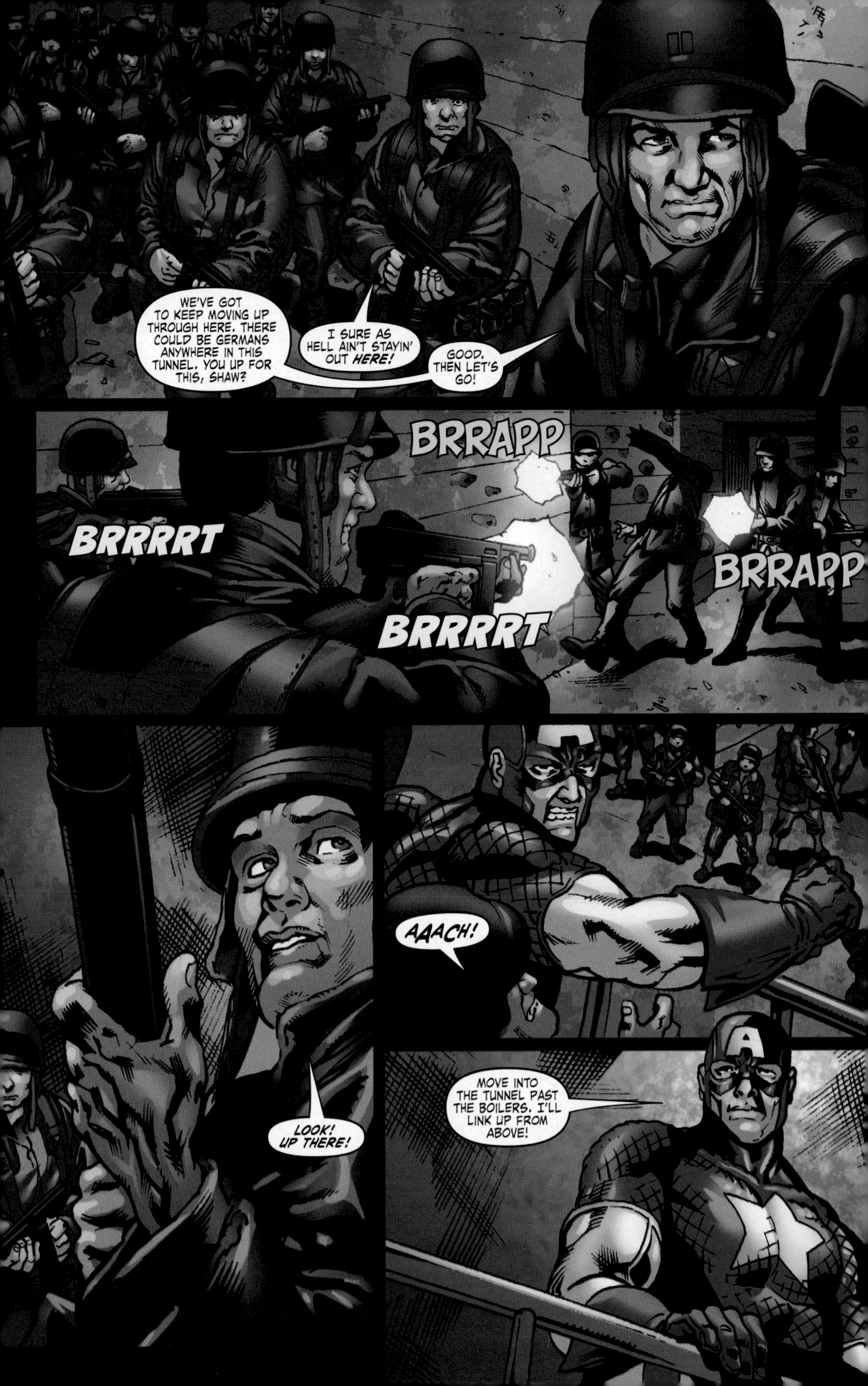
WE'VE GOT TO KEEP MOVING UP THROUGH HERE. THERE COULD BE GERMANS ANYWHERE IN THIS TUNNEL. YOU UP FOR THIS, SHAW?
I SURE AS HELL AIN'T STAYIN' OUT *HERE!*
GOOD. THEN LET'S GO!
BRRAPP
BRRRRT
BRRRRT
BRRAPP
LOOK! UP THERE!
AAACH!
MOVE INTO THE TUNNEL PAST THE BOILERS. I'LL LINK UP FROM ABOVE!

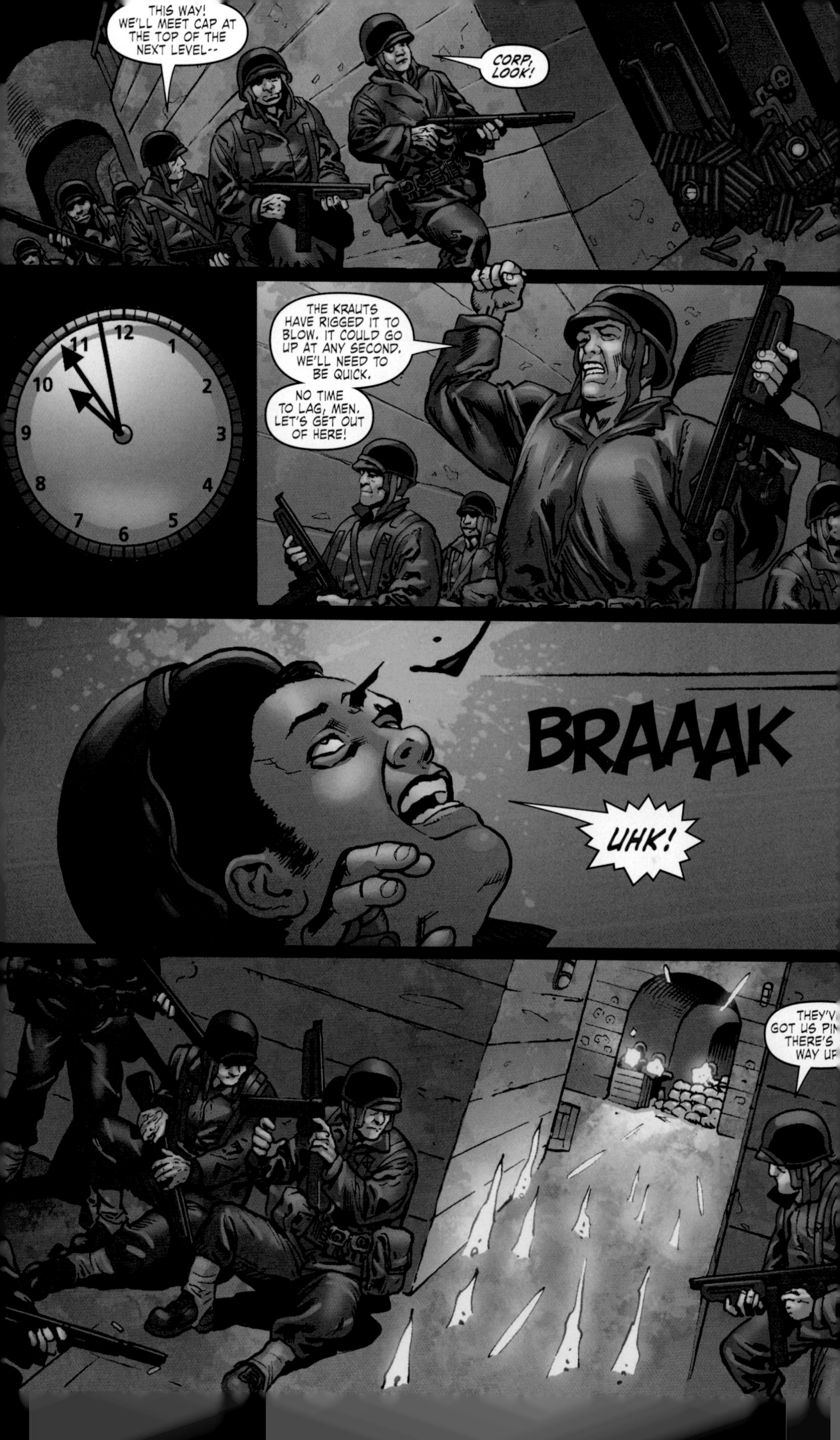
THIS WAY! WE'LL MEET CAP AT THE TOP OF THE NEXT LEVEL--
CORP, LOOK!
THE KRAUTS HAVE RIGGED IT TO BLOW. IT COULD GO UP AT ANY SECOND. WE'LL NEED TO BE QUICK.
NO TIME TO LAG, MEN. LET'S GET OUT OF HERE!
BRAAAK
UHK!
THEY'V
GOT US PIN
THERE'S
WAY UP

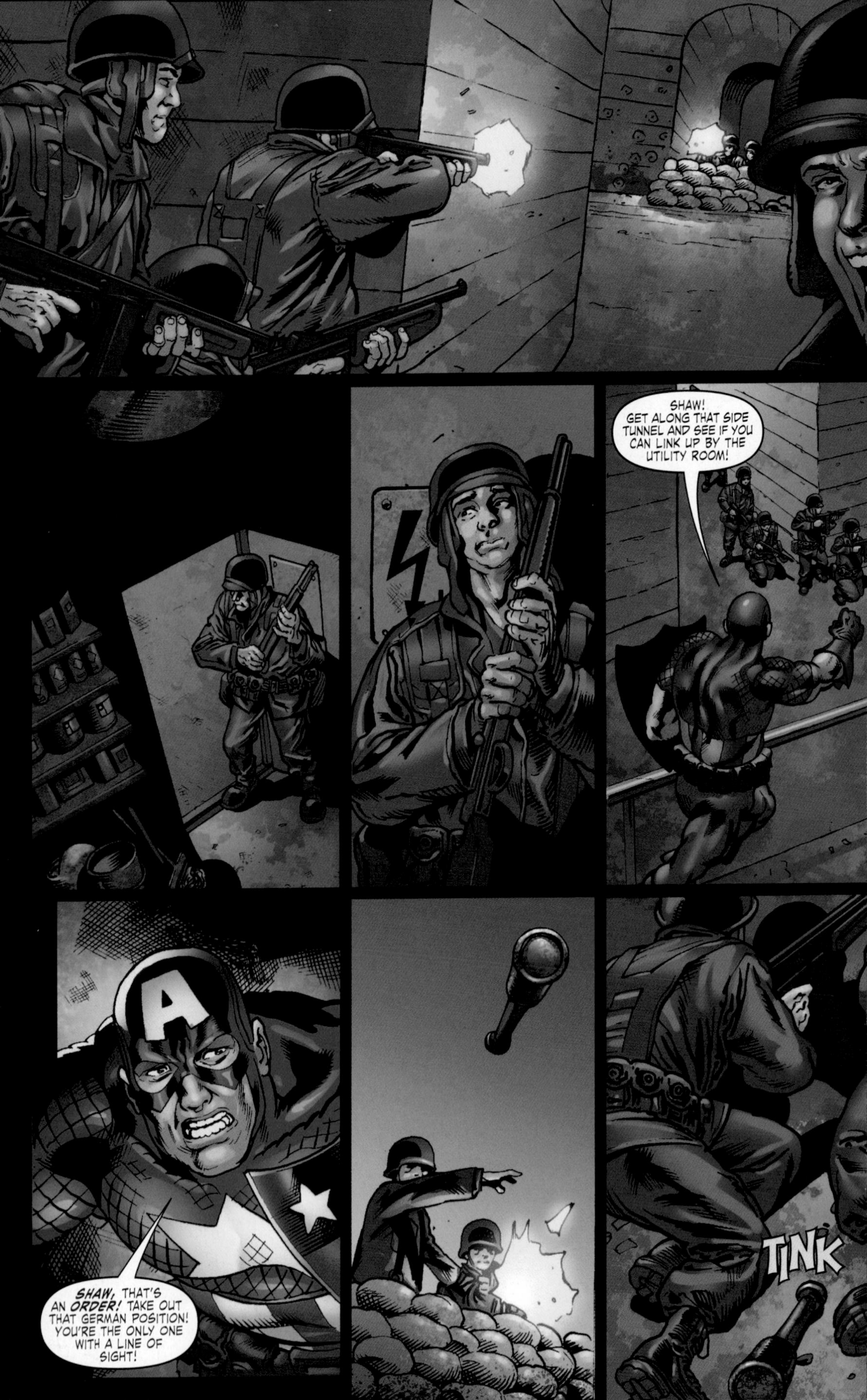
SHAW! GET ALONG THAT SIDE TUNNEL AND SEE IF YOU CAN LINK UP BY THE UTILITY ROOM!
SHAW, THAT'S AN ORDER! TAKE OUT THAT GERMAN POSITION! YOU'RE THE ONLY ONE WITH A LINE OF SIGHT!
TINK

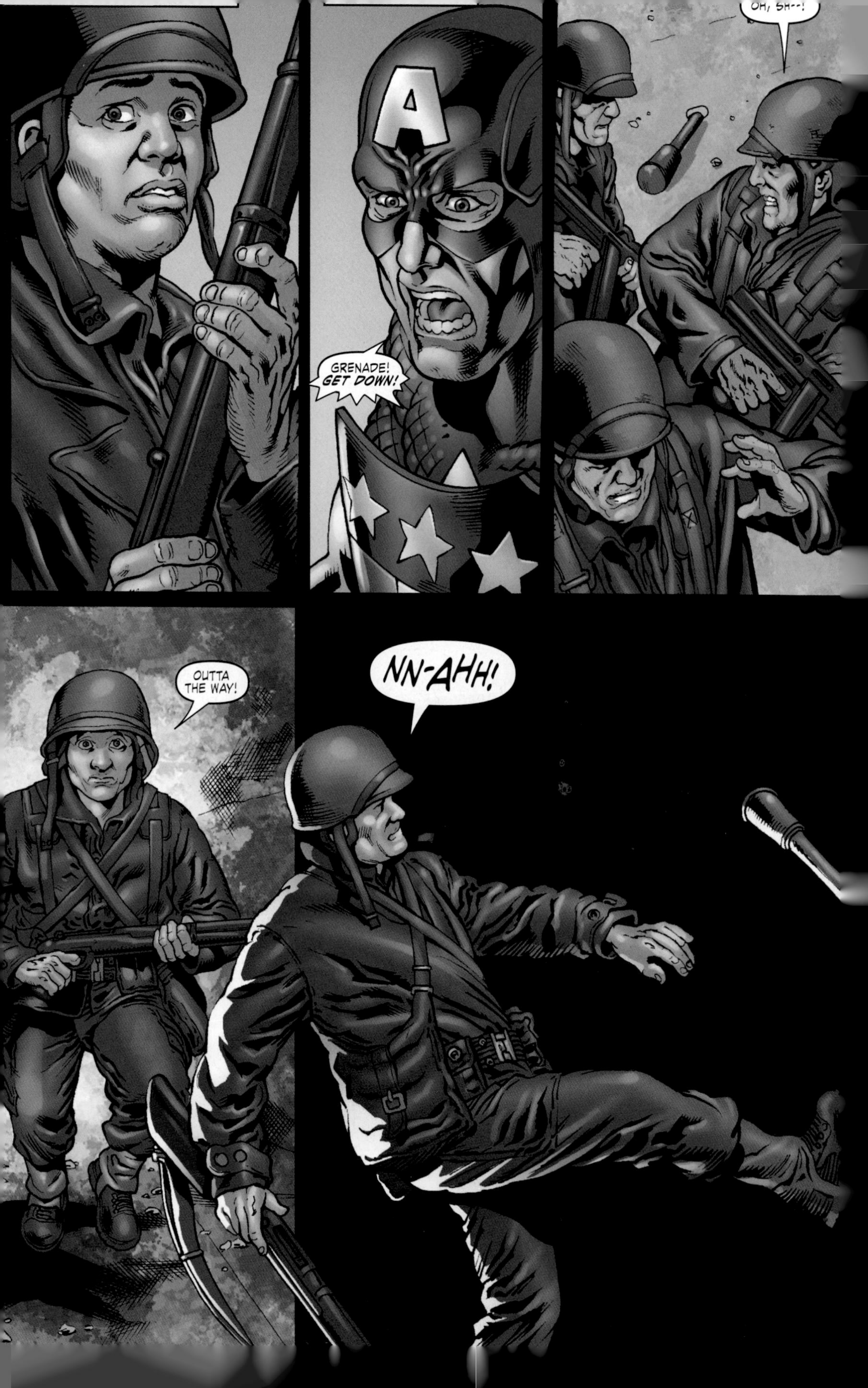
GRENADE! GET DOWN!
OH, SH--!
OUTTA THE WAY!
NN-AHH!

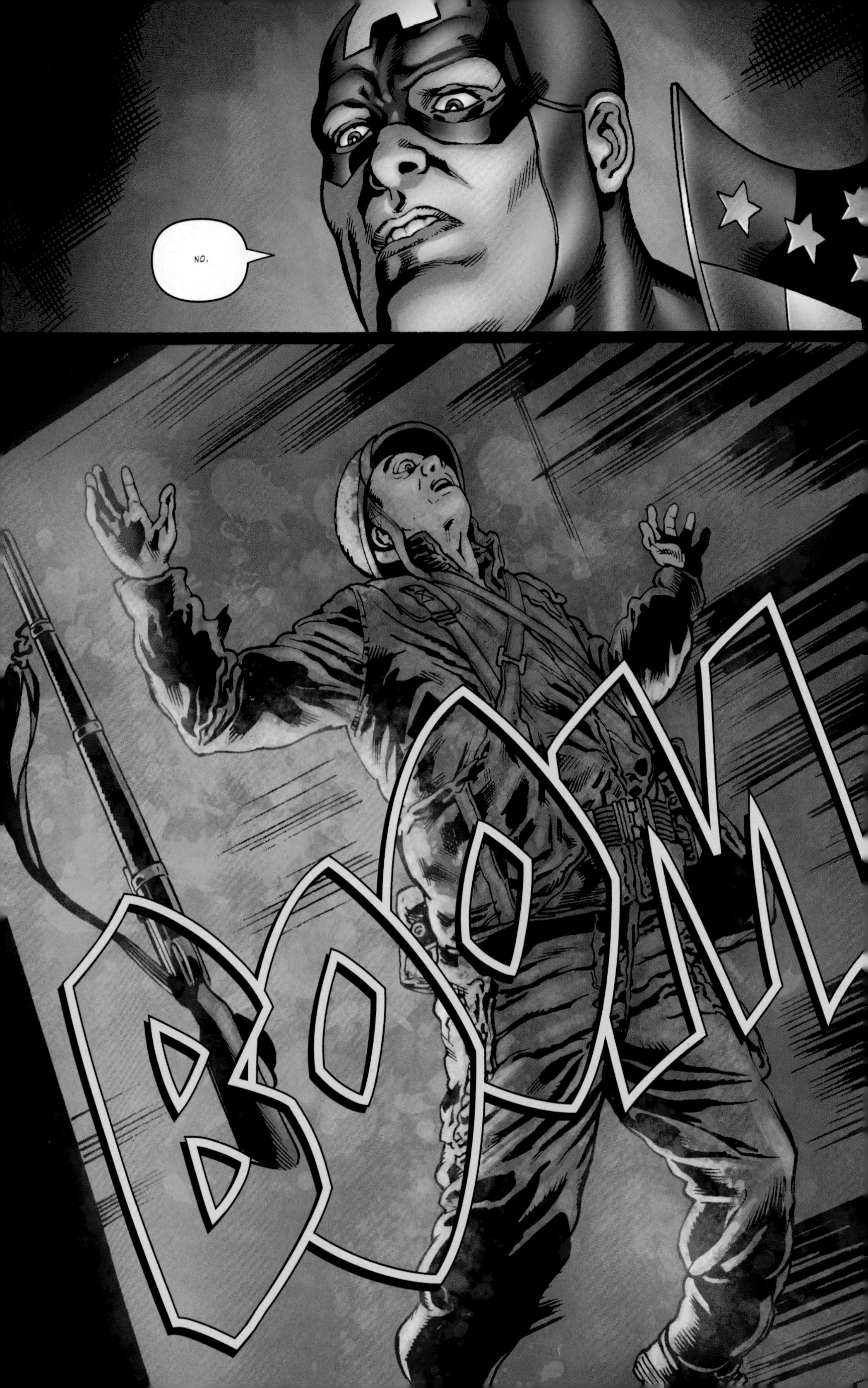
NO.
BOOM

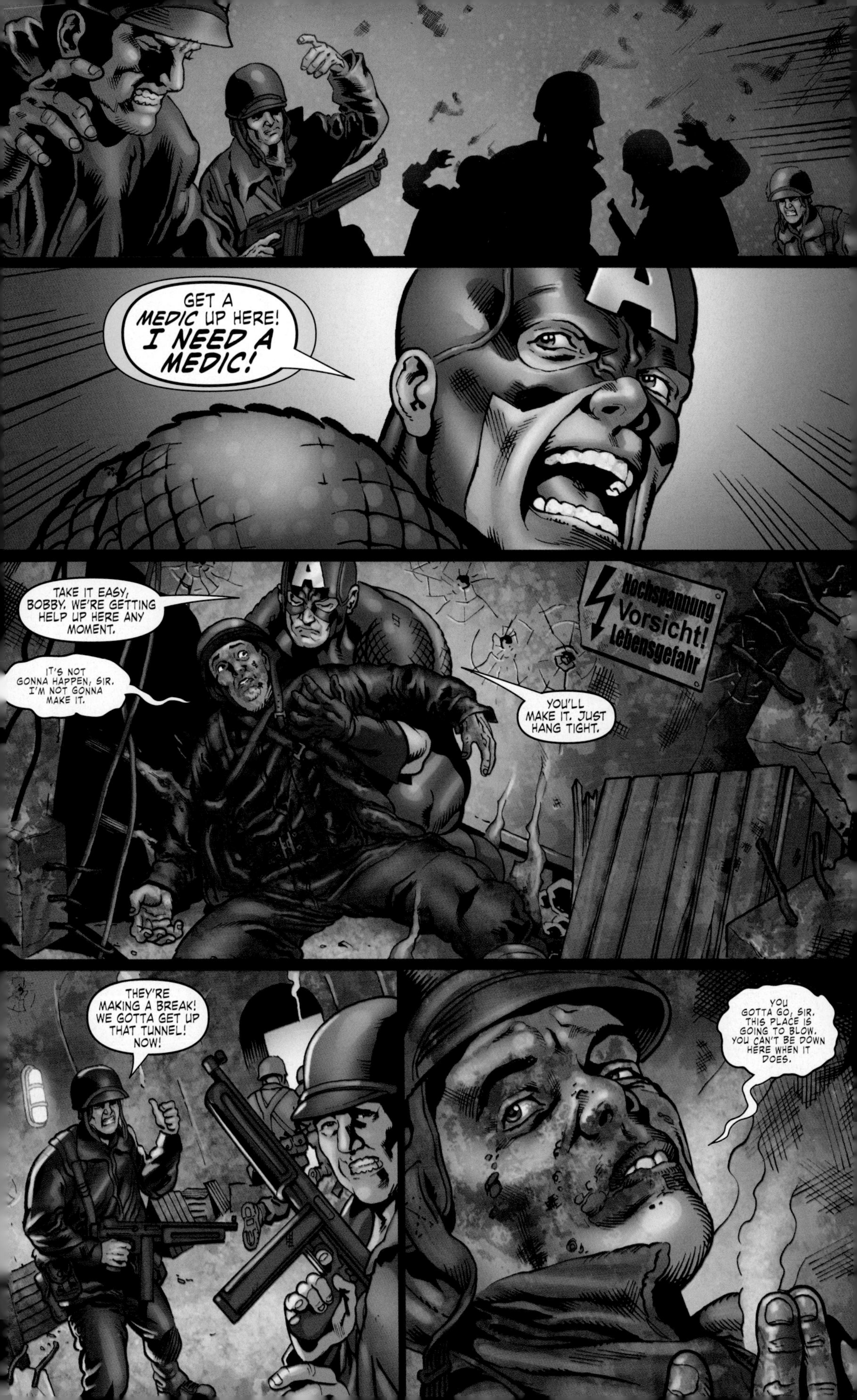
GET A MEDIC UP HERE! I NEED A MEDIC!
TAKE IT EASY, BOBBY. WE'RE GETTING HELP UP HERE ANY MOMENT.
IT'S NOT GONNA HAPPEN, SIR. I'M NOT GONNA MAKE IT.
YOU'LL MAKE IT. JUST HANG TIGHT.
Hochspannung
Vorsicht!
Lebensgefahr
THEY'RE MAKING A BREAK! WE GOTTA GET UP THAT TUNNEL! NOW!
YOU GOTTA GO, SIR. THIS PLACE IS GOING TO BLOW. YOU CAN'T BE DOWN HERE WHEN IT DOES.

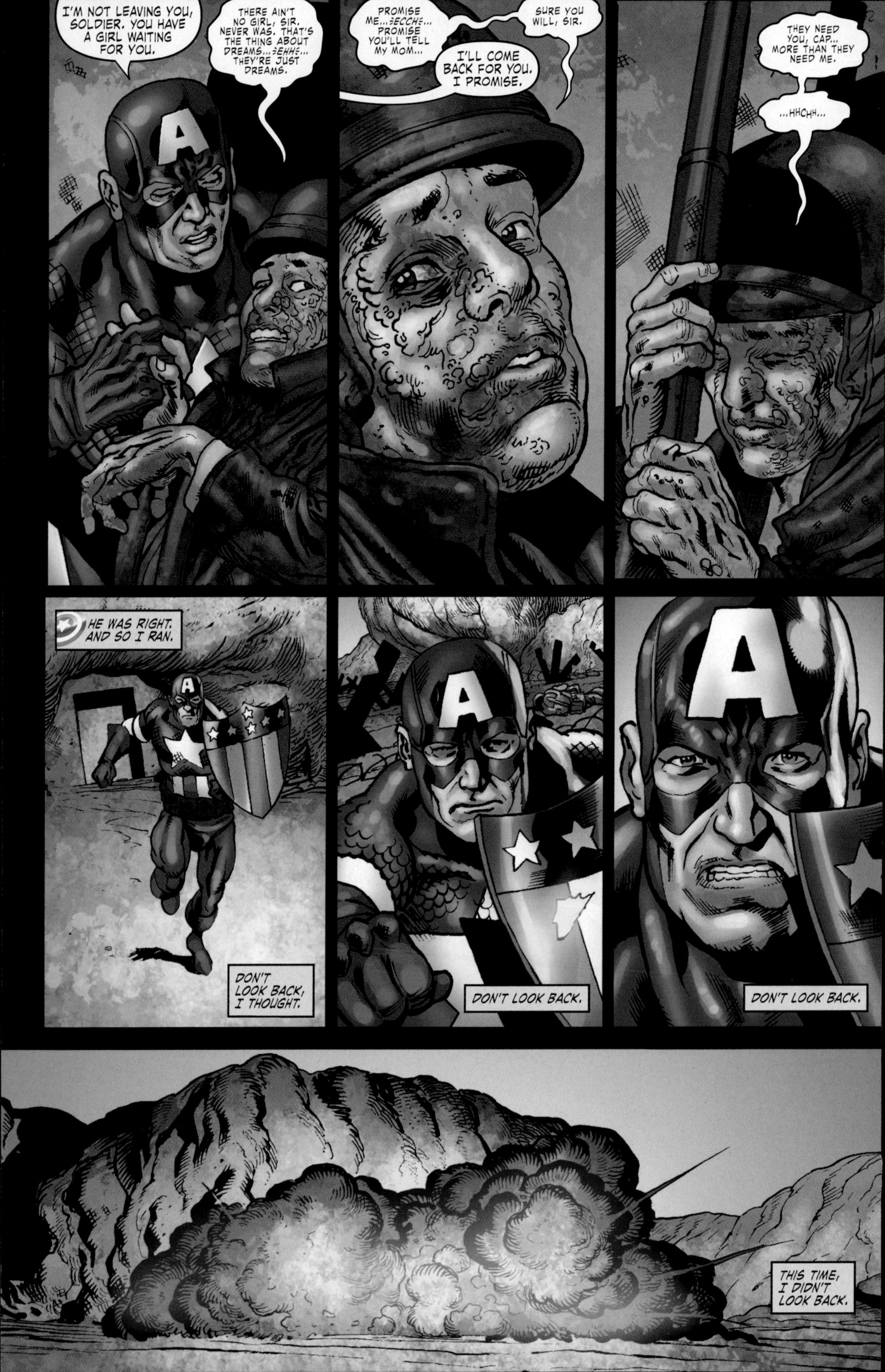
I'M NOT LEAVING YOU, SOLDIER. YOU HAVE A GIRL WAITING FOR YOU.
THERE AIN'T NO GIRL, SIR. NEVER WAS. THAT'S THE THING ABOUT DREAMS... EHHS... THEY'RE JUST DREAMS.
PROMISE ME... ECCHS... PROMISE YOU'LL TELL MY MOM...
SURE YOU WILL, SIR.
I'LL COME BACK FOR YOU. I PROMISE.
THEY NEED YOU, CAP... MORE THAN THEY NEED ME.
...HHCHH...
HE WAS RIGHT. AND SO I RAN.
DON'T LOOK BACK, I THOUGHT.
DON'T LOOK BACK.
DON'T LOOK BACK.
THIS TIME, I DIDN'T LOOK BACK.

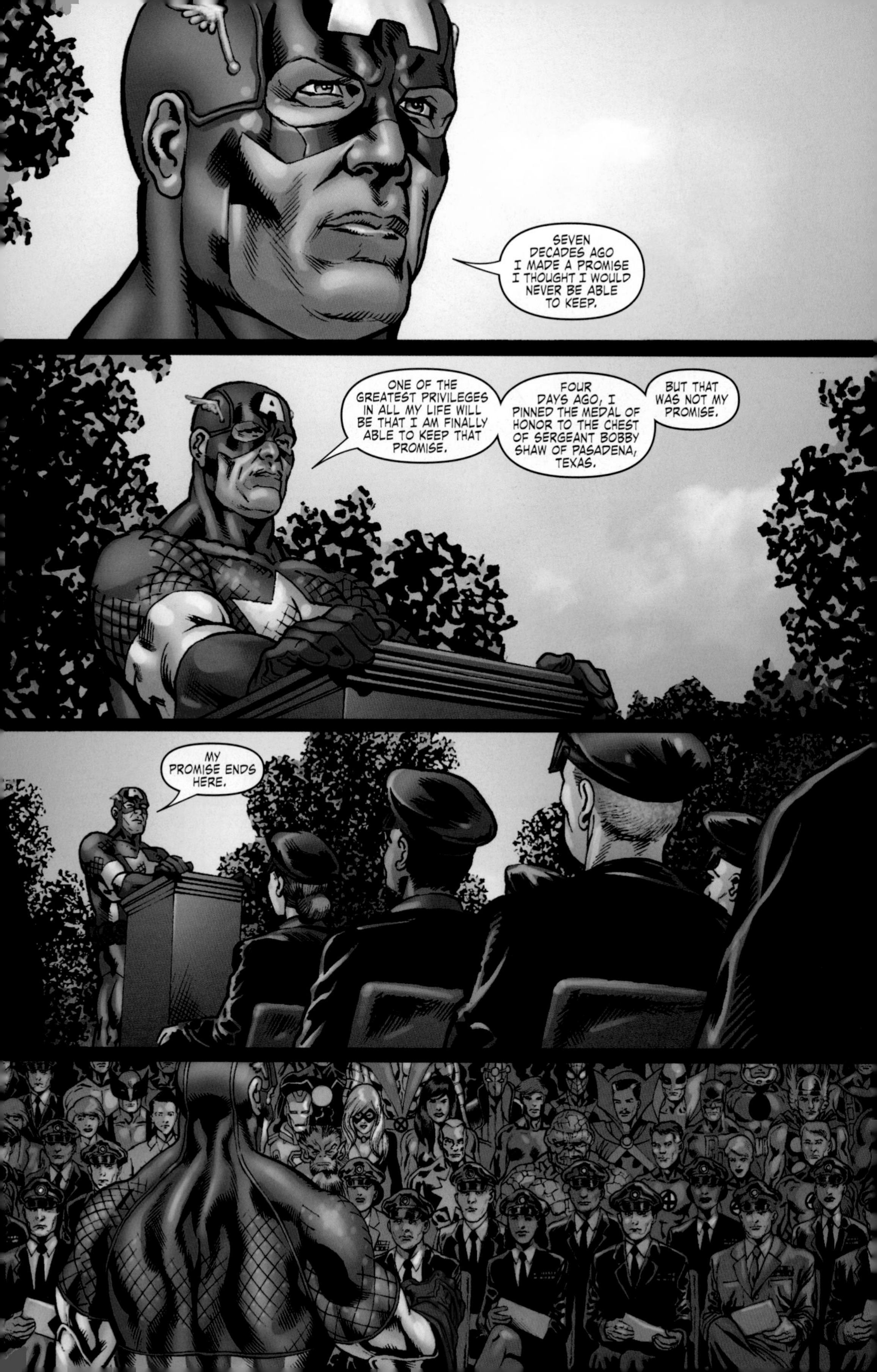
SEVEN DECADES AGO I MADE A PROMISE I THOUGHT I WOULD NEVER BE ABLE TO KEEP.
ONE OF THE GREATEST PRIVILEGES IN ALL MY LIFE WILL BE THAT I AM FINALLY ABLE TO KEEP THAT PROMISE.
FOUR DAYS AGO, I PINNED THE MEDAL OF HONOR TO THE CHEST OF SERGEANT BOBBY SHAW OF PASADENA, TEXAS.
BUT THAT WAS NOT MY PROMISE.
MY PROMISE ENDS HERE.

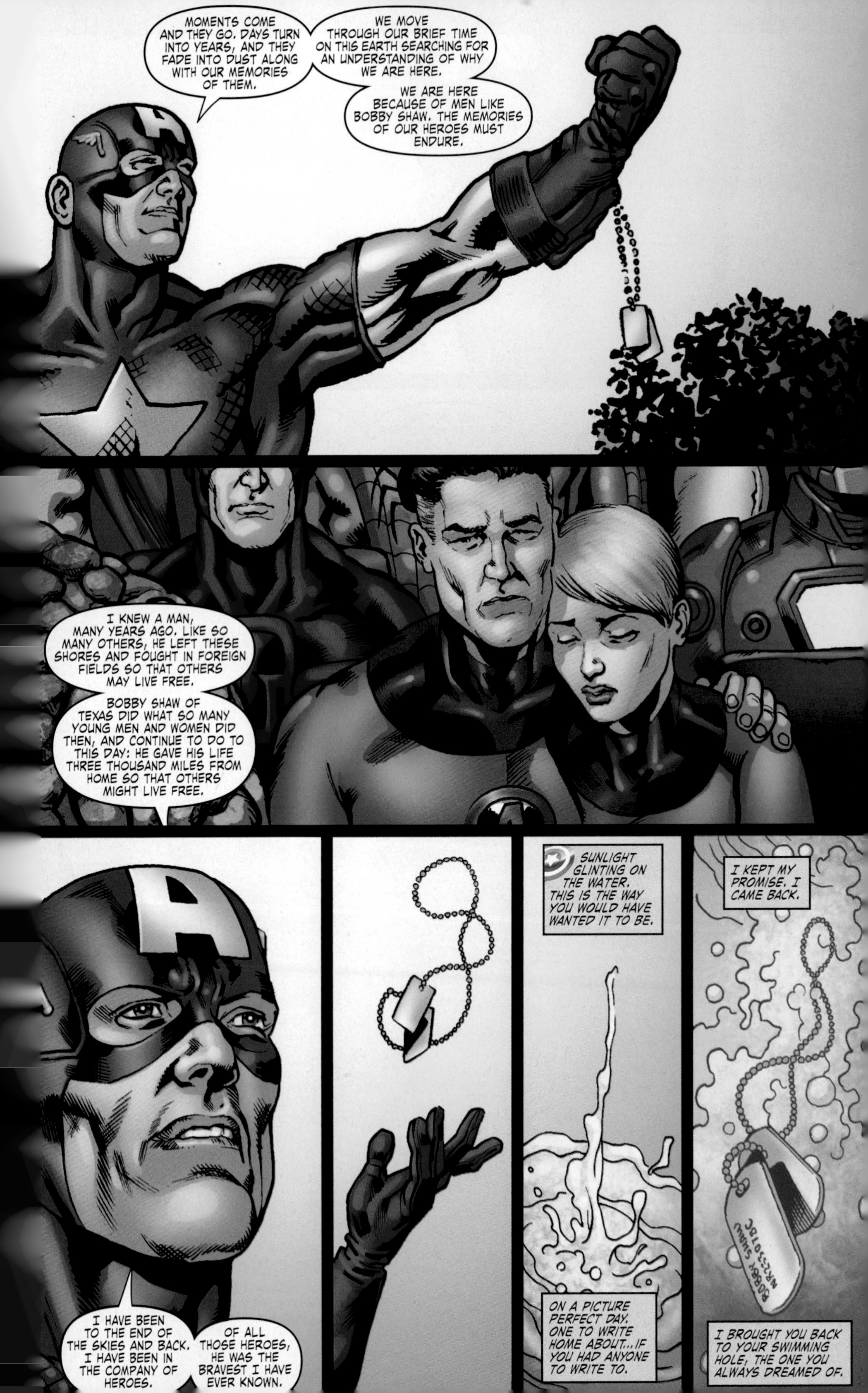
MOMENTS COME AND THEY GO. DAYS TURN INTO YEARS, AND THEY FADE INTO DUST ALONG WITH OUR MEMORIES OF THEM.
WE MOVE THROUGH OUR BRIEF TIME ON THIS EARTH SEARCHING FOR AN UNDERSTANDING OF WHY WE ARE HERE.
WE ARE HERE BECAUSE OF MEN LIKE BOBBY SHAW. THE MEMORIES OF OUR HEROES MUST ENDURE.
I KNEW A MAN, MANY YEARS AGO. LIKE SO MANY OTHERS, HE LEFT THESE SHORES AND FOUGHT IN FOREIGN FIELDS SO THAT OTHERS MAY LIVE FREE.
BOBBY SHAW OF TEXAS DID WHAT SO MANY YOUNG MEN AND WOMEN DID THEN, AND CONTINUE TO DO TO THIS DAY: HE GAVE HIS LIFE THREE THOUSAND MILES FROM HOME SO THAT OTHERS MIGHT LIVE FREE.
I HAVE BEEN TO THE END OF THE SKIES AND BACK. I HAVE BEEN IN THE COMPANY OF HEROES.
OF ALL THOSE HEROES, HE WAS THE BRAVEST I HAVE EVER KNOWN.
SUNLIGHT GLINTING ON THE WATER. THIS IS THE WAY YOU WOULD HAVE WANTED IT TO BE.
ON A PICTURE PERFECT DAY. ONE TO WRITE HOME ABOUT...IF YOU HAD ANYONE TO WRITE TO.
I KEPT MY PROMISE. I CAME BACK.
I BROUGHT YOU BACK TO YOUR SWIMMING HOLE, THE ONE YOU ALWAYS DREAMED OF.

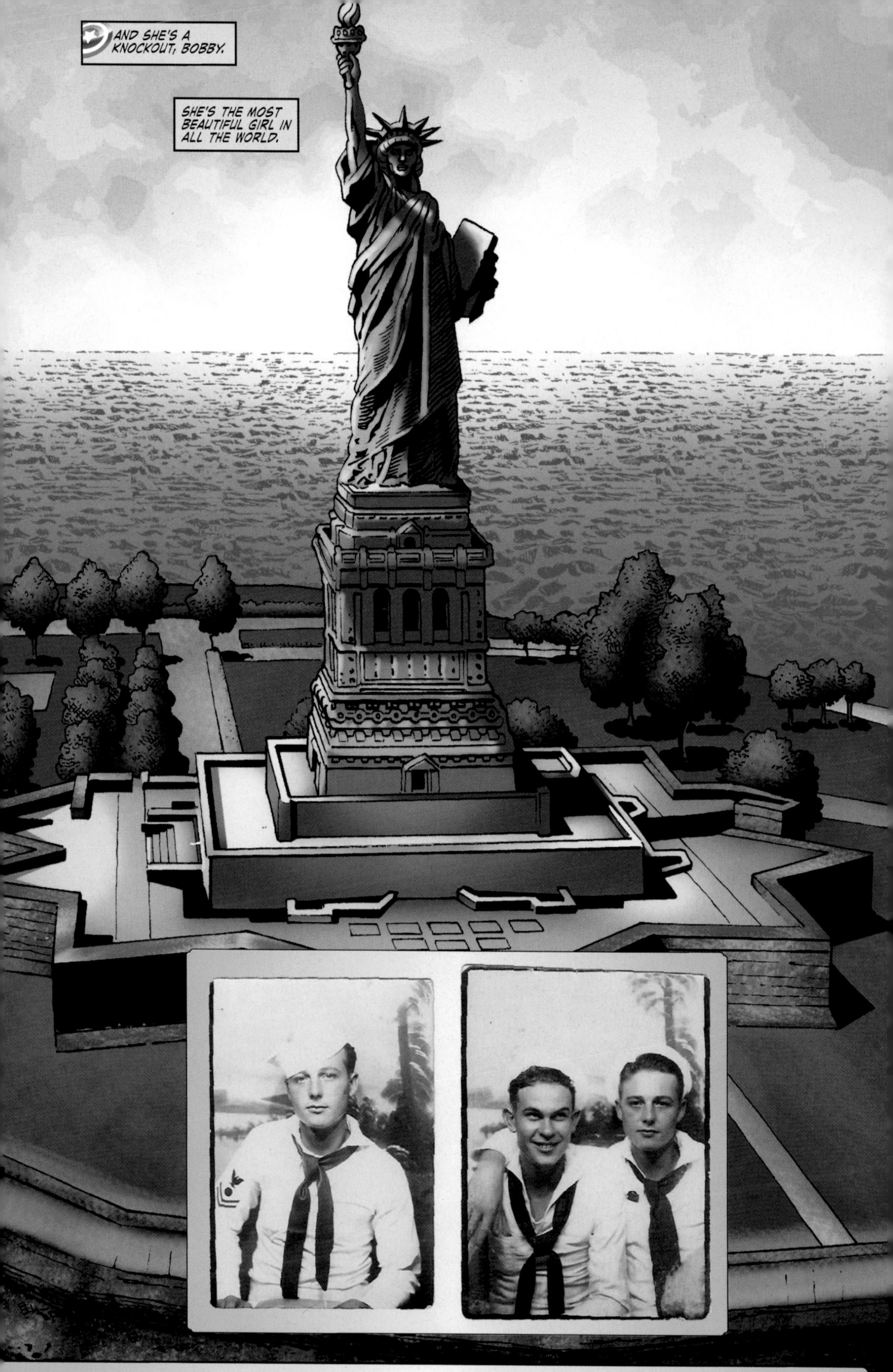
AND SHE'S A KNOCKOUT, BOBBY.
SHE'S THE MOST BEAUTIFUL GIRL IN ALL THE WORLD.

Dedicated with respect and admiration to my friend, J. Douglas Huggins (r) – Electrician's Mate of the USS St. Louis – and to his childhood friend, Musician Second Class Bobby Shaw of Pasadena, Texas (l) who perished on the USS Arizona on December 7th, 1941.

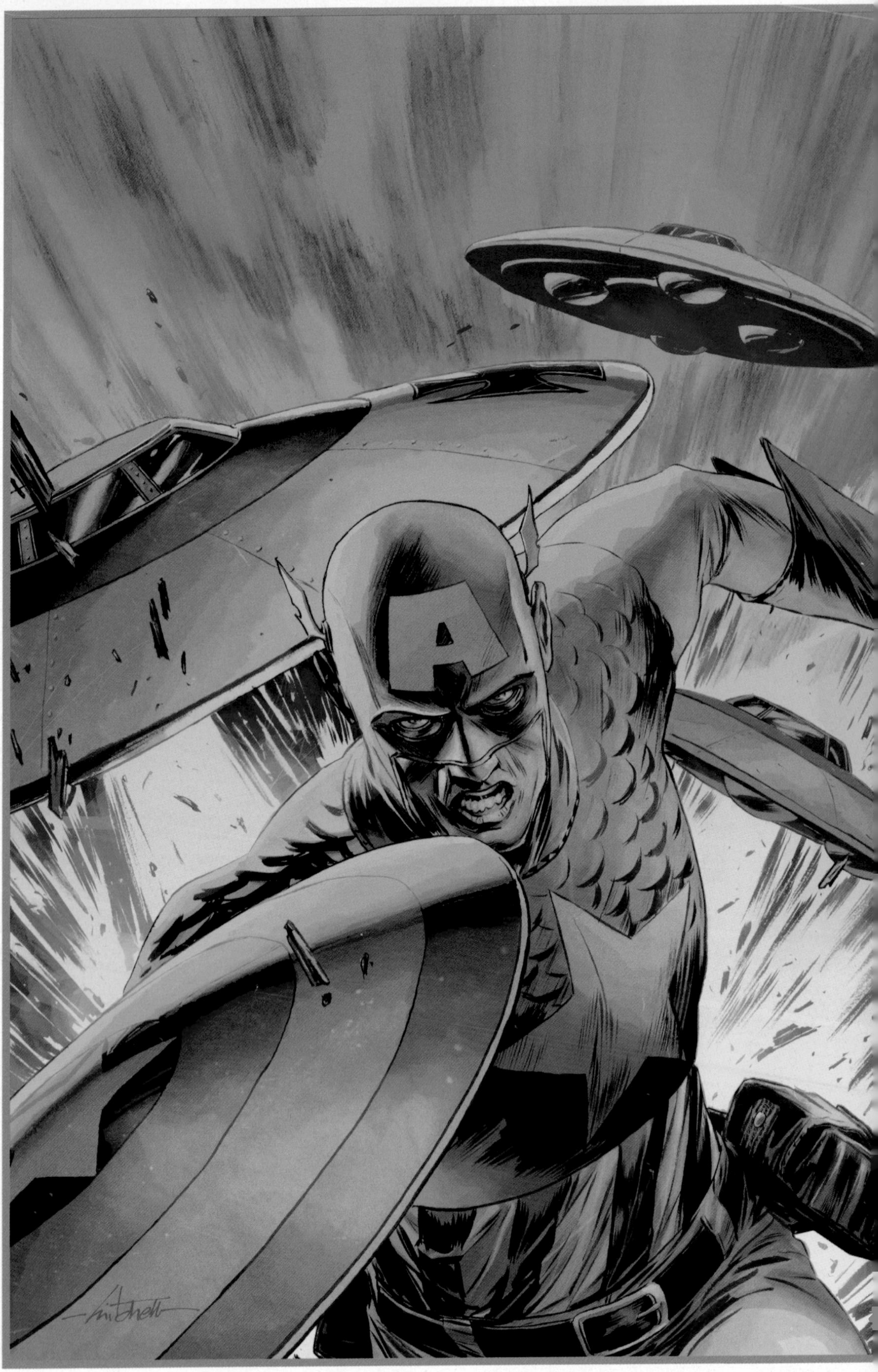

POLAND-- 1944.

THIS WHOLE MISSION SMELLS LIKE A WILD GOOSE CHASE.

...WO DAYS AGO, I'M HAULED OFF ...HE FRONT LINES TO MEET WITH ...OME BOOBOCRATS FROM THE ...FFICE OF STRATEGIC SERVICES.

THEY GIVE ME THE RUB ON A SECRET NAZI PROGRAM IN SOUTHERN POLAND...

SEEMS THE RATZIES HAVE LICKED GRAVITY. THE SCIENTIST IN CHARGE, ONE DOKTOR ERNST FLEISCHER, WANTS TO DEFECT. SAYS HE'LL BUILD US A WHOLE SQUADRON OF FOO-FIGHTERS...

...YEAH, RIGHT.

YOU SAY SOMETHING, CAP?

NO, NOTHING...

BET OLD FLEISCHER'S GOT A BRIDGE IN BROOKLYN TO SELL, TOO. AND THE BOYS IN O.S.S. WOULD PROBABLY BUY *TWO* OF THEM.

SO NOW I'M SUPPOSED TO RENDEZVOUS WITH LIOR ESHEL, AN AGENT WITH THE POLISH RESISTANCE.

WHAT KIND OF A NAME IS "LIOR," ANYWAY?

HUH?

FORGET IT...

FROM THERE, I INFILTR... THE PROJECT BASE--SO... CONVERTED MINE--EXT... FLEISCHER, THEN BLOW... PLACE TO HIGH HEAVEN.

JEEZO, WHENEVER YOU PUT "TOP SECRET" AND "HITLER" TOGETHER, YOU ALWAYS GET SOMETHING RUMMY...

FIVE MINUTES OUT, CAP!

...LAST TIME IT WAS NAZI WEREWOLVES. TIME BEFORE THAT, A HUGE FRIGGIN' ROBOT...

GUY MUST READ *WAY* TOO MANY FUNNY BOOKS...

WHAT'S THAT, CAP?

NOTHING, SOLDIER. I'M JUST TALKING TO MYSELF--

NO! I MEAN...

...WHAT'S THAT?!

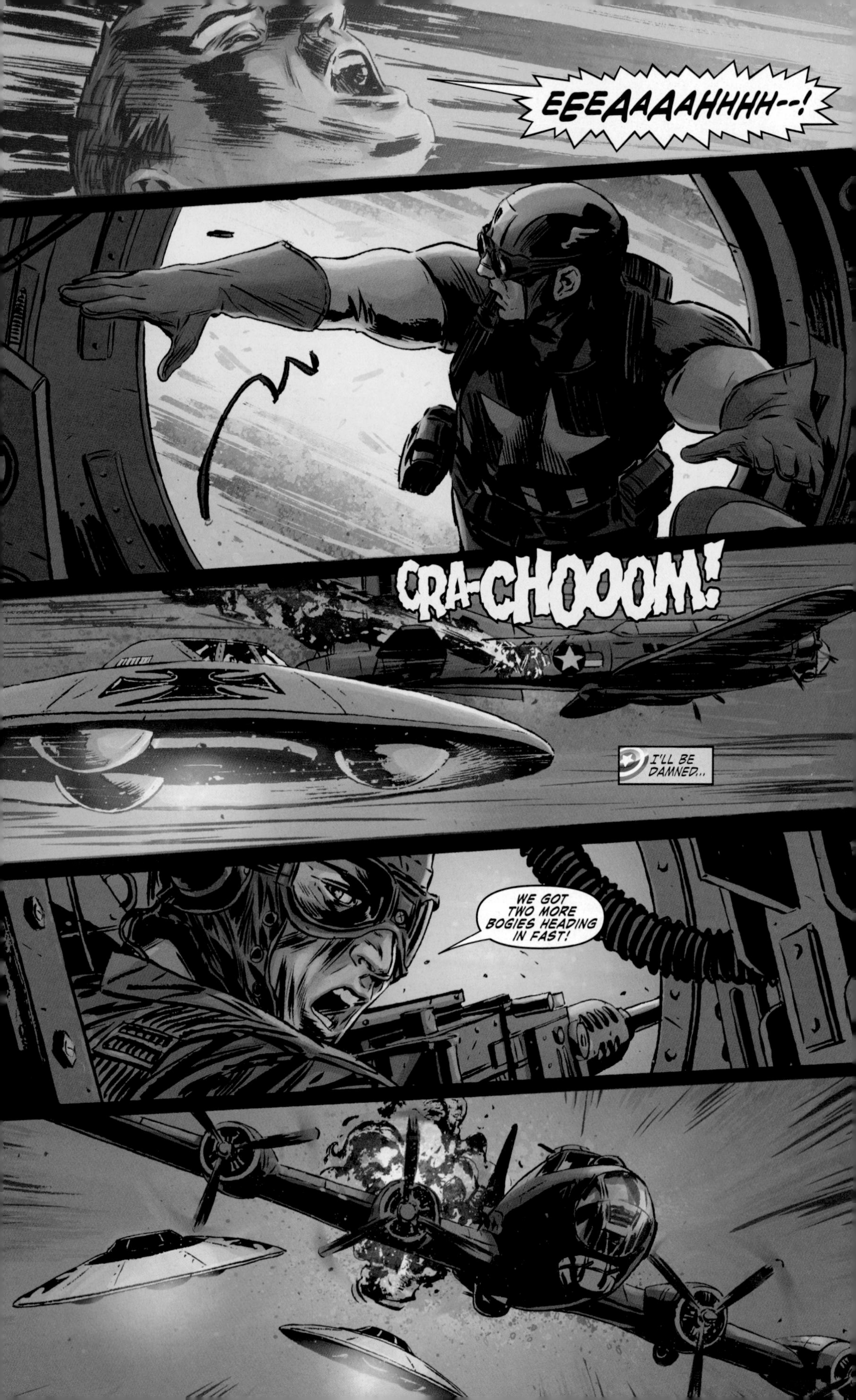
EEEAAAAHHHH--!
CRA-CHOOOM!
I'LL BE DAMNED...
WE GOT TWO MORE BOGIES HEADING IN FAST!

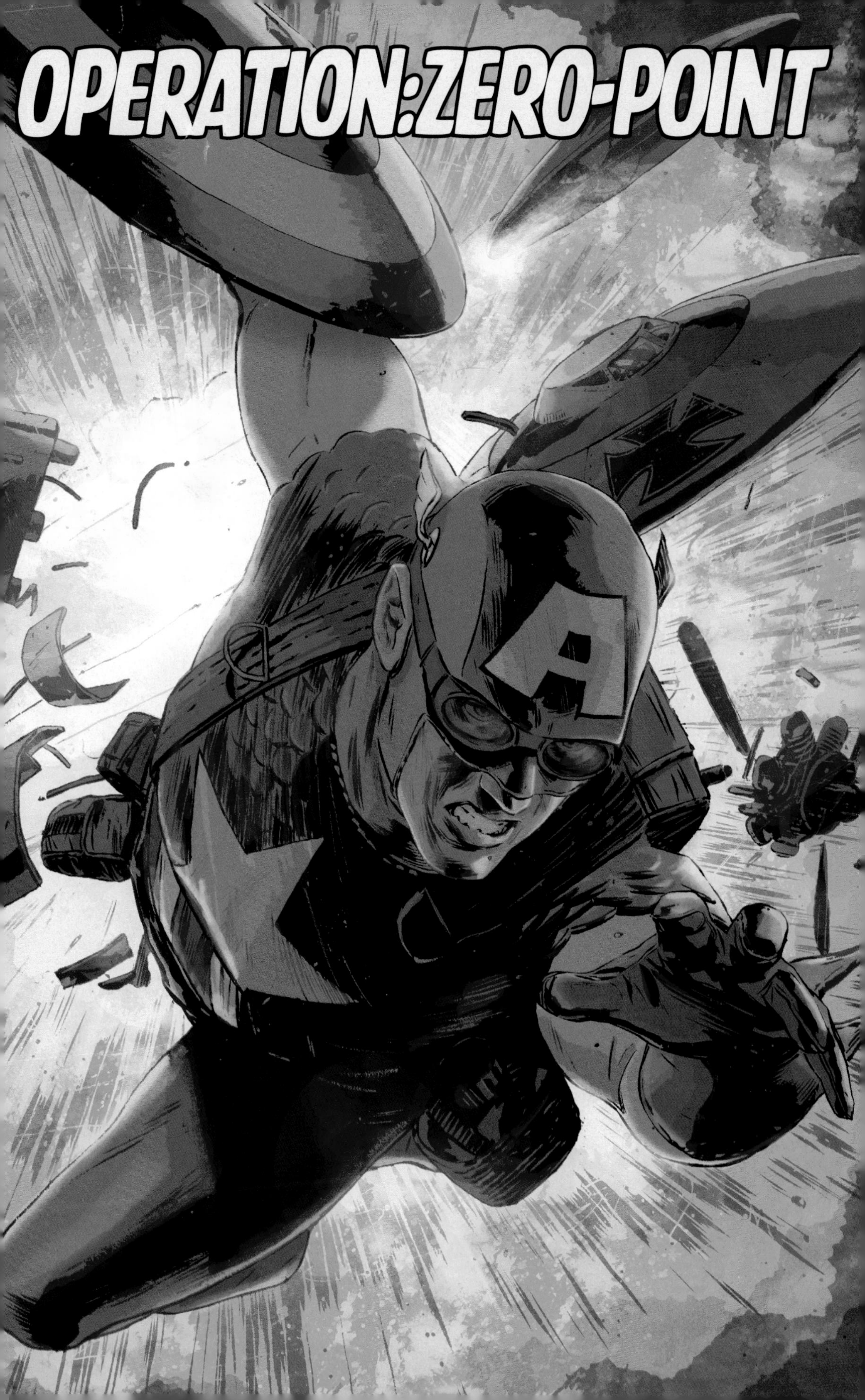
OPERATION: ZERO-POINT

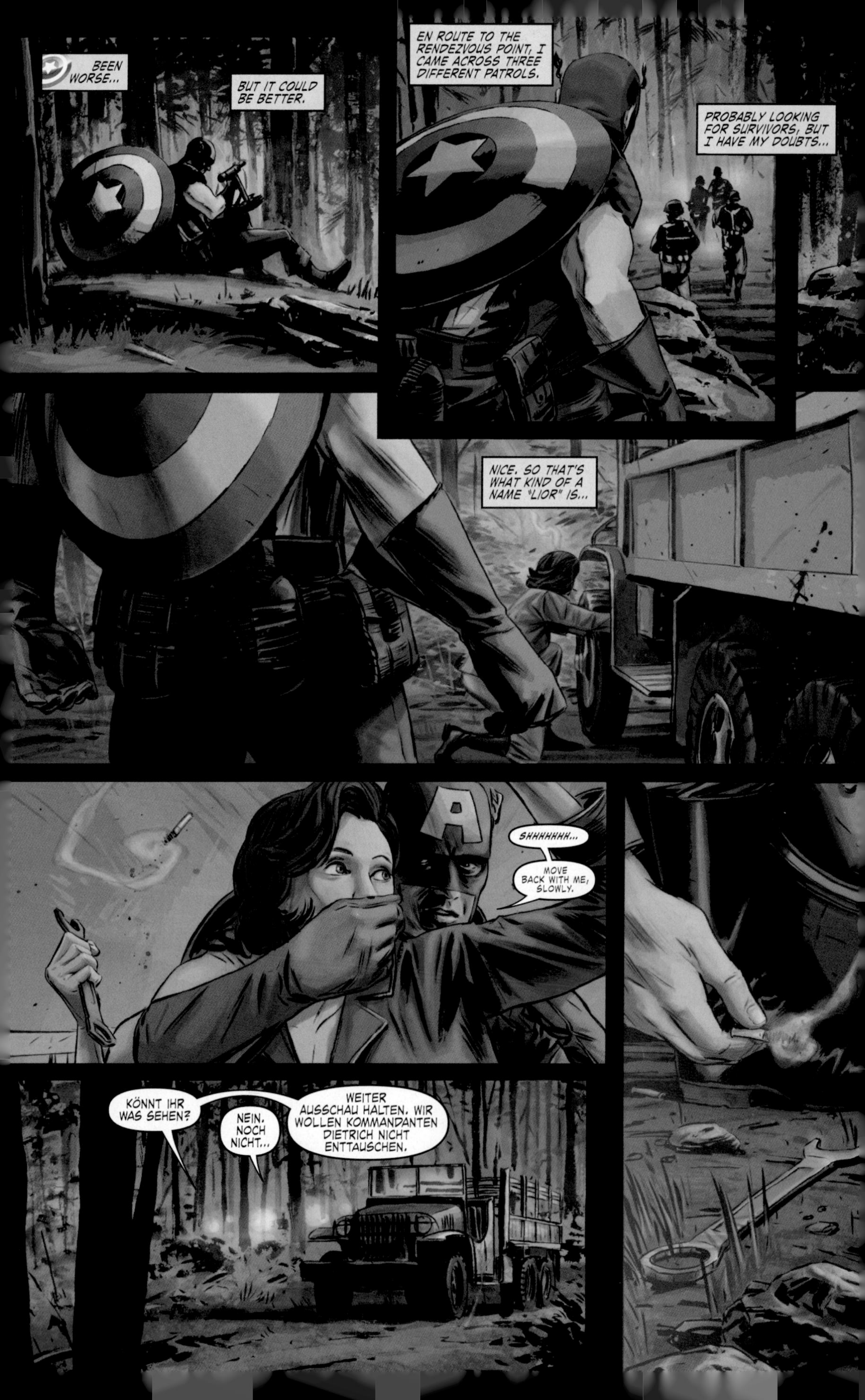
BEEN WORSE...
BUT IT COULD BE BETTER.
EN ROUTE TO THE RENDEZVOUS POINT, I CAME ACROSS THREE DIFFERENT PATROLS.
PROBABLY LOOKING FOR SURVIVORS, BUT I HAVE MY DOUBTS...
NICE. SO THAT'S WHAT KIND OF A NAME "LIOR" IS...
SHHHHHHH...
MOVE BACK WITH ME, SLOWLY.
KÖNNT IHR WAS SEHEN?
NEIN. NOCH NICHT...
WEITER AUSSCHAU HALTEN. WIR WOLLEN KOMMANDANTEN DIETRICH NICHT ENTTAUSCHEN.

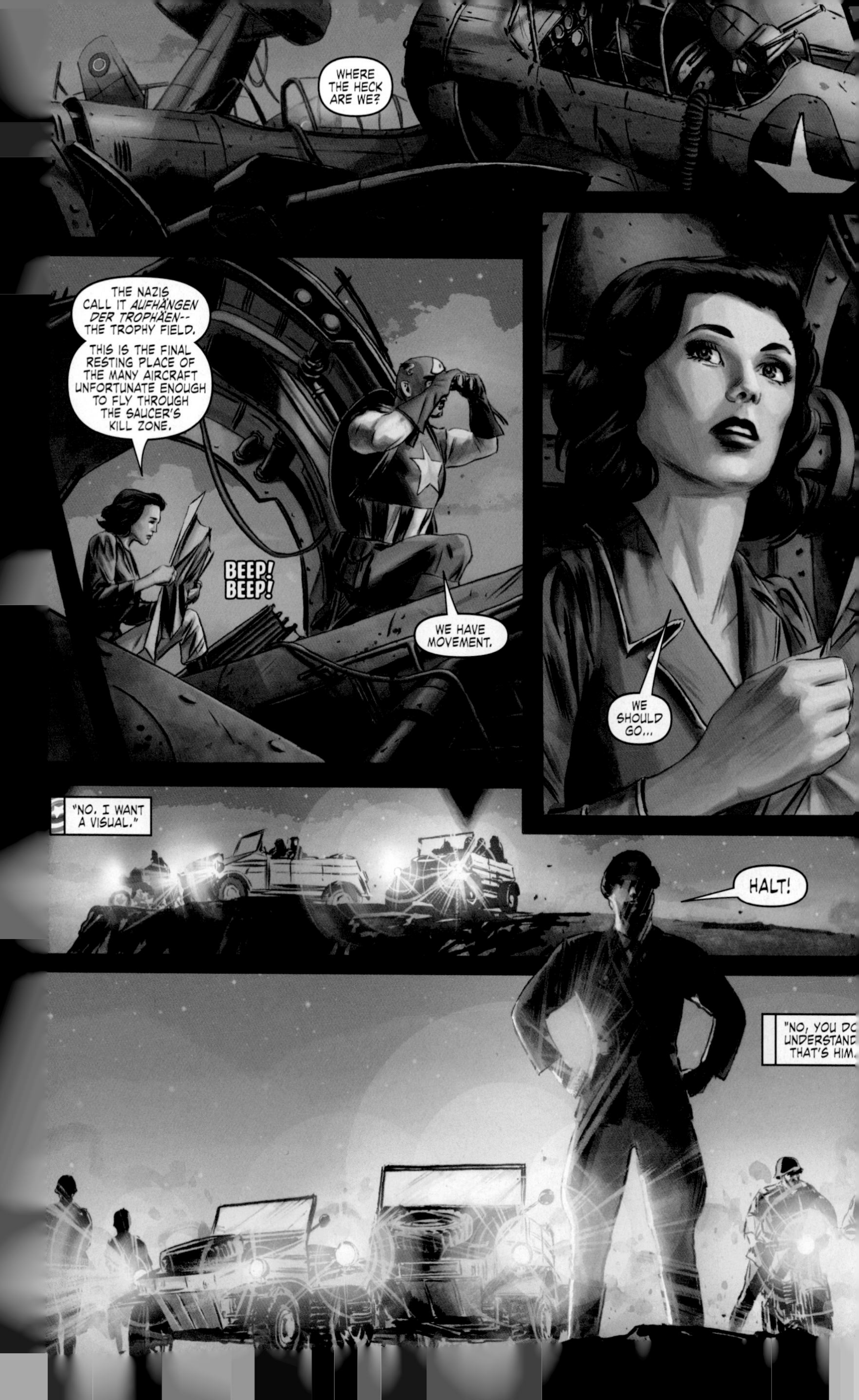
WHERE THE HECK ARE WE?
THE NAZIS CALL IT *AUFHÄNGEN DER TROPHÄEN*-- THE TROPHY FIELD.
THIS IS THE FINAL RESTING PLACE OF THE MANY AIRCRAFT UNFORTUNATE ENOUGH TO FLY THROUGH THE SAUCER'S KILL ZONE.
BEEP! BEEP!
WE HAVE MOVEMENT.
WE SHOULD GO...
"NO. I WANT A VISUAL."
HALT!
"NO, YOU DO UNDERSTAND THAT'S HIM.

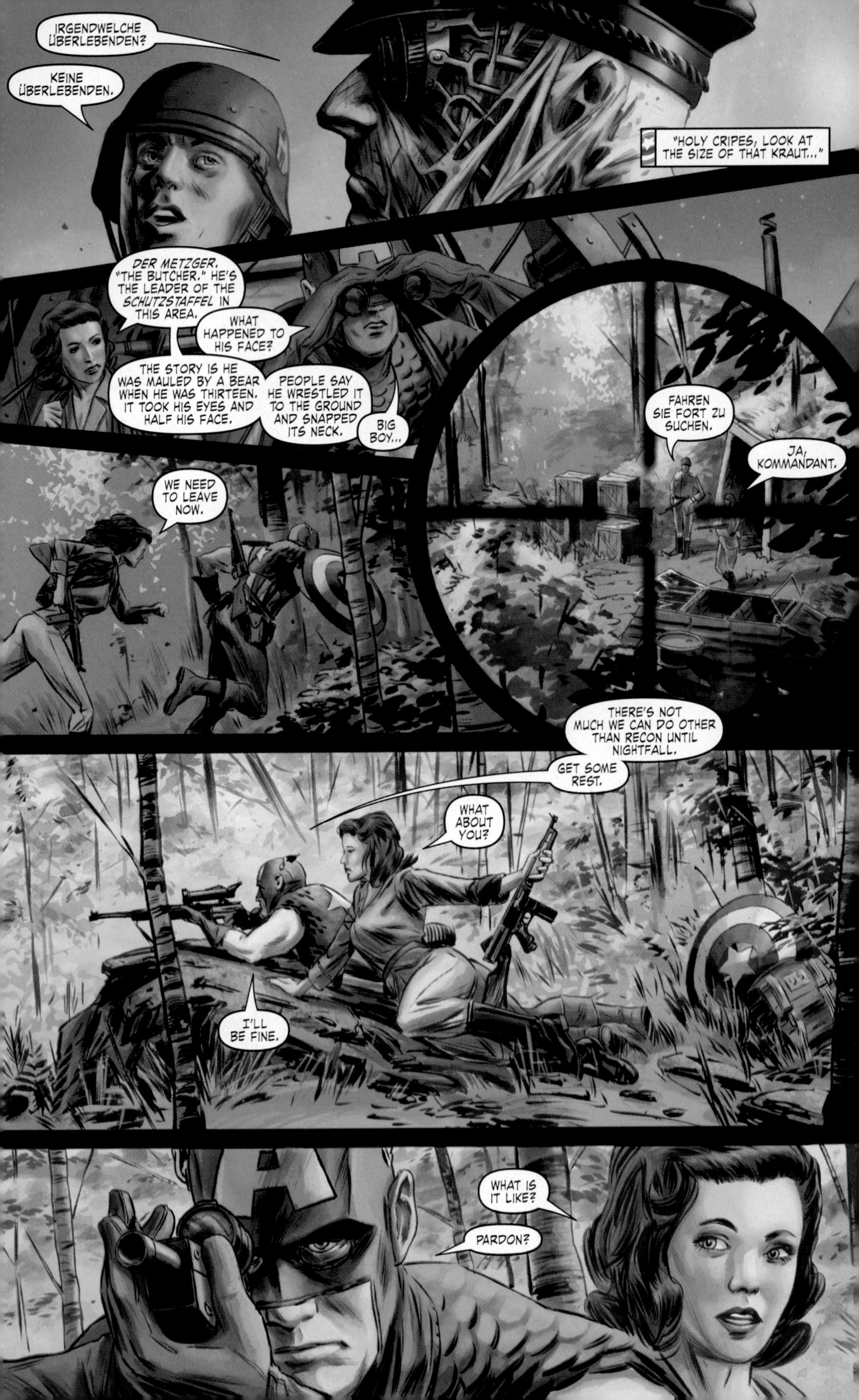
IRGENDWELCHE ÜBERLEBENDEN?
KEINE ÜBERLEBENDEN.
"HOLY CRIPES, LOOK AT THE SIZE OF THAT KRAUT..."
DER METZGER. "THE BUTCHER." HE'S THE LEADER OF THE *SCHUTZSTAFFEL* IN THIS AREA.
WHAT HAPPENED TO HIS FACE?
THE STORY IS HE WAS MAULED BY A BEAR WHEN HE WAS THIRTEEN. IT TOOK HIS EYES AND HALF HIS FACE.
PEOPLE SAY HE WRESTLED IT TO THE GROUND AND SNAPPED ITS NECK.
BIG BOY...
FAHREN SIE FORT ZU SUCHEN.
JA, KOMMANDANT.
WE NEED TO LEAVE NOW.
THERE'S NOT MUCH WE CAN DO OTHER THAN RECON UNTIL NIGHTFALL.
GET SOME REST.
WHAT ABOUT YOU?
I'LL BE FINE.
WHAT IS IT LIKE?
PARDON?

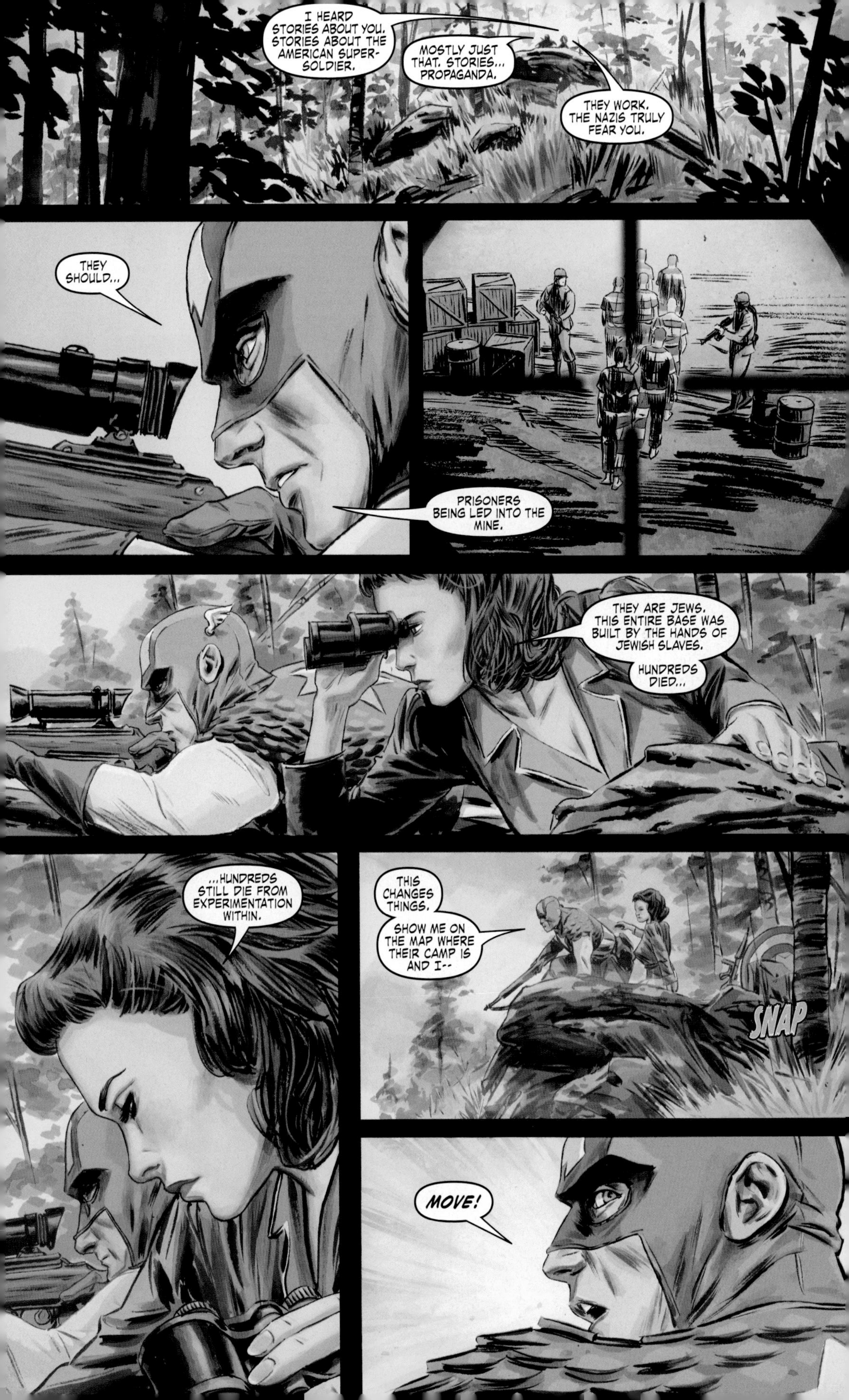
I HEARD STORIES ABOUT YOU. STORIES ABOUT THE AMERICAN SUPER-SOLDIER.
MOSTLY JUST THAT. STORIES... PROPAGANDA.
THEY WORK. THE NAZIS TRULY FEAR YOU.
THEY SHOULD...
PRISONERS BEING LED INTO THE MINE.
THEY ARE JEWS. THIS ENTIRE BASE WAS BUILT BY THE HANDS OF JEWISH SLAVES.
HUNDREDS DIED...
...HUNDREDS STILL DIE FROM EXPERIMENTATION WITHIN.
THIS CHANGES THINGS.
SHOW ME ON THE MAP WHERE THEIR CAMP IS AND I--
SNAP
MOVE!

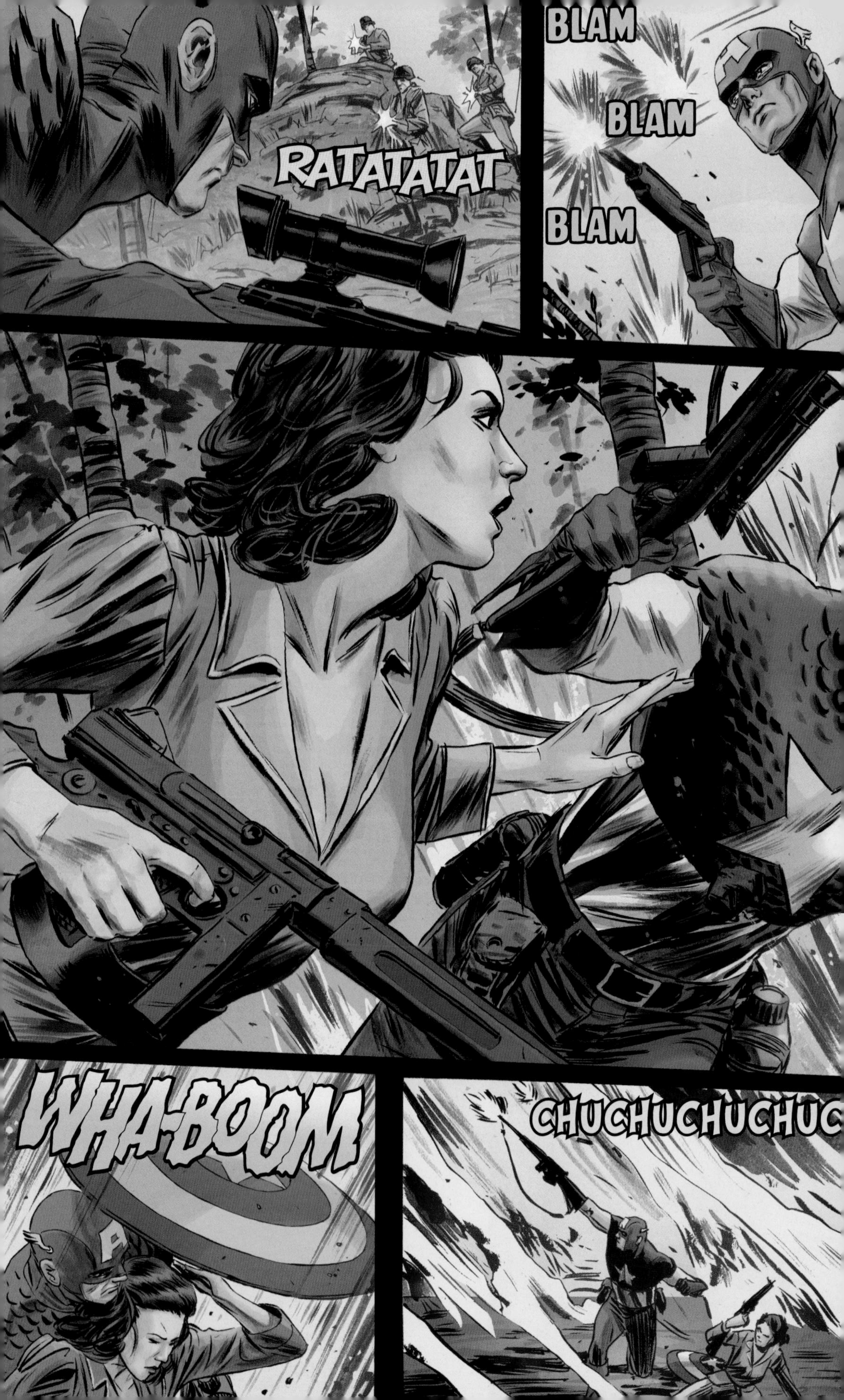
RATATATAT
BLAM
BLAM
BLAM
WHA-BOOM
CHUCHUCHUCHUC

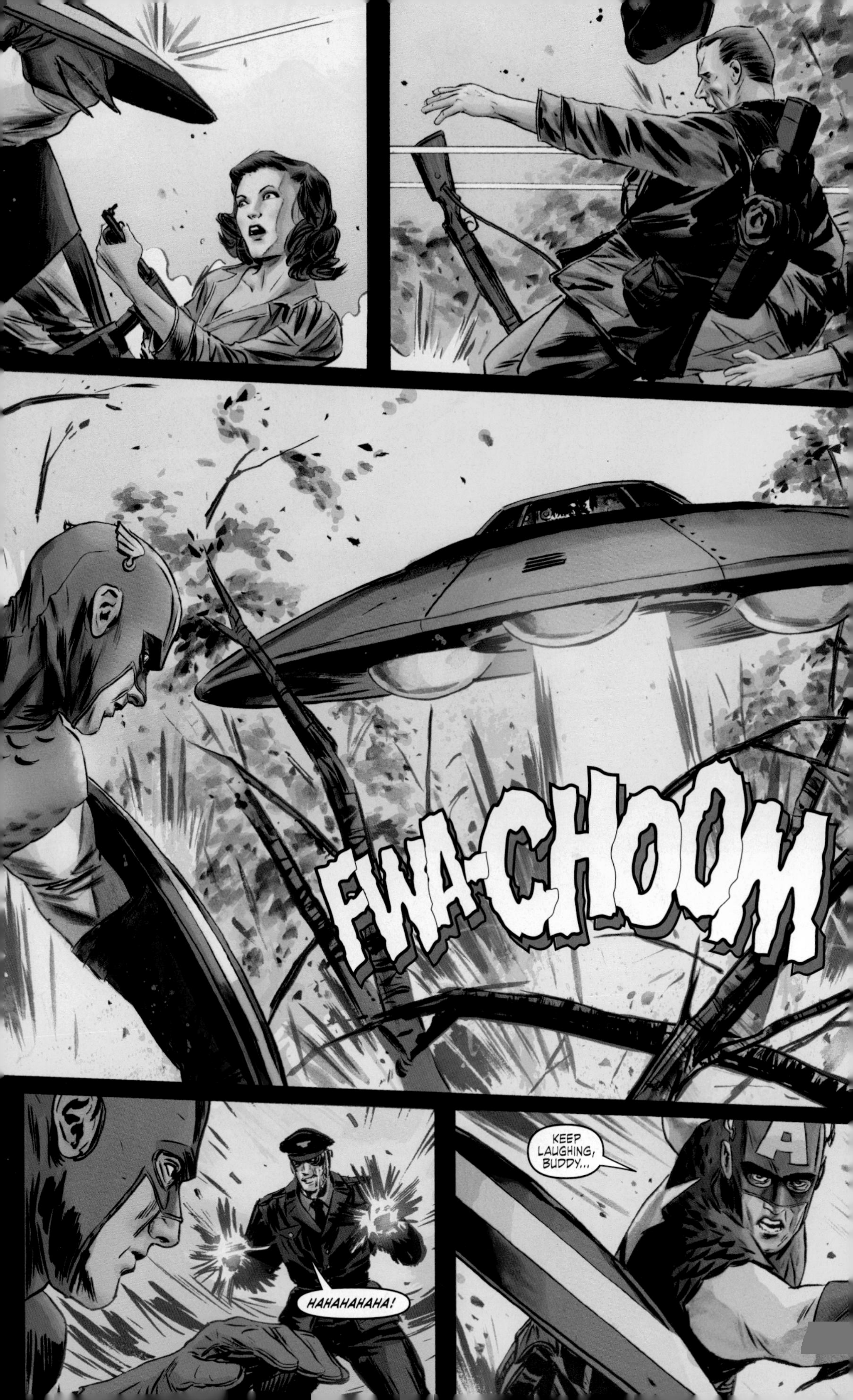
FWA-CHOOM
HAHAHAHAHA!
KEEP LAUGHING, BUDDY...

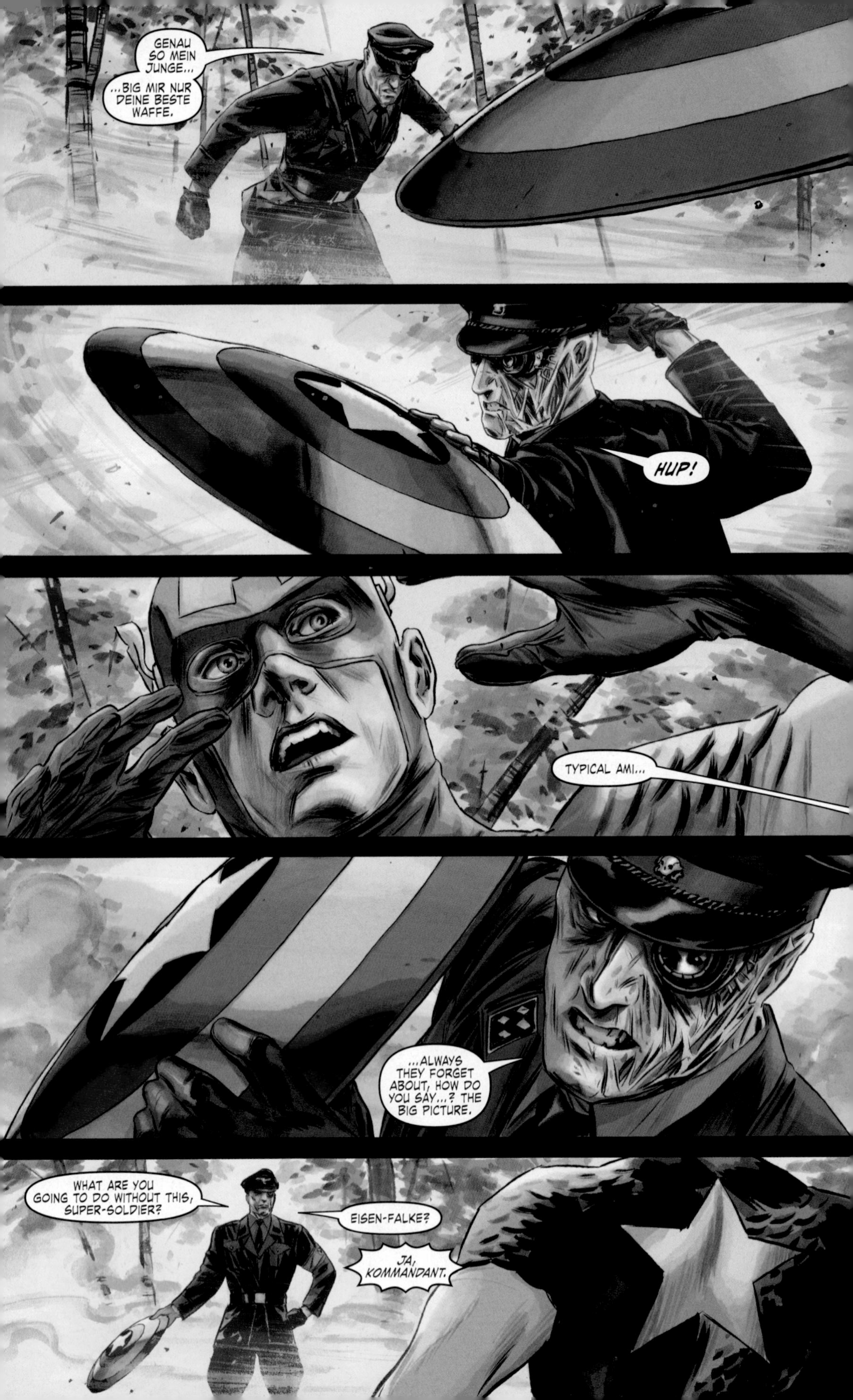
GENAU SO MEIN JUNGE...
...BIG MIR NUR DEINE BESTE WAFFE.
HUP!
TYPICAL AMI...
...ALWAYS THEY FORGET ABOUT, HOW DO YOU SAY...? THE BIG PICTURE.
WHAT ARE YOU GOING TO DO WITHOUT THIS, SUPER-SOLDIER?
EISEN-FALKE?
JA, KOMMANDANT.

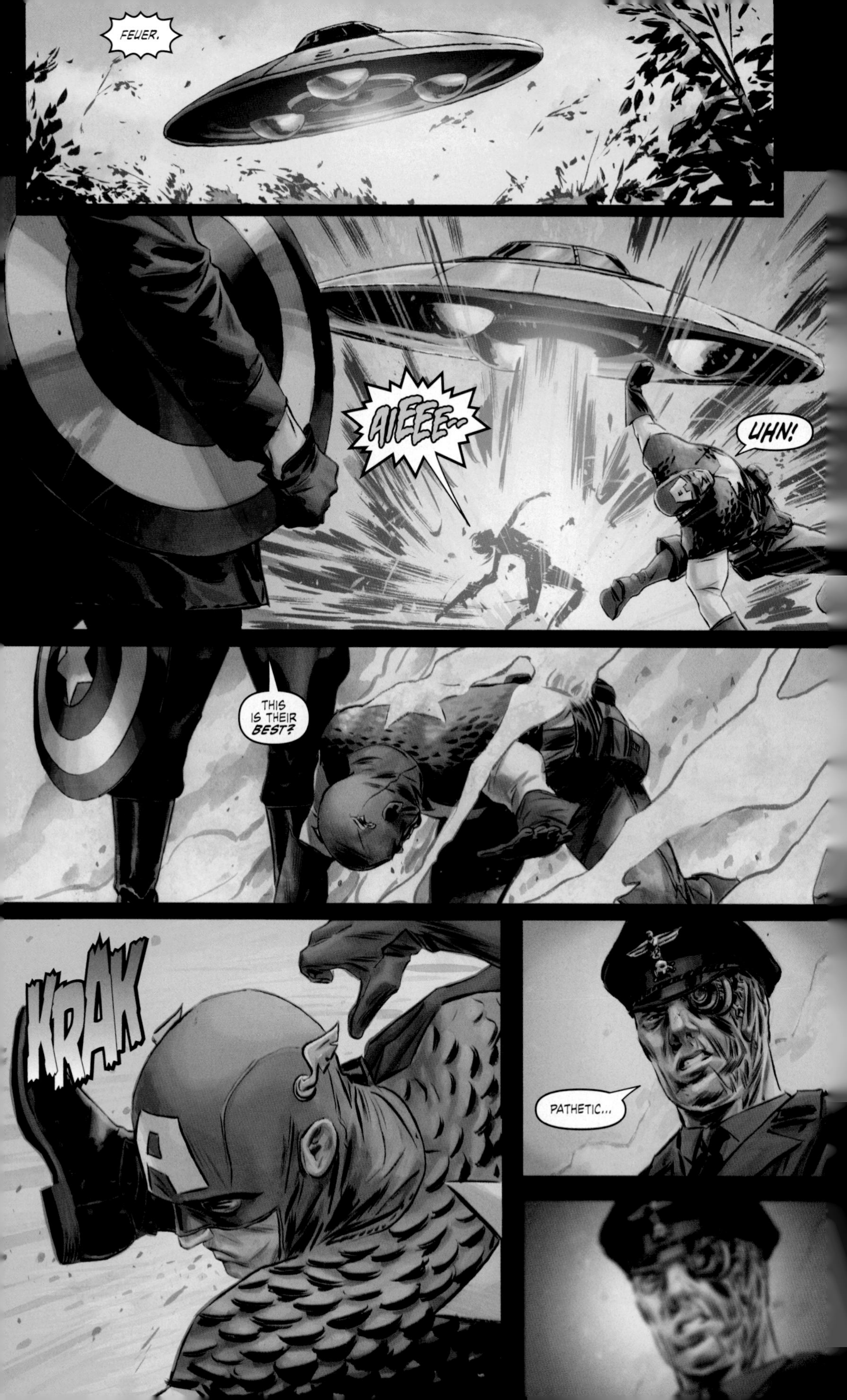
FEUER.
AIEEE--
UHN!
THIS IS THEIR BEST?
KRAK
PATHETIC...

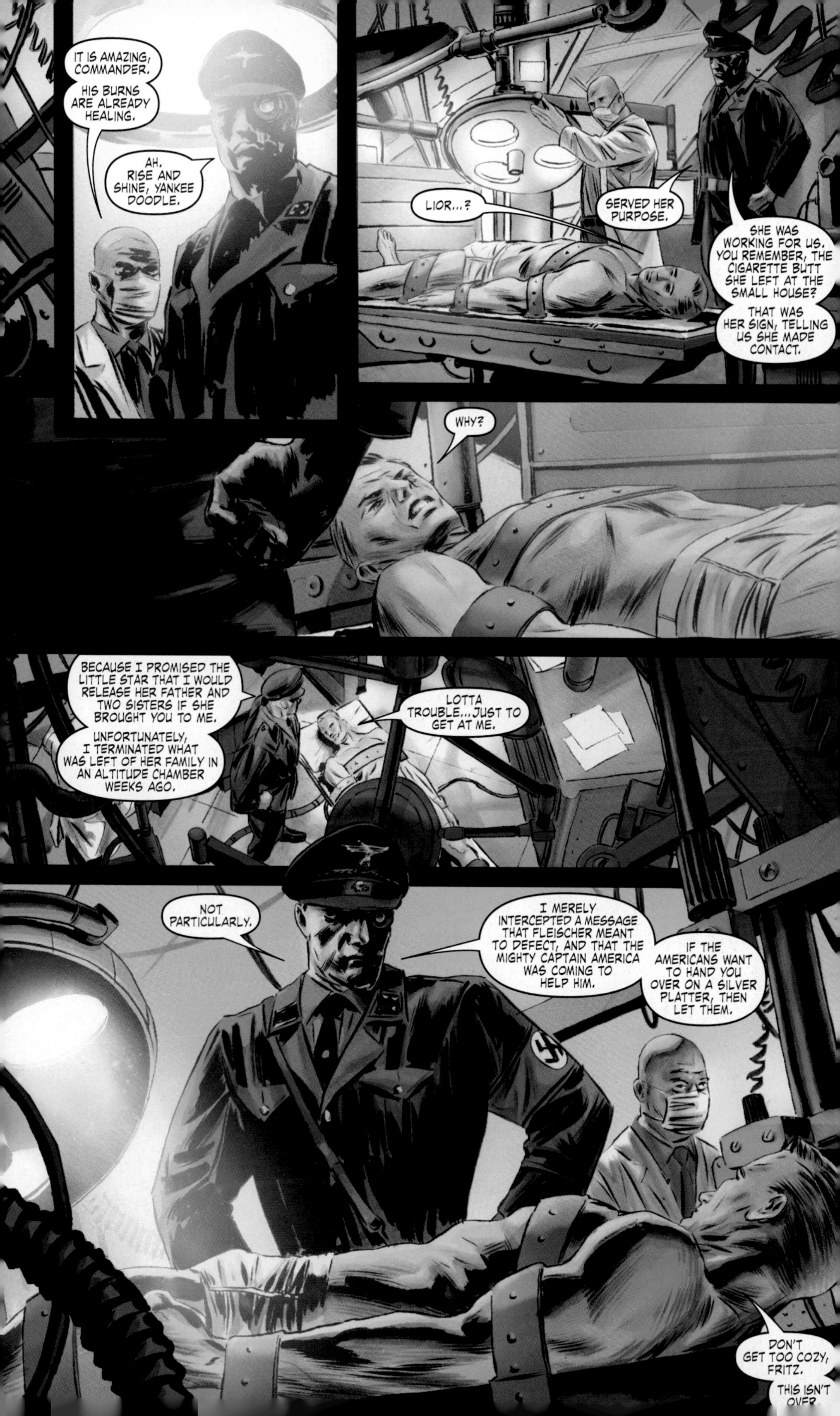
IT IS AMAZING, COMMANDER.
HIS BURNS ARE ALREADY HEALING.
AH. RISE AND SHINE, YANKEE DOODLE.
LIOR...?
SERVED HER PURPOSE.
SHE WAS WORKING FOR US. YOU REMEMBER, THE CIGARETTE BUTT SHE LEFT AT THE SMALL HOUSE?
THAT WAS HER SIGN, TELLING US SHE MADE CONTACT.
WHY?
BECAUSE I PROMISED THE LITTLE STAR THAT I WOULD RELEASE HER FATHER AND TWO SISTERS IF SHE BROUGHT YOU TO ME.
UNFORTUNATELY, I TERMINATED WHAT WAS LEFT OF HER FAMILY IN AN ALTITUDE CHAMBER WEEKS AGO.
LOTTA TROUBLE...JUST TO GET AT ME.
NOT PARTICULARLY.
I MERELY INTERCEPTED A MESSAGE THAT FLEISCHER MEANT TO DEFECT, AND THAT THE MIGHTY CAPTAIN AMERICA WAS COMING TO HELP HIM.
IF THE AMERICANS WANT TO HAND YOU OVER ON A SILVER PLATTER, THEN LET THEM.
DON'T GET TOO COZY, FRITZ.
THIS ISN'T OVER.

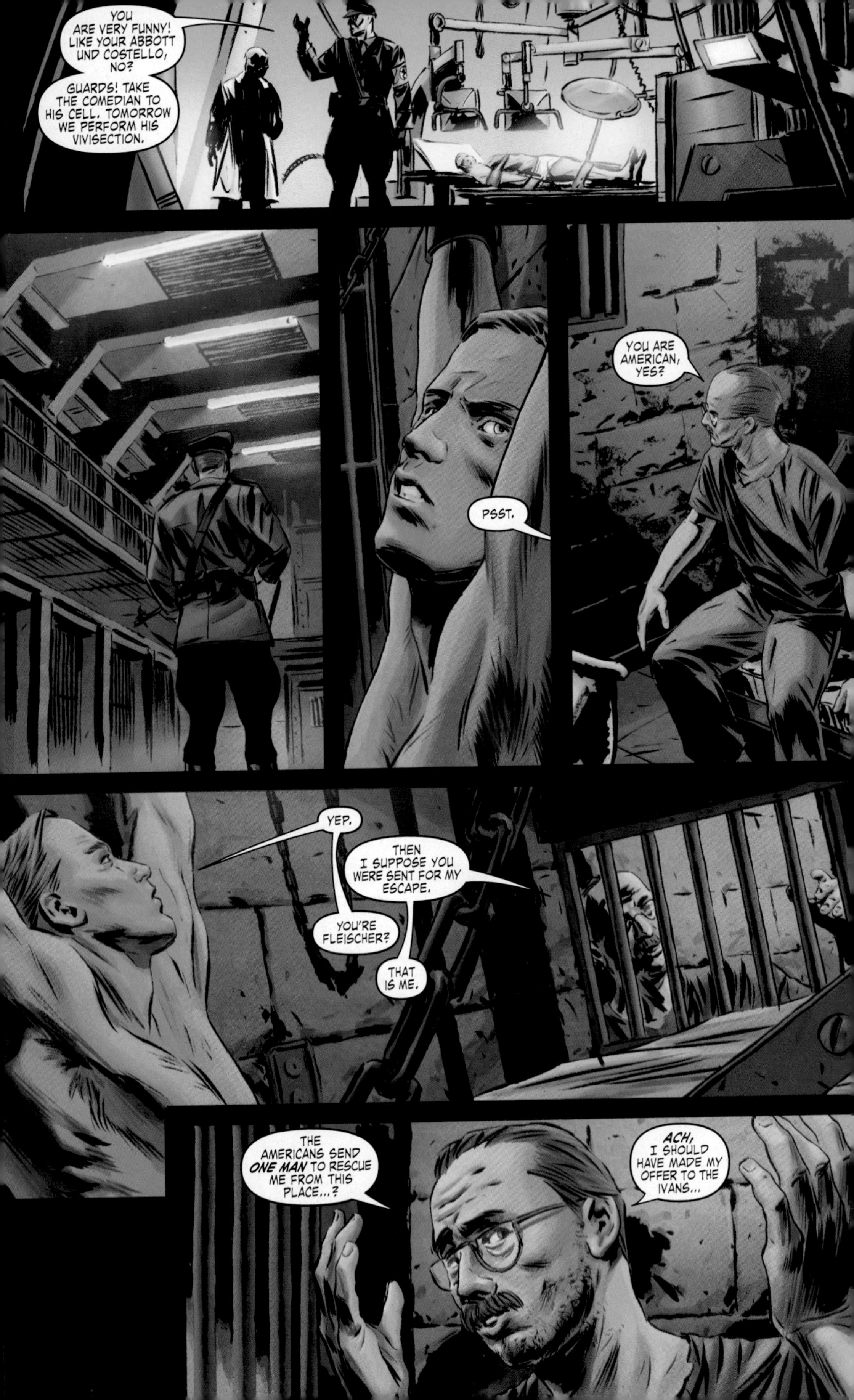

YOU ARE VERY FUNNY! LIKE YOUR ABBOTT UND COSTELLO, NO?
GUARDS! TAKE THE COMEDIAN TO HIS CELL. TOMORROW WE PERFORM HIS VIVISECTION.
PSST.
YOU ARE AMERICAN, YES?
YEP.
THEN I SUPPOSE YOU WERE SENT FOR MY ESCAPE.
YOU'RE FLEISCHER?
THAT IS ME.
THE AMERICANS SEND *ONE MAN* TO RESCUE ME FROM THIS PLACE...?
ACH, I SHOULD HAVE MADE MY OFFER TO THE IVANS...

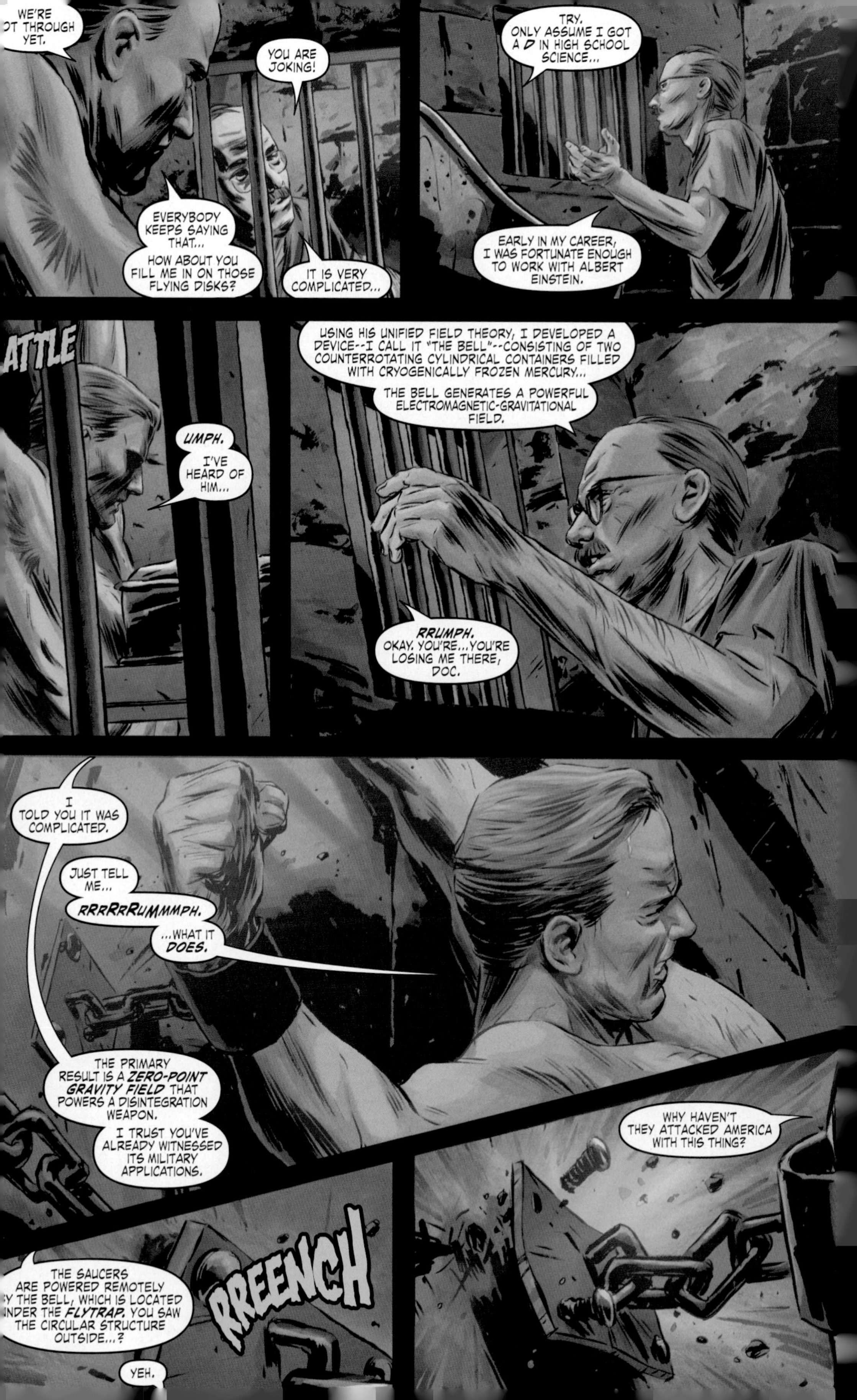
WE'RE OT THROUGH YET.
YOU ARE JOKING!
EVERYBODY KEEPS SAYING THAT...
HOW ABOUT YOU FILL ME IN ON THOSE FLYING DISKS?
IT IS VERY COMPLICATED...
TRY. ONLY ASSUME I GOT A *D* IN HIGH SCHOOL SCIENCE...
EARLY IN MY CAREER, I WAS FORTUNATE ENOUGH TO WORK WITH ALBERT EINSTEIN.
ATTLE
UMPH.
I'VE HEARD OF HIM...
USING HIS UNIFIED FIELD THEORY, I DEVELOPED A DEVICE--I CALL IT "THE BELL"--CONSISTING OF TWO COUNTERROTATING CYLINDRICAL CONTAINERS FILLED WITH CRYOGENICALLY FROZEN MERCURY...
THE BELL GENERATES A POWERFUL ELECTROMAGNETIC-GRAVITATIONAL FIELD.
RRUMPH.
OKAY. YOU'RE...YOU'RE LOSING ME THERE, DOC.
I TOLD YOU IT WAS COMPLICATED.
JUST TELL ME...
RRRRRRUMMMPH.
...WHAT IT *DOES.*
THE PRIMARY RESULT IS A *ZERO-POINT GRAVITY FIELD* THAT POWERS A DISINTEGRATION WEAPON.
I TRUST YOU'VE ALREADY WITNESSED ITS MILITARY APPLICATIONS.
WHY HAVEN'T THEY ATTACKED AMERICA WITH THIS THING?
THE SAUCERS ARE POWERED REMOTELY Y THE BELL, WHICH IS LOCATED NDER THE *FLYTRAP.* YOU SAW THE CIRCULAR STRUCTURE OUTSIDE...?
RREENCH
YEH.

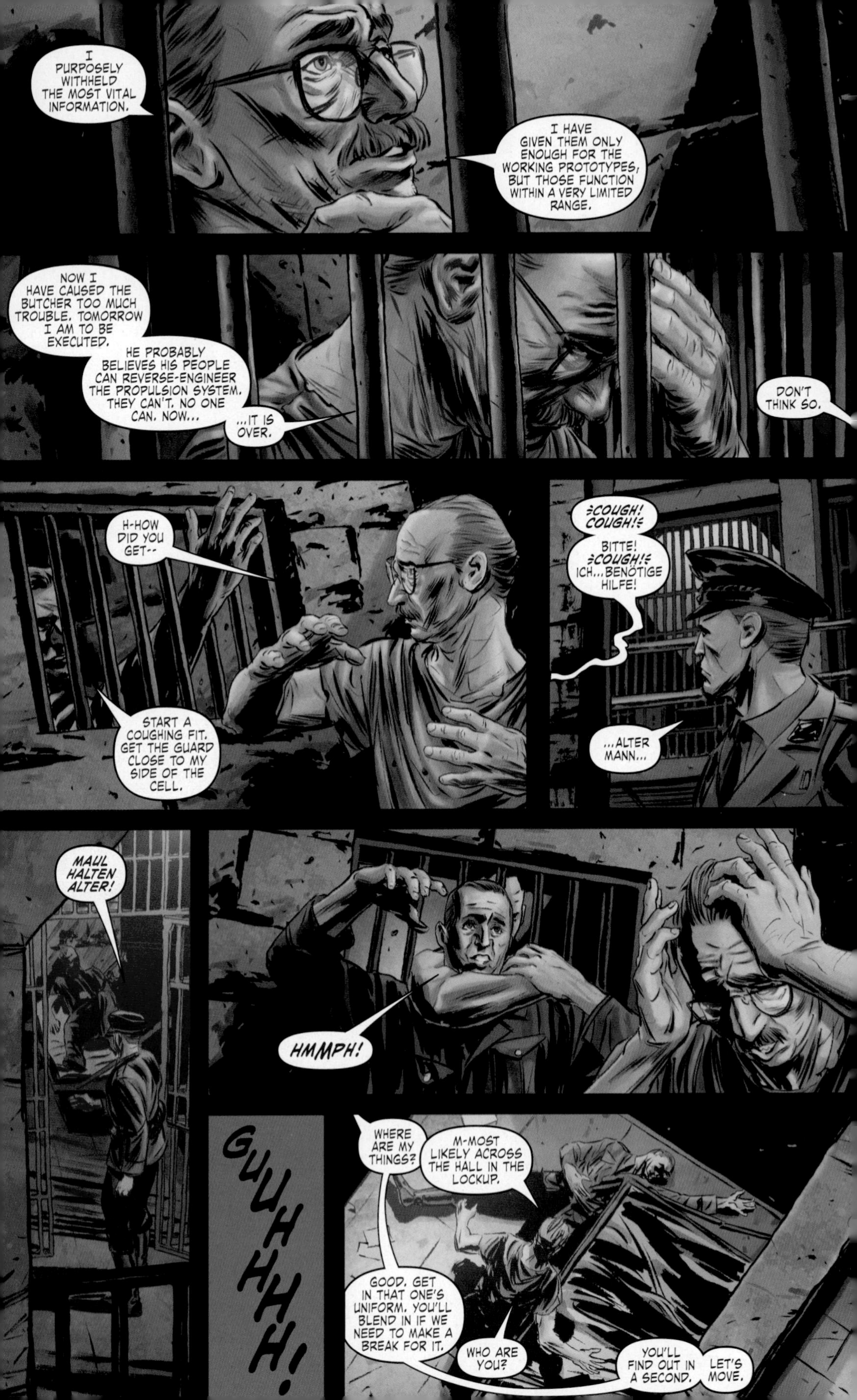
I PURPOSELY WITHHELD THE MOST VITAL INFORMATION.
I HAVE GIVEN THEM ONLY ENOUGH FOR THE WORKING PROTOTYPES, BUT THOSE FUNCTION WITHIN A VERY LIMITED RANGE.
NOW I HAVE CAUSED THE BUTCHER TOO MUCH TROUBLE. TOMORROW I AM TO BE EXECUTED.
HE PROBABLY BELIEVES HIS PEOPLE CAN REVERSE-ENGINEER THE PROPULSION SYSTEM. THEY CAN'T. NO ONE CAN. NOW...
...IT IS OVER.
DON'T THINK SO.
H-HOW DID YOU GET--
START A COUGHING FIT. GET THE GUARD CLOSE TO MY SIDE OF THE CELL.
COUGH! COUGH!
BITTE! COUGH! ICH...BENÖTIGE HILFE!
...ALTER MANN...
MAUL HALTEN ALTER!
HMMPH!
GUUHHH!
WHERE ARE MY THINGS?
M-MOST LIKELY ACROSS THE HALL IN THE LOCKUP.
GOOD. GET IN THAT ONE'S UNIFORM. YOU'LL BLEND IN IF WE NEED TO MAKE A BREAK FOR IT.
WHO ARE YOU?
YOU'LL FIND OUT IN A SECOND.
LET'S MOVE.

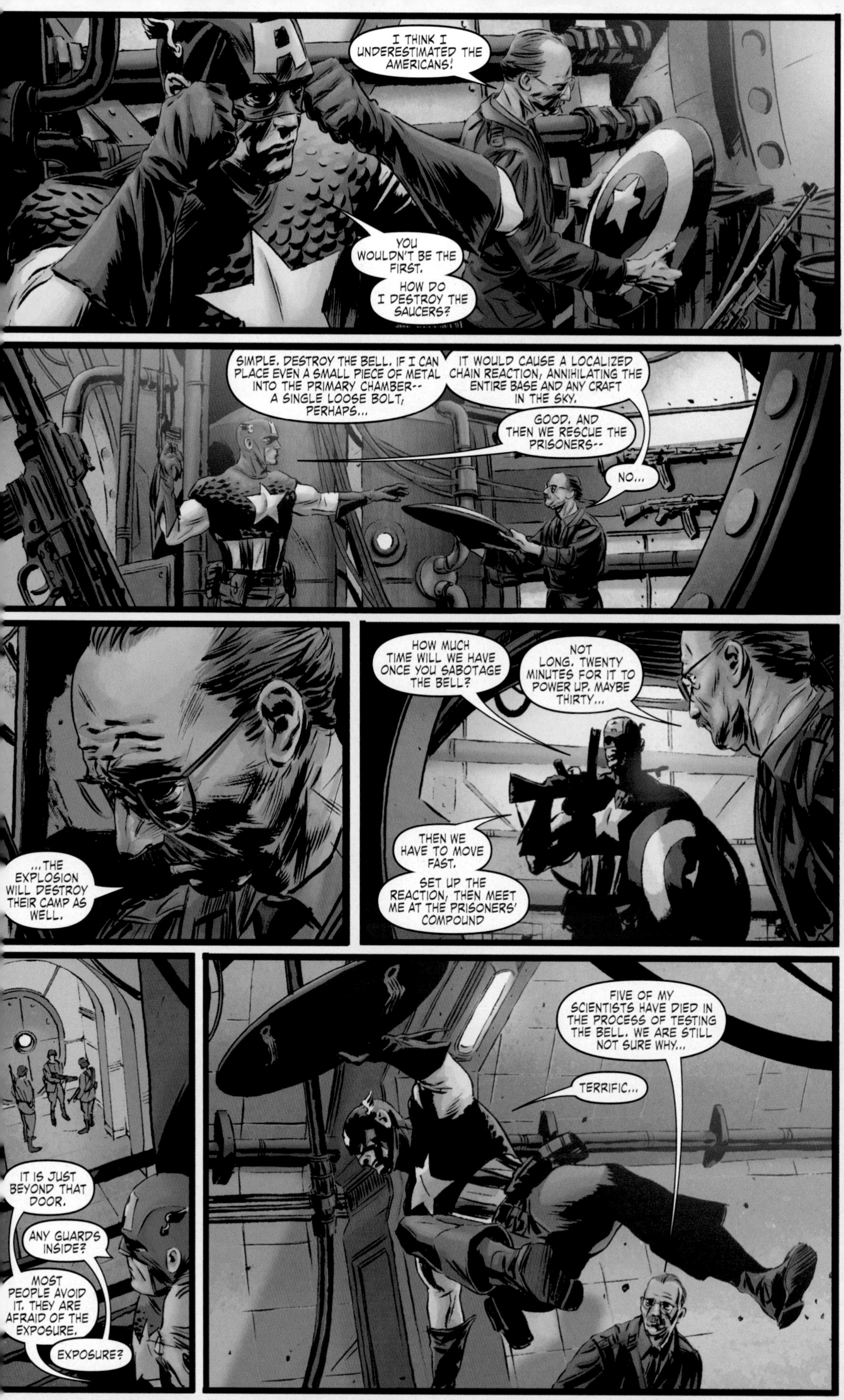
I THINK I UNDERESTIMATED THE AMERICANS!
YOU WOULDN'T BE THE FIRST.
HOW DO I DESTROY THE SAUCERS?
SIMPLE. DESTROY THE BELL. IF I CAN PLACE EVEN A SMALL PIECE OF METAL INTO THE PRIMARY CHAMBER-- A SINGLE LOOSE BOLT, PERHAPS...
IT WOULD CAUSE A LOCALIZED CHAIN REACTION, ANNIHILATING THE ENTIRE BASE AND ANY CRAFT IN THE SKY.
GOOD. AND THEN WE RESCUE THE PRISONERS--
NO...
...THE EXPLOSION WILL DESTROY THEIR CAMP AS WELL.
HOW MUCH TIME WILL WE HAVE ONCE YOU SABOTAGE THE BELL?
NOT LONG. TWENTY MINUTES FOR IT TO POWER UP. MAYBE THIRTY...
THEN WE HAVE TO MOVE FAST.
SET UP THE REACTION, THEN MEET ME AT THE PRISONERS' COMPOUND
IT IS JUST BEYOND THAT DOOR.
ANY GUARDS INSIDE?
MOST PEOPLE AVOID IT. THEY ARE AFRAID OF THE EXPOSURE.
EXPOSURE?
FIVE OF MY SCIENTISTS HAVE DIED IN THE PROCESS OF TESTING THE BELL. WE ARE STILL NOT SURE WHY...
TERRIFIC...

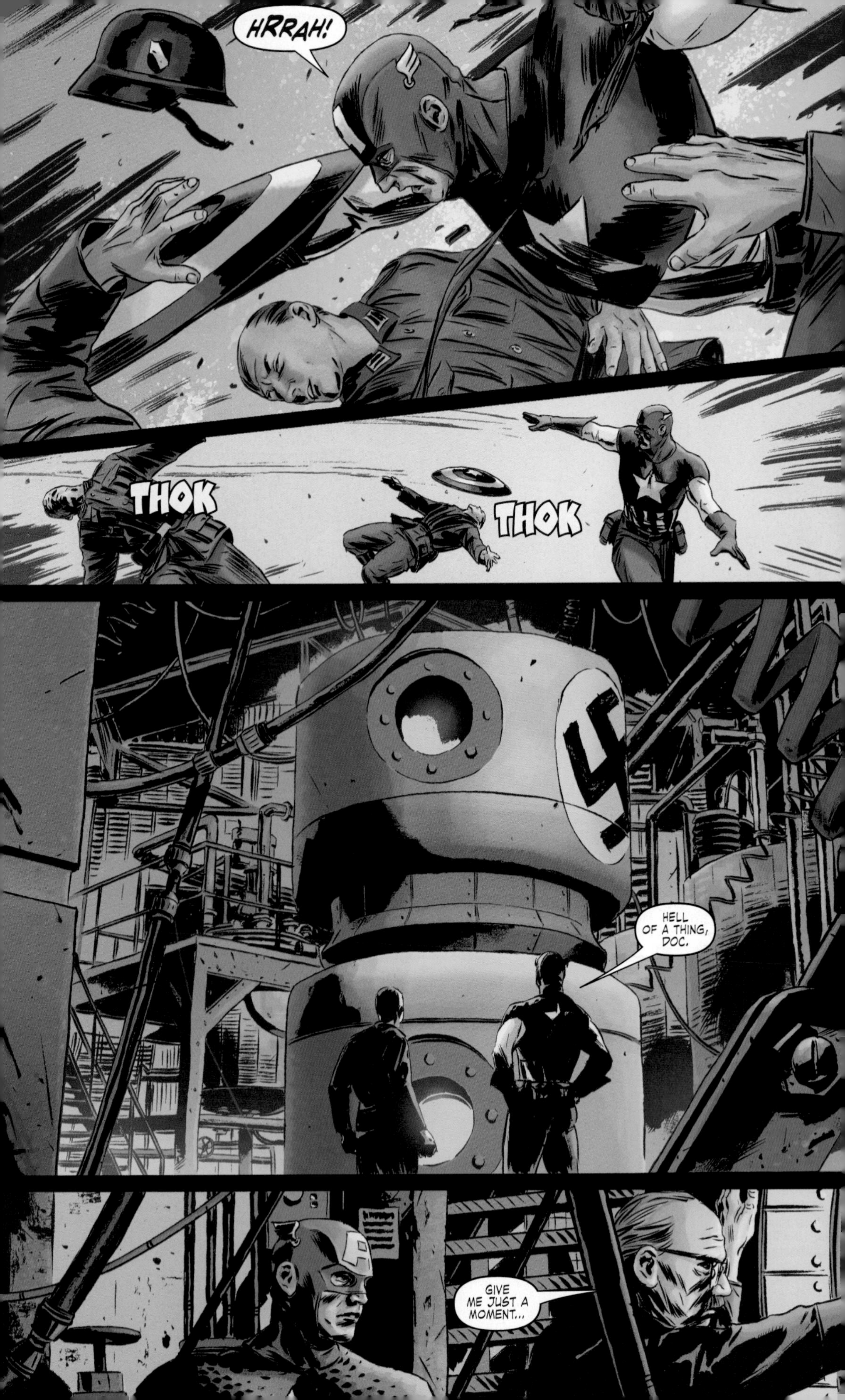
HRRAH!
THOK
THOK
HELL OF A THING, DOC.
GIVE ME JUST A MOMENT...

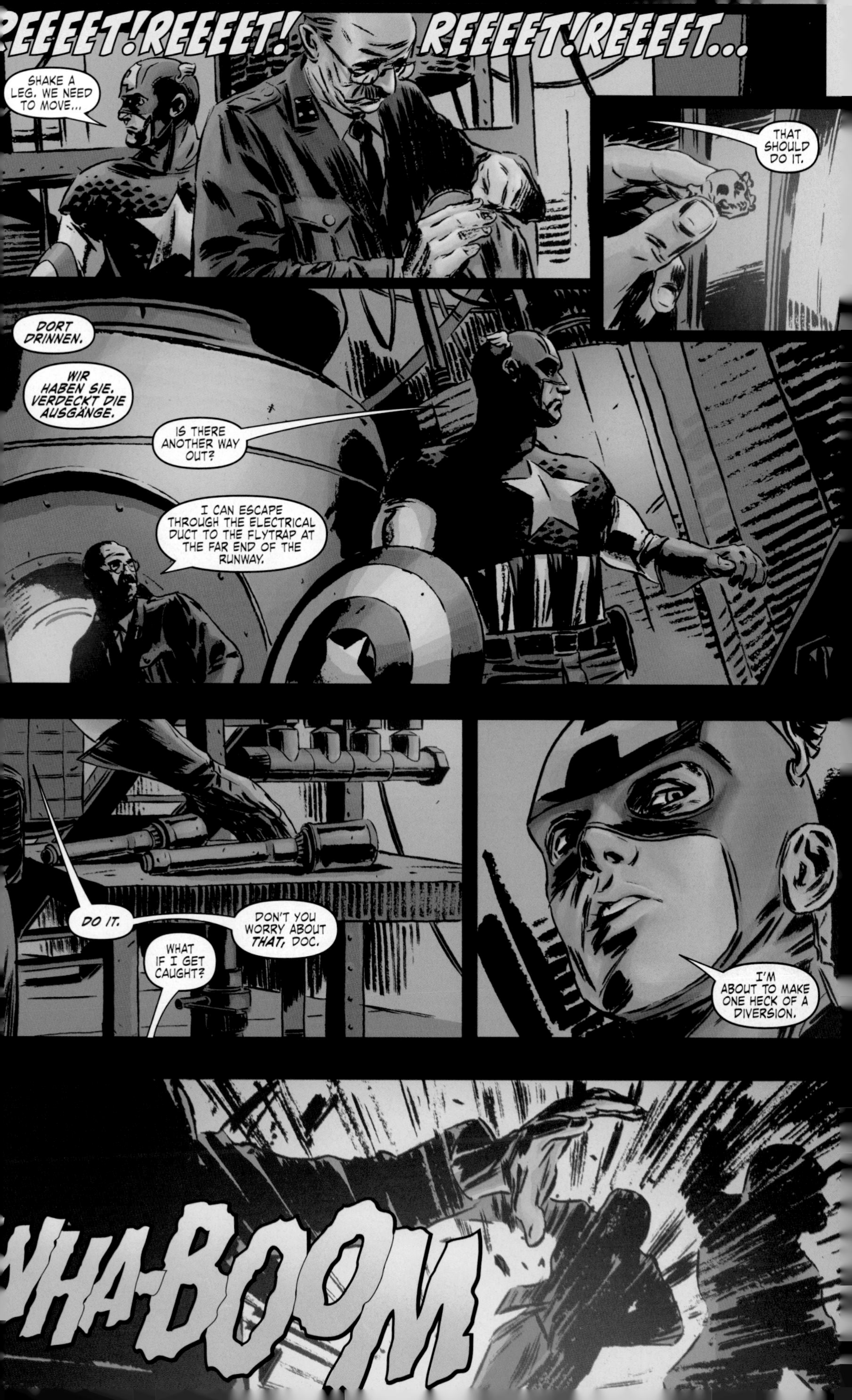
REEEET! REEEET! REEEET! REEEET...
SHAKE A LEG. WE NEED TO MOVE...
THAT SHOULD DO IT.
DORT DRINNEN.
WIR HABEN SIE. VERDECKT DIE AUSGÄNGE.
IS THERE ANOTHER WAY OUT?
I CAN ESCAPE THROUGH THE ELECTRICAL DUCT TO THE FLYTRAP AT THE FAR END OF THE RUNWAY.
DO IT.
WHAT IF I GET CAUGHT?
DON'T YOU WORRY ABOUT *THAT,* DOC.
I'M ABOUT TO MAKE ONE HECK OF A DIVERSION.
HA-BOOM

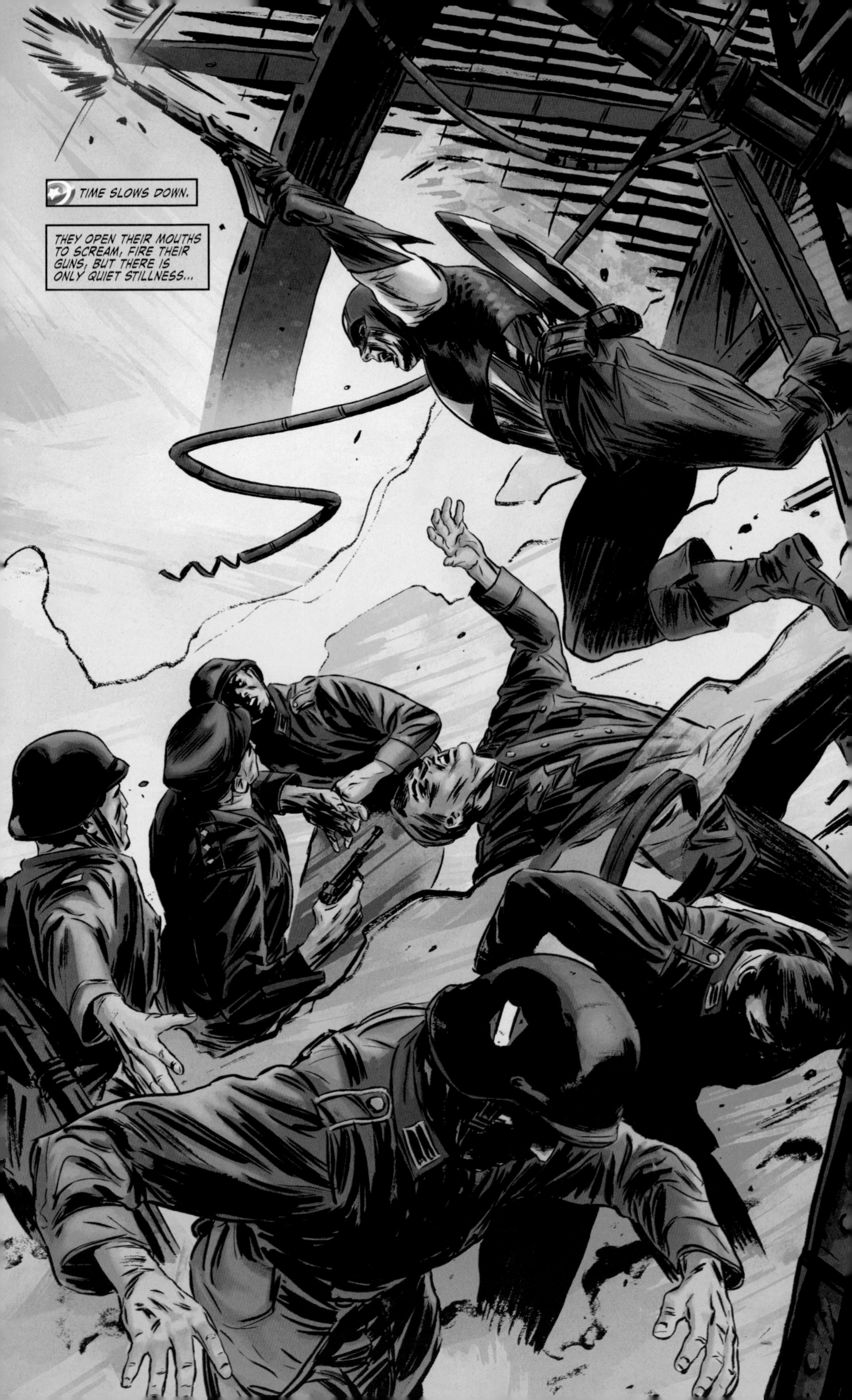
TIME SLOWS DOWN.
THEY OPEN THEIR MOUTHS TO SCREAM, FIRE THEIR GUNS, BUT THERE IS ONLY QUIET STILLNESS...

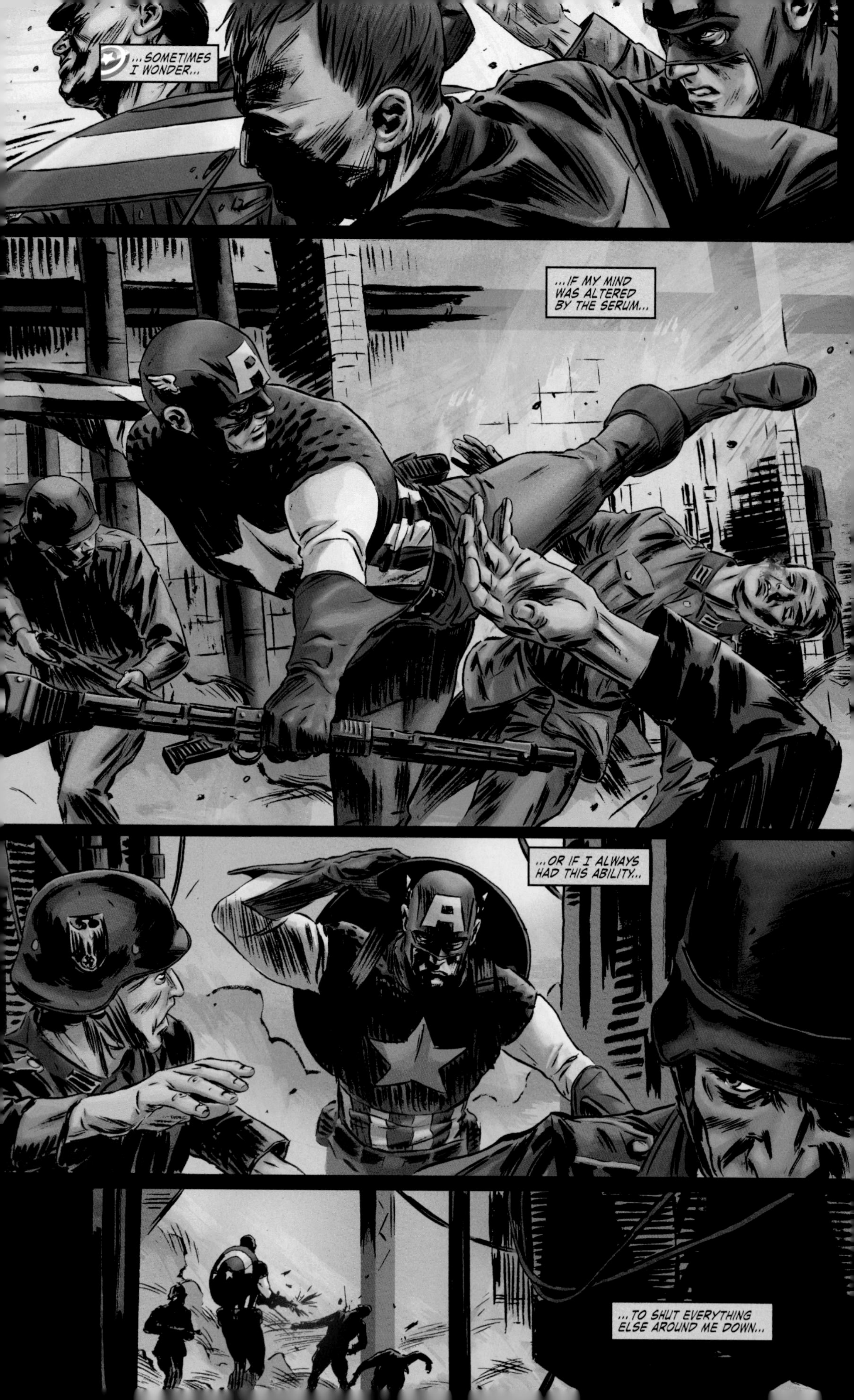
...SOMETIMES I WONDER...
...IF MY MIND WAS ALTERED BY THE SERUM...
...OR IF I ALWAYS HAD THIS ABILITY...
...TO SHUT EVERYTHING ELSE AROUND ME DOWN...

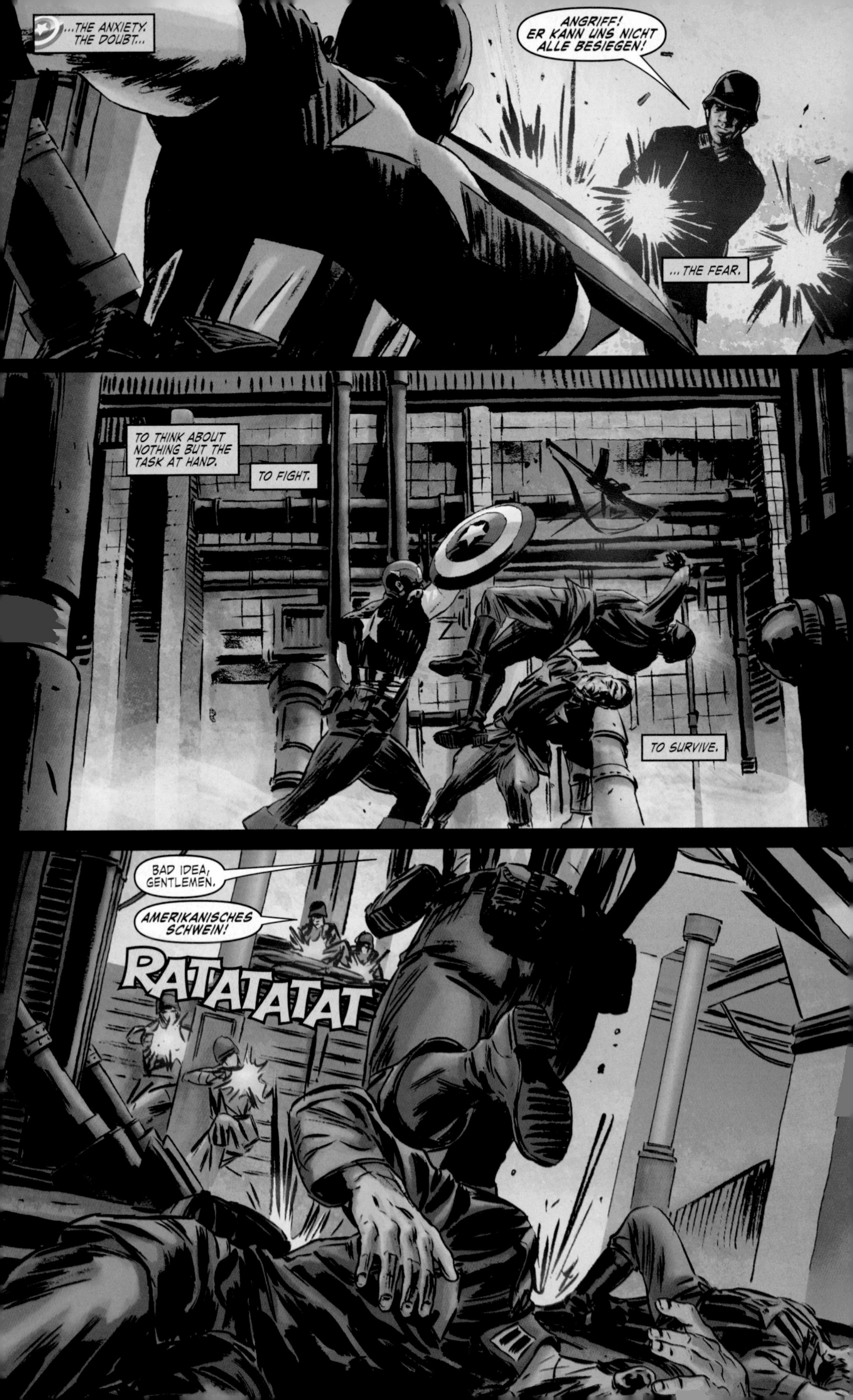
...THE ANXIETY. THE DOUBT...
ANGRIFF! ER KANN UNS NICHT ALLE BESIEGEN!
...THE FEAR.
TO THINK ABOUT NOTHING BUT THE TASK AT HAND.
TO FIGHT.
TO SURVIVE.
BAD IDEA, GENTLEMEN.
AMERIKANISCHES SCHWEIN!
RATATATAT

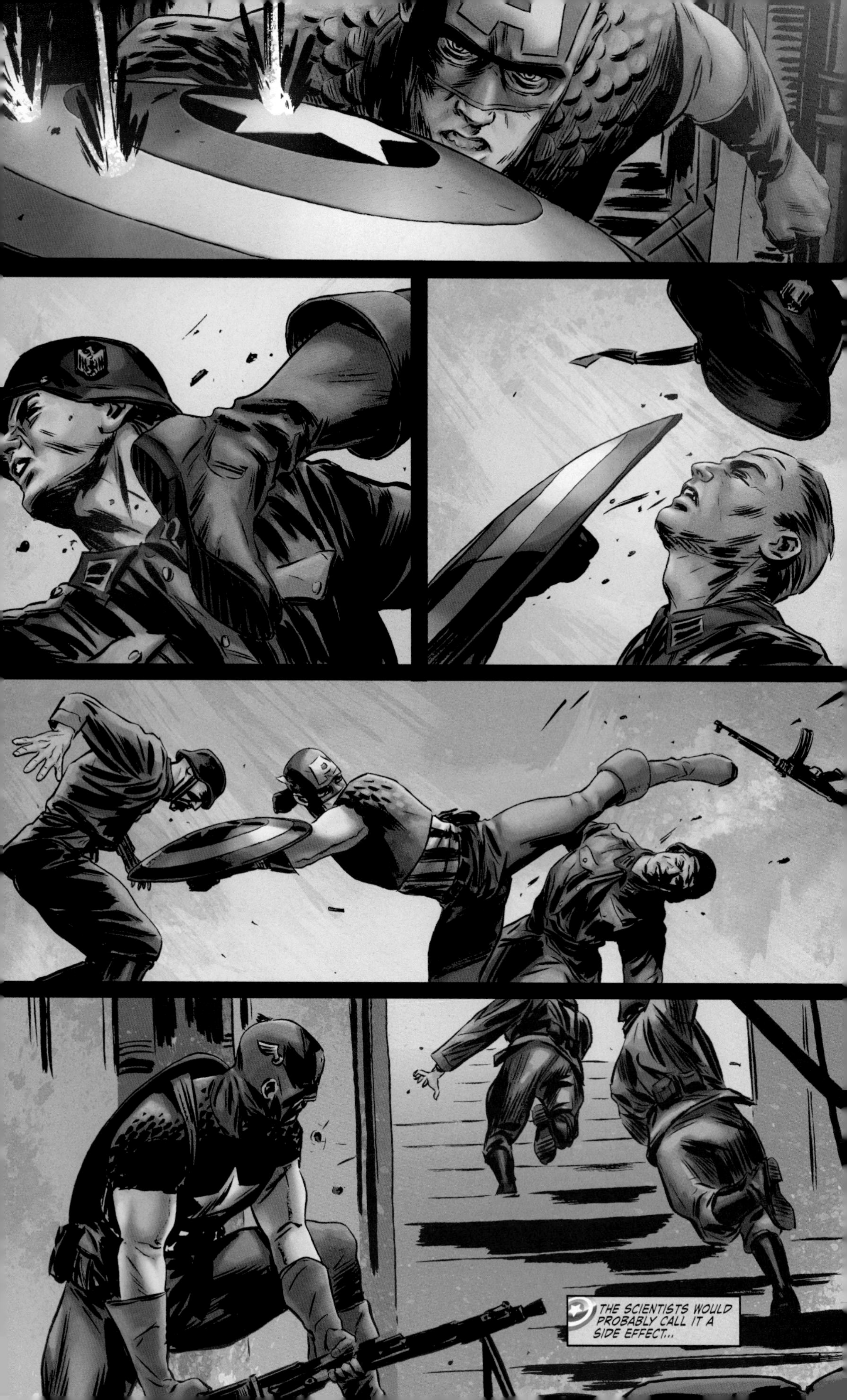
THE SCIENTISTS WOULD PROBABLY CALL IT A SIDE EFFECT...

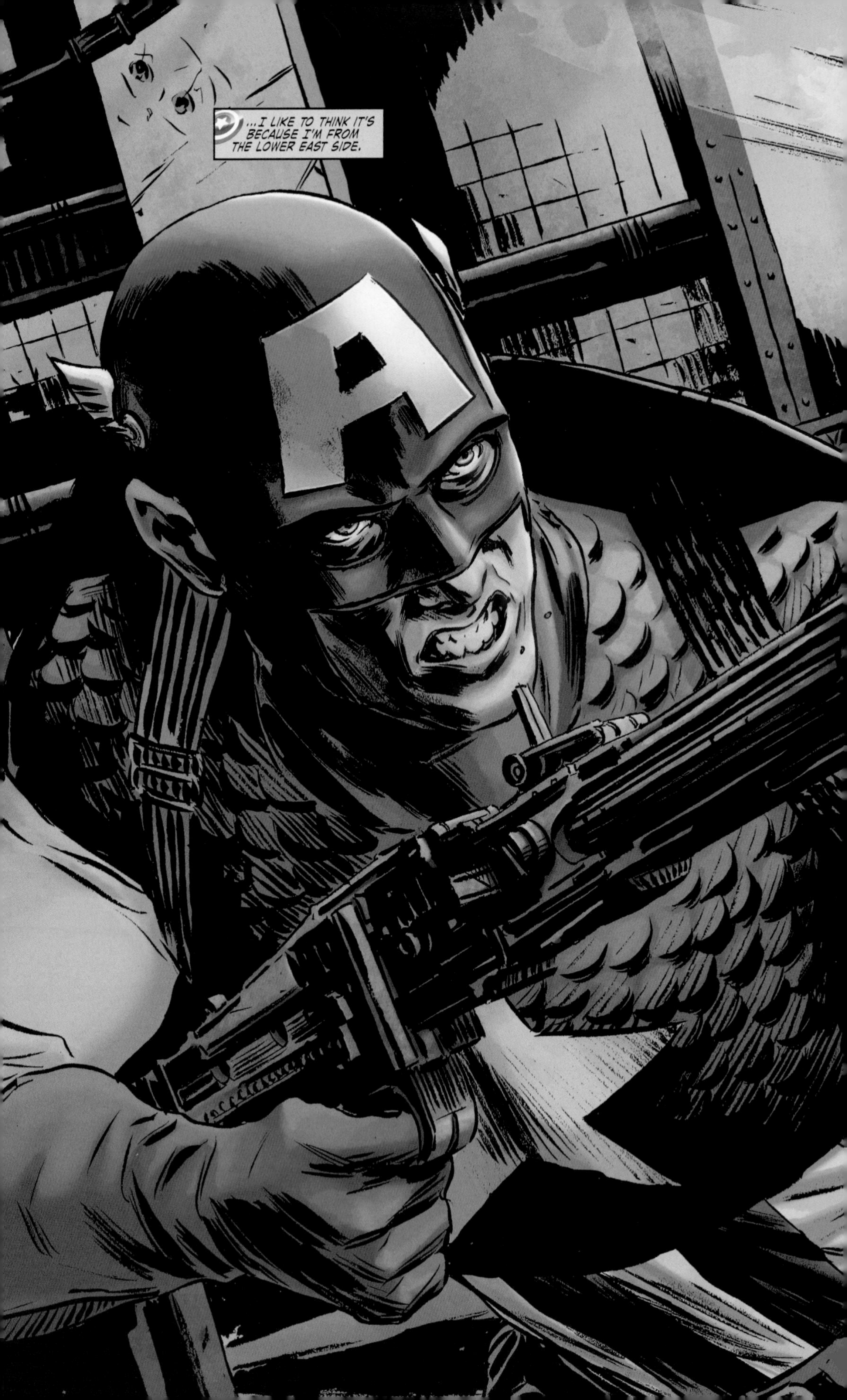
...I LIKE TO THINK IT'S BECAUSE I'M FROM THE LOWER EAST SIDE.

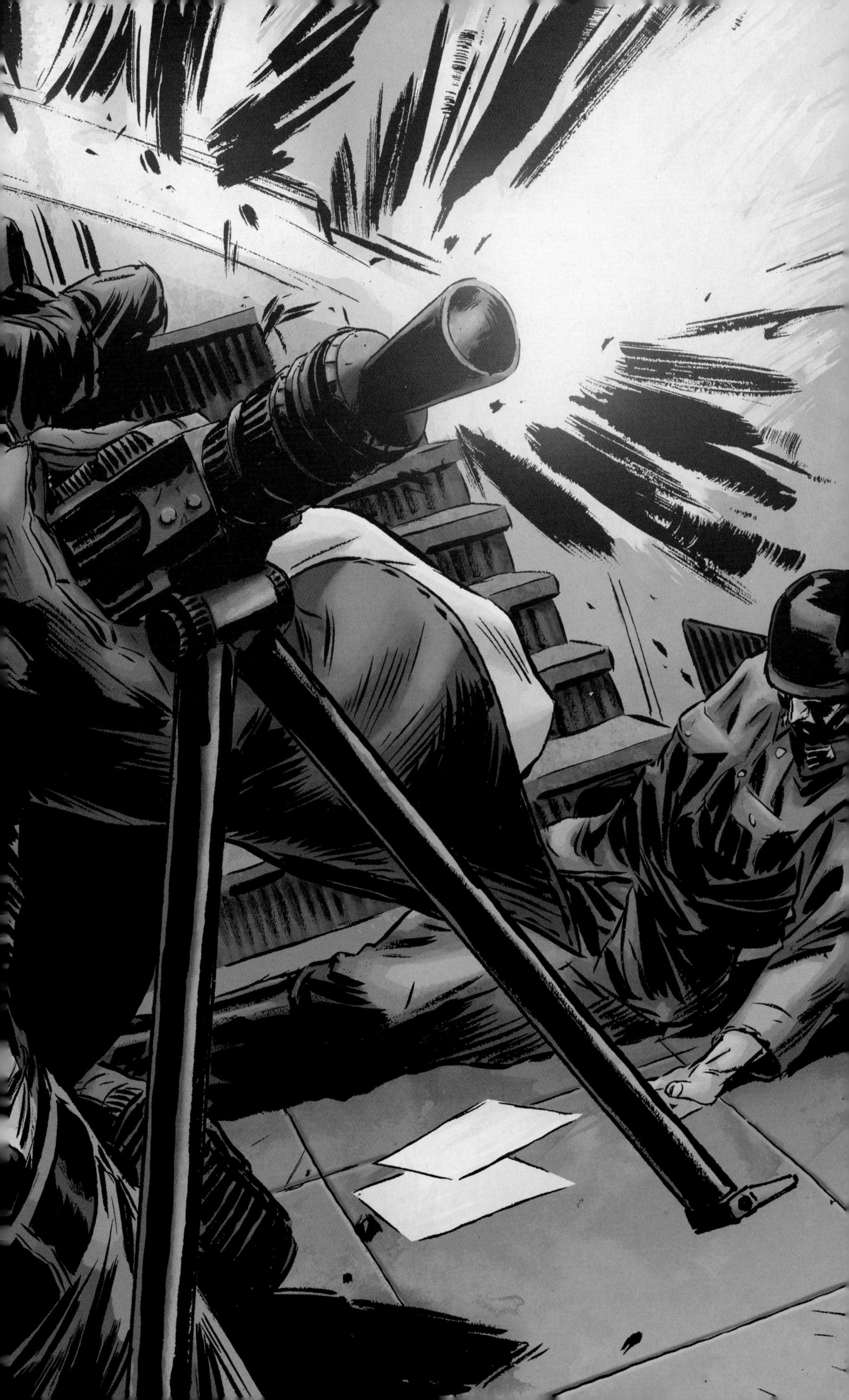

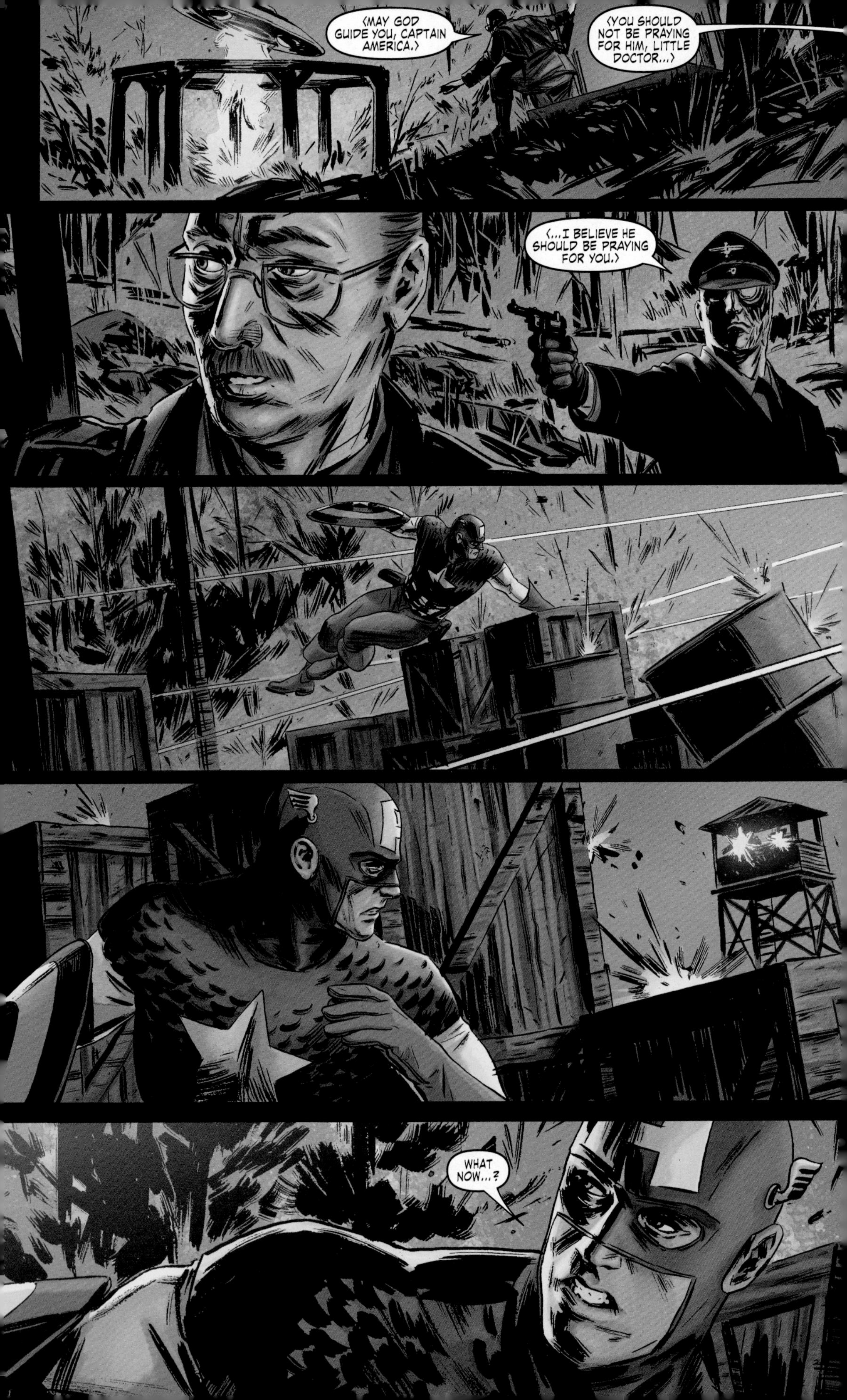
‹MAY GOD GUIDE YOU, CAPTAIN AMERICA.›
‹YOU SHOULD NOT BE PRAYING FOR HIM, LITTLE DOCTOR...›
‹...I BELIEVE HE SHOULD BE PRAYING FOR YOU.›
WHAT NOW...?

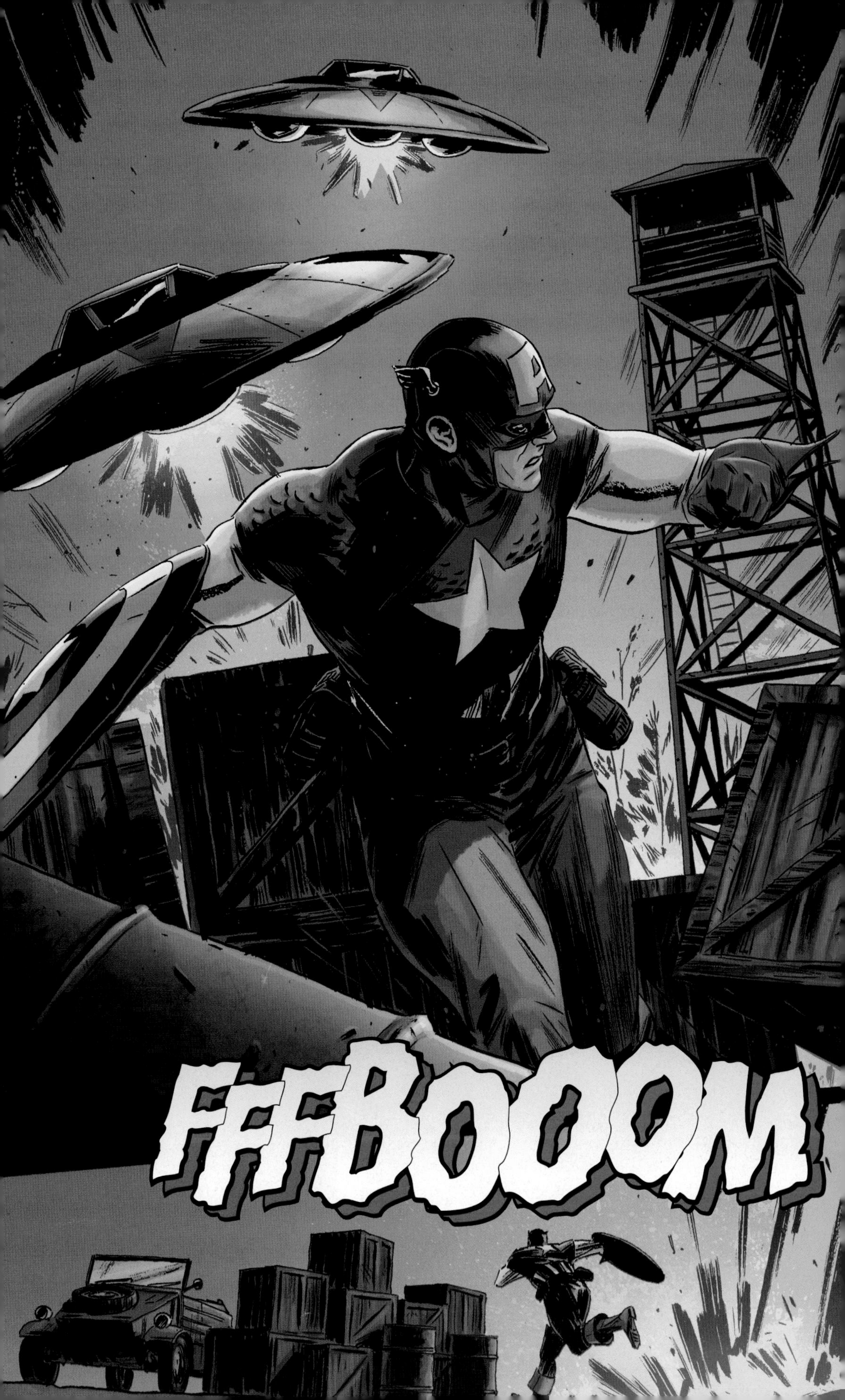
FFFBOOOM

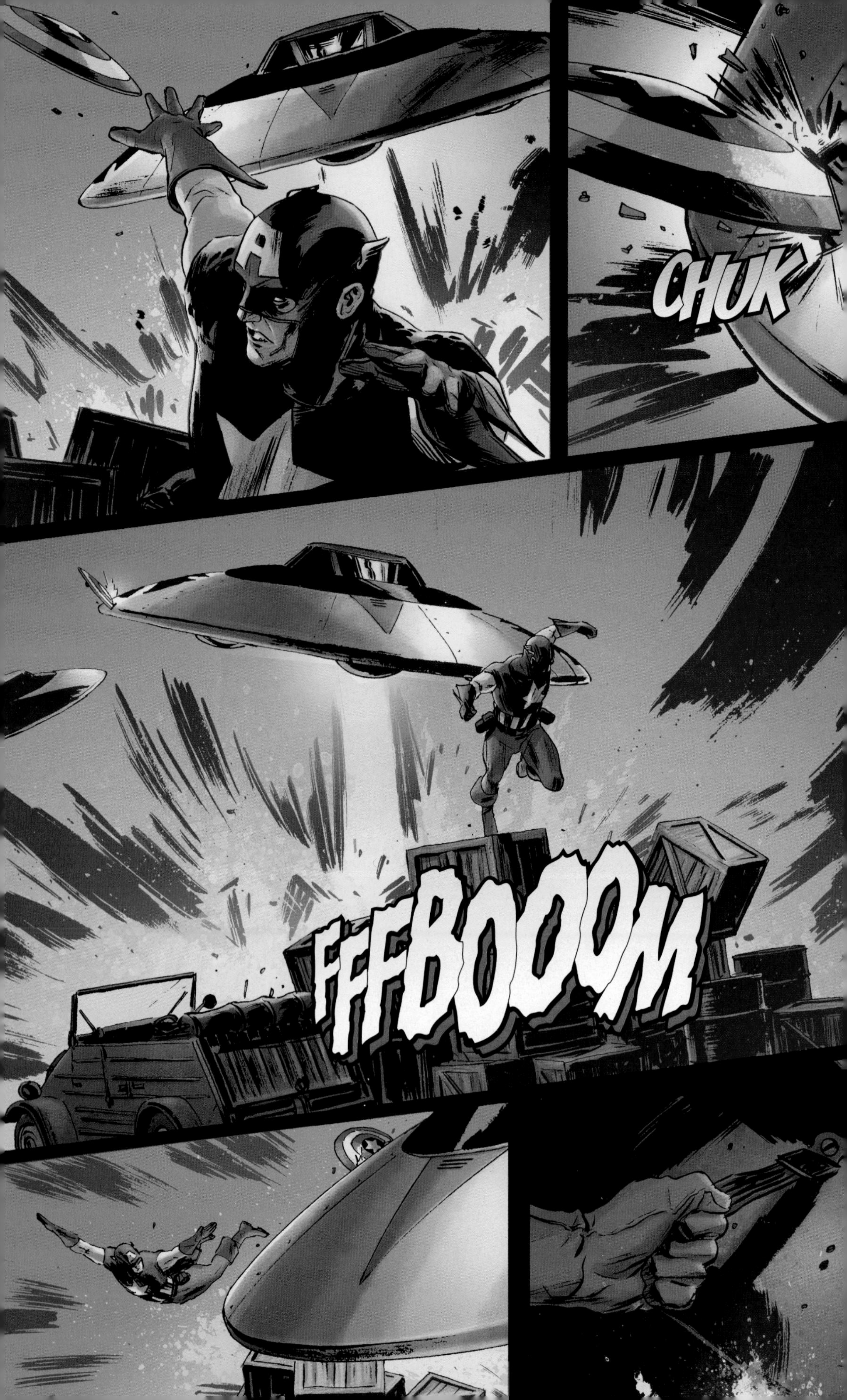
CHUK
FFFBOOOM

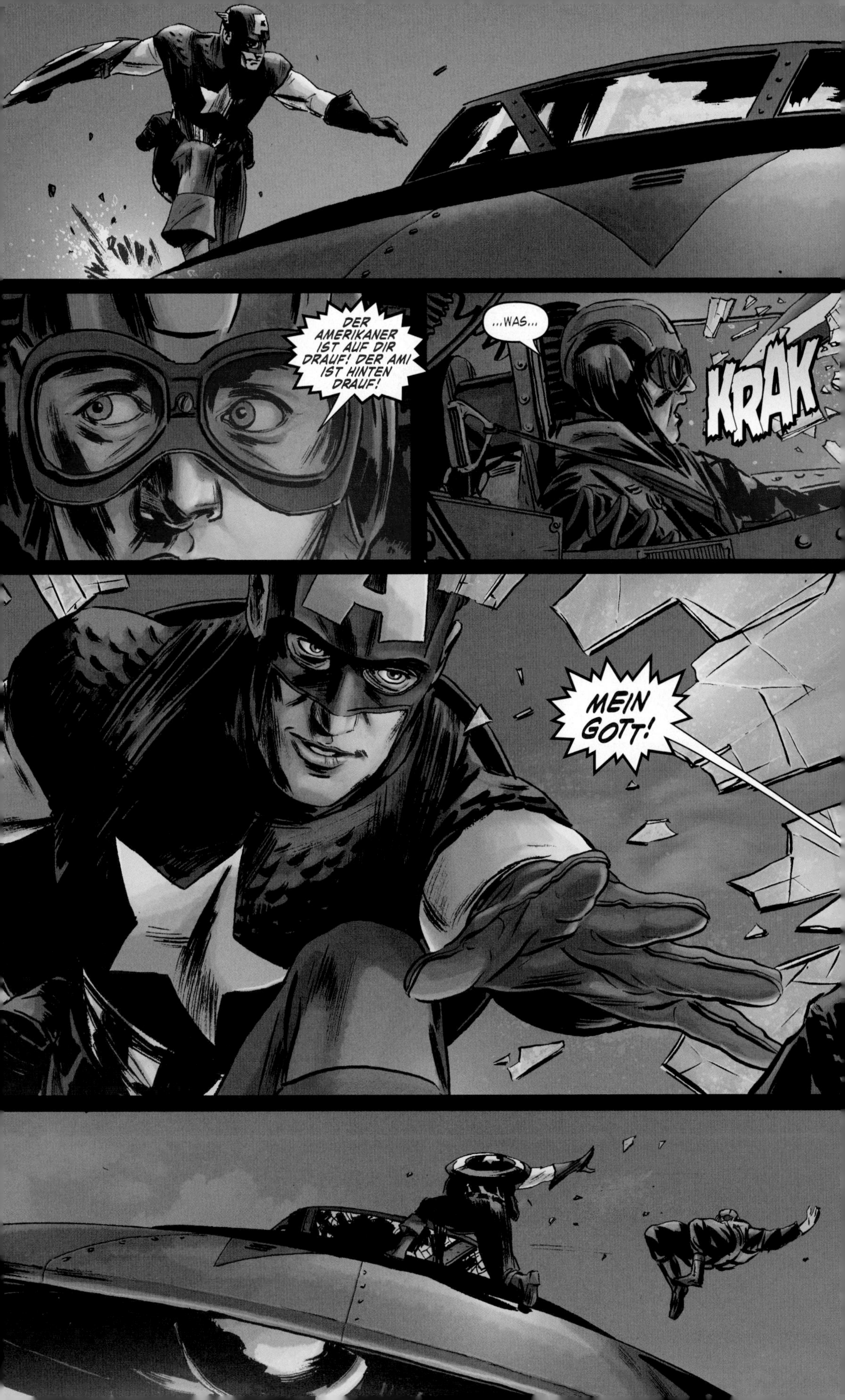
DER AMERIKANER IST AUF DIR DRAUF! DER AMI IST HINTEN DRAUF!
...WAS...
KRAK
MEIN GOTT!

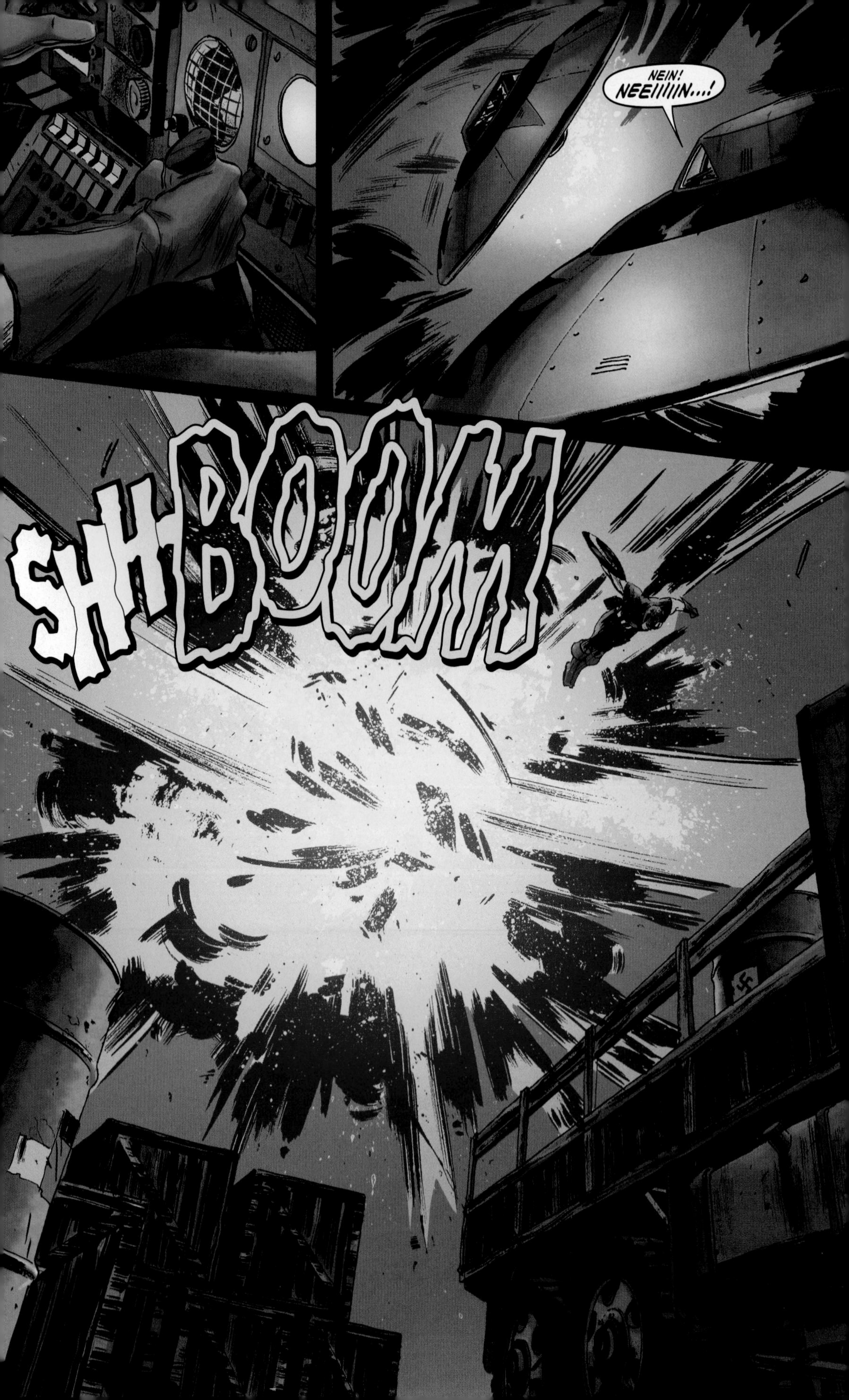
NEIN!
NEE!!!!!N...!
SHHBOOM

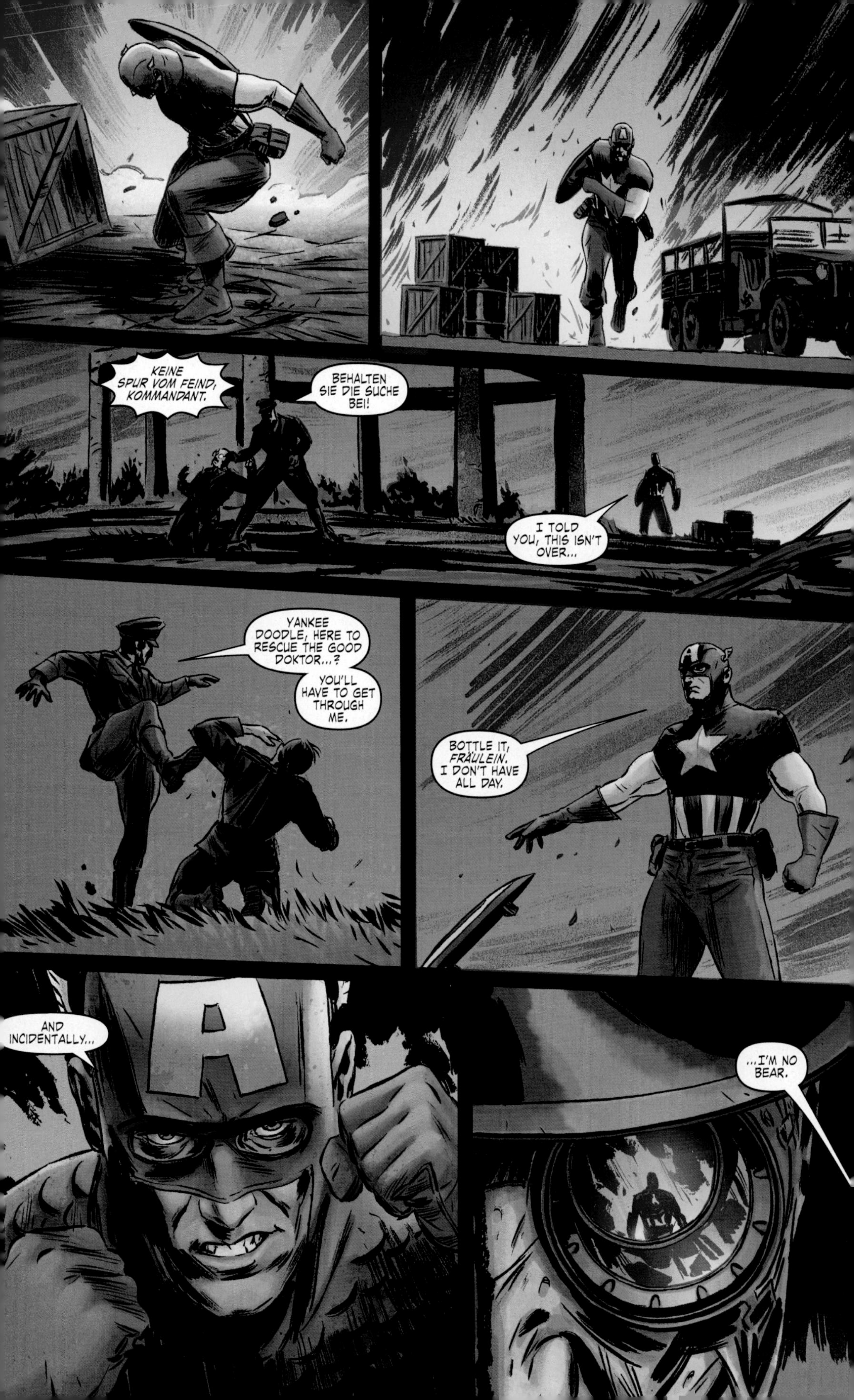
KEINE SPUR VOM FEIND, KOMMANDANT.
BEHALTEN SIE DIE SUCHE BEI!
I TOLD YOU, THIS ISN'T OVER...
YANKEE DOODLE, HERE TO RESCUE THE GOOD DOKTOR...?
YOU'LL HAVE TO GET THROUGH ME.
BOTTLE IT, *FRÄULEIN*. I DON'T HAVE ALL DAY.
AND INCIDENTALLY...
...I'M NO BEAR.

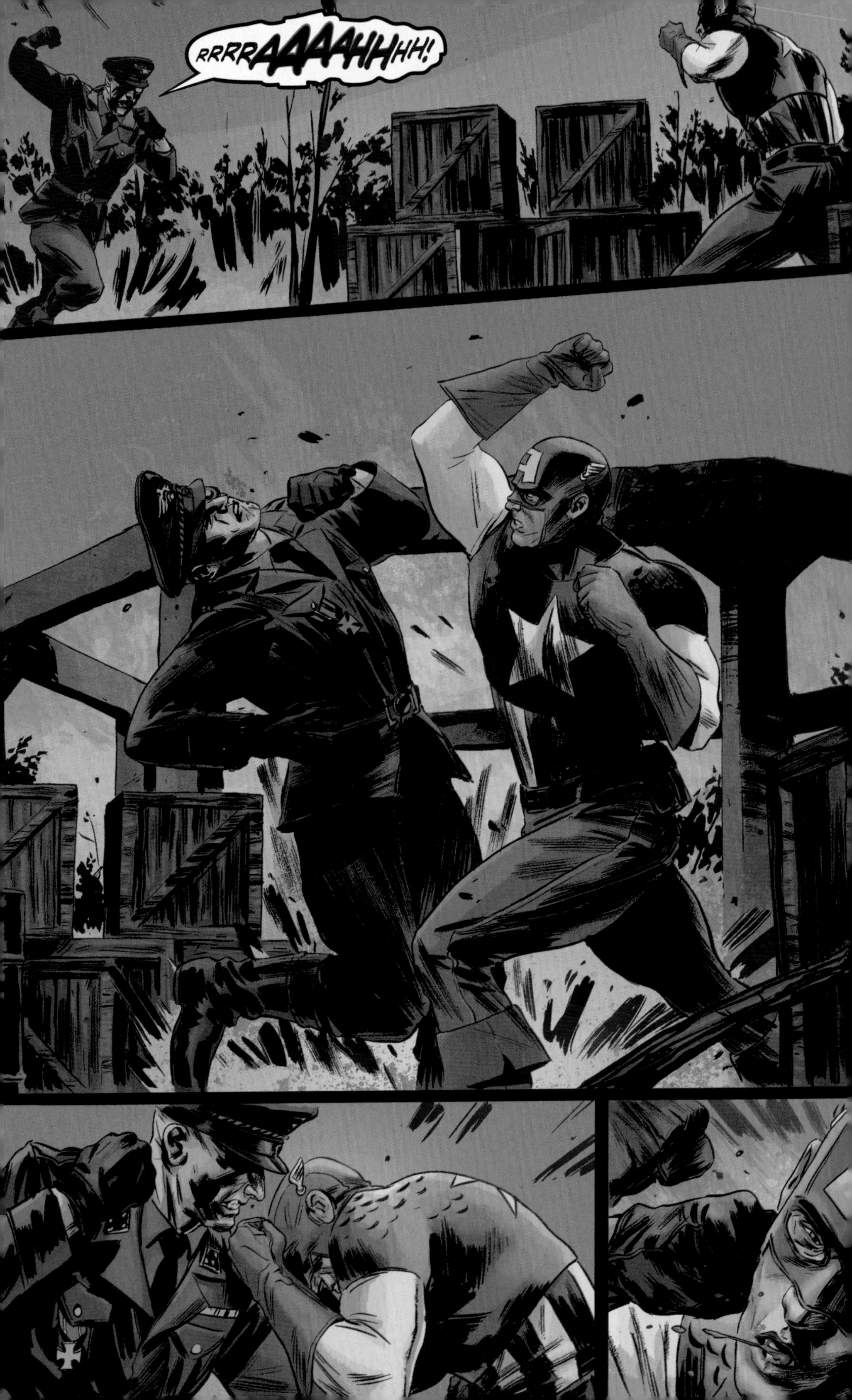
RRRRAAAAHHHH!

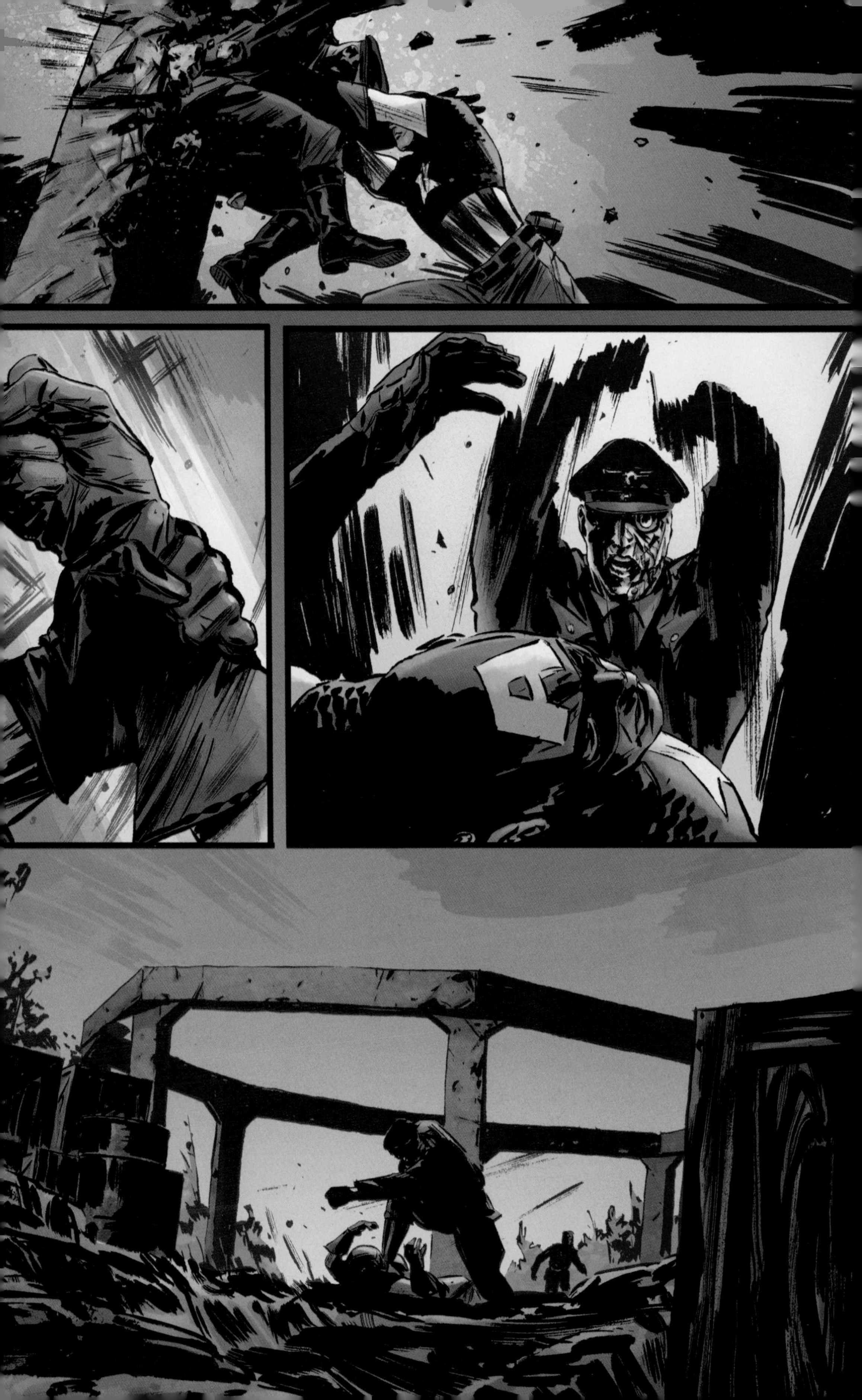

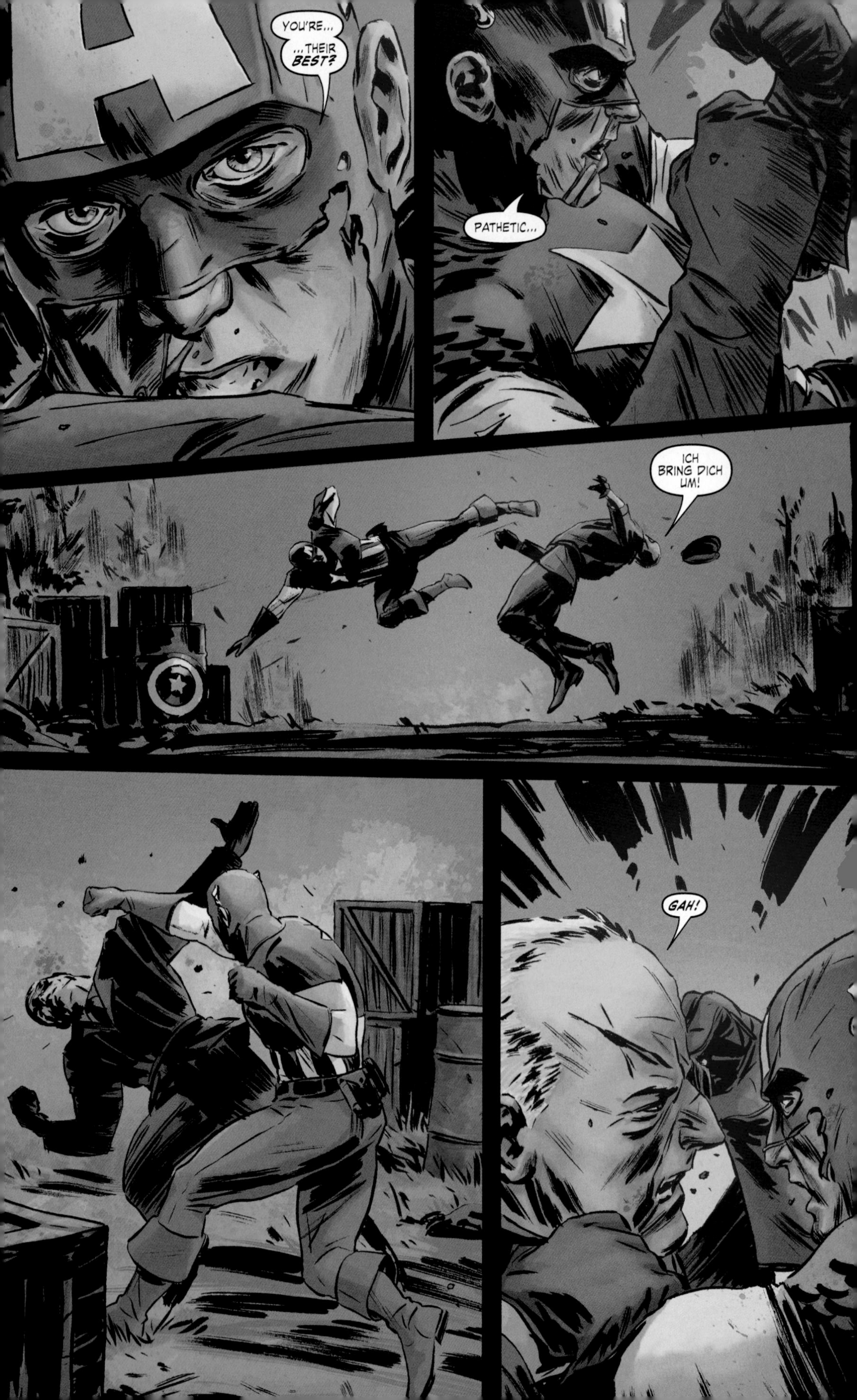
YOU'RE...
...THEIR BEST?
PATHETIC...
ICH BRING DICH UM!
GAH!

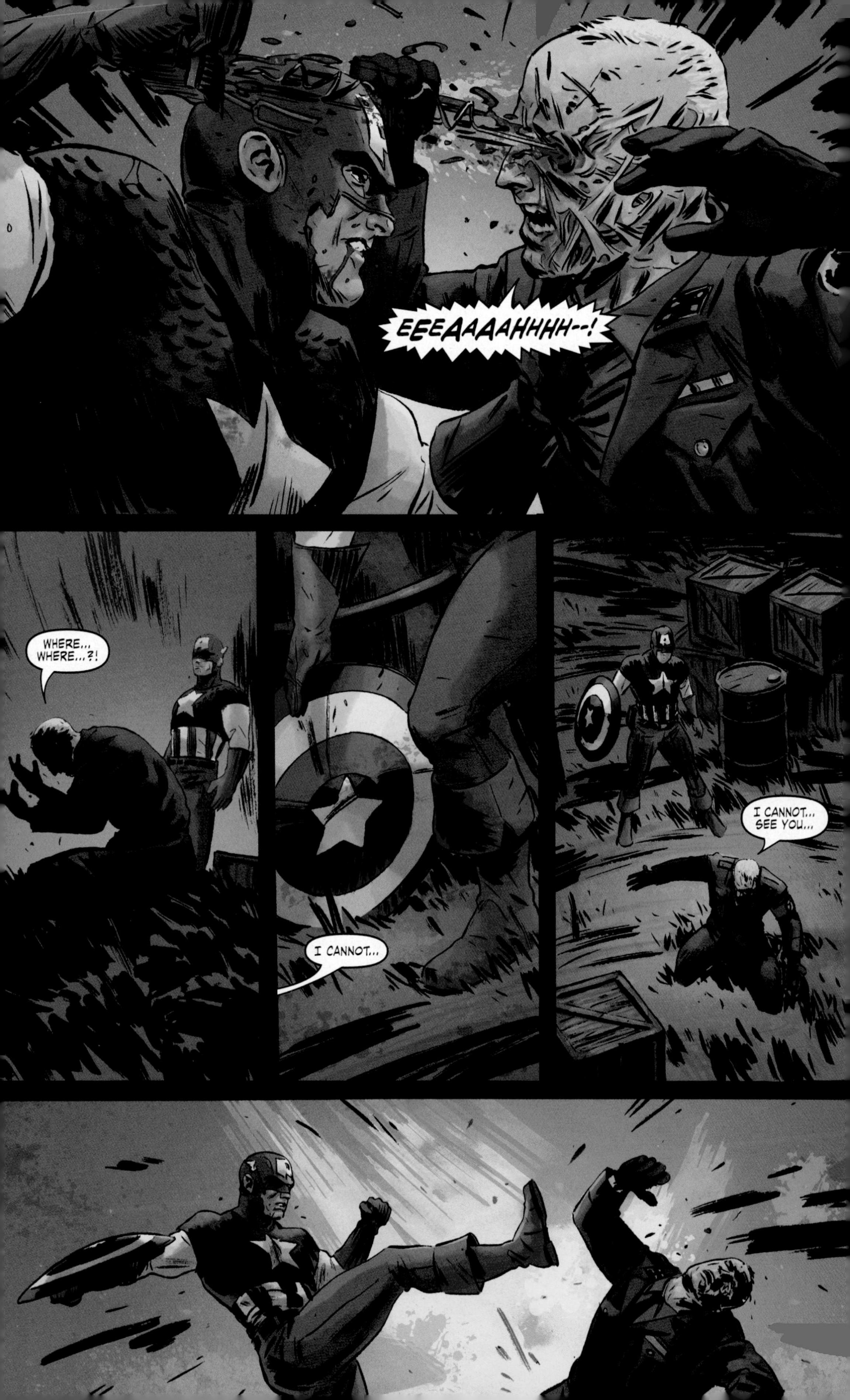
EEEAAAAHHHH--!
WHERE... WHERE...?!
I CANNOT...
I CANNOT... SEE YOU...

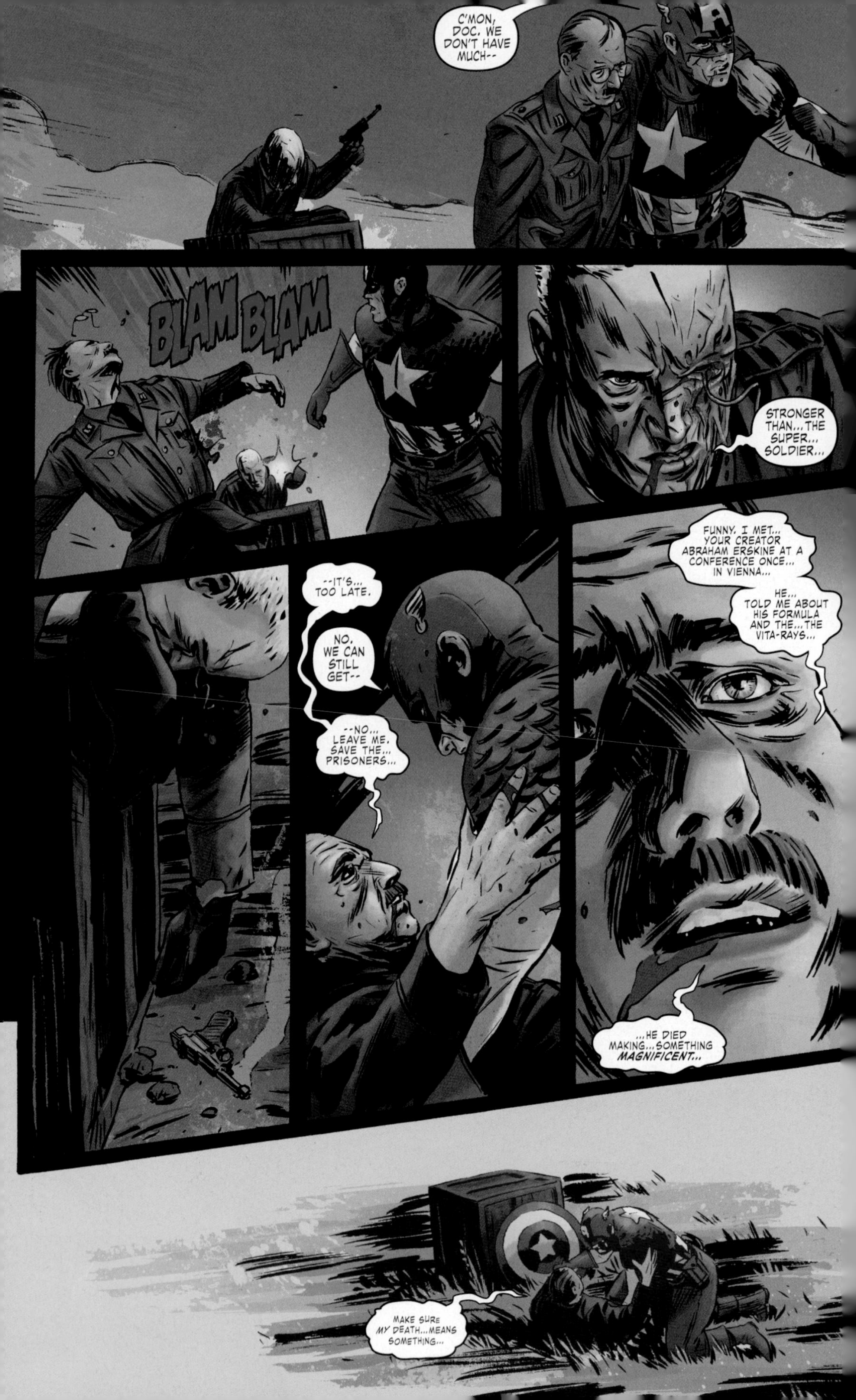
C'MON, DOC. WE DON'T HAVE MUCH--
BLAM BLAM
STRONGER THAN... THE SUPER... SOLDIER...
FUNNY. I MET... YOUR CREATOR ABRAHAM ERSKINE AT A CONFERENCE ONCE... IN VIENNA...
HE... TOLD ME ABOUT HIS FORMULA AND THE... THE VITA-RAYS...
...HE DIED MAKING... SOMETHING MAGNIFICENT...
--IT'S... TOO LATE.
NO. WE CAN STILL GET--
--NO... LEAVE ME. SAVE THE... PRISONERS...
MAKE SURE MY DEATH... MEANS SOMETHING...

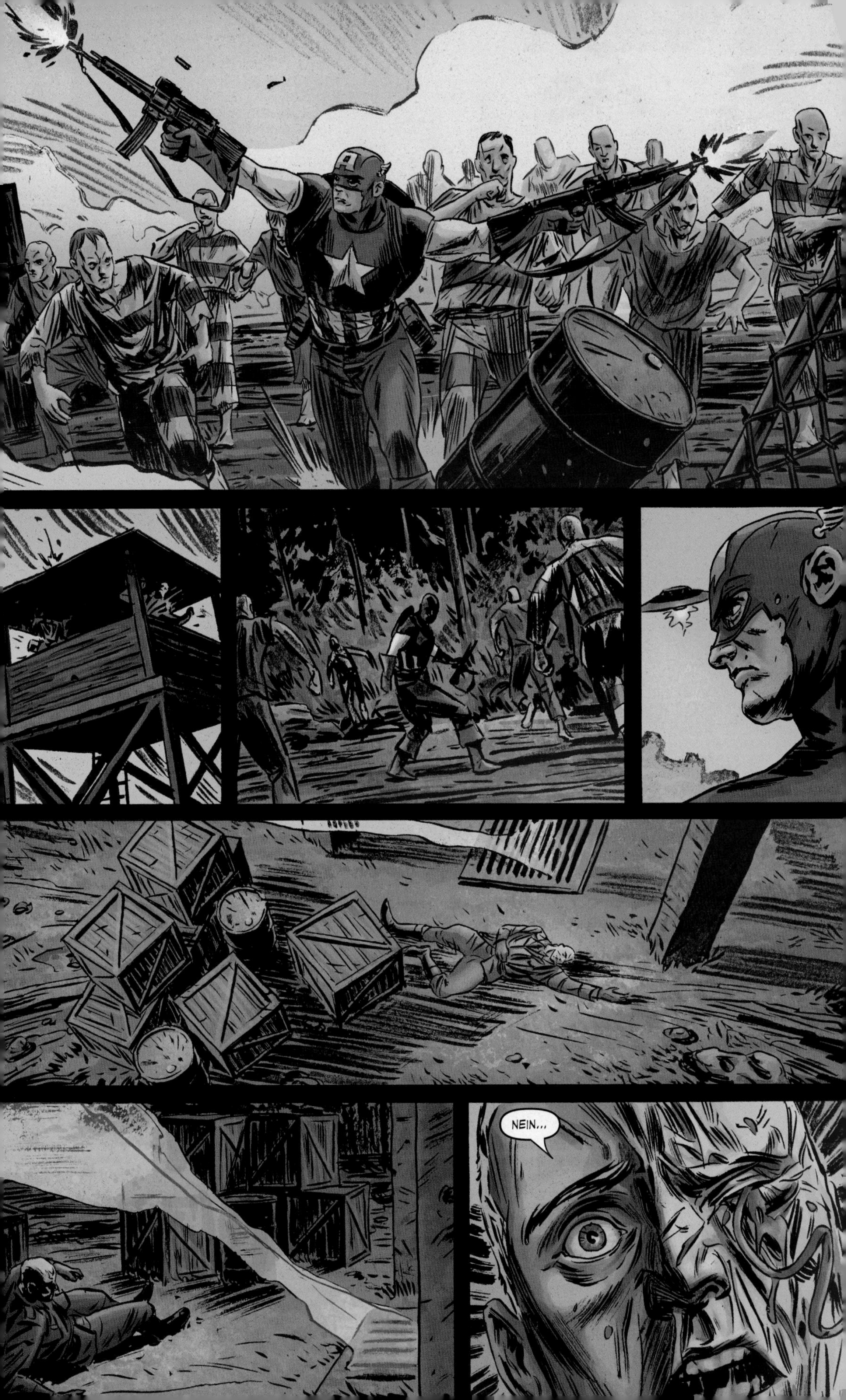
NEIN...

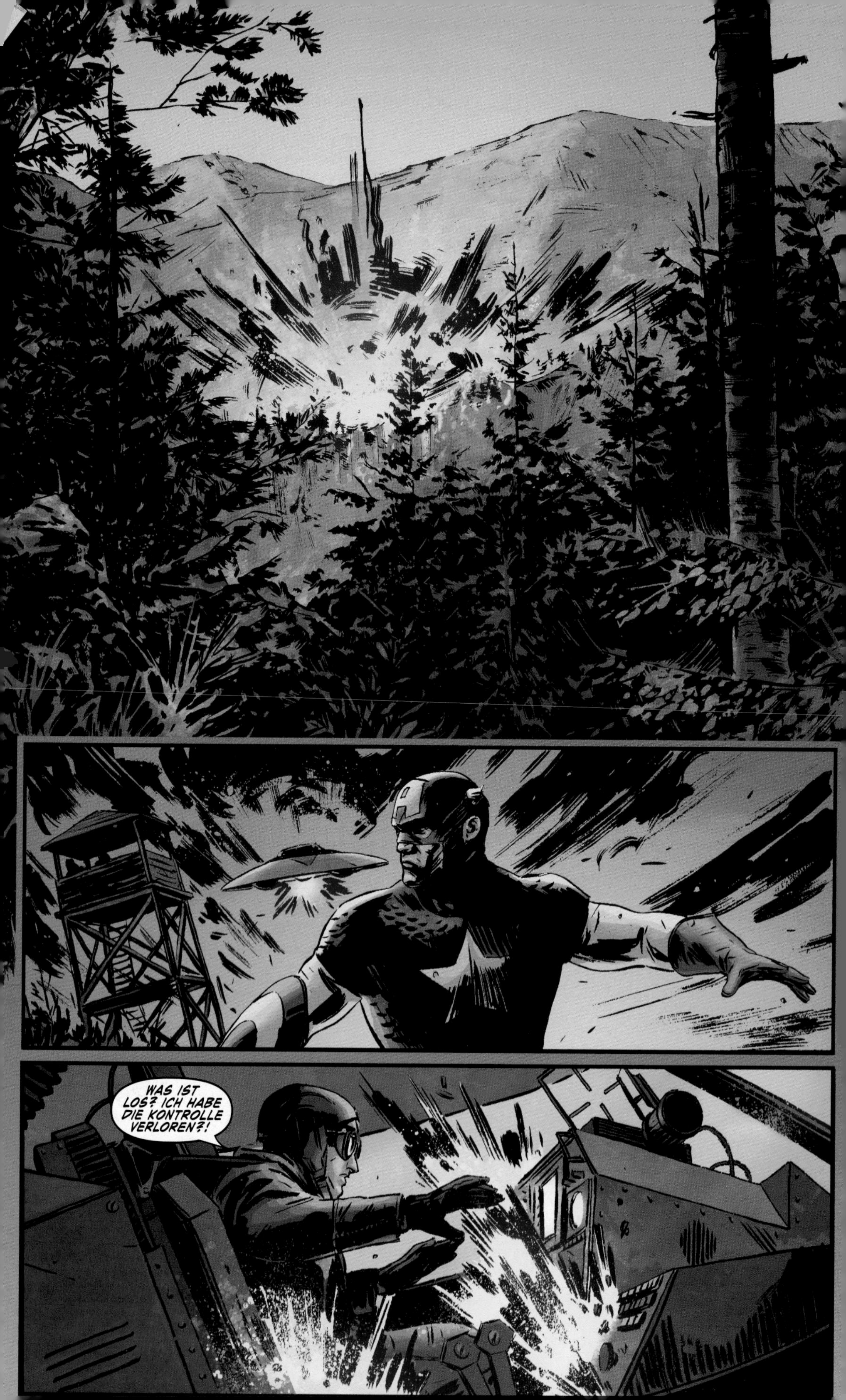
WAS IST LOS? ICH HABE DIE KONTROLLE VERLOREN?!

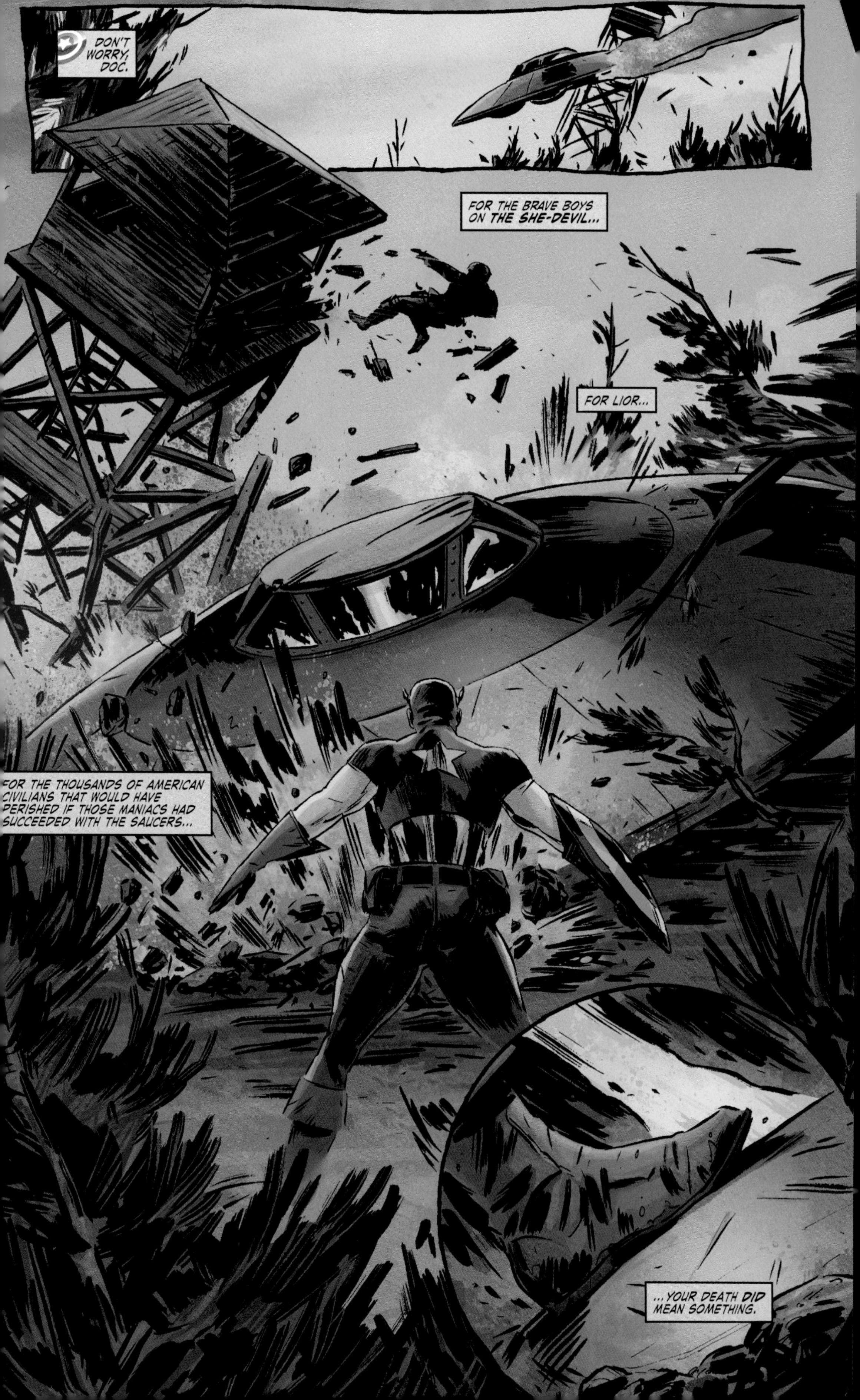
DON'T WORRY, DOC.
FOR THE BRAVE BOYS ON THE SHE-DEVIL...
FOR LIOR...
FOR THE THOUSANDS OF AMERICAN CIVILIANS THAT WOULD HAVE PERISHED IF THOSE MANIACS HAD SUCCEEDED WITH THE SAUCERS...
...YOUR DEATH DID MEAN SOMETHING.

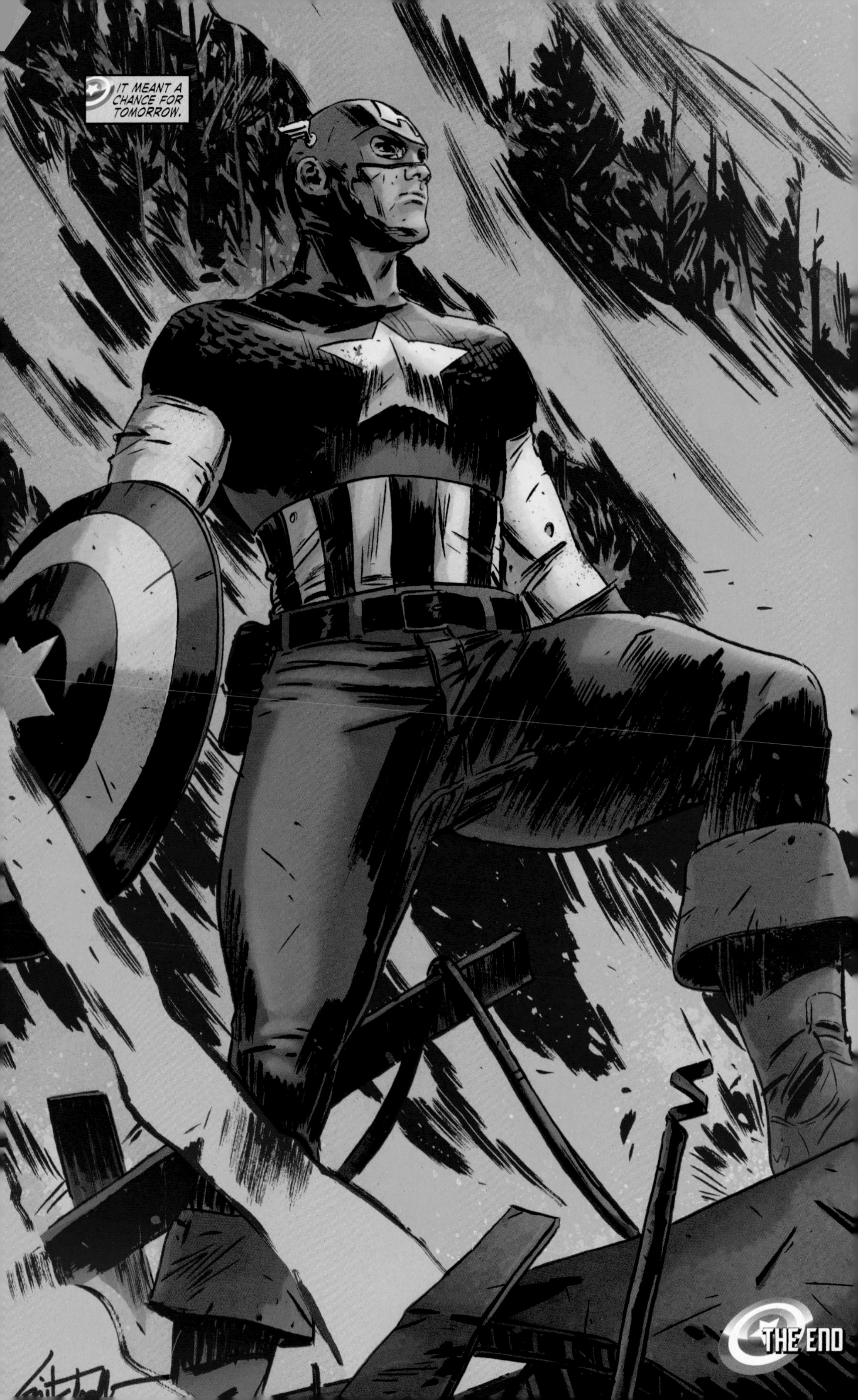
IT MEANT A CHANCE FOR TOMORROW.
THE END

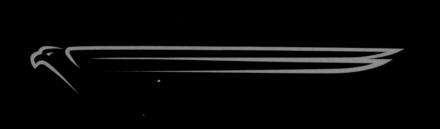

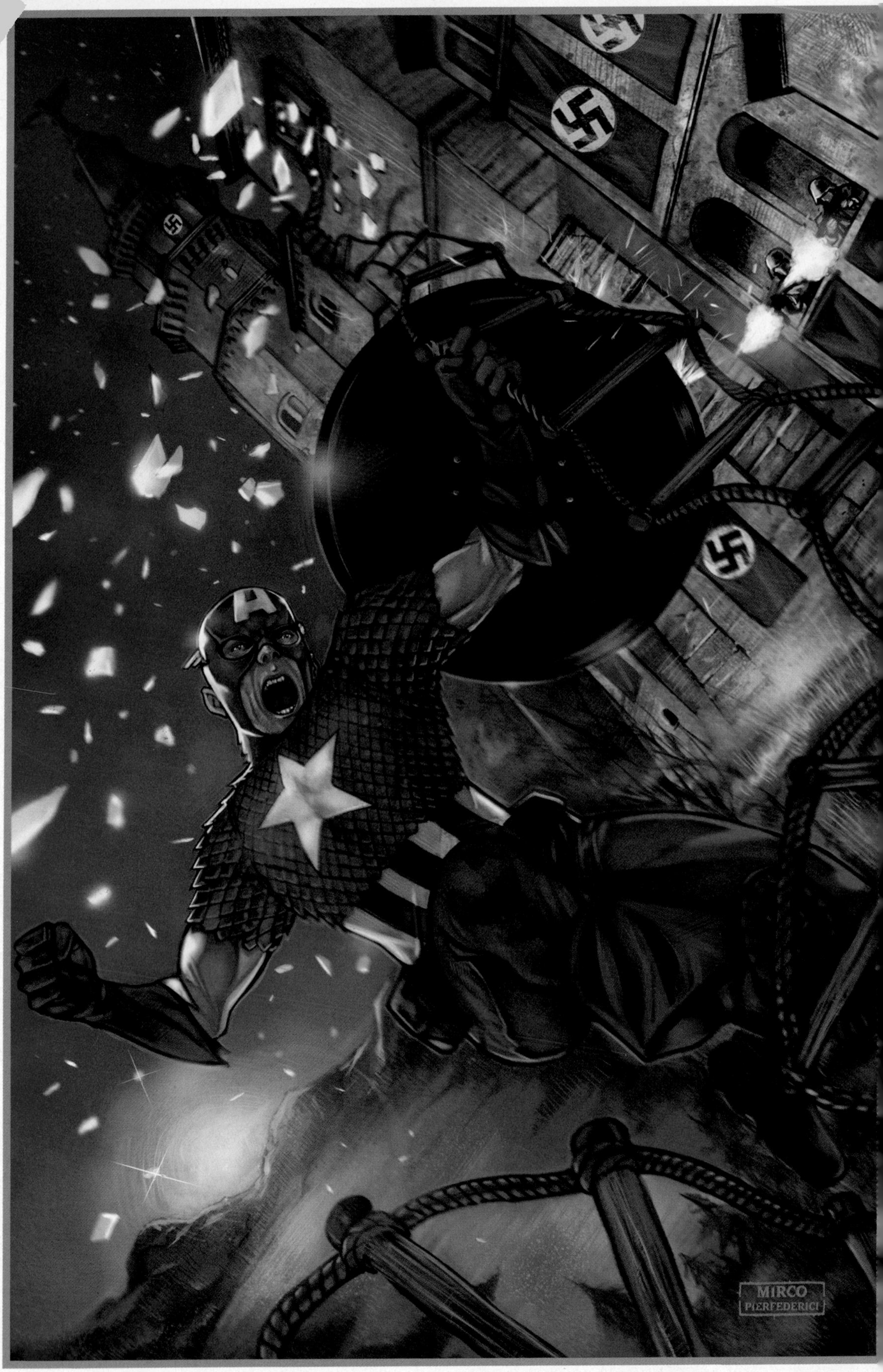
MIRCO
PIERFEDERICI

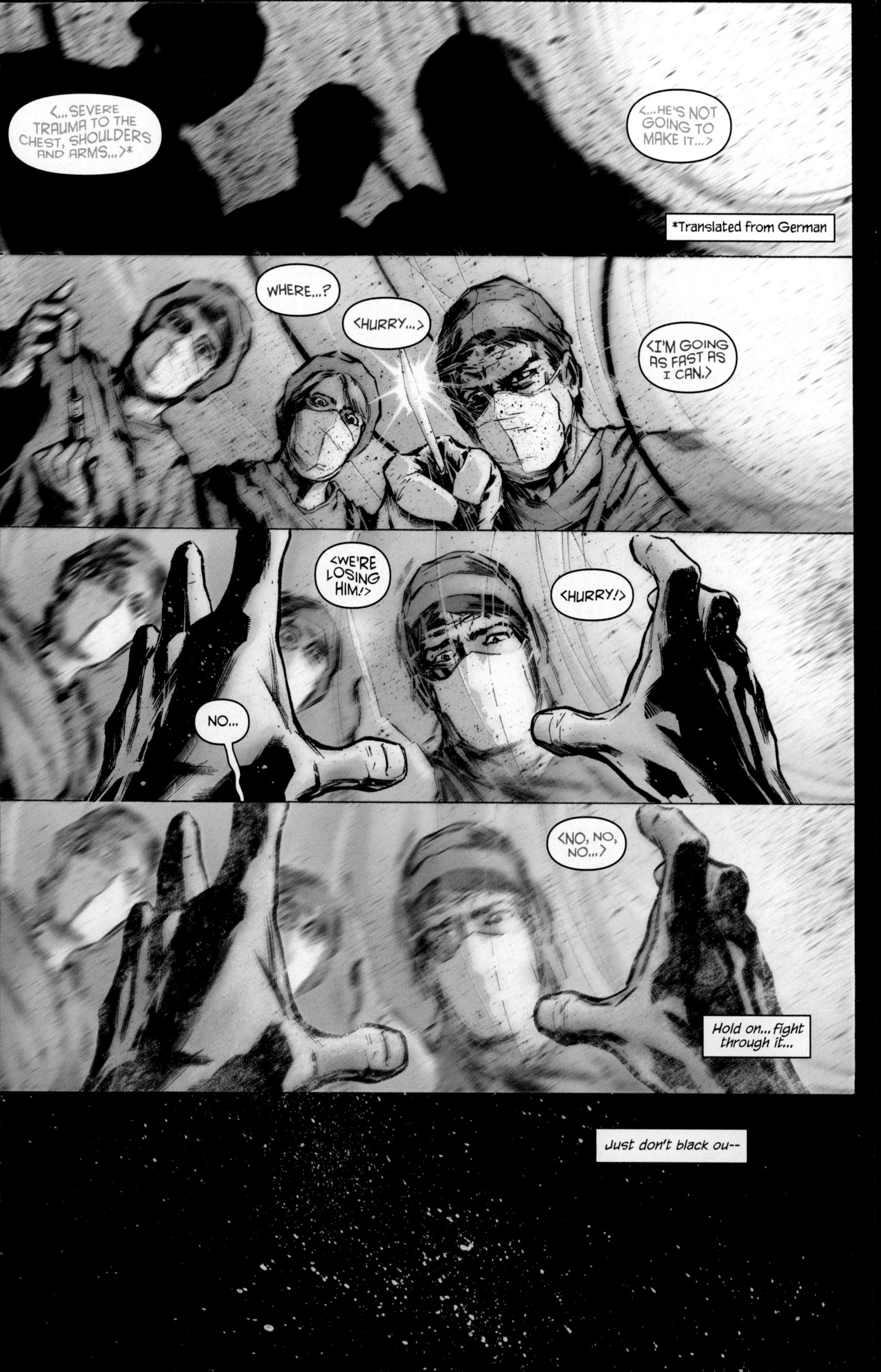
<...SEVERE TRAUMA TO THE CHEST, SHOULDERS AND ARMS...>*
<...HE'S NOT GOING TO MAKE IT...>
*Translated from German
WHERE...?
<HURRY...>
<I'M GOING AS FAST AS I CAN.>
<WE'RE LOSING HIM!>
<HURRY!>
NO...
<NO, NO, NO...>
Hold on... fight through it...
Just don't black ou--

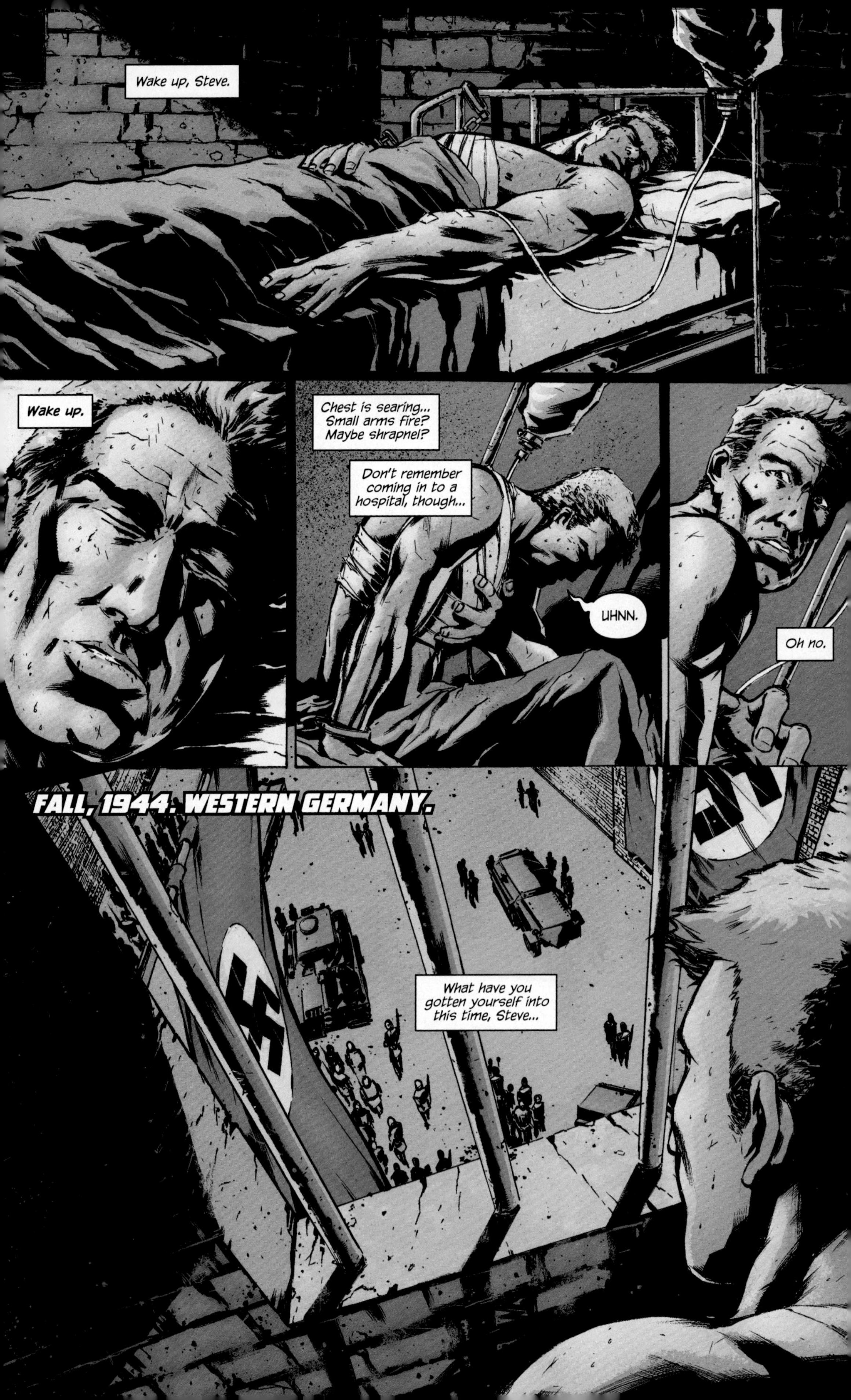
Wake up, Steve.
Wake up.
Chest is searing... Small arms fire? Maybe shrapnel?
Don't remember coming in to a hospital, though...
UHNN.
Oh no.
FALL, 1944. WESTERN GERMANY.
What have you gotten yourself into this time, Steve...

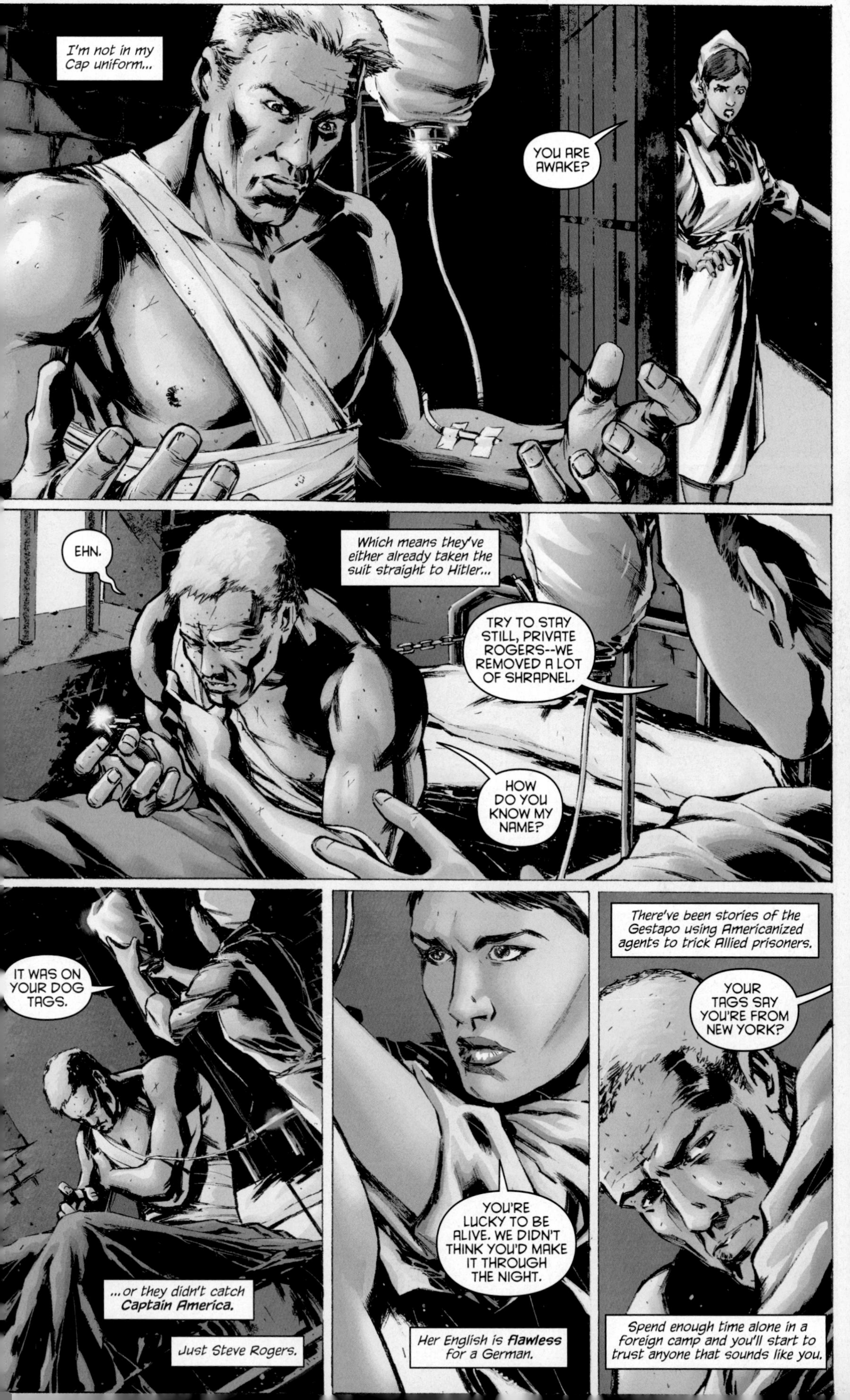
I'm not in my Cap uniform...
YOU ARE AWAKE?
EHN.
Which means they've either already taken the suit straight to Hitler...
TRY TO STAY STILL, PRIVATE ROGERS--WE REMOVED A LOT OF SHRAPNEL.
HOW DO YOU KNOW MY NAME?
IT WAS ON YOUR DOG TAGS.
...or they didn't catch Captain America.
Just Steve Rogers.
YOU'RE LUCKY TO BE ALIVE. WE DIDN'T THINK YOU'D MAKE IT THROUGH THE NIGHT.
Her English is flawless for a German.
There've been stories of the Gestapo using Americanized agents to trick Allied prisoners.
YOUR TAGS SAY YOU'RE FROM NEW YORK?
Spend enough time alone in a foreign camp and you'll start to trust anyone that sounds like you.

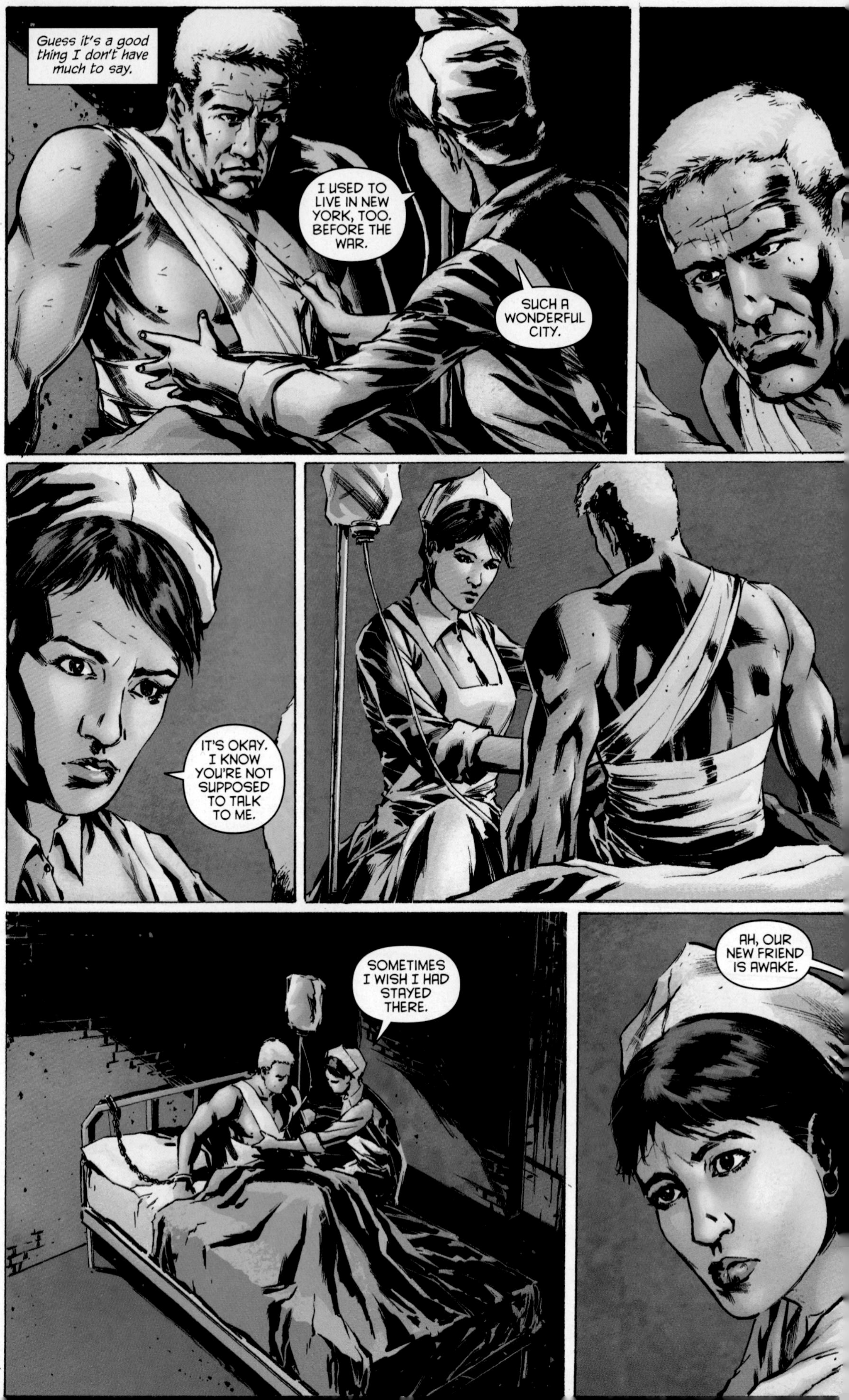
Guess it's a good thing I don't have much to say.
I USED TO LIVE IN NEW YORK, TOO. BEFORE THE WAR.
SUCH A WONDERFUL CITY.
IT'S OKAY. I KNOW YOU'RE NOT SUPPOSED TO TALK TO ME.
SOMETIMES I WISH I HAD STAYED THERE.
AH, OUR NEW FRIEND IS AWAKE.

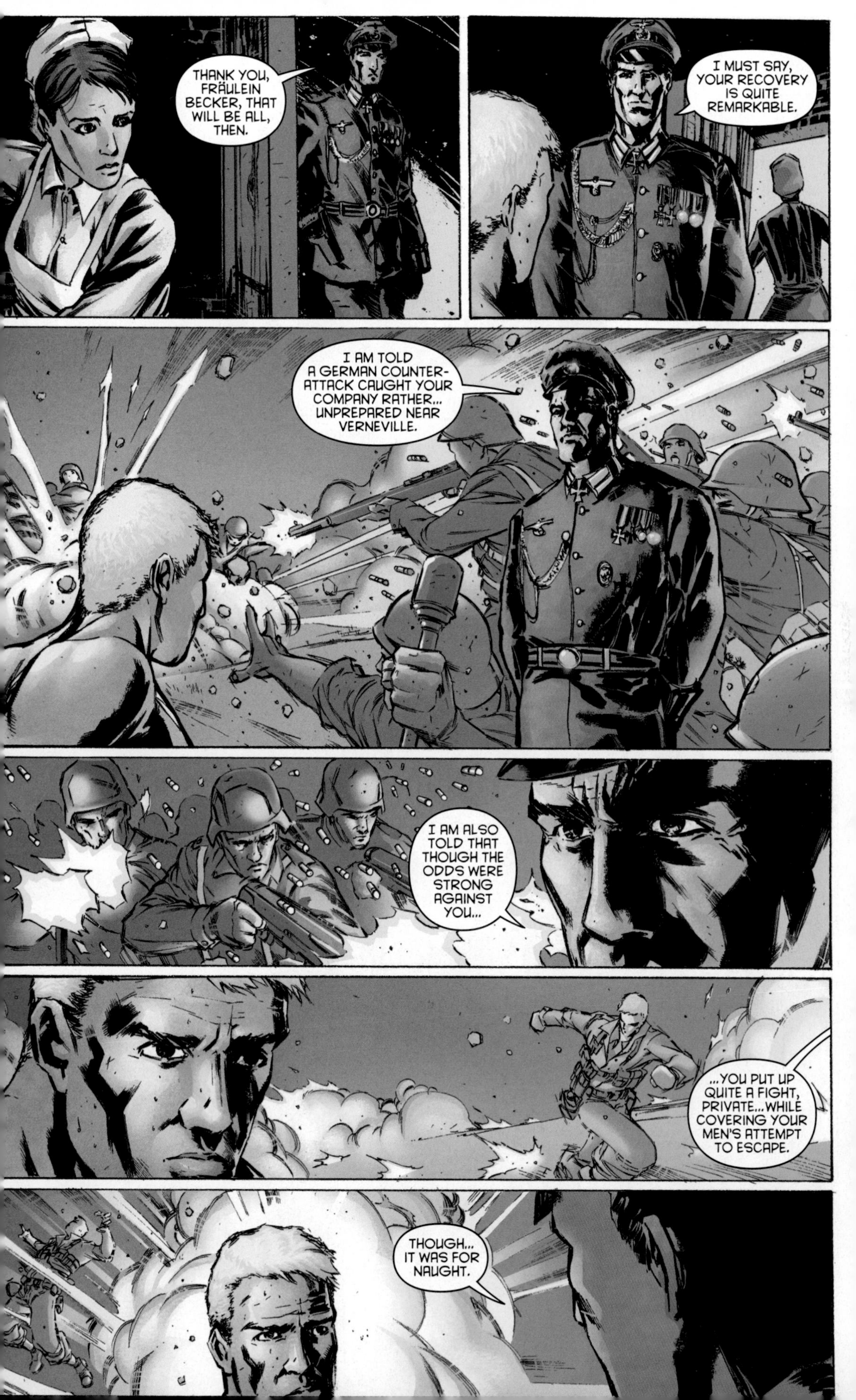
THANK YOU, FRÄULEIN BECKER, THAT WILL BE ALL, THEN.
I MUST SAY, YOUR RECOVERY IS QUITE REMARKABLE.
I AM TOLD A GERMAN COUNTER-ATTACK CAUGHT YOUR COMPANY RATHER... UNPREPARED NEAR VERNEVILLE.
I AM ALSO TOLD THAT THOUGH THE ODDS WERE STRONG AGAINST YOU...
...YOU PUT UP QUITE A FIGHT, PRIVATE...WHILE COVERING YOUR MEN'S ATTEMPT TO ESCAPE.
THOUGH... IT WAS FOR NAUGHT.

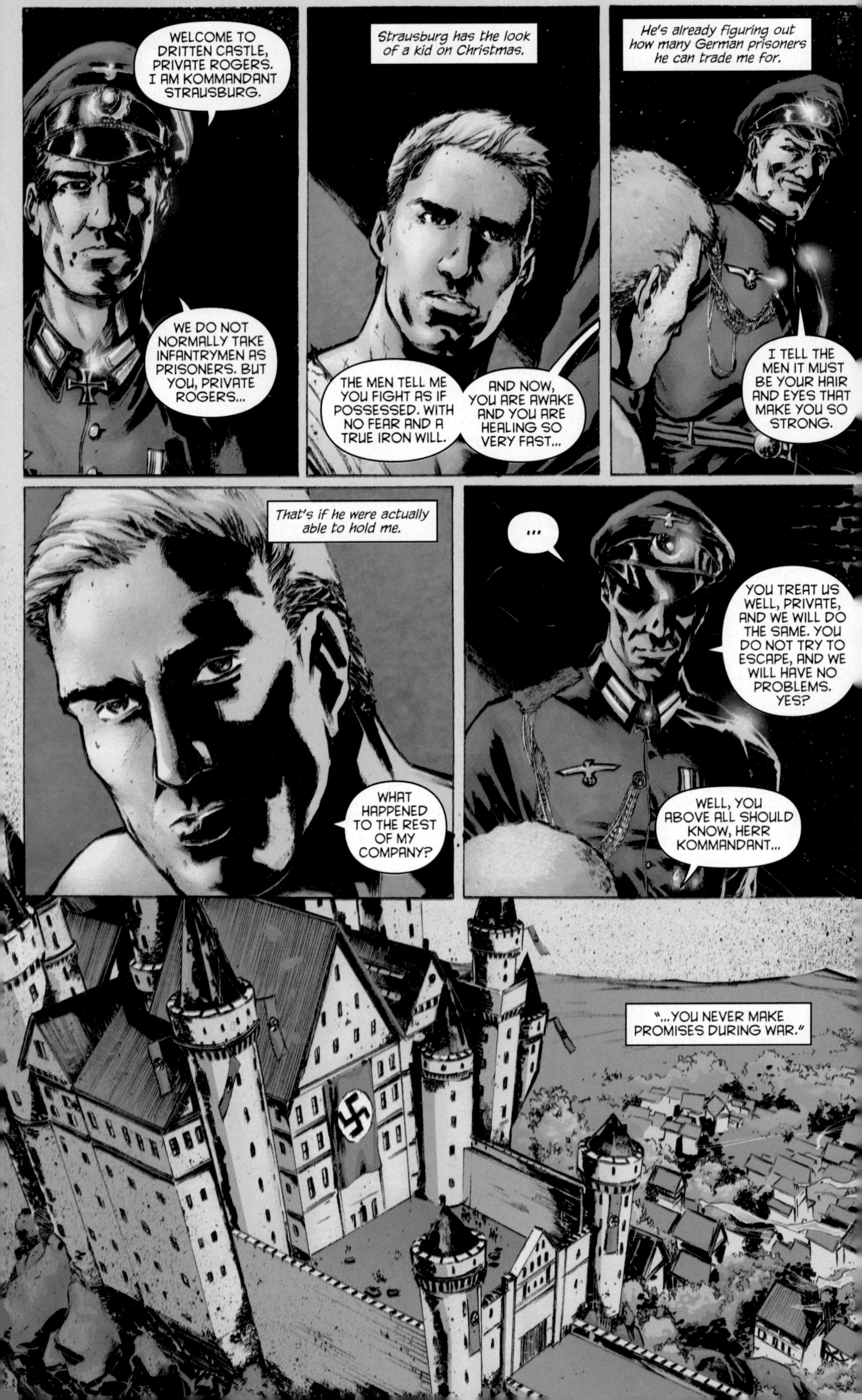
WELCOME TO DRITTEN CASTLE, PRIVATE ROGERS. I AM KOMMANDANT STRAUSBURG.
WE DO NOT NORMALLY TAKE INFANTRYMEN AS PRISONERS. BUT YOU, PRIVATE ROGERS...
Strausburg has the look of a kid on Christmas.
THE MEN TELL ME YOU FIGHT AS IF POSSESSED. WITH NO FEAR AND A TRUE IRON WILL.
AND NOW, YOU ARE AWAKE AND YOU ARE HEALING SO VERY FAST...
He's already figuring out how many German prisoners he can trade me for.
I TELL THE MEN IT MUST BE YOUR HAIR AND EYES THAT MAKE YOU SO STRONG.
That's if he were actually able to hold me.
WHAT HAPPENED TO THE REST OF MY COMPANY?
...
YOU TREAT US WELL, PRIVATE, AND WE WILL DO THE SAME. YOU DO NOT TRY TO ESCAPE, AND WE WILL HAVE NO PROBLEMS. YES?
WELL, YOU ABOVE ALL SHOULD KNOW, HERR KOMMANDANT...
"...YOU NEVER MAKE PROMISES DURING WAR."

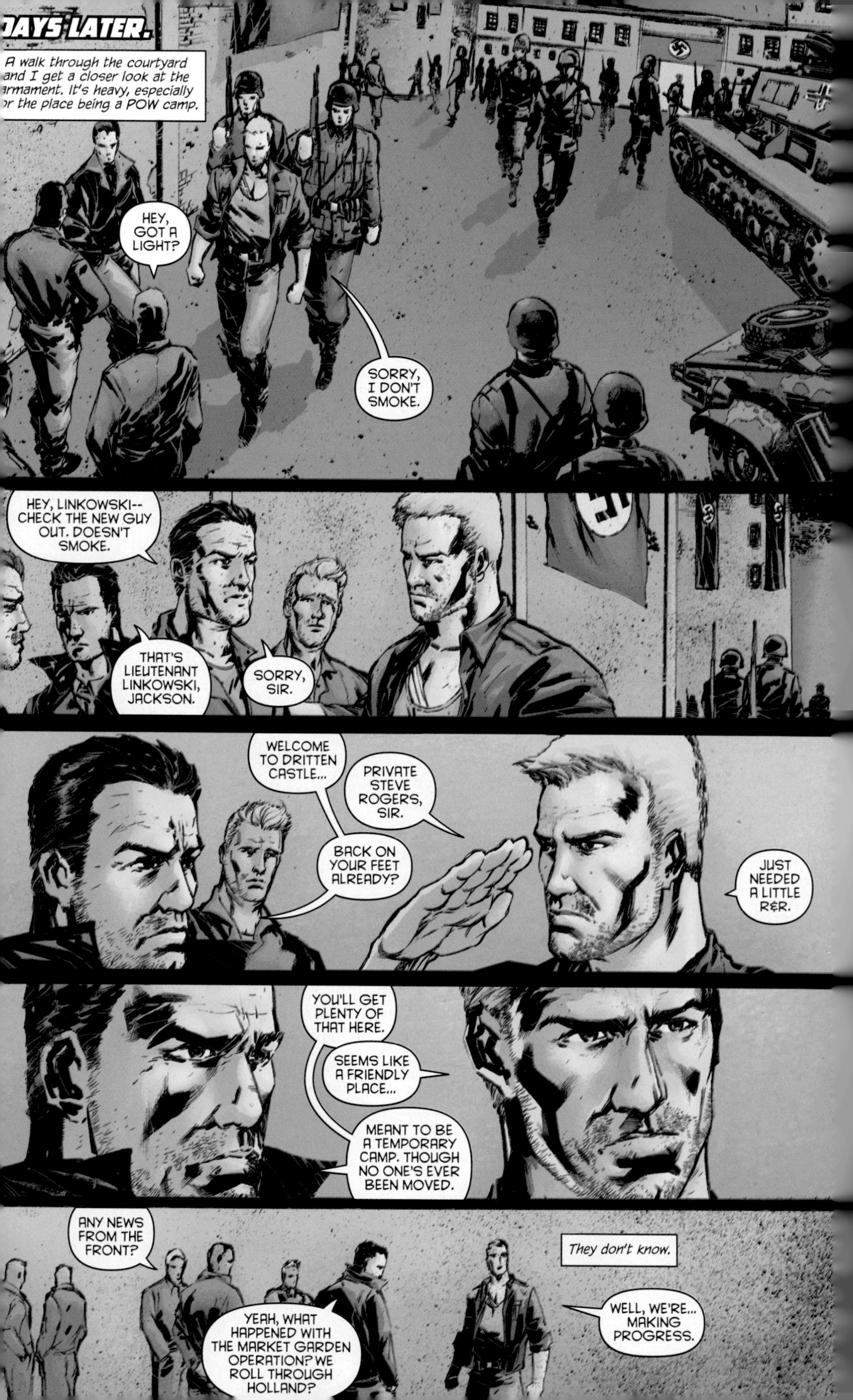
DAYS LATER.
A walk through the courtyard and I get a closer look at the armament. It's heavy, especially for the place being a POW camp.
HEY, GOT A LIGHT?
SORRY, I DON'T SMOKE.
HEY, LINKOWSKI-- CHECK THE NEW GUY OUT. DOESN'T SMOKE.
THAT'S LIEUTENANT LINKOWSKI, JACKSON.
SORRY, SIR.
WELCOME TO DRITTEN CASTLE...
PRIVATE STEVE ROGERS, SIR.
BACK ON YOUR FEET ALREADY?
JUST NEEDED A LITTLE R&R.
YOU'LL GET PLENTY OF THAT HERE.
SEEMS LIKE A FRIENDLY PLACE...
MEANT TO BE A TEMPORARY CAMP. THOUGH NO ONE'S EVER BEEN MOVED.
ANY NEWS FROM THE FRONT?
YEAH, WHAT HAPPENED WITH THE MARKET GARDEN OPERATION? WE ROLL THROUGH HOLLAND?
They don't know.
WELL, WE'RE... MAKING PROGRESS.

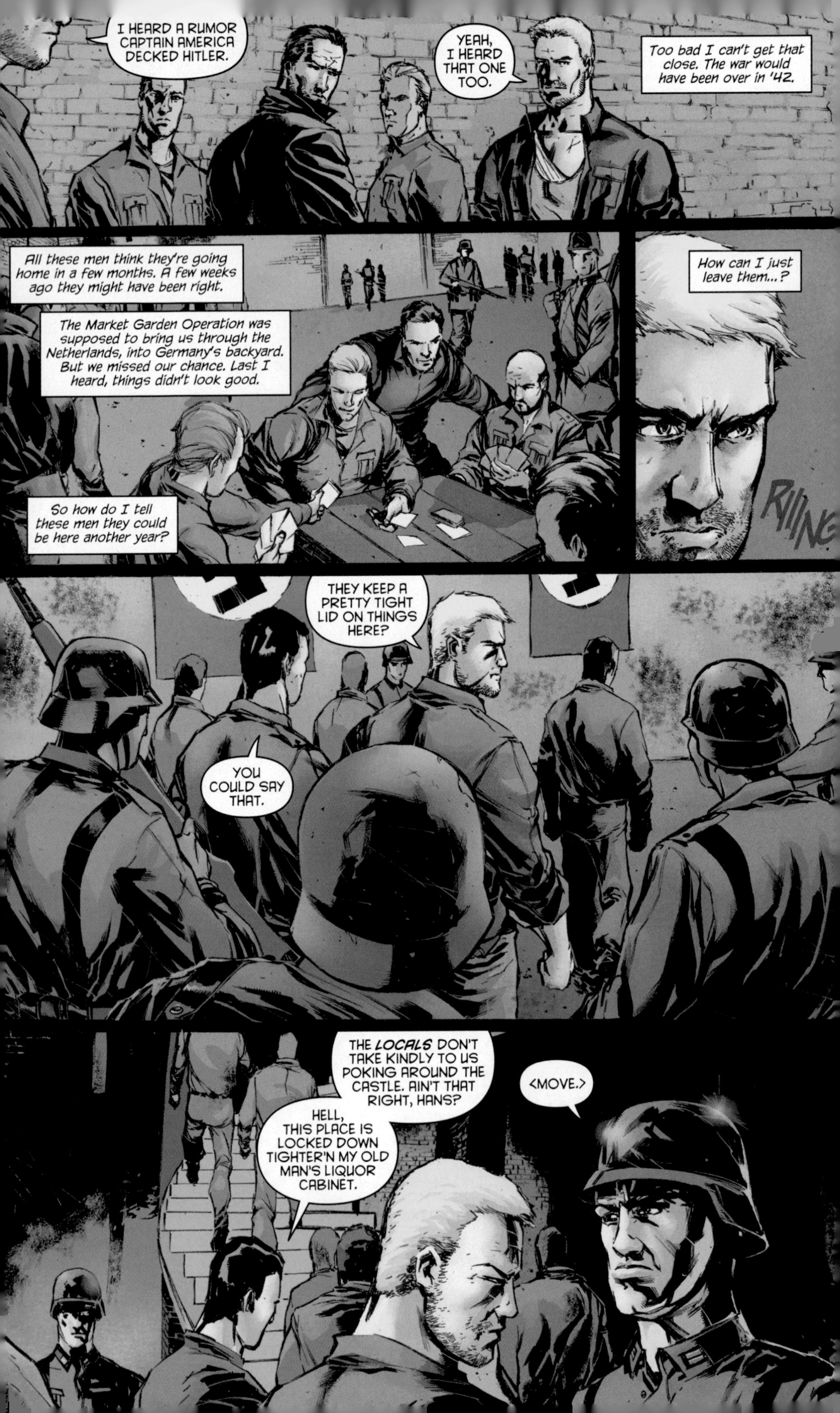
I HEARD A RUMOR CAPTAIN AMERICA DECKED HITLER.
YEAH, I HEARD THAT ONE TOO.
Too bad I can't get that close. The war would have been over in '42.
All these men think they're going home in a few months. A few weeks ago they might have been right.
The Market Garden Operation was supposed to bring us through the Netherlands, into Germany's backyard. But we missed our chance. Last I heard, things didn't look good.
So how do I tell these men they could be here another year?
How can I just leave them...?
RIIING
THEY KEEP A PRETTY TIGHT LID ON THINGS HERE?
YOU COULD SAY THAT.
THE LOCALS DON'T TAKE KINDLY TO US POKING AROUND THE CASTLE. AIN'T THAT RIGHT, HANS?
HELL, THIS PLACE IS LOCKED DOWN TIGHTER'N MY OLD MAN'S LIQUOR CABINET.
<MOVE.>

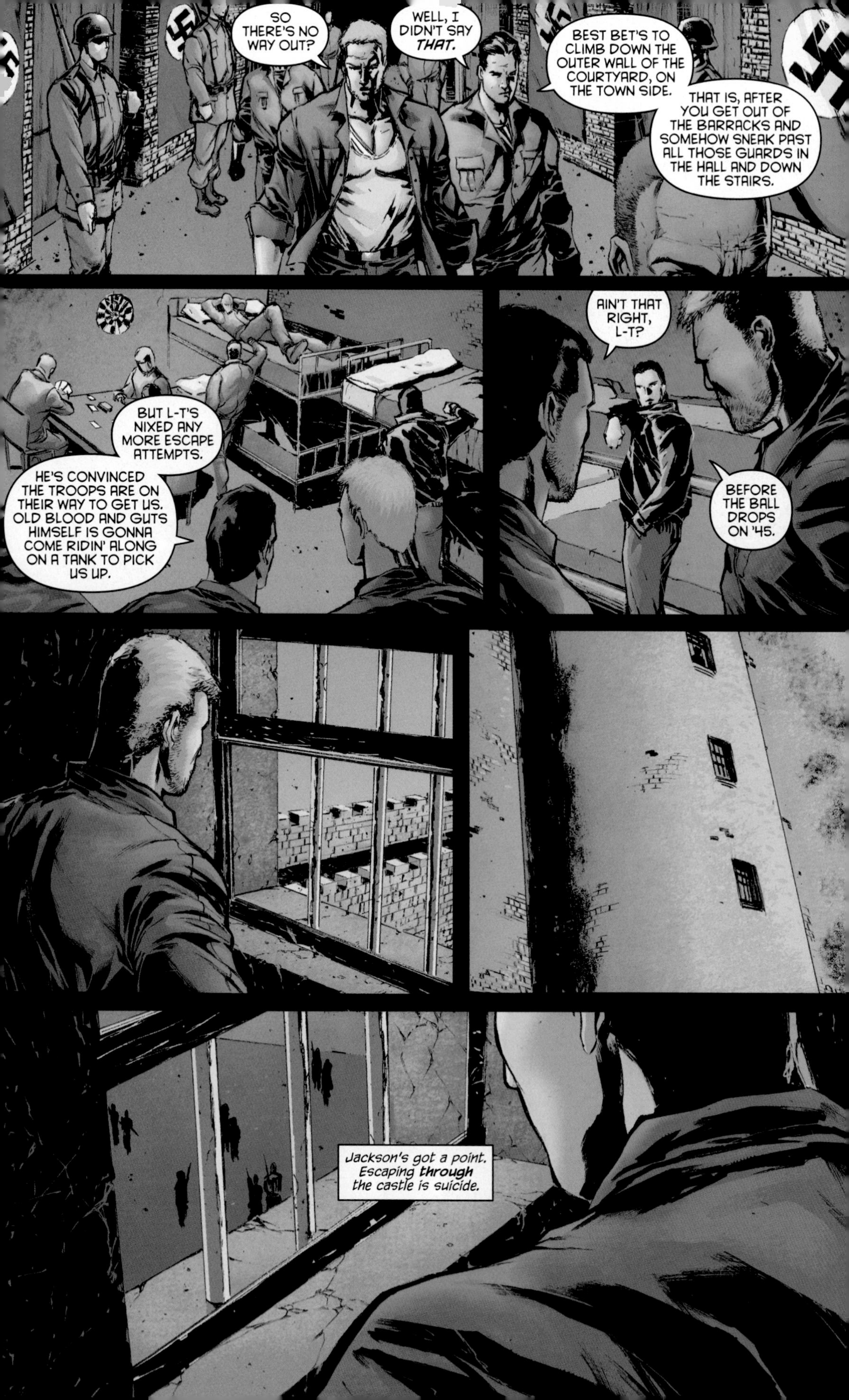
SO THERE'S NO WAY OUT?
WELL, I DIDN'T SAY **THAT.**
BEST BET'S TO CLIMB DOWN THE OUTER WALL OF THE COURTYARD, ON THE TOWN SIDE.
THAT IS, AFTER YOU GET OUT OF THE BARRACKS AND SOMEHOW SNEAK PAST ALL THOSE GUARDS IN THE HALL AND DOWN THE STAIRS.
BUT L-T'S NIXED ANY MORE ESCAPE ATTEMPTS.
HE'S CONVINCED THE TROOPS ARE ON THEIR WAY TO GET US. OLD BLOOD AND GUTS HIMSELF IS GONNA COME RIDIN' ALONG ON A TANK TO PICK US UP.
AIN'T THAT RIGHT, L-T?
BEFORE THE BALL DROPS ON '45.
*Jackson's got a point. Escaping **through** the castle is suicide.*

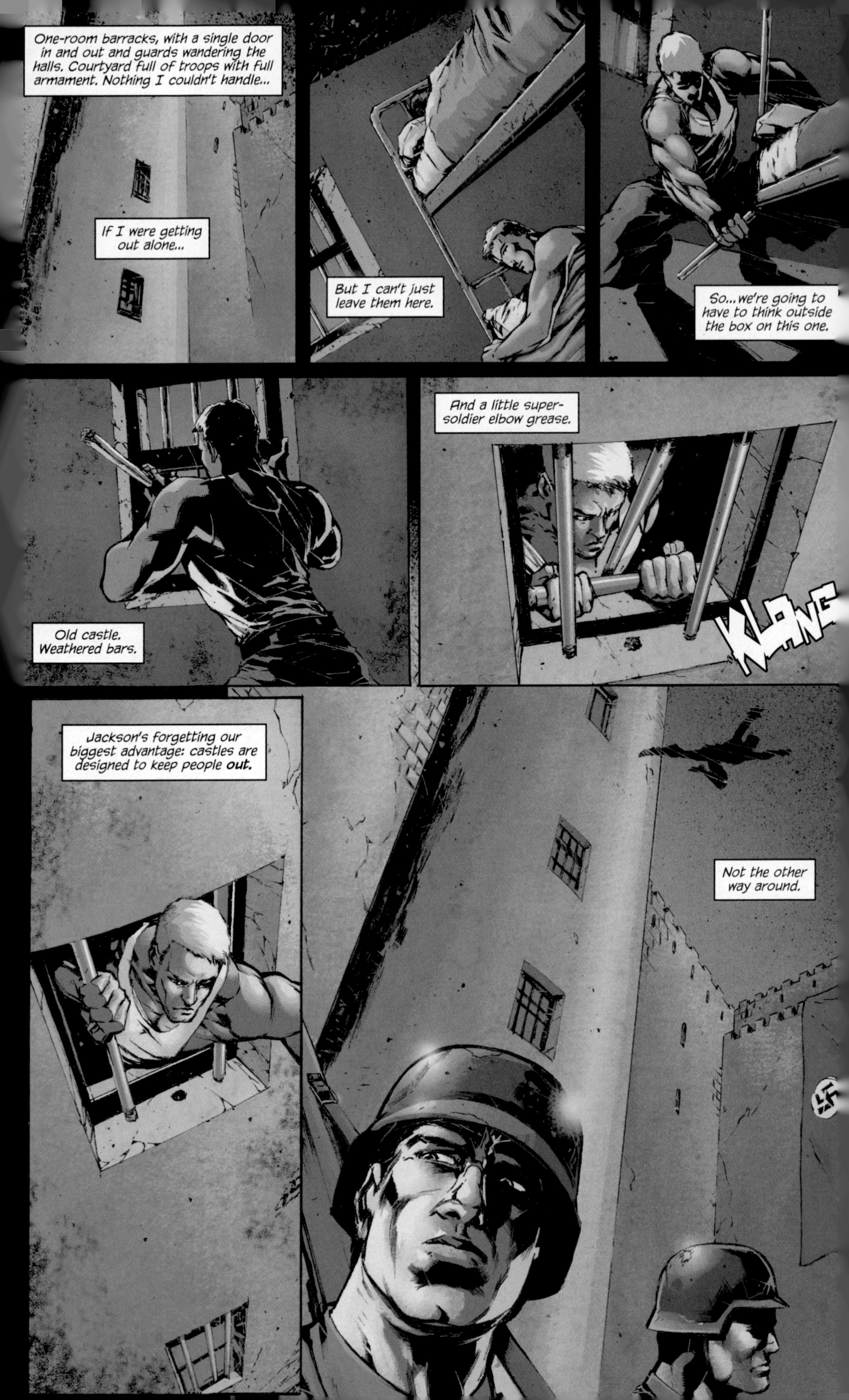
One-room barracks, with a single door in and out and guards wandering the halls. Courtyard full of troops with full armament. Nothing I couldn't handle...
If I were getting out alone...
But I can't just leave them here.
So...we're going to have to think outside the box on this one.
Old castle. Weathered bars.
And a little super-soldier elbow grease.
KLANG
Jackson's forgetting our biggest advantage: castles are designed to keep people out.
Not the other way around.

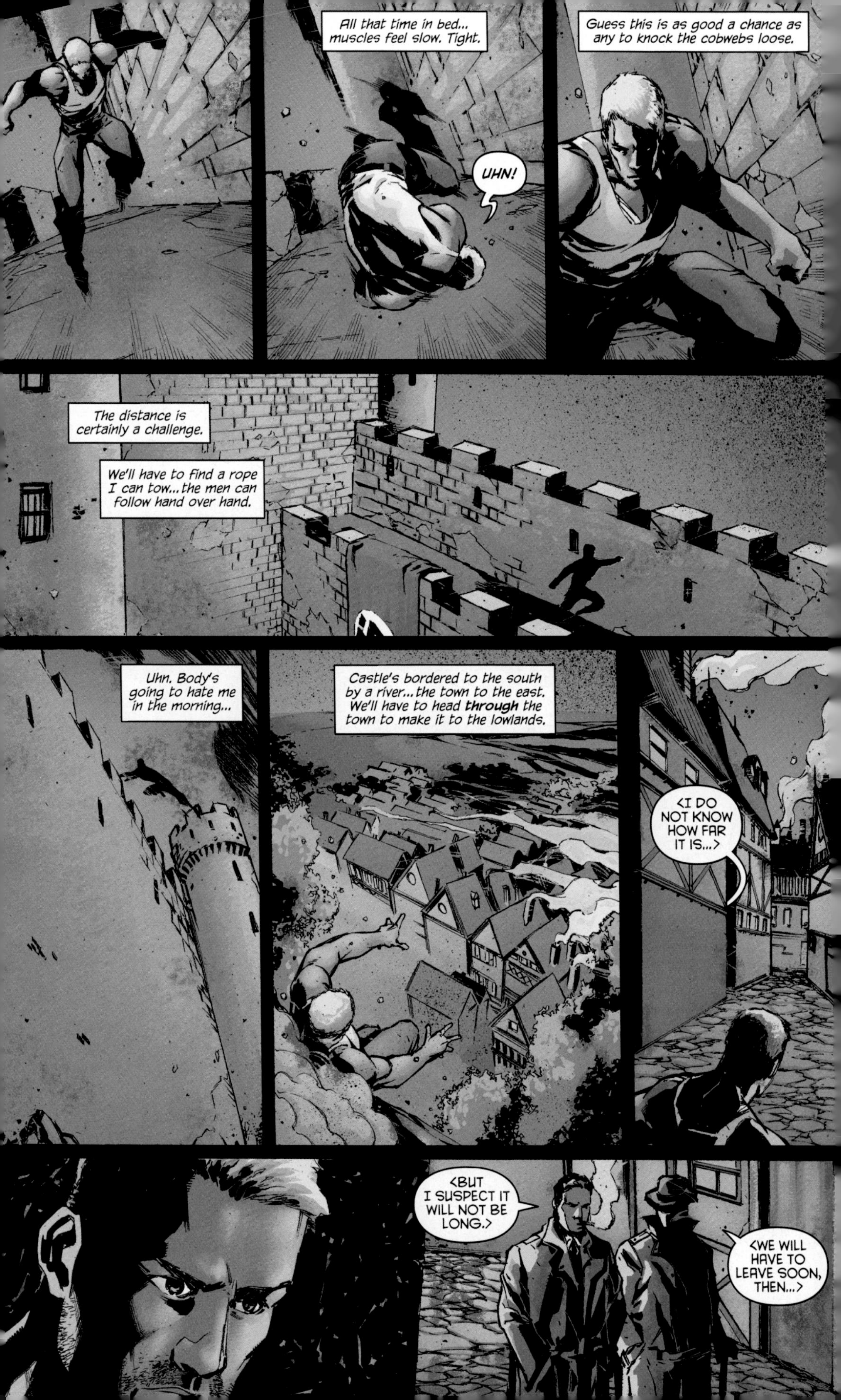
All that time in bed... muscles feel slow. Tight.
UHN!
Guess this is as good a chance as any to knock the cobwebs loose.
The distance is certainly a challenge.
We'll have to find a rope I can tow...the men can follow hand over hand.
Uhn. Body's going to hate me in the morning...
Castle's bordered to the south by a river...the town to the east. We'll have to head **through** the town to make it to the lowlands.
<I DO NOT KNOW HOW FAR IT IS...>
<BUT I SUSPECT IT WILL NOT BE LONG.>
<WE WILL HAVE TO LEAVE SOON, THEN...>

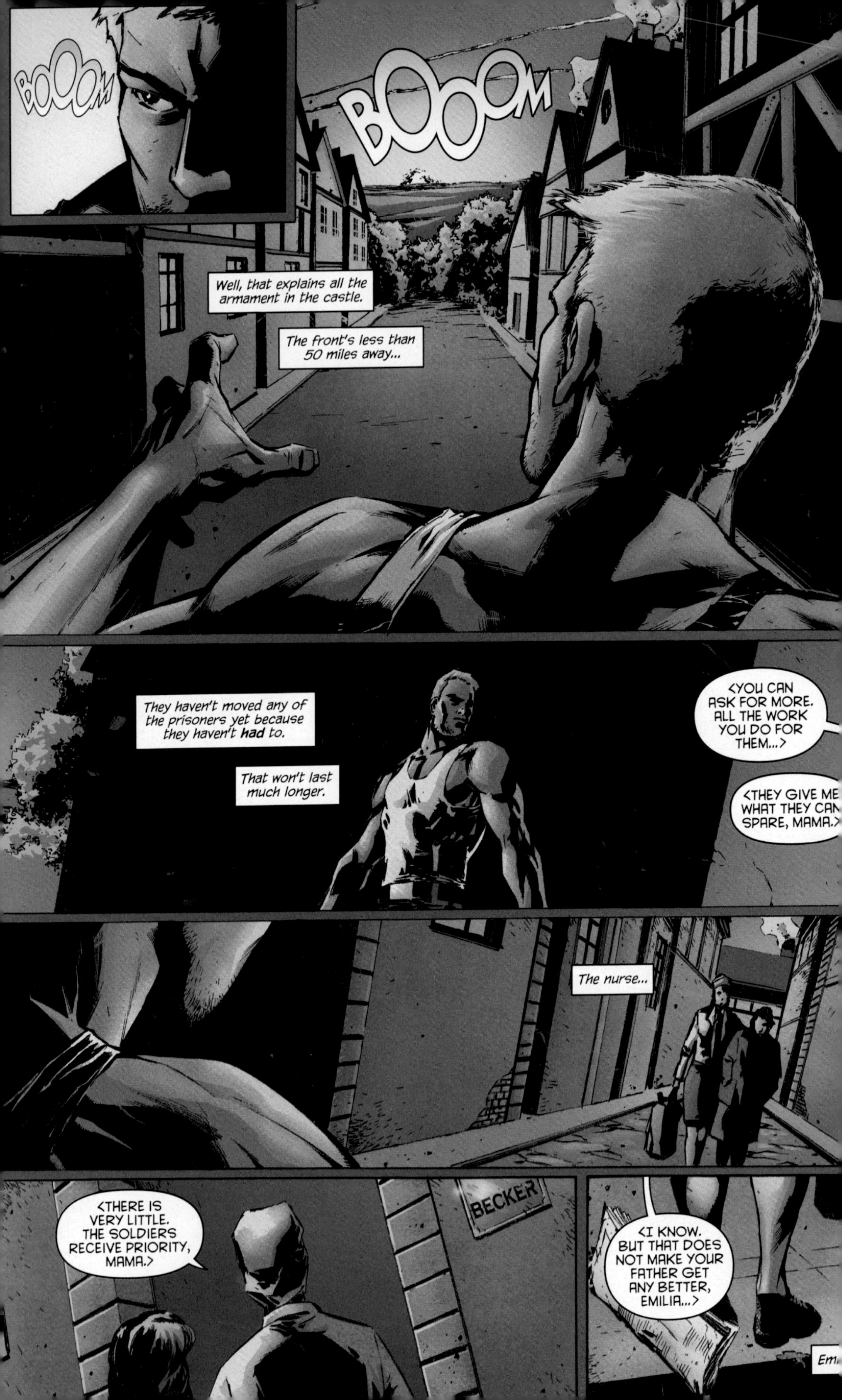
BOOOM
BOOOM
Well, that explains all the armament in the castle.
The front's less than 50 miles away...
They haven't moved any of the prisoners yet because they haven't **had** to.
That won't last much longer.
<YOU CAN ASK FOR MORE. ALL THE WORK YOU DO FOR THEM...>
<THEY GIVE ME WHAT THEY CAN SPARE, MAMA.>
The nurse...
<THERE IS VERY LITTLE. THE SOLDIERS RECEIVE PRIORITY, MAMA.>
BECKER
<I KNOW. BUT THAT DOES NOT MAKE YOUR FATHER GET ANY BETTER, EMILIA...>

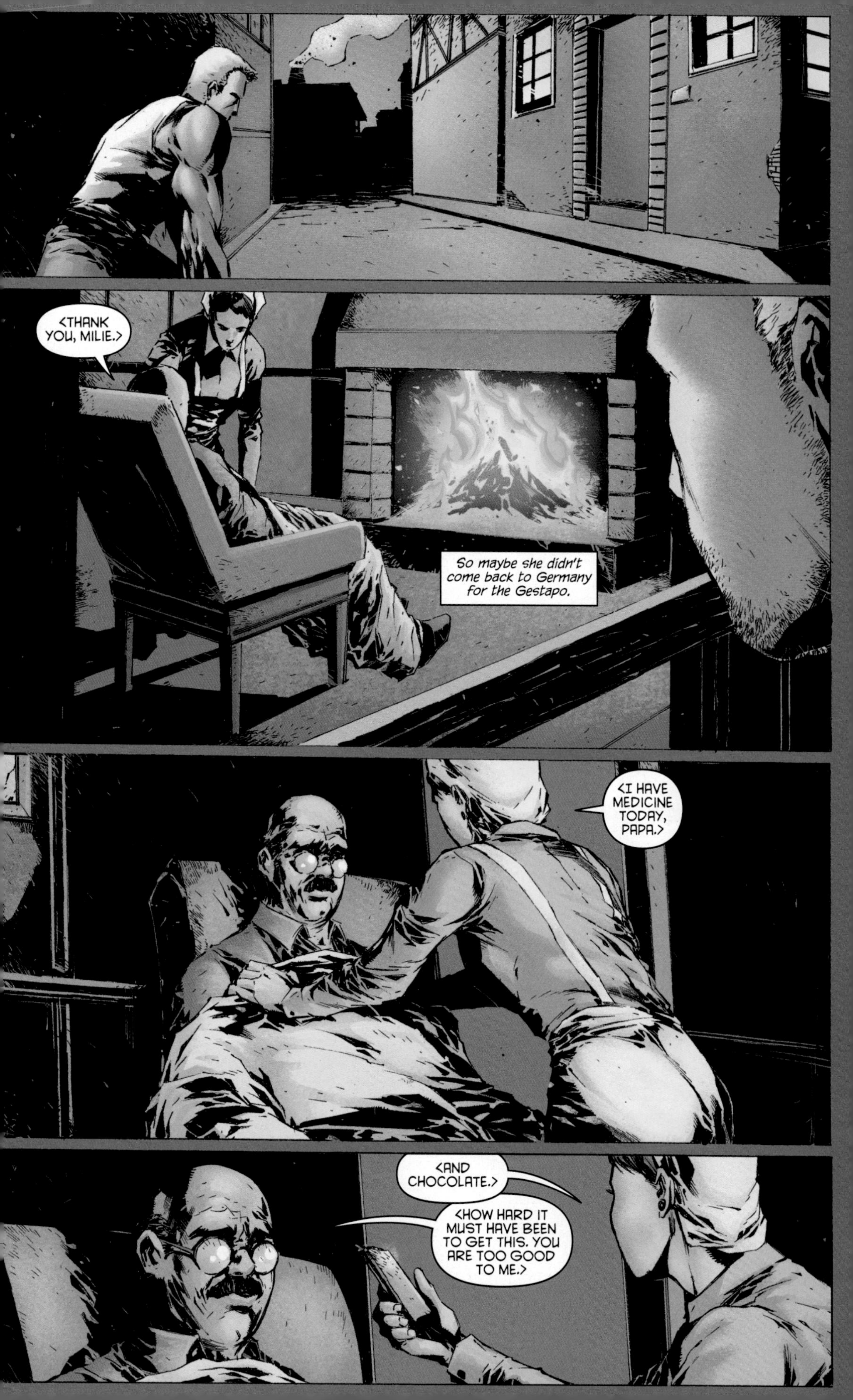
<THANK YOU, MILIE.>
So maybe she didn't come back to Germany for the Gestapo.
<I HAVE MEDICINE TODAY, PAPA.>
<AND CHOCOLATE.>
<HOW HARD IT MUST HAVE BEEN TO GET THIS. YOU ARE TOO GOOD TO ME.>

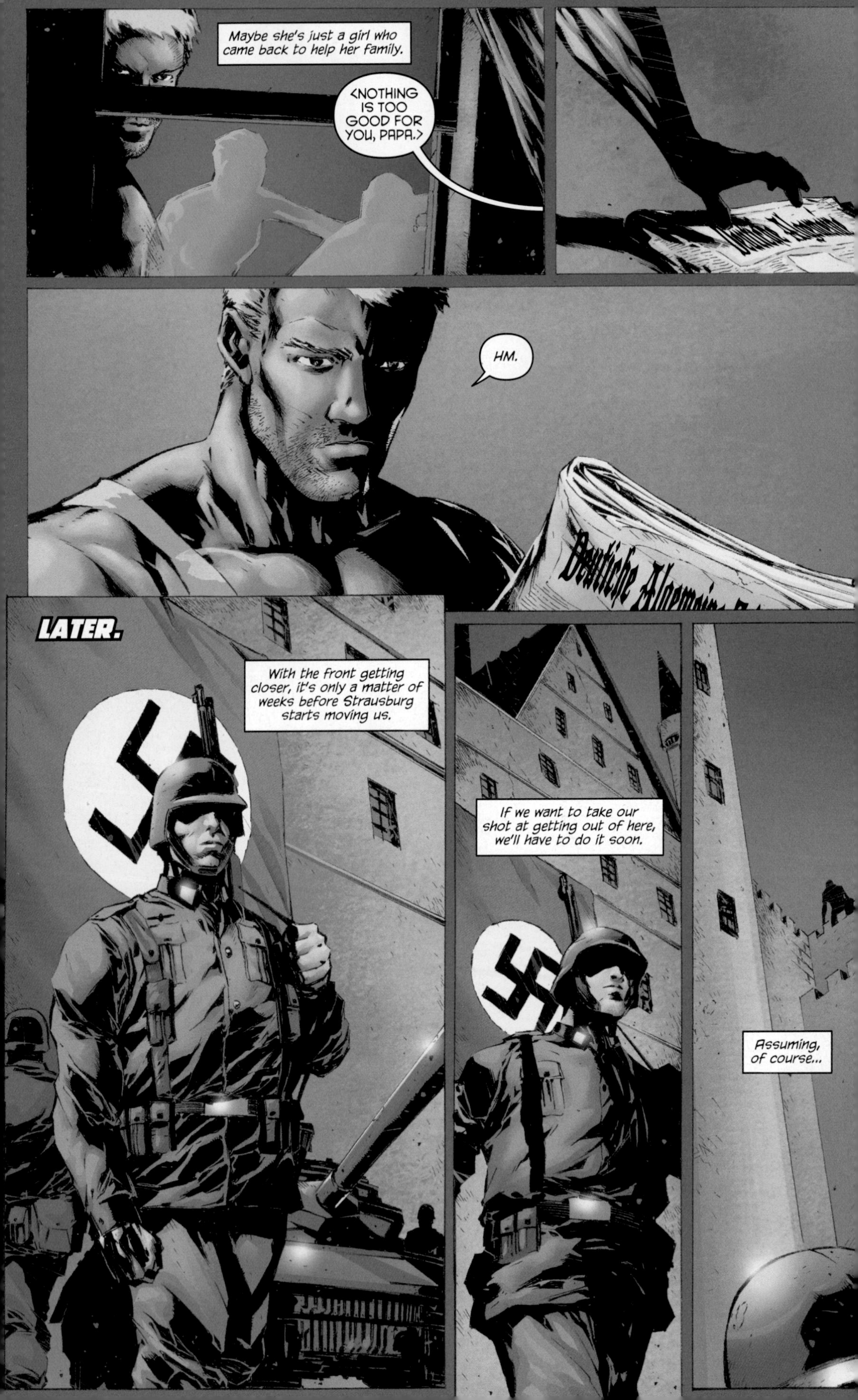
Maybe she's just a girl who came back to help her family.
<NOTHING IS TOO GOOD FOR YOU, PAPA.>
HM.
Deutsche Algemeine
LATER.
With the front getting closer, it's only a matter of weeks before Strausburg starts moving us.
If we want to take our shot at getting out of here, we'll have to do it soon.
Assuming, of course...

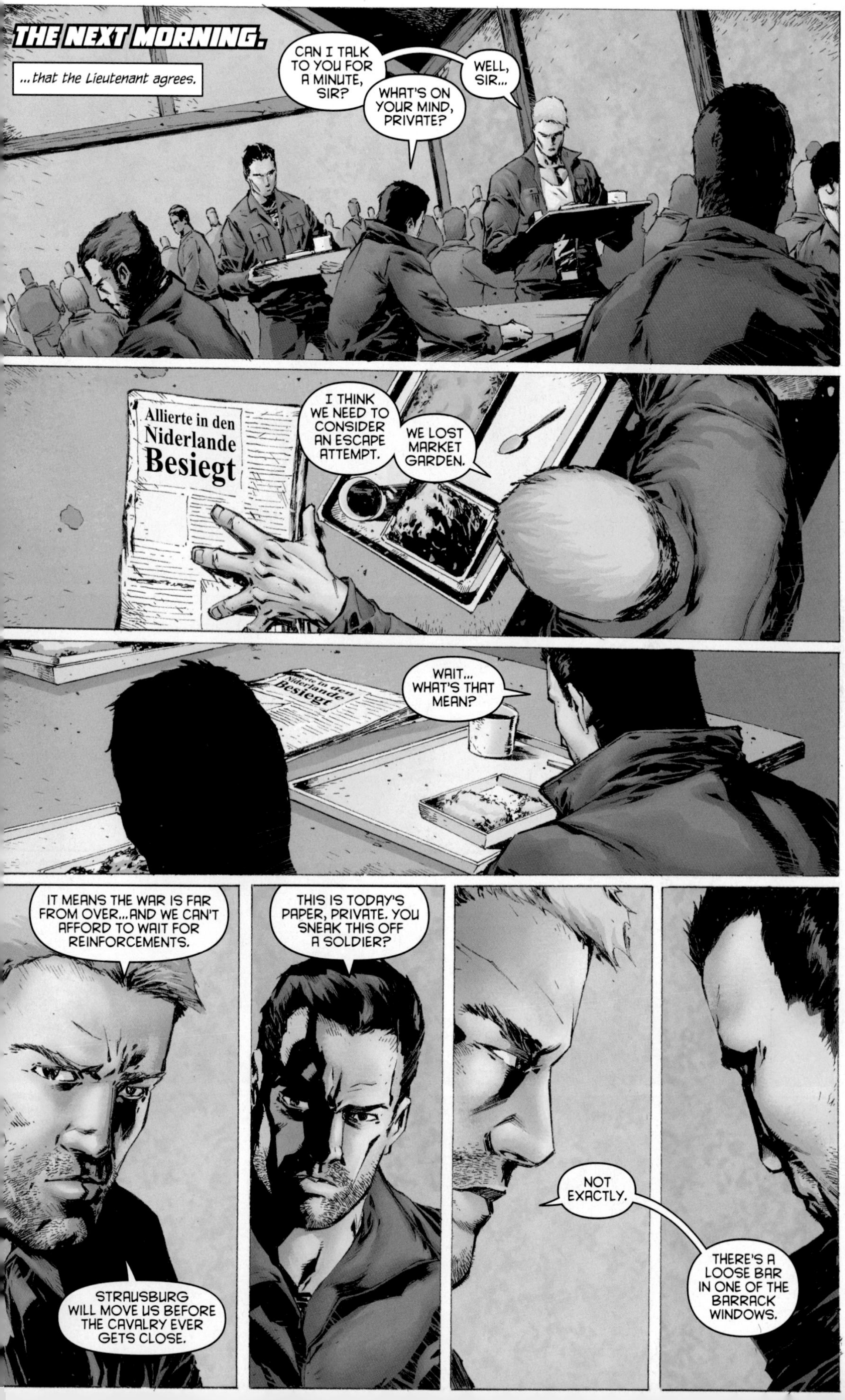
THE NEXT MORNING.
...that the Lieutenant agrees.
CAN I TALK TO YOU FOR A MINUTE, SIR?
WHAT'S ON YOUR MIND, PRIVATE?
WELL, SIR...
Allierte in den Niderlande Besiegt
I THINK WE NEED TO CONSIDER AN ESCAPE ATTEMPT.
WE LOST MARKET GARDEN.
WAIT... WHAT'S THAT MEAN?
IT MEANS THE WAR IS FAR FROM OVER...AND WE CAN'T AFFORD TO WAIT FOR REINFORCEMENTS.
STRAUSBURG WILL MOVE US BEFORE THE CAVALRY EVER GETS CLOSE.
THIS IS TODAY'S PAPER, PRIVATE. YOU SNEAK THIS OFF A SOLDIER?
NOT EXACTLY.
THERE'S A LOOSE BAR IN ONE OF THE BARRACK WINDOWS.

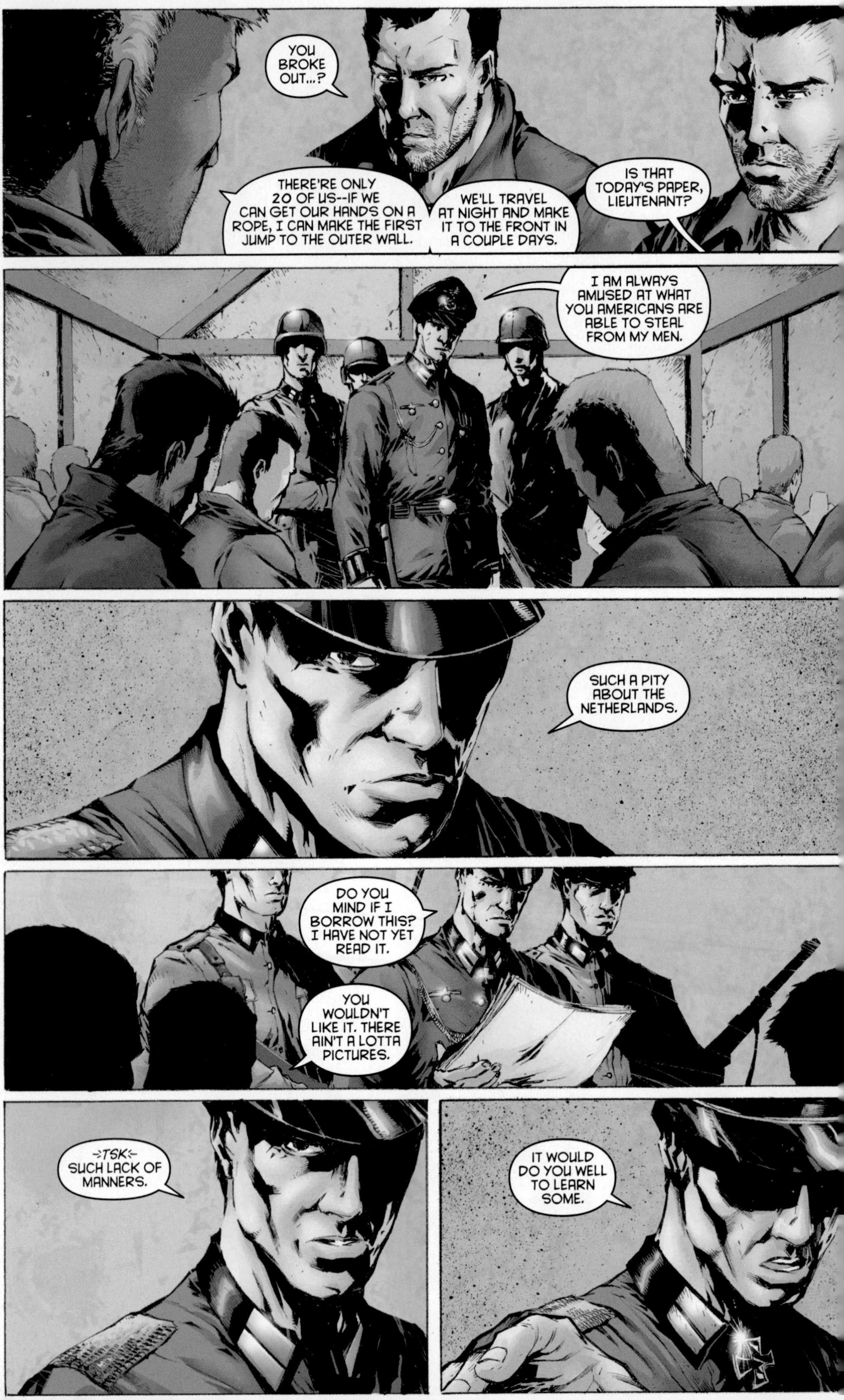
YOU BROKE OUT...?
THERE'RE ONLY 20 OF US--IF WE CAN GET OUR HANDS ON A ROPE, I CAN MAKE THE FIRST JUMP TO THE OUTER WALL.
WE'LL TRAVEL AT NIGHT AND MAKE IT TO THE FRONT IN A COUPLE DAYS.
IS THAT TODAY'S PAPER, LIEUTENANT?
I AM ALWAYS AMUSED AT WHAT YOU AMERICANS ARE ABLE TO STEAL FROM MY MEN.
SUCH A PITY ABOUT THE NETHERLANDS.
DO YOU MIND IF I BORROW THIS? I HAVE NOT YET READ IT.
YOU WOULDN'T LIKE IT. THERE AIN'T A LOTTA PICTURES.
TSK
SUCH LACK OF MANNERS.
IT WOULD DO YOU WELL TO LEARN SOME.

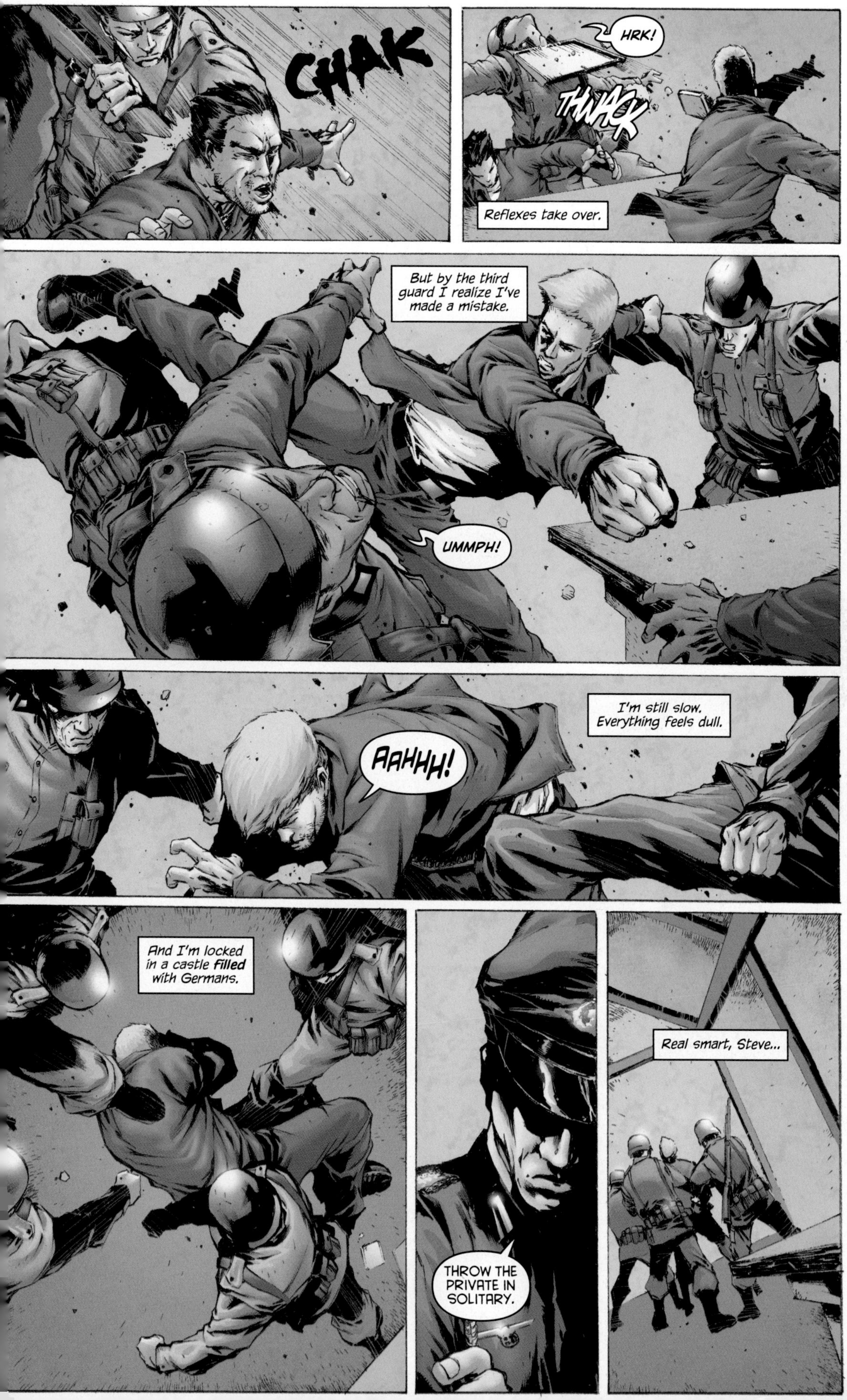
CHAK
HRK!
THWACK
Reflexes take over.
But by the third guard I realize I've made a mistake.
UMMPH!
I'm still slow. Everything feels dull.
AAHHH!
And I'm locked in a castle **filled** with Germans.
THROW THE PRIVATE IN SOLITARY.
Real smart, Steve...

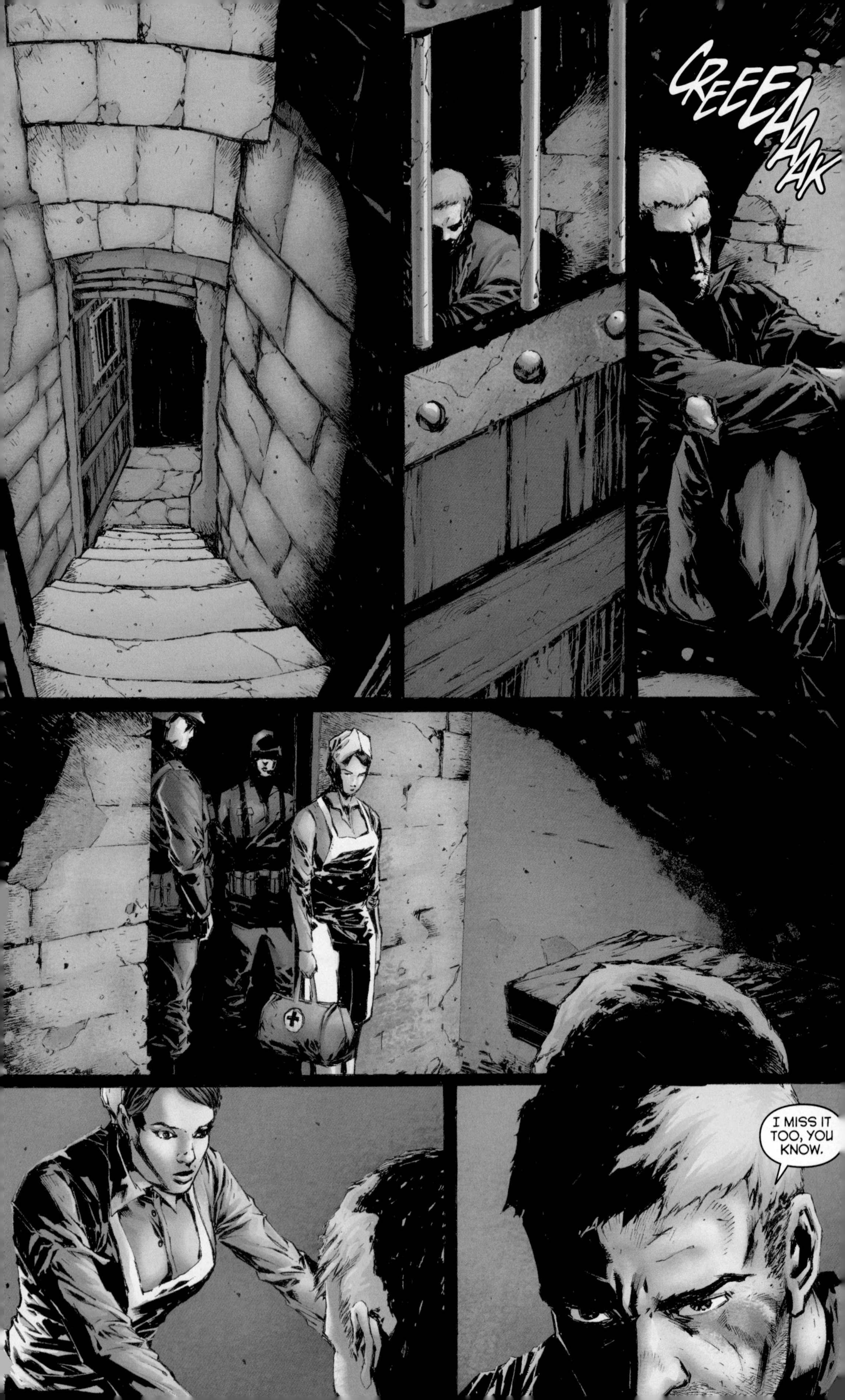
CREEEAAAAK
I MISS IT TOO, YOU KNOW.

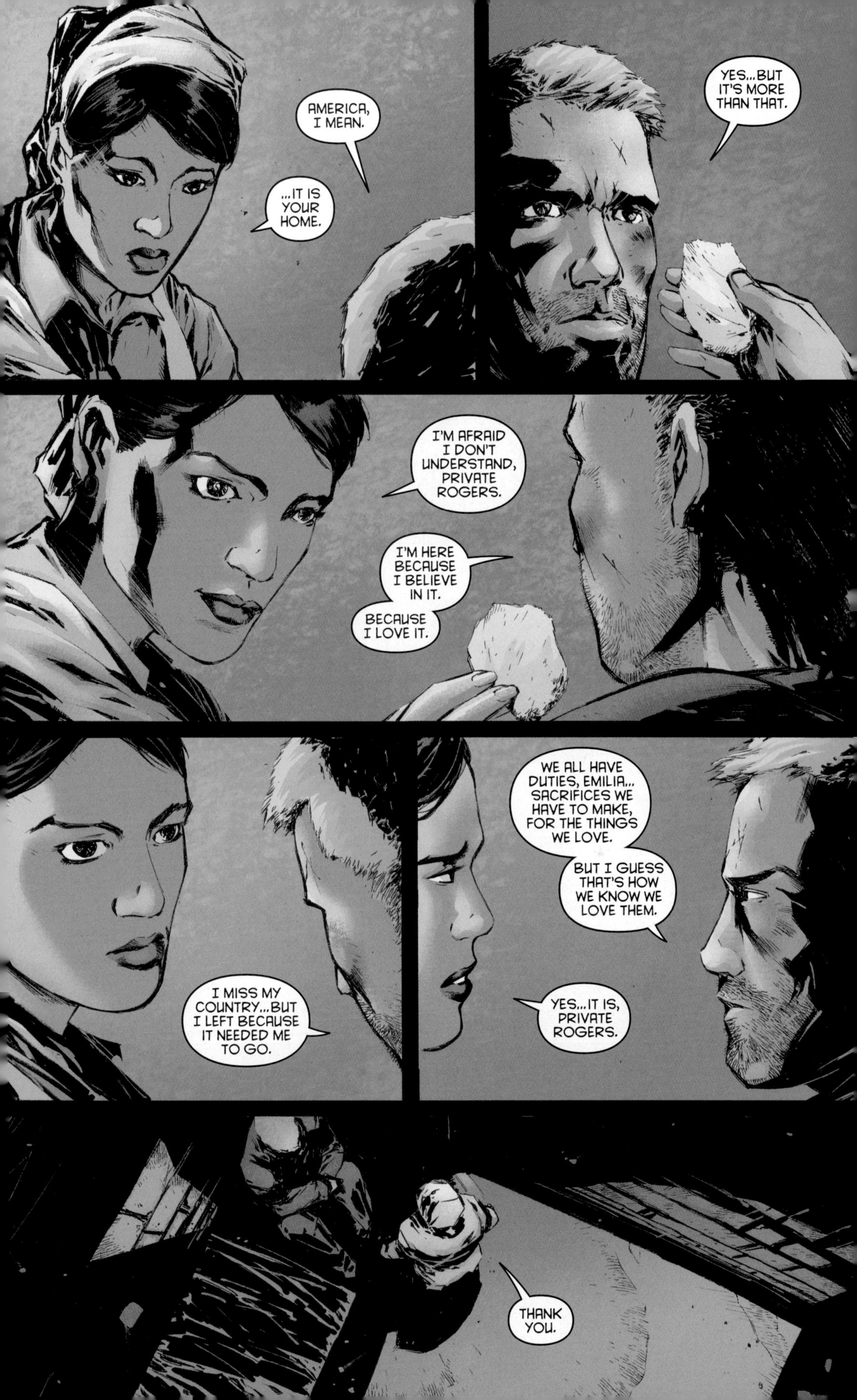
AMERICA, I MEAN.
...IT IS YOUR HOME.
YES...BUT IT'S MORE THAN THAT.
I'M AFRAID I DON'T UNDERSTAND, PRIVATE ROGERS.
I'M HERE BECAUSE I BELIEVE IN IT.
BECAUSE I LOVE IT.
I MISS MY COUNTRY...BUT I LEFT BECAUSE IT NEEDED ME TO GO.
WE ALL HAVE DUTIES, EMILIA... SACRIFICES WE HAVE TO MAKE, FOR THE THINGS WE LOVE.
BUT I GUESS THAT'S HOW WE KNOW WE LOVE THEM.
YES...IT IS, PRIVATE ROGERS.
THANK YOU.

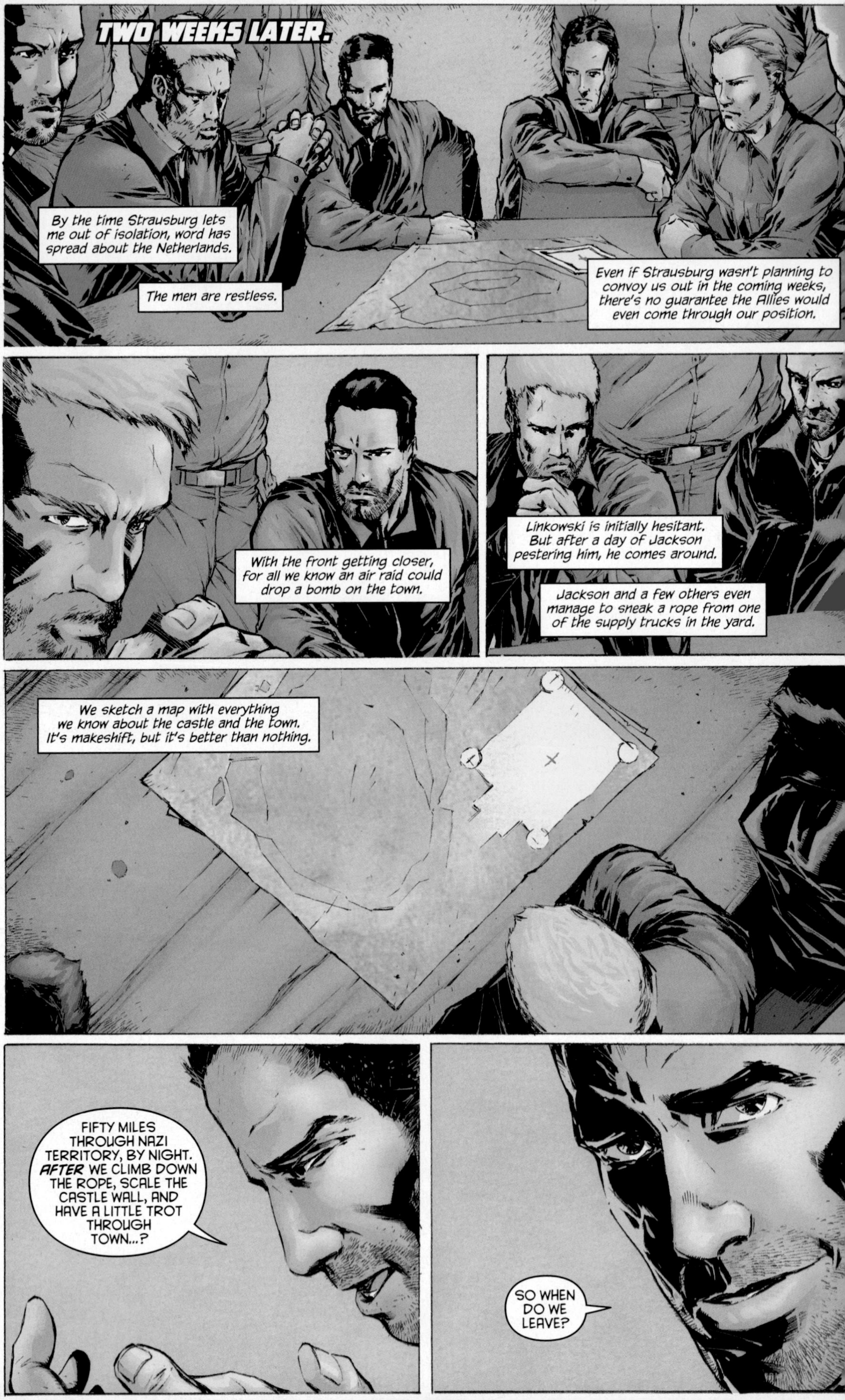
TWO WEEKS LATER.
By the time Strausburg lets me out of isolation, word has spread about the Netherlands.
The men are restless.
Even if Strausburg wasn't planning to convoy us out in the coming weeks, there's no guarantee the Allies would even come through our position.
With the front getting closer, for all we know an air raid could drop a bomb on the town.
Linkowski is initially hesitant. But after a day of Jackson pestering him, he comes around.
Jackson and a few others even manage to sneak a rope from one of the supply trucks in the yard.
We sketch a map with everything we know about the castle and the town. It's makeshift, but it's better than nothing.
FIFTY MILES THROUGH NAZI TERRITORY, BY NIGHT. AFTER WE CLIMB DOWN THE ROPE, SCALE THE CASTLE WALL, AND HAVE A LITTLE TROT THROUGH TOWN...?
SO WHEN DO WE LEAVE?

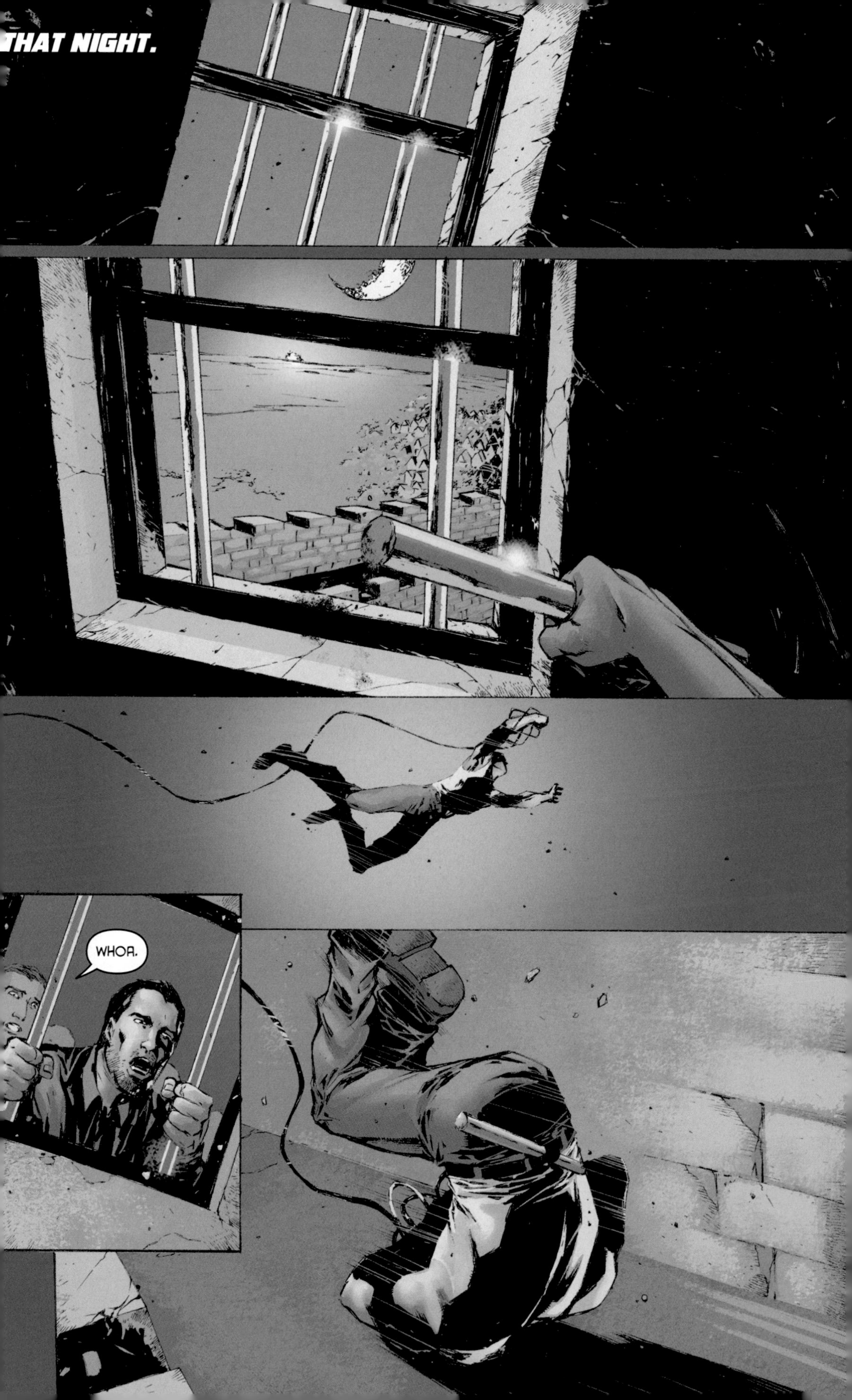
THAT NIGHT.
WHOA.

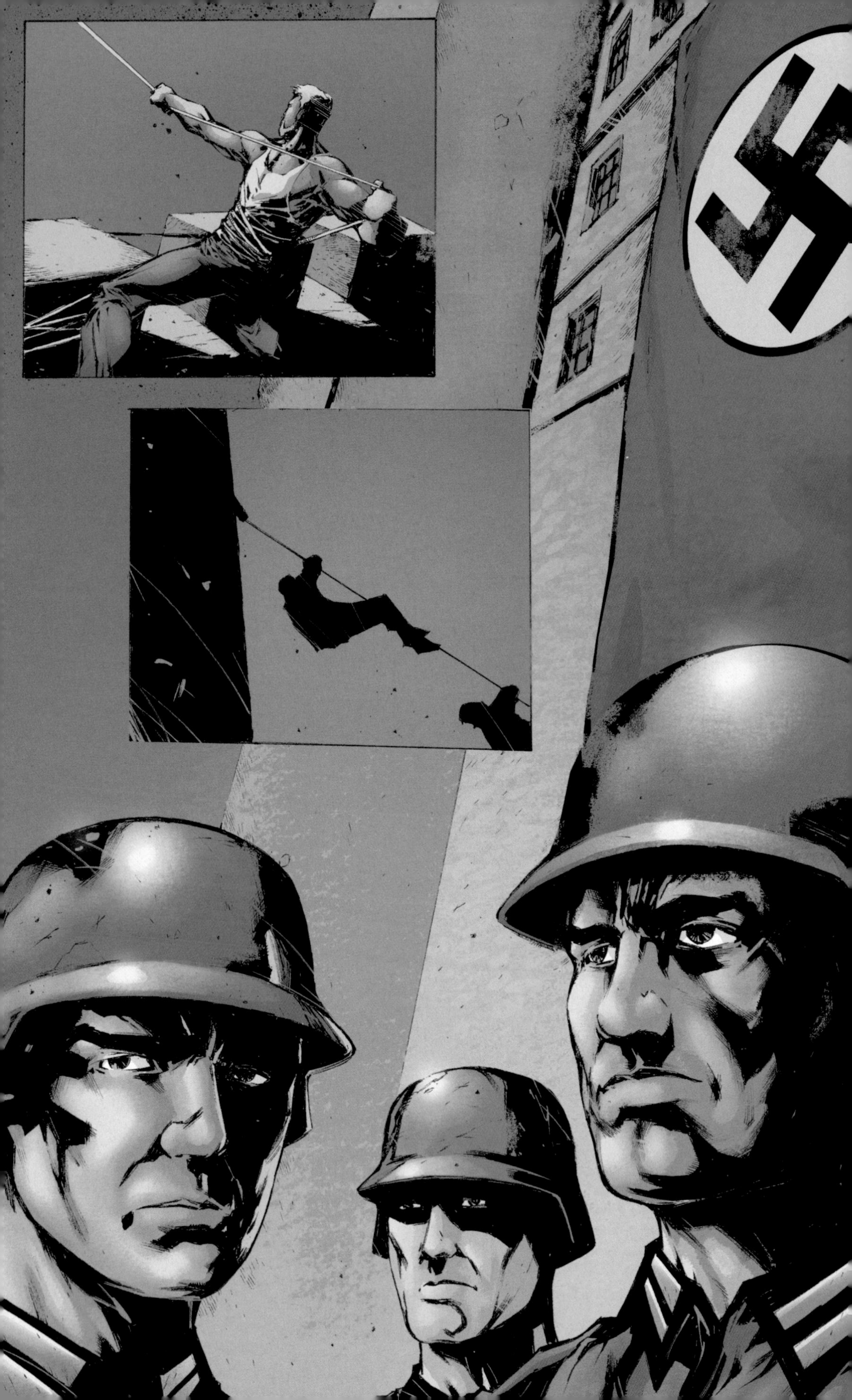

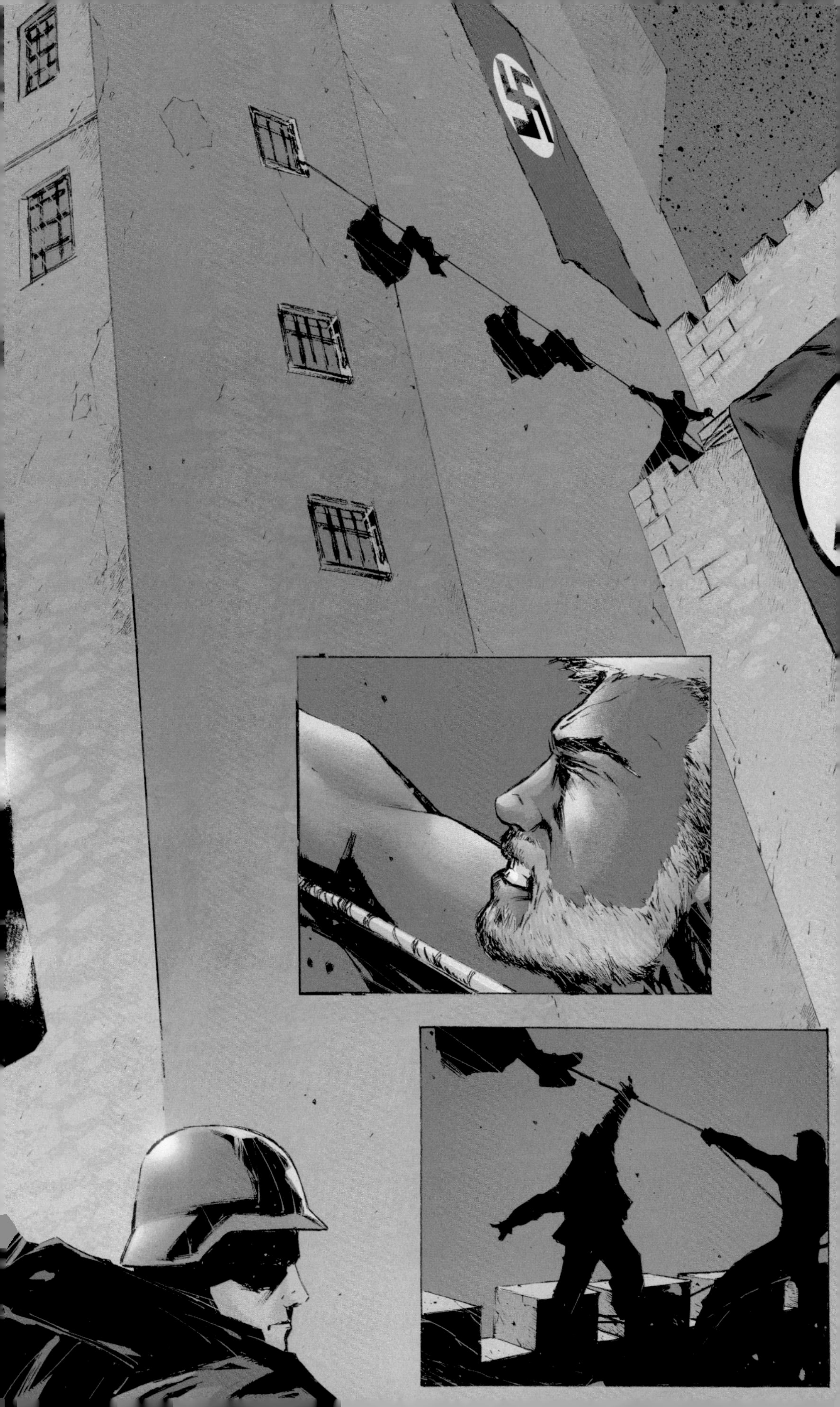

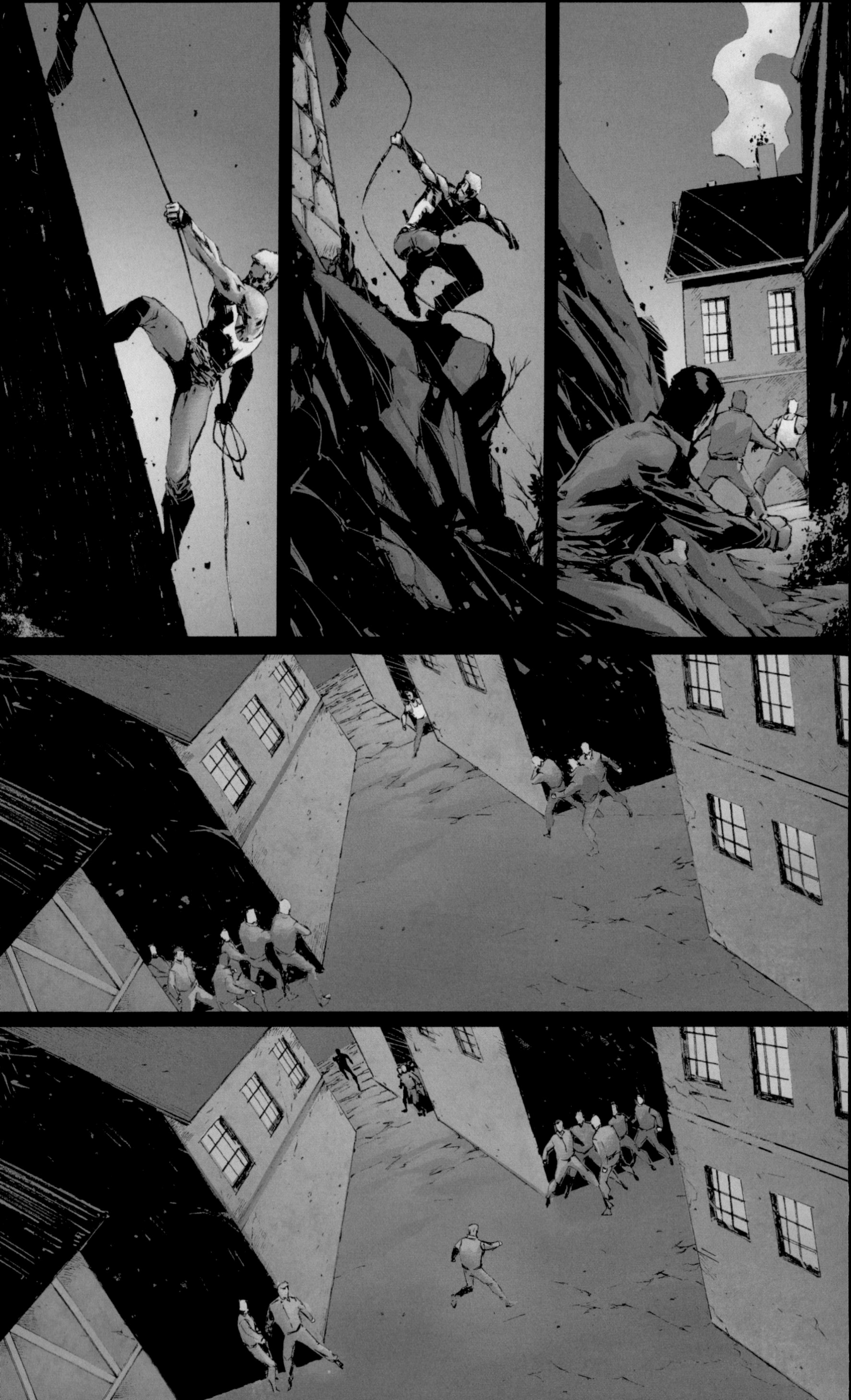

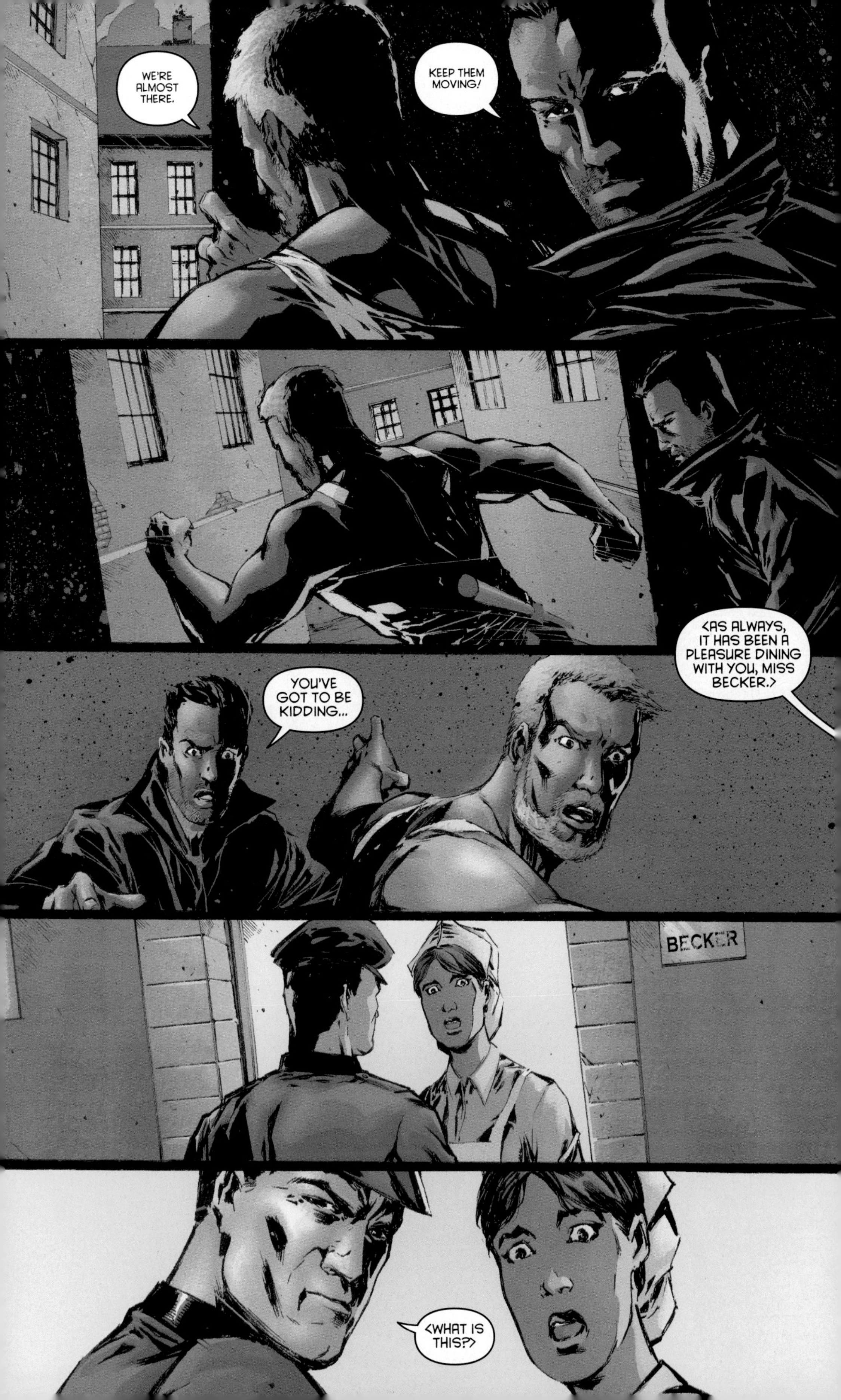
WE'RE ALMOST THERE.
KEEP THEM MOVING!
YOU'VE GOT TO BE KIDDING...
<AS ALWAYS, IT HAS BEEN A PLEASURE DINING WITH YOU, MISS BECKER.>
BECKER
<WHAT IS THIS?>

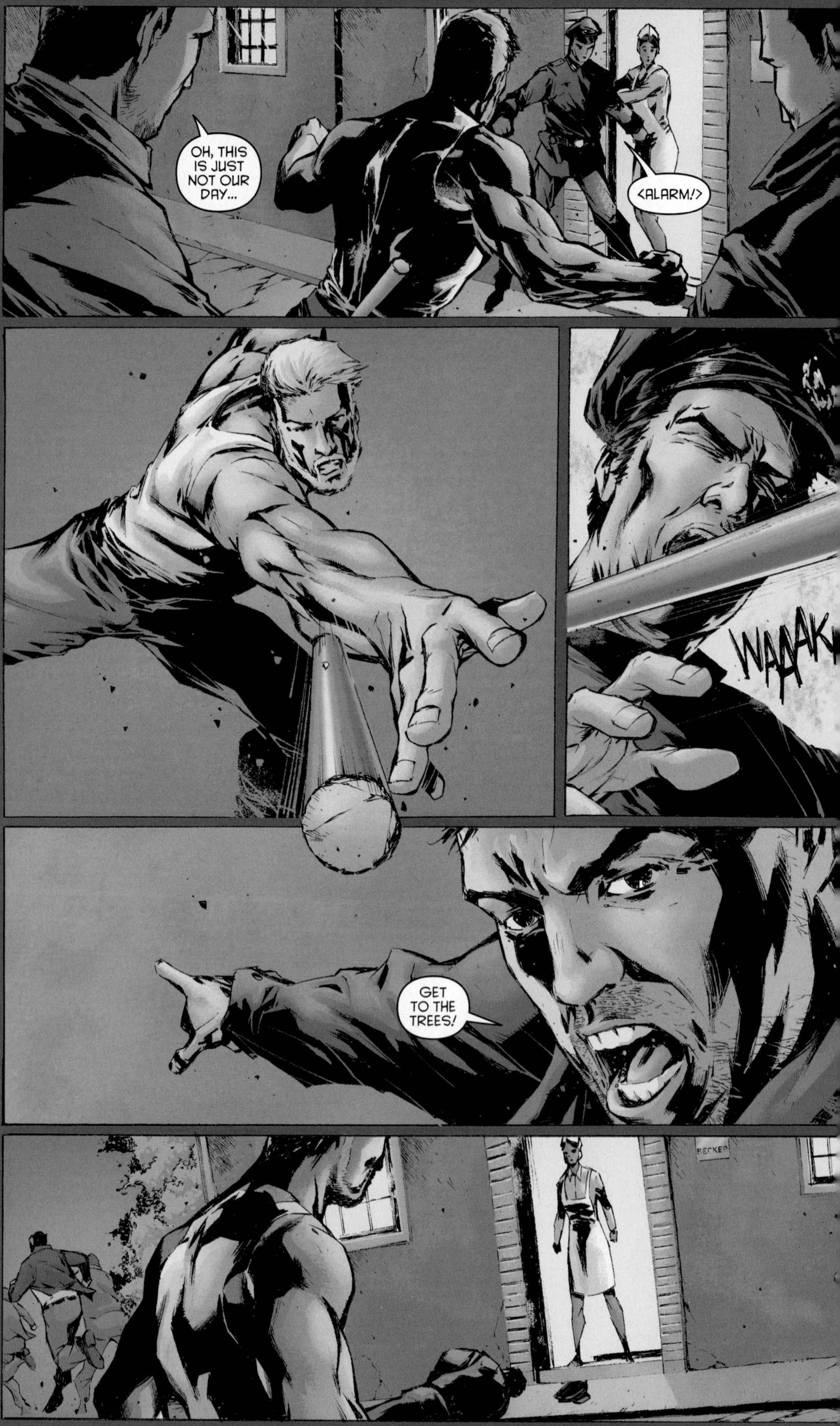
OH, THIS IS JUST NOT OUR DAY...
<ALARM!>
WAAAK
GET TO THE TREES!
BECKER

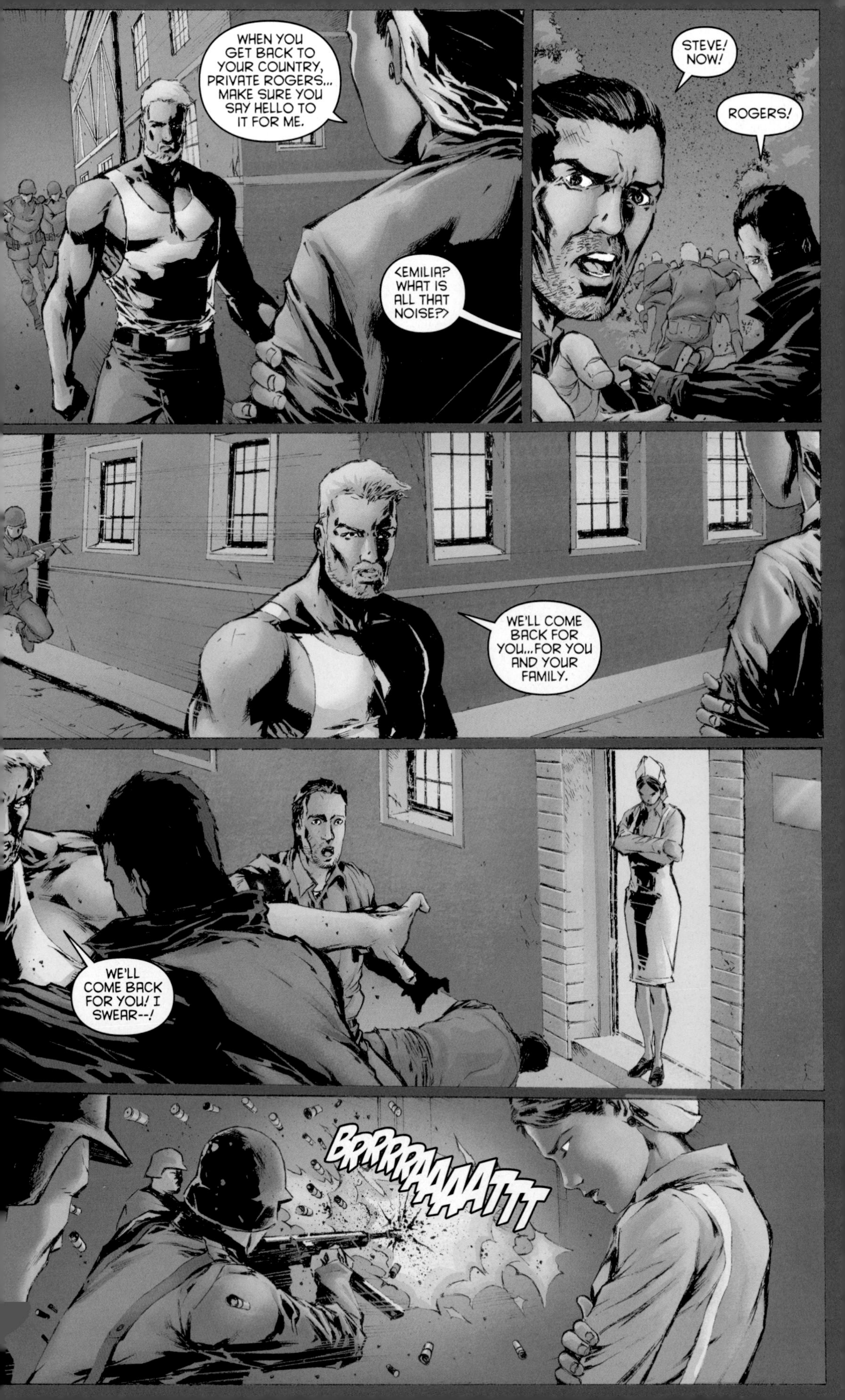
WHEN YOU GET BACK TO YOUR COUNTRY, PRIVATE ROGERS... MAKE SURE YOU SAY HELLO TO IT FOR ME.
<EMILIA? WHAT IS ALL THAT NOISE?>
STEVE! NOW!
ROGERS!
WE'LL COME BACK FOR YOU...FOR YOU AND YOUR FAMILY.
WE'LL COME BACK FOR YOU! I SWEAR--!
BRRRRAAAATTT

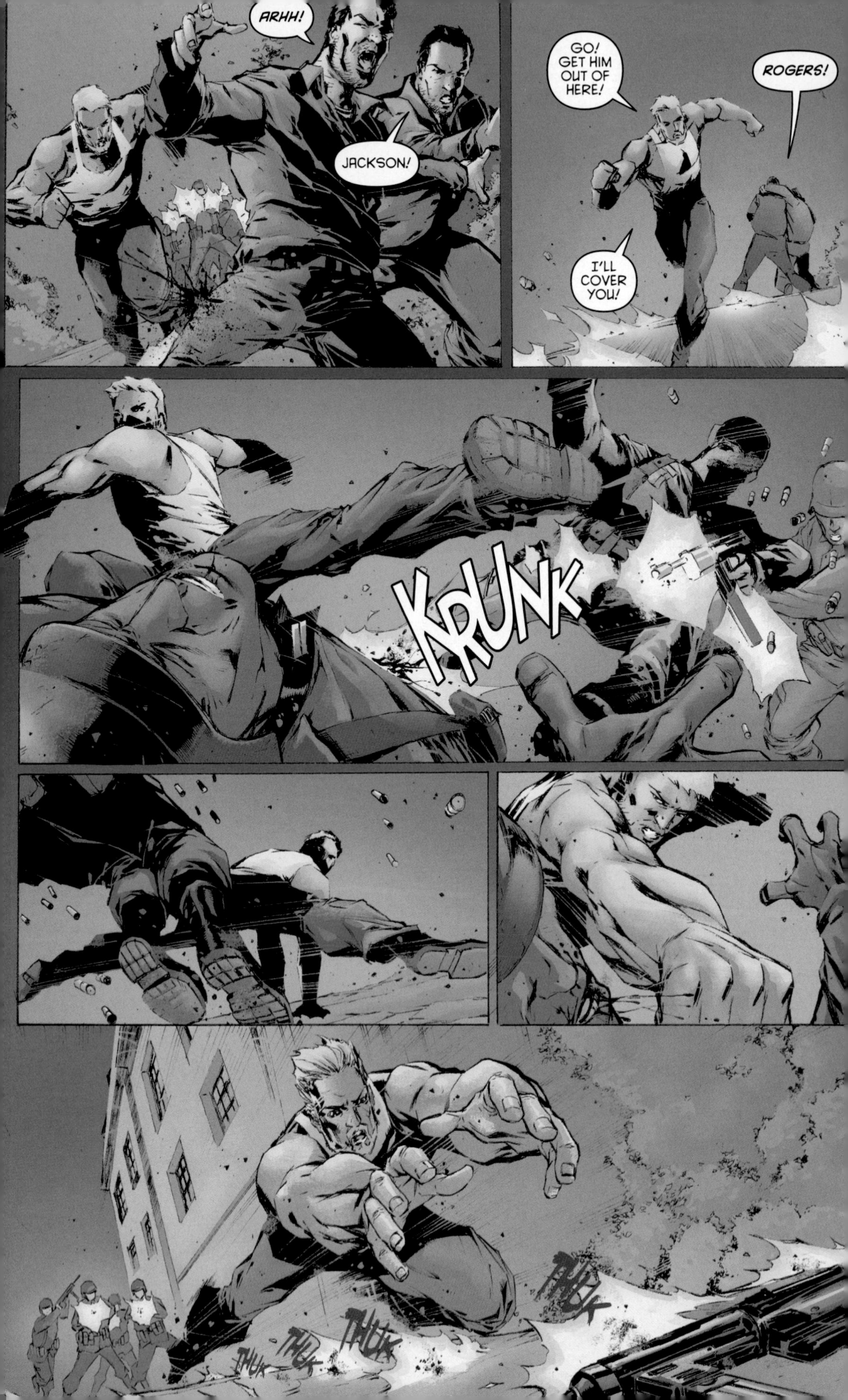

ARRHH!
JACKSON!
GO! GET HIM OUT OF HERE!
ROGERS!
I'LL COVER YOU!
KRUNK
THUK
THUK
THUK
THUK

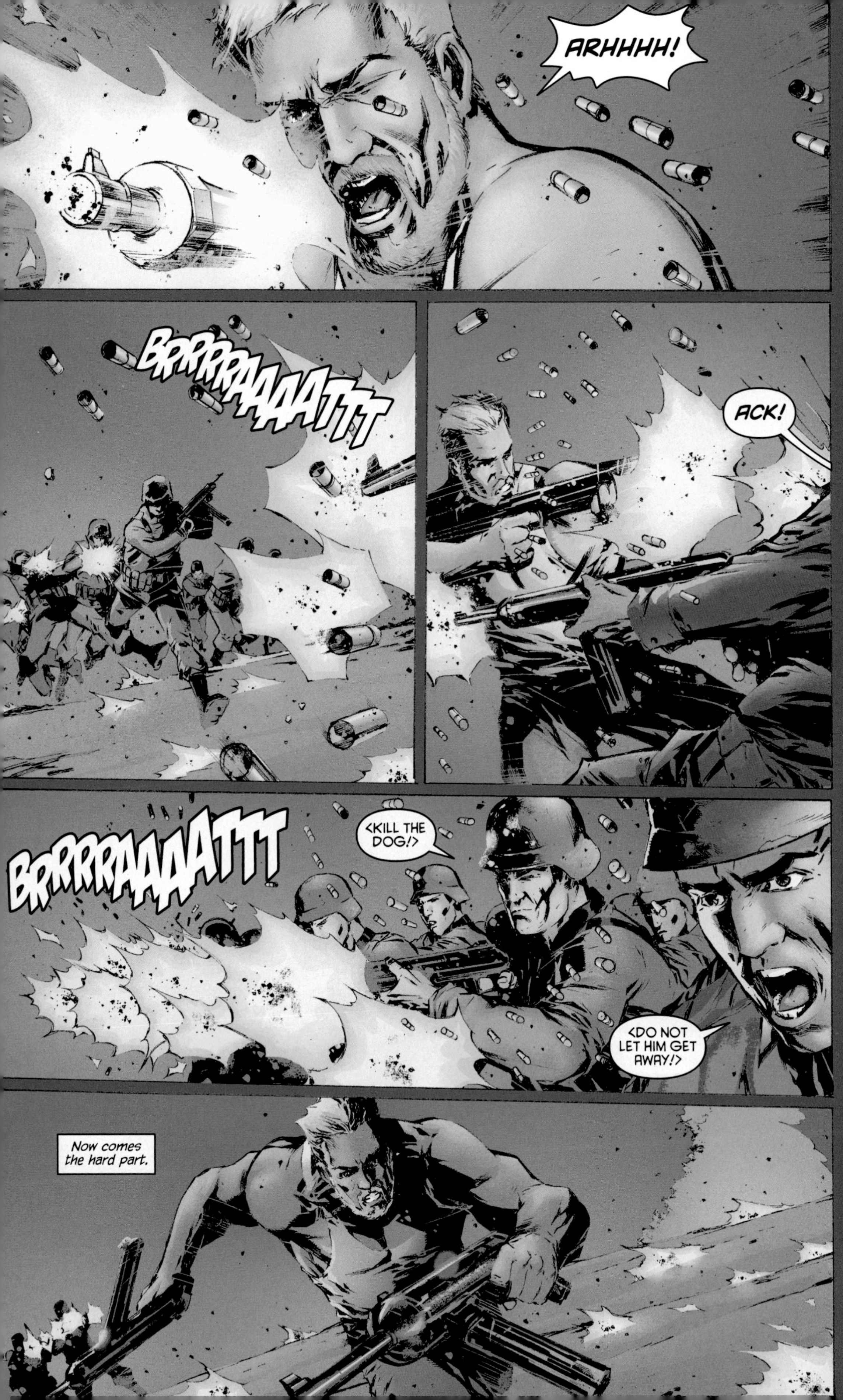
ARHHHH!
BRRRRAAAATTT
ACK!
BRRRRAAAATTT
<KILL THE DOG!>
<DO NOT LET HIM GET AWAY!>
Now comes the hard part.

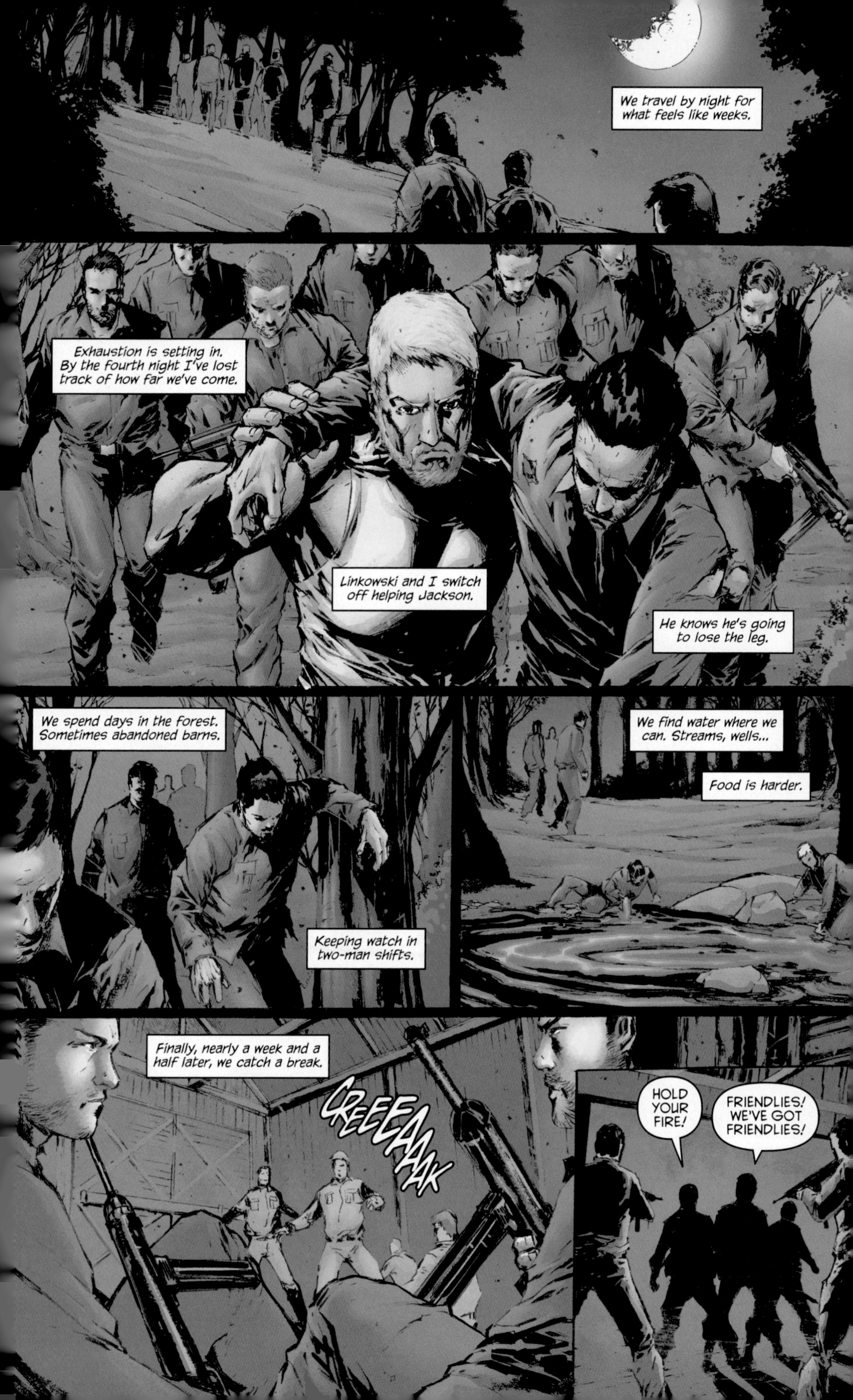
We travel by night for what feels like weeks.
Exhaustion is setting in. By the fourth night I've lost track of how far we've come.
Linkowski and I switch off helping Jackson.
He knows he's going to lose the leg.
We spend days in the forest. Sometimes abandoned barns.
Keeping watch in two-man shifts.
We find water where we can. Streams, wells...
Food is harder.
Finally, nearly a week and a half later, we catch a break.
CREEEAAAK
HOLD YOUR FIRE!
FRIENDLIES! WE'VE GOT FRIENDLIES!

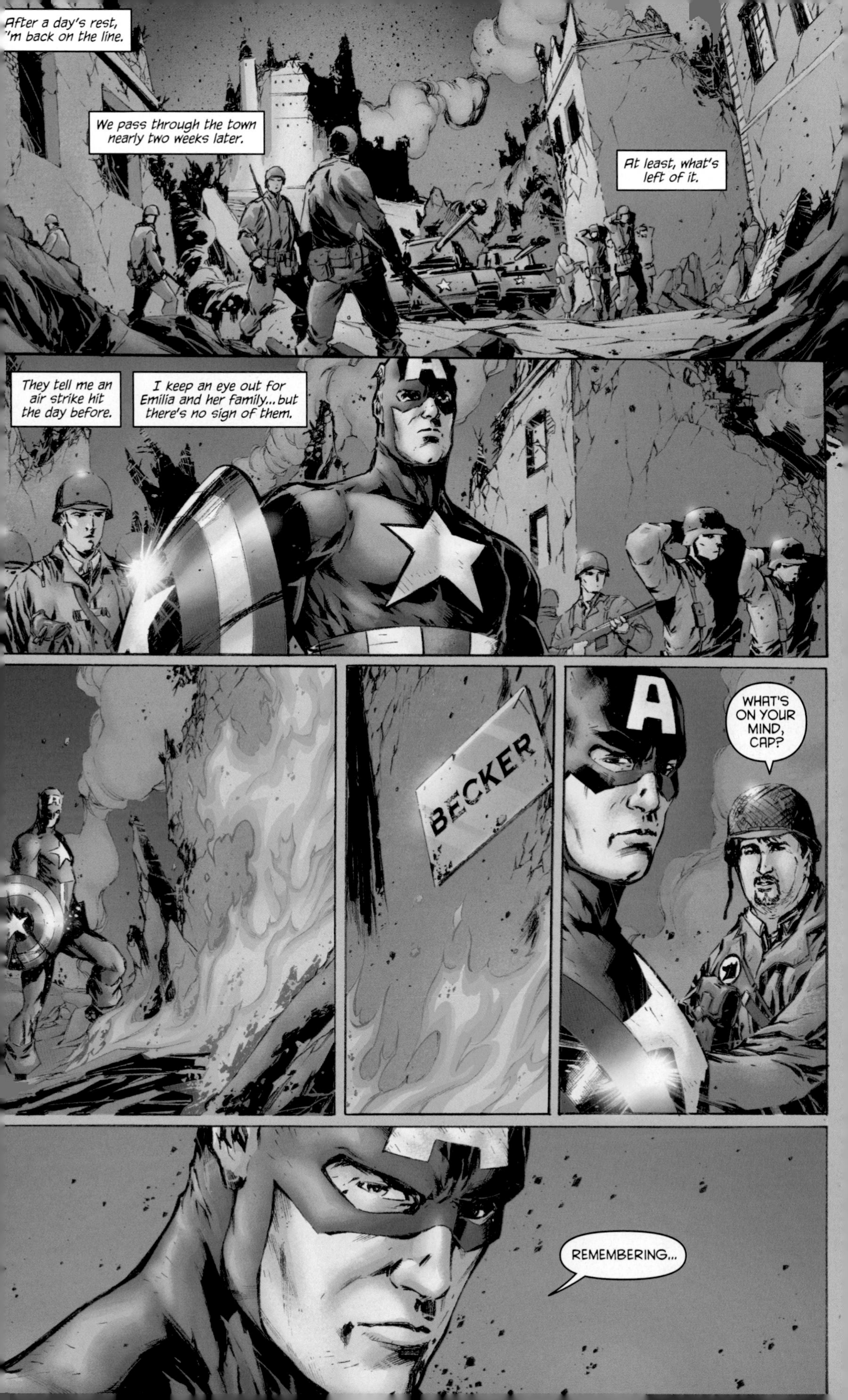
After a day's rest,
'm back on the line.
We pass through the town nearly two weeks later.
At least, what's left of it.
They tell me an air strike hit the day before.
I keep an eye out for Emilia and her family... but there's no sign of them.
BECKER
WHAT'S ON YOUR MIND, CAP?
REMEMBERING...

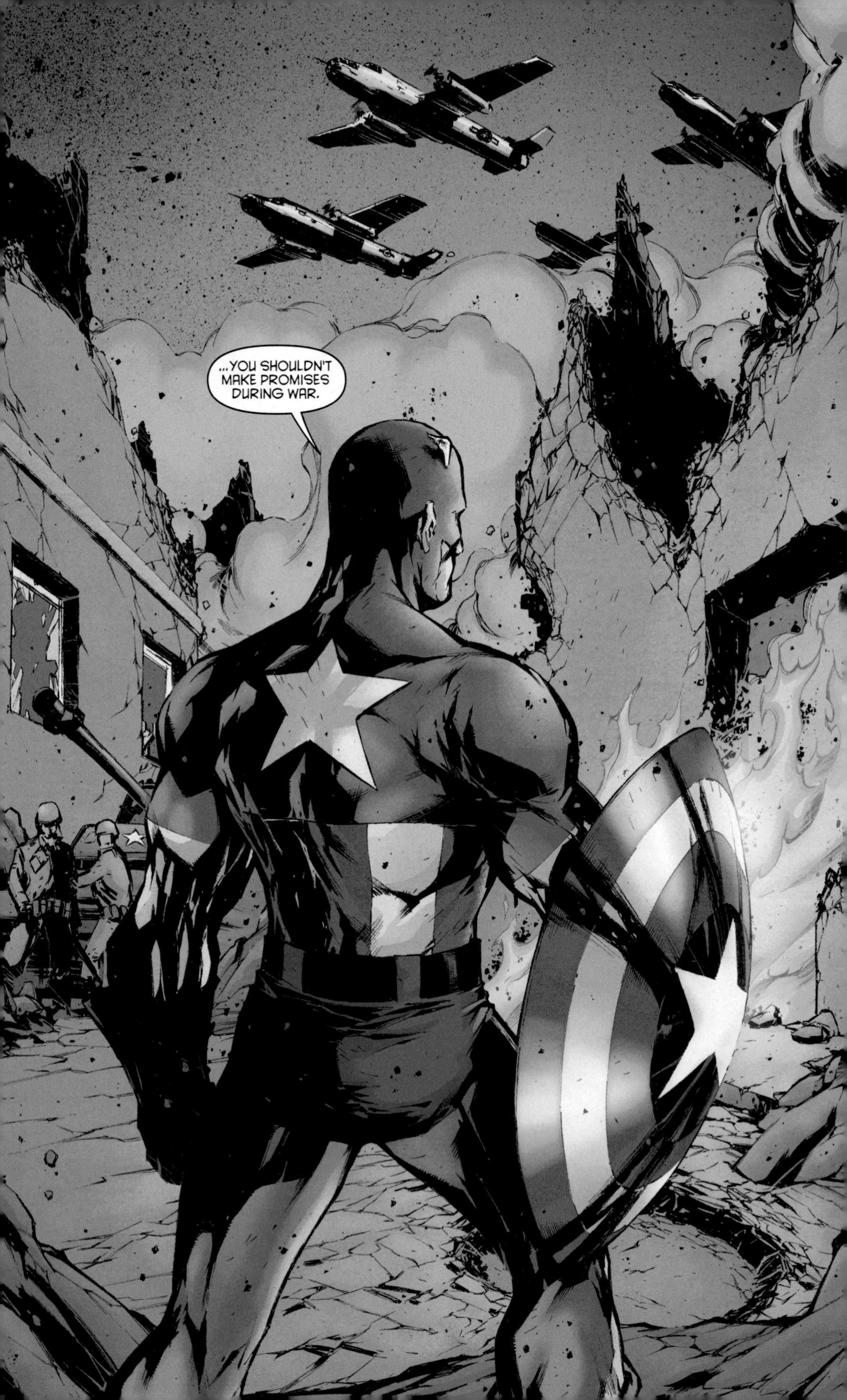
...YOU SHOULDN'T MAKE PROMISES DURING WAR.

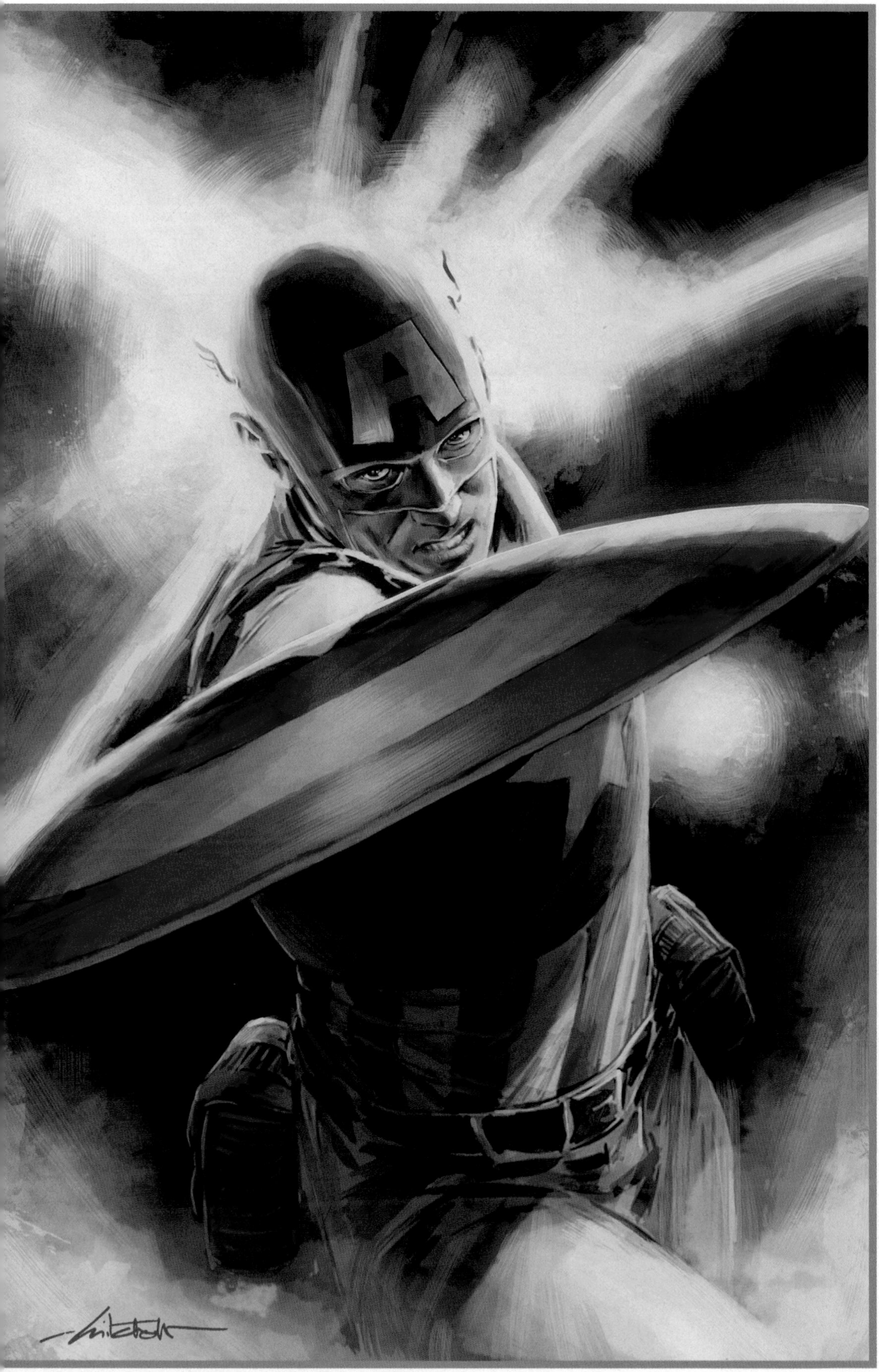

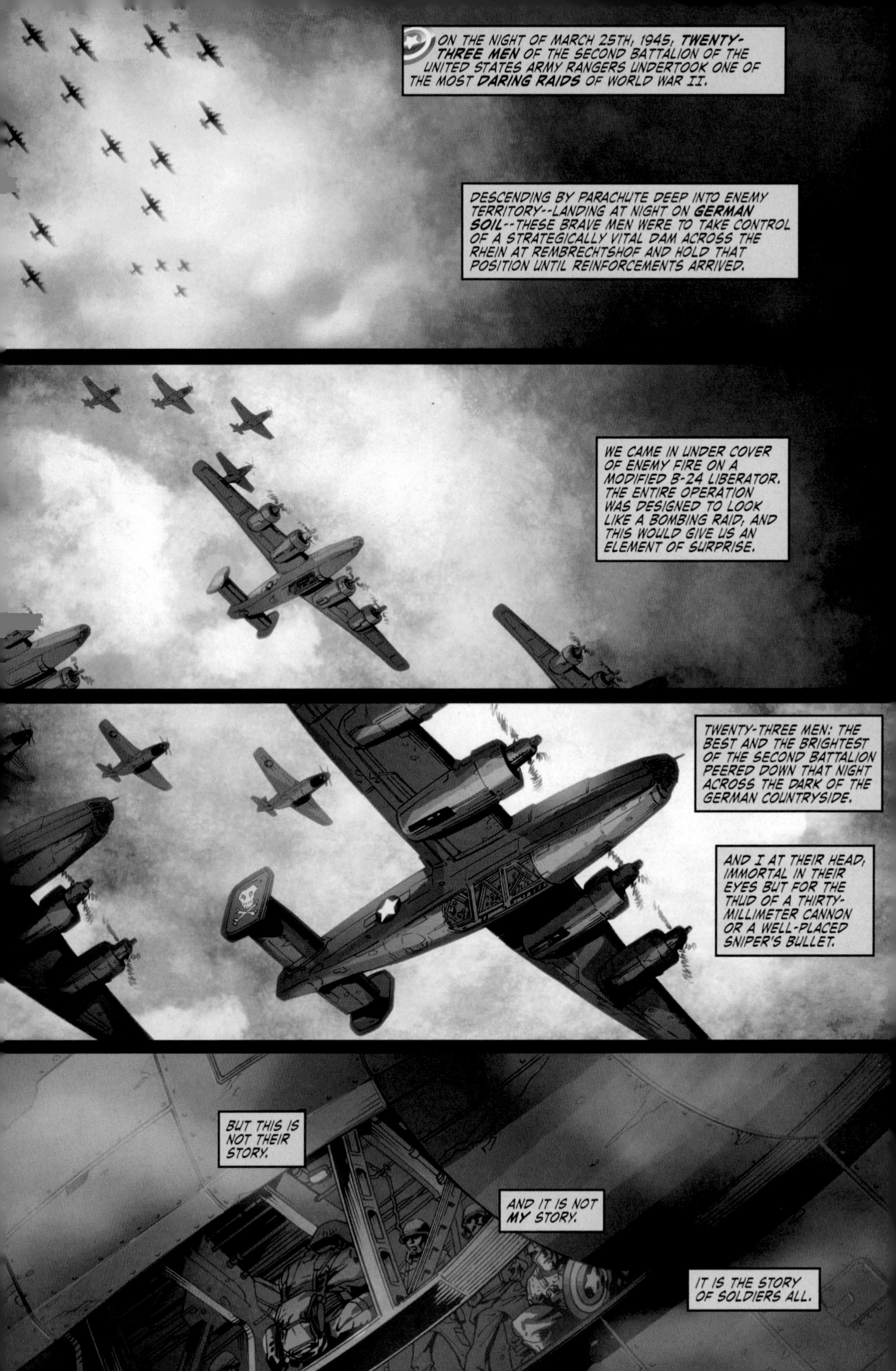
ON THE NIGHT OF MARCH 25TH, 1945, TWENTY-THREE MEN OF THE SECOND BATTALION OF THE UNITED STATES ARMY RANGERS UNDERTOOK ONE OF THE MOST DARING RAIDS OF WORLD WAR II.
DESCENDING BY PARACHUTE DEEP INTO ENEMY TERRITORY--LANDING AT NIGHT ON GERMAN SOIL--THESE BRAVE MEN WERE TO TAKE CONTROL OF A STRATEGICALLY VITAL DAM ACROSS THE RHEIN AT REMBRECHTSHOF AND HOLD THAT POSITION UNTIL REINFORCEMENTS ARRIVED.
WE CAME IN UNDER COVER OF ENEMY FIRE ON A MODIFIED B-24 LIBERATOR. THE ENTIRE OPERATION WAS DESIGNED TO LOOK LIKE A BOMBING RAID, AND THIS WOULD GIVE US AN ELEMENT OF SURPRISE.
TWENTY-THREE MEN: THE BEST AND THE BRIGHTEST OF THE SECOND BATTALION PEERED DOWN THAT NIGHT ACROSS THE DARK OF THE GERMAN COUNTRYSIDE.
AND I AT THEIR HEAD, IMMORTAL IN THEIR EYES BUT FOR THE THUD OF A THIRTY-MILLIMETER CANNON OR A WELL-PLACED SNIPER'S BULLET.
BUT THIS IS NOT THEIR STORY.
AND IT IS NOT MY STORY.
IT IS THE STORY OF SOLDIERS ALL.

A BROTHER IN ARMS

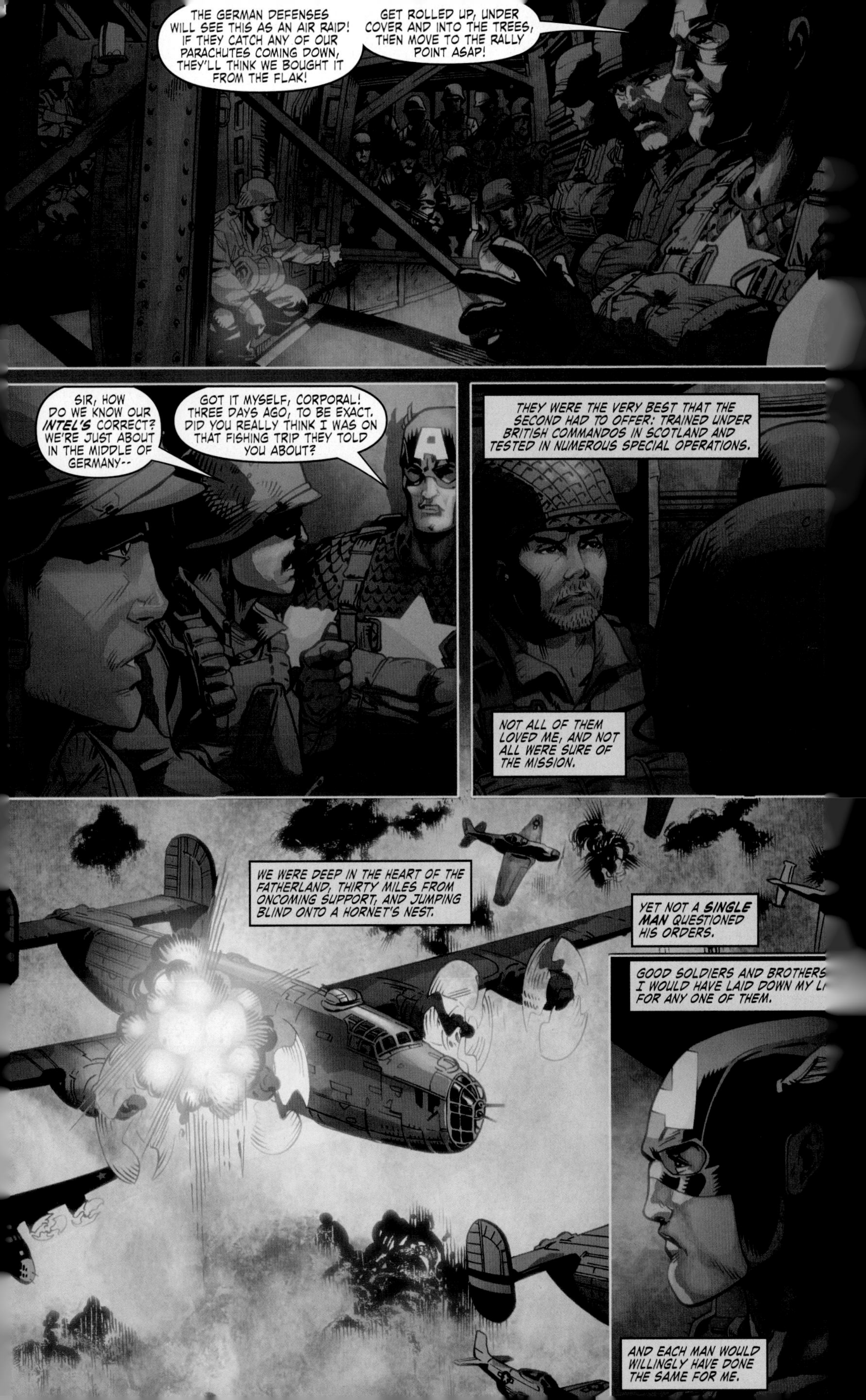
THE GERMAN DEFENSES WILL SEE THIS AS AN AIR RAID! IF THEY CATCH ANY OF OUR PARACHUTES COMING DOWN, THEY'LL THINK WE BOUGHT IT FROM THE FLAK!
GET ROLLED UP, UNDER COVER AND INTO THE TREES, THEN MOVE TO THE RALLY POINT ASAP!
SIR, HOW DO WE KNOW OUR INTEL'S CORRECT? WE'RE JUST ABOUT IN THE MIDDLE OF GERMANY--
GOT IT MYSELF, CORPORAL! THREE DAYS AGO, TO BE EXACT. DID YOU REALLY THINK I WAS ON THAT FISHING TRIP THEY TOLD YOU ABOUT?
THEY WERE THE VERY BEST THAT THE SECOND HAD TO OFFER: TRAINED UNDER BRITISH COMMANDOS IN SCOTLAND AND TESTED IN NUMEROUS SPECIAL OPERATIONS.
NOT ALL OF THEM LOVED ME, AND NOT ALL WERE SURE OF THE MISSION.
WE WERE DEEP IN THE HEART OF THE FATHERLAND, THIRTY MILES FROM ONCOMING SUPPORT, AND JUMPING BLIND ONTO A HORNET'S NEST.
YET NOT A SINGLE MAN QUESTIONED HIS ORDERS.
GOOD SOLDIERS AND BROTHERS I WOULD HAVE LAID DOWN MY L FOR ANY ONE OF THEM.
AND EACH MAN WOULD WILLINGLY HAVE DONE THE SAME FOR ME.

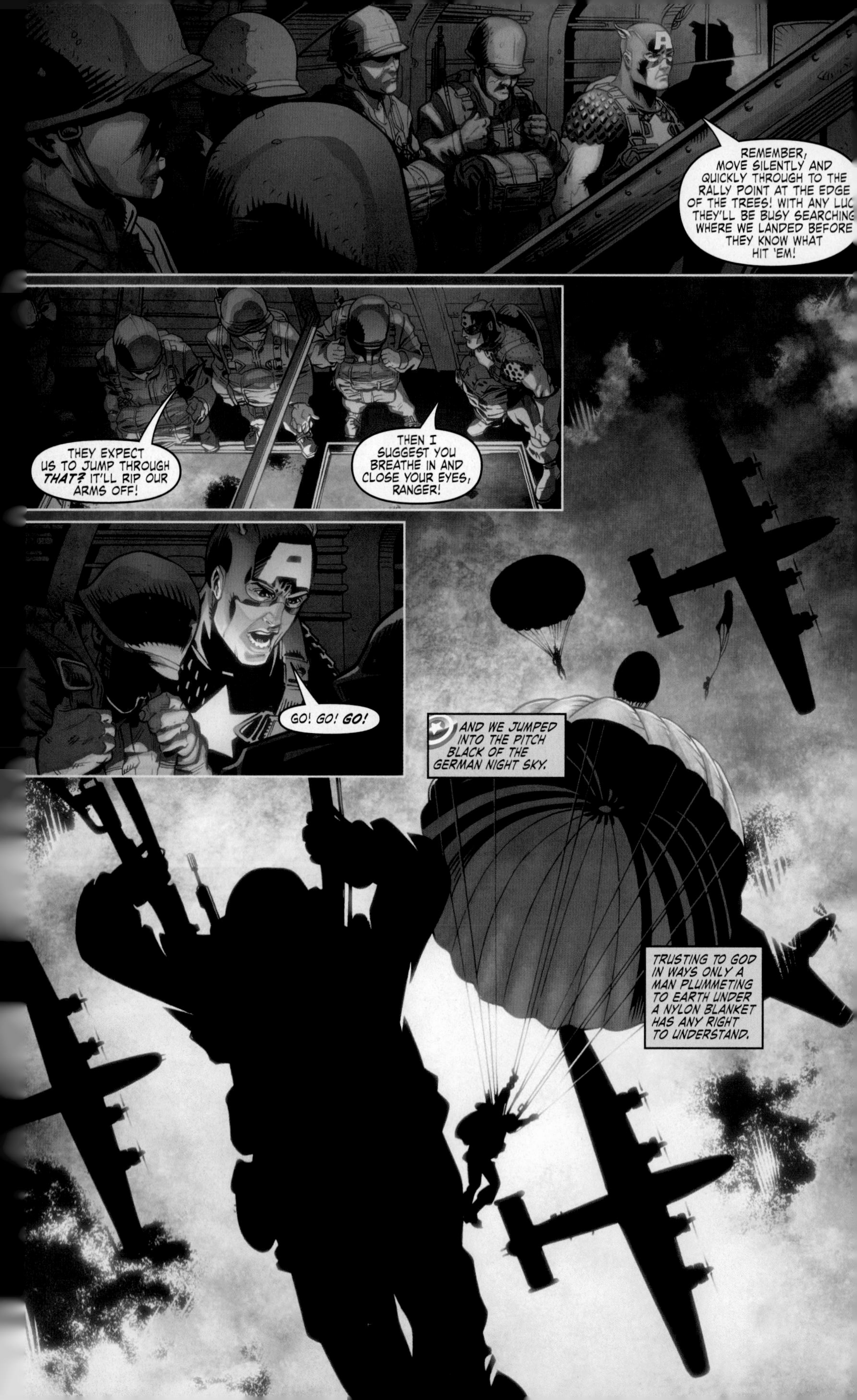
REMEMBER, MOVE SILENTLY AND QUICKLY THROUGH TO THE RALLY POINT AT THE EDGE OF THE TREES! WITH ANY LUC THEY'LL BE BUSY SEARCHING WHERE WE LANDED BEFORE THEY KNOW WHAT HIT 'EM!
THEY EXPECT US TO JUMP THROUGH THAT? IT'LL RIP OUR ARMS OFF!
THEN I SUGGEST YOU BREATHE IN AND CLOSE YOUR EYES, RANGER!
GO! GO! GO!
AND WE JUMPED INTO THE PITCH BLACK OF THE GERMAN NIGHT SKY.
TRUSTING TO GOD IN WAYS ONLY A MAN PLUMMETING TO EARTH UNDER A NYLON BLANKET HAS ANY RIGHT TO UNDERSTAND.

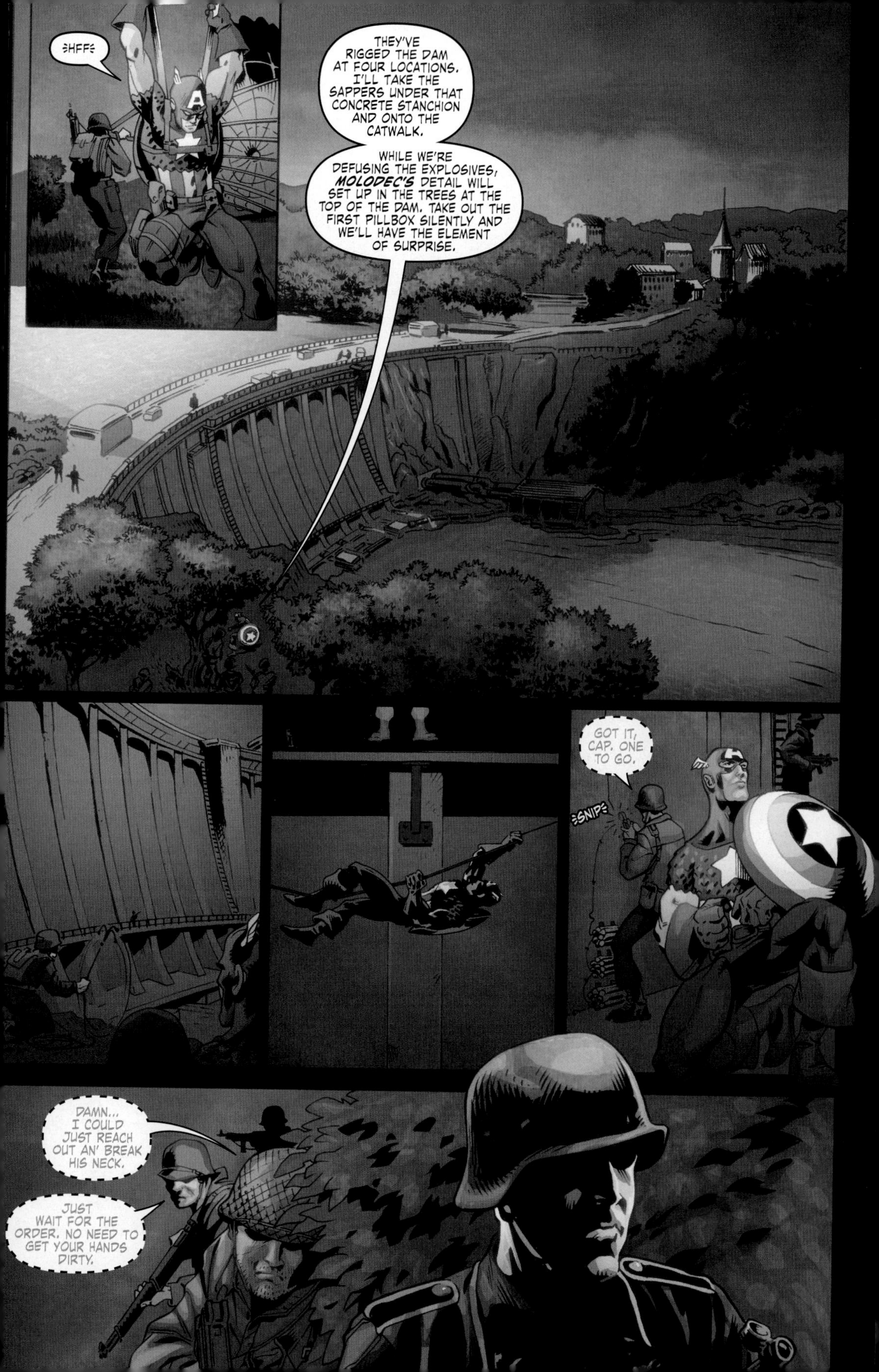
HFF
THEY'VE RIGGED THE DAM AT FOUR LOCATIONS. I'LL TAKE THE SAPPERS UNDER THAT CONCRETE STANCHION AND ONTO THE CATWALK.
WHILE WE'RE DEFUSING THE EXPLOSIVES, MOLODEC'S DETAIL WILL SET UP IN THE TREES AT THE TOP OF THE DAM. TAKE OUT THE FIRST PILLBOX SILENTLY AND WE'LL HAVE THE ELEMENT OF SURPRISE.
GOT IT, CAP. ONE TO GO.
SNIP
DAMN... I COULD JUST REACH OUT AN' BREAK HIS NECK.
JUST WAIT FOR THE ORDER. NO NEED TO GET YOUR HANDS DIRTY.

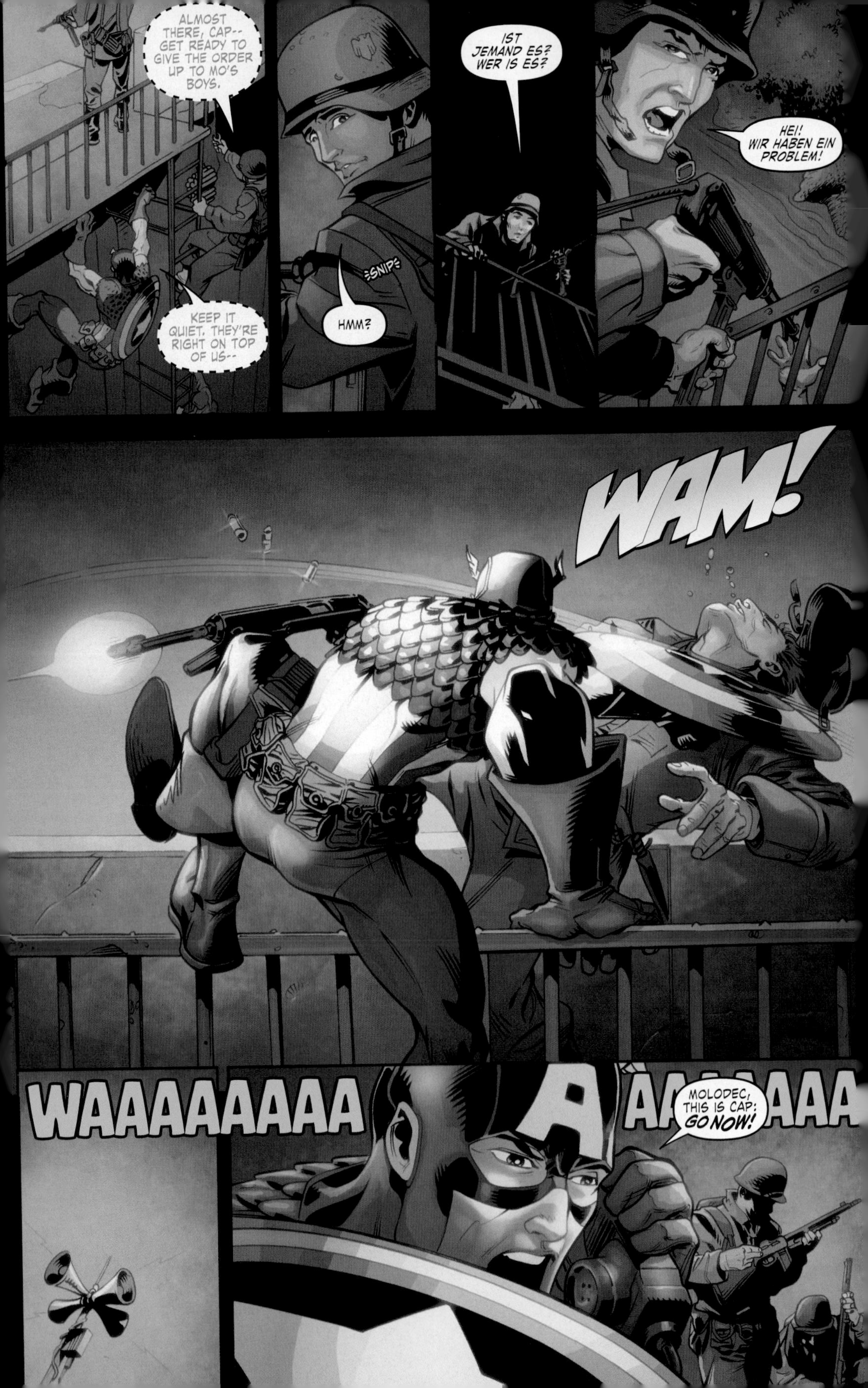
ALMOST THERE, CAP-- GET READY TO GIVE THE ORDER UP TO MO'S BOYS.
KEEP IT QUIET. THEY'RE RIGHT ON TOP OF US--
SNIP
HMM?
IST JEMAND ES? WER IS ES?
HEI! WIR HABEN EIN PROBLEM!
WAM!
WAAAAAAAA
AAAAAA
MOLODEC, THIS IS CAP: GO NOW!

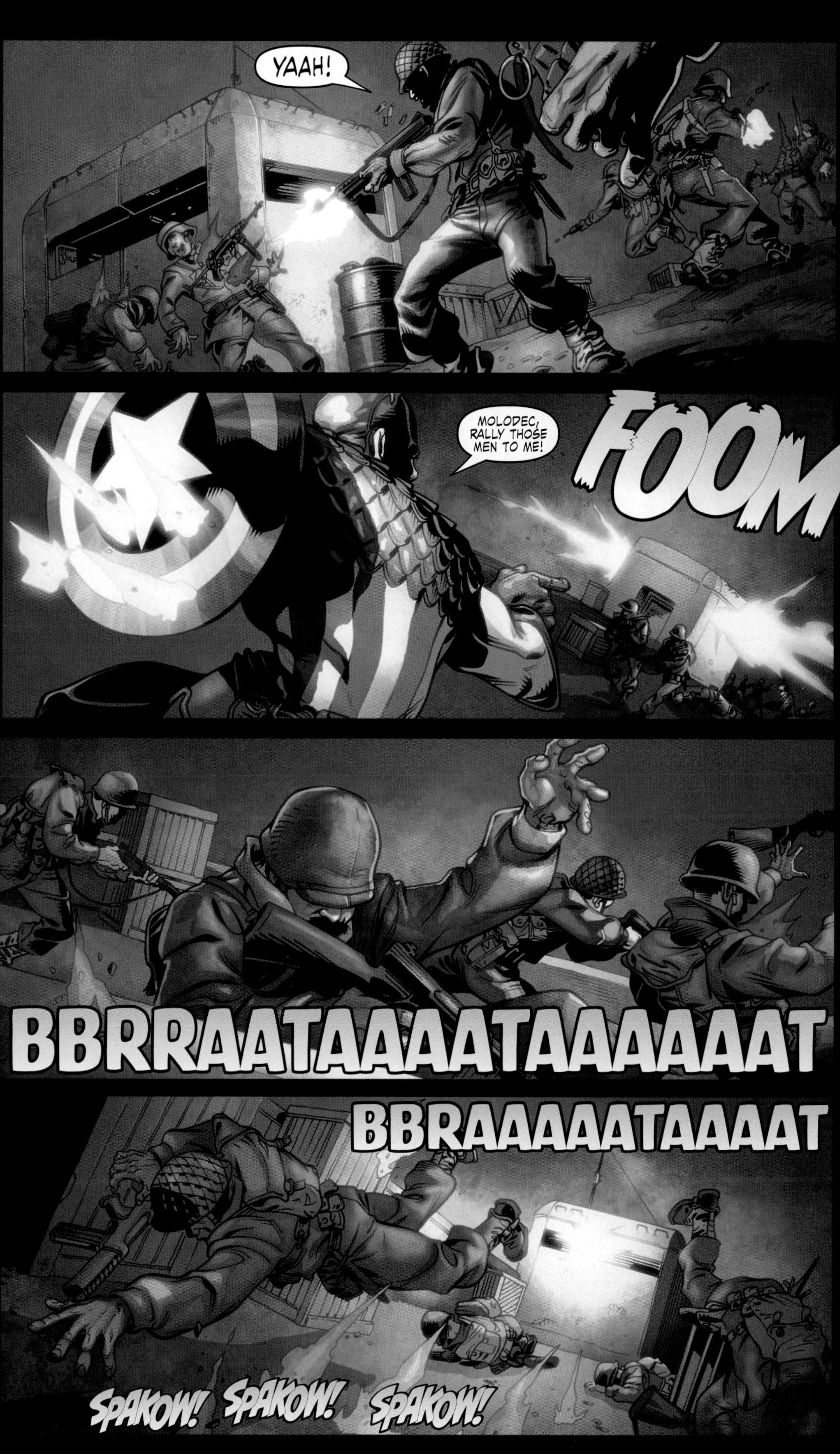
YAAH!
MOLODEC, RALLY THOSE MEN TO ME!
FOOM
BBRRAATAAAATAAAAAAT
BBRAAAAAATAAAAT
SPAKOW! SPAKOW! SPAKOW!

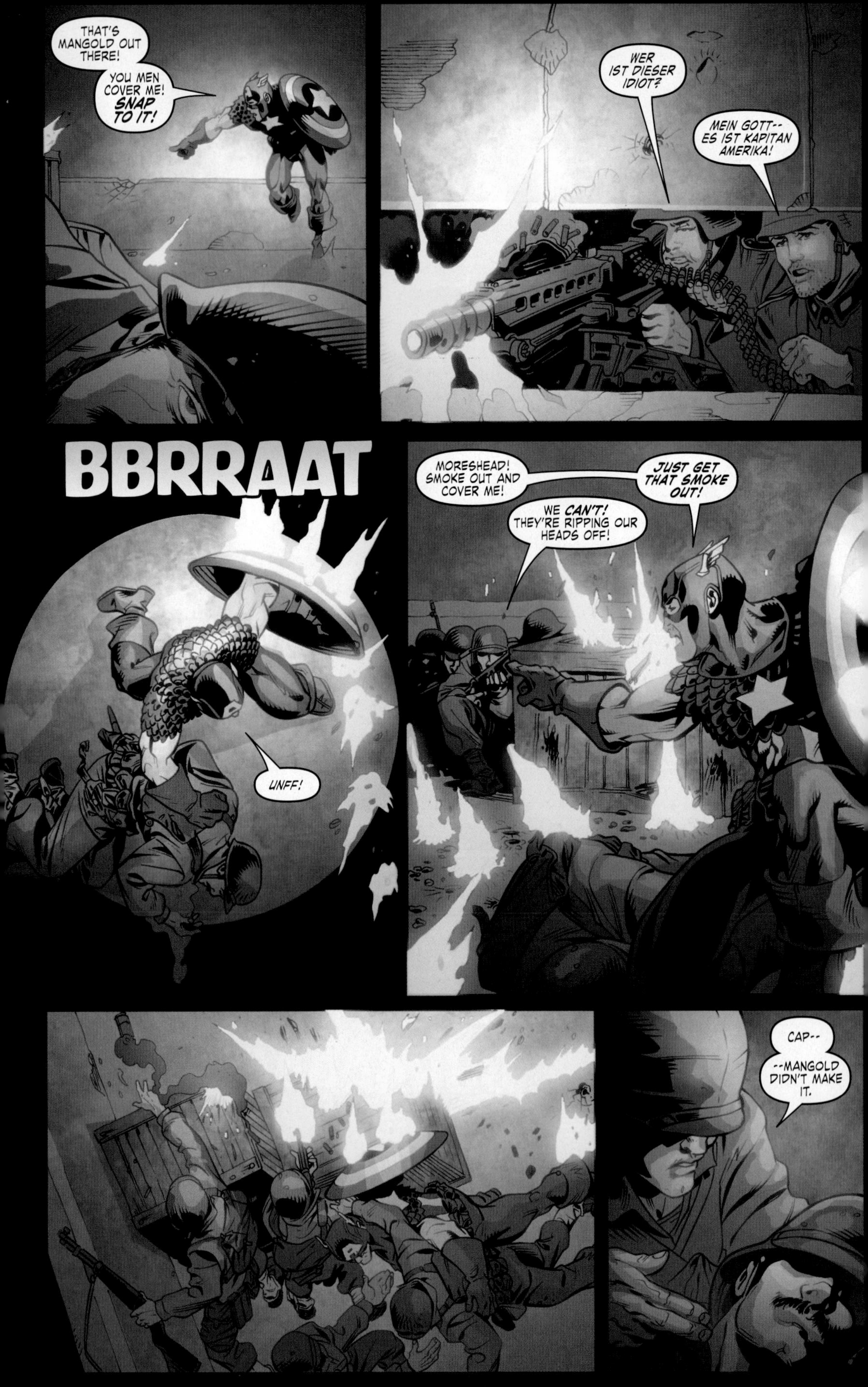
THAT'S MANGOLD OUT THERE!
YOU MEN COVER ME! SNAP TO IT!
WER IST DIESER IDIOT?
MEIN GOTT-- ES IST KAPITAN AMERIKA!
BBRRAAT
UNFF!
MORESHEAD! SMOKE OUT AND COVER ME!
WE CAN'T! THEY'RE RIPPING OUR HEADS OFF!
JUST GET THAT SMOKE OUT!
CAP--
--MANGOLD DIDN'T MAKE IT.

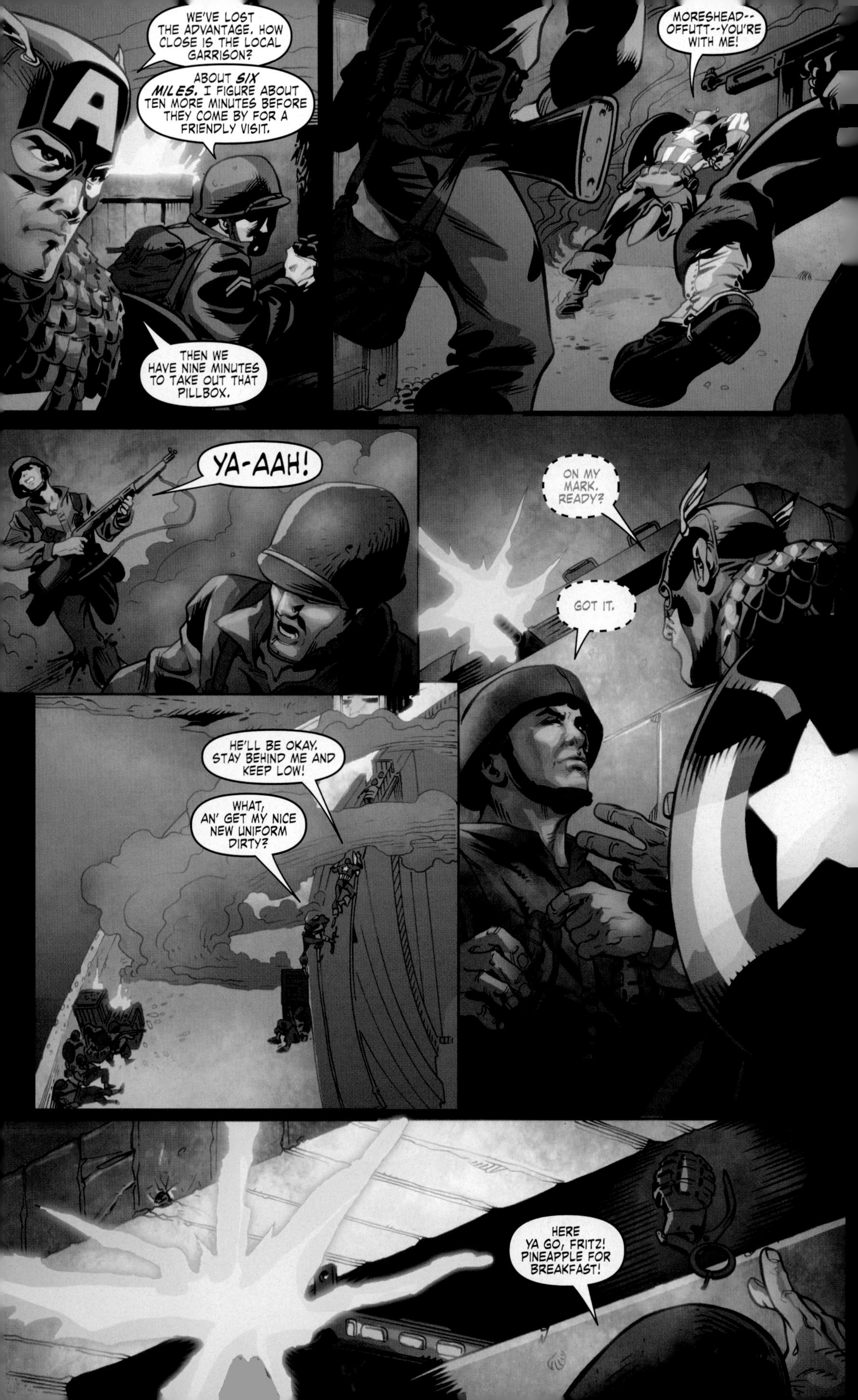
WE'VE LOST THE ADVANTAGE. HOW CLOSE IS THE LOCAL GARRISON?
ABOUT SIX MILES. I FIGURE ABOUT TEN MORE MINUTES BEFORE THEY COME BY FOR A FRIENDLY VISIT.
THEN WE HAVE NINE MINUTES TO TAKE OUT THAT PILLBOX.
MORESHEAD--OFFUTT--YOU'RE WITH ME!
YA-AAH!
ON MY MARK. READY?
GOT IT.
HE'LL BE OKAY. STAY BEHIND ME AND KEEP LOW!
WHAT, AN' GET MY NICE NEW UNIFORM DIRTY?
HERE YA GO, FRITZ! PINEAPPLE FOR BREAKFAST!

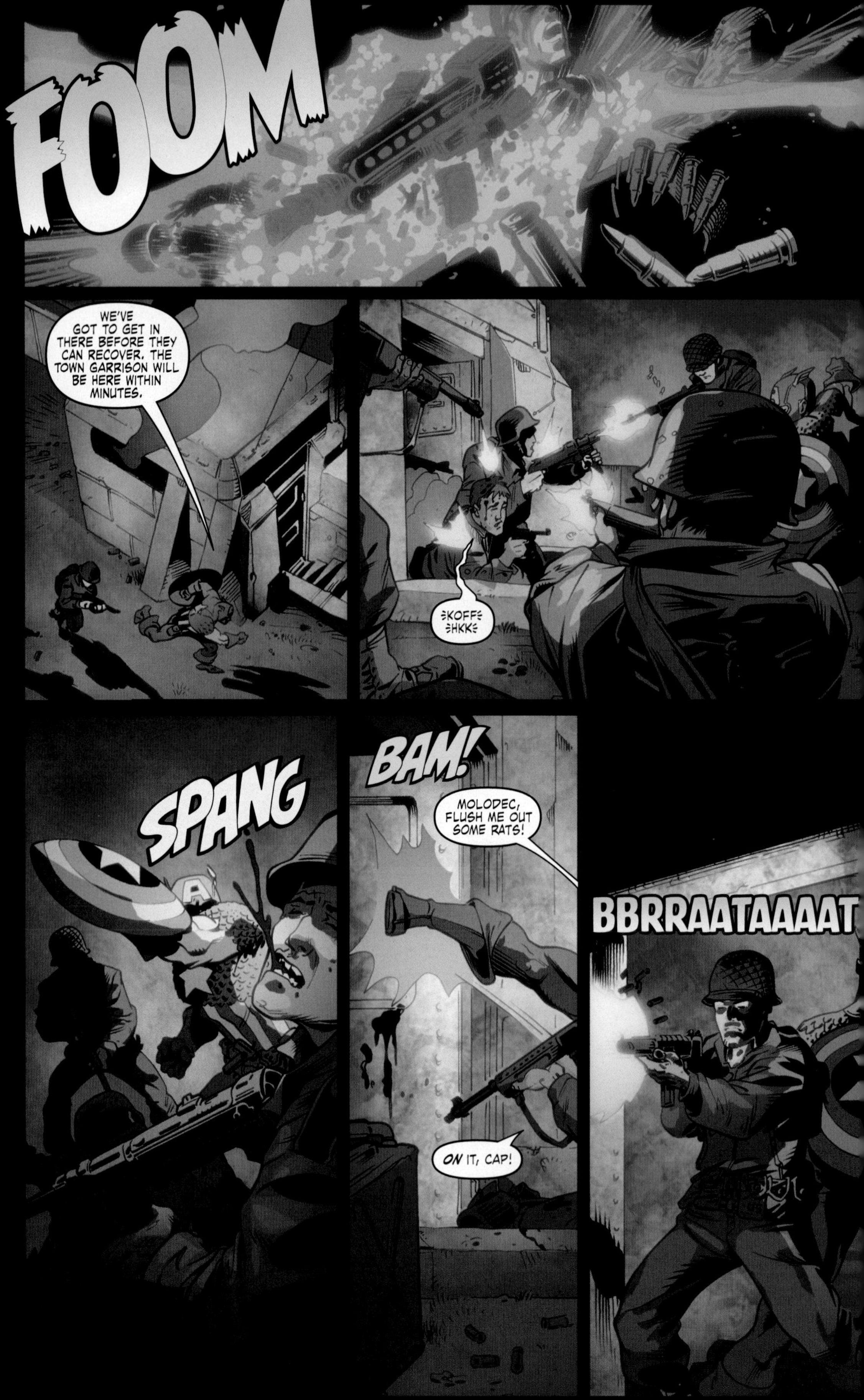
FOOM
WE'VE GOT TO GET IN THERE BEFORE THEY CAN RECOVER. THE TOWN GARRISON WILL BE HERE WITHIN MINUTES.
KOFF HKK
SPANG
BAM!
MOLODEC, FLUSH ME OUT SOME RATS!
ON IT, CAP!
BBRRAATAAAAT

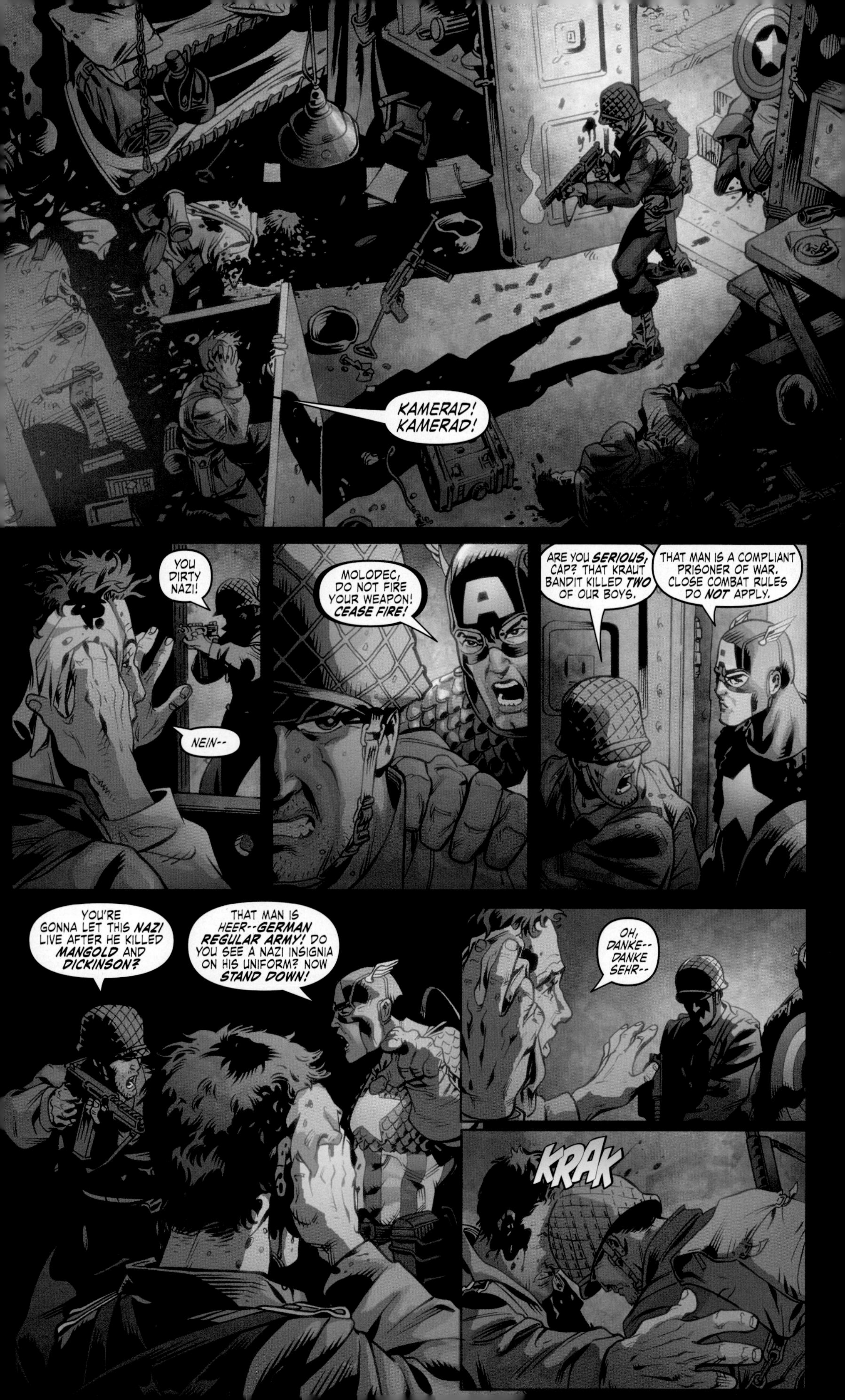
KAMERAD! KAMERAD!
YOU DIRTY NAZI!
NEIN--
MOLODEC, DO NOT FIRE YOUR WEAPON! CEASE FIRE!
ARE YOU SERIOUS, CAP? THAT KRAUT BANDIT KILLED TWO OF OUR BOYS.
THAT MAN IS A COMPLIANT PRISONER OF WAR. CLOSE COMBAT RULES DO NOT APPLY.
YOU'RE GONNA LET THIS NAZI LIVE AFTER HE KILLED MANGOLD AND DICKINSON?
THAT MAN IS HEER--GERMAN REGULAR ARMY! DO YOU SEE A NAZI INSIGNIA ON HIS UNIFORM? NOW STAND DOWN!
OH, DANKE--DANKE SEHR--
KRAK

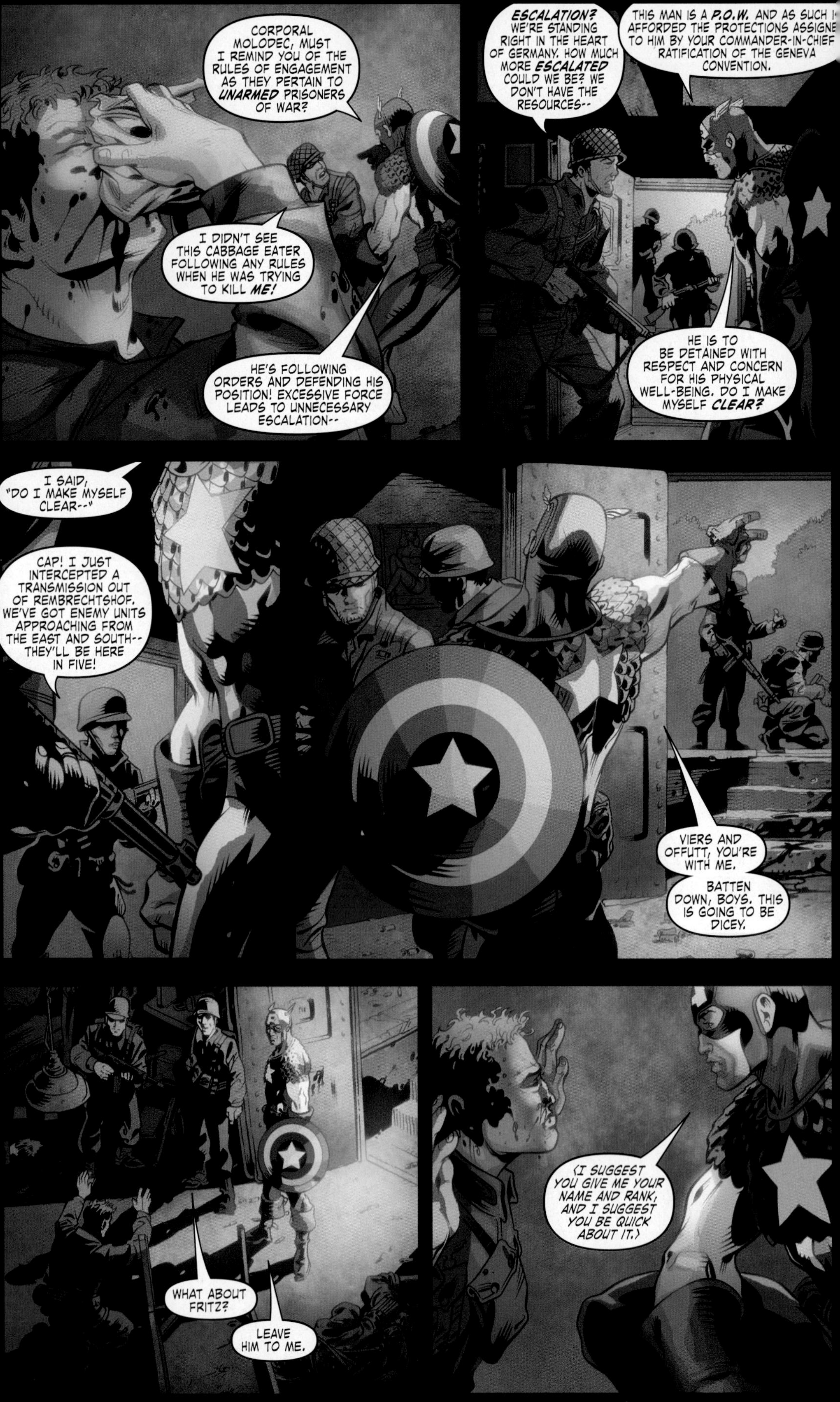

CORPORAL MOLODEC, MUST I REMIND YOU OF THE RULES OF ENGAGEMENT AS THEY PERTAIN TO UNARMED PRISONERS OF WAR?
I DIDN'T SEE THIS CABBAGE EATER FOLLOWING ANY RULES WHEN HE WAS TRYING TO KILL ME!
HE'S FOLLOWING ORDERS AND DEFENDING HIS POSITION! EXCESSIVE FORCE LEADS TO UNNECESSARY ESCALATION--
ESCALATION? WE'RE STANDING RIGHT IN THE HEART OF GERMANY. HOW MUCH MORE ESCALATED COULD WE BE? WE DON'T HAVE THE RESOURCES--
THIS MAN IS A P.O.W. AND AS SUCH I AFFORDED THE PROTECTIONS ASSIGNE TO HIM BY YOUR COMMANDER-IN-CHIEF RATIFICATION OF THE GENEVA CONVENTION.
HE IS TO BE DETAINED WITH RESPECT AND CONCERN FOR HIS PHYSICAL WELL-BEING. DO I MAKE MYSELF CLEAR?
I SAID, "DO I MAKE MYSELF CLEAR--"
CAP! I JUST INTERCEPTED A TRANSMISSION OUT OF REMBRECHTSHOF. WE'VE GOT ENEMY UNITS APPROACHING FROM THE EAST AND SOUTH-- THEY'LL BE HERE IN FIVE!
VIERS AND OFFUTT, YOU'RE WITH ME.
BATTEN DOWN, BOYS. THIS IS GOING TO BE DICEY.
WHAT ABOUT FRITZ?
LEAVE HIM TO ME.
(I SUGGEST YOU GIVE ME YOUR NAME AND RANK, AND I SUGGEST YOU BE QUICK ABOUT IT.)

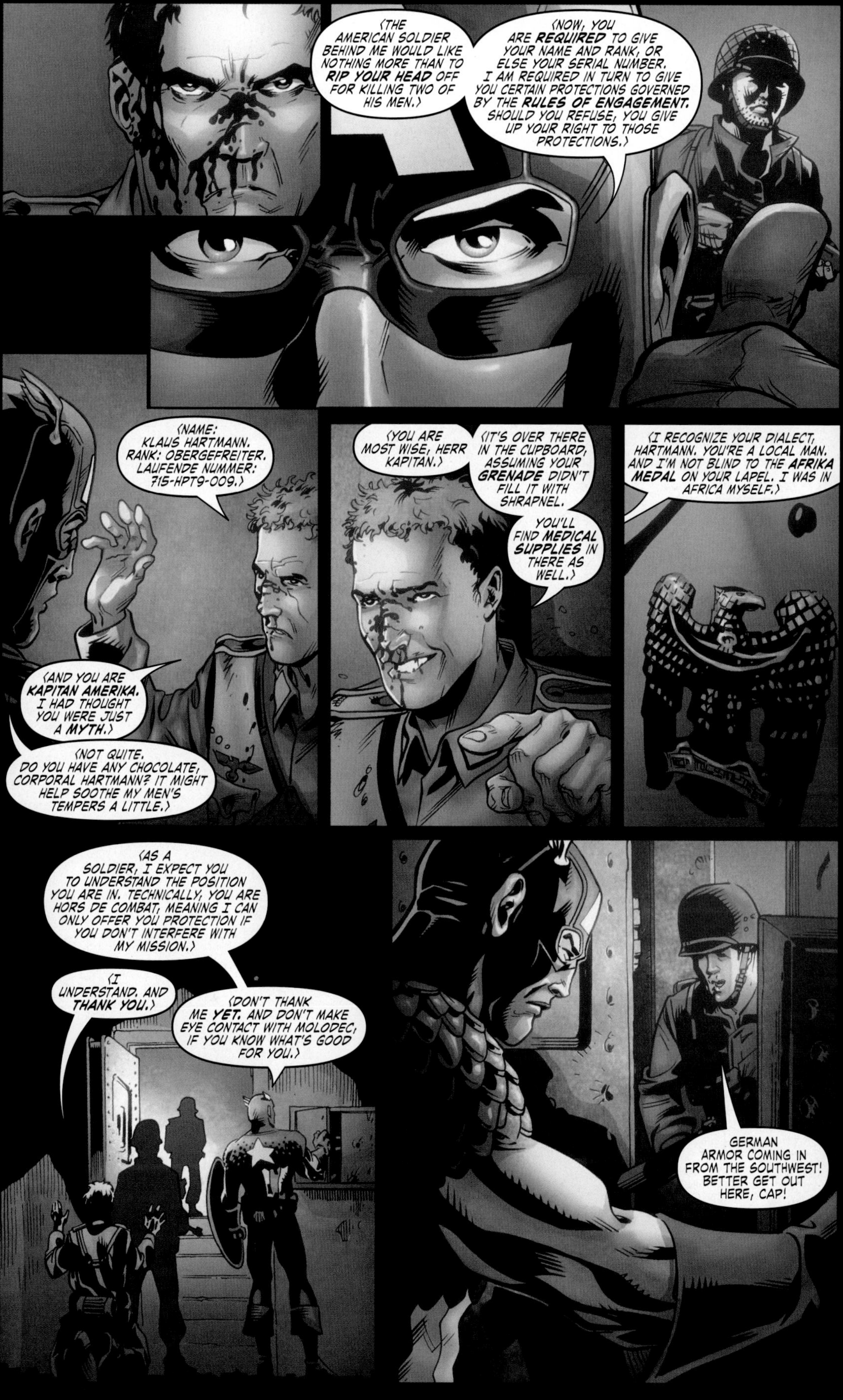
⟨THE AMERICAN SOLDIER BEHIND ME WOULD LIKE NOTHING MORE THAN TO RIP YOUR HEAD OFF FOR KILLING TWO OF HIS MEN.⟩
⟨NOW, YOU ARE REQUIRED TO GIVE YOUR NAME AND RANK, OR ELSE YOUR SERIAL NUMBER. I AM REQUIRED IN TURN TO GIVE YOU CERTAIN PROTECTIONS GOVERNED BY THE RULES OF ENGAGEMENT. SHOULD YOU REFUSE, YOU GIVE UP YOUR RIGHT TO THOSE PROTECTIONS.⟩
⟨NAME: KLAUS HARTMANN. RANK: OBERGEFREITER. LAUFENDE NUMMER: 715-HPT9-009.⟩
⟨AND YOU ARE KAPITAN AMERIKA. I HAD THOUGHT YOU WERE JUST A MYTH.⟩
⟨NOT QUITE. DO YOU HAVE ANY CHOCOLATE, CORPORAL HARTMANN? IT MIGHT HELP SOOTHE MY MEN'S TEMPERS A LITTLE.⟩
⟨YOU ARE MOST WISE, HERR KAPITAN.⟩
⟨IT'S OVER THERE IN THE CUPBOARD, ASSUMING YOUR GRENADE DIDN'T FILL IT WITH SHRAPNEL.
YOU'LL FIND MEDICAL SUPPLIES IN THERE AS WELL.⟩
⟨I RECOGNIZE YOUR DIALECT, HARTMANN. YOU'RE A LOCAL MAN. AND I'M NOT BLIND TO THE AFRIKA MEDAL ON YOUR LAPEL. I WAS IN AFRICA MYSELF.⟩
⟨AS A SOLDIER, I EXPECT YOU TO UNDERSTAND THE POSITION YOU ARE IN. TECHNICALLY, YOU ARE HORS DE COMBAT, MEANING I CAN ONLY OFFER YOU PROTECTION IF YOU DON'T INTERFERE WITH MY MISSION.⟩
⟨I UNDERSTAND. AND THANK YOU.⟩
⟨DON'T THANK ME YET. AND DON'T MAKE EYE CONTACT WITH MOLODEC, IF YOU KNOW WHAT'S GOOD FOR YOU.⟩
GERMAN ARMOR COMING IN FROM THE SOUTHWEST! BETTER GET OUT HERE, CAP!

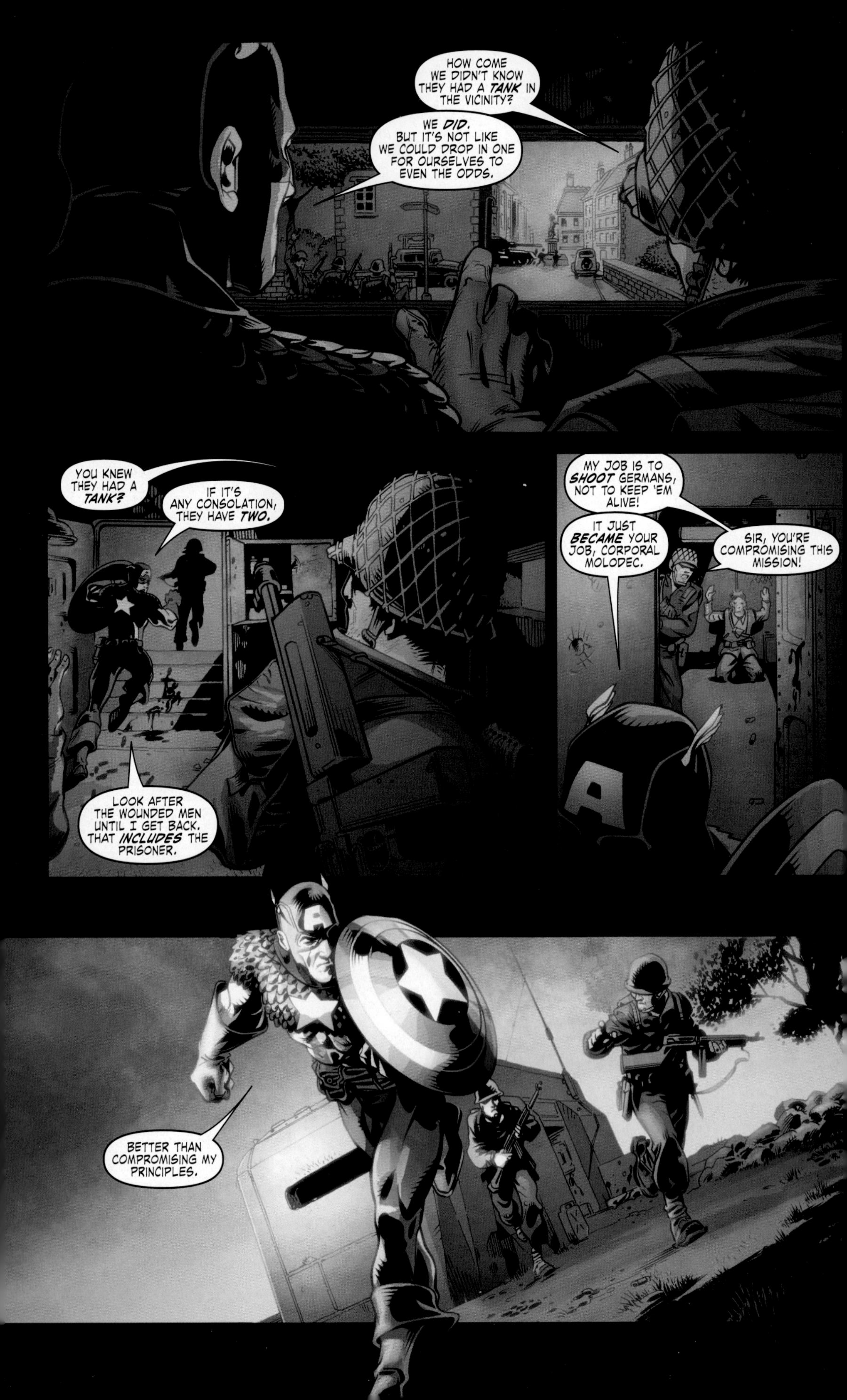
HOW COME WE DIDN'T KNOW THEY HAD A TANK IN THE VICINITY?
WE DID. BUT IT'S NOT LIKE WE COULD DROP IN ONE FOR OURSELVES TO EVEN THE ODDS.
YOU KNEW THEY HAD A TANK?
IF IT'S ANY CONSOLATION, THEY HAVE TWO.
LOOK AFTER THE WOUNDED MEN UNTIL I GET BACK. THAT INCLUDES THE PRISONER.
MY JOB IS TO SHOOT GERMANS, NOT TO KEEP 'EM ALIVE!
IT JUST BECAME YOUR JOB, CORPORAL MOLODEC.
SIR, YOU'RE COMPROMISING THIS MISSION!
BETTER THAN COMPROMISING MY PRINCIPLES.

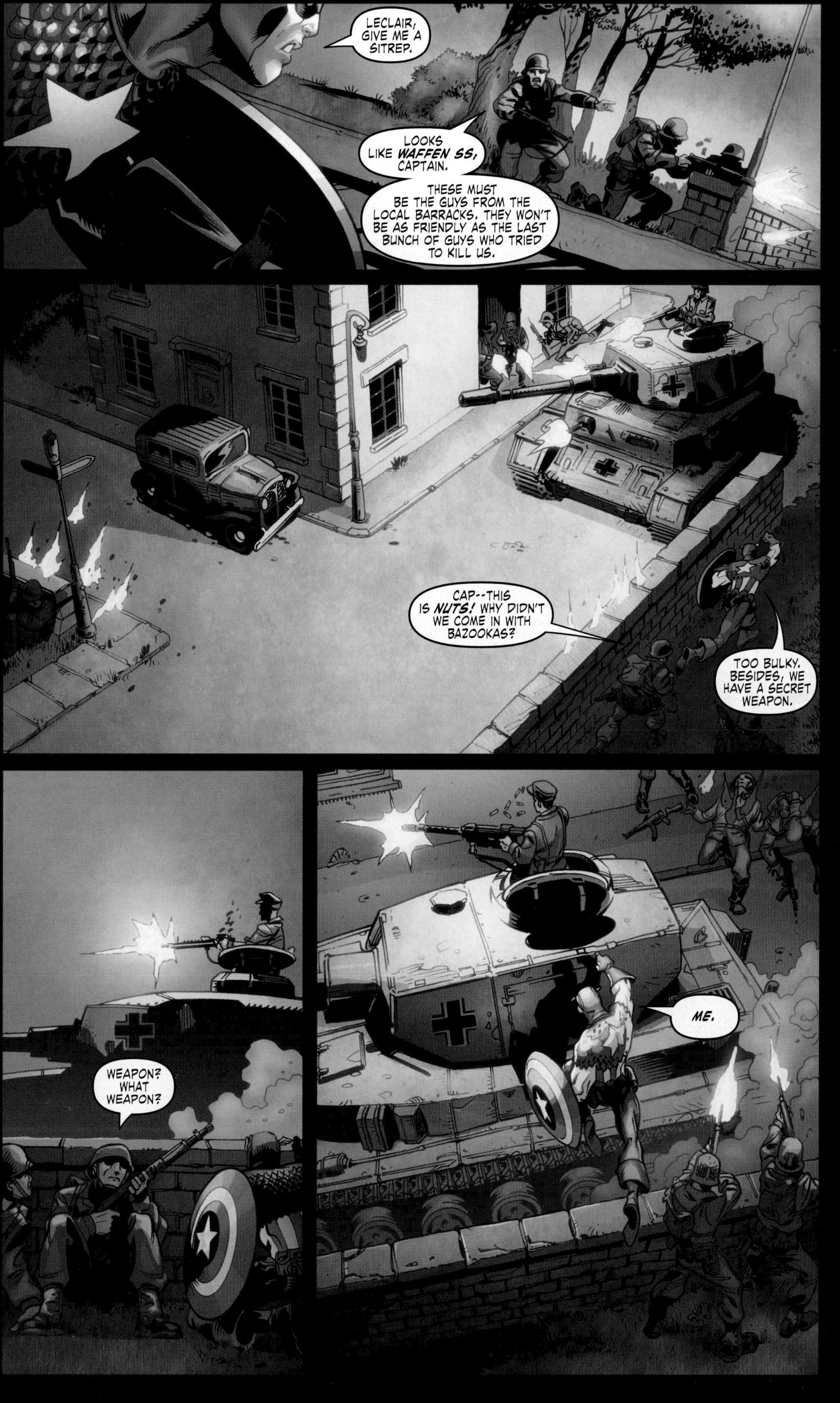
LECLAIR, GIVE ME A SITREP.
LOOKS LIKE WAFFEN SS, CAPTAIN.
THESE MUST BE THE GUYS FROM THE LOCAL BARRACKS. THEY WON'T BE AS FRIENDLY AS THE LAST BUNCH OF GUYS WHO TRIED TO KILL US.
CAP--THIS IS NUTS! WHY DIDN'T WE COME IN WITH BAZOOKAS?
TOO BULKY. BESIDES, WE HAVE A SECRET WEAPON.
WEAPON? WHAT WEAPON?
ME.

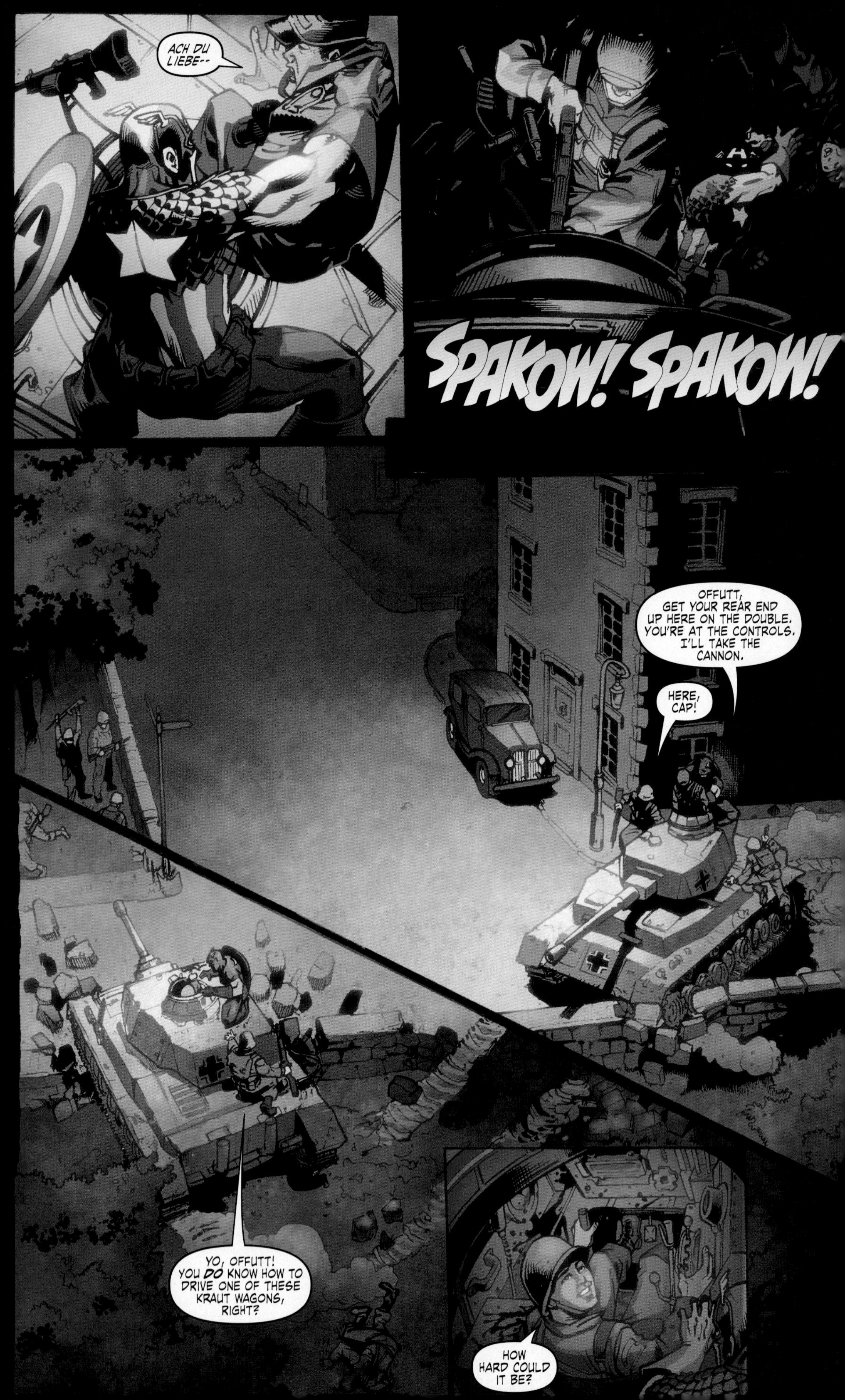
ACH DU LIEBE--
SPAKOW! SPAKOW!
OFFUTT, GET YOUR REAR END UP HERE ON THE DOUBLE. YOU'RE AT THE CONTROLS. I'LL TAKE THE CANNON.
HERE, CAP!
YO, OFFUTT! YOU DO KNOW HOW TO DRIVE ONE OF THESE KRAUT WAGONS, RIGHT?
HOW HARD COULD IT BE?

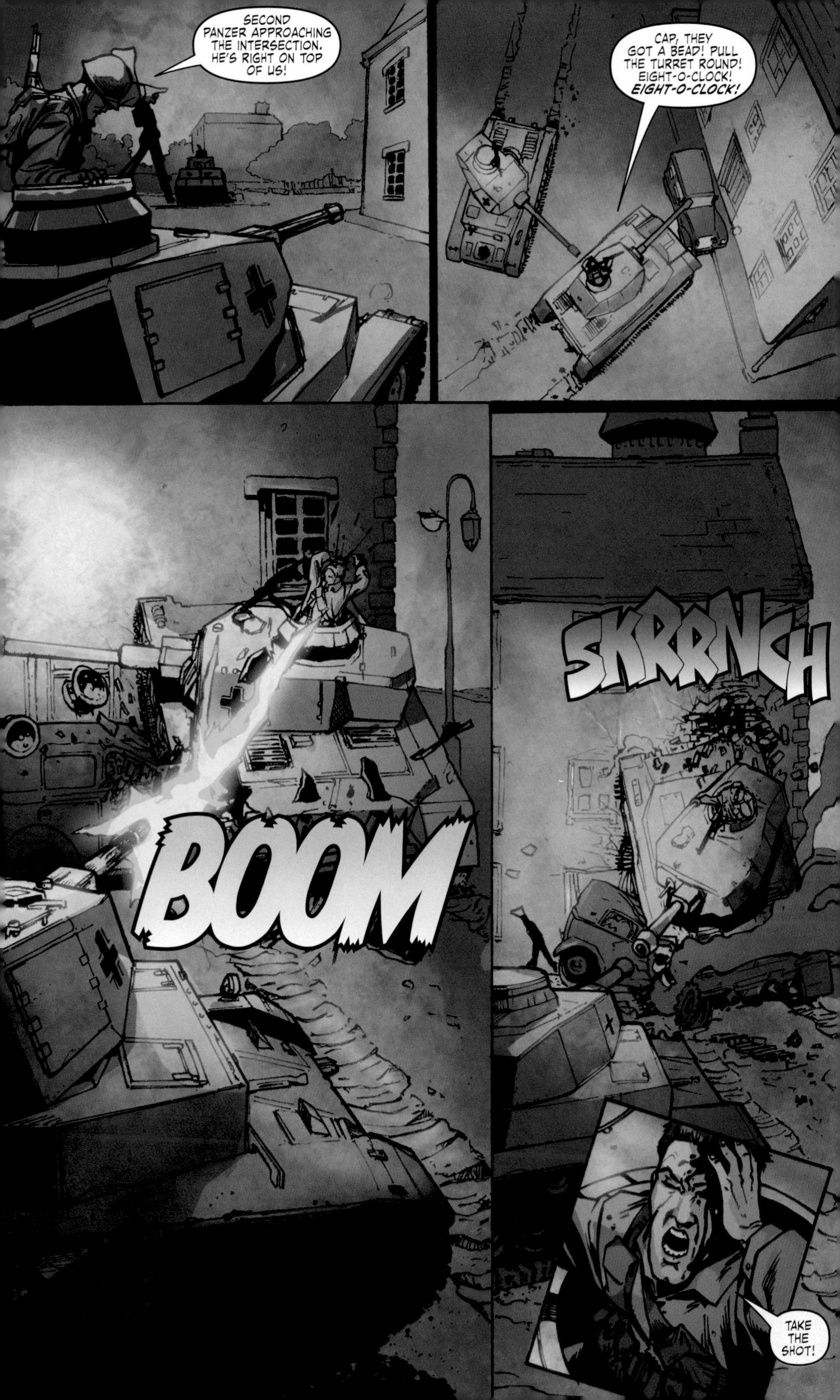
SECOND PANZER APPROACHING THE INTERSECTION. HE'S RIGHT ON TOP OF US!
CAP, THEY GOT A BEAD! PULL THE TURRET ROUND! EIGHT-O-CLOCK! EIGHT-O-CLOCK!
BOOM
SKRRNCH
TAKE THE SHOT!

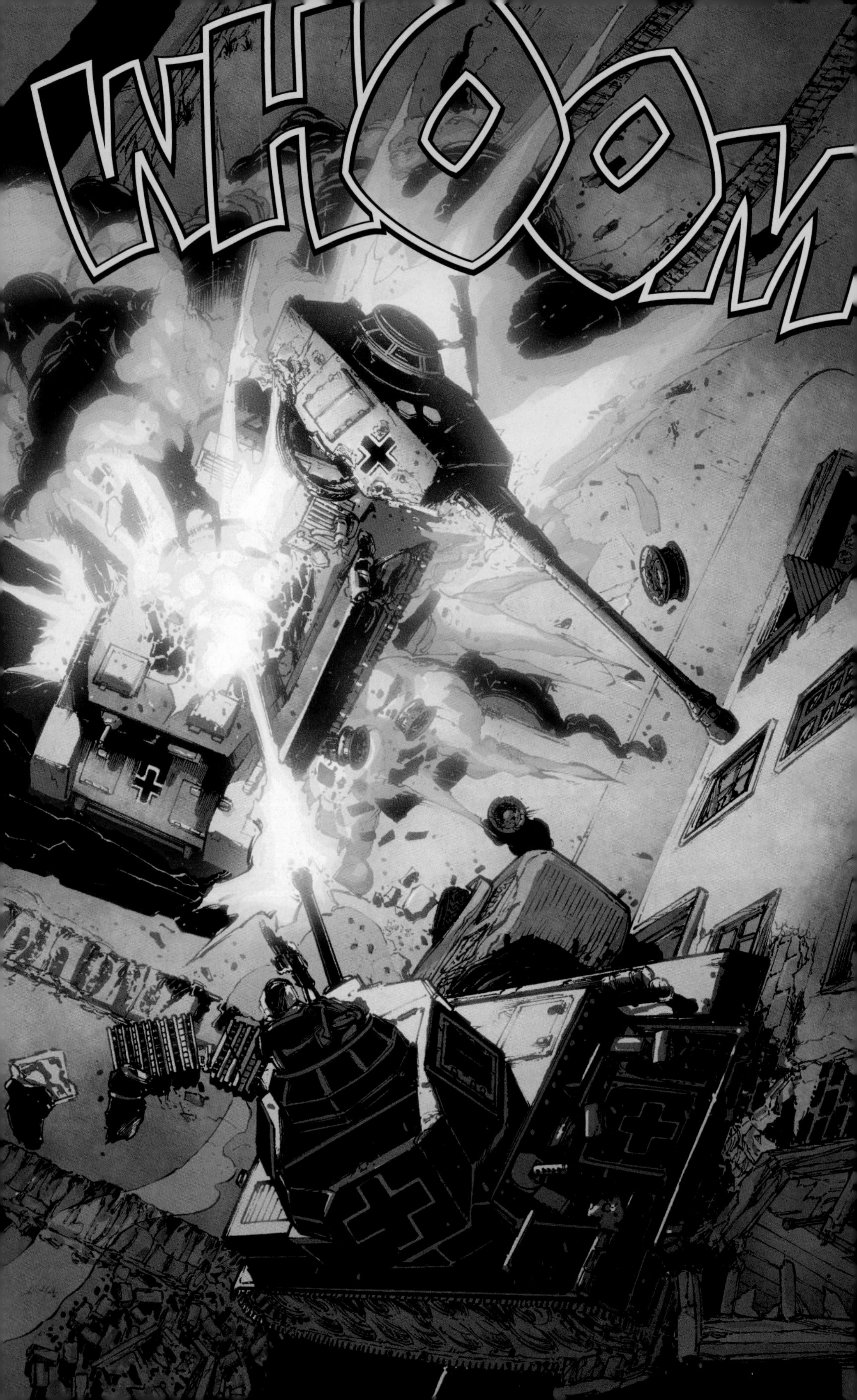
WHOOM

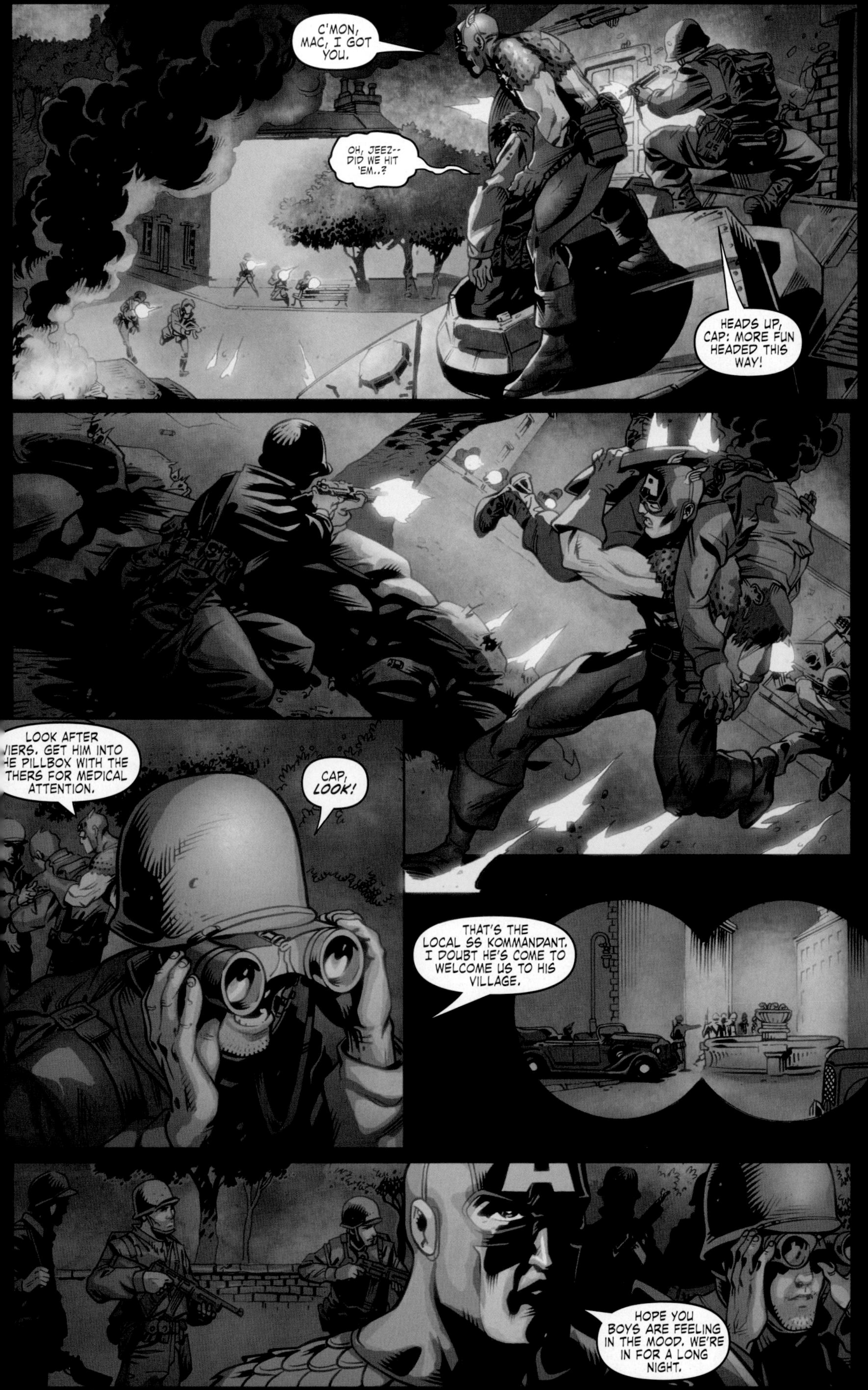
C'MON, MAC, I GOT YOU.
OH, JEEZ-- DID WE HIT 'EM..?
HEADS UP, CAP: MORE FUN HEADED THIS WAY!
LOOK AFTER IERS. GET HIM INTO E PILLBOX WITH THE THERS FOR MEDICAL ATTENTION.
CAP, LOOK!
THAT'S THE LOCAL SS KOMMANDANT. I DOUBT HE'S COME TO WELCOME US TO HIS VILLAGE.
HOPE YOU BOYS ARE FEELING IN THE MOOD. WE'RE IN FOR A LONG NIGHT.

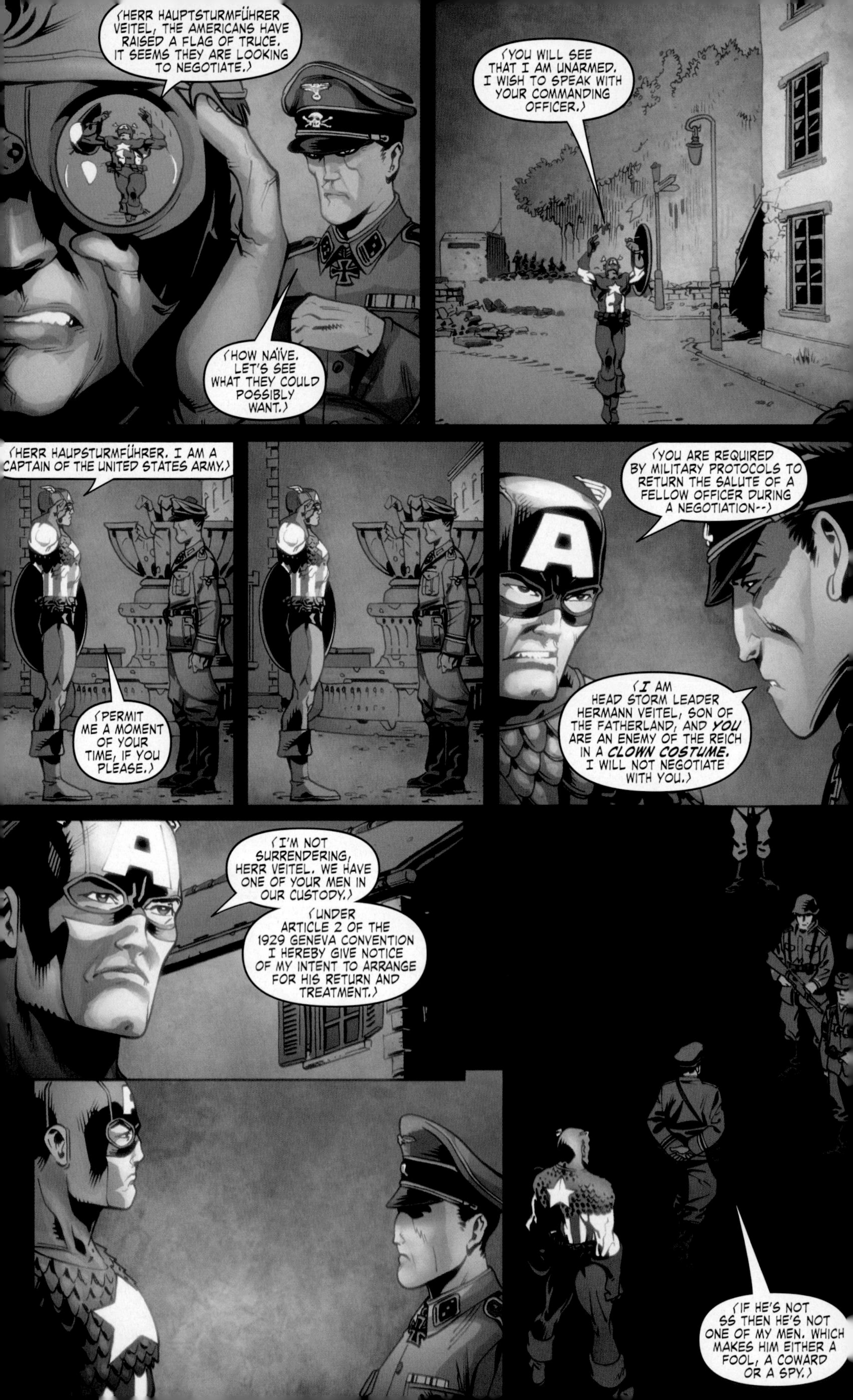
‹HERR HAUPTSTURMFÜHRER VEITEL, THE AMERICANS HAVE RAISED A FLAG OF TRUCE. IT SEEMS THEY ARE LOOKING TO NEGOTIATE.›
‹HOW NAÏVE. LET'S SEE WHAT THEY COULD POSSIBLY WANT.›
‹YOU WILL SEE THAT I AM UNARMED. I WISH TO SPEAK WITH YOUR COMMANDING OFFICER.›
‹HERR HAUPSTURMFÜHRER. I AM A CAPTAIN OF THE UNITED STATES ARMY.›
‹PERMIT ME A MOMENT OF YOUR TIME, IF YOU PLEASE.›
‹YOU ARE REQUIRED BY MILITARY PROTOCOLS TO RETURN THE SALUTE OF A FELLOW OFFICER DURING A NEGOTIATION--›
‹*I* AM HEAD STORM LEADER HERMANN VEITEL, SON OF THE FATHERLAND, AND *YOU* ARE AN ENEMY OF THE REICH IN A ***CLOWN COSTUME.*** I WILL NOT NEGOTIATE WITH YOU.›
‹I'M NOT SURRENDERING, HERR VEITEL. WE HAVE ONE OF YOUR MEN IN OUR CUSTODY.›
‹UNDER ARTICLE 2 OF THE 1929 GENEVA CONVENTION I HEREBY GIVE NOTICE OF MY INTENT TO ARRANGE FOR HIS RETURN AND TREATMENT.›
‹IF HE'S NOT SS THEN HE'S NOT ONE OF MY MEN. WHICH MAKES HIM EITHER A FOOL, A COWARD OR A SPY.›

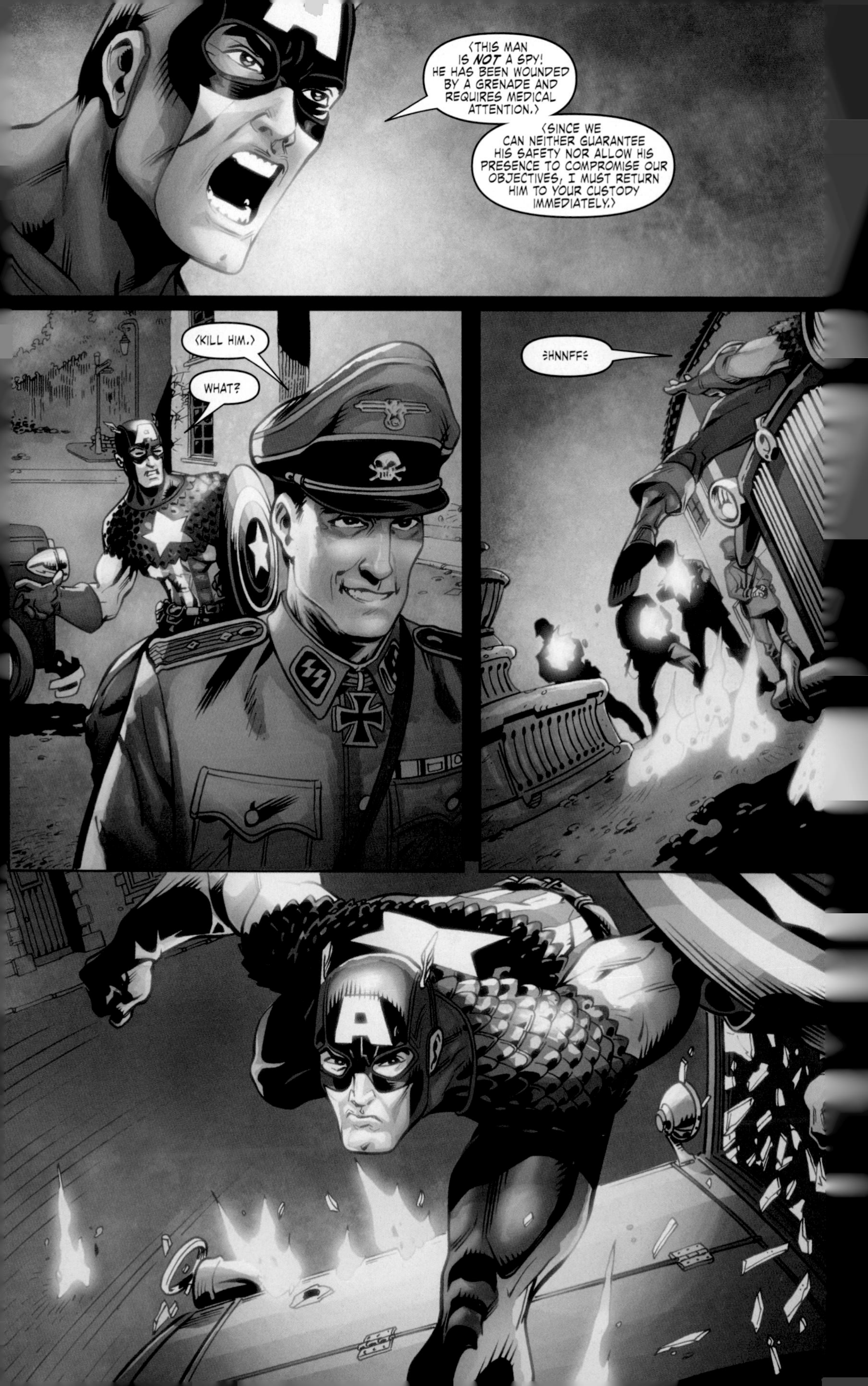

<THIS MAN IS *NOT* A SPY! HE HAS BEEN WOUNDED BY A GRENADE AND REQUIRES MEDICAL ATTENTION.>
<SINCE WE CAN NEITHER GUARANTEE HIS SAFETY NOR ALLOW HIS PRESENCE TO COMPROMISE OUR OBJECTIVES, I MUST RETURN HIM TO YOUR CUSTODY IMMEDIATELY.>
<KILL HIM.>
WHAT?
HNNFF

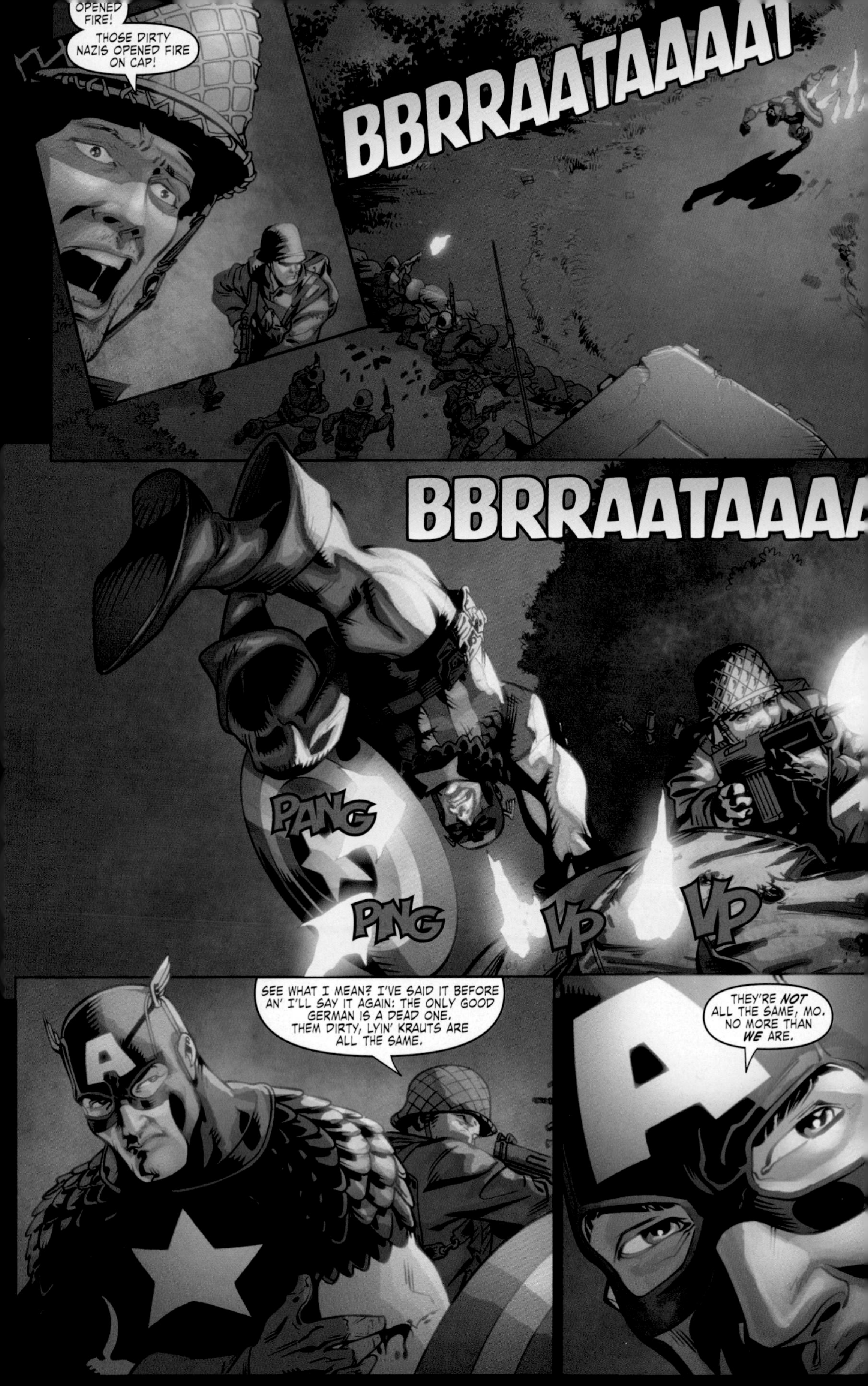
OPENED FIRE!
THOSE DIRTY NAZIS OPENED FIRE ON CAP!
BBRRAATAAAAT
BBRRAATAAAA
PANG
PNG
VP
VP
SEE WHAT I MEAN? I'VE SAID IT BEFORE AN' I'LL SAY IT AGAIN: THE ONLY GOOD GERMAN IS A DEAD ONE. THEM DIRTY, LYIN' KRAUTS ARE ALL THE SAME.
THEY'RE NOT ALL THE SAME, MO. NO MORE THAN WE ARE.

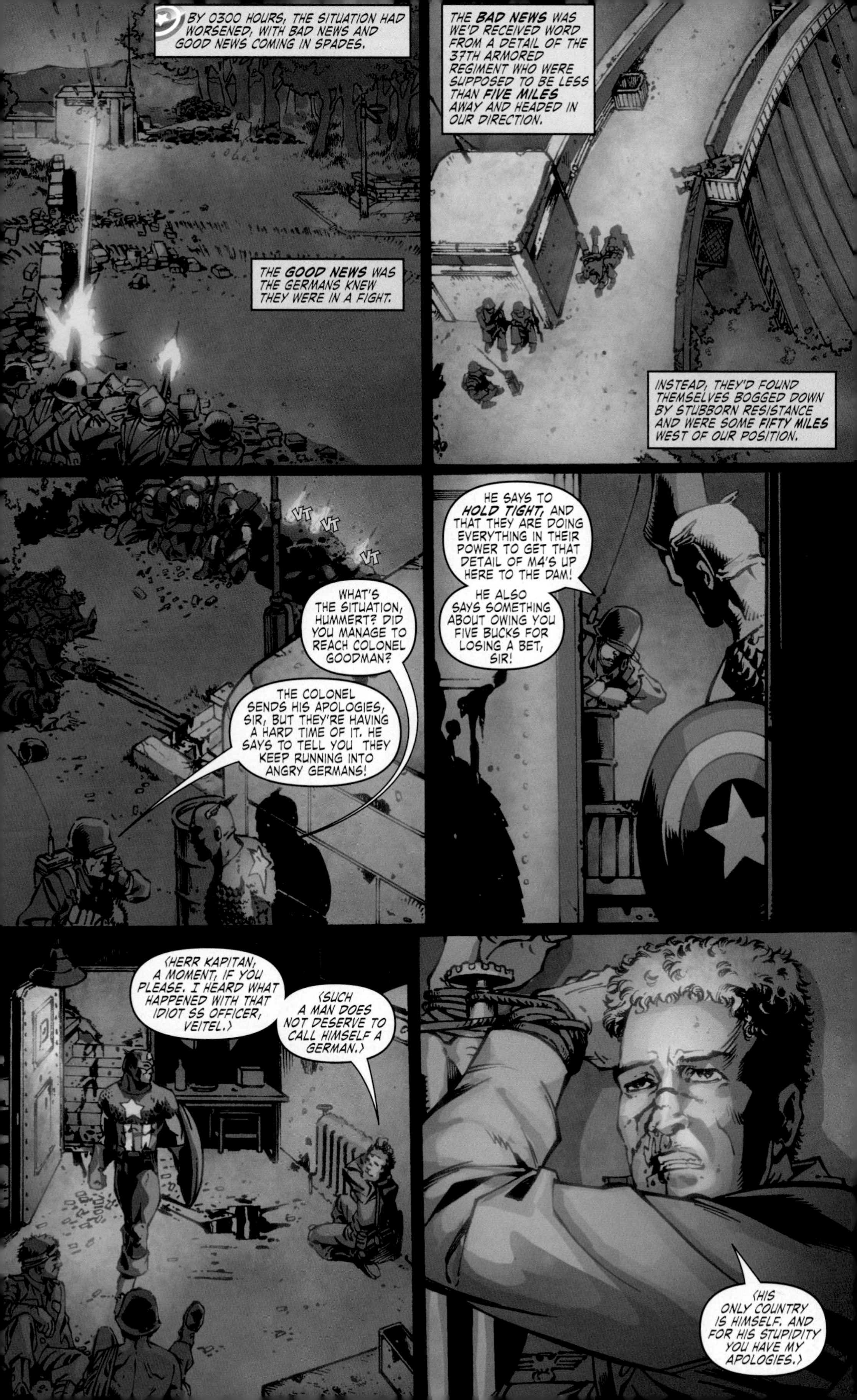
BY 0300 HOURS, THE SITUATION HAD WORSENED, WITH BAD NEWS AND GOOD NEWS COMING IN SPADES.
THE GOOD NEWS WAS THE GERMANS KNEW THEY WERE IN A FIGHT.
THE BAD NEWS WAS WE'D RECEIVED WORD FROM A DETAIL OF THE 37TH ARMORED REGIMENT WHO WERE SUPPOSED TO BE LESS THAN FIVE MILES AWAY AND HEADED IN OUR DIRECTION.
INSTEAD, THEY'D FOUND THEMSELVES BOGGED DOWN BY STUBBORN RESISTANCE AND WERE SOME FIFTY MILES WEST OF OUR POSITION.
VT VT VT
WHAT'S THE SITUATION, HUMMERT? DID YOU MANAGE TO REACH COLONEL GOODMAN?
THE COLONEL SENDS HIS APOLOGIES, SIR, BUT THEY'RE HAVING A HARD TIME OF IT. HE SAYS TO TELL YOU THEY KEEP RUNNING INTO ANGRY GERMANS!
HE SAYS TO HOLD TIGHT, AND THAT THEY ARE DOING EVERYTHING IN THEIR POWER TO GET THAT DETAIL OF M4'S UP HERE TO THE DAM!
HE ALSO SAYS SOMETHING ABOUT OWING YOU FIVE BUCKS FOR LOSING A BET, SIR!
(HERR KAPITAN, A MOMENT, IF YOU PLEASE. I HEARD WHAT HAPPENED WITH THAT IDIOT SS OFFICER, VEITEL.)
(SUCH A MAN DOES NOT DESERVE TO CALL HIMSELF A GERMAN.)
(HIS ONLY COUNTRY IS HIMSELF. AND FOR HIS STUPIDITY YOU HAVE MY APOLOGIES.)

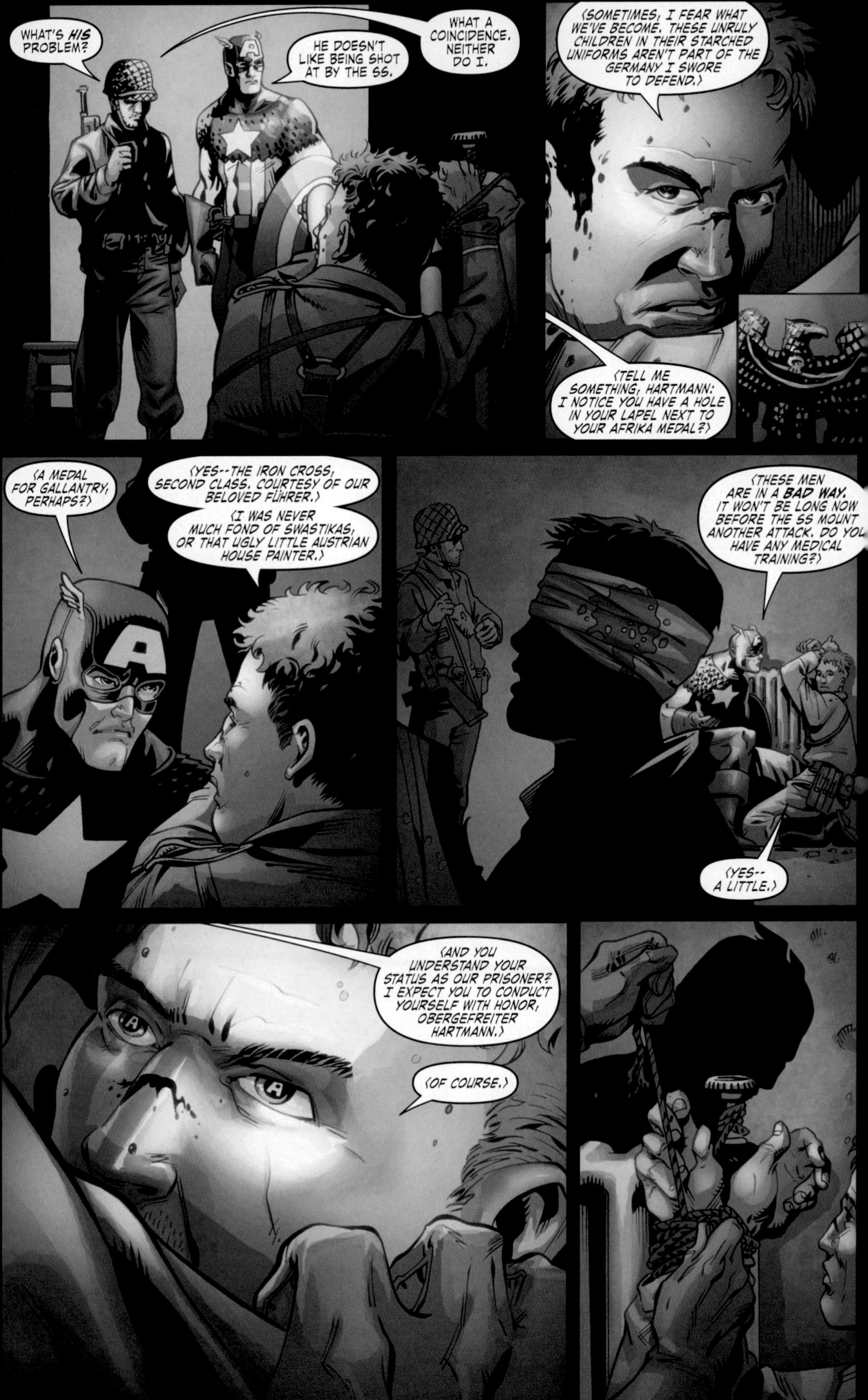
WHAT'S HIS PROBLEM?
HE DOESN'T LIKE BEING SHOT AT BY THE SS.
WHAT A COINCIDENCE. NEITHER DO I.
‹SOMETIMES, I FEAR WHAT WE'VE BECOME. THESE UNRULY CHILDREN IN THEIR STARCHED UNIFORMS AREN'T PART OF THE GERMANY I SWORE TO DEFEND.›
‹TELL ME SOMETHING, HARTMANN: I NOTICE YOU HAVE A HOLE IN YOUR LAPEL NEXT TO YOUR AFRIKA MEDAL?›
‹A MEDAL FOR GALLANTRY, PERHAPS?›
‹YES--THE IRON CROSS, SECOND CLASS. COURTESY OF OUR BELOVED FÜHRER.›
‹I WAS NEVER MUCH FOND OF SWASTIKAS, OR THAT UGLY LITTLE AUSTRIAN HOUSE PAINTER.›
‹THESE MEN ARE IN A BAD WAY. IT WON'T BE LONG NOW BEFORE THE SS MOUNT ANOTHER ATTACK. DO YOU HAVE ANY MEDICAL TRAINING?›
‹YES-- A LITTLE.›
‹AND YOU UNDERSTAND YOUR STATUS AS OUR PRISONER? I EXPECT YOU TO CONDUCT YOURSELF WITH HONOR, OBERGEFREITER HARTMANN.›
‹OF COURSE.›

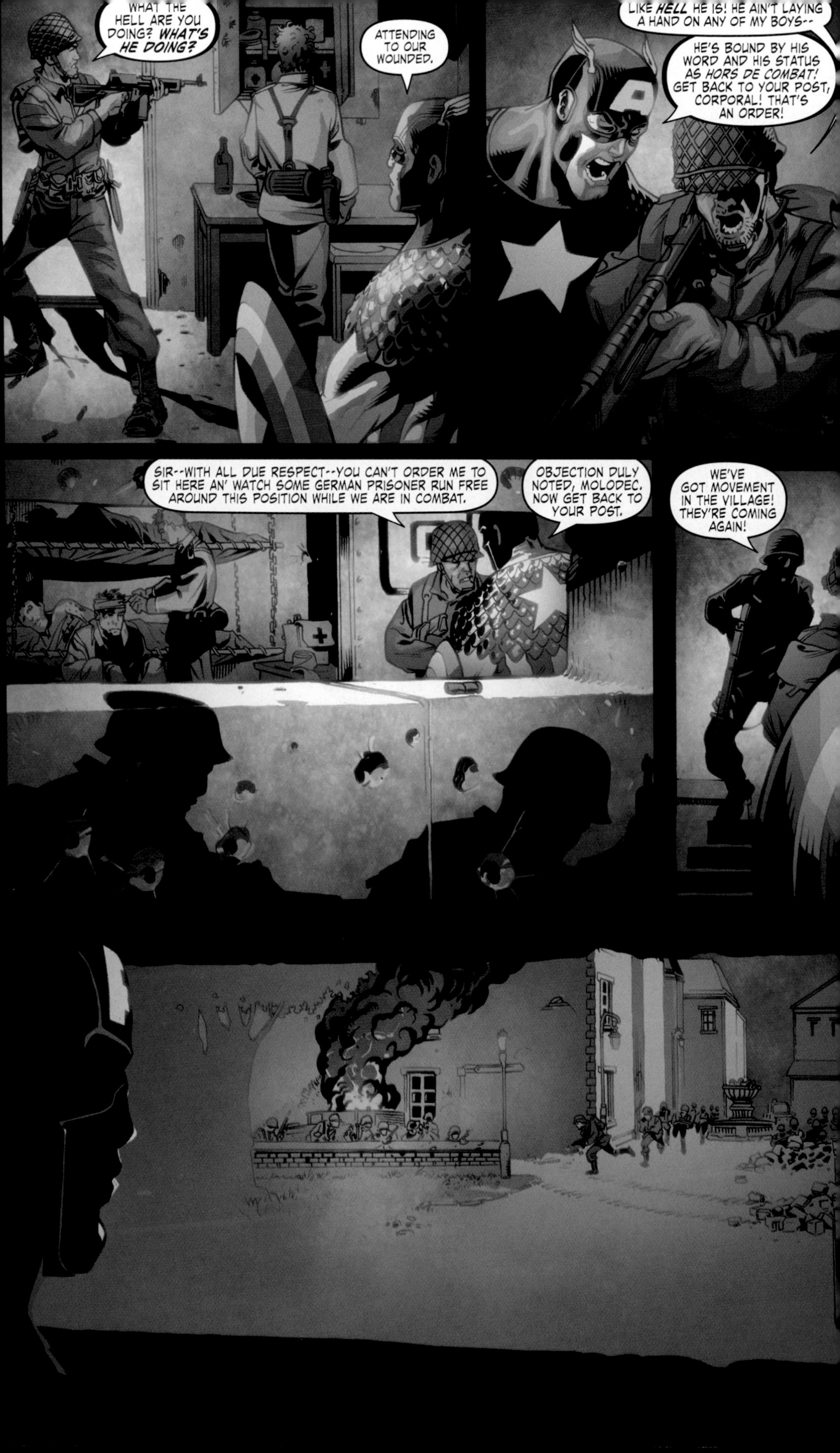
WHAT THE HELL ARE YOU DOING? WHAT'S HE DOING?
ATTENDING TO OUR WOUNDED.
LIKE HELL HE IS! HE AIN'T LAYING A HAND ON ANY OF MY BOYS--
HE'S BOUND BY HIS WORD AND HIS STATUS AS HORS DE COMBAT! GET BACK TO YOUR POST, CORPORAL! THAT'S AN ORDER!
SIR--WITH ALL DUE RESPECT--YOU CAN'T ORDER ME TO SIT HERE AN' WATCH SOME GERMAN PRISONER RUN FREE AROUND THIS POSITION WHILE WE ARE IN COMBAT.
OBJECTION DULY NOTED, MOLODEC. NOW GET BACK TO YOUR POST.
WE'VE GOT MOVEMENT IN THE VILLAGE! THEY'RE COMING AGAIN!

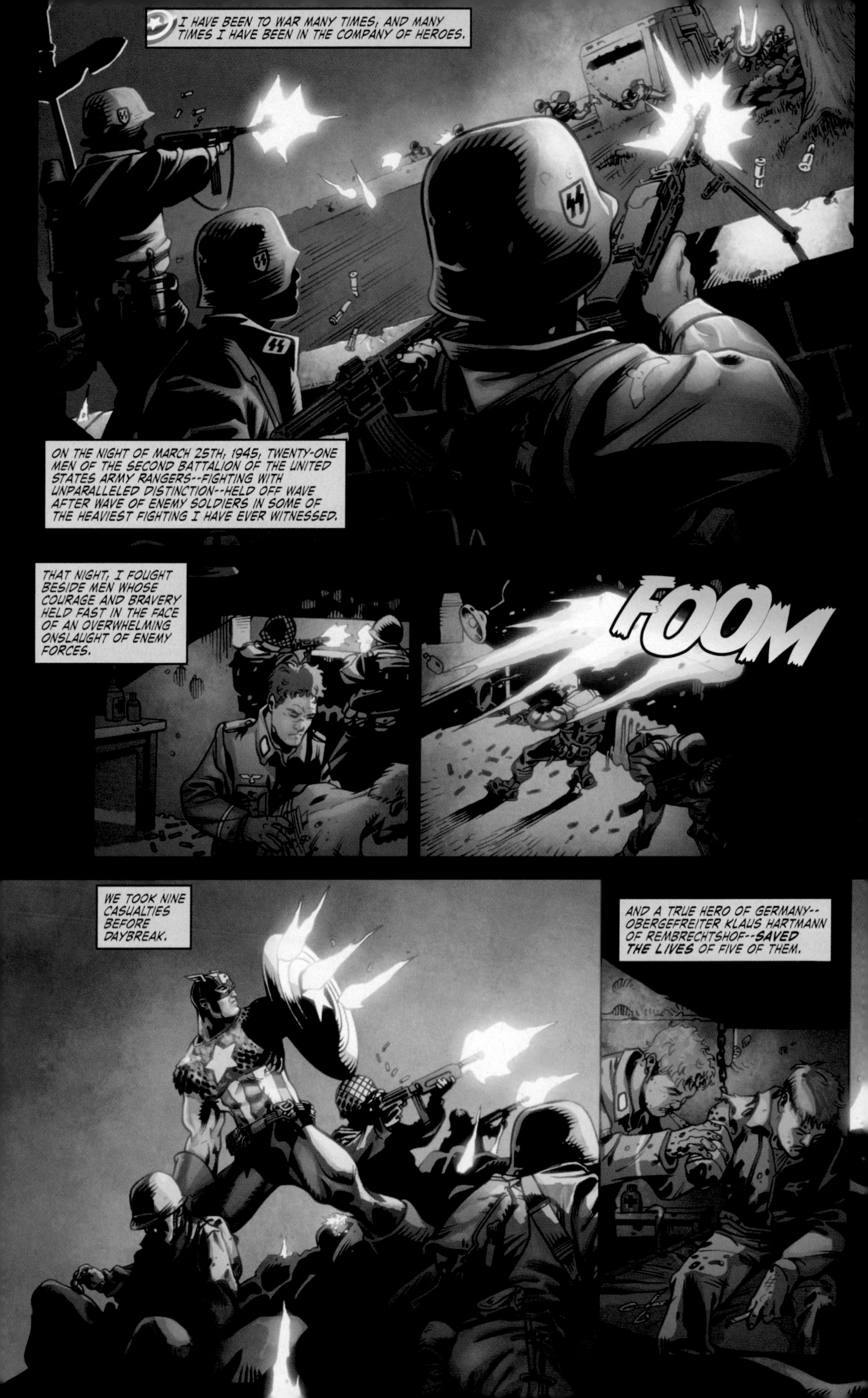
I HAVE BEEN TO WAR MANY TIMES, AND MANY TIMES I HAVE BEEN IN THE COMPANY OF HEROES.
ON THE NIGHT OF MARCH 25TH, 1945, TWENTY-ONE MEN OF THE SECOND BATTALION OF THE UNITED STATES ARMY RANGERS--FIGHTING WITH UNPARALLELED DISTINCTION--HELD OFF WAVE AFTER WAVE OF ENEMY SOLDIERS IN SOME OF THE HEAVIEST FIGHTING I HAVE EVER WITNESSED.
THAT NIGHT, I FOUGHT BESIDE MEN WHOSE COURAGE AND BRAVERY HELD FAST IN THE FACE OF AN OVERWHELMING ONSLAUGHT OF ENEMY FORCES.
FOOM
WE TOOK NINE CASUALTIES BEFORE DAYBREAK.
AND A TRUE HERO OF GERMANY--OBERGEFREITER KLAUS HARTMANN OF REMBRECHTSHOF--SAVED THE LIVES OF FIVE OF THEM.

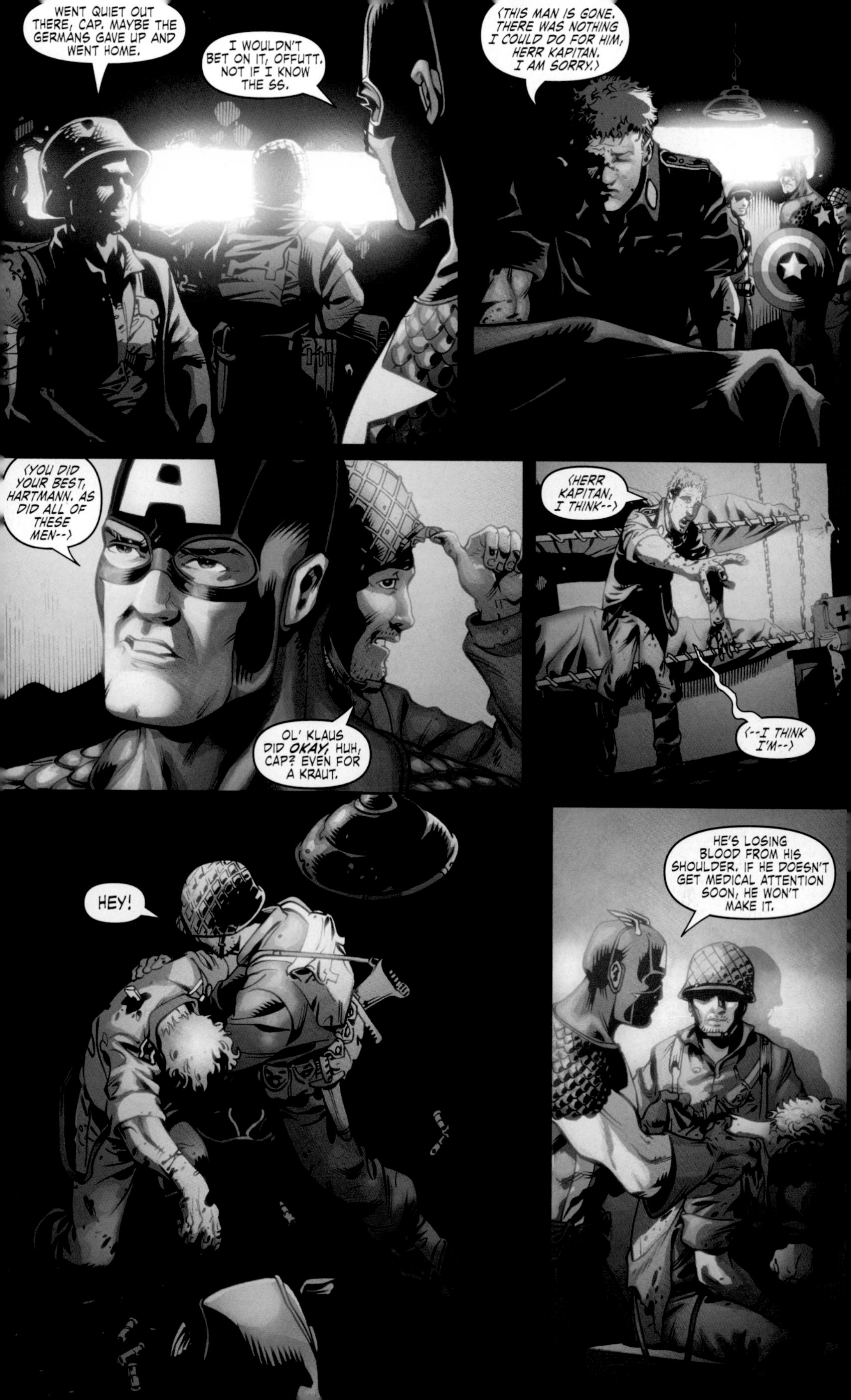
WENT QUIET OUT THERE, CAP. MAYBE THE GERMANS GAVE UP AND WENT HOME.
I WOULDN'T BET ON IT, OFFUTT. NOT IF I KNOW THE SS.
‹THIS MAN IS GONE. THERE WAS NOTHING I COULD DO FOR HIM, HERR KAPITAN. I AM SORRY.›
‹YOU DID YOUR BEST, HARTMANN. AS DID ALL OF THESE MEN--›
OL' KLAUS DID OKAY, HUH, CAP? EVEN FOR A KRAUT.
‹HERR KAPITAN, I THINK--›
‹--I THINK I'M--›
HEY!
HE'S LOSING BLOOD FROM HIS SHOULDER. IF HE DOESN'T GET MEDICAL ATTENTION SOON, HE WON'T MAKE IT.

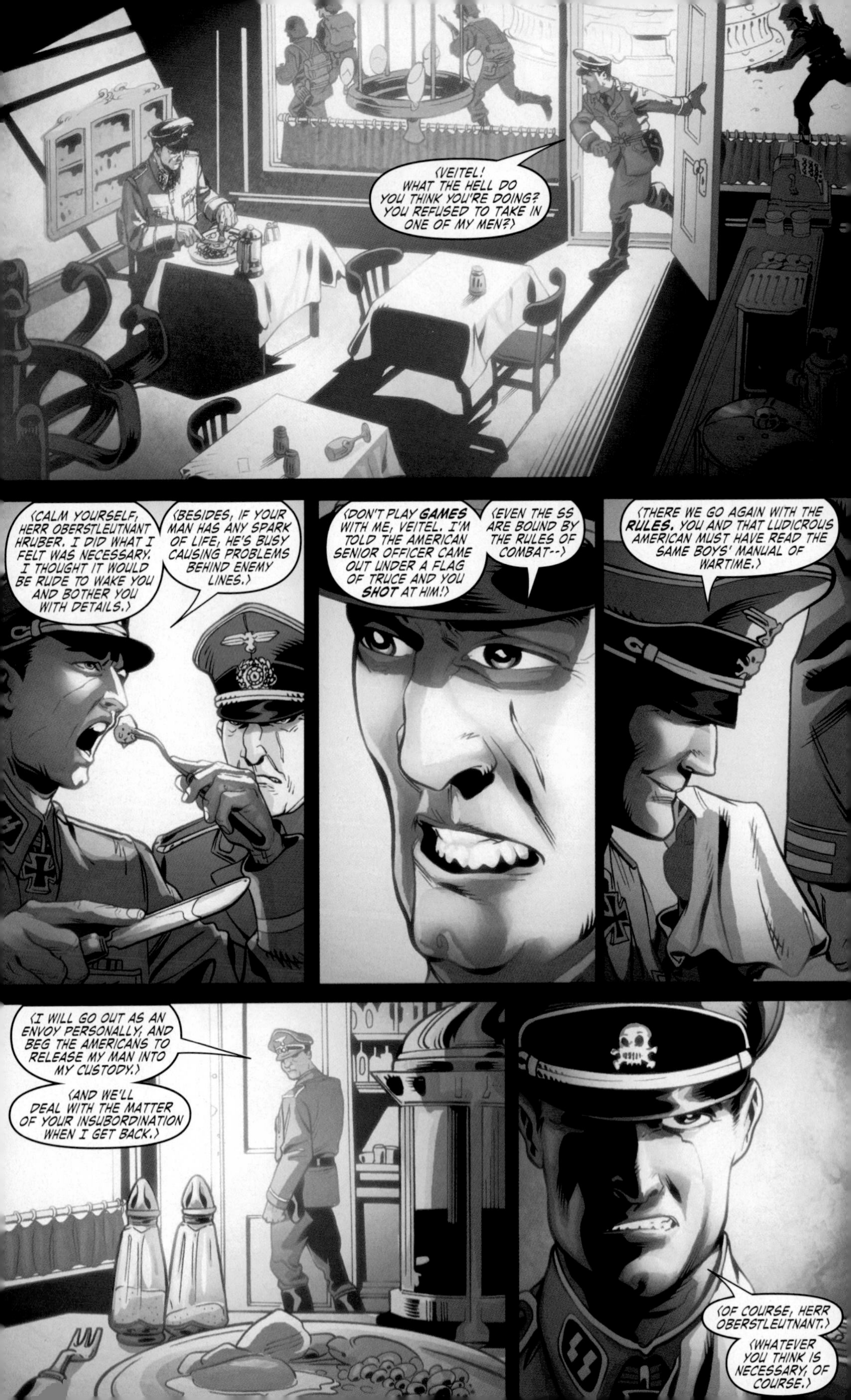

⟨VEITEL! WHAT THE HELL DO YOU THINK YOU'RE DOING? YOU REFUSED TO TAKE IN ONE OF MY MEN?⟩
⟨CALM YOURSELF, HERR OBERSTLEUTNANT HRUBER. I DID WHAT I FELT WAS NECESSARY. I THOUGHT IT WOULD BE RUDE TO WAKE YOU AND BOTHER YOU WITH DETAILS.⟩
⟨BESIDES, IF YOUR MAN HAS ANY SPARK OF LIFE, HE'S BUSY CAUSING PROBLEMS BEHIND ENEMY LINES.⟩
⟨DON'T PLAY GAMES WITH ME, VEITEL. I'M TOLD THE AMERICAN SENIOR OFFICER CAME OUT UNDER A FLAG OF TRUCE AND YOU SHOT AT HIM!⟩
⟨EVEN THE SS ARE BOUND BY THE RULES OF COMBAT--⟩
⟨THERE WE GO AGAIN WITH THE RULES. YOU AND THAT LUDICROUS AMERICAN MUST HAVE READ THE SAME BOYS' MANUAL OF WARTIME.⟩
⟨I WILL GO OUT AS AN ENVOY PERSONALLY, AND BEG THE AMERICANS TO RELEASE MY MAN INTO MY CUSTODY.⟩
⟨AND WE'LL DEAL WITH THE MATTER OF YOUR INSUBORDINATION WHEN I GET BACK.⟩
⟨OF COURSE, HERR OBERSTLEUTNANT.⟩
⟨WHATEVER YOU THINK IS NECESSARY, OF COURSE.⟩

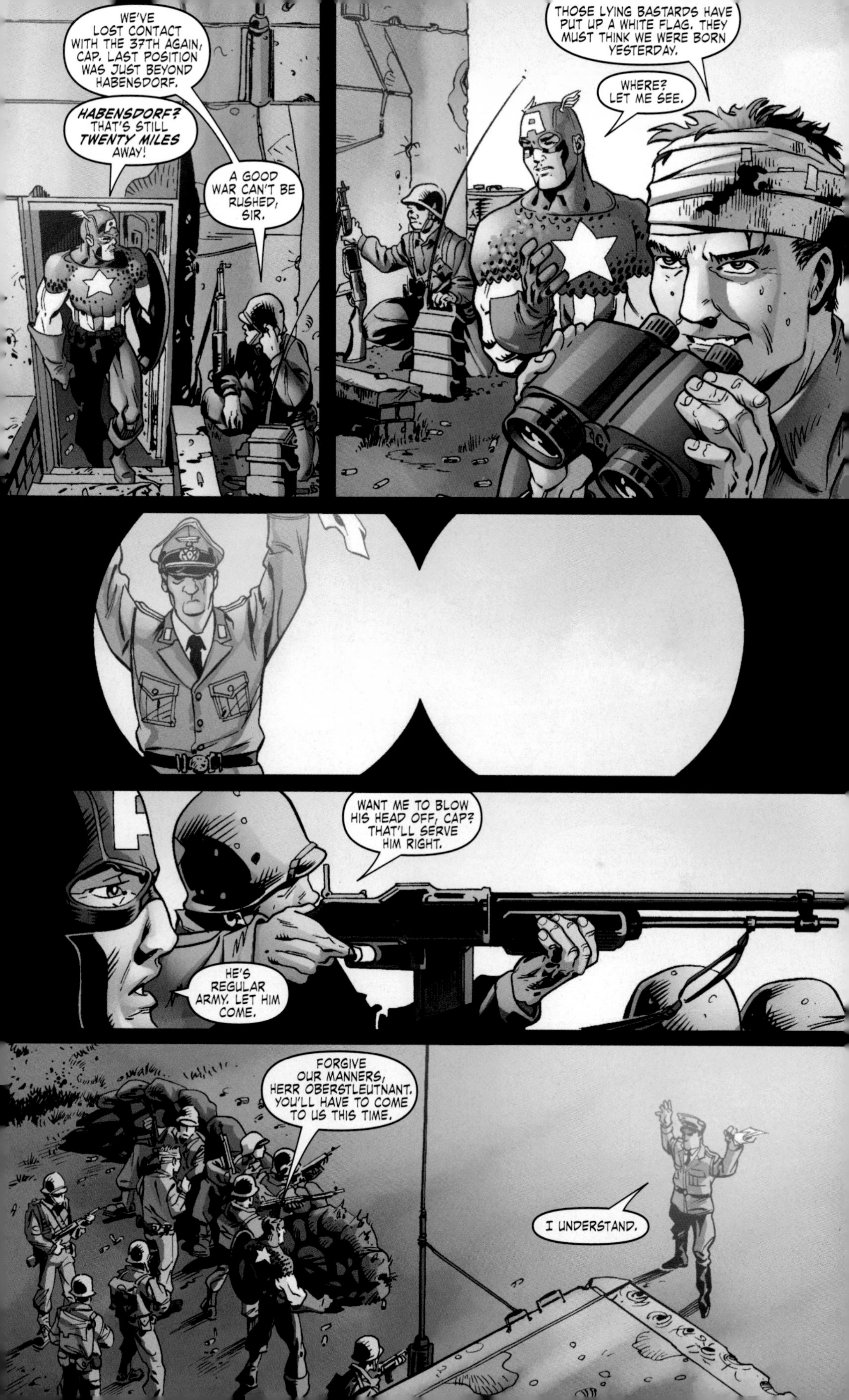
WE'VE LOST CONTACT WITH THE 37TH AGAIN, CAP. LAST POSITION WAS JUST BEYOND HABENSDORF.
HABENSDORF? THAT'S STILL TWENTY MILES AWAY!
A GOOD WAR CAN'T BE RUSHED, SIR.
THOSE LYING BASTARDS HAVE PUT UP A WHITE FLAG. THEY MUST THINK WE WERE BORN YESTERDAY.
WHERE? LET ME SEE.
WANT ME TO BLOW HIS HEAD OFF, CAP? THAT'LL SERVE HIM RIGHT.
HE'S REGULAR ARMY. LET HIM COME.
FORGIVE OUR MANNERS, HERR OBERSTLEUTNANT. YOU'LL HAVE TO COME TO US THIS TIME.
I UNDERSTAND.

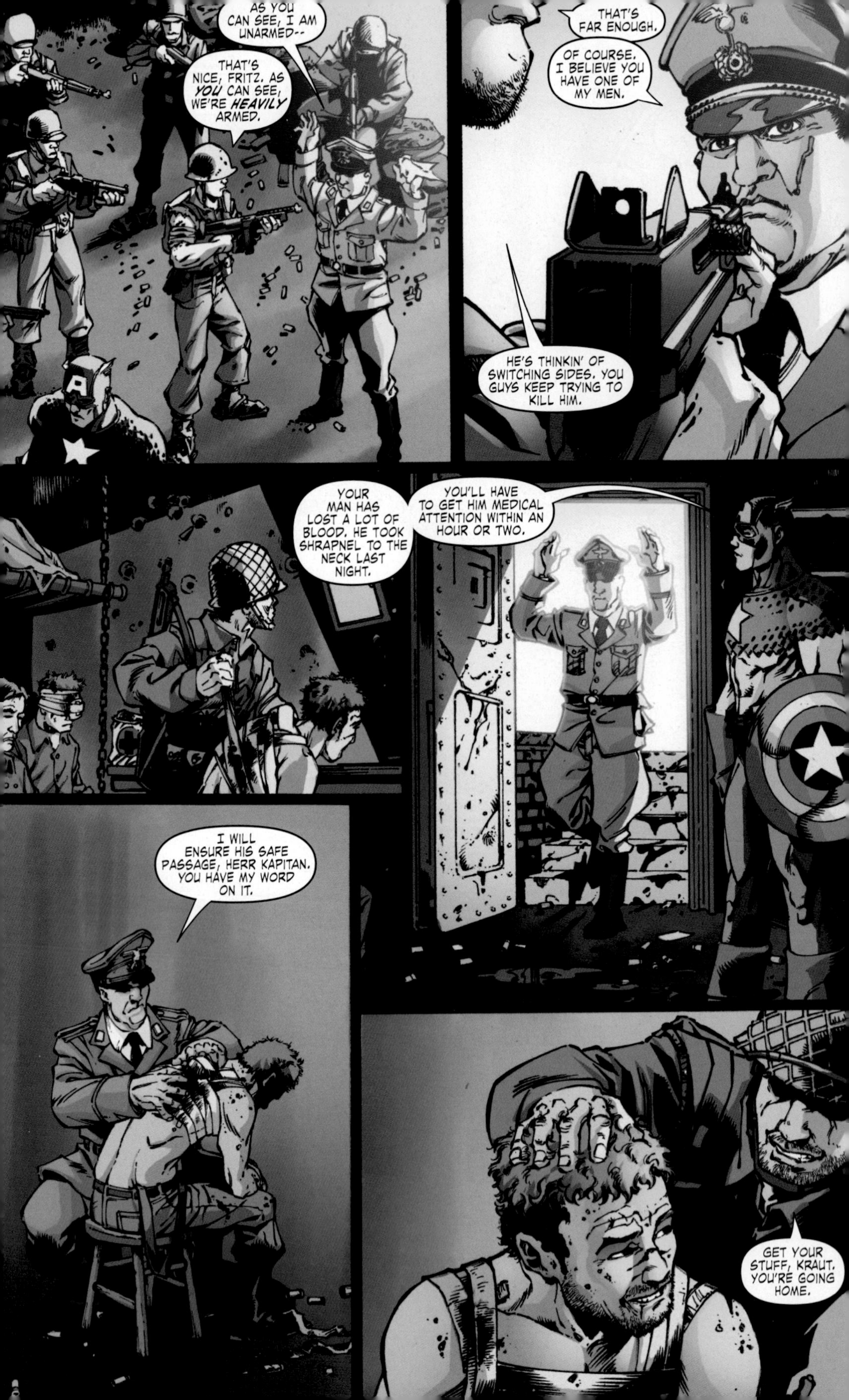
AS YOU CAN SEE, I AM UNARMED--
THAT'S NICE, FRITZ. AS YOU CAN SEE, WE'RE HEAVILY ARMED.
THAT'S FAR ENOUGH.
OF COURSE. I BELIEVE YOU HAVE ONE OF MY MEN.
HE'S THINKIN' OF SWITCHING SIDES. YOU GUYS KEEP TRYING TO KILL HIM.
YOUR MAN HAS LOST A LOT OF BLOOD. HE TOOK SHRAPNEL TO THE NECK LAST NIGHT.
YOU'LL HAVE TO GET HIM MEDICAL ATTENTION WITHIN AN HOUR OR TWO.
I WILL ENSURE HIS SAFE PASSAGE, HERR KAPITAN. YOU HAVE MY WORD ON IT.
GET YOUR STUFF, KRAUT. YOU'RE GOING HOME.

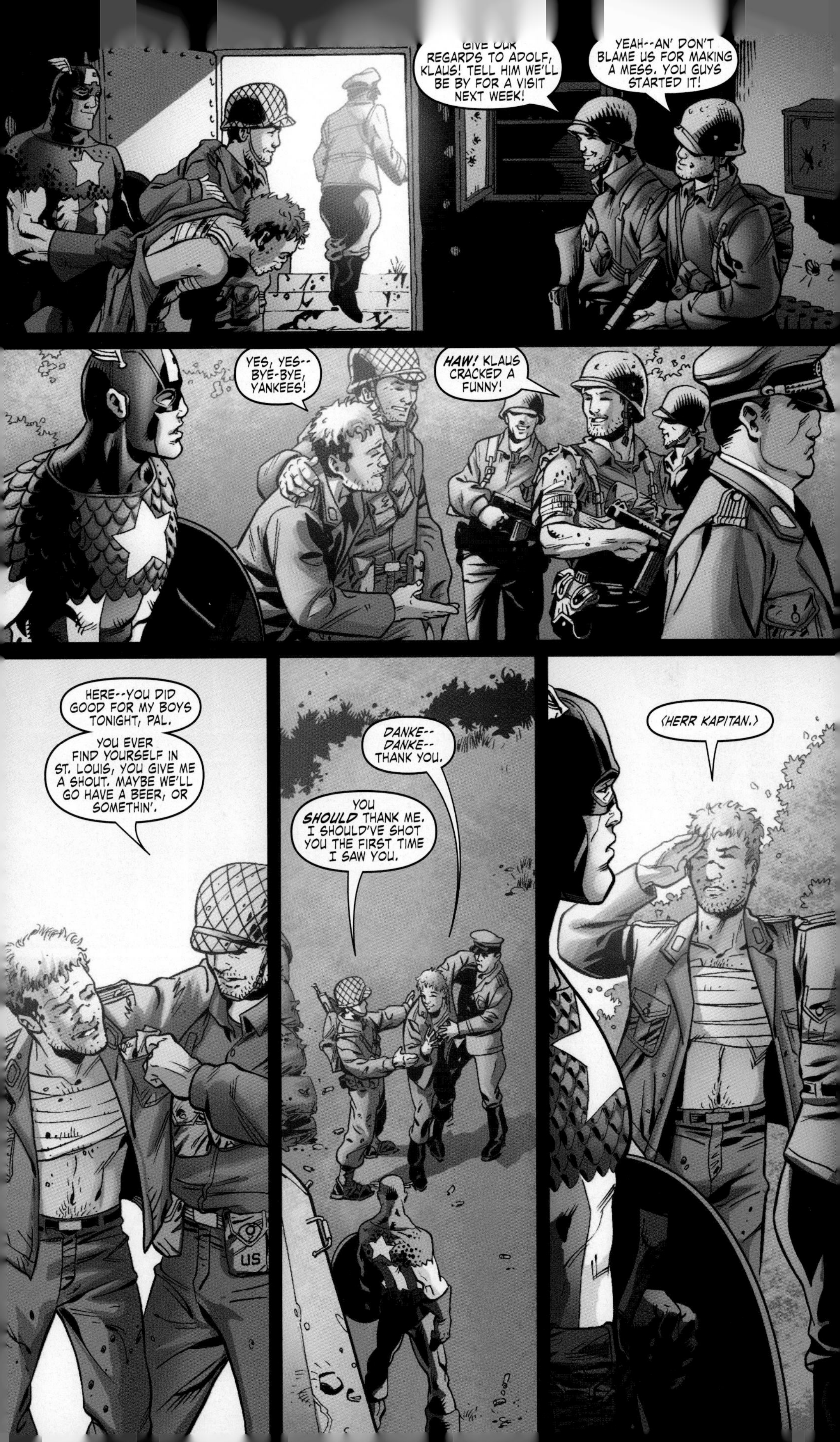
GIVE OUR REGARDS TO ADOLF, KLAUS! TELL HIM WE'LL BE BY FOR A VISIT NEXT WEEK!
YEAH--AN' DON'T BLAME US FOR MAKING A MESS. YOU GUYS STARTED IT!
YES, YES-- BYE-BYE, YANKEES!
HAW! KLAUS CRACKED A FUNNY!
HERE--YOU DID GOOD FOR MY BOYS TONIGHT, PAL.
YOU EVER FIND YOURSELF IN ST. LOUIS, YOU GIVE ME A SHOUT. MAYBE WE'LL GO HAVE A BEER, OR SOMETHIN'.
DANKE-- DANKE-- THANK YOU.
YOU SHOULD THANK ME. I SHOULD'VE SHOT YOU THE FIRST TIME I SAW YOU.
<HERR KAPITAN.>
US

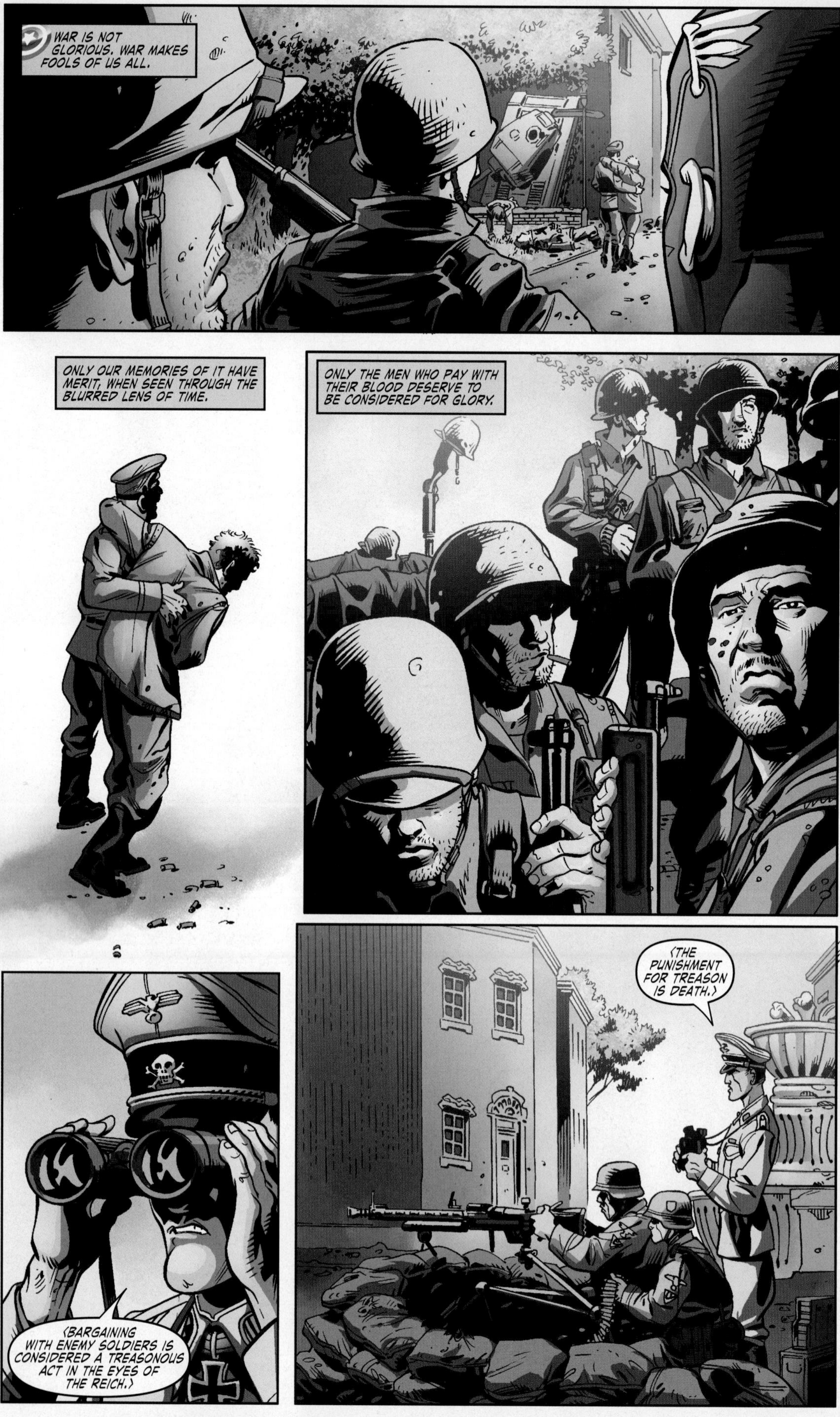
WAR IS NOT GLORIOUS. WAR MAKES FOOLS OF US ALL.
ONLY OUR MEMORIES OF IT HAVE MERIT, WHEN SEEN THROUGH THE BLURRED LENS OF TIME.
ONLY THE MEN WHO PAY WITH THEIR BLOOD DESERVE TO BE CONSIDERED FOR GLORY.
‹BARGAINING WITH ENEMY SOLDIERS IS CONSIDERED A TREASONOUS ACT IN THE EYES OF THE REICH.›
‹THE PUNISHMENT FOR TREASON IS DEATH.›

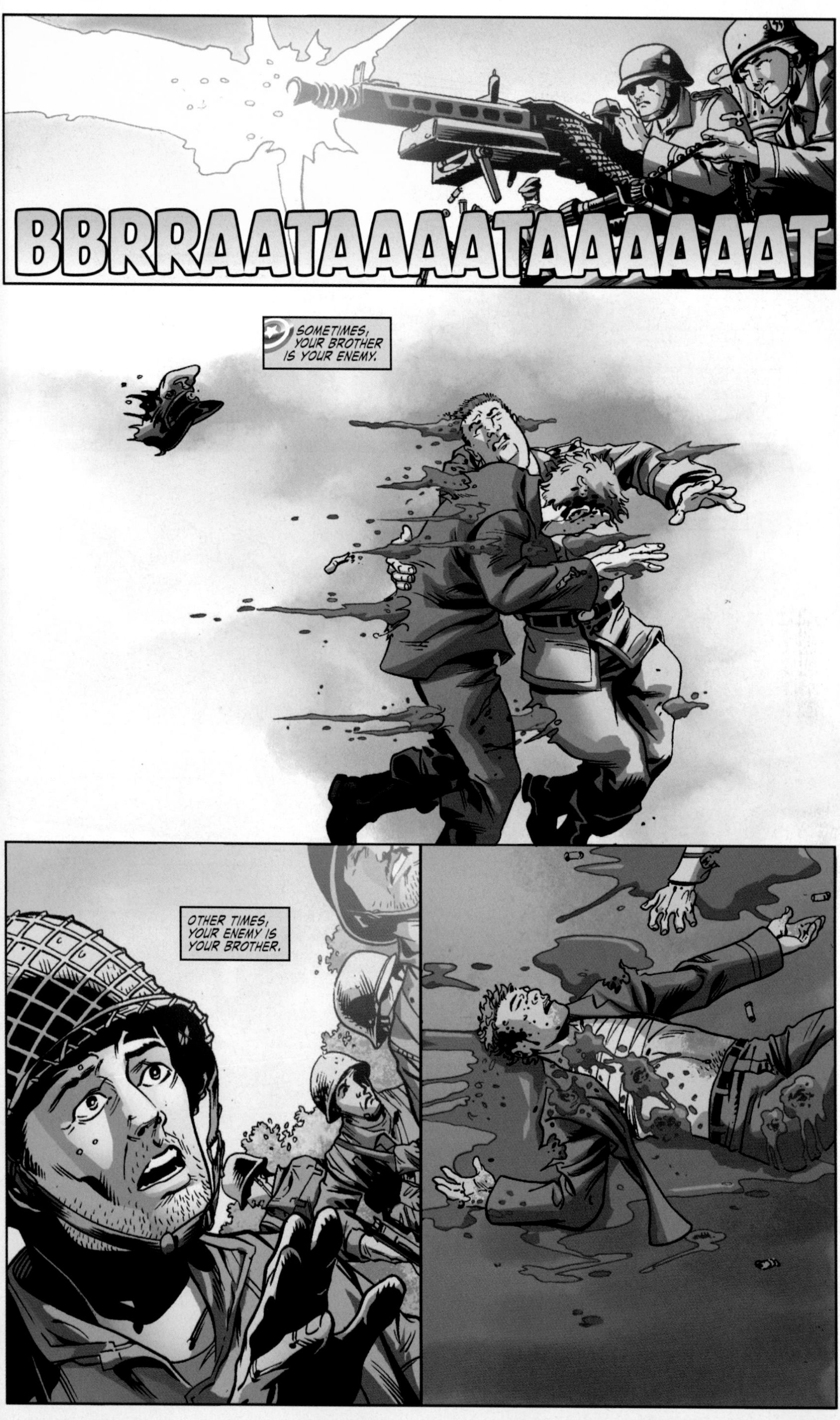
BBRRAATAAAATAAAAAAT
SOMETIMES, YOUR BROTHER IS YOUR ENEMY.
OTHER TIMES, YOUR ENEMY IS YOUR BROTHER.

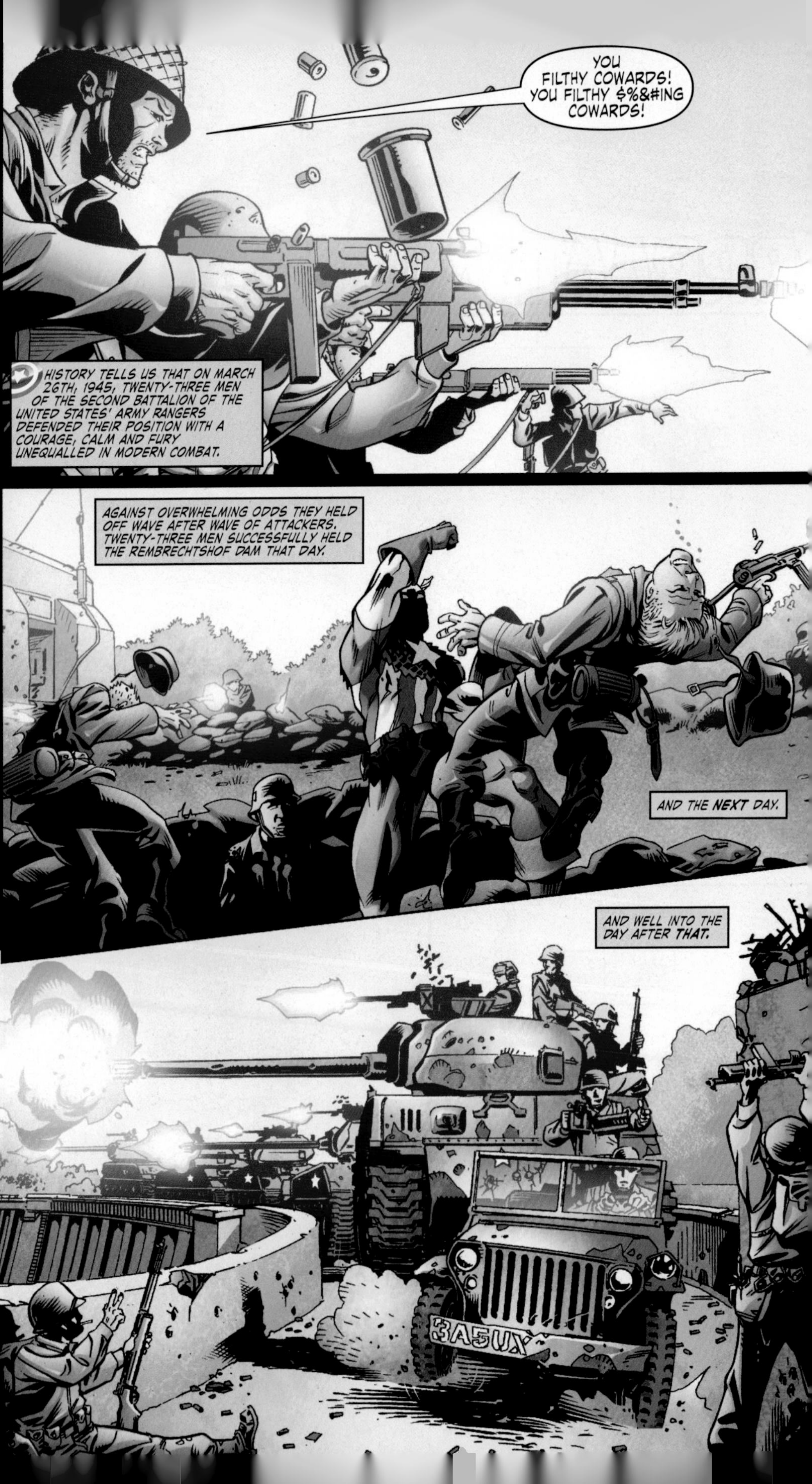
YOU FILTHY COWARDS! YOU FILTHY $%&#ING COWARDS!
HISTORY TELLS US THAT ON MARCH 26TH, 1945, TWENTY-THREE MEN OF THE SECOND BATTALION OF THE UNITED STATES' ARMY RANGERS DEFENDED THEIR POSITION WITH A COURAGE, CALM AND FURY UNEQUALLED IN MODERN COMBAT.
AGAINST OVERWHELMING ODDS THEY HELD OFF WAVE AFTER WAVE OF ATTACKERS. TWENTY-THREE MEN SUCCESSFULLY HELD THE REMBRECHTSHOF DAM THAT DAY.
AND THE NEXT DAY.
AND WELL INTO THE DAY AFTER THAT.
3A5UX

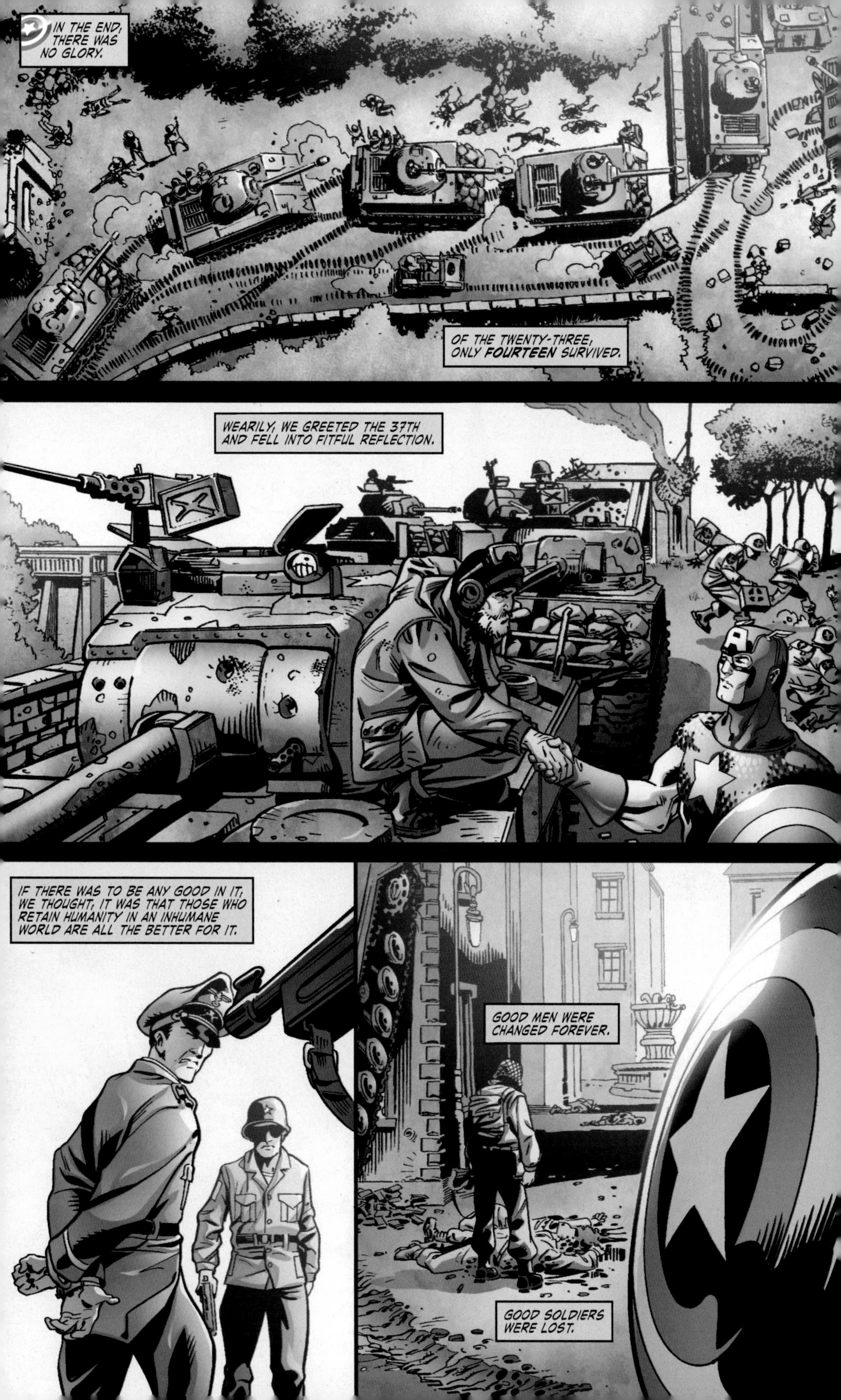
IN THE END, THERE WAS NO GLORY.
OF THE TWENTY-THREE, ONLY FOURTEEN SURVIVED.
WEARILY, WE GREETED THE 37TH AND FELL INTO FITFUL REFLECTION.
IF THERE WAS TO BE ANY GOOD IN IT, WE THOUGHT, IT WAS THAT THOSE WHO RETAIN HUMANITY IN AN INHUMANE WORLD ARE ALL THE BETTER FOR IT.
GOOD MEN WERE CHANGED FOREVER.
GOOD SOLDIERS WERE LOST.

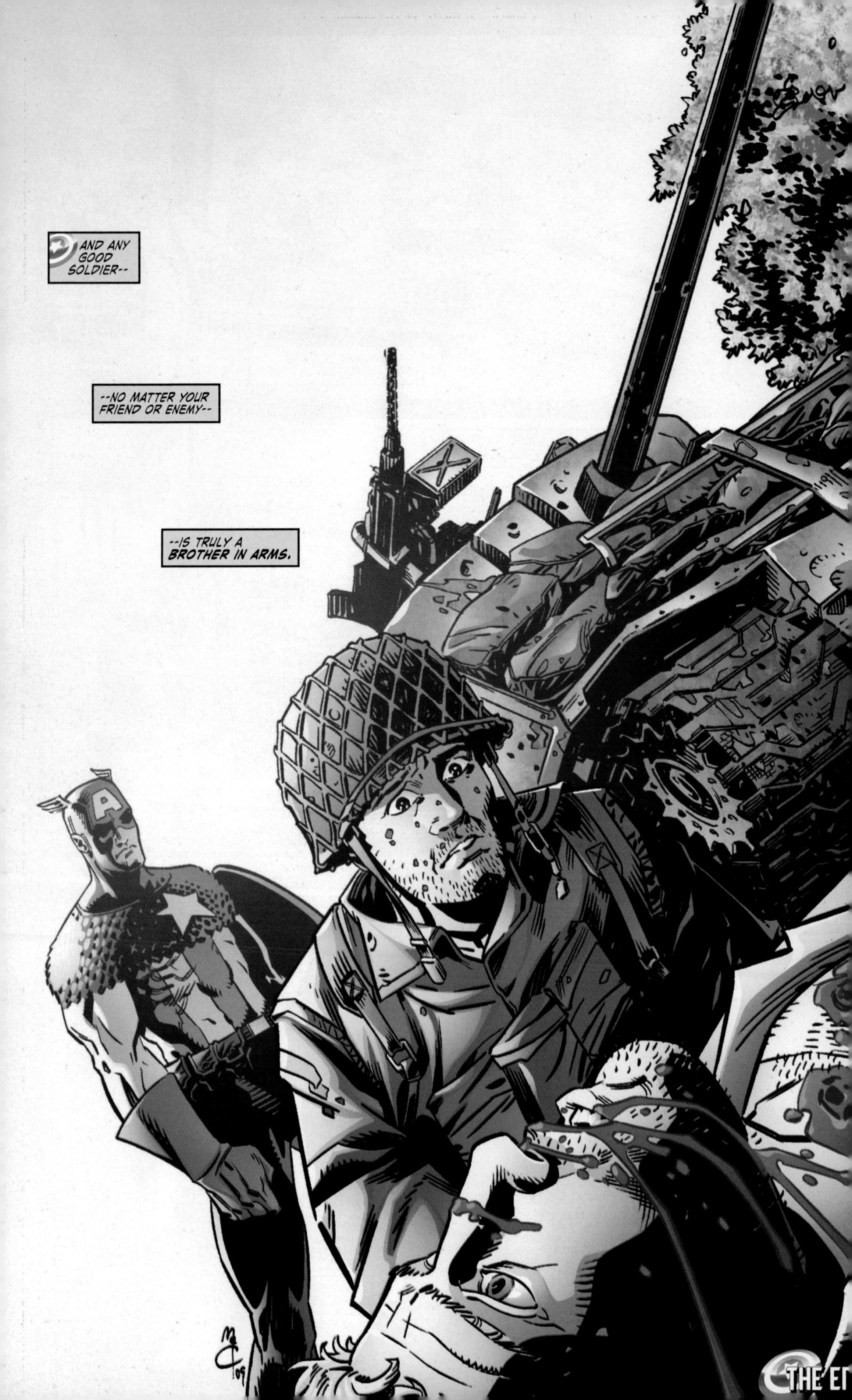
AND ANY GOOD SOLDIER--
--NO MATTER YOUR FRIEND OR ENEMY--
--IS TRULY A BROTHER IN ARMS.
THE EN

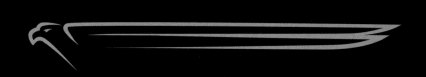

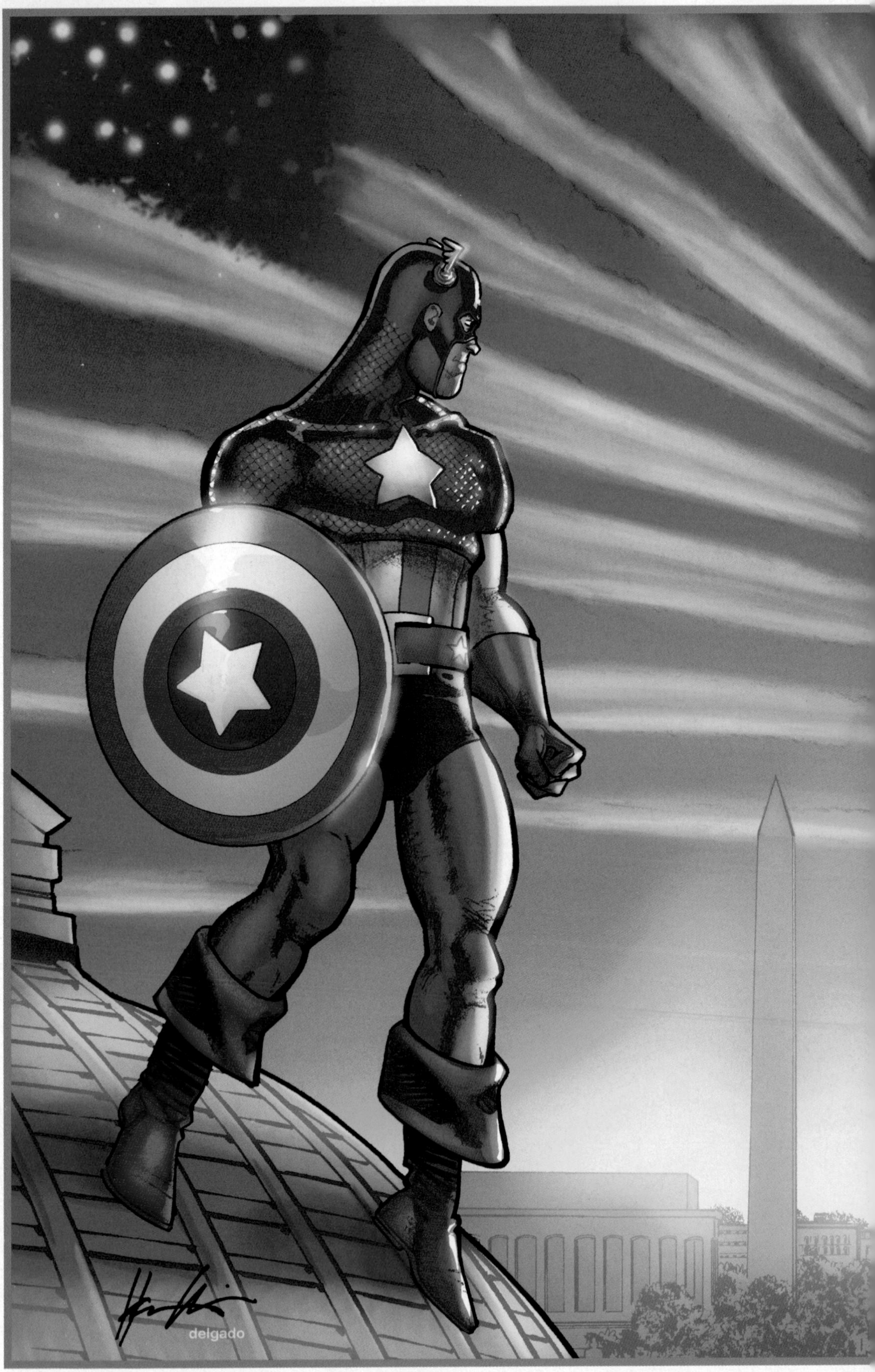

delgado

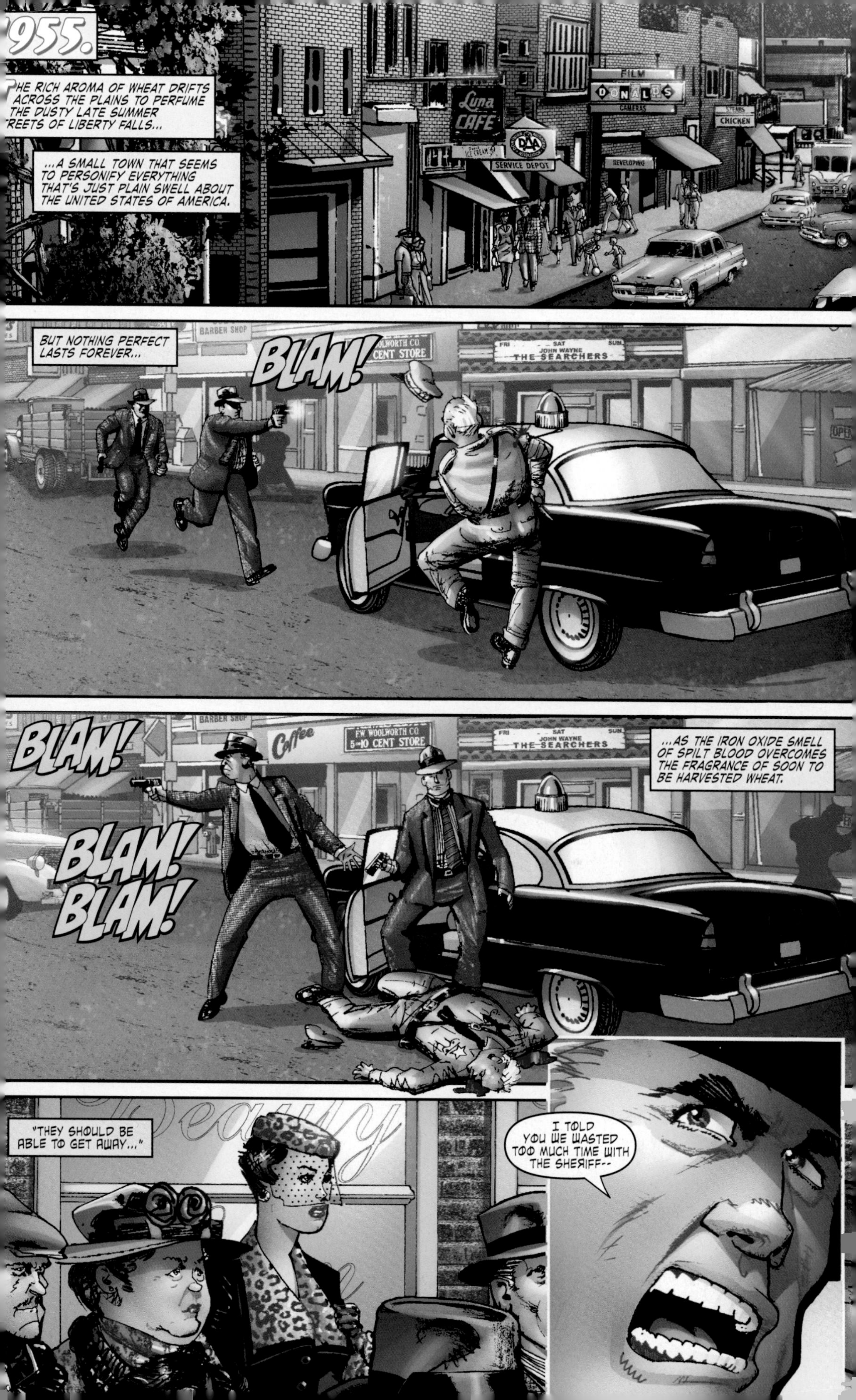

1955.
THE RICH AROMA OF WHEAT DRIFTS ACROSS THE PLAINS TO PERFUME THE DUSTY LATE SUMMER STREETS OF LIBERTY FALLS...
...A SMALL TOWN THAT SEEMS TO PERSONIFY EVERYTHING THAT'S JUST PLAIN SWELL ABOUT THE UNITED STATES OF AMERICA.
Luna CAFE
FILM
DONALDS
CAMERAS
SERVICE DEPOT
DEVELOPING
CHICKEN
BUT NOTHING PERFECT LASTS FOREVER...
BLAM!
BARBER SHOP
WOOLWORTH CO. CENT STORE
FRI SAT SUN
JOHN WAYNE
THE SEARCHERS
BLAM!
BLAM! BLAM!
F.W. WOOLWORTH CO. 5-10 CENT STORE
...AS THE IRON OXIDE SMELL OF SPILT BLOOD OVERCOMES THE FRAGRANCE OF SOON TO BE HARVESTED WHEAT.
"THEY SHOULD BE ABLE TO GET AWAY..."
I TOLD YOU WE WASTED TOO MUCH TIME WITH THE SHERIFF--

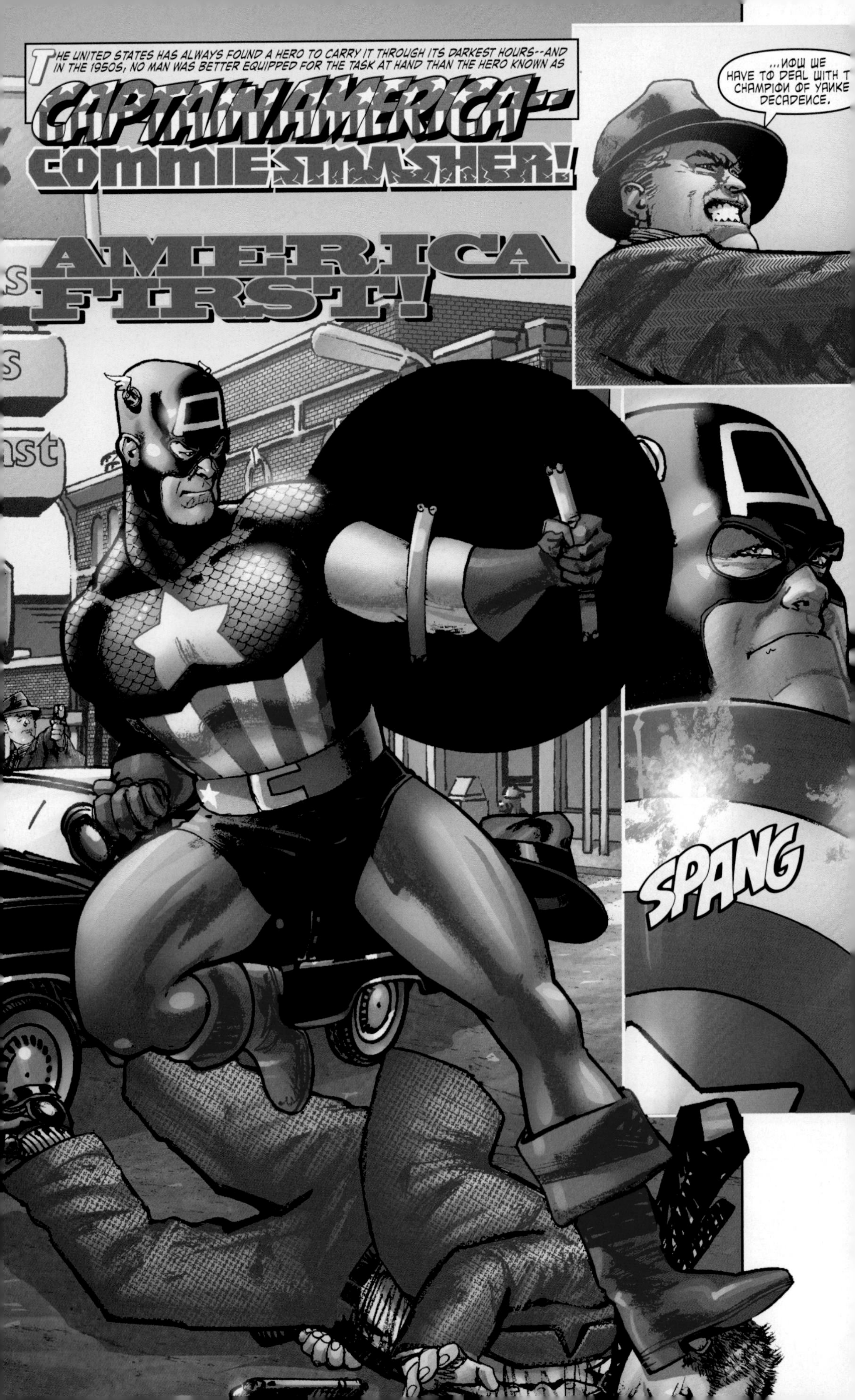
THE UNITED STATES HAS ALWAYS FOUND A HERO TO CARRY IT THROUGH ITS DARKEST HOURS--AND IN THE 1950S, NO MAN WAS BETTER EQUIPPED FOR THE TASK AT HAND THAN THE HERO KNOWN AS
CAPTAIN AMERICA--
COMMIE SMASHER!
AMERICA FIRST!
...NOW WE HAVE TO DEAL WITH T CHAMPION OF YANKE DECADENCE.
SPANG

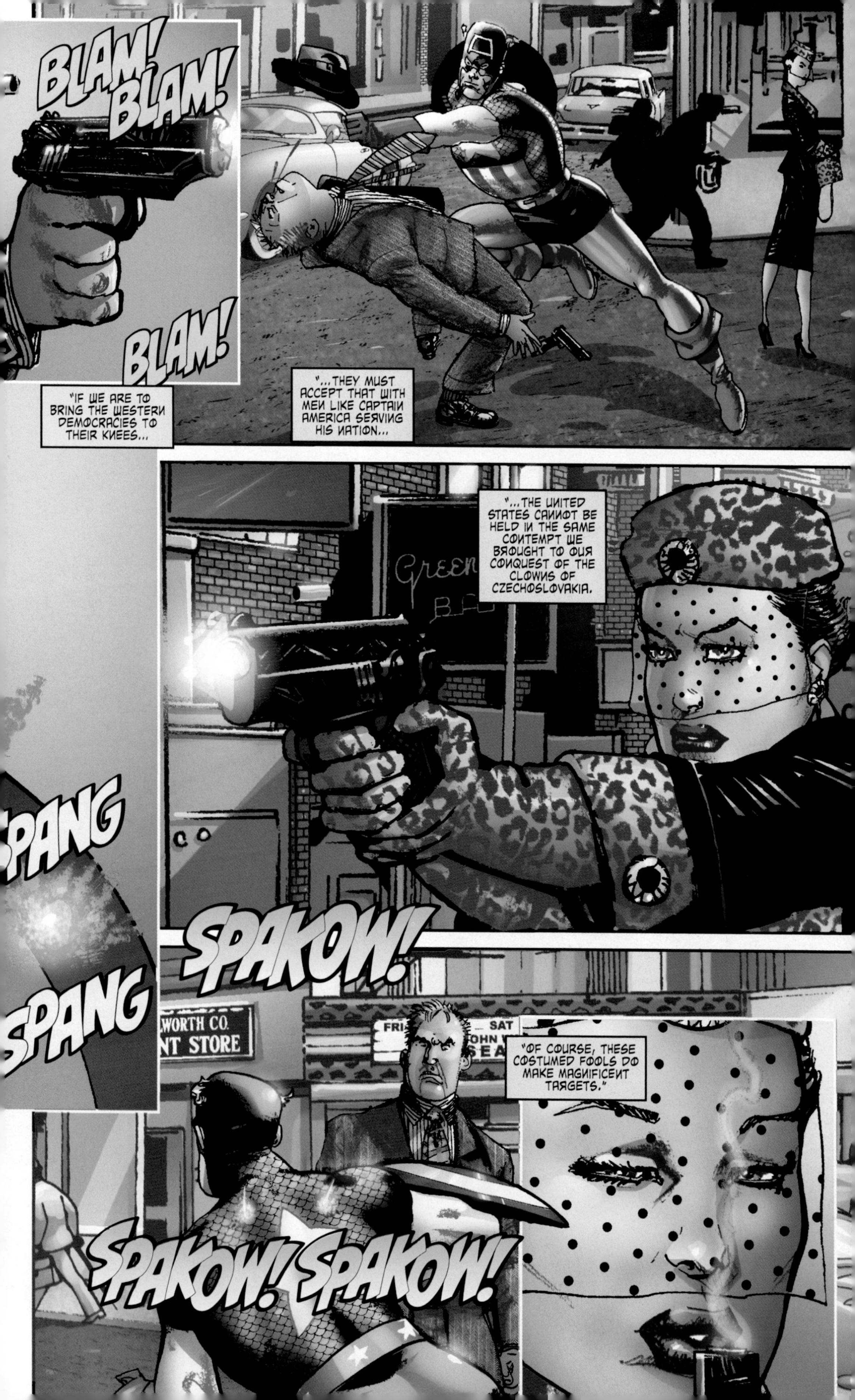
BLAM! BLAM!
BLAM!
"IF WE ARE TO BRING THE WESTERN DEMOCRACIES TO THEIR KNEES...
"...THEY MUST ACCEPT THAT WITH MEN LIKE CAPTAIN AMERICA SERVING HIS NATION...
"...THE UNITED STATES CANNOT BE HELD IN THE SAME CONTEMPT WE BROUGHT TO OUR CONQUEST OF THE CLOWNS OF CZECHOSLOVAKIA.
SPANG
SPAKOW!
SPANG
LWORTH CO.
NT STORE
FRI
SAT
"OF COURSE, THESE COSTUMED FOOLS DO MAKE MAGNIFICENT TARGETS."
SPAKOW! SPAKOW!

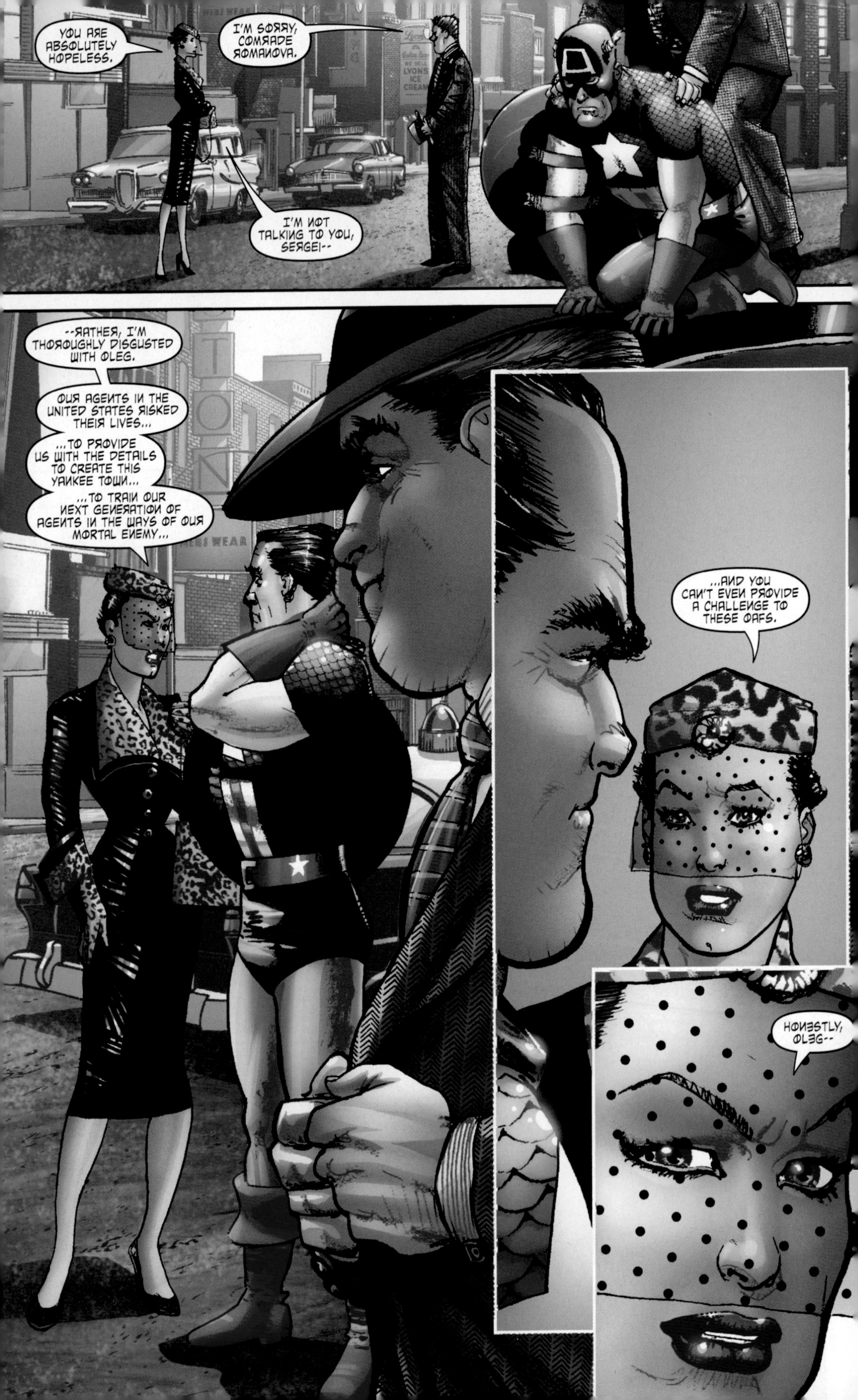
YOU ARE ABSOLUTELY HOPELESS.
I'M SORRY, COMRADE ROMANOVA.
I'M NOT TALKING TO YOU, SERGEI--
LYONS ICE CREAM
--RATHER, I'M THOROUGHLY DISGUSTED WITH OLEG.
OUR AGENTS IN THE UNITED STATES RISKED THEIR LIVES...
...TO PROVIDE US WITH THE DETAILS TO CREATE THIS YANKEE TOWN...
...TO TRAIN OUR NEXT GENERATION OF AGENTS IN THE WAYS OF OUR MORTAL ENEMY...
...AND YOU CAN'T EVEN PROVIDE A CHALLENGE TO THESE OAFS.
HONESTLY, OLEG--

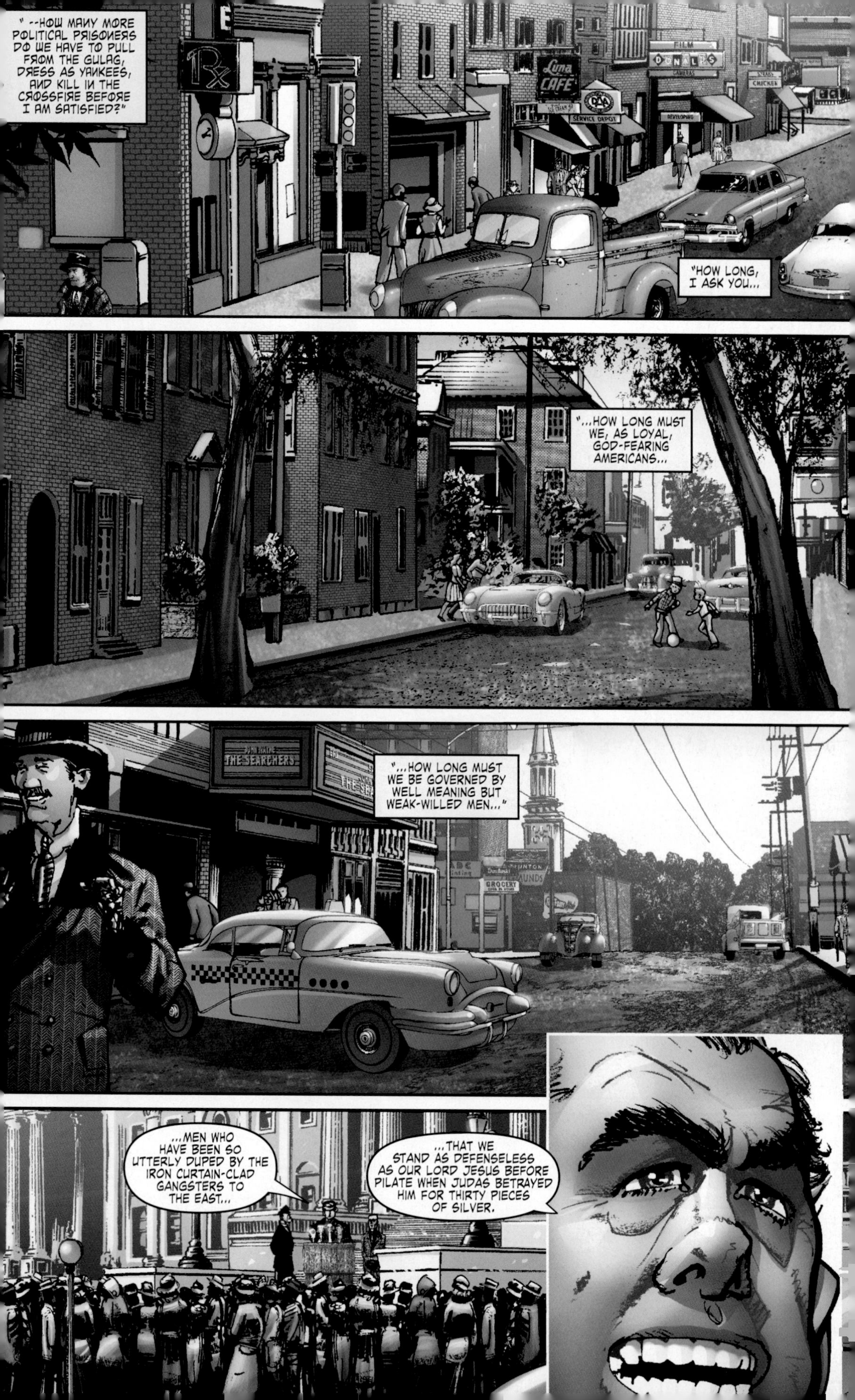
" --HOW MANY MORE POLITICAL PRISONERS DO WE HAVE TO PULL FROM THE GULAG, DRESS AS YANKEES, AND KILL IN THE CROSSFIRE BEFORE I AM SATISFIED?"
Luna CAFE
SERVICE DEPOT
DEVELOPING
"HOW LONG, I ASK YOU...
"...HOW LONG MUST WE, AS LOYAL, GOD-FEARING AMERICANS...
THE SEARCHERS
"...HOW LONG MUST WE BE GOVERNED BY WELL MEANING BUT WEAK-WILLED MEN..."
GROCERY
...MEN WHO HAVE BEEN SO UTTERLY DUPED BY THE IRON CURTAIN-CLAD GANGSTERS TO THE EAST...
...THAT WE STAND AS DEFENSELESS AS OUR LORD JESUS BEFORE PILATE WHEN JUDAS BETRAYED HIM FOR THIRTY PIECES OF SILVER.

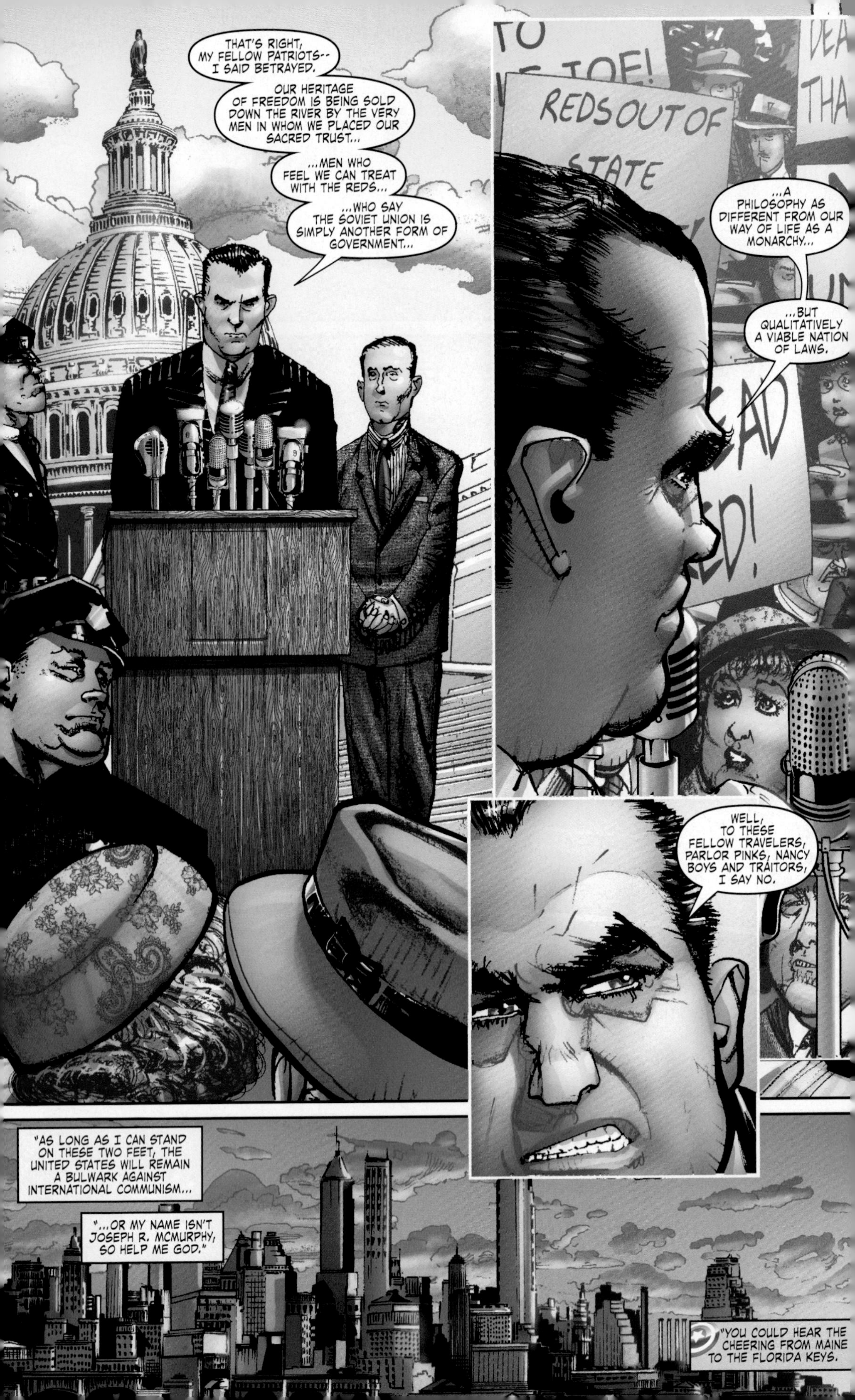
THAT'S RIGHT, MY FELLOW PATRIOTS-- I SAID BETRAYED.
OUR HERITAGE OF FREEDOM IS BEING SOLD DOWN THE RIVER BY THE VERY MEN IN WHOM WE PLACED OUR SACRED TRUST...
...MEN WHO FEEL WE CAN TREAT WITH THE REDS...
...WHO SAY THE SOVIET UNION IS SIMPLY ANOTHER FORM OF GOVERNMENT...
REDS OUT OF STATE
...A PHILOSOPHY AS DIFFERENT FROM OUR WAY OF LIFE AS A MONARCHY...
...BUT QUALITATIVELY A VIABLE NATION OF LAWS.
WELL, TO THESE FELLOW TRAVELERS, PARLOR PINKS, NANCY BOYS AND TRAITORS, I SAY NO.
"AS LONG AS I CAN STAND ON THESE TWO FEET, THE UNITED STATES WILL REMAIN A BULWARK AGAINST INTERNATIONAL COMMUNISM...
"...OR MY NAME ISN'T JOSEPH R. MCMURPHY, SO HELP ME GOD."
"YOU COULD HEAR THE CHEERING FROM MAINE TO THE FLORIDA KEYS.

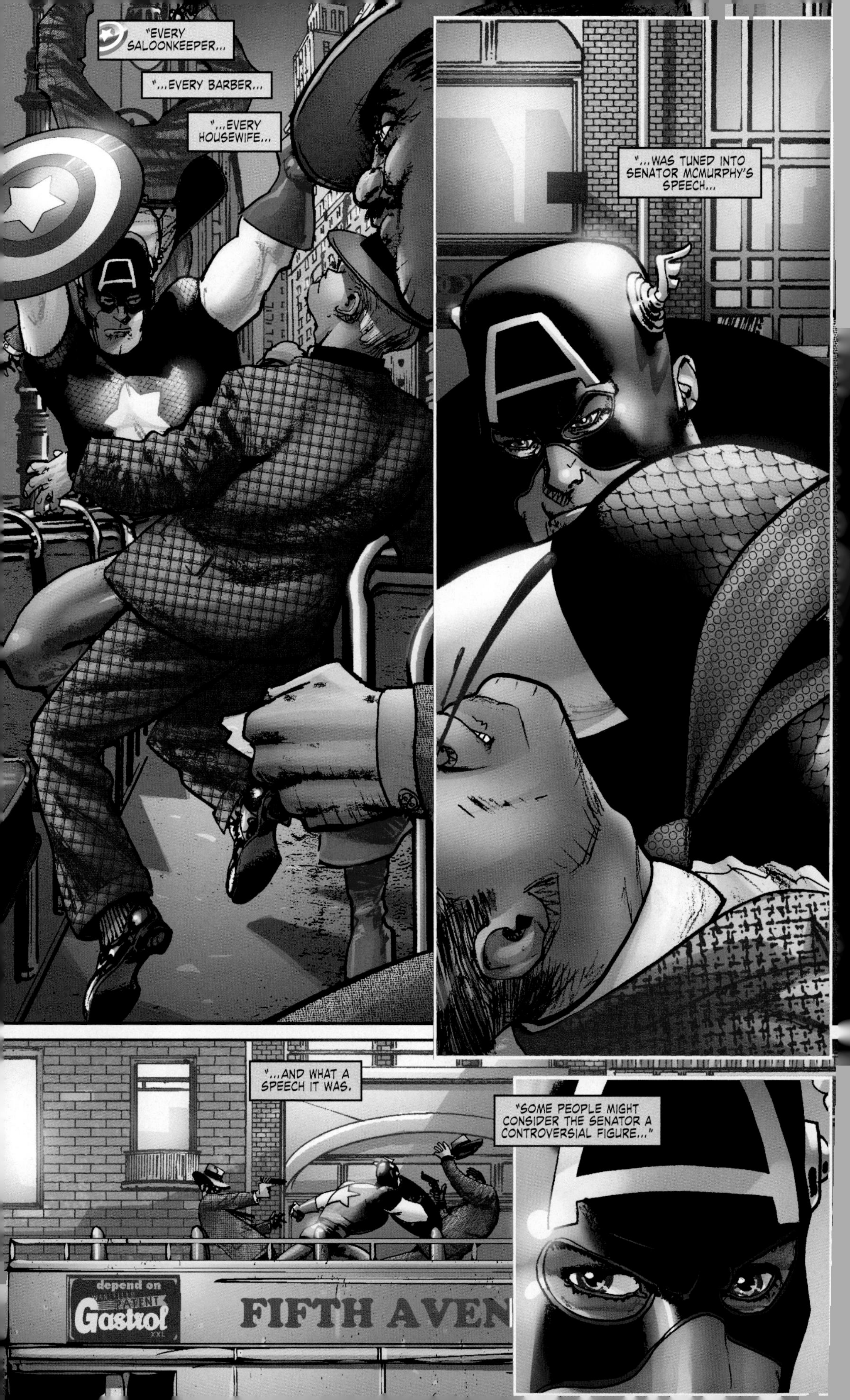

"EVERY SALOONKEEPER...
"...EVERY BARBER...
"...EVERY HOUSEWIFE...
"...WAS TUNED INTO SENATOR MCMURPHY'S SPEECH...
"...AND WHAT A SPEECH IT WAS.
"SOME PEOPLE MIGHT CONSIDER THE SENATOR A CONTROVERSIAL FIGURE..."
depend on
Gastrol
FIFTH AVEN

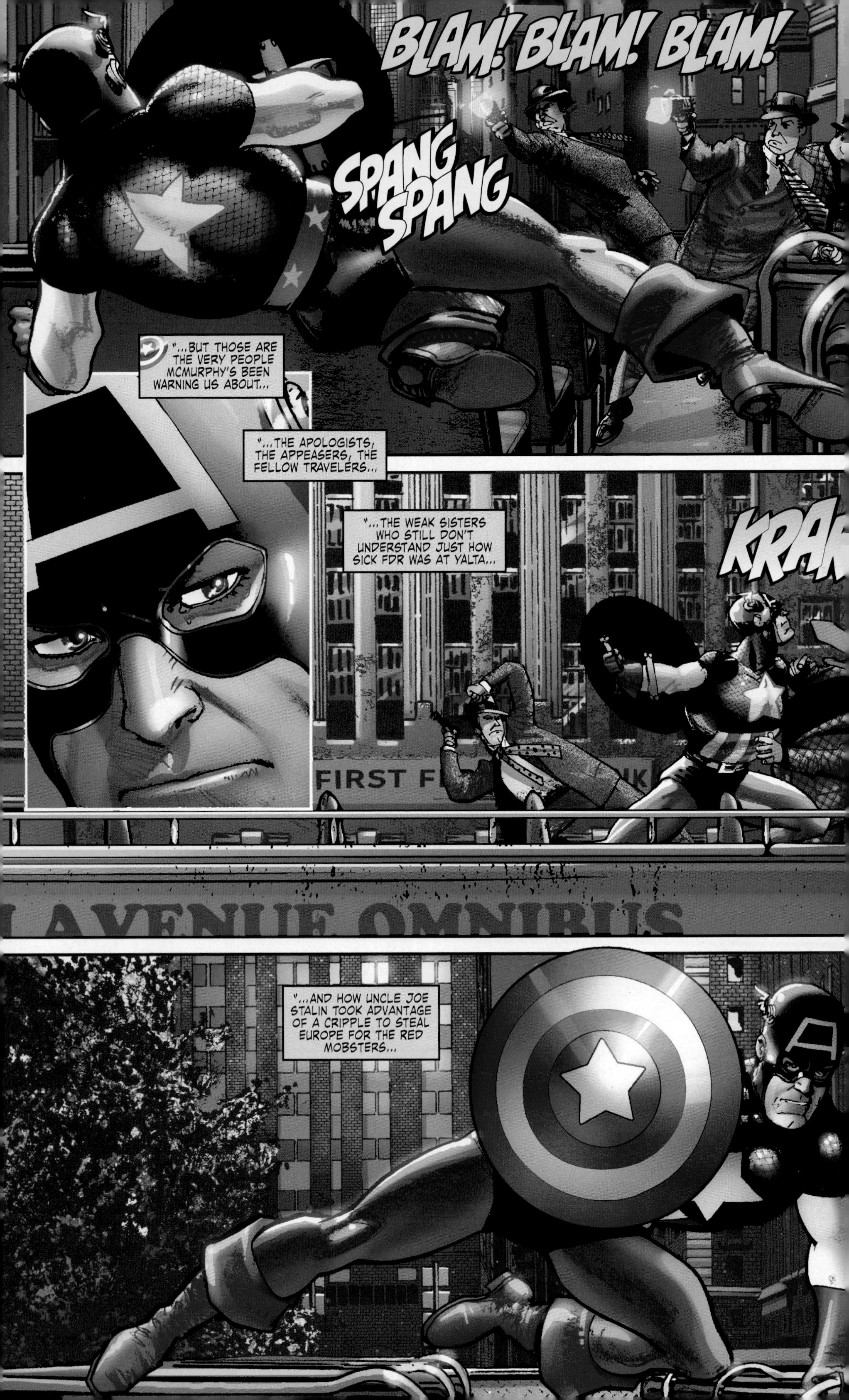
BLAM! BLAM! BLAM!
SPANG SPANG
"...BUT THOSE ARE THE VERY PEOPLE MCMURPHY'S BEEN WARNING US ABOUT...
"...THE APOLOGISTS, THE APPEASERS, THE FELLOW TRAVELERS...
"...THE WEAK SISTERS WHO STILL DON'T UNDERSTAND JUST HOW SICK FDR WAS AT YALTA...
FIRST F
"...AND HOW UNCLE JOE STALIN TOOK ADVANTAGE OF A CRIPPLE TO STEAL EUROPE FOR THE RED MOBSTERS...

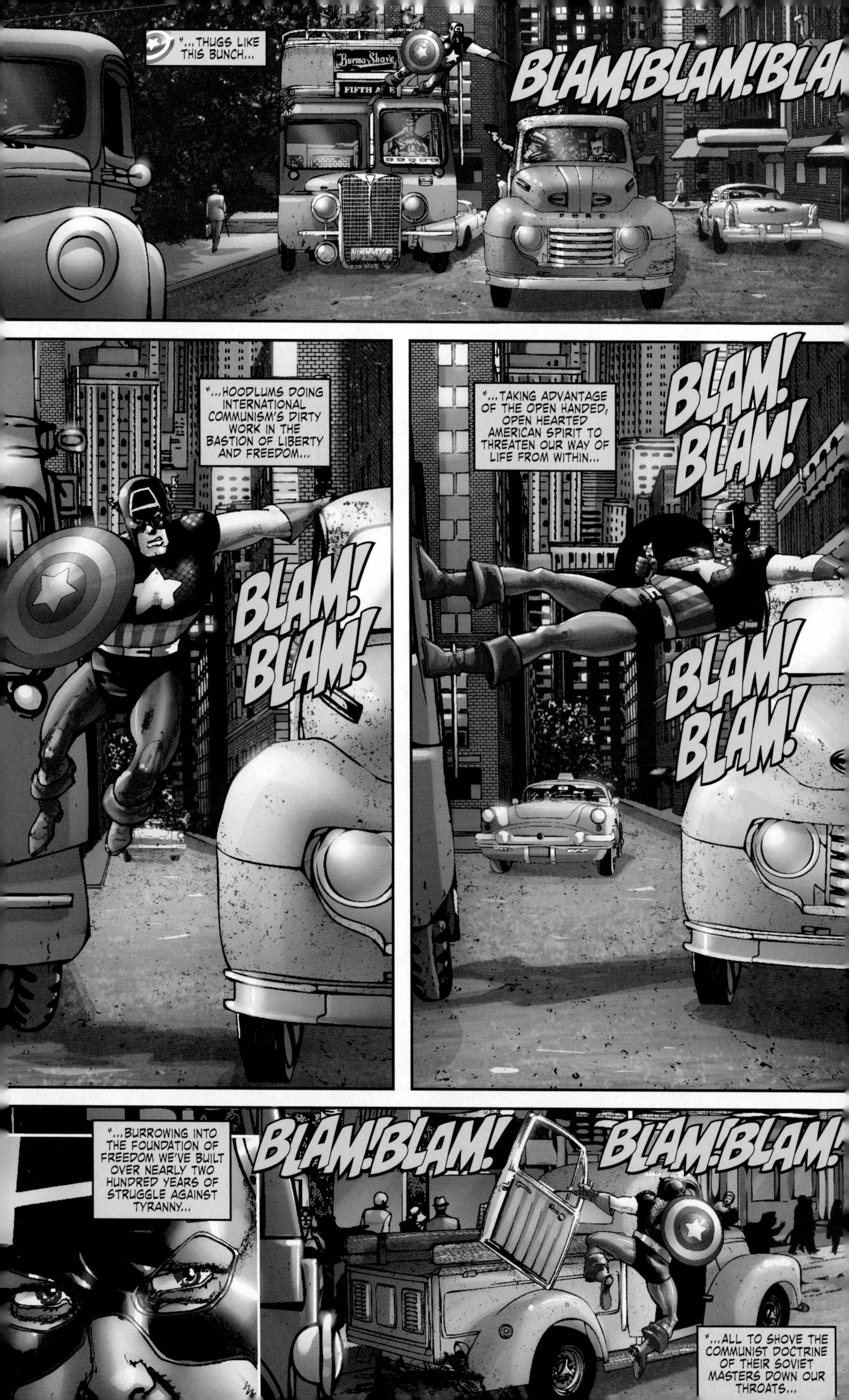
"...THUGS LIKE THIS BUNCH...
Burma-Shave
FIFTH AVE
BLAM! BLAM! BLAM!
"...HOODLUMS DOING INTERNATIONAL COMMUNISM'S DIRTY WORK IN THE BASTION OF LIBERTY AND FREEDOM...
BLAM! BLAM!
"...TAKING ADVANTAGE OF THE OPEN HANDED, OPEN HEARTED AMERICAN SPIRIT TO THREATEN OUR WAY OF LIFE FROM WITHIN...
BLAM! BLAM!
BLAM! BLAM!
"...BURROWING INTO THE FOUNDATION OF FREEDOM WE'VE BUILT OVER NEARLY TWO HUNDRED YEARS OF STRUGGLE AGAINST TYRANNY...
BLAM! BLAM!
BLAM! BLAM!
"...ALL TO SHOVE THE COMMUNIST DOCTRINE OF THEIR SOVIET MASTERS DOWN OUR THROATS...

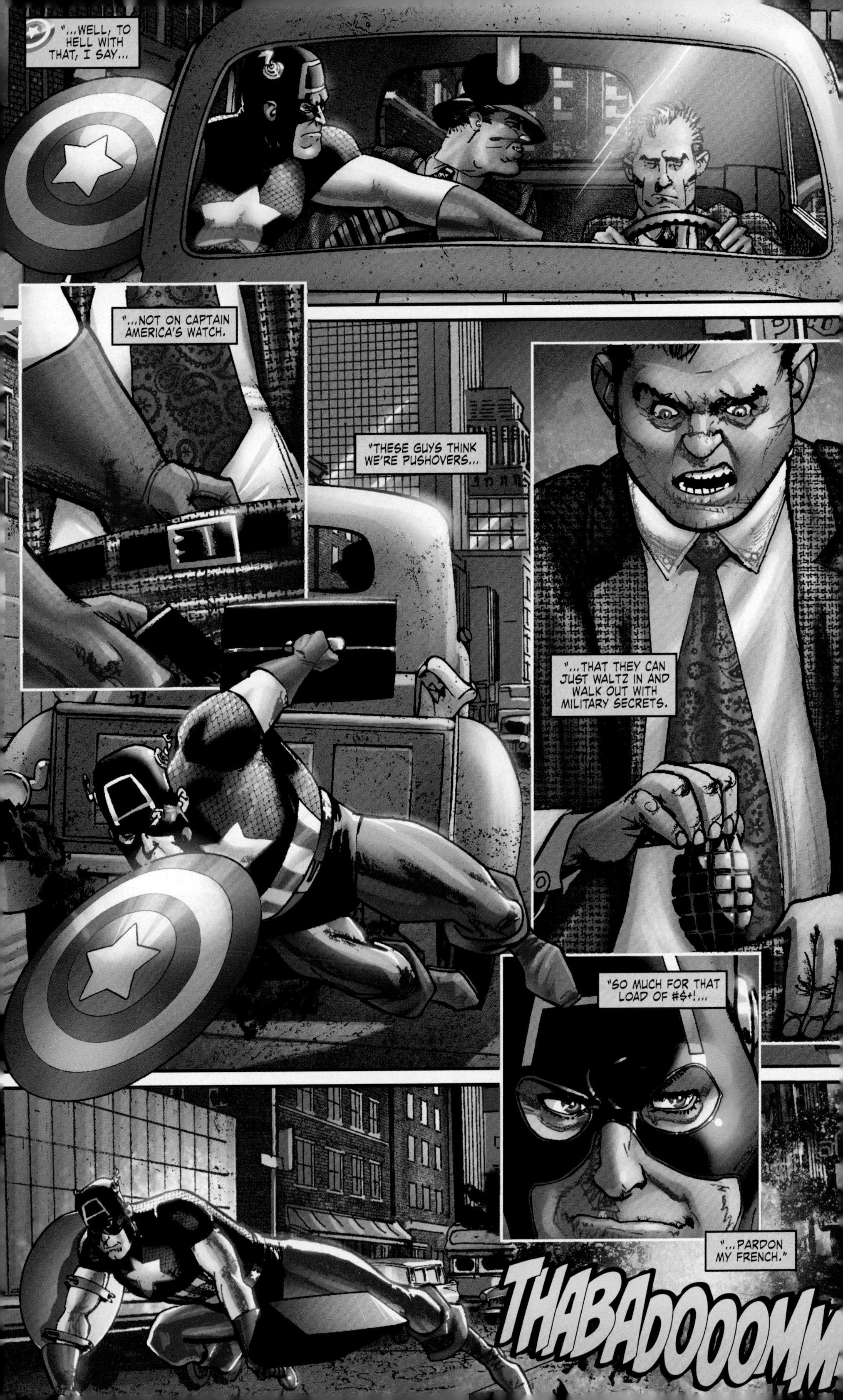
"...WELL, TO HELL WITH THAT, I SAY...
"...NOT ON CAPTAIN AMERICA'S WATCH.
"THESE GUYS THINK WE'RE PUSHOVERS...
"...THAT THEY CAN JUST WALTZ IN AND WALK OUT WITH MILITARY SECRETS.
"SO MUCH FOR THAT LOAD OF #$+!...
"...PARDON MY FRENCH."
THABADOOOMM

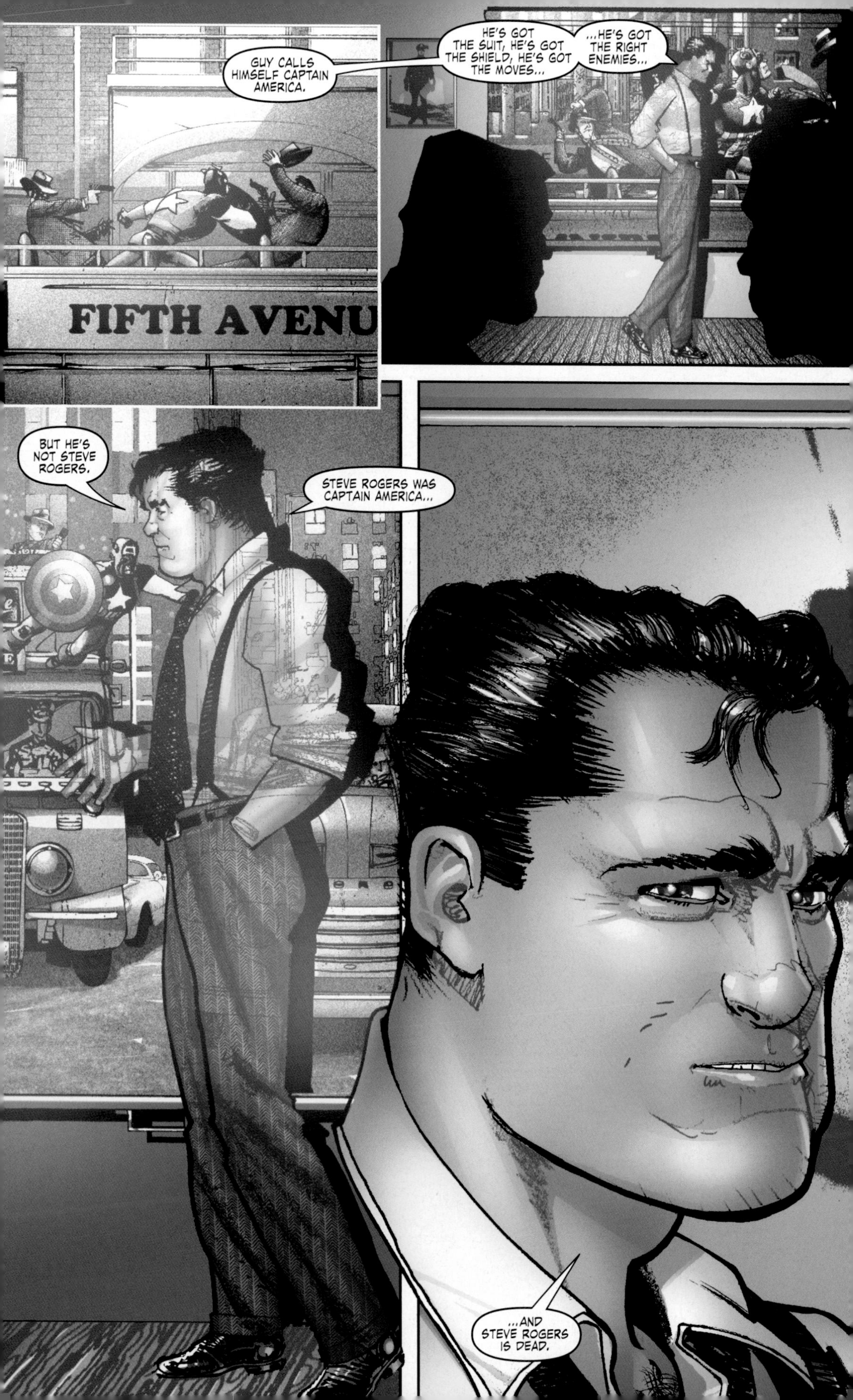
GUY CALLS HIMSELF CAPTAIN AMERICA.
FIFTH AVENU
HE'S GOT THE SUIT, HE'S GOT THE SHIELD, HE'S GOT THE MOVES...
...HE'S GOT THE RIGHT ENEMIES...
BUT HE'S NOT STEVE ROGERS.
STEVE ROGERS WAS CAPTAIN AMERICA...
...AND STEVE ROGERS IS DEAD.

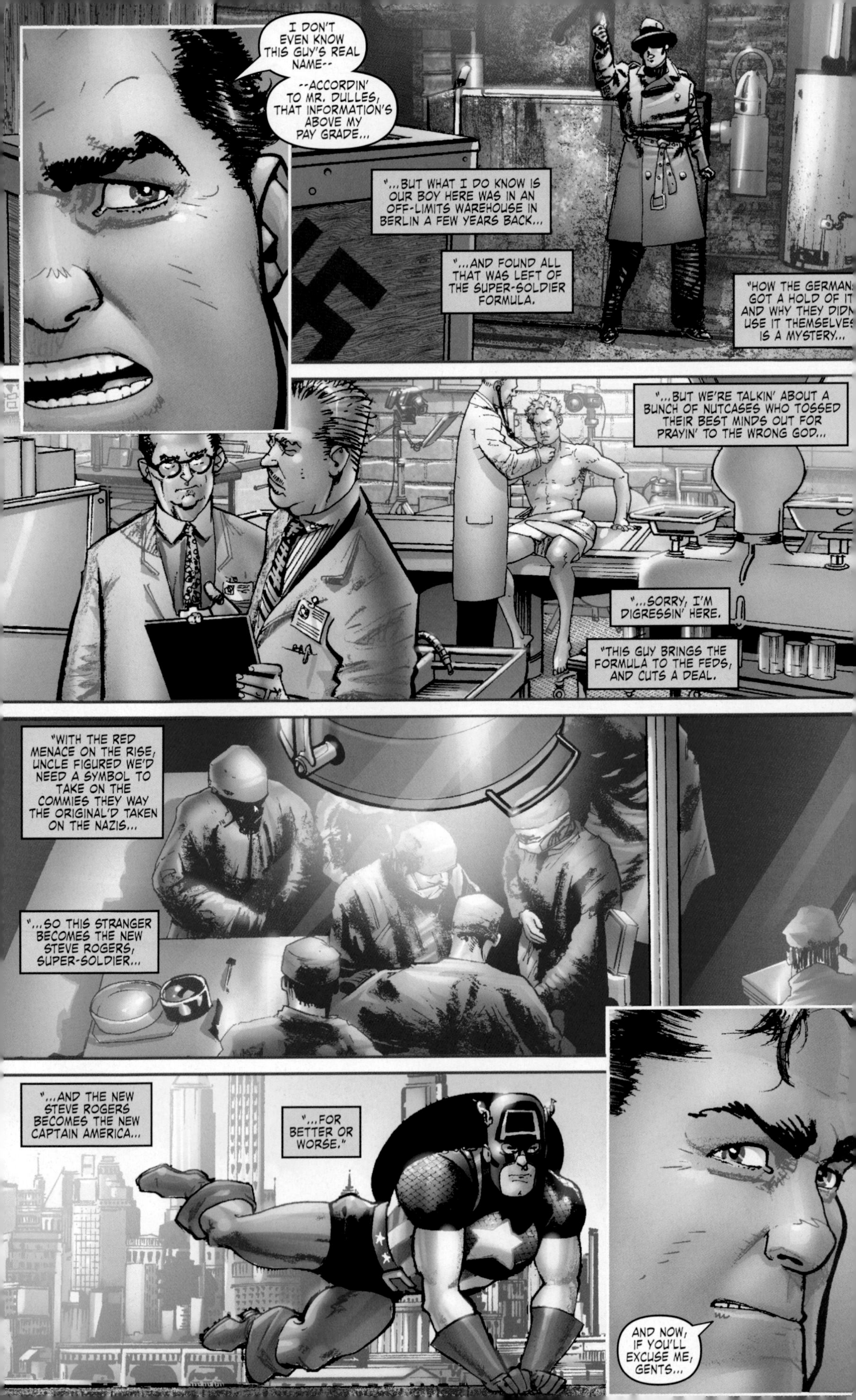
I DON'T EVEN KNOW THIS GUY'S REAL NAME--
--ACCORDIN' TO MR. DULLES, THAT INFORMATION'S ABOVE MY PAY GRADE...
"...BUT WHAT I DO KNOW IS OUR BOY HERE WAS IN AN OFF-LIMITS WAREHOUSE IN BERLIN A FEW YEARS BACK...
"...AND FOUND ALL THAT WAS LEFT OF THE SUPER-SOLDIER FORMULA.
"HOW THE GERMANS GOT A HOLD OF IT AND WHY THEY DIDN' USE IT THEMSELVES IS A MYSTERY...
"...BUT WE'RE TALKIN' ABOUT A BUNCH OF NUTCASES WHO TOSSED THEIR BEST MINDS OUT FOR PRAYIN' TO THE WRONG GOD...
"...SORRY, I'M DIGRESSIN' HERE.
"THIS GUY BRINGS THE FORMULA TO THE FEDS, AND CUTS A DEAL.
"WITH THE RED MENACE ON THE RISE, UNCLE FIGURED WE'D NEED A SYMBOL TO TAKE ON THE COMMIES THEY WAY THE ORIGINAL'D TAKEN ON THE NAZIS...
"...SO THIS STRANGER BECOMES THE NEW STEVE ROGERS, SUPER-SOLDIER...
"...AND THE NEW STEVE ROGERS BECOMES THE NEW CAPTAIN AMERICA...
"...FOR BETTER OR WORSE."
AND NOW, IF YOU'LL EXCUSE ME, GENTS...

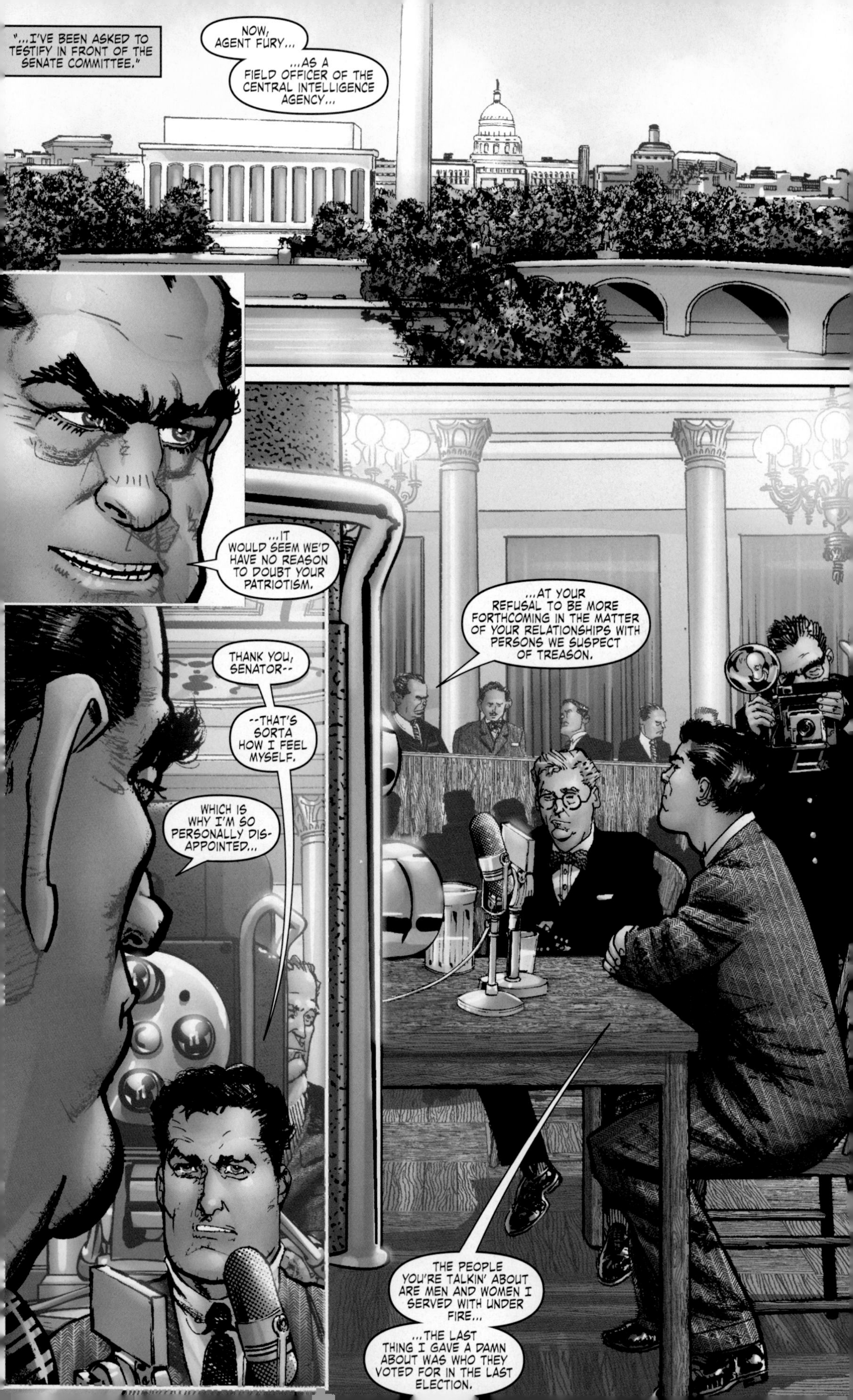
"...I'VE BEEN ASKED TO TESTIFY IN FRONT OF THE SENATE COMMITTEE."
NOW, AGENT FURY...
...AS A FIELD OFFICER OF THE CENTRAL INTELLIGENCE AGENCY...
...IT WOULD SEEM WE'D HAVE NO REASON TO DOUBT YOUR PATRIOTISM.
THANK YOU, SENATOR--
--THAT'S SORTA HOW I FEEL MYSELF.
WHICH IS WHY I'M SO PERSONALLY DIS-APPOINTED...
...AT YOUR REFUSAL TO BE MORE FORTHCOMING IN THE MATTER OF YOUR RELATIONSHIPS WITH PERSONS WE SUSPECT OF TREASON.
THE PEOPLE YOU'RE TALKIN' ABOUT ARE MEN AND WOMEN I SERVED WITH UNDER FIRE...
...THE LAST THING I GAVE A DAMN ABOUT WAS WHO THEY VOTED FOR IN THE LAST ELECTION.

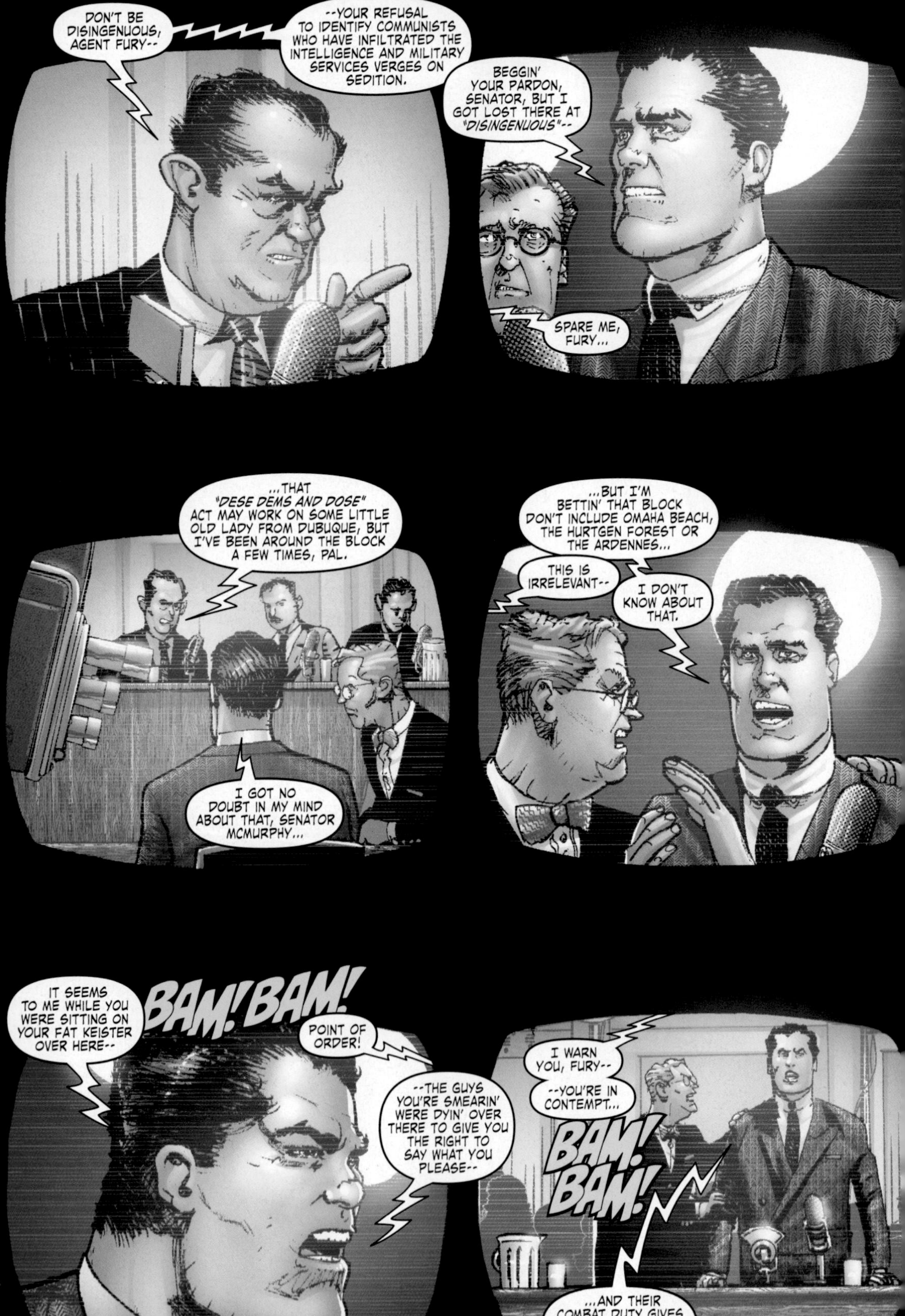
DON'T BE DISINGENUOUS, AGENT FURY--
--YOUR REFUSAL TO IDENTIFY COMMUNISTS WHO HAVE INFILTRATED THE INTELLIGENCE AND MILITARY SERVICES VERGES ON SEDITION.
BEGGIN' YOUR PARDON, SENATOR, BUT I GOT LOST THERE AT "DISINGENUOUS"--
SPARE ME, FURY...
...THAT "DESE DEMS AND DOSE" ACT MAY WORK ON SOME LITTLE OLD LADY FROM DUBUQUE, BUT I'VE BEEN AROUND THE BLOCK A FEW TIMES, PAL.
I GOT NO DOUBT IN MY MIND ABOUT THAT, SENATOR MCMURPHY...
...BUT I'M BETTIN' THAT BLOCK DON'T INCLUDE OMAHA BEACH, THE HURTGEN FOREST OR THE ARDENNES...
THIS IS IRRELEVANT--
I DON'T KNOW ABOUT THAT.
IT SEEMS TO ME WHILE YOU WERE SITTING ON YOUR FAT KEISTER OVER HERE--
BAM! BAM!
POINT OF ORDER!
--THE GUYS YOU'RE SMEARIN' WERE DYIN' OVER THERE TO GIVE YOU THE RIGHT TO SAY WHAT YOU PLEASE--
I WARN YOU, FURY--
--YOU'RE IN CONTEMPT...
BAM! BAM!
...AND THEIR COMBAT DUTY GIVES THEM THE RIGHT TO VOTE HOWEVER THEY PLEASE, TOO.

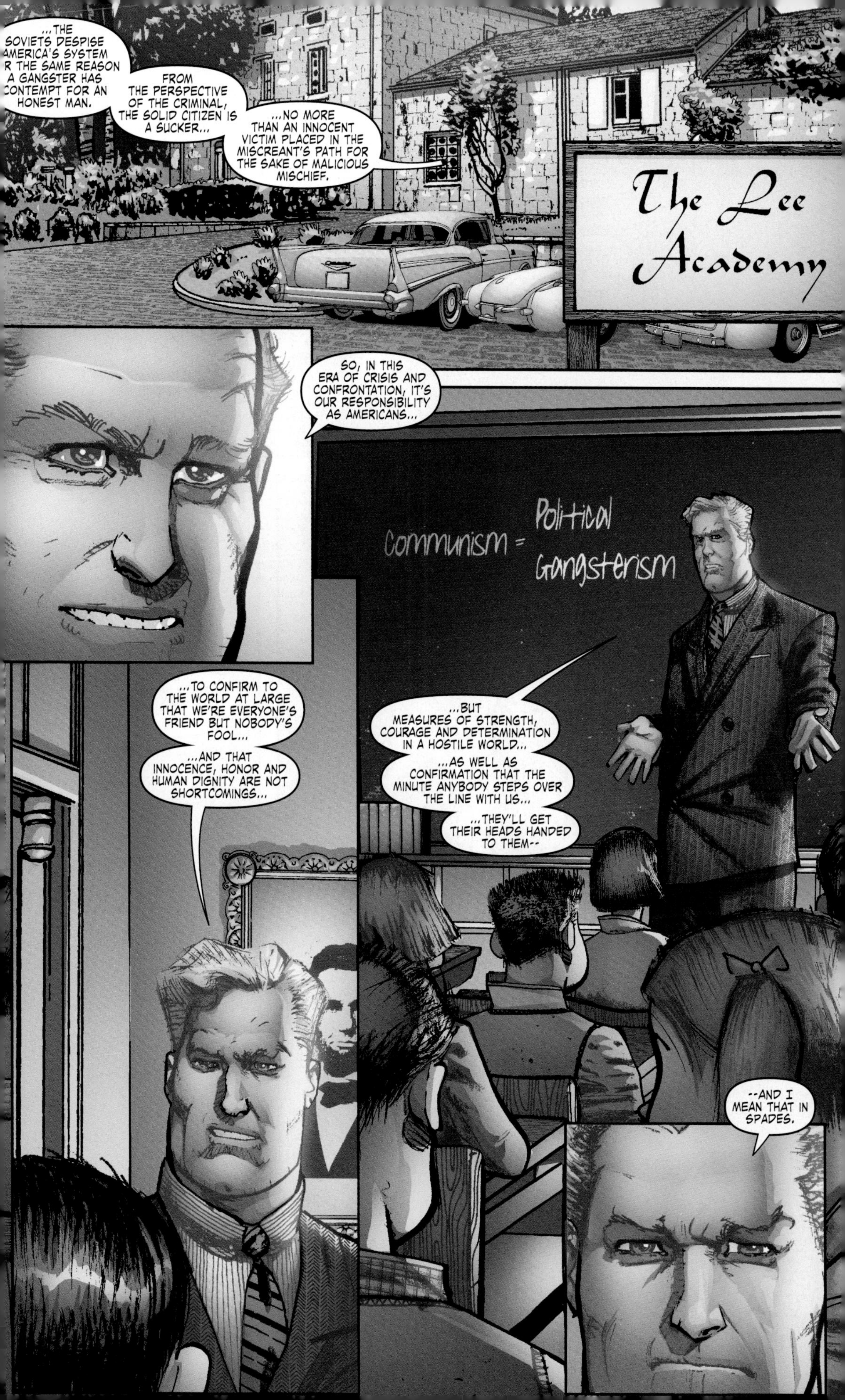
...THE SOVIETS DESPISE AMERICA'S SYSTEM R THE SAME REASON A GANGSTER HAS CONTEMPT FOR AN HONEST MAN.
FROM THE PERSPECTIVE OF THE CRIMINAL, THE SOLID CITIZEN IS A SUCKER...
...NO MORE THAN AN INNOCENT VICTIM PLACED IN THE MISCREANT'S PATH FOR THE SAKE OF MALICIOUS MISCHIEF.
The Lee Academy
SO, IN THIS ERA OF CRISIS AND CONFRONTATION, IT'S OUR RESPONSIBILITY AS AMERICANS...
Communism = Political Gangsterism
...TO CONFIRM TO THE WORLD AT LARGE THAT WE'RE EVERYONE'S FRIEND BUT NOBODY'S FOOL...
...AND THAT INNOCENCE, HONOR AND HUMAN DIGNITY ARE NOT SHORTCOMINGS...
...BUT MEASURES OF STRENGTH, COURAGE AND DETERMINATION IN A HOSTILE WORLD...
...AS WELL AS CONFIRMATION THAT THE MINUTE ANYBODY STEPS OVER THE LINE WITH US...
...THEY'LL GET THEIR HEADS HANDED TO THEM--
--AND I MEAN THAT IN SPADES.

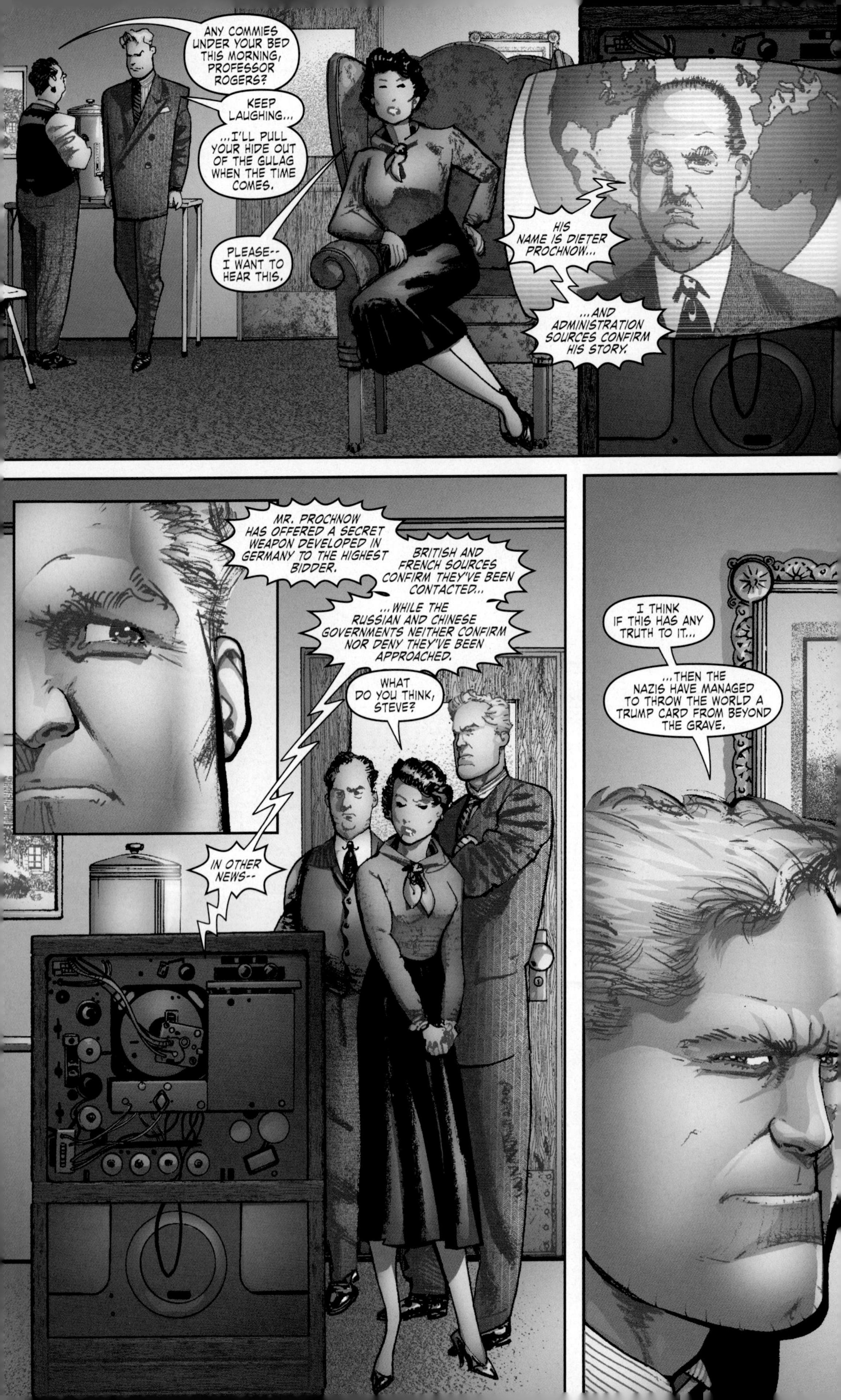
ANY COMMIES UNDER YOUR BED THIS MORNING, PROFESSOR ROGERS?
KEEP LAUGHING...
...I'LL PULL YOUR HIDE OUT OF THE GULAG WHEN THE TIME COMES.
PLEASE-- I WANT TO HEAR THIS.
HIS NAME IS DIETER PROCHNOW...
...AND ADMINISTRATION SOURCES CONFIRM HIS STORY.
MR. PROCHNOW HAS OFFERED A SECRET WEAPON DEVELOPED IN GERMANY TO THE HIGHEST BIDDER.
BRITISH AND FRENCH SOURCES CONFIRM THEY'VE BEEN CONTACTED...
...WHILE THE RUSSIAN AND CHINESE GOVERNMENTS NEITHER CONFIRM NOR DENY THEY'VE BEEN APPROACHED.
WHAT DO YOU THINK, STEVE?
IN OTHER NEWS--
I THINK IF THIS HAS ANY TRUTH TO IT...
...THEN THE NAZIS HAVE MANAGED TO THROW THE WORLD A TRUMP CARD FROM BEYOND THE GRAVE.

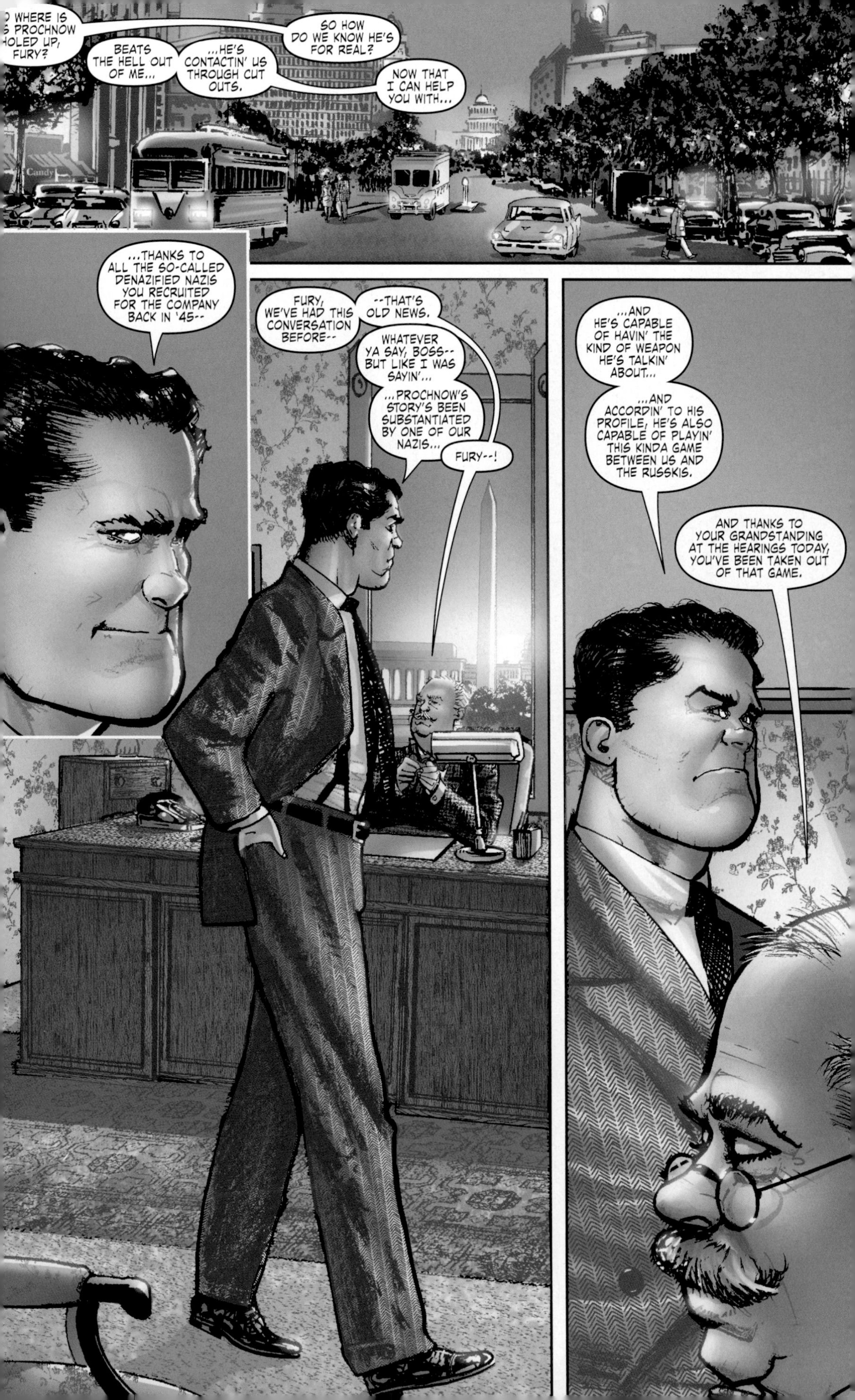

O WHERE IS
S PROCHNOW
HOLED UP,
FURY?
BEATS
THE HELL OUT
OF ME...
...HE'S
CONTACTIN' US
THROUGH CUT
OUTS.
SO HOW
DO WE KNOW HE'S
FOR REAL?
NOW THAT
I CAN HELP
YOU WITH...
Candy
...THANKS TO
ALL THE SO-CALLED
DENAZIFIED NAZIS
YOU RECRUITED
FOR THE COMPANY
BACK IN '45--
FURY,
WE'VE HAD THIS
CONVERSATION
BEFORE--
--THAT'S
OLD NEWS.
WHATEVER
YA SAY, BOSS--
BUT LIKE I WAS
SAYIN'...
...PROCHNOW'S
STORY'S BEEN
SUBSTANTIATED
BY ONE OF OUR
NAZIS...
FURY--!
...AND
HE'S CAPABLE
OF HAVIN' THE
KIND OF WEAPON
HE'S TALKIN'
ABOUT...
...AND
ACCORDIN' TO HIS
PROFILE, HE'S ALSO
CAPABLE OF PLAYIN'
THIS KINDA GAME
BETWEEN US AND
THE RUSSKIS.
AND THANKS TO
YOUR GRANDSTANDING
AT THE HEARINGS TODAY,
YOU'VE BEEN TAKEN OUT
OF THAT GAME.

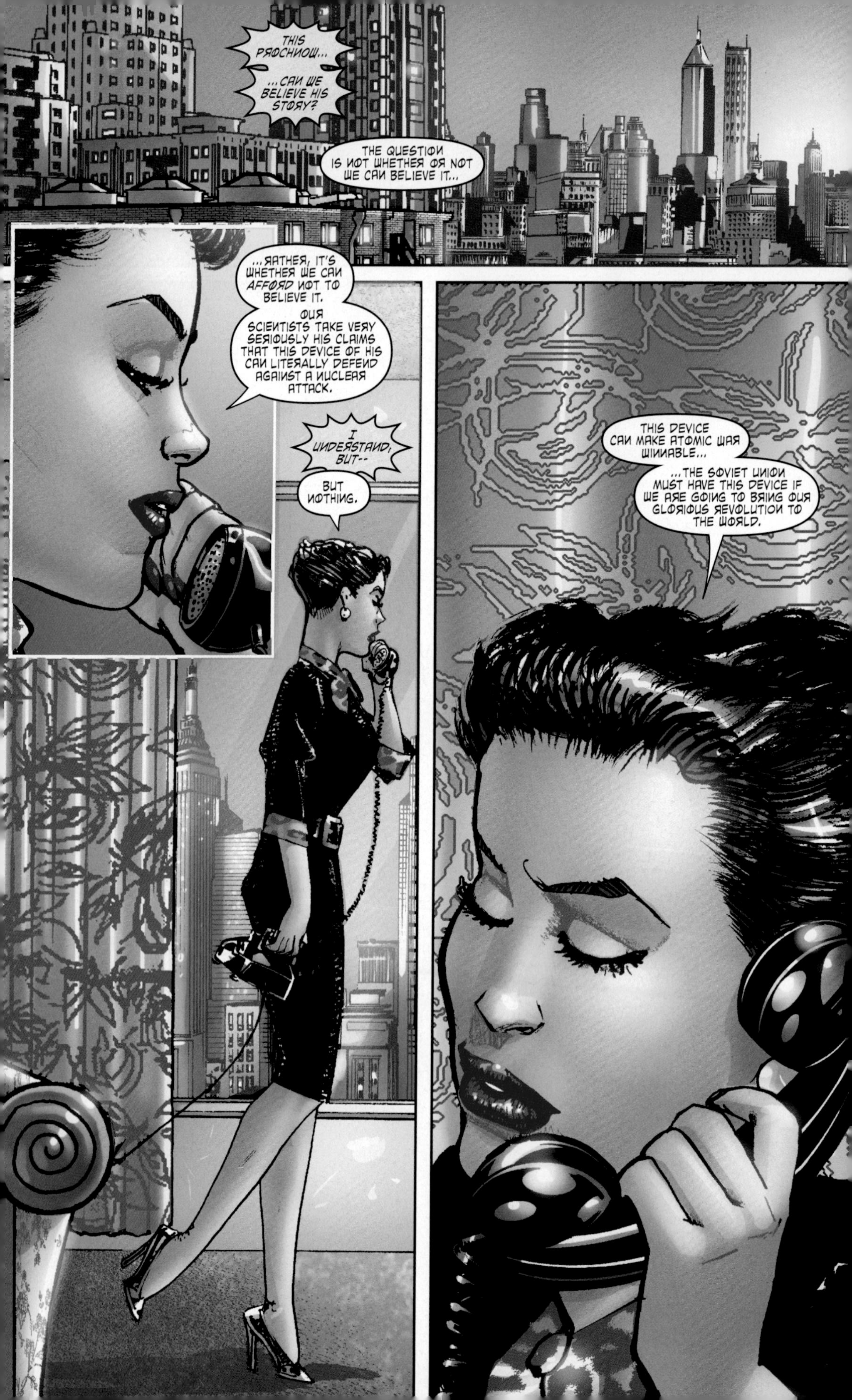
THIS PROCHNOW...
...CAN WE BELIEVE HIS STORY?
THE QUESTION IS NOT WHETHER OR NOT WE CAN BELIEVE IT...
...RATHER, IT'S WHETHER WE CAN *AFFORD* NOT TO BELIEVE IT.
OUR SCIENTISTS TAKE VERY SERIOUSLY HIS CLAIMS THAT THIS DEVICE OF HIS CAN LITERALLY DEFEND AGAINST A NUCLEAR ATTACK.
I *UNDERSTAND,* BUT--
BUT NOTHING.
THIS DEVICE CAN MAKE ATOMIC WAR WINNABLE...
...THE SOVIET UNION MUST HAVE THIS DEVICE IF WE ARE GOING TO BRING OUR GLORIOUS REVOLUTION TO THE WORLD.

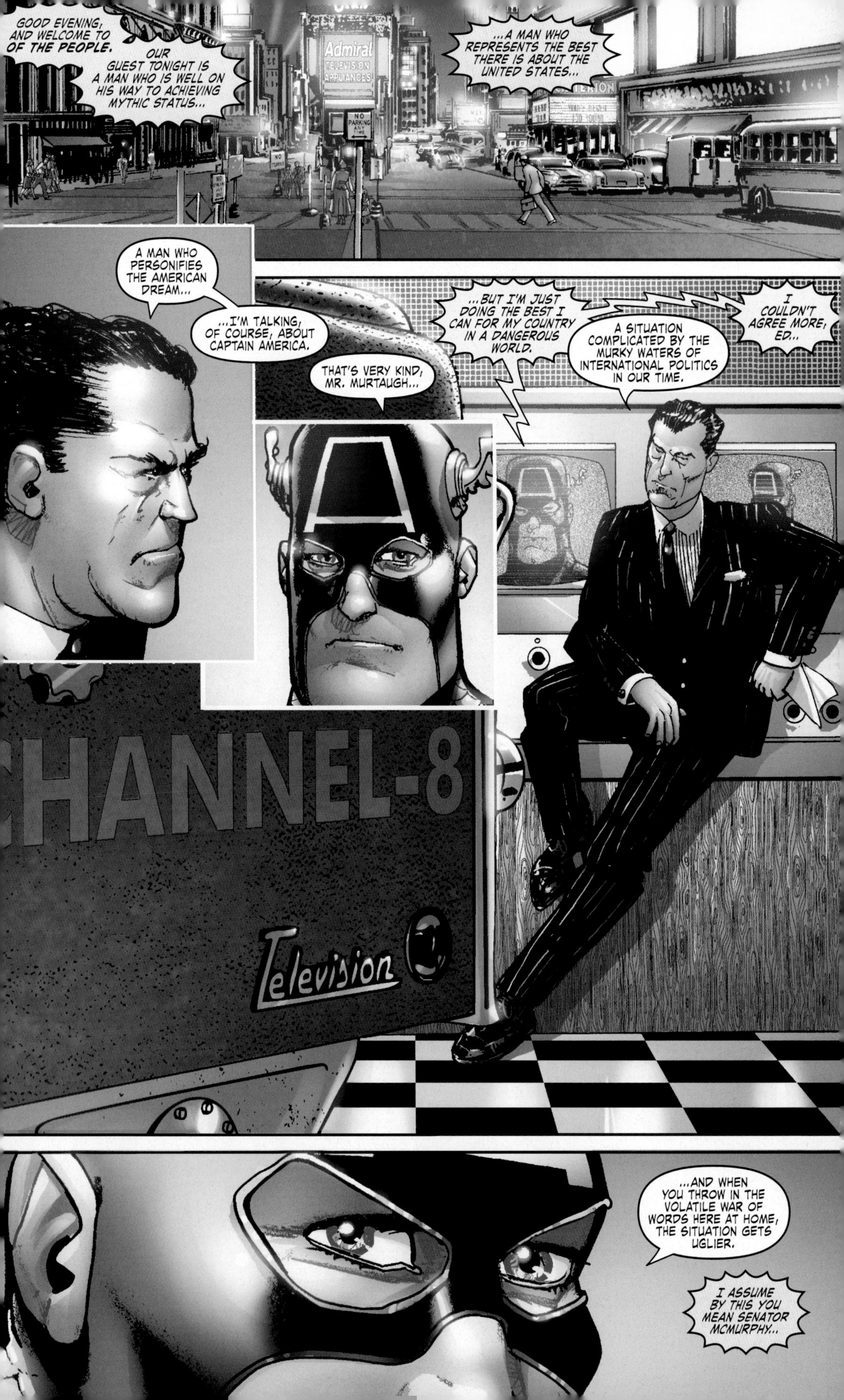
GOOD EVENING, AND WELCOME TO **OF THE PEOPLE.**
OUR GUEST TONIGHT IS A MAN WHO IS WELL ON HIS WAY TO ACHIEVING MYTHIC STATUS...
...A MAN WHO REPRESENTS THE BEST THERE IS ABOUT THE UNITED STATES...
Admiral
TELEVISION APPLIANCES
NO PARKING ANY TIME
A MAN WHO PERSONIFIES THE AMERICAN DREAM...
...I'M TALKING, OF COURSE, ABOUT CAPTAIN AMERICA.
THAT'S VERY KIND, MR. MURTAUGH...
...BUT I'M JUST DOING THE BEST I CAN FOR MY COUNTRY IN A DANGEROUS WORLD.
A SITUATION COMPLICATED BY THE MURKY WATERS OF INTERNATIONAL POLITICS IN OUR TIME.
I COULDN'T AGREE MORE, ED...
CHANNEL-8
Television
...AND WHEN YOU THROW IN THE VOLATILE WAR OF WORDS HERE AT HOME, THE SITUATION GETS UGLIER.
I ASSUME BY THIS YOU MEAN SENATOR MCMURPHY...

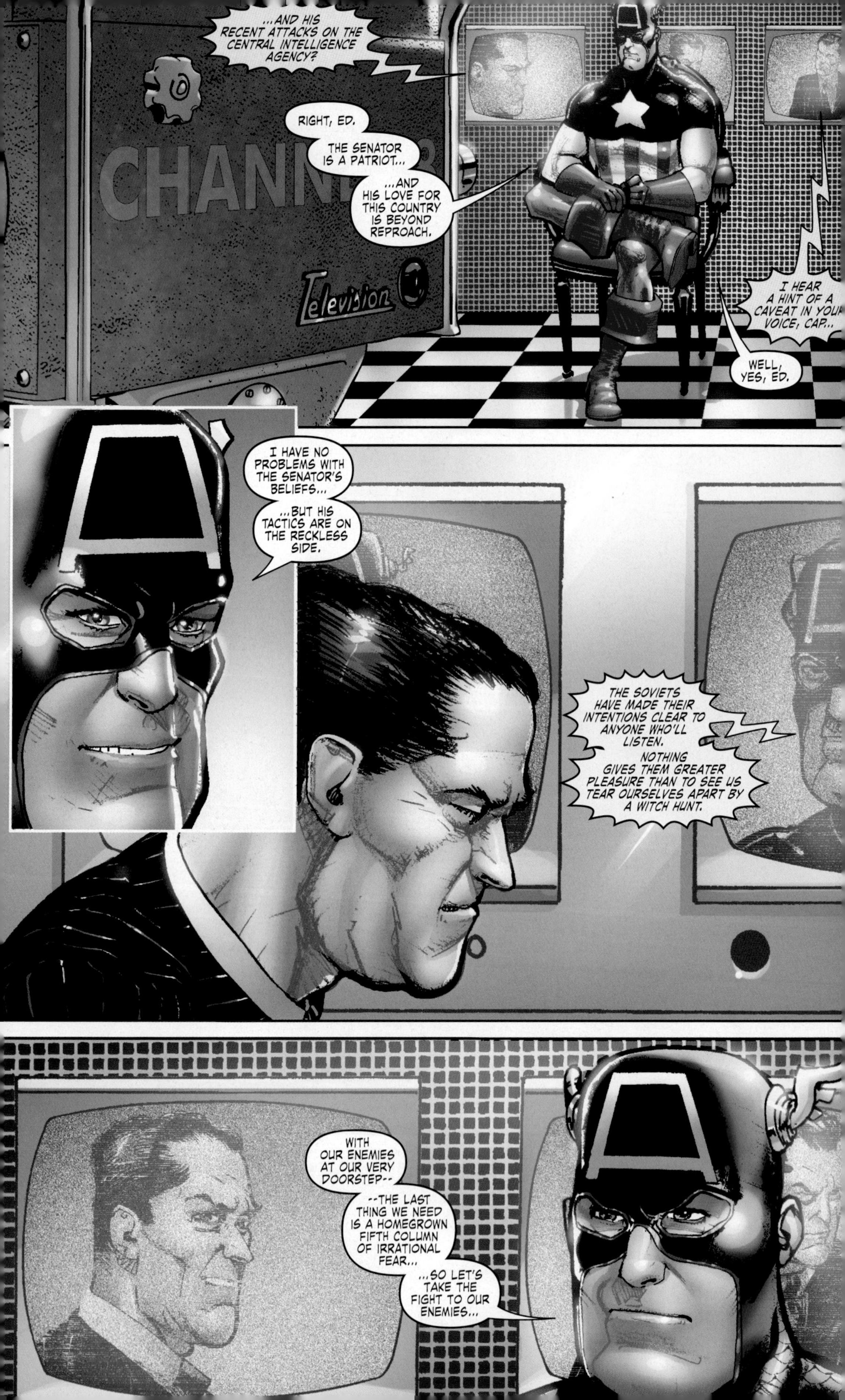
...AND HIS RECENT ATTACKS ON THE CENTRAL INTELLIGENCE AGENCY?
RIGHT, ED.
THE SENATOR IS A PATRIOT...
...AND HIS LOVE FOR THIS COUNTRY IS BEYOND REPROACH.
I HEAR A HINT OF A CAVEAT IN YOUR VOICE, CAP...
WELL, YES, ED.
I HAVE NO PROBLEMS WITH THE SENATOR'S BELIEFS...
...BUT HIS TACTICS ARE ON THE RECKLESS SIDE.
THE SOVIETS HAVE MADE THEIR INTENTIONS CLEAR TO ANYONE WHO'LL LISTEN.
NOTHING GIVES THEM GREATER PLEASURE THAN TO SEE US TEAR OURSELVES APART BY A WITCH HUNT.
WITH OUR ENEMIES AT OUR VERY DOORSTEP--
--THE LAST THING WE NEED IS A HOMEGROWN FIFTH COLUMN OF IRRATIONAL FEAR...
...SO LET'S TAKE THE FIGHT TO OUR ENEMIES...

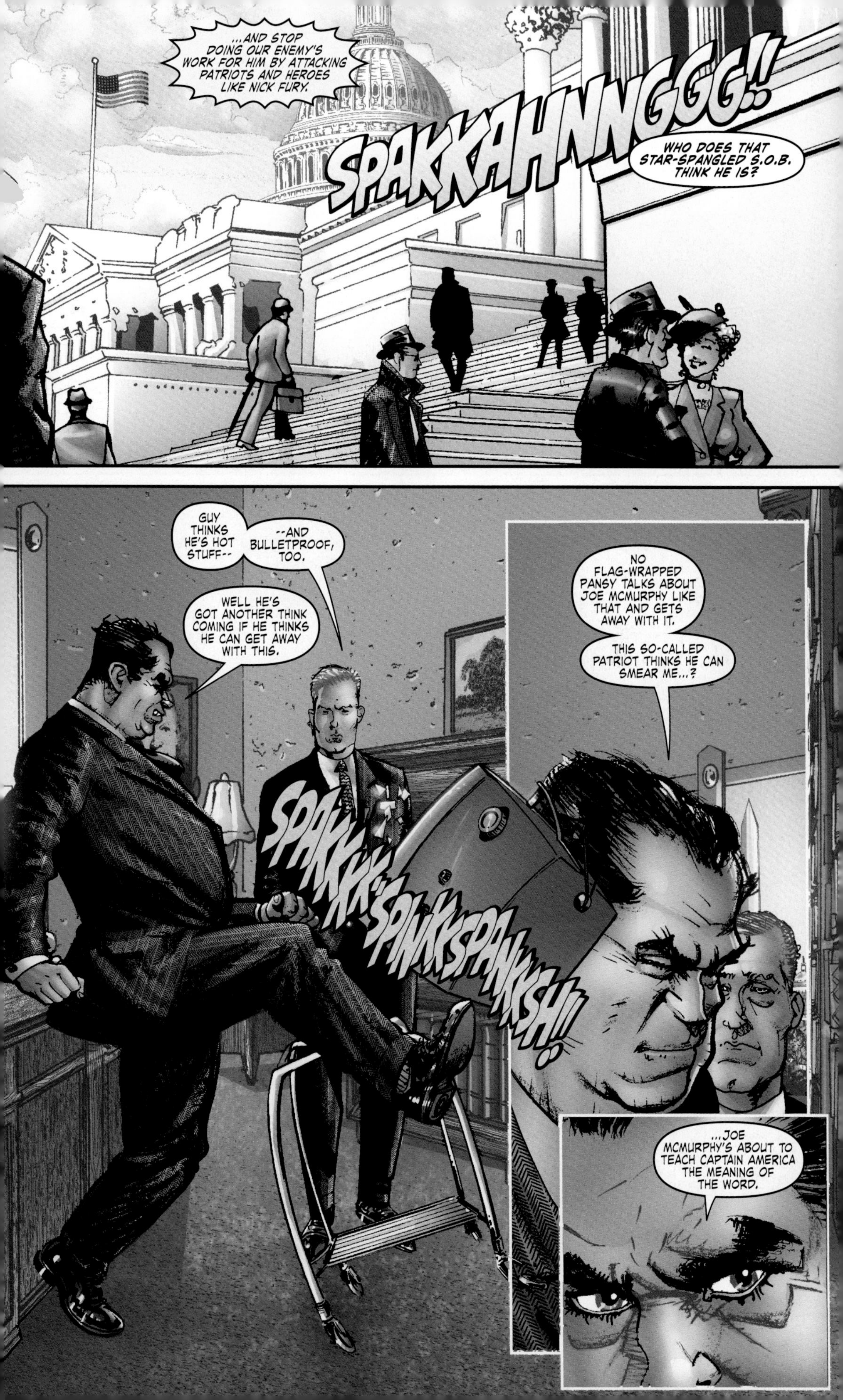
...AND STOP DOING OUR ENEMY'S WORK FOR HIM BY ATTACKING PATRIOTS AND HEROES LIKE NICK FURY.
SPAKKAHNNGGG!!
WHO DOES THAT STAR-SPANGLED S.O.B. THINK HE IS?
GUY THINKS HE'S HOT STUFF--
--AND BULLETPROOF, TOO.
WELL HE'S GOT ANOTHER THINK COMING IF HE THINKS HE CAN GET AWAY WITH THIS.
SPAKKK!! SPINKKSPANKKSH!!
NO FLAG-WRAPPED PANSY TALKS ABOUT JOE MCMURPHY LIKE THAT AND GETS AWAY WITH IT.
THIS SO-CALLED PATRIOT THINKS HE CAN SMEAR ME...?
...JOE MCMURPHY'S ABOUT TO TEACH CAPTAIN AMERICA THE MEANING OF THE WORD.

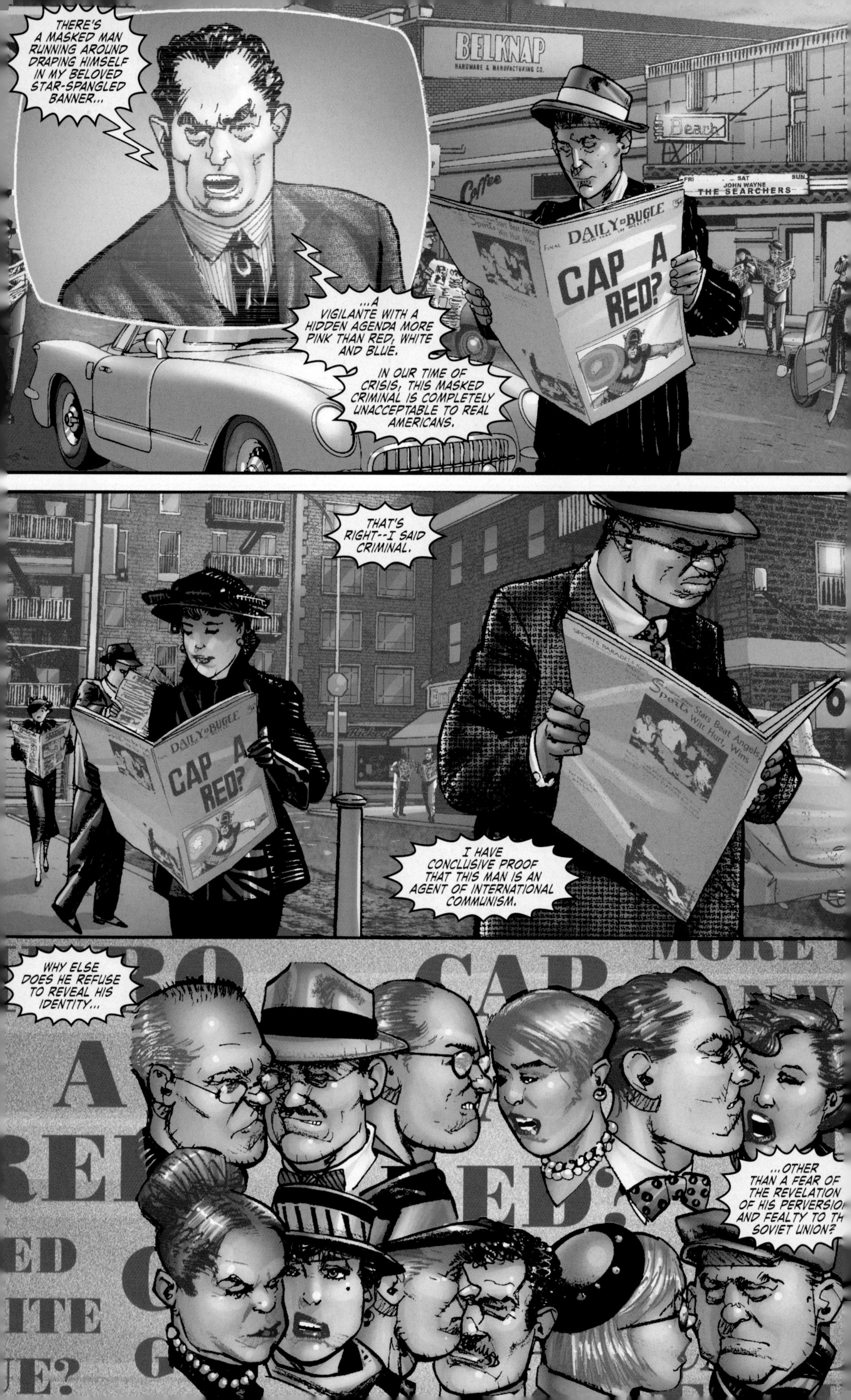

THERE'S A MASKED MAN RUNNING AROUND DRAPING HIMSELF IN MY BELOVED STAR-SPANGLED BANNER...
BELKNAP HARDWARE & MANUFACTURING CO.
Beach
FRI SAT SUN JOHN WAYNE THE SEARCHERS
Coffee
DAILY BUGLE
CAP A RED?
...A VIGILANTE WITH A HIDDEN AGENDA MORE PINK THAN RED, WHITE AND BLUE.
IN OUR TIME OF CRISIS, THIS MASKED CRIMINAL IS COMPLETELY UNACCEPTABLE TO REAL AMERICANS.
THAT'S RIGHT--I SAID CRIMINAL.
DAILY BUGLE
CAP A RED?
Sports Stars Beat Angels, Witt Hurt, Wins
I HAVE CONCLUSIVE PROOF THAT THIS MAN IS AN AGENT OF INTERNATIONAL COMMUNISM.
WHY ELSE DOES HE REFUSE TO REVEAL HIS IDENTITY...
...OTHER THAN A FEAR OF THE REVELATION OF HIS PERVERSIO AND FEALTY TO TH SOVIET UNION?

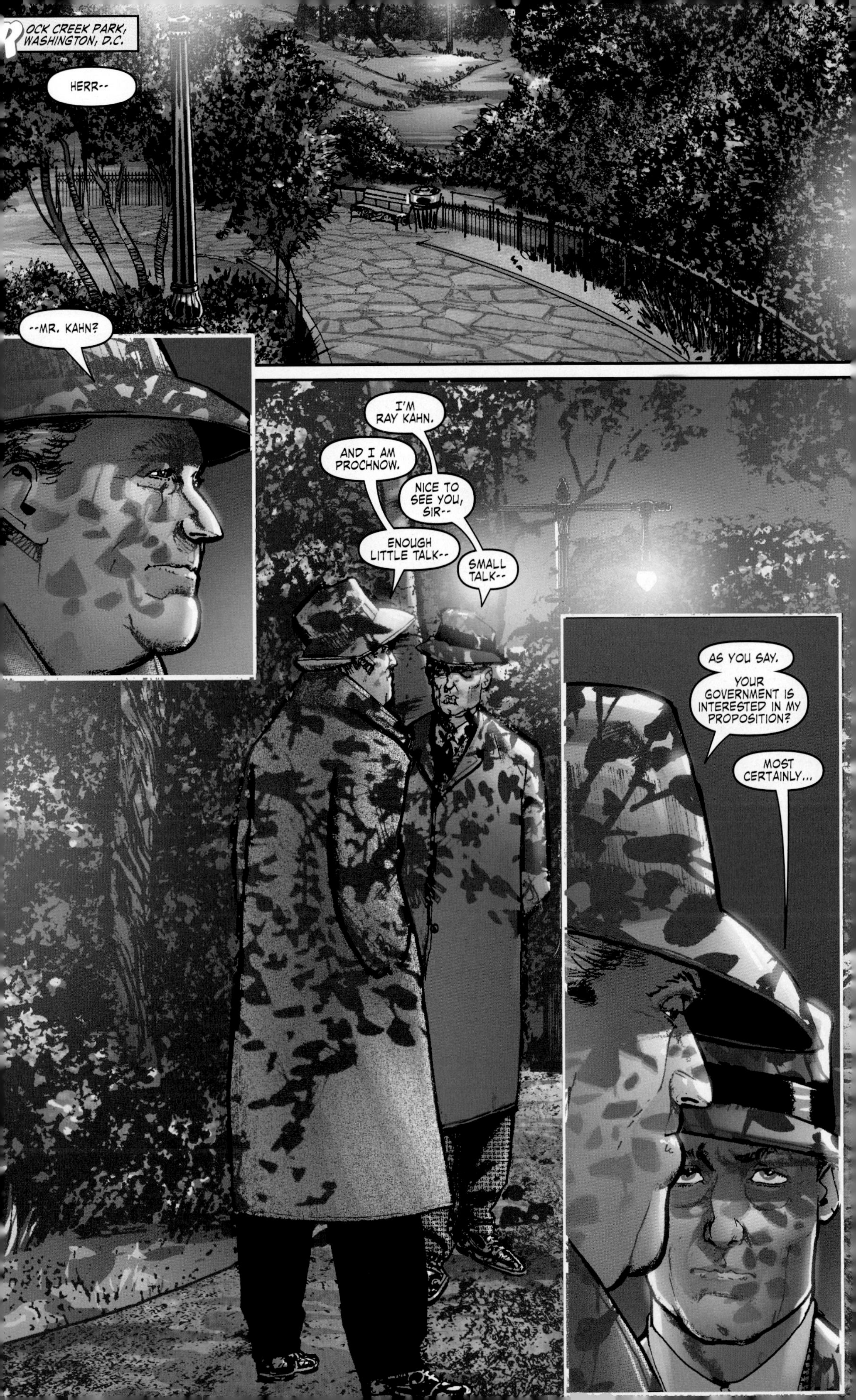
ROCK CREEK PARK, WASHINGTON, D.C.
HERR--
--MR. KAHN?
I'M RAY KAHN.
AND I AM PROCHNOW.
NICE TO SEE YOU, SIR--
ENOUGH LITTLE TALK--
SMALL TALK--
AS YOU SAY.
YOUR GOVERNMENT IS INTERESTED IN MY PROPOSITION?
MOST CERTAINLY...

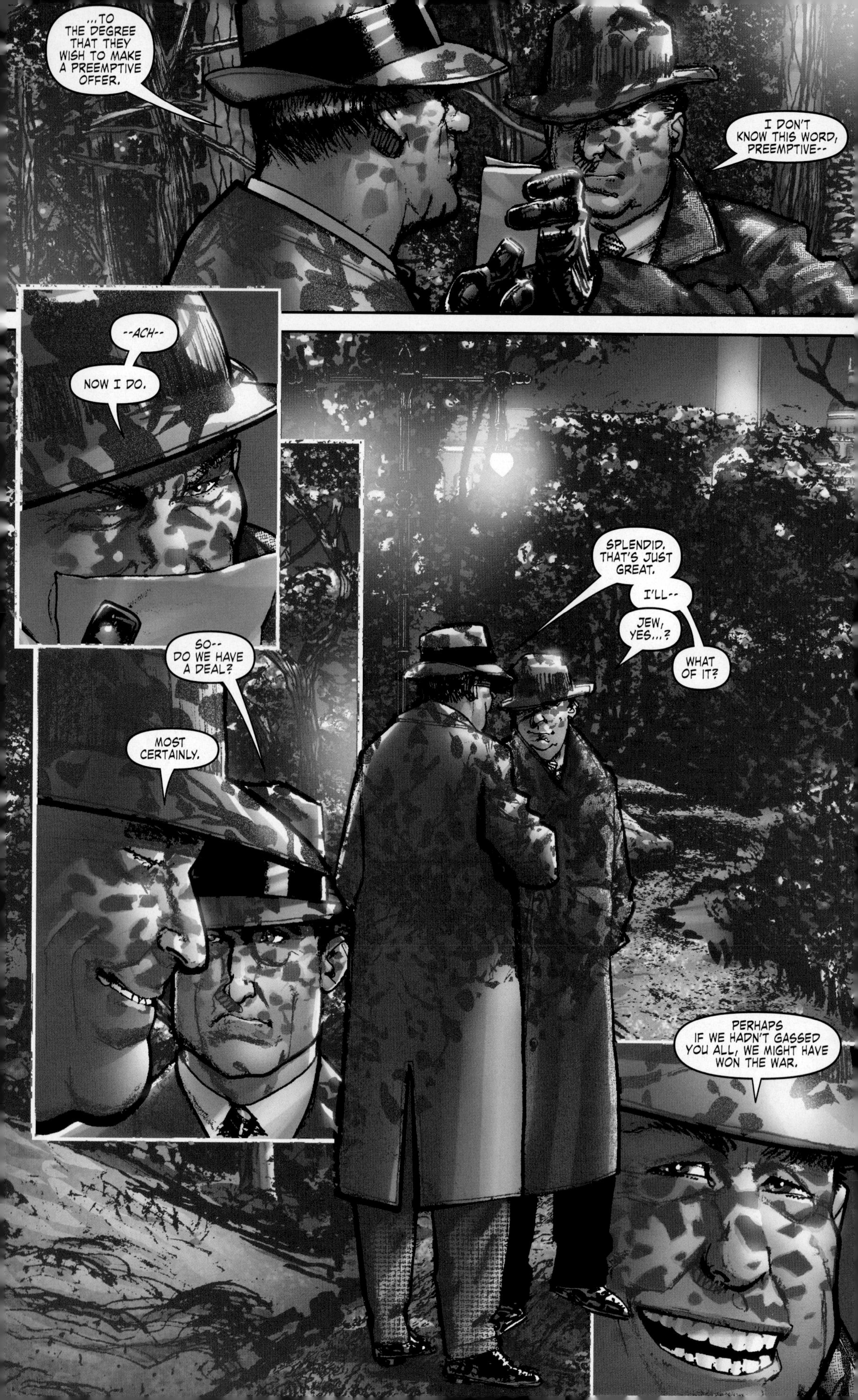
...TO THE DEGREE THAT THEY WISH TO MAKE A PREEMPTIVE OFFER.
I DON'T KNOW THIS WORD, PREEMPTIVE--
--ACH--
NOW I DO.
SO-- DO WE HAVE A DEAL?
MOST CERTAINLY.
SPLENDID. THAT'S JUST GREAT.
I'LL--
JEW, YES...?
WHAT OF IT?
PERHAPS IF WE HADN'T GASSED YOU ALL, WE MIGHT HAVE WON THE WAR.

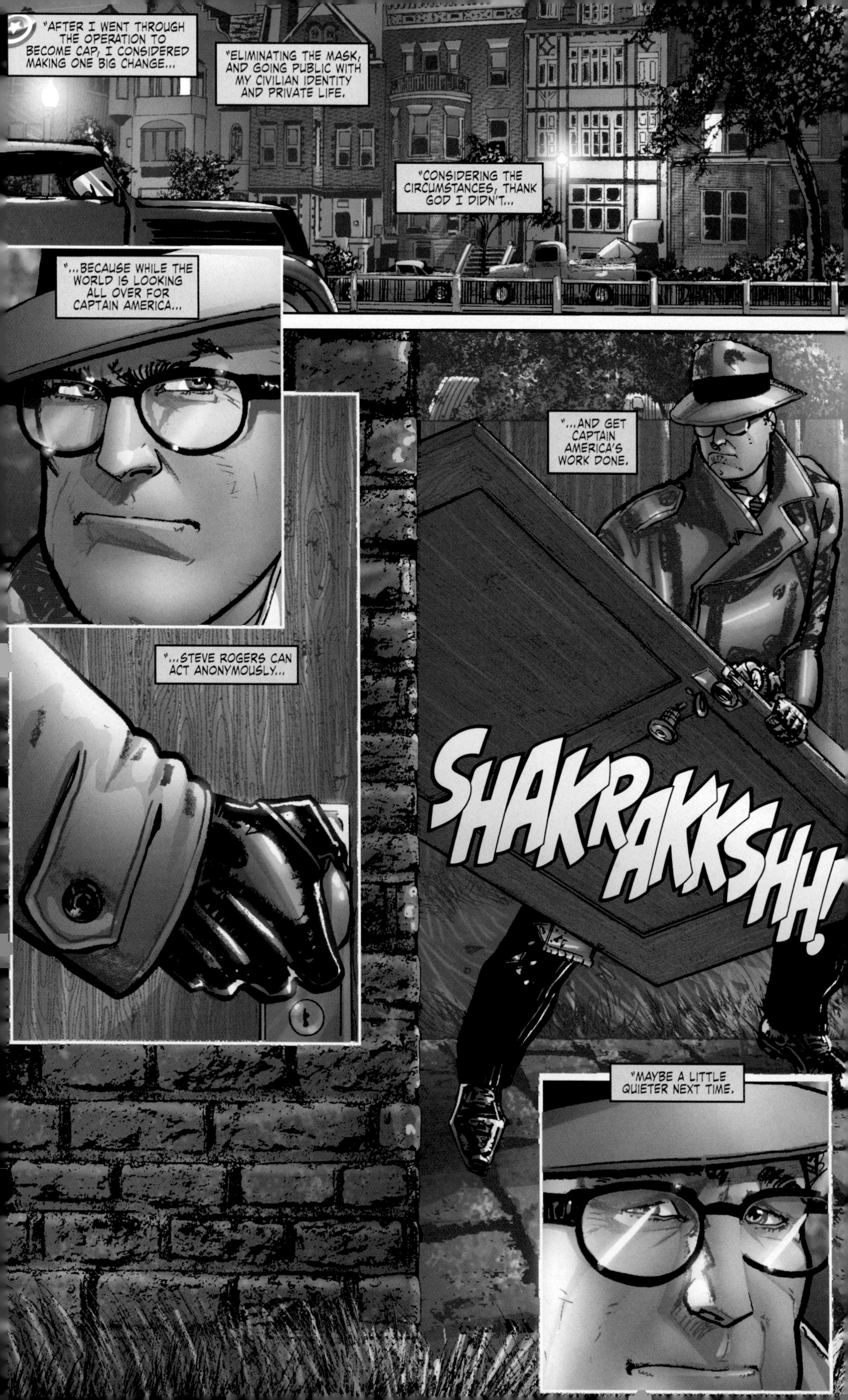
"AFTER I WENT THROUGH THE OPERATION TO BECOME CAP, I CONSIDERED MAKING ONE BIG CHANGE...
"ELIMINATING THE MASK, AND GOING PUBLIC WITH MY CIVILIAN IDENTITY AND PRIVATE LIFE.
"CONSIDERING THE CIRCUMSTANCES, THANK GOD I DIDN'T...
"...BECAUSE WHILE THE WORLD IS LOOKING ALL OVER FOR CAPTAIN AMERICA...
"...STEVE ROGERS CAN ACT ANONYMOUSLY...
"...AND GET CAPTAIN AMERICA'S WORK DONE.
SHAKRAKKSHH!
"MAYBE A LITTLE QUIETER NEXT TIME.

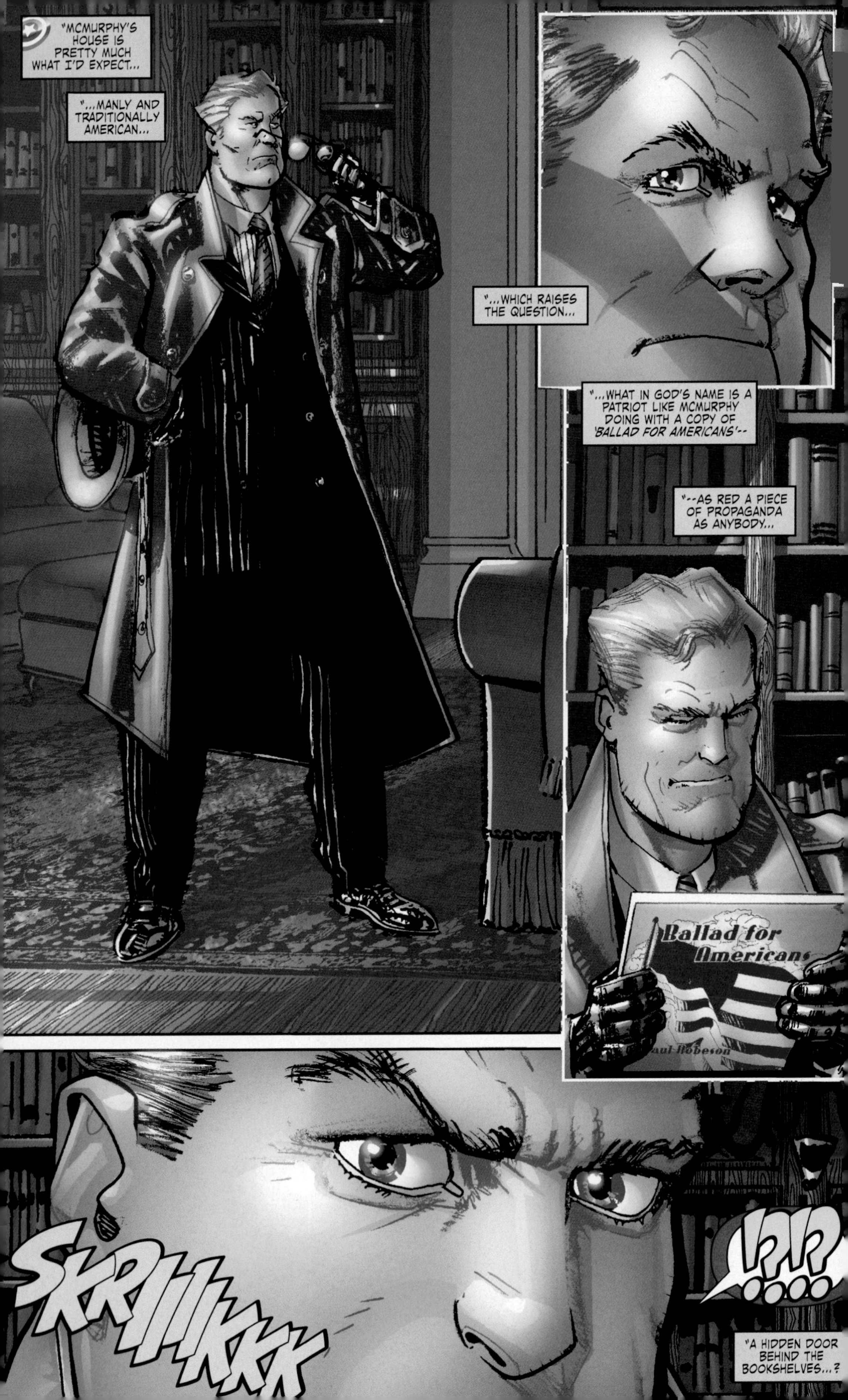
"MCMURPHY'S HOUSE IS PRETTY MUCH WHAT I'D EXPECT...
"...MANLY AND TRADITIONALLY AMERICAN...
"...WHICH RAISES THE QUESTION...
"...WHAT IN GOD'S NAME IS A PATRIOT LIKE MCMURPHY DOING WITH A COPY OF 'BALLAD FOR AMERICANS'--
"--AS RED A PIECE OF PROPAGANDA AS ANYBODY...
Ballad for Americans
SKRIIKKK
!?!?
"A HIDDEN DOOR BEHIND THE BOOKSHELVES...?

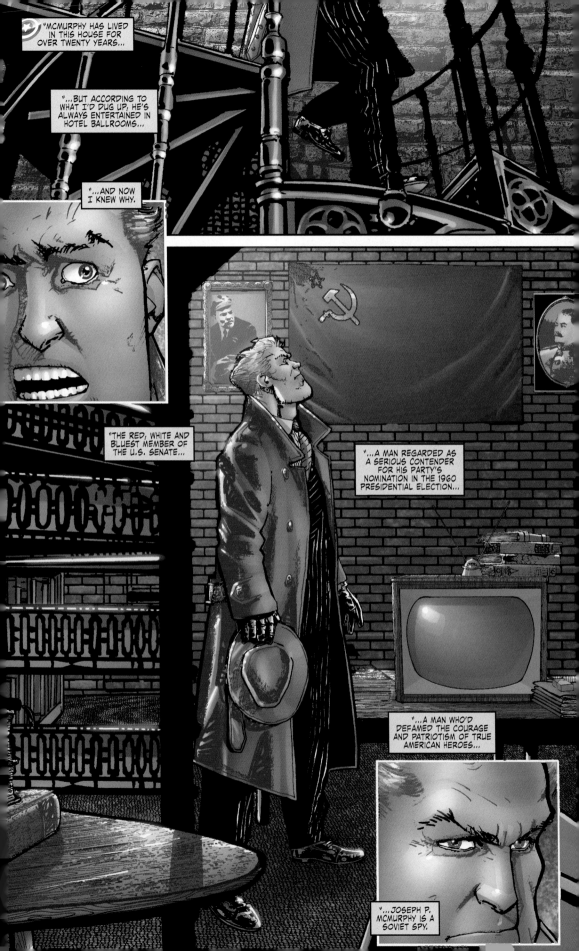

"MCMURPHY HAS LIVED IN THIS HOUSE FOR OVER TWENTY YEARS...

"...BUT ACCORDING TO WHAT I'D DUG UP, HE'S ALWAYS ENTERTAINED IN HOTEL BALLROOMS...

"...AND NOW I KNEW WHY.

"THE RED, WHITE AND BLUEST MEMBER OF THE U.S. SENATE...

"...A MAN REGARDED AS A SERIOUS CONTENDER FOR HIS PARTY'S NOMINATION IN THE 1960 PRESIDENTIAL ELECTION...

"...A MAN WHO'D DEFAMED THE COURAGE AND PATRIOTISM OF TRUE AMERICAN HEROES...

"...JOSEPH P. MCMURPHY IS A SOVIET SPY.

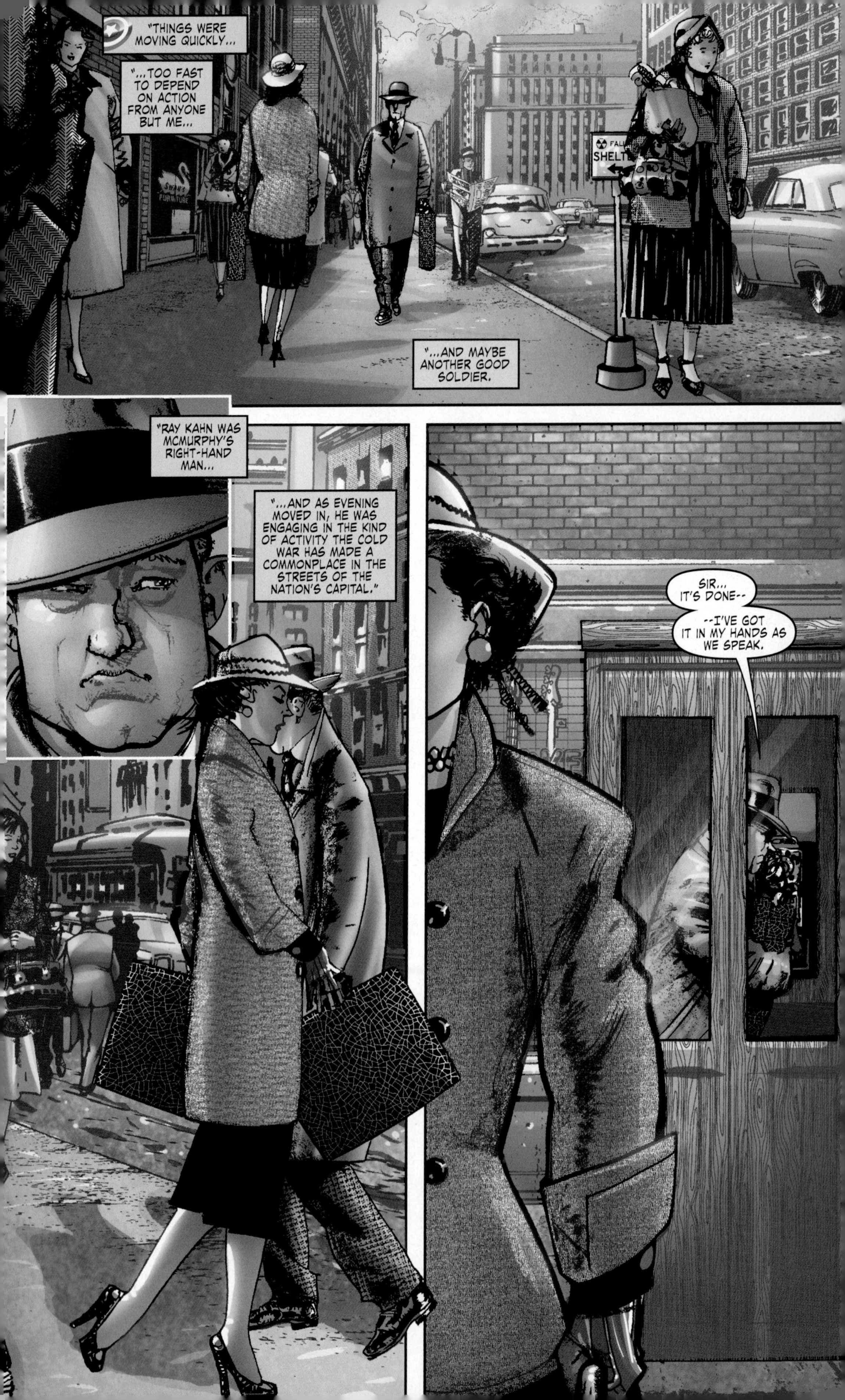
"THINGS WERE MOVING QUICKLY...
"...TOO FAST TO DEPEND ON ACTION FROM ANYONE BUT ME...
"...AND MAYBE ANOTHER GOOD SOLDIER.
SHELT
SWAN'S FURNITURE
"RAY KAHN WAS MCMURPHY'S RIGHT-HAND MAN...
"...AND AS EVENING MOVED IN, HE WAS ENGAGING IN THE KIND OF ACTIVITY THE COLD WAR HAS MADE A COMMONPLACE IN THE STREETS OF THE NATION'S CAPITAL."
SIR... IT'S DONE--
--I'VE GOT IT IN MY HANDS AS WE SPEAK.

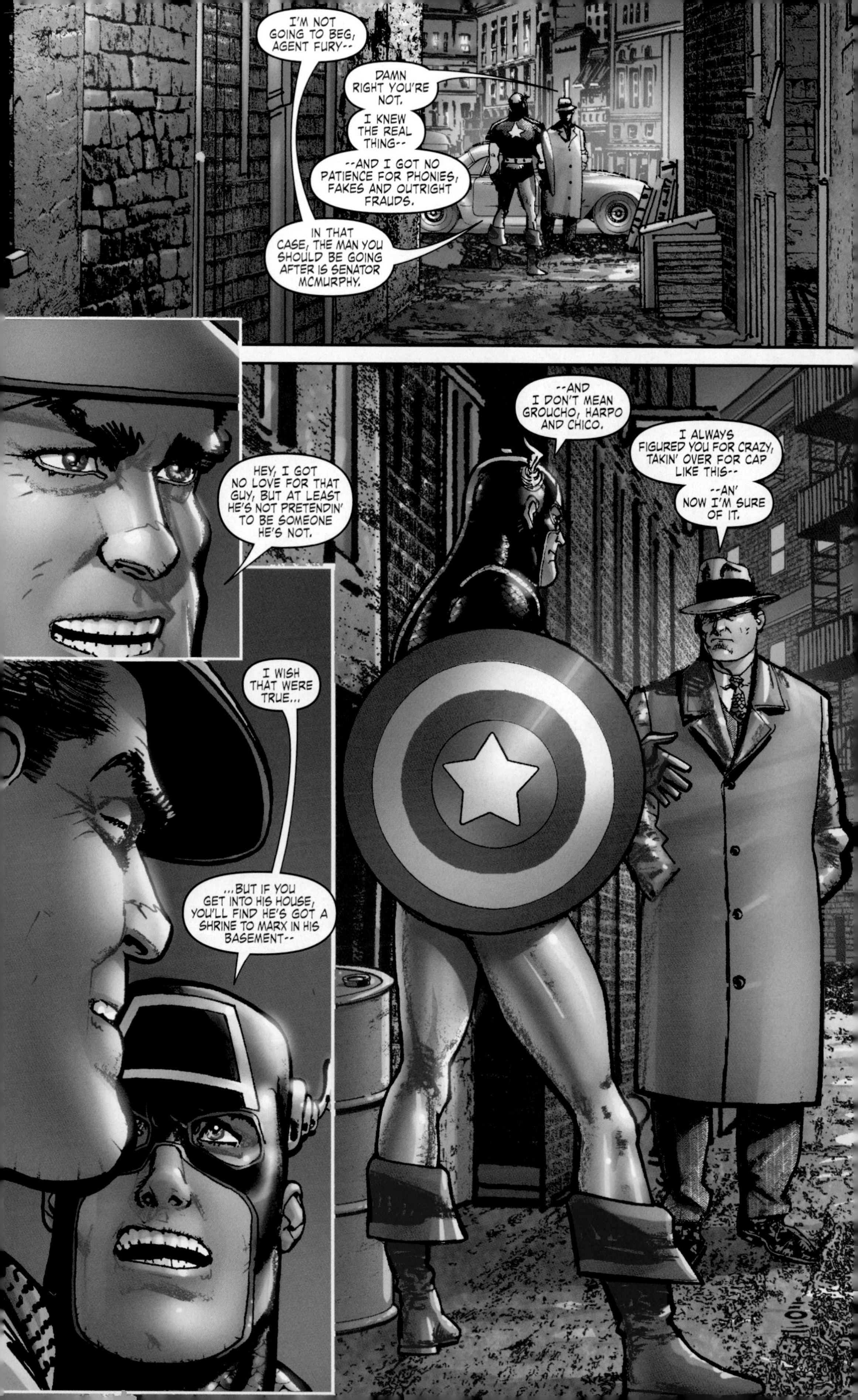
I'M NOT GOING TO BEG, AGENT FURY--
DAMN RIGHT YOU'RE NOT.
I KNEW THE REAL THING--
--AND I GOT NO PATIENCE FOR PHONIES, FAKES AND OUTRIGHT FRAUDS.
IN THAT CASE, THE MAN YOU SHOULD BE GOING AFTER IS SENATOR MCMURPHY.
HEY, I GOT NO LOVE FOR THAT GUY, BUT AT LEAST HE'S NOT PRETENDIN' TO BE SOMEONE HE'S NOT.
I WISH THAT WERE TRUE...
...BUT IF YOU GET INTO HIS HOUSE, YOU'LL FIND HE'S GOT A SHRINE TO MARX IN HIS BASEMENT--
--AND I DON'T MEAN GROUCHO, HARPO AND CHICO.
I ALWAYS FIGURED YOU FOR CRAZY, TAKIN' OVER FOR CAP LIKE THIS--
--AN' NOW I'M SURE OF IT.

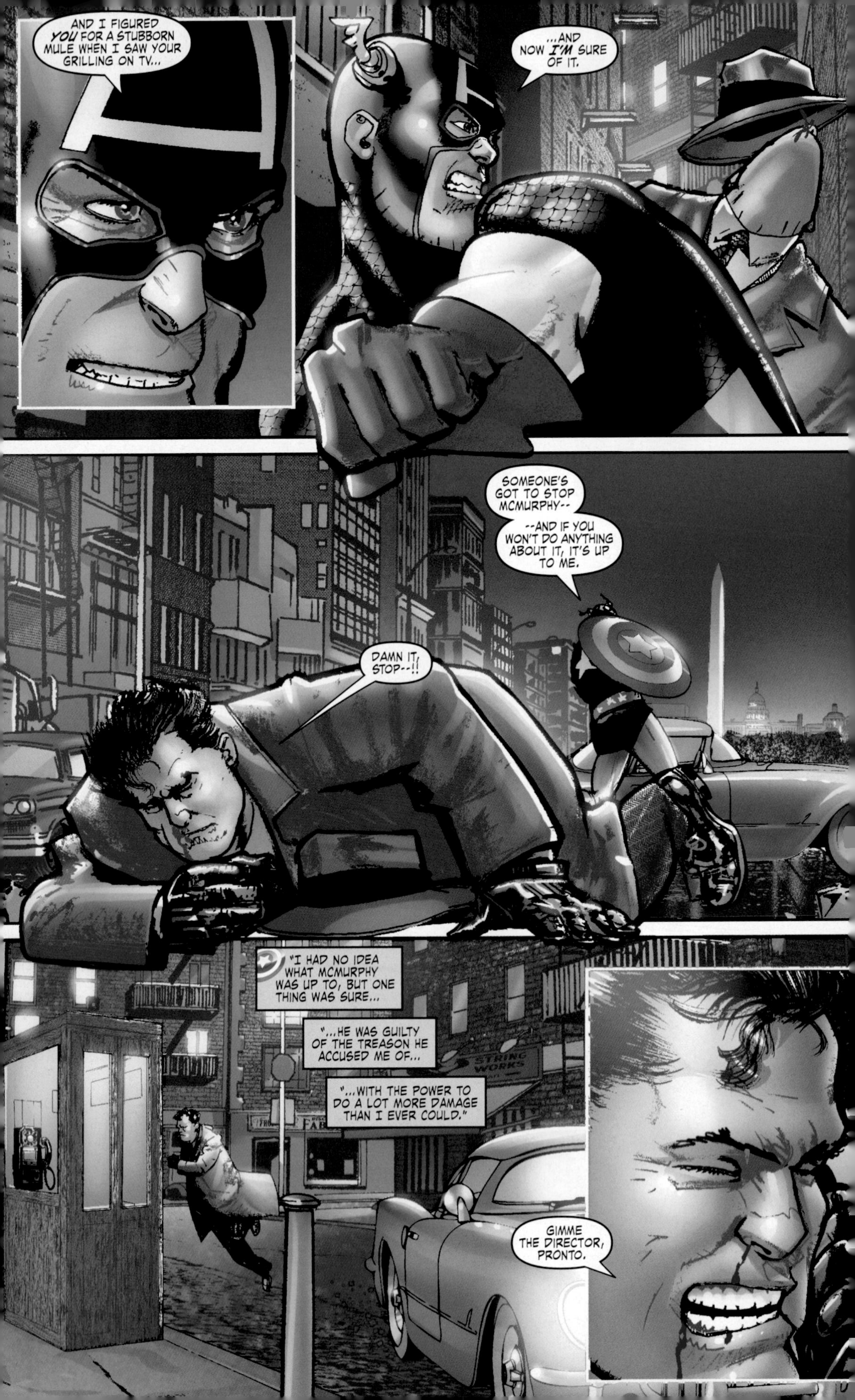
AND I FIGURED YOU FOR A STUBBORN MULE WHEN I SAW YOUR GRILLING ON TV...
...AND NOW I'M SURE OF IT.
SOMEONE'S GOT TO STOP MCMURPHY--
--AND IF YOU WON'T DO ANYTHING ABOUT IT, IT'S UP TO ME.
DAMN IT, STOP--!!
"I HAD NO IDEA WHAT MCMURPHY WAS UP TO, BUT ONE THING WAS SURE...
"...HE WAS GUILTY OF THE TREASON HE ACCUSED ME OF...
"...WITH THE POWER TO DO A LOT MORE DAMAGE THAN I EVER COULD."
STRING WORKS
GIMME THE DIRECTOR, PRONTO.

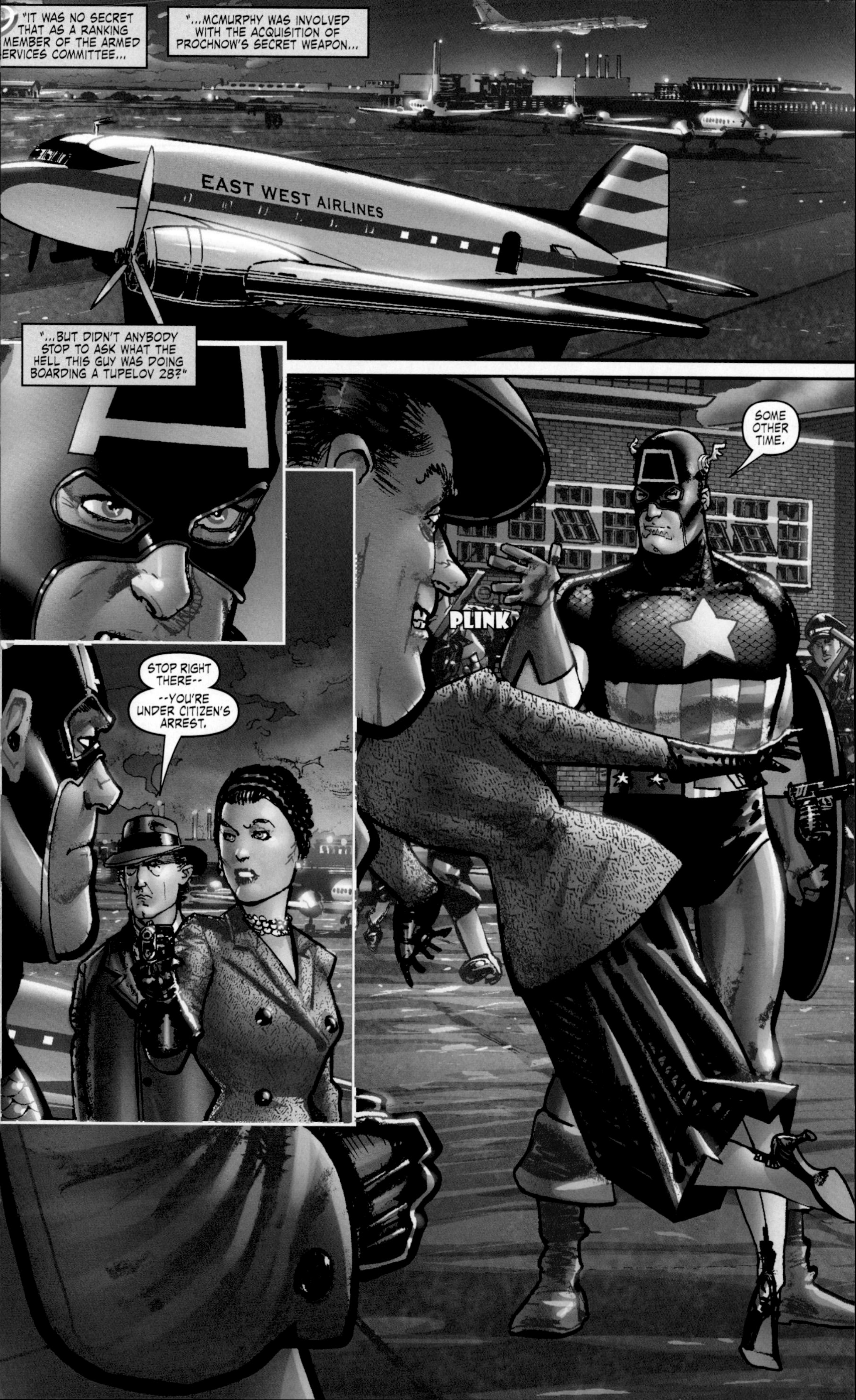
"IT WAS NO SECRET THAT AS A RANKING MEMBER OF THE ARMED SERVICES COMMITTEE...
"...MCMURPHY WAS INVOLVED WITH THE ACQUISITION OF PROCHNOW'S SECRET WEAPON...
EAST WEST AIRLINES
"...BUT DIDN'T ANYBODY STOP TO ASK WHAT THE HELL THIS GUY WAS DOING BOARDING A TUPELOV 28?"
STOP RIGHT THERE--
--YOU'RE UNDER CITIZEN'S ARREST.
PLINK
SOME OTHER TIME.

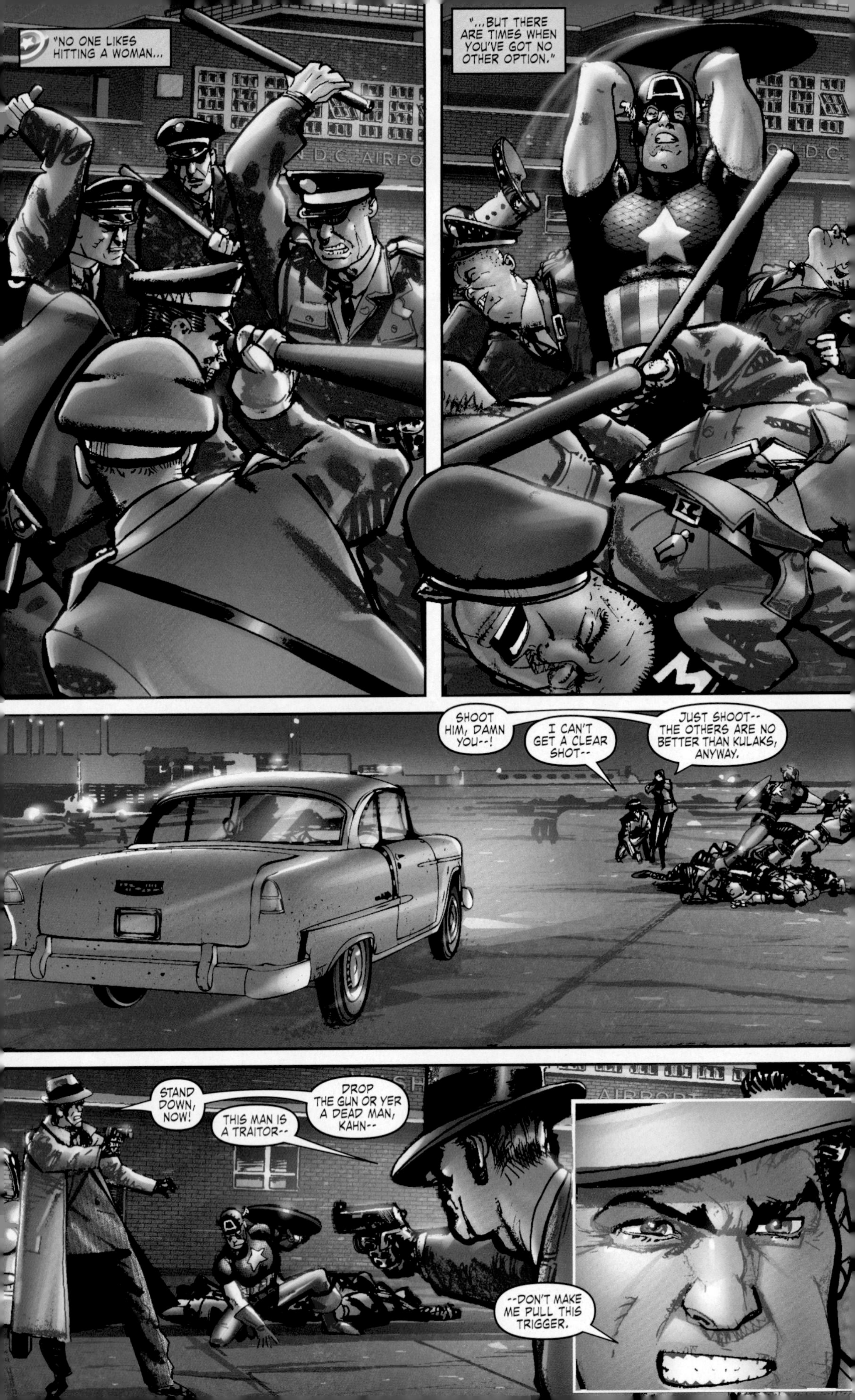
"NO ONE LIKES HITTING A WOMAN...
"...BUT THERE ARE TIMES WHEN YOU'VE GOT NO OTHER OPTION."
SHOOT HIM, DAMN YOU--!
I CAN'T GET A CLEAR SHOT--
JUST SHOOT-- THE OTHERS ARE NO BETTER THAN KULAKS, ANYWAY.
STAND DOWN, NOW!
THIS MAN IS A TRAITOR--
DROP THE GUN OR YER A DEAD MAN, KAHN--
--DON'T MAKE ME PULL THIS TRIGGER.

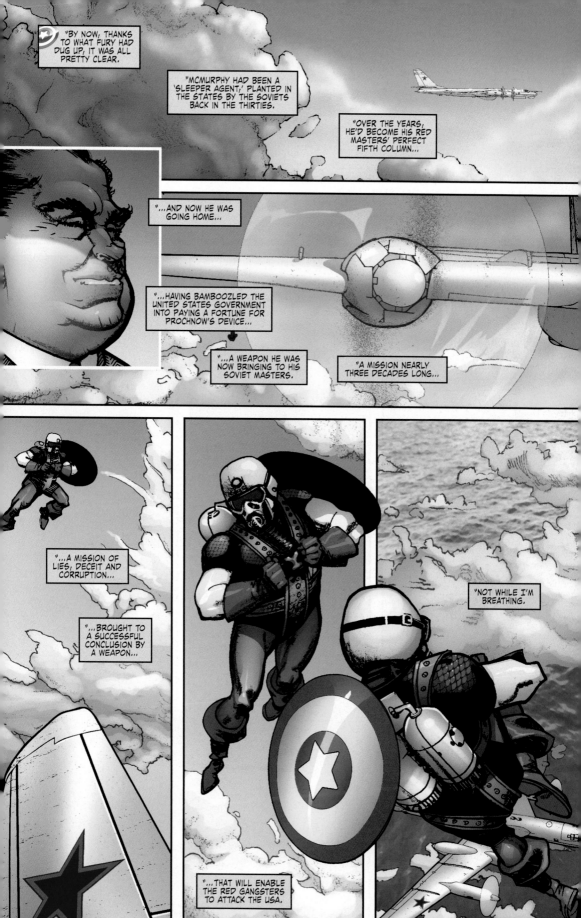

"BY NOW, THANKS TO WHAT FURY HAD DUG UP, IT WAS ALL PRETTY CLEAR.

"MCMURPHY HAD BEEN A 'SLEEPER AGENT,' PLANTED IN THE STATES BY THE SOVIETS BACK IN THE THIRTIES.

"OVER THE YEARS, HE'D BECOME HIS RED MASTERS' PERFECT FIFTH COLUMN...

"...AND NOW HE WAS GOING HOME...

"...HAVING BAMBOOZLED THE UNITED STATES GOVERNMENT INTO PAYING A FORTUNE FOR PROCHNOW'S DEVICE...

"...A WEAPON HE WAS NOW BRINGING TO HIS SOVIET MASTERS.

"A MISSION NEARLY THREE DECADES LONG...

"...A MISSION OF LIES, DECEIT AND CORRUPTION...

"...BROUGHT TO A SUCCESSFUL CONCLUSION BY A WEAPON...

"NOT WHILE I'M BREATHING.

"...THAT WILL ENABLE THE RED GANGSTERS TO ATTACK THE USA.

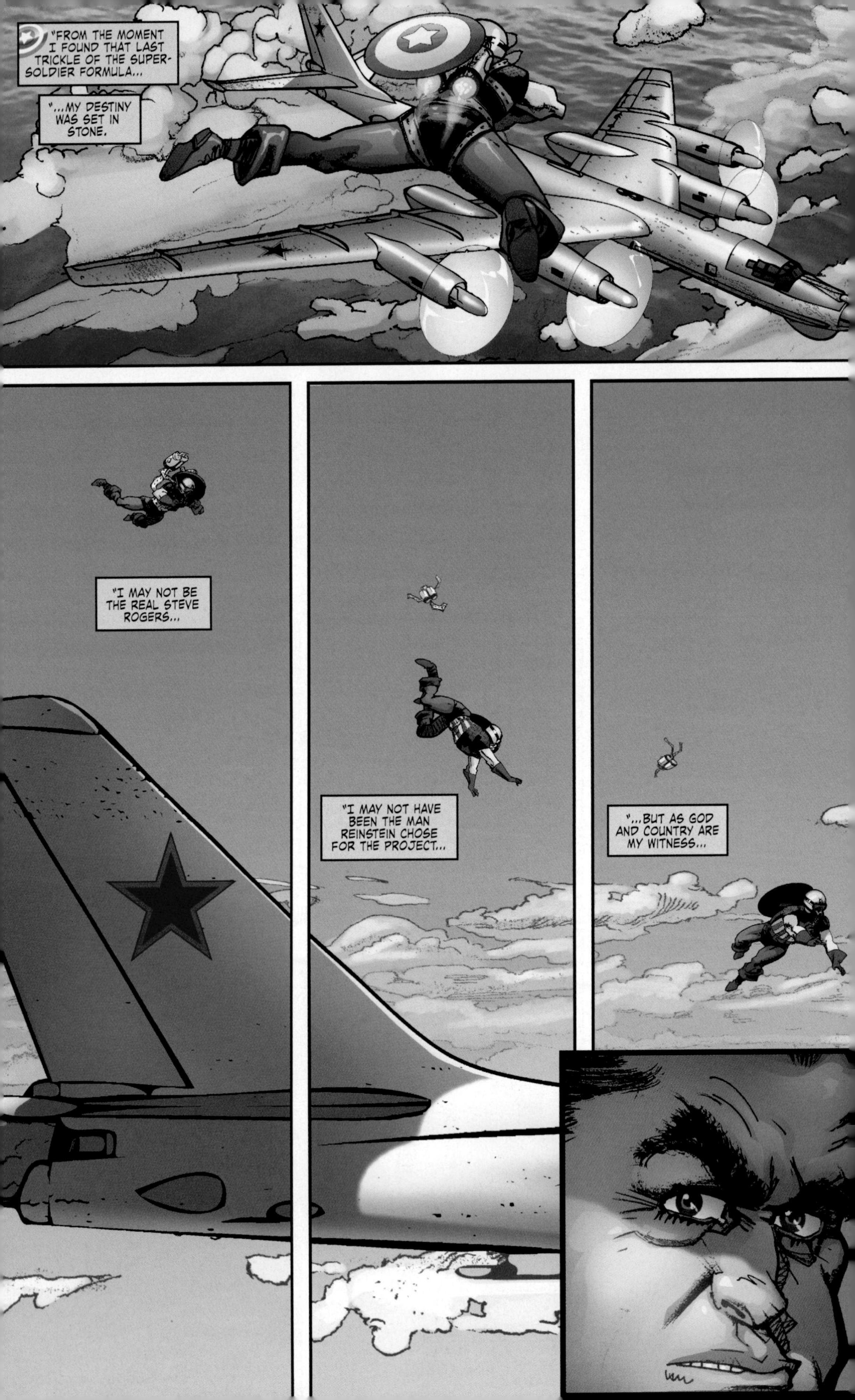
"FROM THE MOMENT I FOUND THAT LAST TRICKLE OF THE SUPER-SOLDIER FORMULA...
"...MY DESTINY WAS SET IN STONE.
"I MAY NOT BE THE REAL STEVE ROGERS...
"I MAY NOT HAVE BEEN THE MAN REINSTEIN CHOSE FOR THE PROJECT...
"...BUT AS GOD AND COUNTRY ARE MY WITNESS...

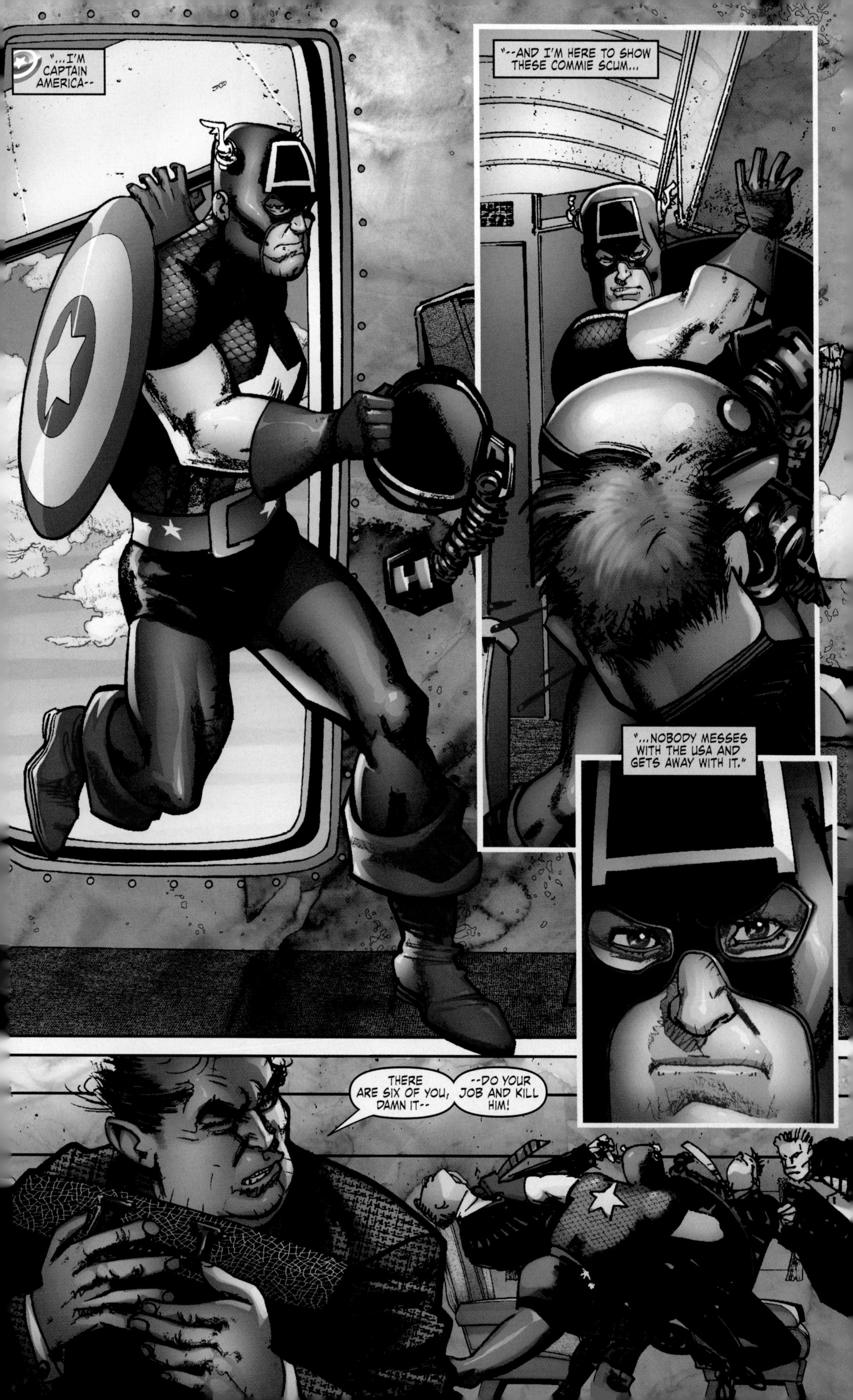
"...I'M CAPTAIN AMERICA--
"--AND I'M HERE TO SHOW THESE COMMIE SCUM...
"...NOBODY MESSES WITH THE USA AND GETS AWAY WITH IT."
THERE ARE SIX OF YOU, DAMN IT--
--DO YOUR JOB AND KILL HIM!

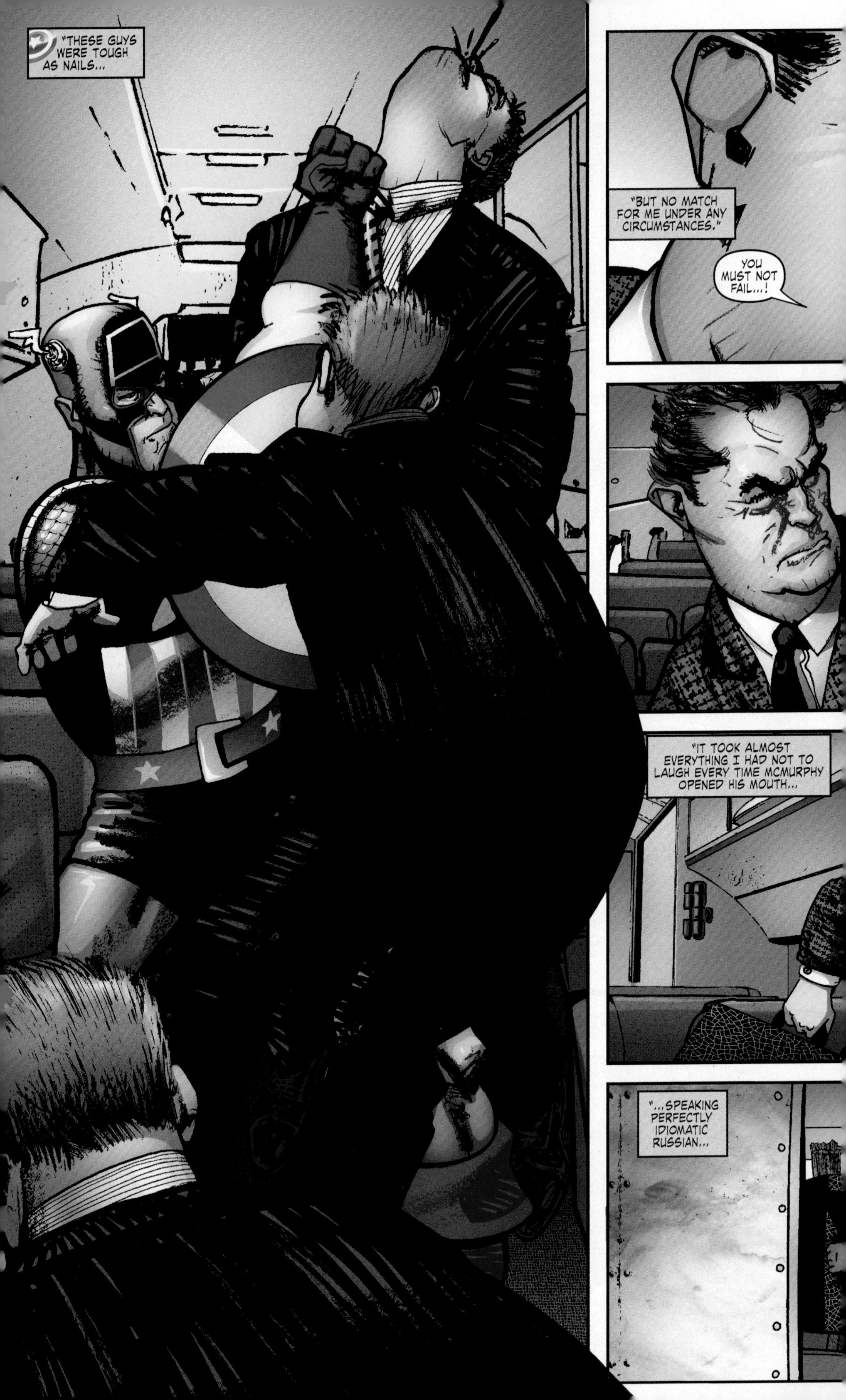
"THESE GUYS WERE TOUGH AS NAILS...
"BUT NO MATCH FOR ME UNDER ANY CIRCUMSTANCES."
YOU MUST NOT FAIL...!
"IT TOOK ALMOST EVERYTHING I HAD NOT TO LAUGH EVERY TIME MCMURPHY OPENED HIS MOUTH...
"...SPEAKING PERFECTLY IDIOMATIC RUSSIAN...

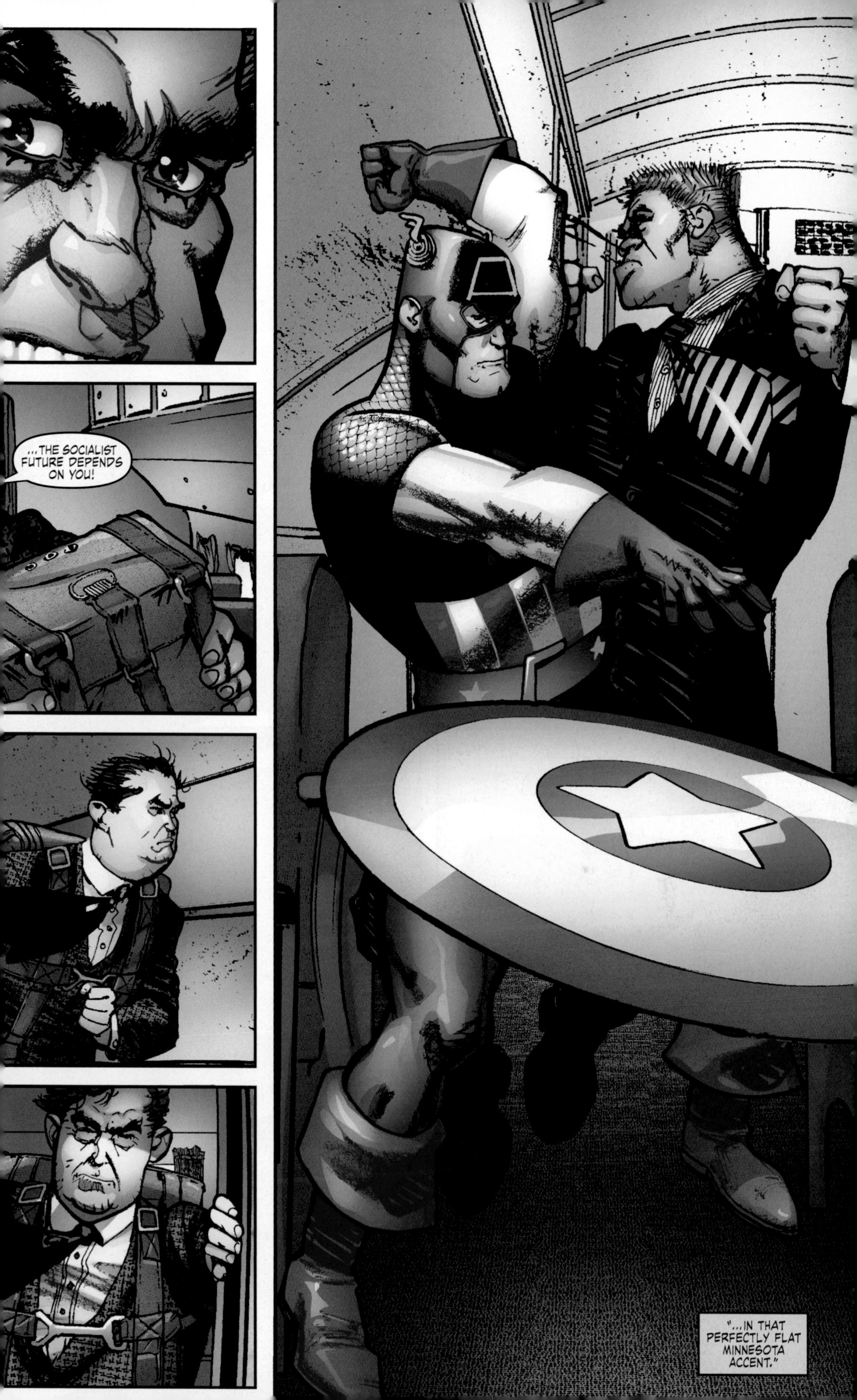
...THE SOCIALIST FUTURE DEPENDS ON YOU!
"...IN THAT PERFECTLY FLAT MINNESOTA ACCENT."

NO!!

CALLING TUPELOV TRANSCON 121--

--THIS IS NICK FURY OF THE CENTRAL INTELLIGENCE AGENCY...

"SURE, IT'S ALL ABOUT EGO...

...DO YOU READ ME, OVER...

"...BUT THANK GOD NOBODY SAW THAT."

I REPEAT, TUPELOV TRANSCON--

I READ YOU LOUD A CLEAR, FUR

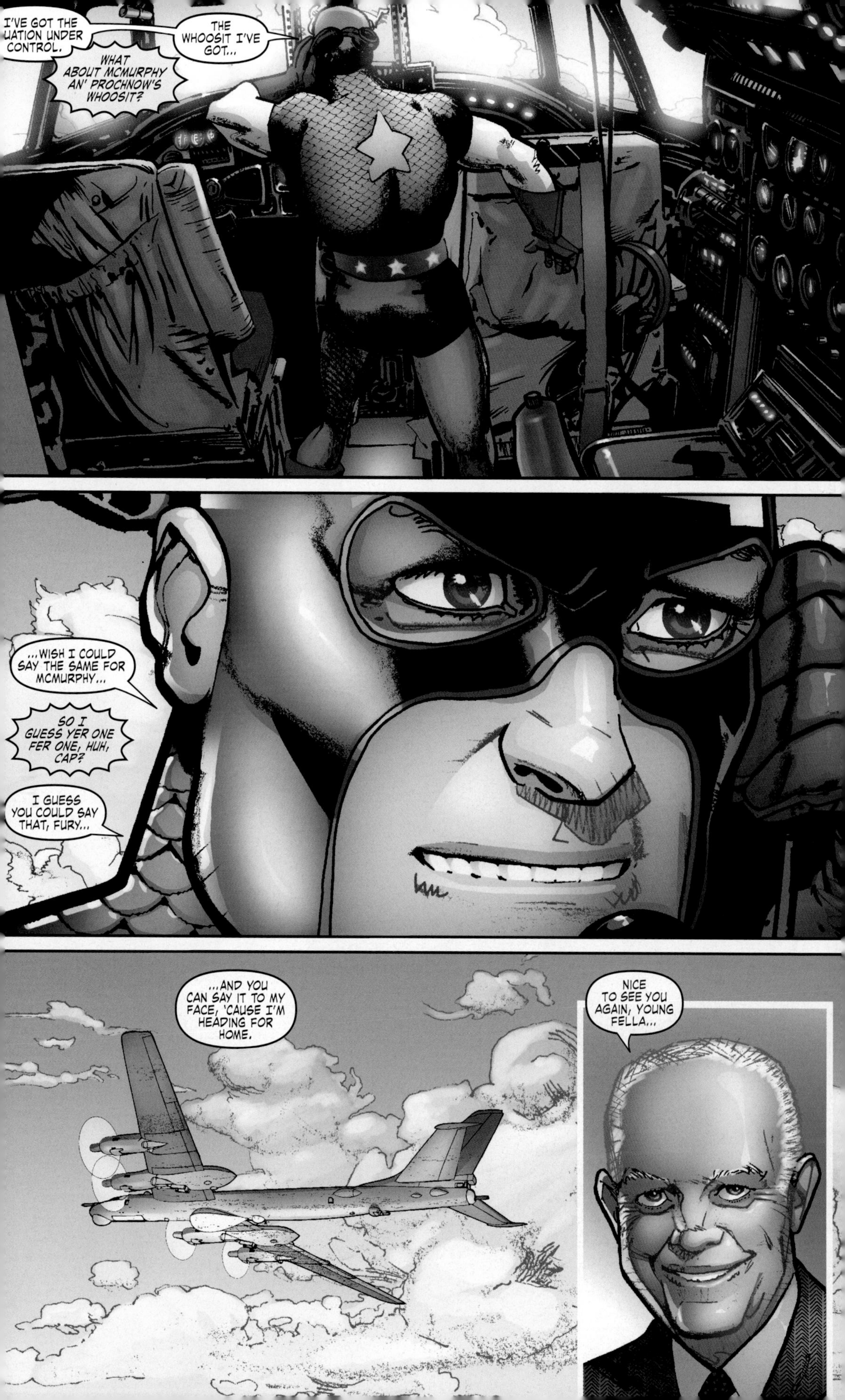

I'VE GOT THE
UATION UNDER CONTROL.
THE WHOOSIT I'VE GOT...
WHAT ABOUT MCMURPHY AN' PROCHNOW'S WHOOSIT?
...WISH I COULD SAY THE SAME FOR MCMURPHY...
SO I GUESS YER ONE FER ONE, HUH, CAP?
I GUESS YOU COULD SAY THAT, FURY...
...AND YOU CAN SAY IT TO MY FACE, 'CAUSE I'M HEADING FOR HOME.
NICE TO SEE YOU AGAIN, YOUNG FELLA...

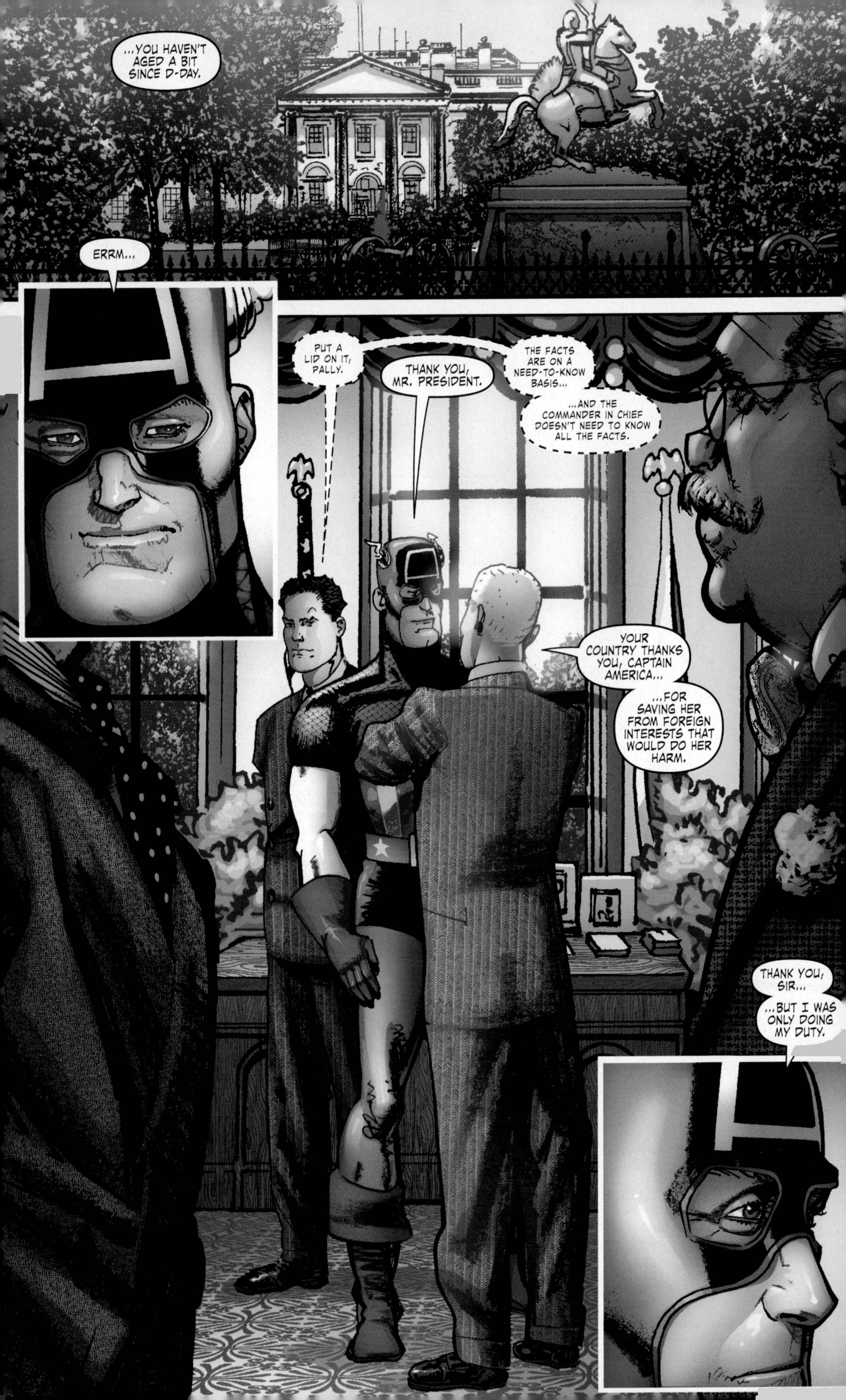
...YOU HAVEN'T AGED A BIT SINCE D-DAY.
ERRM...
PUT A LID ON IT, PALLY.
THANK YOU, MR. PRESIDENT.
THE FACTS ARE ON A NEED-TO-KNOW BASIS...
...AND THE COMMANDER IN CHIEF DOESN'T NEED TO KNOW ALL THE FACTS.
YOUR COUNTRY THANKS YOU, CAPTAIN AMERICA...
...FOR SAVING HER FROM FOREIGN INTERESTS THAT WOULD DO HER HARM.
THANK YOU, SIR...
...BUT I WAS ONLY DOING MY DUTY.

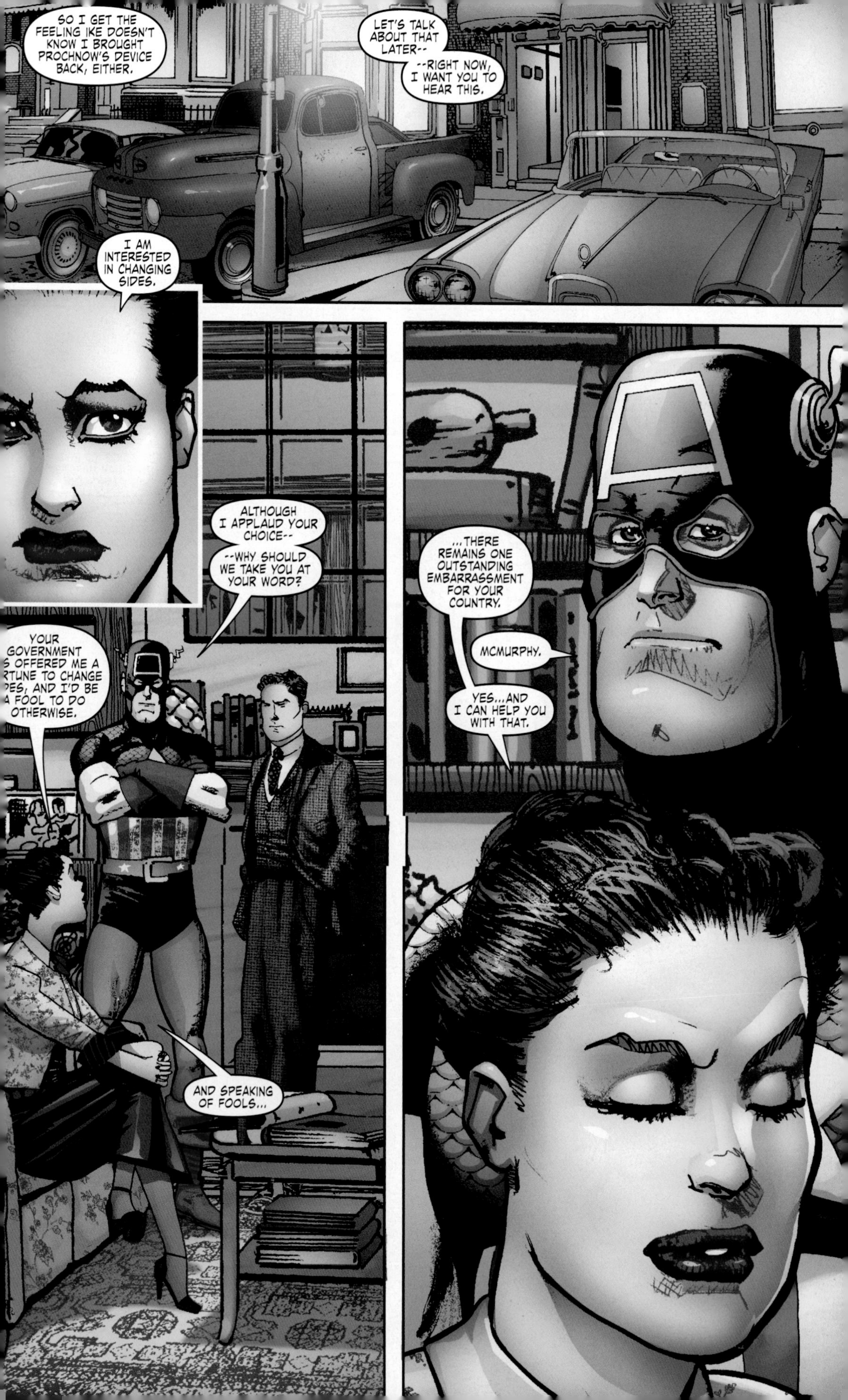
SO I GET THE FEELING IKE DOESN'T KNOW I BROUGHT PROCHNOW'S DEVICE BACK, EITHER.
LET'S TALK ABOUT THAT LATER--
--RIGHT NOW, I WANT YOU TO HEAR THIS.
I AM INTERESTED IN CHANGING SIDES.
ALTHOUGH I APPLAUD YOUR CHOICE--
--WHY SHOULD WE TAKE YOU AT YOUR WORD?
YOUR GOVERNMENT S OFFERED ME A RTUNE TO CHANGE DES, AND I'D BE A FOOL TO DO OTHERWISE.
AND SPEAKING OF FOOLS...
...THERE REMAINS ONE OUTSTANDING EMBARRASSMENT FOR YOUR COUNTRY.
MCMURPHY.
YES...AND I CAN HELP YOU WITH THAT.

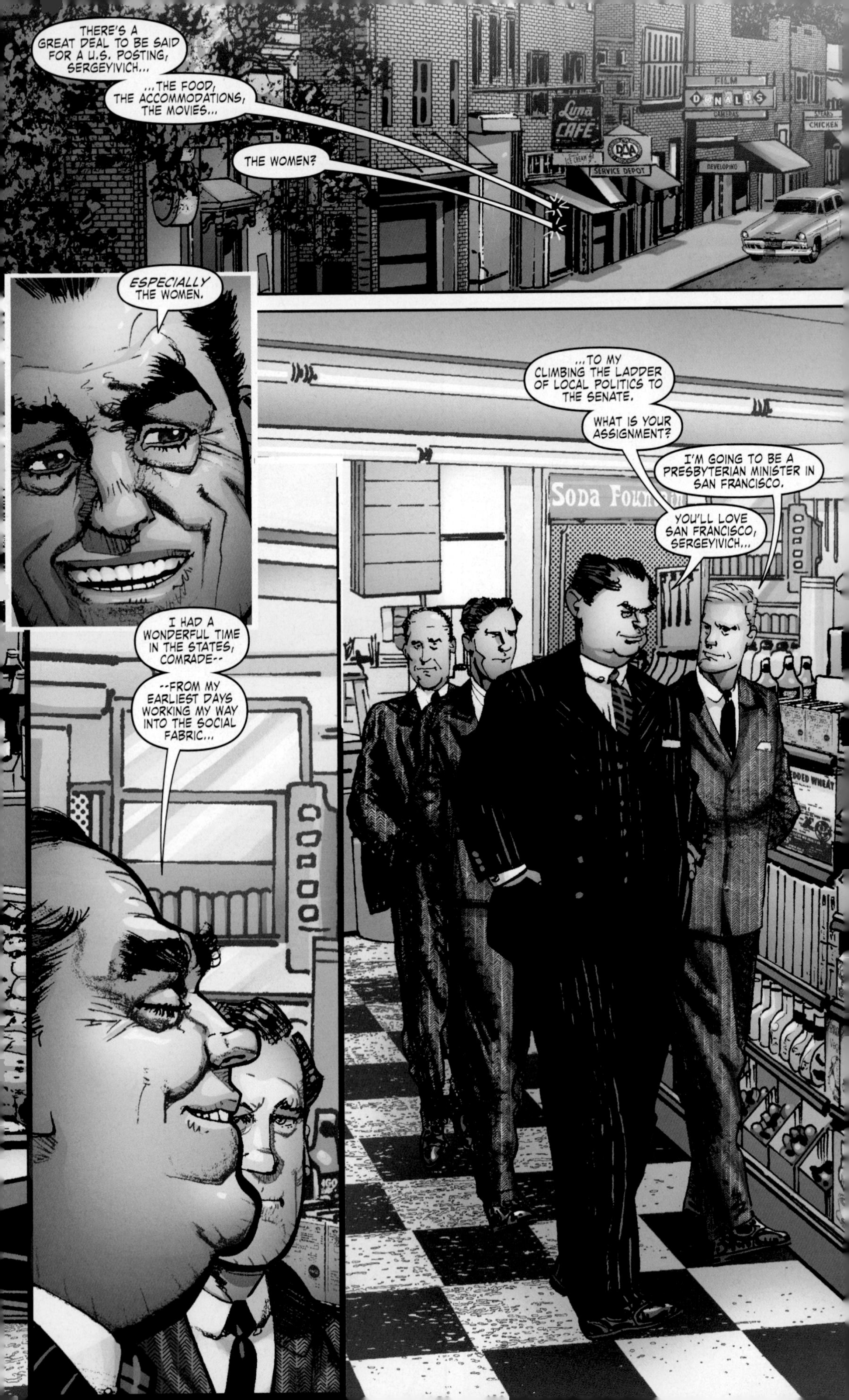
THERE'S A GREAT DEAL TO BE SAID FOR A U.S. POSTING, SERGEYIVICH...
...THE FOOD, THE ACCOMMODATIONS, THE MOVIES...
THE WOMEN?
Luna CAFE
SERVICE DEPOT
FILM
CAMERAS
DEVELOPING
STEAKS
CHICKEN
ESPECIALLY THE WOMEN.
I HAD A WONDERFUL TIME IN THE STATES, COMRADE--
--FROM MY EARLIEST DAYS WORKING MY WAY INTO THE SOCIAL FABRIC...
...TO MY CLIMBING THE LADDER OF LOCAL POLITICS TO THE SENATE.
WHAT IS YOUR ASSIGNMENT?
I'M GOING TO BE A PRESBYTERIAN MINISTER IN SAN FRANCISCO.
YOU'LL LOVE SAN FRANCISCO, SERGEYIVICH...

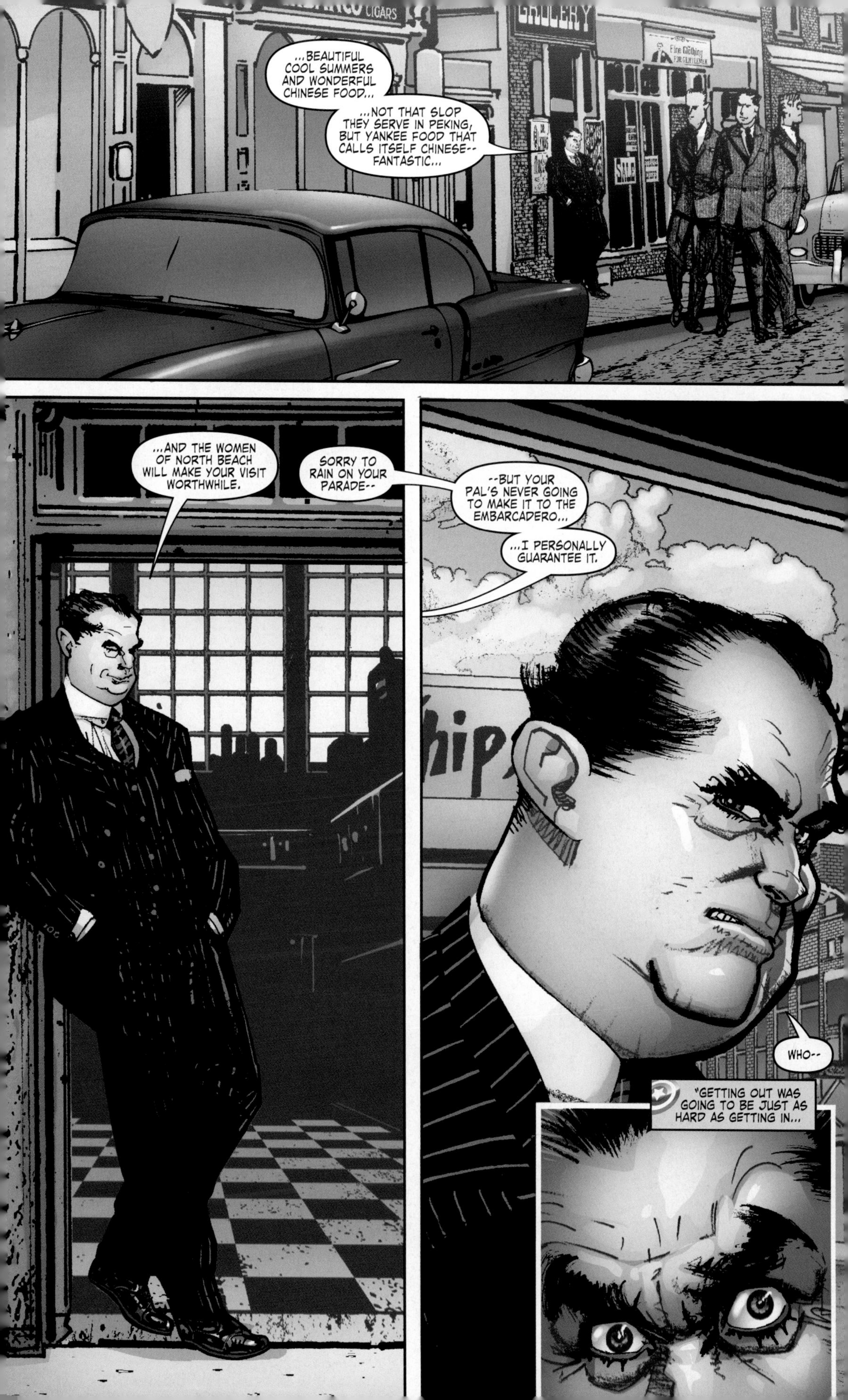
...BEAUTIFUL COOL SUMMERS AND WONDERFUL CHINESE FOOD...
...NOT THAT SLOP THEY SERVE IN PEKING, BUT YANKEE FOOD THAT CALLS ITSELF CHINESE--FANTASTIC...
...AND THE WOMEN OF NORTH BEACH WILL MAKE YOUR VISIT WORTHWHILE.
SORRY TO RAIN ON YOUR PARADE--
--BUT YOUR PAL'S NEVER GOING TO MAKE IT TO THE EMBARCADERO...
...I PERSONALLY GUARANTEE IT.
WHO--
"GETTING OUT WAS GOING TO BE JUST AS HARD AS GETTING IN...

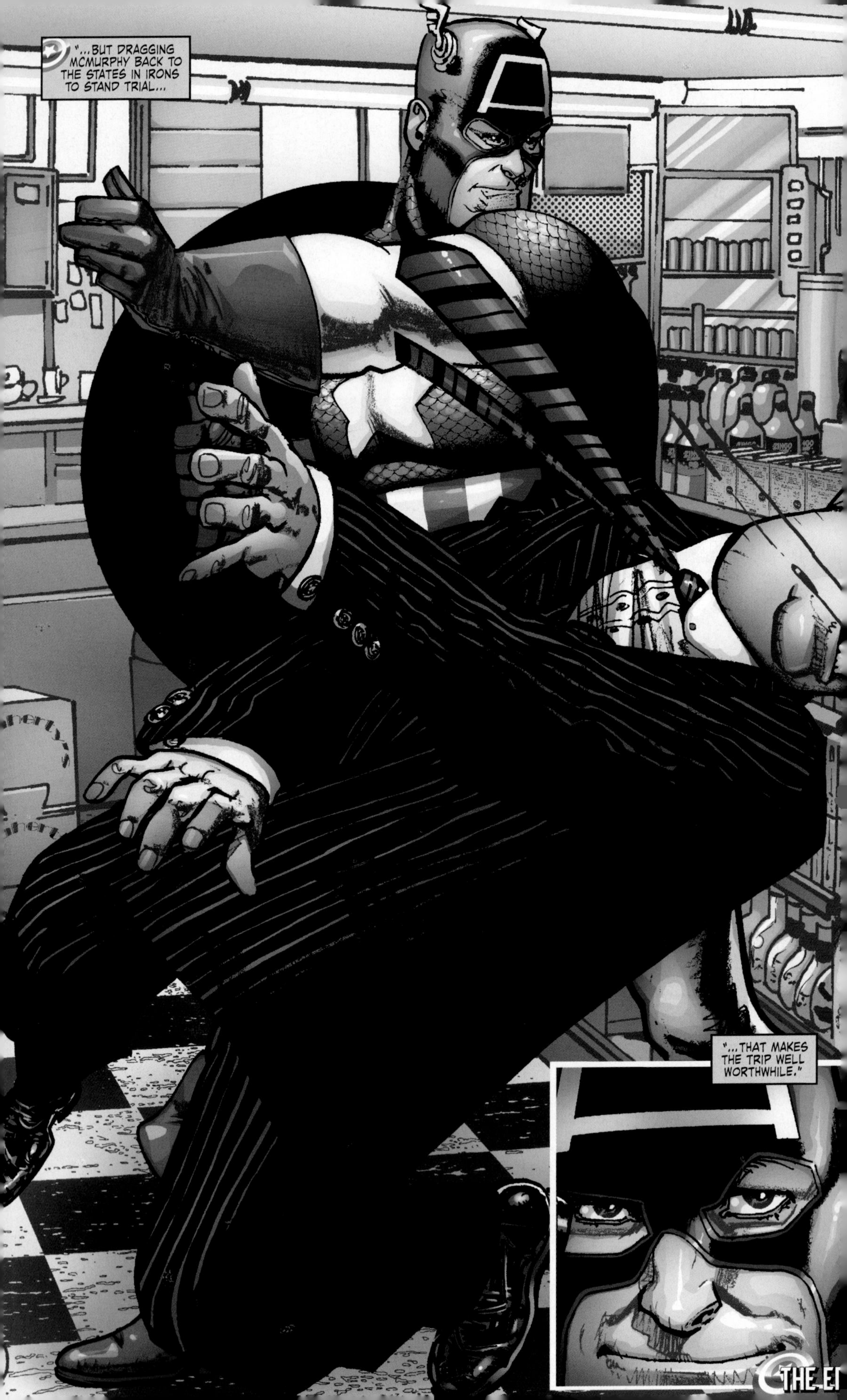
"...BUT DRAGGING MCMURPHY BACK TO THE STATES IN IRONS TO STAND TRIAL...
"...THAT MAKES THE TRIP WELL WORTHWHILE."

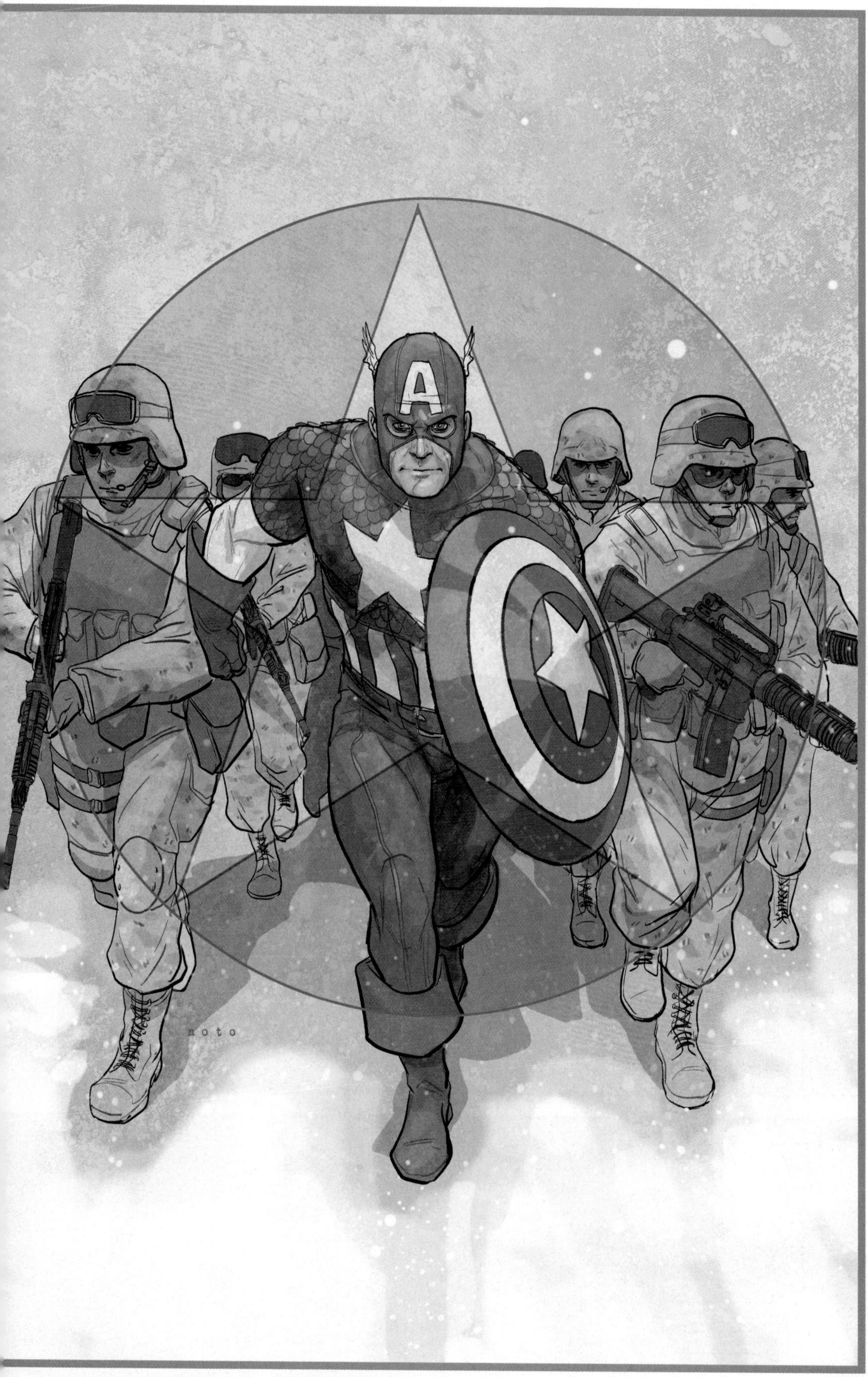
noto

TO SOLDIER ON

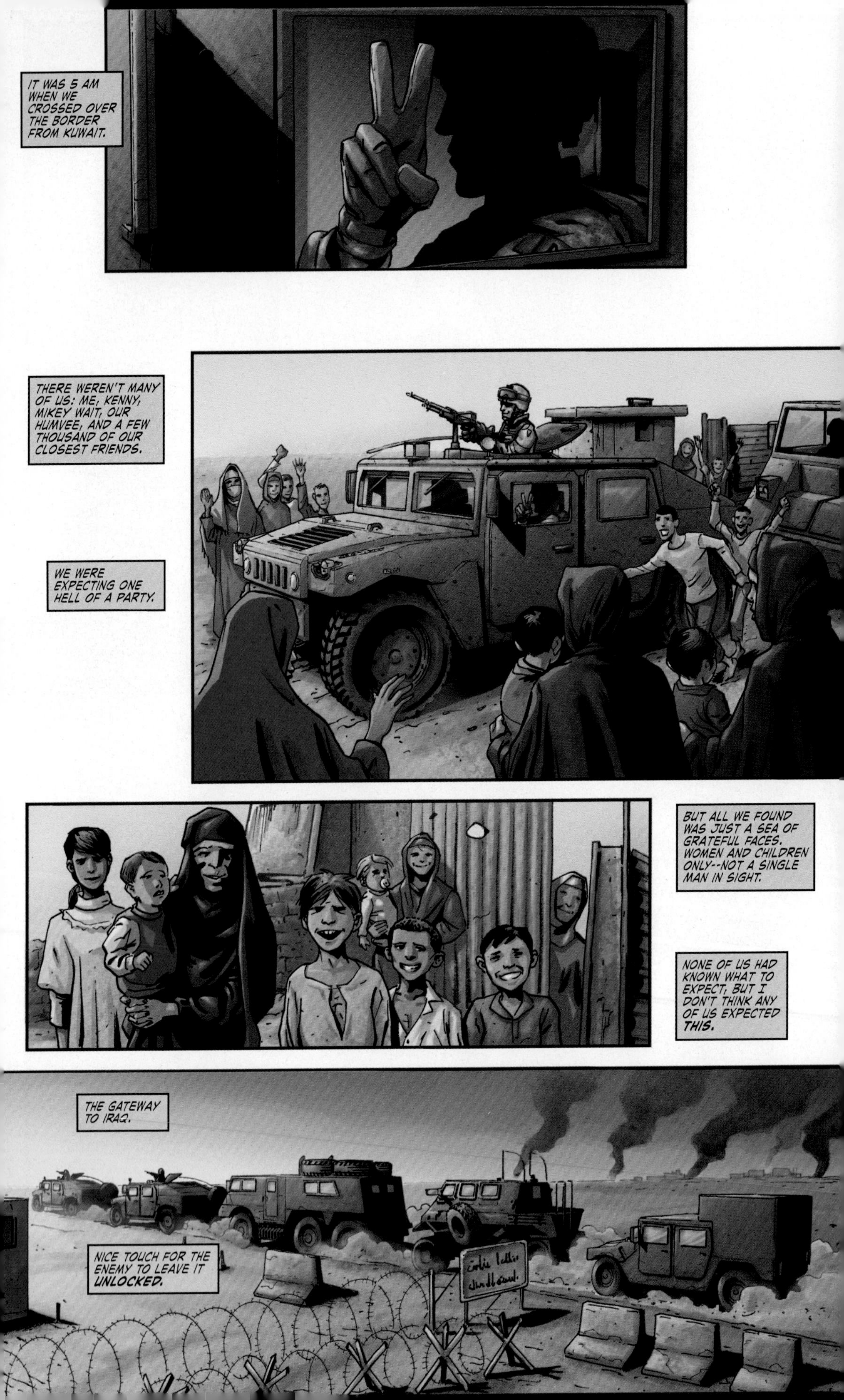
IT WAS 5 AM WHEN WE CROSSED OVER THE BORDER FROM KUWAIT.
THERE WEREN'T MANY OF US: ME, KENNY, MIKEY WAIT, OUR HUMVEE, AND A FEW THOUSAND OF OUR CLOSEST FRIENDS.
WE WERE EXPECTING ONE HELL OF A PARTY.
BUT ALL WE FOUND WAS JUST A SEA OF GRATEFUL FACES. WOMEN AND CHILDREN ONLY--NOT A SINGLE MAN IN SIGHT.
NONE OF US HAD KNOWN WHAT TO EXPECT, BUT I DON'T THINK ANY OF US EXPECTED **THIS.**
THE GATEWAY TO IRAQ.
NICE TOUCH FOR THE ENEMY TO LEAVE IT **UNLOCKED.**

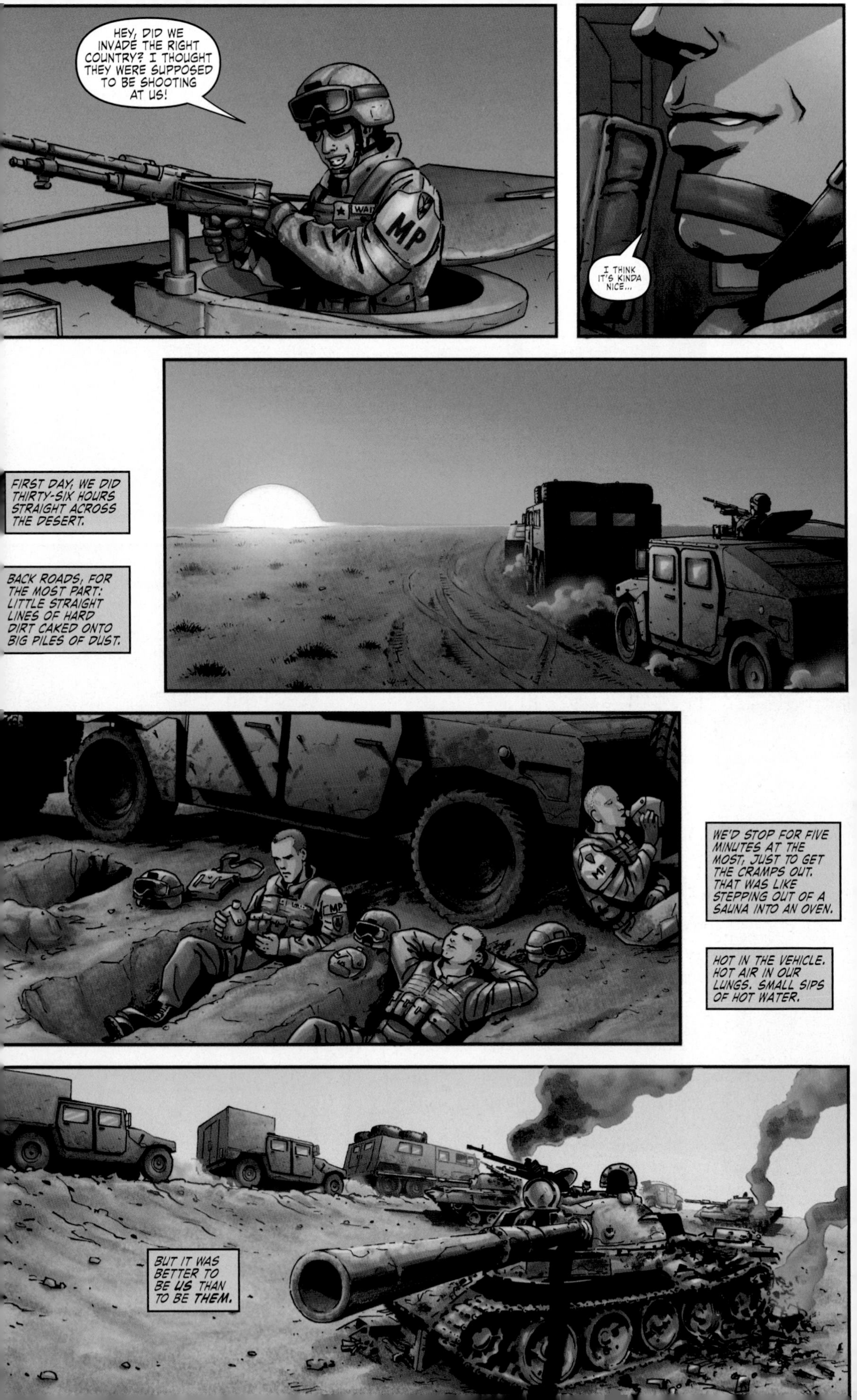
HEY, DID WE INVADE THE RIGHT COUNTRY? I THOUGHT THEY WERE SUPPOSED TO BE SHOOTING AT US!
I THINK IT'S KINDA NICE...
FIRST DAY, WE DID THIRTY-SIX HOURS STRAIGHT ACROSS THE DESERT.
BACK ROADS, FOR THE MOST PART: LITTLE STRAIGHT LINES OF HARD DIRT CAKED ONTO BIG PILES OF DUST.
WE'D STOP FOR FIVE MINUTES AT THE MOST, JUST TO GET THE CRAMPS OUT. THAT WAS LIKE STEPPING OUT OF A SAUNA INTO AN OVEN.
HOT IN THE VEHICLE. HOT AIR IN OUR LUNGS. SMALL SIPS OF HOT WATER.
BUT IT WAS BETTER TO BE US THAN TO BE THEM.

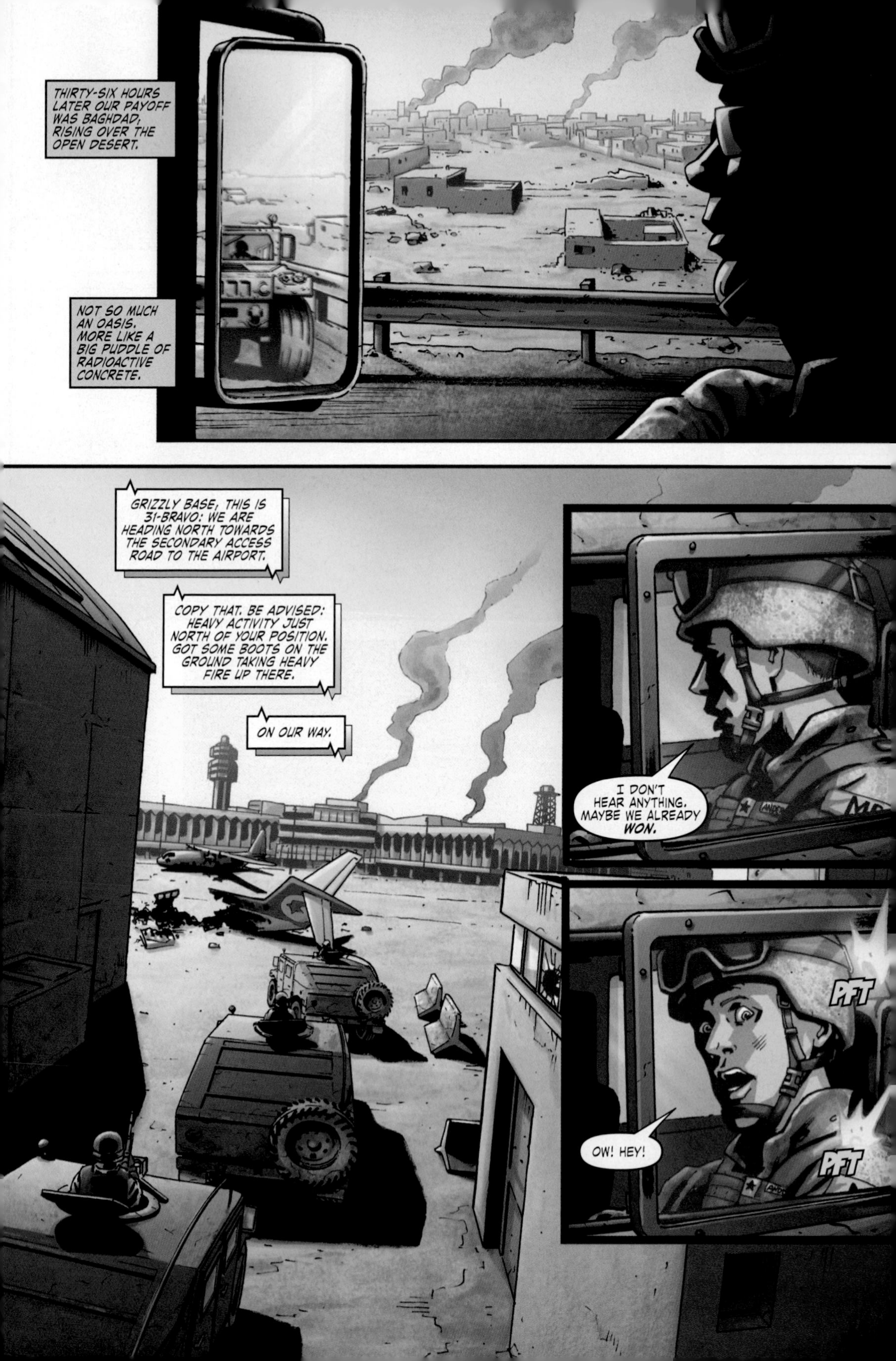
THIRTY-SIX HOURS LATER OUR PAYOFF WAS BAGHDAD, RISING OVER THE OPEN DESERT.
NOT SO MUCH AN OASIS. MORE LIKE A BIG PUDDLE OF RADIOACTIVE CONCRETE.
GRIZZLY BASE, THIS IS 31-BRAVO: WE ARE HEADING NORTH TOWARDS THE SECONDARY ACCESS ROAD TO THE AIRPORT.
COPY THAT. BE ADVISED: HEAVY ACTIVITY JUST NORTH OF YOUR POSITION. GOT SOME BOOTS ON THE GROUND TAKING HEAVY FIRE UP THERE.
ON OUR WAY.
I DON'T HEAR ANYTHING. MAYBE WE ALREADY WON.
PFT
OW! HEY!
PFT

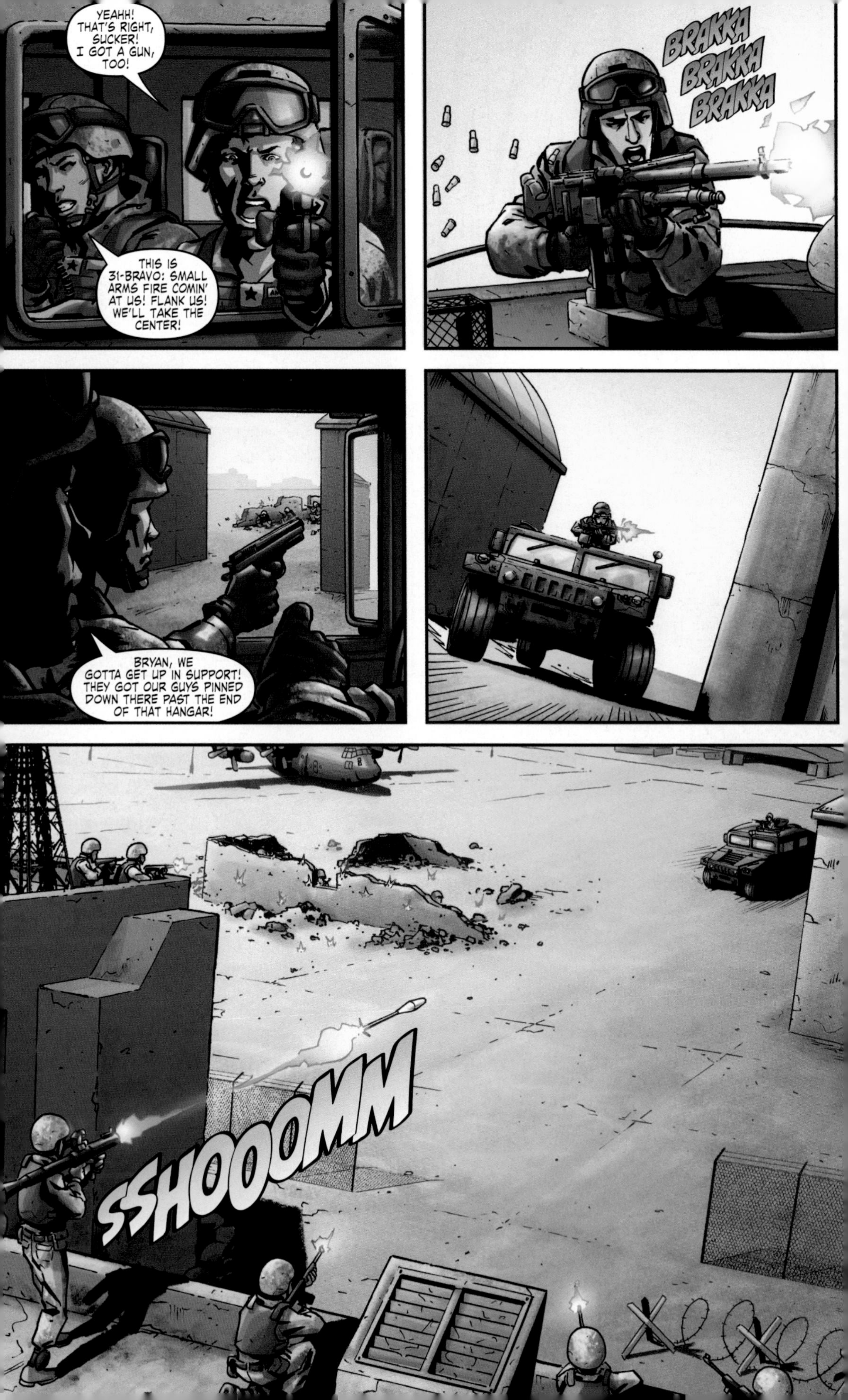
YEAHH! THAT'S RIGHT, SUCKER! I GOT A GUN, TOO!
THIS IS 31-BRAVO: SMALL ARMS FIRE COMIN' AT US! FLANK US! WE'LL TAKE THE CENTER!
BRAKKA BRAKKA BRAKKA
BRYAN, WE GOTTA GET UP IN SUPPORT! THEY GOT OUR GUYS PINNED DOWN THERE PAST THE END OF THAT HANGAR!
SSHOOOMM

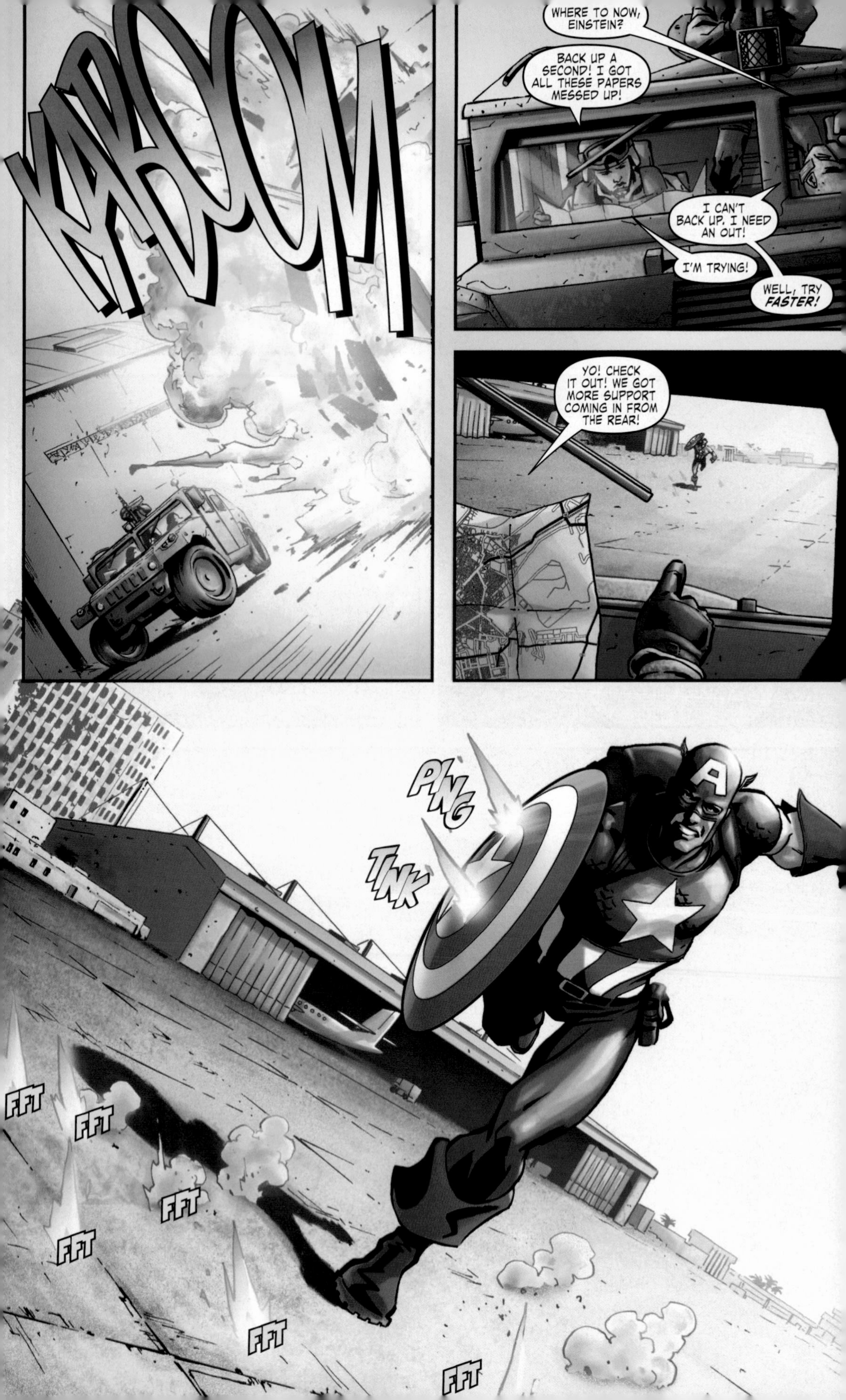
KABOOM
WHERE TO NOW, EINSTEIN?
BACK UP A SECOND! I GOT ALL THESE PAPERS MESSED UP!
I CAN'T BACK UP. I NEED AN OUT!
I'M TRYING!
WELL, TRY *FASTER!*
YO! CHECK IT OUT! WE GOT MORE SUPPORT COMING IN FROM THE REAR!
PING
TINK
FFT
FFT
FFT
FFT
FFT
FFT

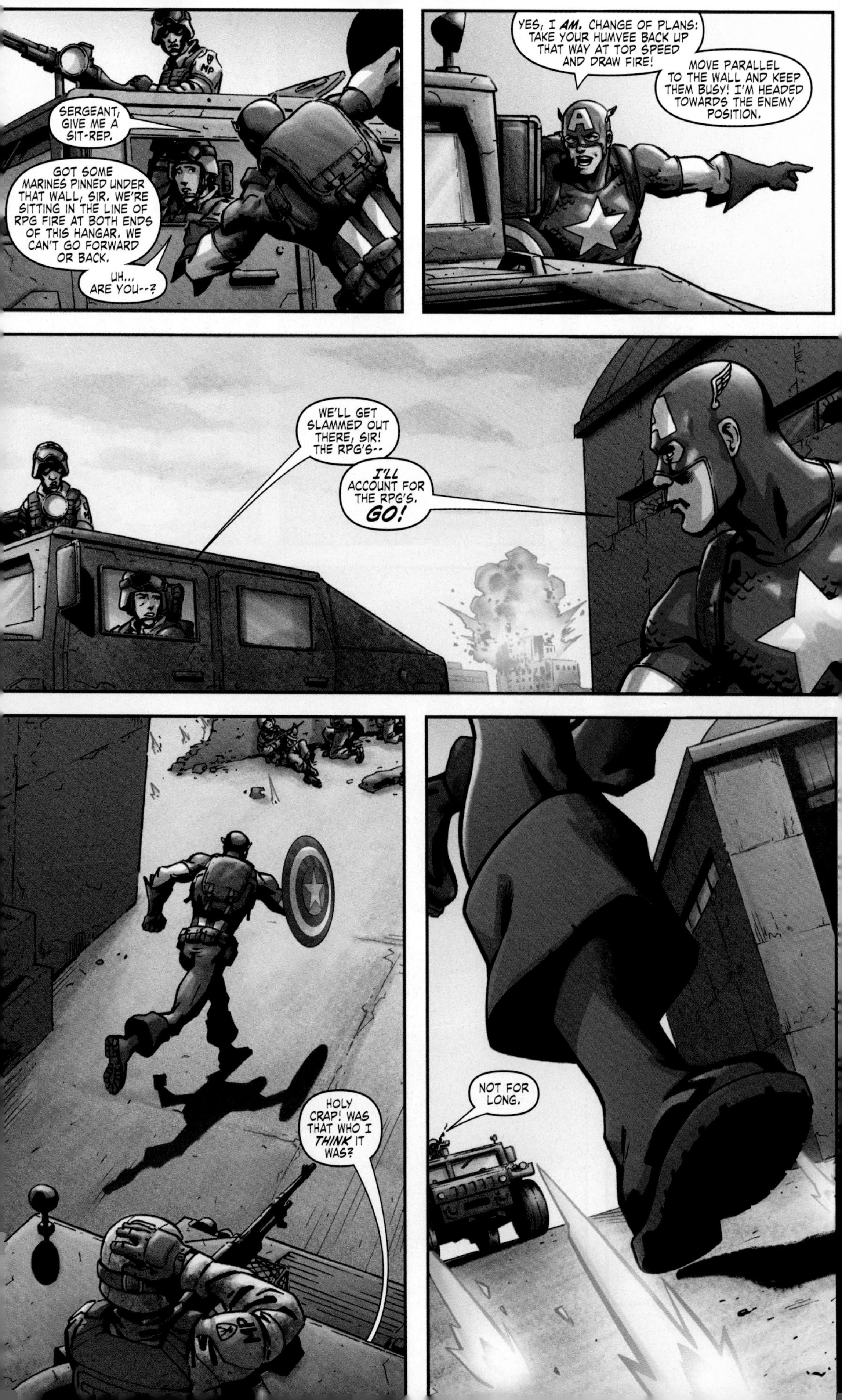

SERGEANT, GIVE ME A SIT-REP.
GOT SOME MARINES PINNED UNDER THAT WALL, SIR. WE'RE SITTING IN THE LINE OF RPG FIRE AT BOTH ENDS OF THIS HANGAR. WE CAN'T GO FORWARD OR BACK.
UH... ARE YOU--?
YES, I AM. CHANGE OF PLANS: TAKE YOUR HUMVEE BACK UP THAT WAY AT TOP SPEED AND DRAW FIRE!
MOVE PARALLEL TO THE WALL AND KEEP THEM BUSY! I'M HEADED TOWARDS THE ENEMY POSITION.
WE'LL GET SLAMMED OUT THERE, SIR! THE RPG'S--
I'LL ACCOUNT FOR THE RPG'S. GO!
HOLY CRAP! WAS THAT WHO I THINK IT WAS?
NOT FOR LONG.

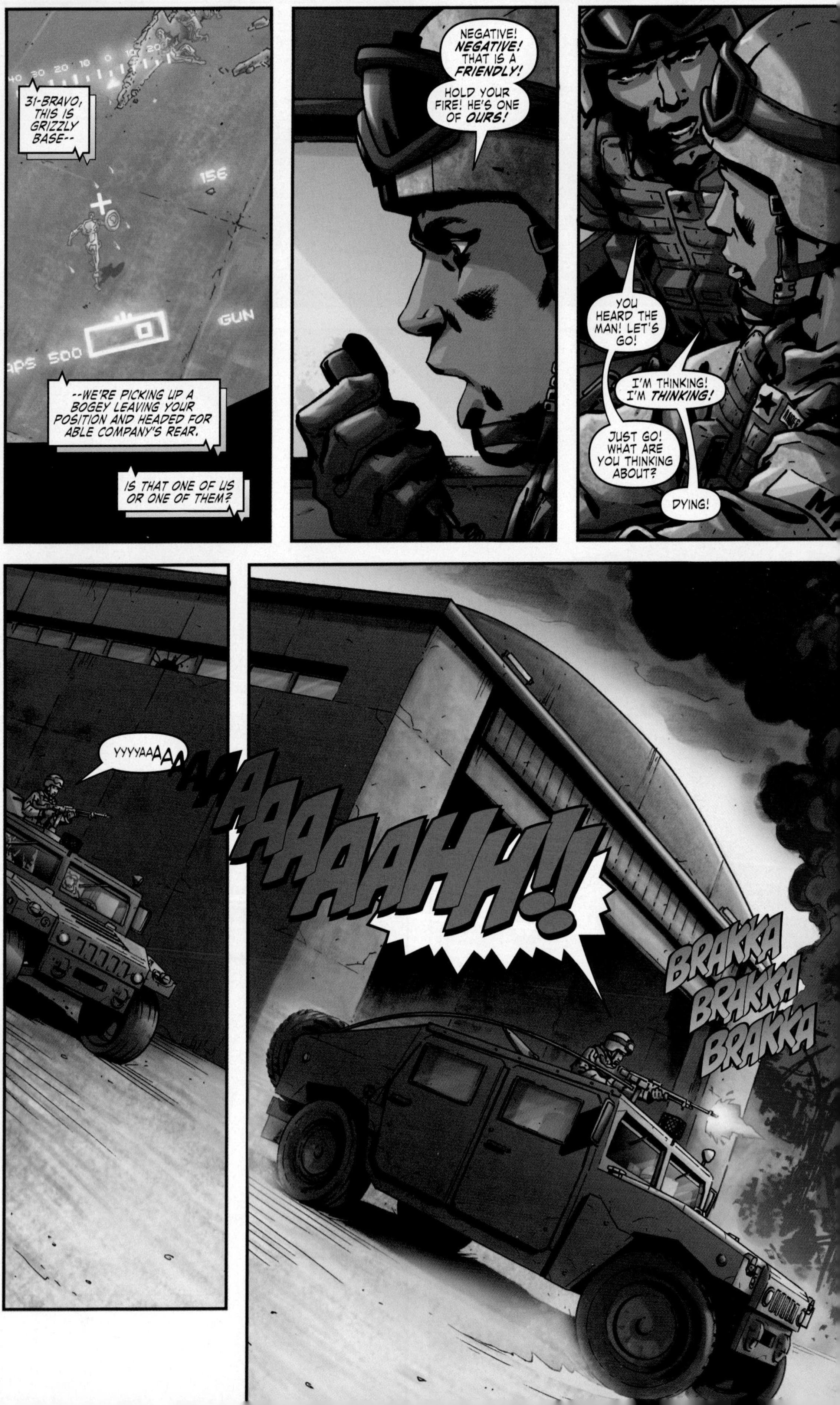

40 30 20 10 0 10 20
156
GUN
APS 500
31-BRAVO, THIS IS GRIZZLY BASE--
--WE'RE PICKING UP A BOGEY LEAVING YOUR POSITION AND HEADED FOR ABLE COMPANY'S REAR.
IS THAT ONE OF US OR ONE OF THEM?
NEGATIVE! NEGATIVE! THAT IS A FRIENDLY!
HOLD YOUR FIRE! HE'S ONE OF OURS!
YOU HEARD THE MAN! LET'S GO!
I'M THINKING! I'M THINKING!
JUST GO! WHAT ARE YOU THINKING ABOUT?
DYING!
YYYYAAAAAAAAAAAAHH!!
BRAKKA BRAKKA BRAKKA

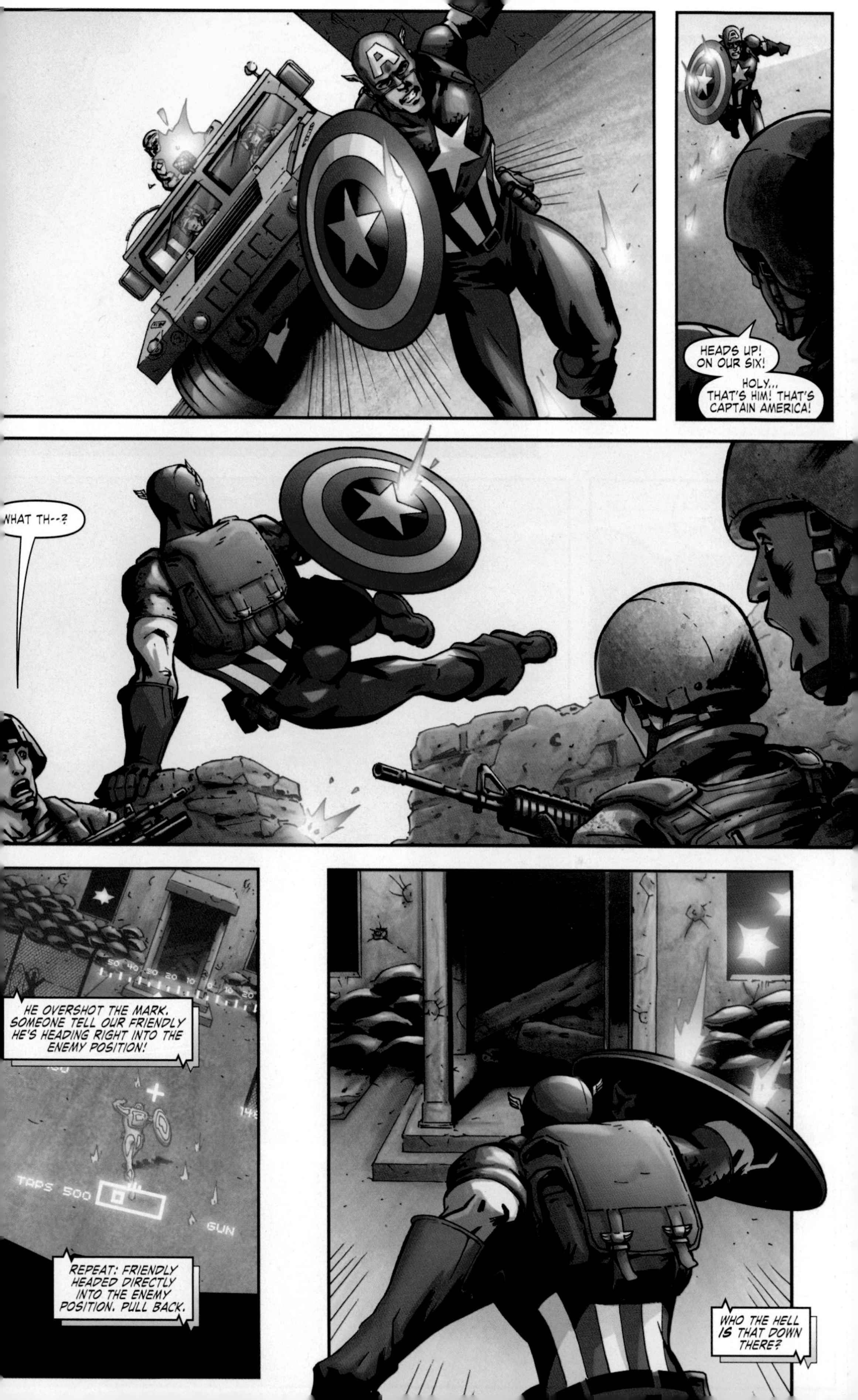
HEADS UP! ON OUR SIX!
HOLY... THAT'S HIM! THAT'S CAPTAIN AMERICA!
WHAT TH--?
HE OVERSHOT THE MARK. SOMEONE TELL OUR FRIENDLY HE'S HEADING RIGHT INTO THE ENEMY POSITION!
TAPS 500
GUN
REPEAT: FRIENDLY HEADED DIRECTLY INTO THE ENEMY POSITION. PULL BACK.
WHO THE HELL IS THAT DOWN THERE?

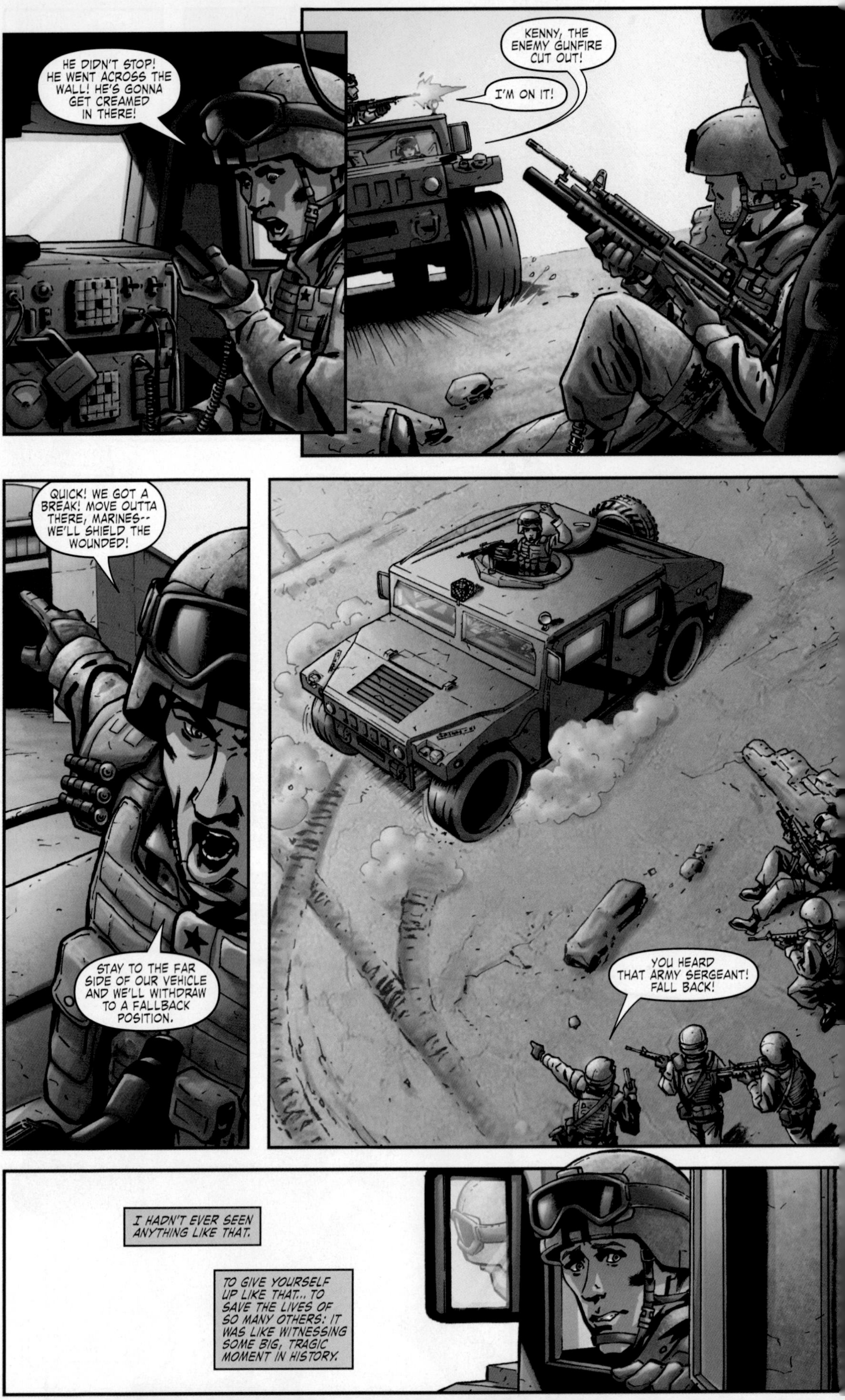

HE DIDN'T STOP! HE WENT ACROSS THE WALL! HE'S GONNA GET CREAMED IN THERE!
KENNY, THE ENEMY GUNFIRE CUT OUT!
I'M ON IT!
QUICK! WE GOT A BREAK! MOVE OUTTA THERE, MARINES-- WE'LL SHIELD THE WOUNDED!
STAY TO THE FAR SIDE OF OUR VEHICLE AND WE'LL WITHDRAW TO A FALLBACK POSITION.
YOU HEARD THAT ARMY SERGEANT! FALL BACK!
I HADN'T EVER SEEN ANYTHING LIKE THAT.
TO GIVE YOURSELF UP LIKE THAT... TO SAVE THE LIVES OF SO MANY OTHERS: IT WAS LIKE WITNESSING SOME BIG, TRAGIC MOMENT IN HISTORY.

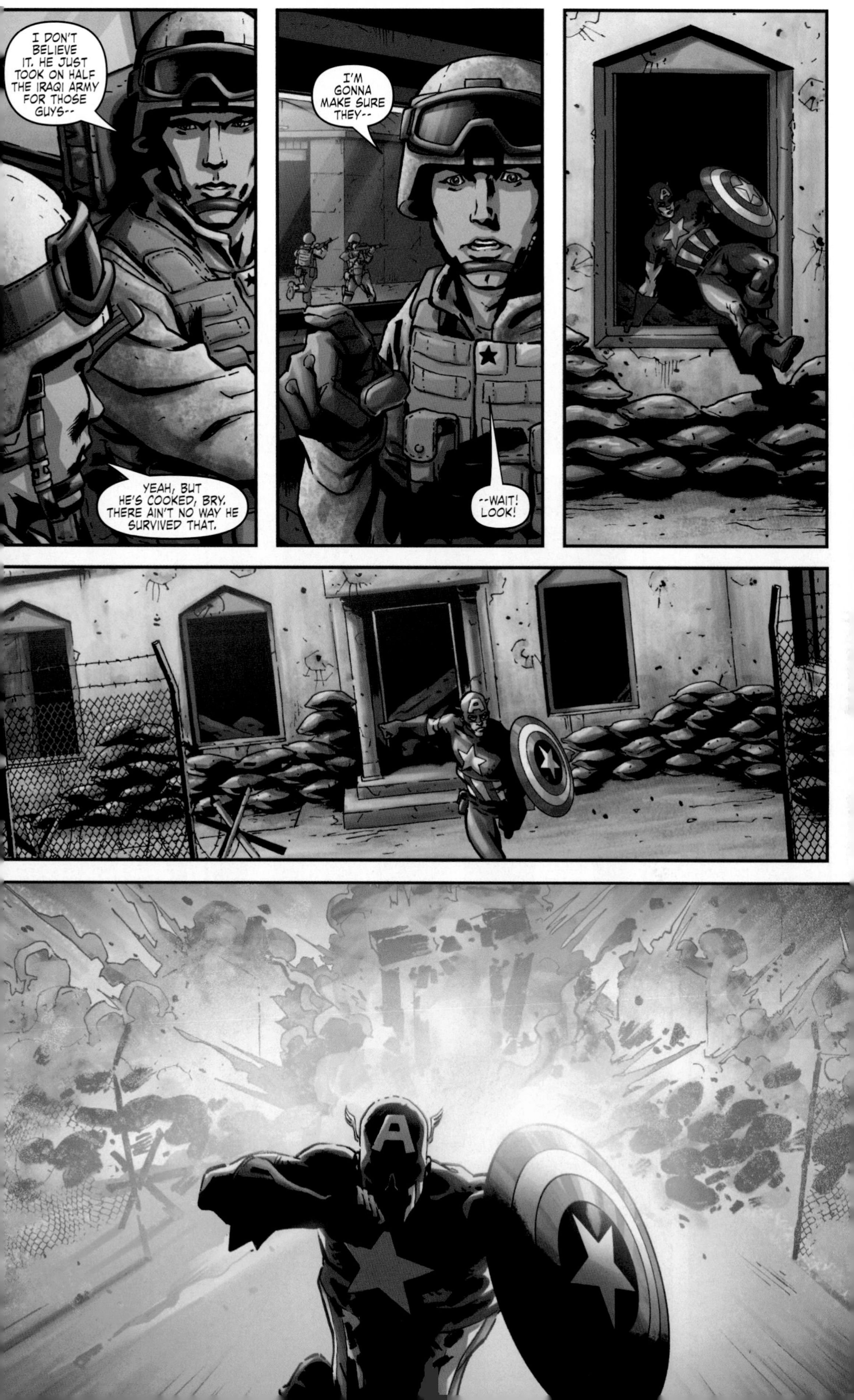
I DON'T BELIEVE IT. HE JUST TOOK ON HALF THE IRAQI ARMY FOR THOSE GUYS--
YEAH, BUT HE'S COOKED, BRY. THERE AIN'T NO WAY HE SURVIVED THAT.
I'M GONNA MAKE SURE THEY--
--WAIT! LOOK!

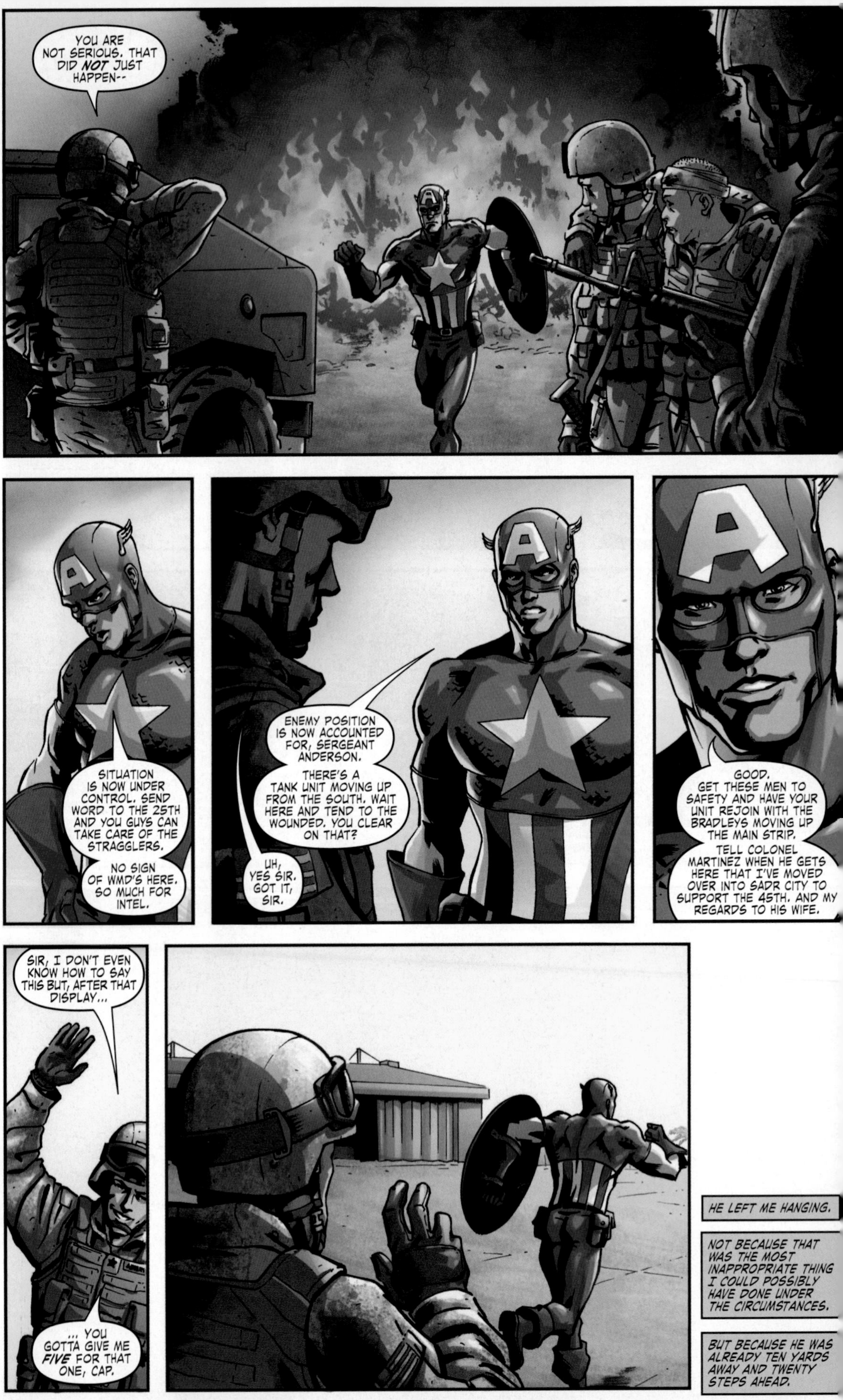
YOU ARE NOT SERIOUS. THAT DID NOT JUST HAPPEN--
SITUATION IS NOW UNDER CONTROL. SEND WORD TO THE 25TH AND YOU GUYS CAN TAKE CARE OF THE STRAGGLERS.
NO SIGN OF WMD'S HERE. SO MUCH FOR INTEL.
ENEMY POSITION IS NOW ACCOUNTED FOR, SERGEANT ANDERSON.
THERE'S A TANK UNIT MOVING UP FROM THE SOUTH. WAIT HERE AND TEND TO THE WOUNDED. YOU CLEAR ON THAT?
UH, YES SIR. GOT IT, SIR.
GOOD. GET THESE MEN TO SAFETY AND HAVE YOUR UNIT REJOIN WITH THE BRADLEYS MOVING UP THE MAIN STRIP.
TELL COLONEL MARTINEZ WHEN HE GETS HERE THAT I'VE MOVED OVER INTO SADR CITY TO SUPPORT THE 45TH. AND MY REGARDS TO HIS WIFE.
SIR, I DON'T EVEN KNOW HOW TO SAY THIS BUT, AFTER THAT DISPLAY...
... YOU GOTTA GIVE ME FIVE FOR THAT ONE, CAP.
HE LEFT ME HANGING.
NOT BECAUSE THAT WAS THE MOST INAPPROPRIATE THING I COULD POSSIBLY HAVE DONE UNDER THE CIRCUMSTANCES.
BUT BECAUSE HE WAS ALREADY TEN YARDS AWAY AND TWENTY STEPS AHEAD.

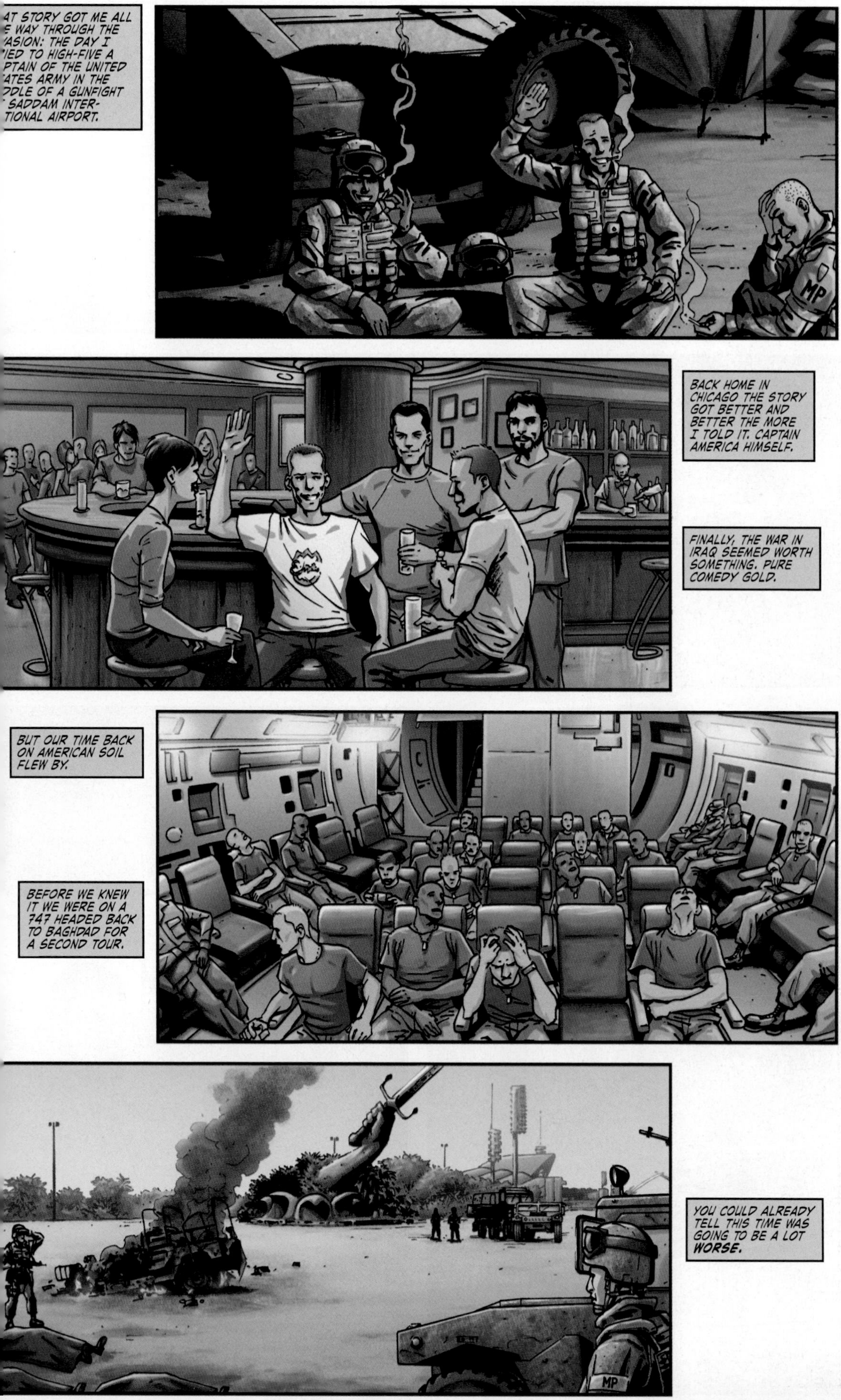
AT STORY GOT ME ALL E WAY THROUGH THE VASION: THE DAY I IED TO HIGH-FIVE A PTAIN OF THE UNITED ATES ARMY IN THE DDLE OF A GUNFIGHT SADDAM INTER-TIONAL AIRPORT.
BACK HOME IN CHICAGO THE STORY GOT BETTER AND BETTER THE MORE I TOLD IT. CAPTAIN AMERICA HIMSELF.
FINALLY, THE WAR IN IRAQ SEEMED WORTH SOMETHING. PURE COMEDY GOLD.
BUT OUR TIME BACK ON AMERICAN SOIL FLEW BY.
BEFORE WE KNEW IT WE WERE ON A 747 HEADED BACK TO BAGHDAD FOR A SECOND TOUR.
YOU COULD ALREADY TELL THIS TIME WAS GOING TO BE A LOT WORSE.

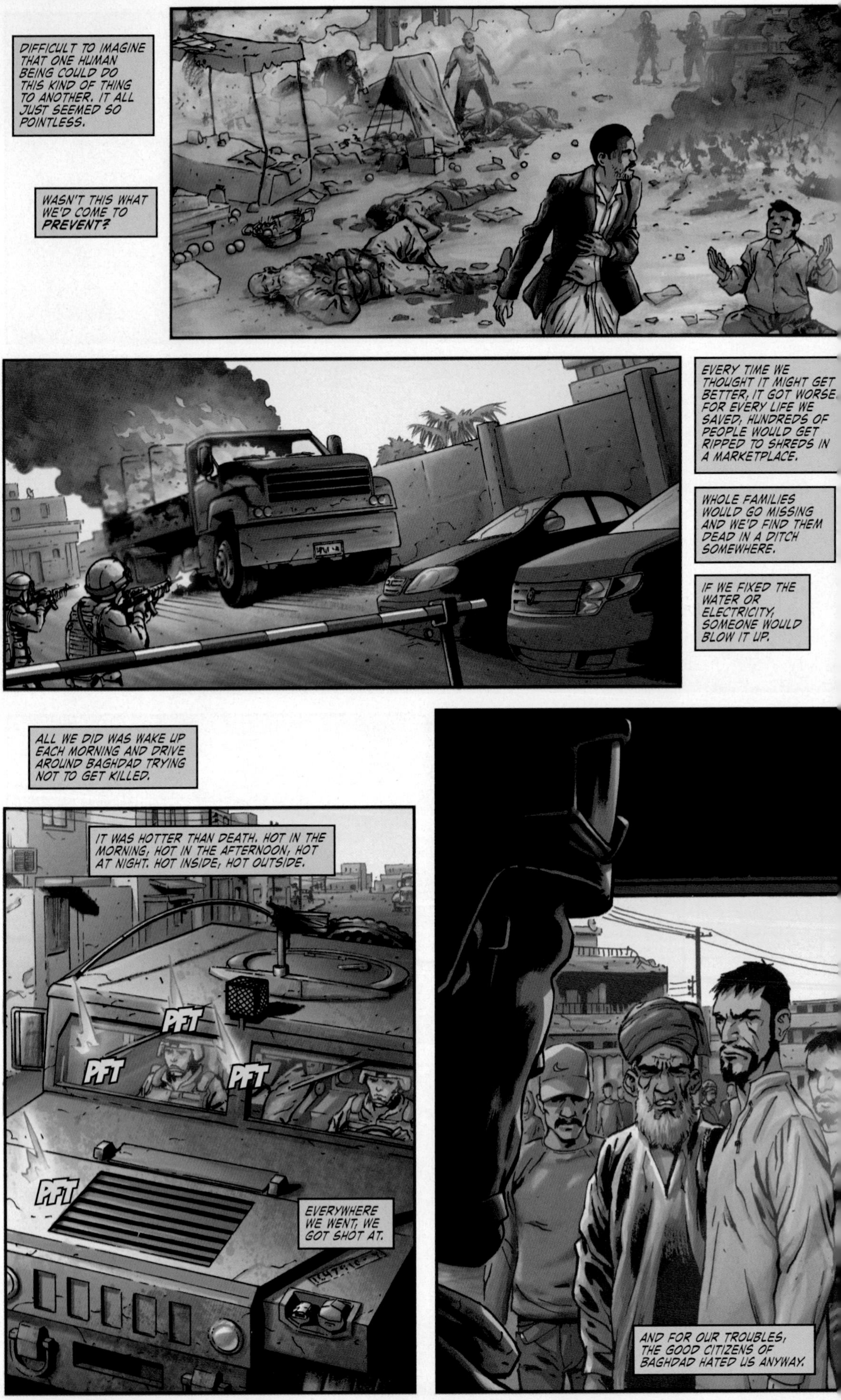
DIFFICULT TO IMAGINE THAT ONE HUMAN BEING COULD DO THIS KIND OF THING TO ANOTHER. IT ALL JUST SEEMED SO POINTLESS.
WASN'T THIS WHAT WE'D COME TO PREVENT?
EVERY TIME WE THOUGHT IT MIGHT GET BETTER, IT GOT WORSE. FOR EVERY LIFE WE SAVED, HUNDREDS OF PEOPLE WOULD GET RIPPED TO SHREDS IN A MARKETPLACE.
WHOLE FAMILIES WOULD GO MISSING AND WE'D FIND THEM DEAD IN A DITCH SOMEWHERE.
IF WE FIXED THE WATER OR ELECTRICITY, SOMEONE WOULD BLOW IT UP.
ALL WE DID WAS WAKE UP EACH MORNING AND DRIVE AROUND BAGHDAD TRYING NOT TO GET KILLED.
IT WAS HOTTER THAN DEATH. HOT IN THE MORNING, HOT IN THE AFTERNOON, HOT AT NIGHT. HOT INSIDE, HOT OUTSIDE.
PFT
PFT
PFT
PFT
EVERYWHERE WE WENT, WE GOT SHOT AT.
AND FOR OUR TROUBLES, THE GOOD CITIZENS OF BAGHDAD HATED US ANYWAY.

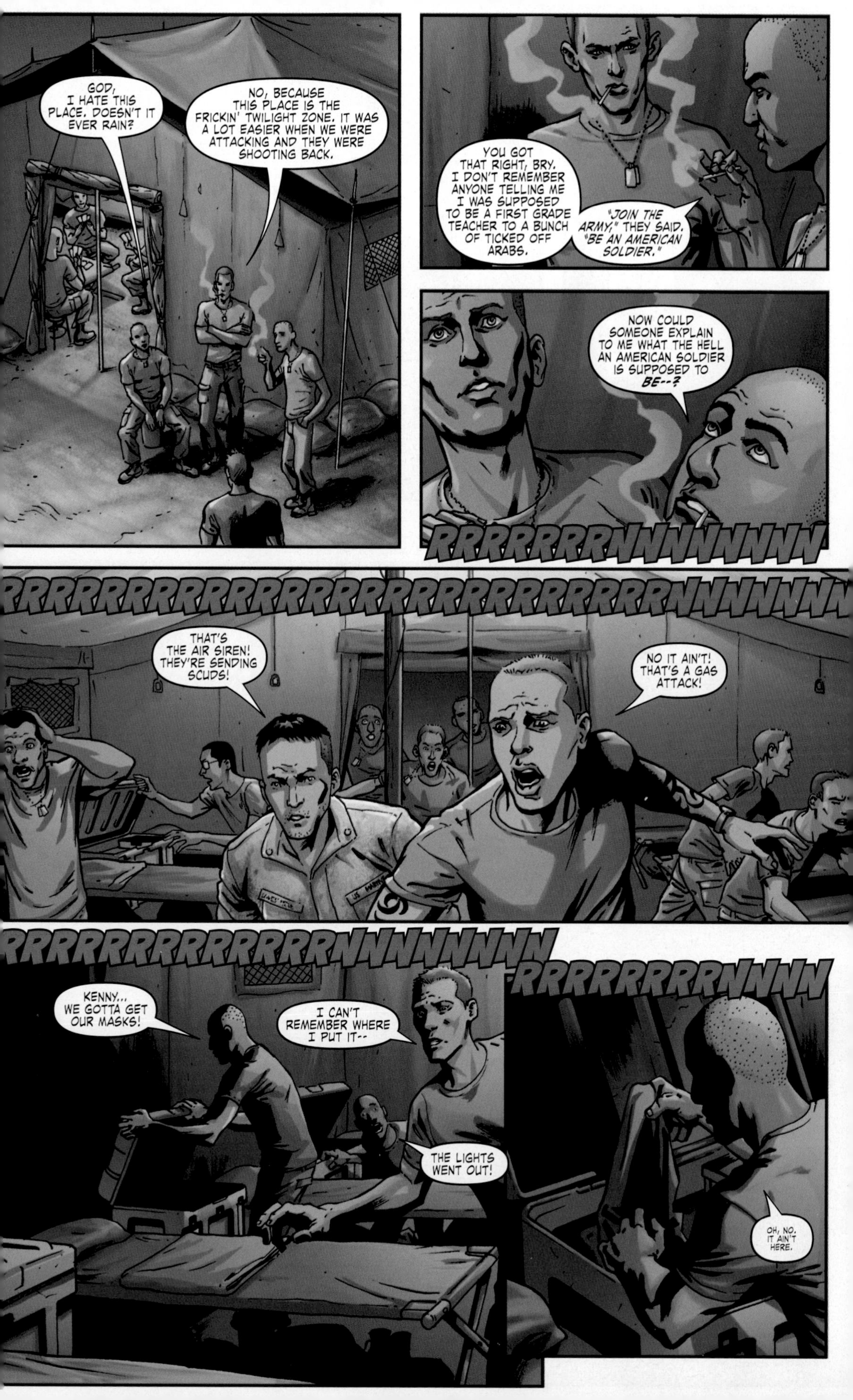
GOD, I HATE THIS PLACE. DOESN'T IT EVER RAIN?
NO, BECAUSE THIS PLACE IS THE FRICKIN' TWILIGHT ZONE. IT WAS A LOT EASIER WHEN WE WERE ATTACKING AND THEY WERE SHOOTING BACK.
YOU GOT THAT RIGHT, BRY. I DON'T REMEMBER ANYONE TELLING ME I WAS SUPPOSED TO BE A FIRST GRADE TEACHER TO A BUNCH OF TICKED OFF ARABS.
"JOIN THE ARMY," THEY SAID. "BE AN AMERICAN SOLDIER."
NOW COULD SOMEONE EXPLAIN TO ME WHAT THE HELL AN AMERICAN SOLDIER IS SUPPOSED TO BE--?
RRRRRRRNNNNNNNN
RRRRRRRRRRRRRRRRRRRRRRRRRNNNNNNN
THAT'S THE AIR SIREN! THEY'RE SENDING SCUDS!
NO IT AIN'T! THAT'S A GAS ATTACK!
RRRRRRRRRRRRRRNNNNNNNN
RRRRRRRRRNNNNN
KENNY... WE GOTTA GET OUR MASKS!
I CAN'T REMEMBER WHERE I PUT IT--
THE LIGHTS WENT OUT!
OH, NO. IT AIN'T HERE.

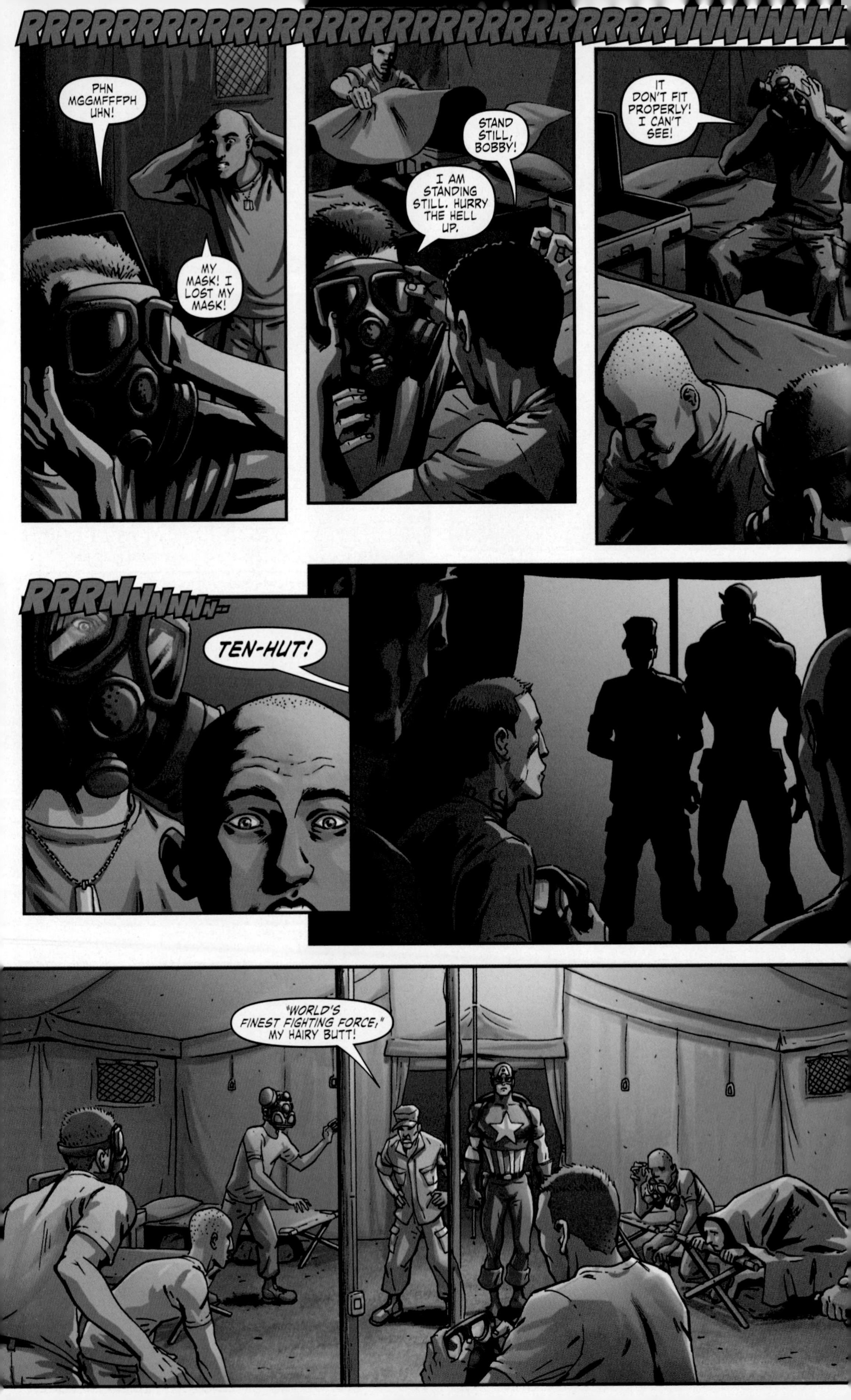
RRRRRRRRRRRRRRRRRRRRRRRRRRRRRNNNNNNNNN
PHN MGGMFFFPH UHN!
MY MASK! I LOST MY MASK!
STAND STILL, BOBBY!
I AM STANDING STILL. HURRY THE HELL UP.
IT DON'T FIT PROPERLY! I CAN'T SEE!
RRRNNNNNN--
TEN-HUT!
"WORLD'S FINEST FIGHTING FORCE," MY HAIRY BUTT!

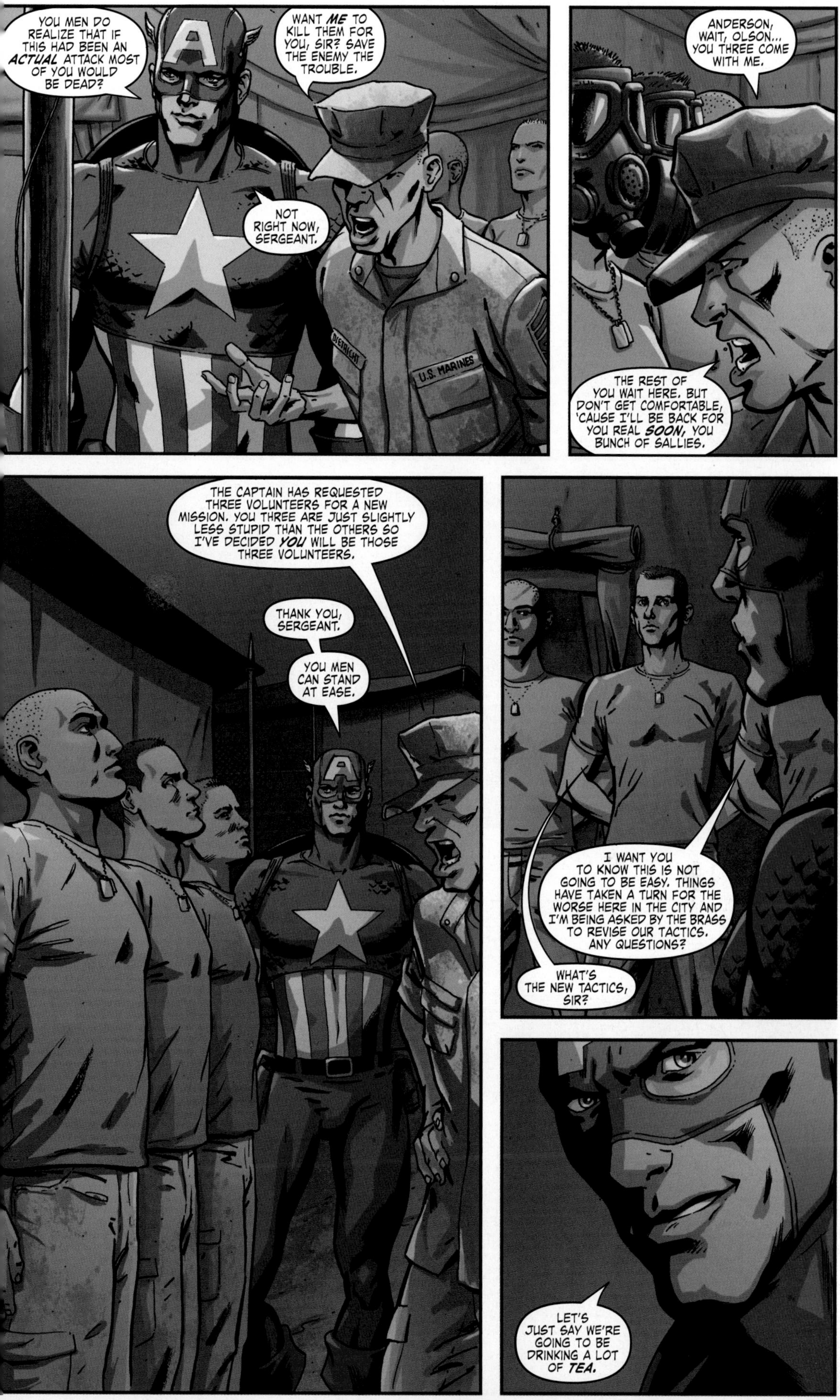
YOU MEN DO REALIZE THAT IF THIS HAD BEEN AN ACTUAL ATTACK MOST OF YOU WOULD BE DEAD?
WANT ME TO KILL THEM FOR YOU, SIR? SAVE THE ENEMY THE TROUBLE.
NOT RIGHT NOW, SERGEANT.
DIETRICHT
U.S. MARINES
ANDERSON, WAIT, OLSON... YOU THREE COME WITH ME.
THE REST OF YOU WAIT HERE. BUT DON'T GET COMFORTABLE, 'CAUSE I'LL BE BACK FOR YOU REAL SOON, YOU BUNCH OF SALLIES.
THE CAPTAIN HAS REQUESTED THREE VOLUNTEERS FOR A NEW MISSION. YOU THREE ARE JUST SLIGHTLY LESS STUPID THAN THE OTHERS SO I'VE DECIDED YOU WILL BE THOSE THREE VOLUNTEERS.
THANK YOU, SERGEANT.
YOU MEN CAN STAND AT EASE.
I WANT YOU TO KNOW THIS IS NOT GOING TO BE EASY. THINGS HAVE TAKEN A TURN FOR THE WORSE HERE IN THE CITY AND I'M BEING ASKED BY THE BRASS TO REVISE OUR TACTICS. ANY QUESTIONS?
WHAT'S THE NEW TACTICS, SIR?
LET'S JUST SAY WE'RE GOING TO BE DRINKING A LOT OF TEA.

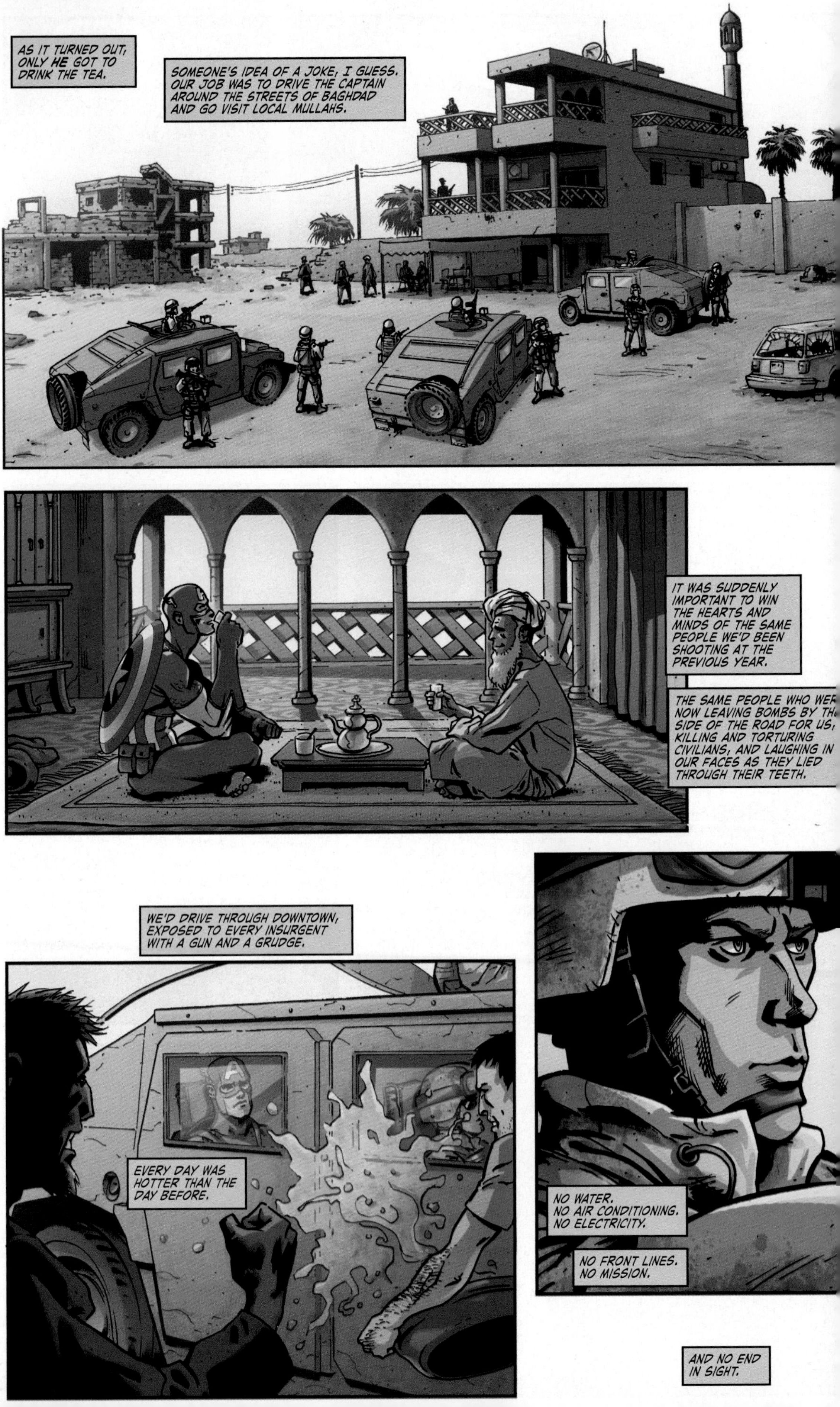
AS IT TURNED OUT, ONLY HE GOT TO DRINK THE TEA.
SOMEONE'S IDEA OF A JOKE, I GUESS. OUR JOB WAS TO DRIVE THE CAPTAIN AROUND THE STREETS OF BAGHDAD AND GO VISIT LOCAL MULLAHS.
IT WAS SUDDENLY IMPORTANT TO WIN THE HEARTS AND MINDS OF THE SAME PEOPLE WE'D BEEN SHOOTING AT THE PREVIOUS YEAR.
THE SAME PEOPLE WHO WER NOW LEAVING BOMBS BY TH SIDE OF THE ROAD FOR US, KILLING AND TORTURING CIVILIANS, AND LAUGHING IN OUR FACES AS THEY LIED THROUGH THEIR TEETH.
WE'D DRIVE THROUGH DOWNTOWN, EXPOSED TO EVERY INSURGENT WITH A GUN AND A GRUDGE.
EVERY DAY WAS HOTTER THAN THE DAY BEFORE.
NO WATER. NO AIR CONDITIONING. NO ELECTRICITY.
NO FRONT LINES. NO MISSION.
AND NO END IN SIGHT.

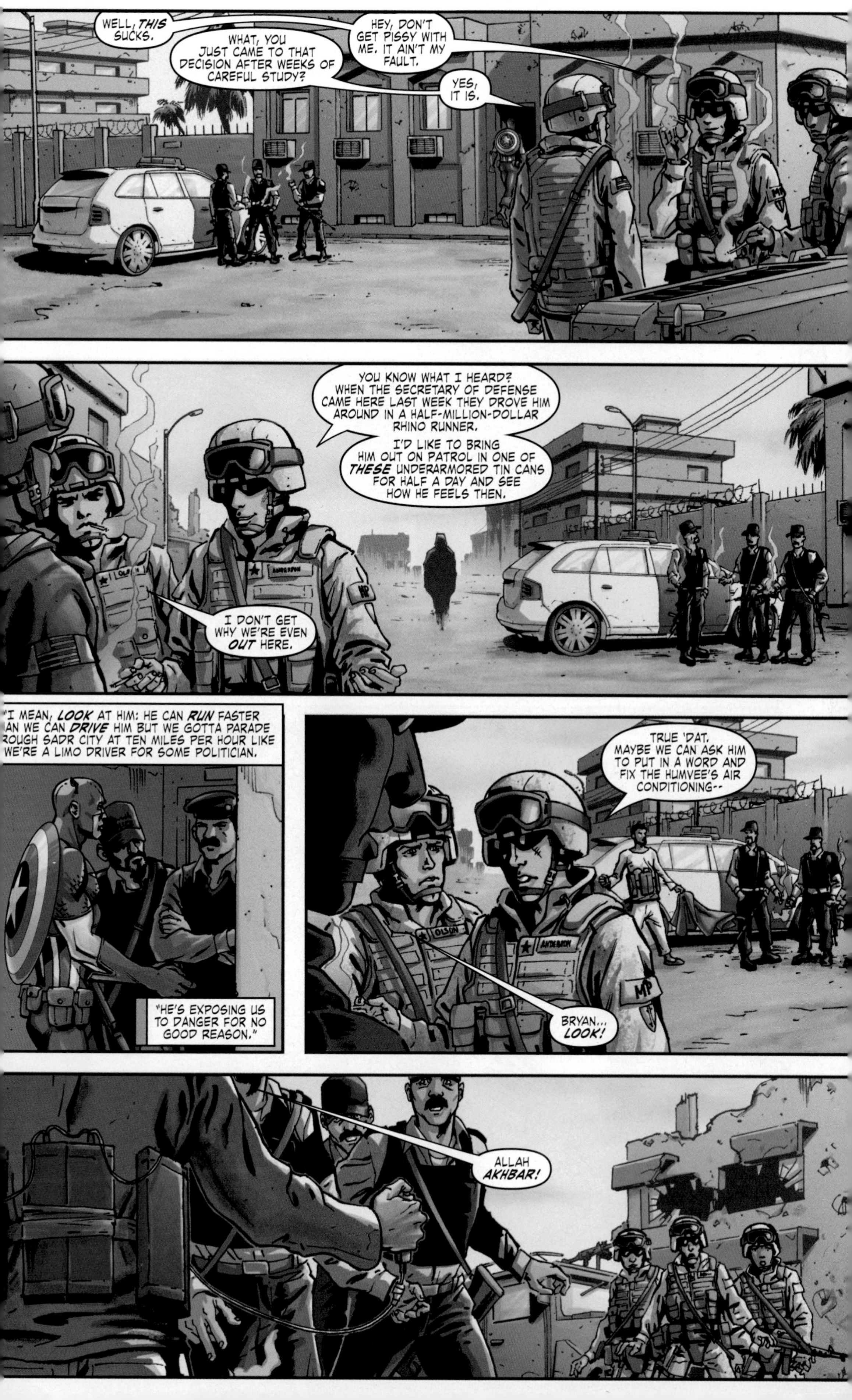
WELL, THIS SUCKS.
HEY, DON'T GET PISSY WITH ME. IT AIN'T MY FAULT.
WHAT, YOU JUST CAME TO THAT DECISION AFTER WEEKS OF CAREFUL STUDY?
YES, IT IS.
YOU KNOW WHAT I HEARD? WHEN THE SECRETARY OF DEFENSE CAME HERE LAST WEEK THEY DROVE HIM AROUND IN A HALF-MILLION-DOLLAR RHINO RUNNER.
I'D LIKE TO BRING HIM OUT ON PATROL IN ONE OF THESE UNDERARMORED TIN CANS FOR HALF A DAY AND SEE HOW HE FEELS THEN.
I DON'T GET WHY WE'RE EVEN OUT HERE.
"I MEAN, LOOK AT HIM: HE CAN RUN FASTER IAN WE CAN DRIVE HIM BUT WE GOTTA PARADE ROUGH SADR CITY AT TEN MILES PER HOUR LIKE WE'RE A LIMO DRIVER FOR SOME POLITICIAN.
"HE'S EXPOSING US TO DANGER FOR NO GOOD REASON."
TRUE 'DAT. MAYBE WE CAN ASK HIM TO PUT IN A WORD AND FIX THE HUMVEE'S AIR CONDITIONING--
BRYAN... LOOK!
ALLAH AKHBAR!

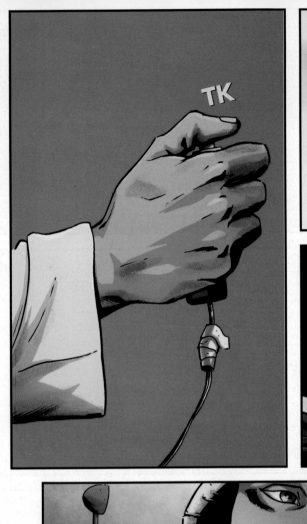

TK

ALLAH...

...UH...

...ALLAH AKHBAR...

IT DIDN'T GO OFF.

HOLY #@%! NOW WHAT?

NOW WE SIT BACK AN' WATCH THE IRAQI POLICE FORCE SHOW US EVERYTHING THEY'VE LEARNED.

THE IRAQIS BEAT THE GUY UNTIL HIS FACE WAS UNRECOGNIZABLE. I MEAN, SO BAD THAT HE DIDN'T EVEN LOOK HUMAN.

CAP WENT BERSERK BECAUSE WE DIDN'T TRY TO STOP THEM. AND THEN HE MADE US DRIVE BACK THROUGH THE SADR GAUNTLET JUST TO PUT ON A SHOW OF FORCE.

FRICKING BOY SCOUT! LIKE WE SHOULD HAVE HELPED SOME GUY WHO JUST TRIED TO BLOW US TO PIECES--

CAREFUL, KENNY, HE'S GOT BIONIC EARS.

THIS IS RIDICULOUS. WE AIN'T GETTIN' *NOWHERE* OUT HERE LIKE THIS.

EVERY TIME WE COME OUT THEY RESENT IT MORE AN' MORE. WE SHOULD JUST GO HOME AN' LET THEM PUT EACH OTHER OUT OF THE WORLD'S MISERY.

I SWEAR, BRY... I THOUGHT WE WERE DEAD FOR *SURE*. WHY DIDN'T IT GO *OFF*, D'YOU THINK?

I DUNNO. *LUCKY*, I GUESS.

FLIK FLIK

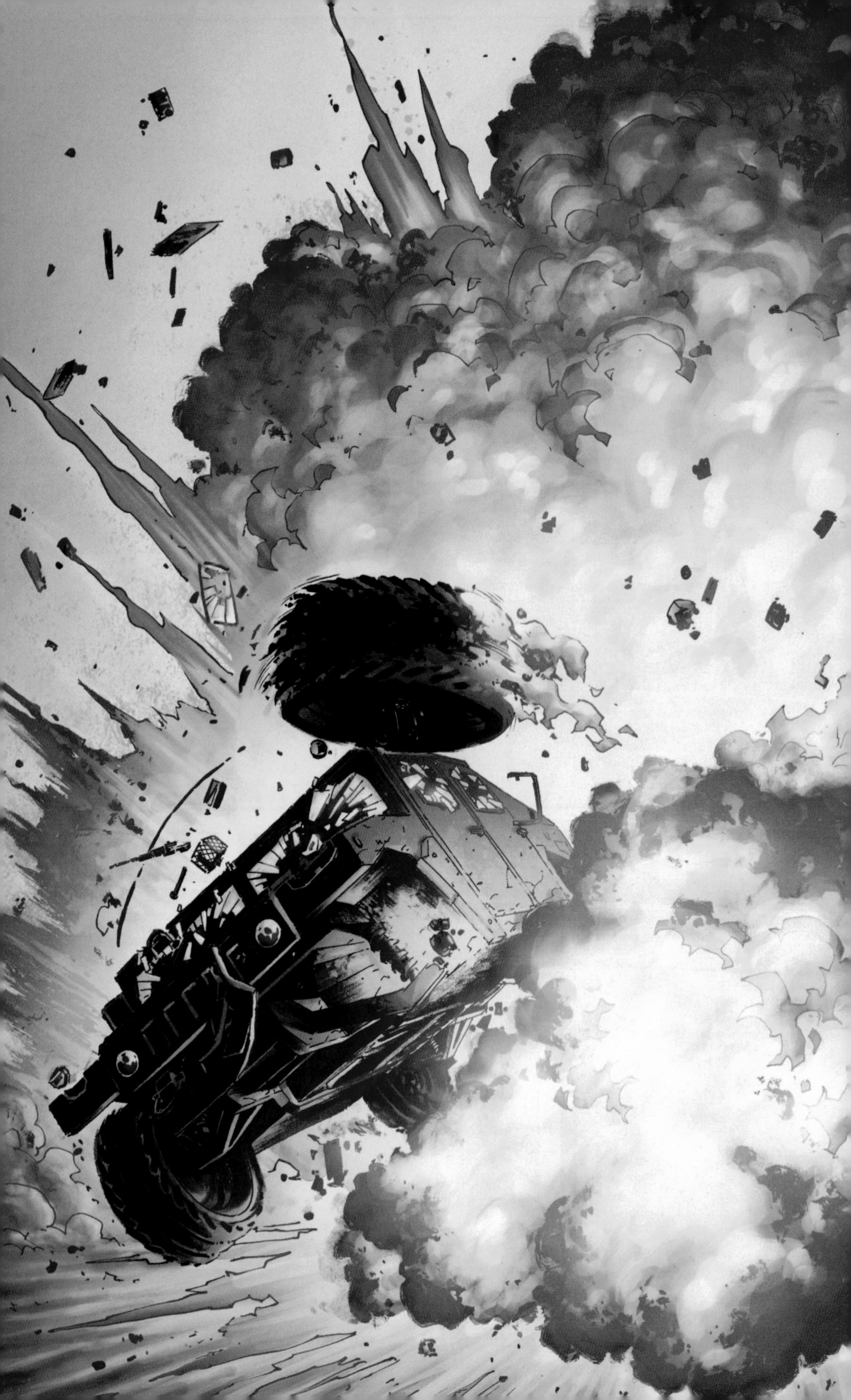

I REMEMBER SEEING GREEN.

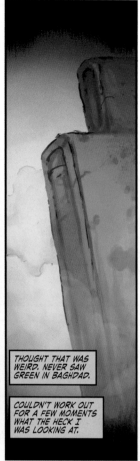

THOUGHT THAT WAS WEIRD. NEVER SAW GREEN IN BAGHDAD.

COULDN'T WORK OUT FOR A FEW MOMENTS WHAT THE HECK I WAS LOOKING AT.

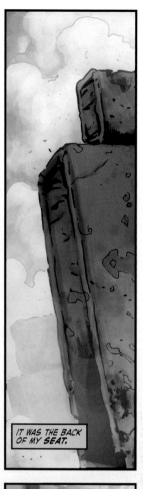

IT WAS THE BACK OF MY *SEAT.*

ξKAFFξ... OHH...GOD, BRYAN...YOU THERE...?

YEAH, I THINK I HURT MY THUMB.

MIKEY, YOU THERE? MIKEY?

UHH...

I HAD BLOOD ON MY FACE. I REMEMBER I WENT TO WIPE IT OFF, AND *MISSED.*

THAT'S HOW I FOUND OUT MY RIGHT HAND WAS MISSING.

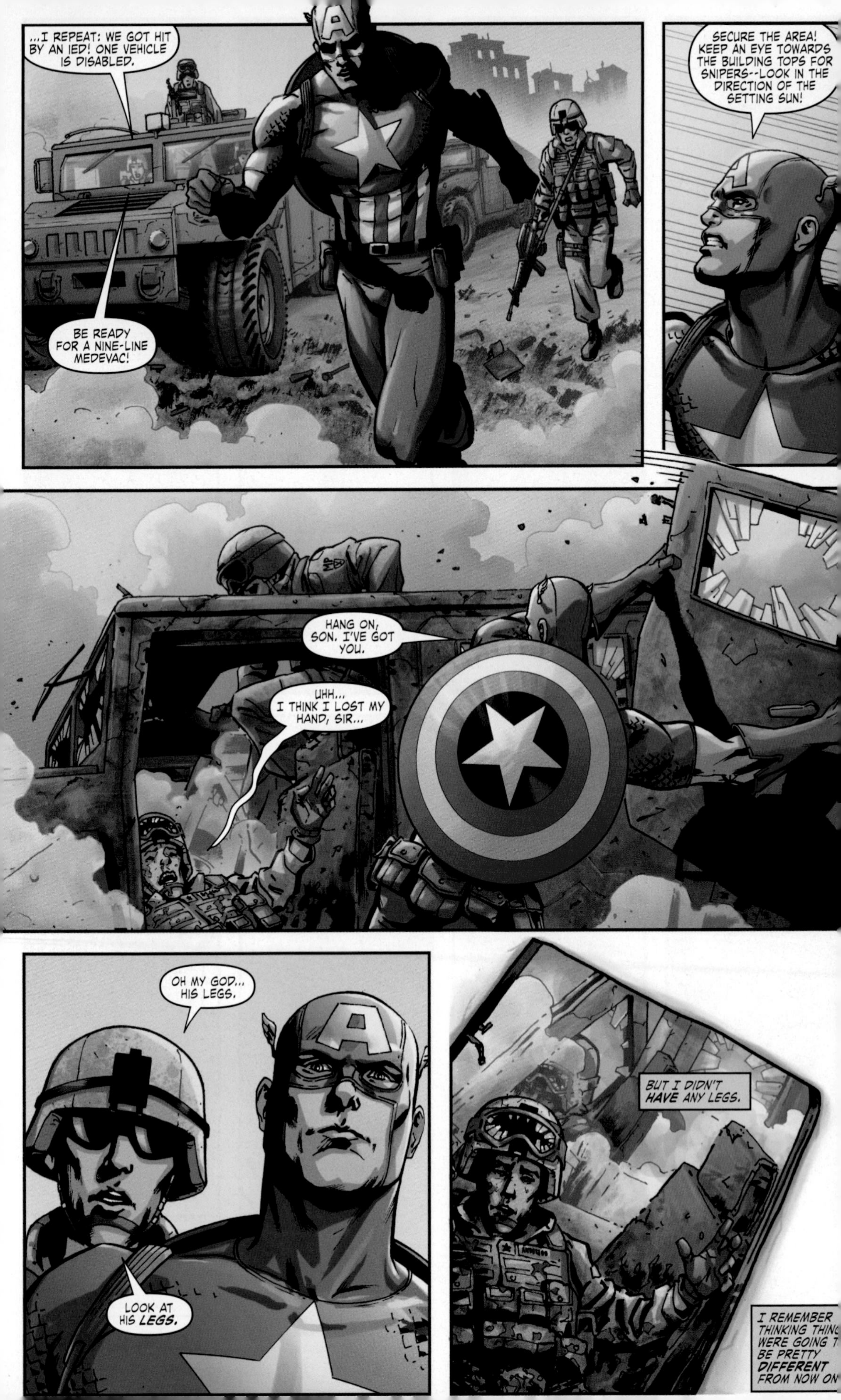
...I REPEAT: WE GOT HIT BY AN IED! ONE VEHICLE IS DISABLED.
BE READY FOR A NINE-LINE MEDEVAC!
SECURE THE AREA! KEEP AN EYE TOWARDS THE BUILDING TOPS FOR SNIPERS--LOOK IN THE DIRECTION OF THE SETTING SUN!
HANG ON, SON. I'VE GOT YOU.
UHH... I THINK I LOST MY HAND, SIR...
OH MY GOD... HIS LEGS.
LOOK AT HIS LEGS.
BUT I DIDN'T HAVE ANY LEGS.
I REMEMBER THINKING THING WERE GOING T BE PRETTY DIFFERENT FROM NOW ON

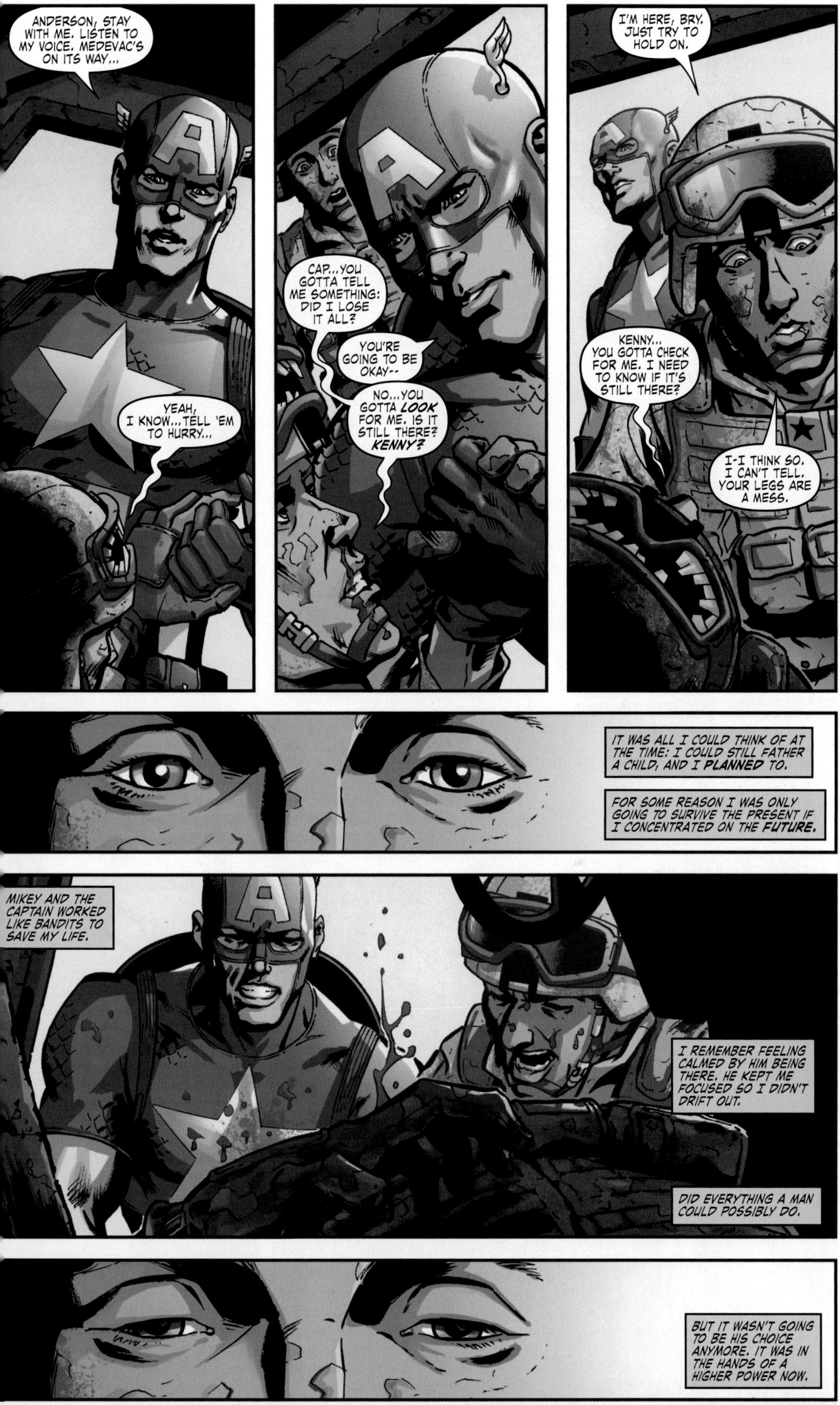
ANDERSON, STAY WITH ME. LISTEN TO MY VOICE. MEDEVAC'S ON ITS WAY...
YEAH, I KNOW...TELL 'EM TO HURRY...
CAP...YOU GOTTA TELL ME SOMETHING: DID I LOSE IT ALL?
YOU'RE GOING TO BE OKAY--
NO...YOU GOTTA **LOOK** FOR ME. IS IT STILL THERE? ***KENNY?***
I'M HERE, BRY. JUST TRY TO HOLD ON.
KENNY... YOU GOTTA CHECK FOR ME. I NEED TO KNOW IF IT'S STILL THERE?
I-I THINK SO. I CAN'T TELL. YOUR LEGS ARE A MESS.
*IT WAS ALL I COULD THINK OF AT THE TIME: I COULD STILL FATHER A CHILD, AND I **PLANNED** TO.*
*FOR SOME REASON I WAS ONLY GOING TO SURVIVE THE PRESENT IF I CONCENTRATED ON THE **FUTURE.***
MIKEY AND THE CAPTAIN WORKED LIKE BANDITS TO SAVE MY LIFE.
I REMEMBER FEELING CALMED BY HIM BEING THERE. HE KEPT ME FOCUSED SO I DIDN'T DRIFT OUT.
DID EVERYTHING A MAN COULD POSSIBLY DO.
BUT IT WASN'T GOING TO BE HIS CHOICE ANYMORE. IT WAS IN THE HANDS OF A HIGHER POWER NOW.

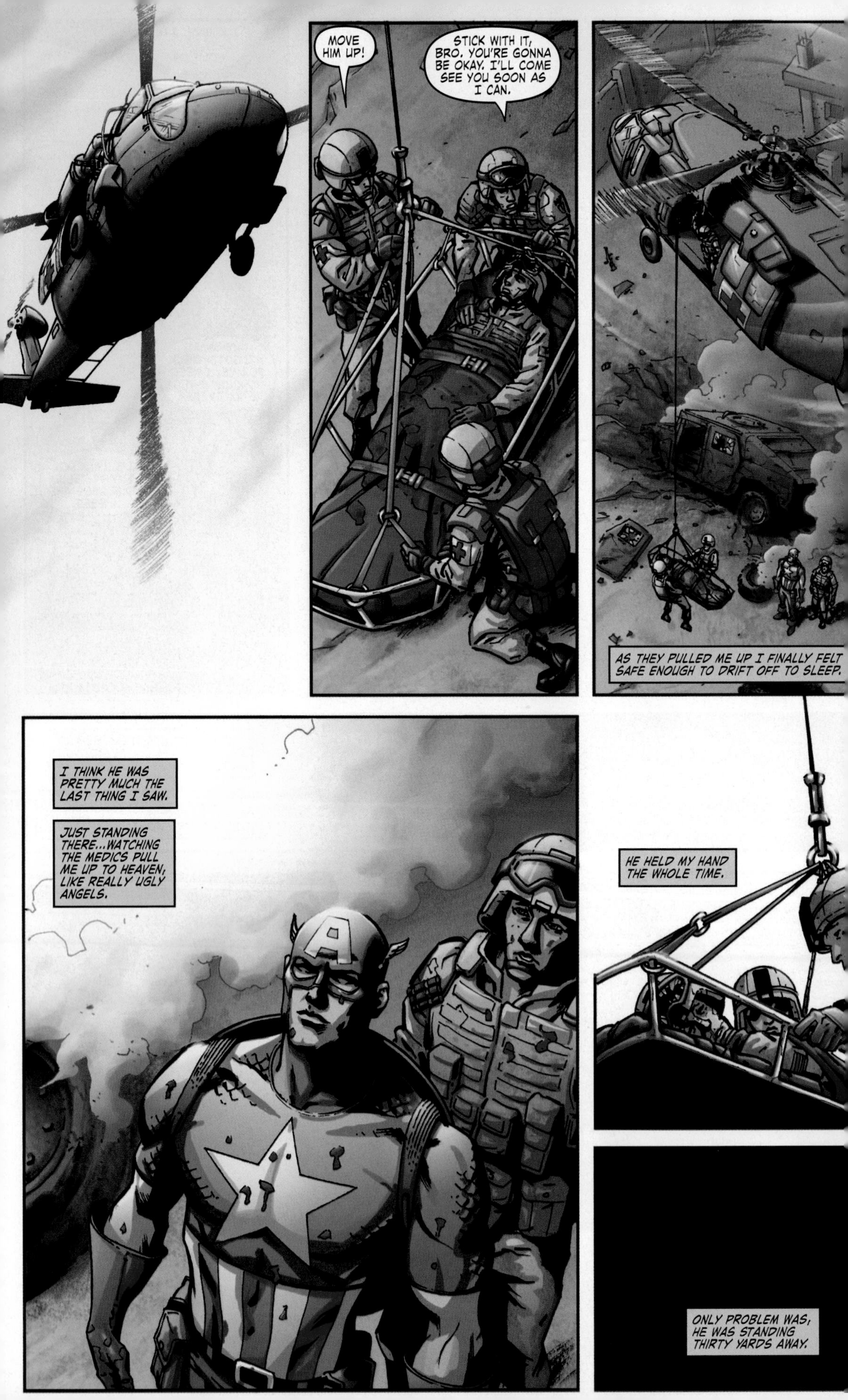
MOVE HIM UP!
STICK WITH IT, BRO. YOU'RE GONNA BE OKAY. I'LL COME SEE YOU SOON AS I CAN.
AS THEY PULLED ME UP I FINALLY FELT SAFE ENOUGH TO DRIFT OFF TO SLEEP.
I THINK HE WAS PRETTY MUCH THE LAST THING I SAW.
JUST STANDING THERE...WATCHING THE MEDICS PULL ME UP TO HEAVEN, LIKE REALLY UGLY ANGELS.
HE HELD MY HAND THE WHOLE TIME.
ONLY PROBLEM WAS, HE WAS STANDING THIRTY YARDS AWAY.

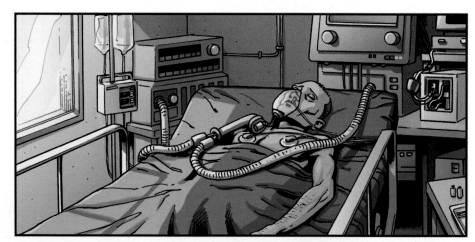

THEY KEPT ME IN AN INDUCED COMA FOR ALMOST TWO MONTHS.

THE ARMY BROUGHT MY MOM AND DAD OVER TO BE WITH ME. MY BROTHER CAME TOO.

DAD DIDN'T LEAVE MY SIDE FOR A MOMENT, EVEN IF THEY TOLD HIM TO. HE HELPED PACK AND DRESS MY WOUNDS.

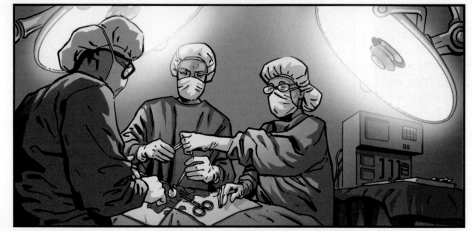

FORTY-SEVEN SURGERIES IN THE FIRST THREE WEEKS. TWELVE MORE AFTER THAT.

THEY DID ALL THEY COULD TO SAVE ALL THE PIECES OF ME THAT WERE LEFT.

WAKING UP WAS A LOT HARDER THAN IT HAD ANY RIGHT TO BE.

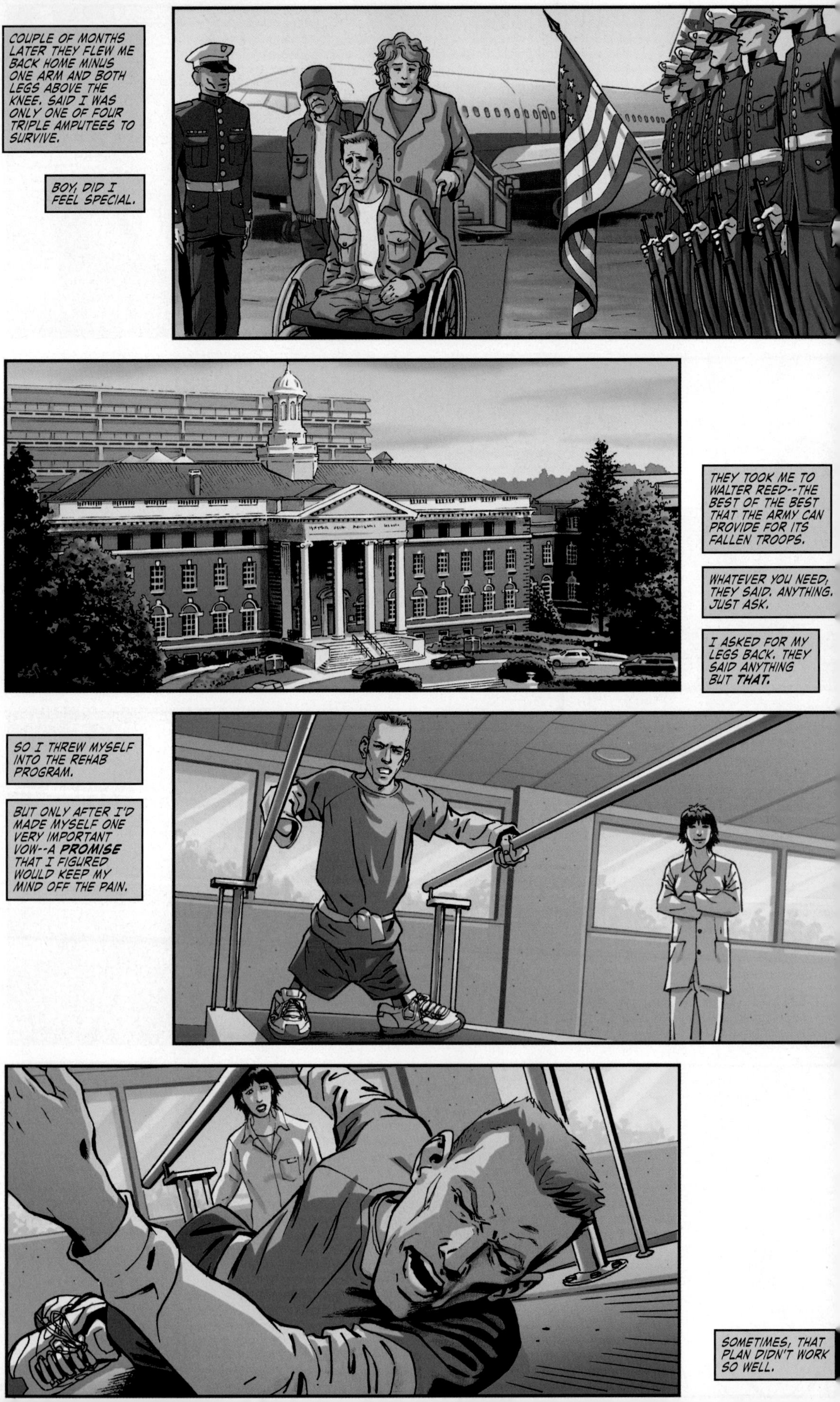
COUPLE OF MONTHS LATER THEY FLEW ME BACK HOME MINUS ONE ARM AND BOTH LEGS ABOVE THE KNEE. SAID I WAS ONLY ONE OF FOUR TRIPLE AMPUTEES TO SURVIVE.
BOY, DID I FEEL SPECIAL.
THEY TOOK ME TO WALTER REED--THE BEST OF THE BEST THAT THE ARMY CAN PROVIDE FOR ITS FALLEN TROOPS.
WHATEVER YOU NEED, THEY SAID. ANYTHING. JUST ASK.
I ASKED FOR MY LEGS BACK. THEY SAID ANYTHING BUT THAT.
SO I THREW MYSELF INTO THE REHAB PROGRAM.
BUT ONLY AFTER I'D MADE MYSELF ONE VERY IMPORTANT VOW--A PROMISE THAT I FIGURED WOULD KEEP MY MIND OFF THE PAIN.
SOMETIMES, THAT PLAN DIDN'T WORK SO WELL.

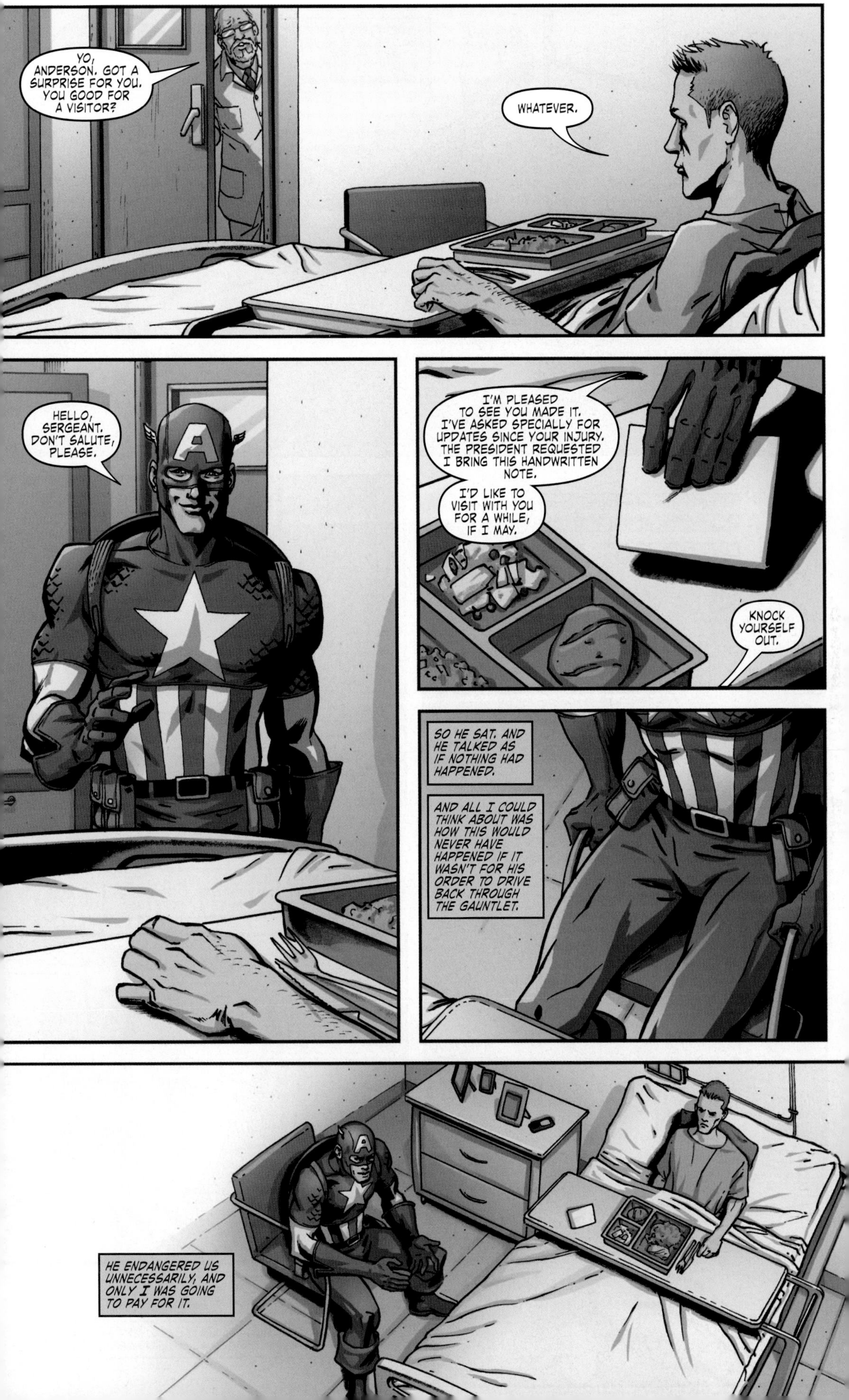

YO, ANDERSON. GOT A SURPRISE FOR YOU. YOU GOOD FOR A VISITOR?
WHATEVER.
HELLO, SERGEANT. DON'T SALUTE, PLEASE.
I'M PLEASED TO SEE YOU MADE IT. I'VE ASKED SPECIALLY FOR UPDATES SINCE YOUR INJURY. THE PRESIDENT REQUESTED I BRING THIS HANDWRITTEN NOTE.
I'D LIKE TO VISIT WITH YOU FOR A WHILE, IF I MAY.
KNOCK YOURSELF OUT.
SO HE SAT. AND HE TALKED AS IF NOTHING HAD HAPPENED.
AND ALL I COULD THINK ABOUT WAS HOW THIS WOULD NEVER HAVE HAPPENED IF IT WASN'T FOR HIS ORDER TO DRIVE BACK THROUGH THE GAUNTLET.
HE ENDANGERED US UNNECESSARILY, AND ONLY I WAS GOING TO PAY FOR IT.

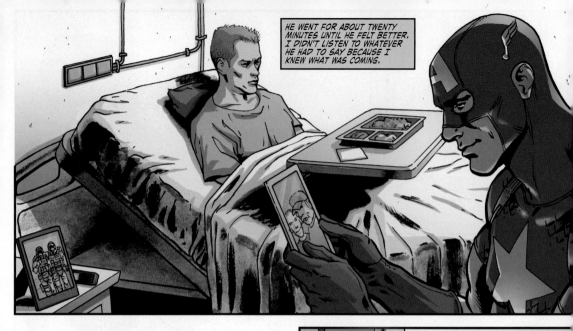

HE WENT FOR ABOUT TWENTY MINUTES UNTIL HE FELT BETTER. I DIDN'T LISTEN TO WHATEVER HE HAD TO SAY BECAUSE I KNEW WHAT WAS COMING.

WHEN HE WAS DONE, HE STOOD UP TO WALK OUT OF THE ROOM.

BECAUSE HE *COULD.*

I KEPT THINKING, "TELL HIM. TELL HIM." BUT WHAT WAS I GOING TO SAY?

THERE'S NO PLACE TO TELL A CAPTAIN THAT HE PUT YOUR LIFE IN JEOPARDY AND COST YOU THREE OF YOUR LIMBS.

DESPITE HIS GENEROUS REQUEST I SALUTED AS HE LEFT.

WITH MY HAND MISSING YOU COULDN'T EVEN SEE WHICH FINGER I WAS HOLDING UP.

I STAYED AT WALTER REED FOR AN ENTIRE YEAR. WENT TO A PRETTY DARK PLACE THAT I ALMOST DIDN'T CLIMB OUT OF.

GOT FIT WITH AN ELECTRIC HAND THAT COULD SWIVEL ALL THE WAY AROUND, LIKE A FRICKIN' OWL.

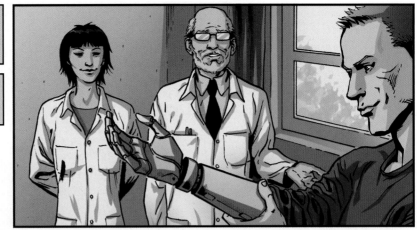

THEN I GOT BACK TO THE REHAB, DRIVEN BY THE PROMISE I'D MADE TO MYSELF.

AAHW!

THAT WHOLE TIME DOING REHAB MADE ME THINK OF THIS SHERYL CROW SONG: "NO ONE SAID IT WOULD BE EASY.

"NO ONE SAID IT WOULD BE THIS HARD."

WHEN THE YEAR WAS UP I WENT BACK HOME. IT WAS KIND OF EMOTIONAL LEAVING ALL THOSE DOCTORS AND NURSES.

I HAD NO IDEA WHAT I WAS GOING HOME TO.

THANKS BRYAN

WELLCOME HOME

TRULY...

I HAD NO IDEA.

...TODAY, A HEARTWARMING HOMECOMING FOR ARMY SERGEANT BRYAN ANDERSON. WE'RE HERE AT CHICAGO'S O'HARE AIRPORT WHERE HUNDREDS HAVE GATHERED AT THE GATE TO WELCOME BACK AN AMERICAN HERO...

BRYAN OUR HERO

THANK YOU

LIFE HAS A FUNNY WAY OF EVENING OUT SOMETIMES. FOR EVERYTHING YOU LOSE, THERE'S SOMETHING YOU GAIN.

I HAD LOST TWO LEGS AND MY RIGHT ARM. YET I HAD THE LOVE AND ADMIRATION OF ALL THESE PEOPLE.

COUPLE OF WEEKS AFTER I GOT HOME I THREW OUT THE FIRST PITCH AT THE CUBBIES. IT WAS FUNNY 'CAUSE MY DAD WAS SO IMPRESSED.

I ASKED HIM IF HE WASN'T IMPRESSED WHEN I GOT BLOWN UP AND HE SAID, "NO, I WAS *ANNOYED*."

The Meanin... Esq...
MAN AT HIS BEST
WISDOM & DAMNGOOD ADVICE

SOMEONE AT A MAGAZINE SAW IT ON TV, AND THEY CALLED ME IN TO DO AN ARTICLE.

I THOUGHT IT WOULD BE IN THE MIDDLE SOMEWHERE. AND INSTEAD, THEY PUT ME ON THE COVER.

NEXT THING YOU KNOW, I'D BECOME A CERTIFIED *CELEBRITY*.

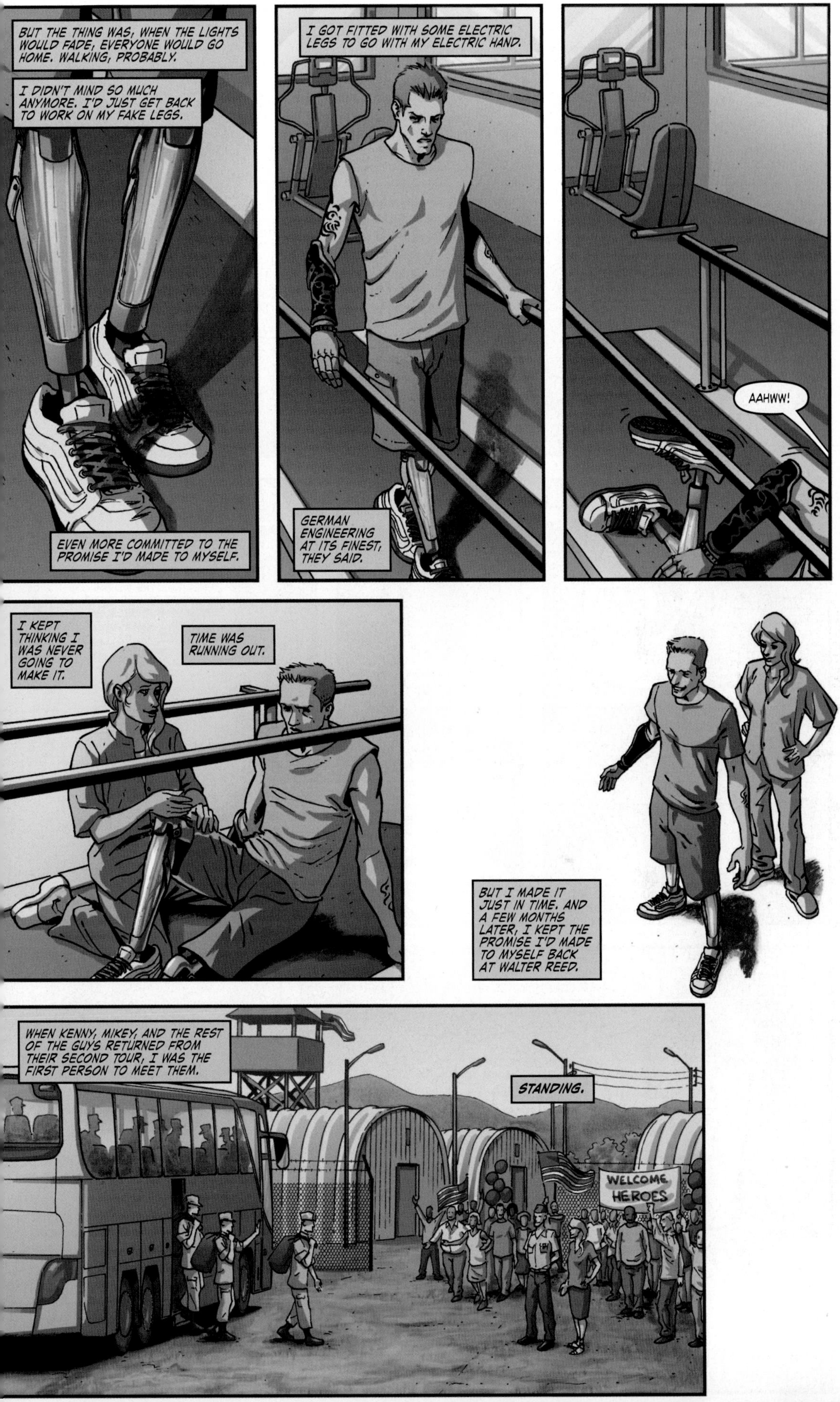

BUT THE THING WAS, WHEN THE LIGHTS WOULD FADE, EVERYONE WOULD GO HOME. WALKING, PROBABLY.
I DIDN'T MIND SO MUCH ANYMORE. I'D JUST GET BACK TO WORK ON MY FAKE LEGS.
EVEN MORE COMMITTED TO THE PROMISE I'D MADE TO MYSELF.
I GOT FITTED WITH SOME ELECTRIC LEGS TO GO WITH MY ELECTRIC HAND.
GERMAN ENGINEERING AT ITS FINEST, THEY SAID.
AAHWW!
I KEPT THINKING I WAS NEVER GOING TO MAKE IT.
TIME WAS RUNNING OUT.
BUT I MADE IT JUST IN TIME. AND A FEW MONTHS LATER, I KEPT THE PROMISE I'D MADE TO MYSELF BACK AT WALTER REED.
WHEN KENNY, MIKEY, AND THE REST OF THE GUYS RETURNED FROM THEIR SECOND TOUR, I WAS THE FIRST PERSON TO MEET THEM.
STANDING.
WELCOME HEROES

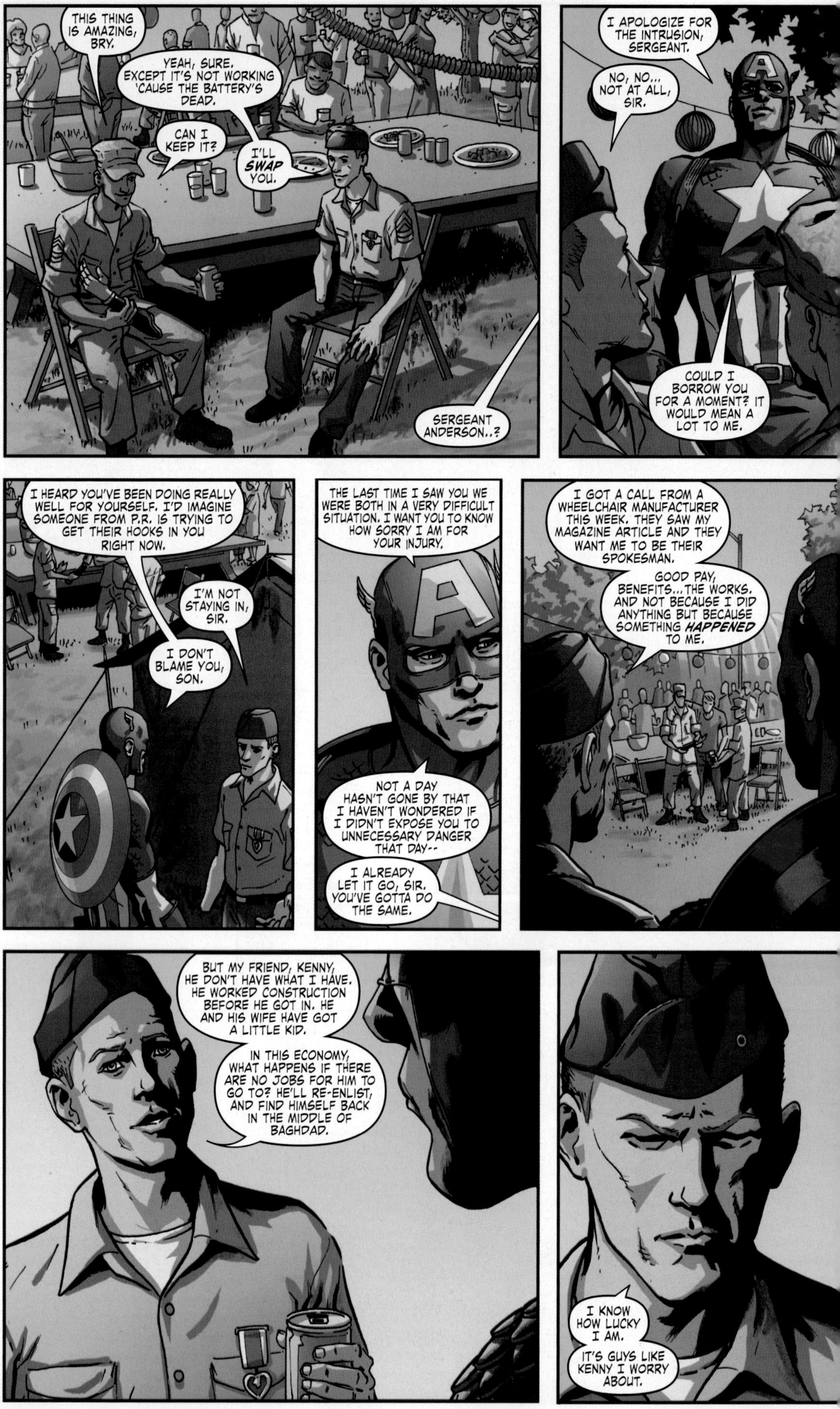

THIS THING IS AMAZING, BRY.
YEAH, SURE. EXCEPT IT'S NOT WORKING 'CAUSE THE BATTERY'S DEAD.
CAN I KEEP IT?
I'LL SWAP YOU.
SERGEANT ANDERSON..?
I APOLOGIZE FOR THE INTRUSION, SERGEANT.
NO, NO... NOT AT ALL, SIR.
COULD I BORROW YOU FOR A MOMENT? IT WOULD MEAN A LOT TO ME.
I HEARD YOU'VE BEEN DOING REALLY WELL FOR YOURSELF. I'D IMAGINE SOMEONE FROM P.R. IS TRYING TO GET THEIR HOOKS IN YOU RIGHT NOW.
I'M NOT STAYING IN, SIR.
I DON'T BLAME YOU, SON.
THE LAST TIME I SAW YOU WE WERE BOTH IN A VERY DIFFICULT SITUATION. I WANT YOU TO KNOW HOW SORRY I AM FOR YOUR INJURY.
NOT A DAY HASN'T GONE BY THAT I HAVEN'T WONDERED IF I DIDN'T EXPOSE YOU TO UNNECESSARY DANGER THAT DAY--
I ALREADY LET IT GO, SIR. YOU'VE GOTTA DO THE SAME.
I GOT A CALL FROM A WHEELCHAIR MANUFACTURER THIS WEEK. THEY SAW MY MAGAZINE ARTICLE AND THEY WANT ME TO BE THEIR SPOKESMAN.
GOOD PAY, BENEFITS...THE WORKS. AND NOT BECAUSE I DID ANYTHING BUT BECAUSE SOMETHING HAPPENED TO ME.
BUT MY FRIEND, KENNY, HE DON'T HAVE WHAT I HAVE. HE WORKED CONSTRUCTION BEFORE HE GOT IN. HE AND HIS WIFE HAVE GOT A LITTLE KID.
IN THIS ECONOMY, WHAT HAPPENS IF THERE ARE NO JOBS FOR HIM TO GO TO? HE'LL RE-ENLIST, AND FIND HIMSELF BACK IN THE MIDDLE OF BAGHDAD.
I KNOW HOW LUCKY I AM.
IT'S GUYS LIKE KENNY I WORRY ABOUT.

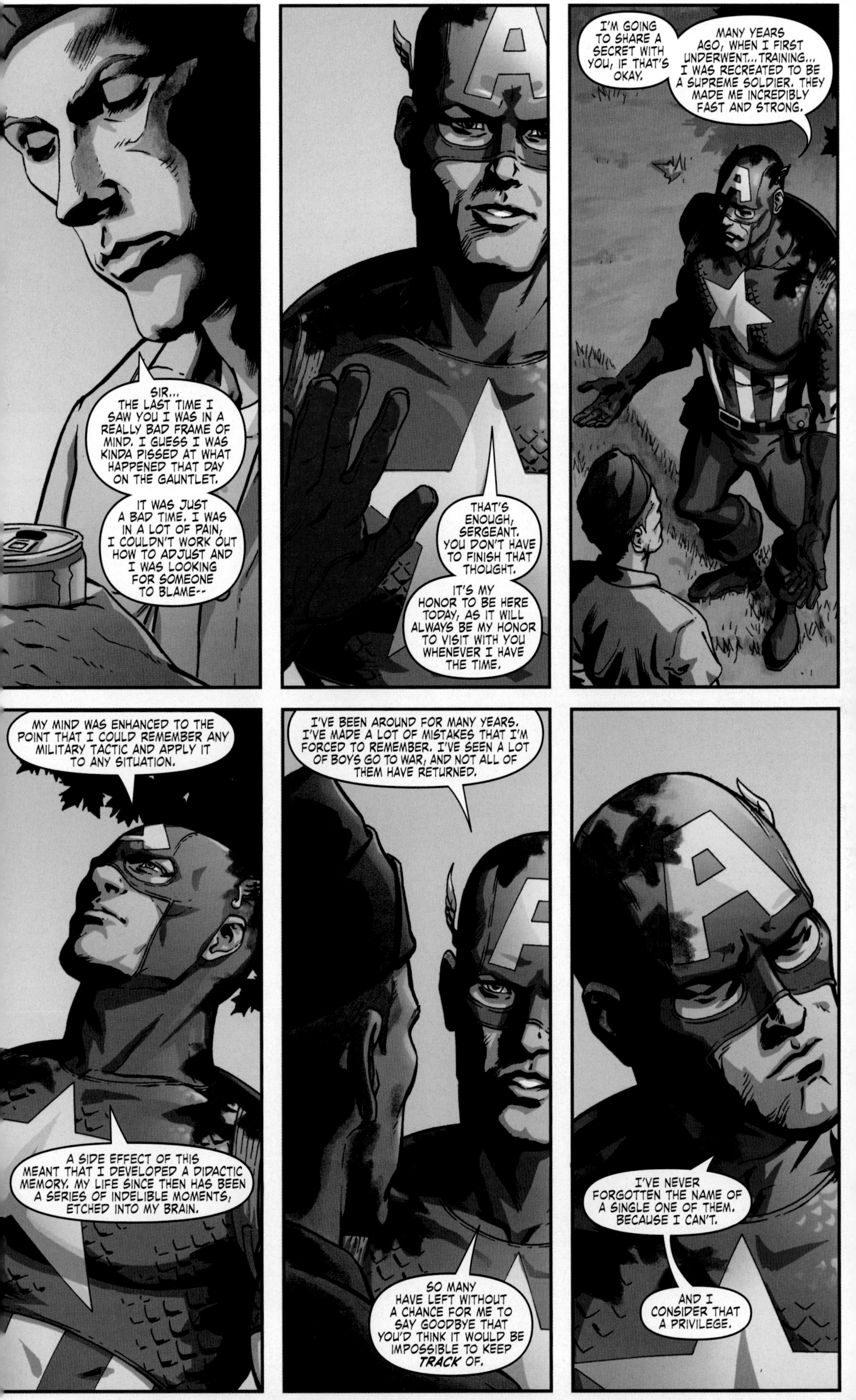
SIR... THE LAST TIME I SAW YOU I WAS IN A REALLY BAD FRAME OF MIND. I GUESS I WAS KINDA PISSED AT WHAT HAPPENED THAT DAY ON THE GAUNTLET.
IT WAS JUST A BAD TIME. I WAS IN A LOT OF PAIN, I COULDN'T WORK OUT HOW TO ADJUST AND I WAS LOOKING FOR SOMEONE TO BLAME--
THAT'S ENOUGH, SERGEANT. YOU DON'T HAVE TO FINISH THAT THOUGHT.
IT'S MY HONOR TO BE HERE TODAY, AS IT WILL ALWAYS BE MY HONOR TO VISIT WITH YOU WHENEVER I HAVE THE TIME.
I'M GOING TO SHARE A SECRET WITH YOU, IF THAT'S OKAY.
MANY YEARS AGO, WHEN I FIRST UNDERWENT...TRAINING... I WAS RECREATED TO BE A SUPREME SOLDIER. THEY MADE ME INCREDIBLY FAST AND STRONG.
MY MIND WAS ENHANCED TO THE POINT THAT I COULD REMEMBER ANY MILITARY TACTIC AND APPLY IT TO ANY SITUATION.
A SIDE EFFECT OF THIS MEANT THAT I DEVELOPED A DIDACTIC MEMORY. MY LIFE SINCE THEN HAS BEEN A SERIES OF INDELIBLE MOMENTS, ETCHED INTO MY BRAIN.
I'VE BEEN AROUND FOR MANY YEARS. I'VE MADE A LOT OF MISTAKES THAT I'M FORCED TO REMEMBER. I'VE SEEN A LOT OF BOYS GO TO WAR, AND NOT ALL OF THEM HAVE RETURNED.
SO MANY HAVE LEFT WITHOUT A CHANCE FOR ME TO SAY GOODBYE THAT YOU'D THINK IT WOULD BE IMPOSSIBLE TO KEEP *TRACK* OF.
I'VE NEVER FORGOTTEN THE NAME OF A SINGLE ONE OF THEM. BECAUSE I CAN'T.
AND I CONSIDER THAT A PRIVILEGE.

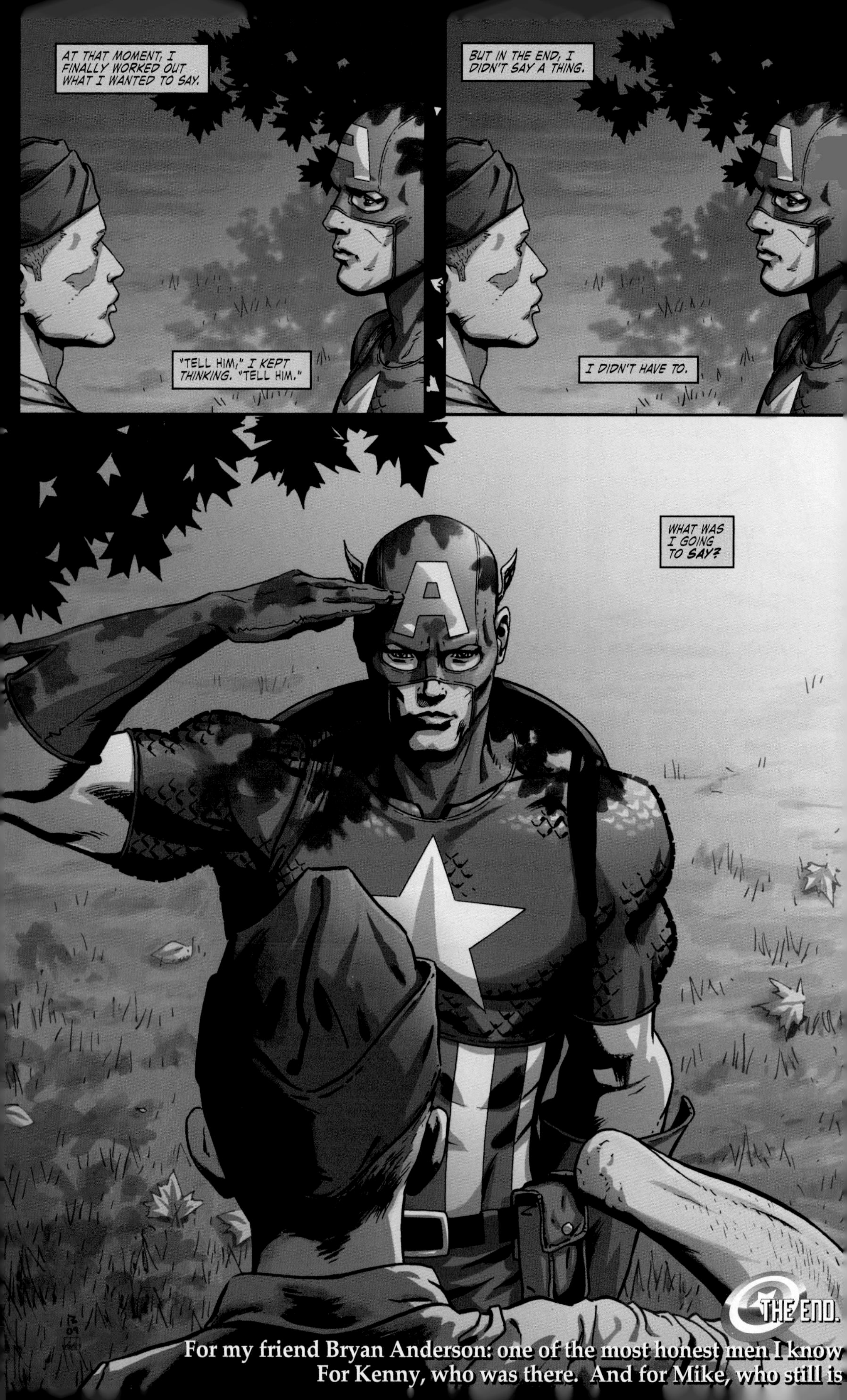
AT THAT MOMENT, I FINALLY WORKED OUT WHAT I WANTED TO SAY.
"TELL HIM," I KEPT THINKING. "TELL HIM."
BUT IN THE END, I DIDN'T SAY A THING.
I DIDN'T HAVE TO.
WHAT WAS I GOING TO SAY?
THE END.
For my friend Bryan Anderson: one of the most honest men I know
For Kenny, who was there. And for Mike, who still is

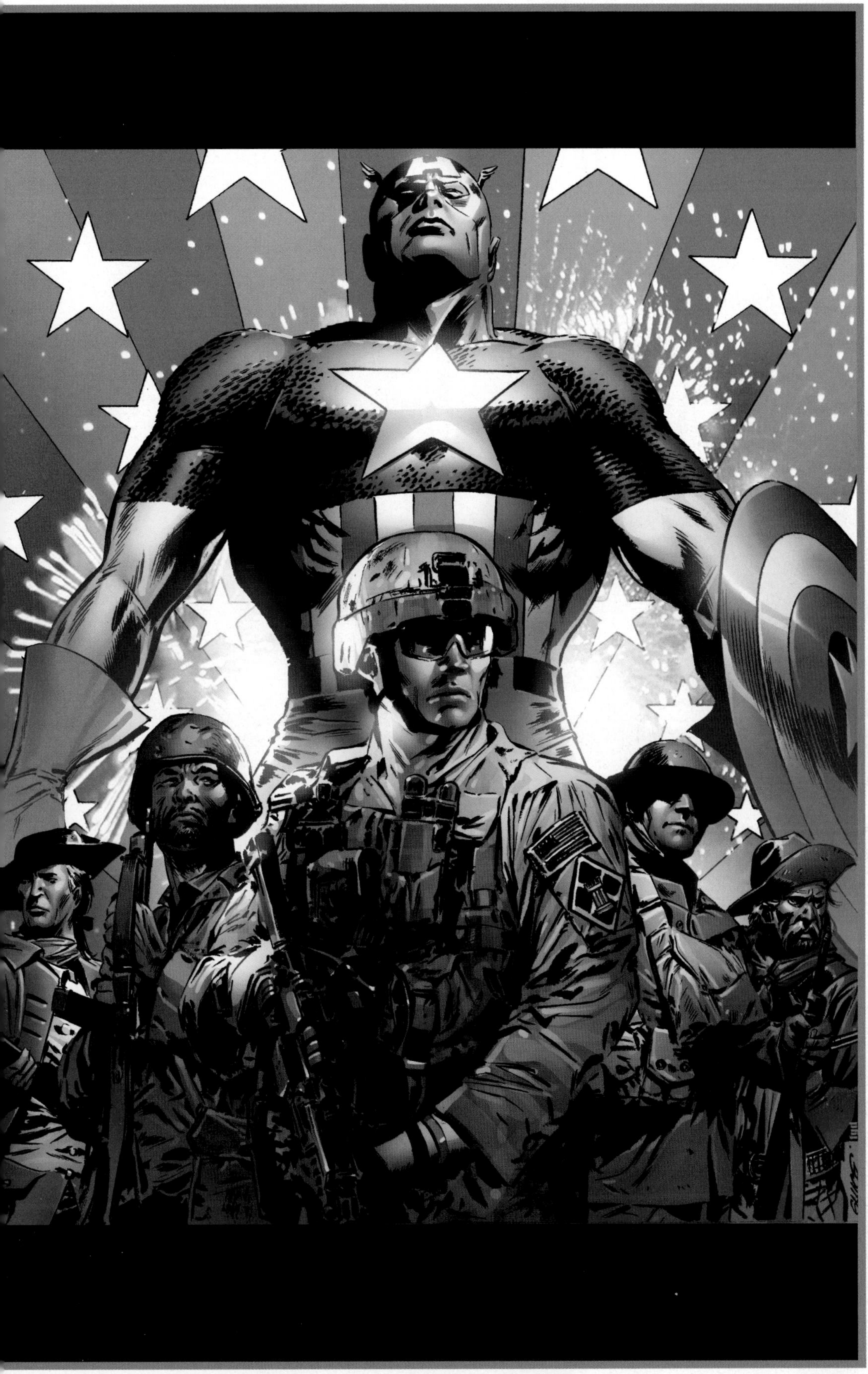

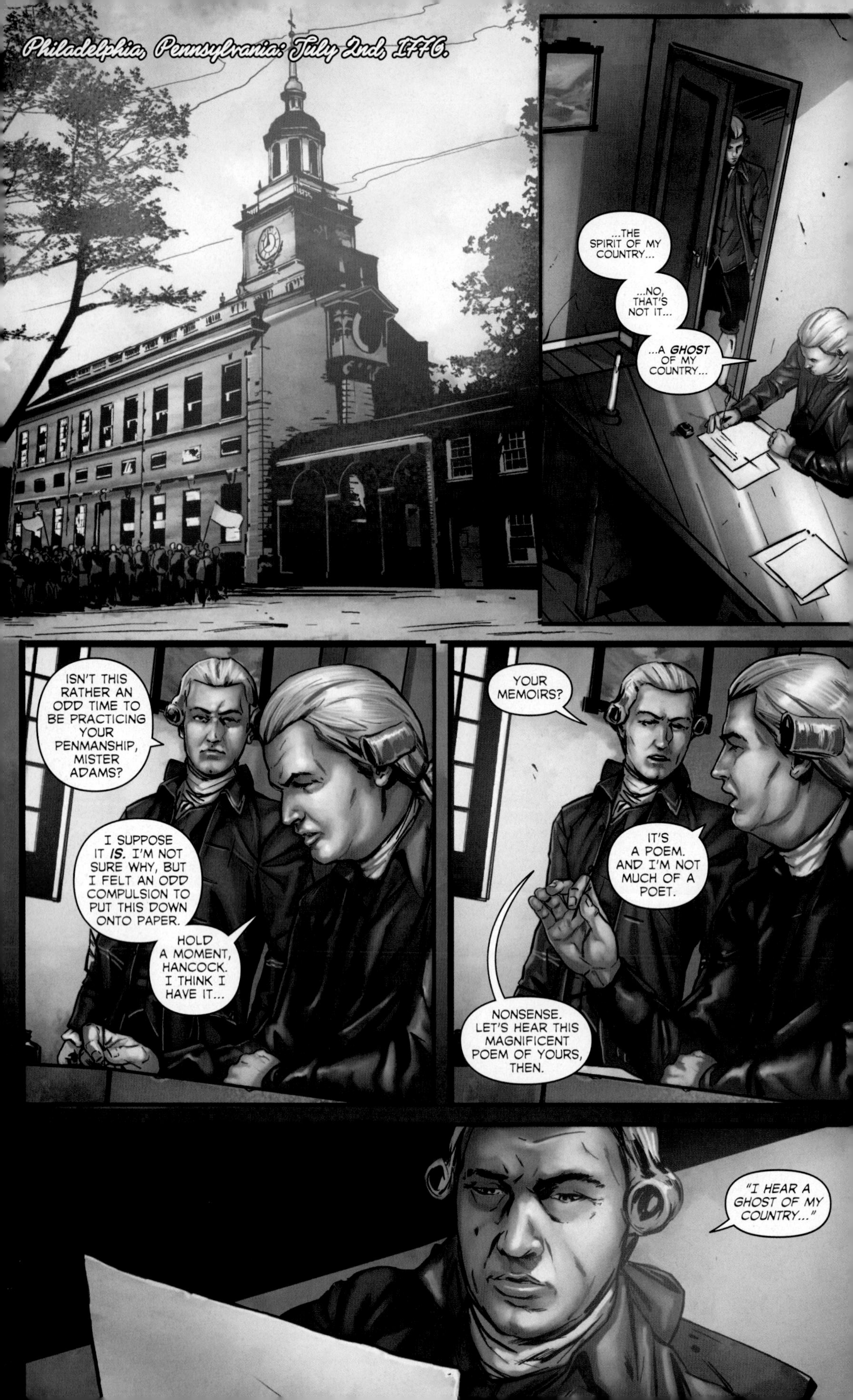
Philadelphia, Pennsylvania: July 2nd, 1776.
...THE SPIRIT OF MY COUNTRY...
...NO, THAT'S NOT IT...
...A GHOST OF MY COUNTRY...
ISN'T THIS RATHER AN ODD TIME TO BE PRACTICING YOUR PENMANSHIP, MISTER ADAMS?
I SUPPOSE IT IS. I'M NOT SURE WHY, BUT I FELT AN ODD COMPULSION TO PUT THIS DOWN ONTO PAPER.
HOLD A MOMENT, HANCOCK. I THINK I HAVE IT...
YOUR MEMOIRS?
IT'S A POEM. AND I'M NOT MUCH OF A POET.
NONSENSE. LET'S HEAR THIS MAGNIFICENT POEM OF YOURS, THEN.
"I HEAR A GHOST OF MY COUNTRY..."

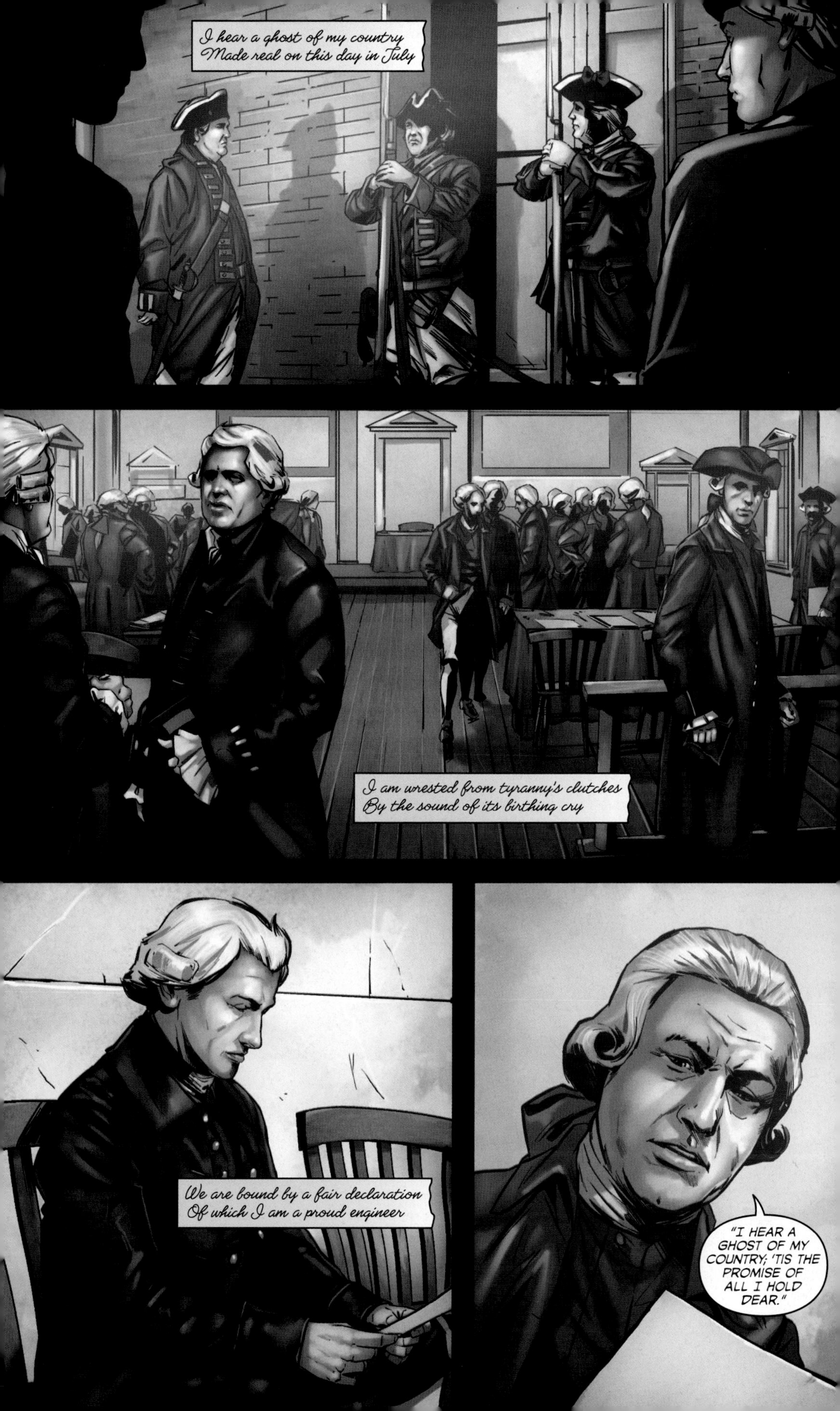
I hear a ghost of my country
Made real on this day in July
I am wrested from tyranny's clutches
By the sound of its birthing cry
We are bound by a fair declaration
Of which I am a proud engineer
"I HEAR A GHOST OF MY COUNTRY; 'TIS THE PROMISE OF ALL I HOLD DEAR."

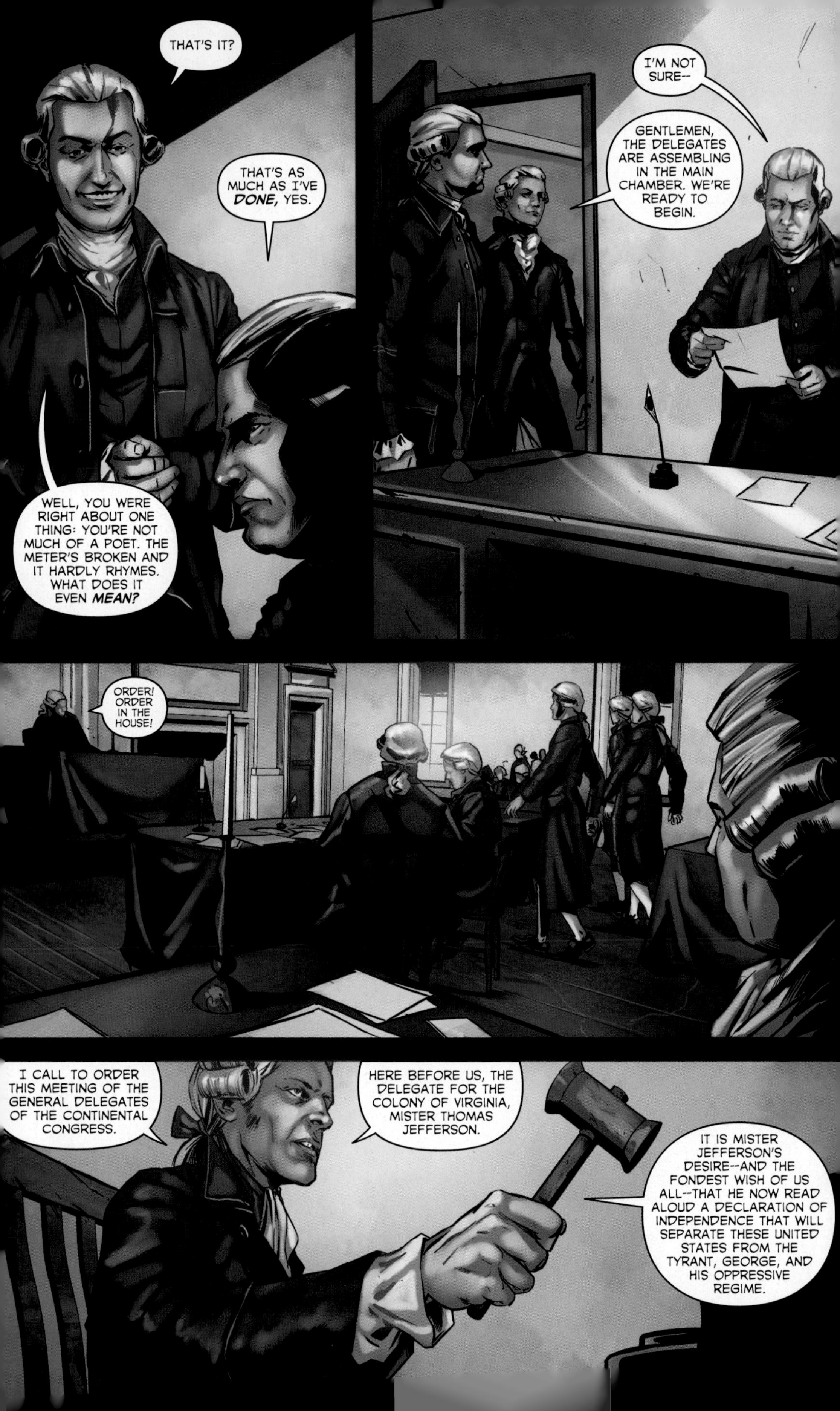
THAT'S IT?
THAT'S AS MUCH AS I'VE *DONE,* YES.
WELL, YOU WERE RIGHT ABOUT ONE THING: YOU'RE NOT MUCH OF A POET. THE METER'S BROKEN AND IT HARDLY RHYMES. WHAT DOES IT EVEN *MEAN?*
I'M NOT SURE--
GENTLEMEN, THE DELEGATES ARE ASSEMBLING IN THE MAIN CHAMBER. WE'RE READY TO BEGIN.
ORDER! ORDER IN THE HOUSE!
I CALL TO ORDER THIS MEETING OF THE GENERAL DELEGATES OF THE CONTINENTAL CONGRESS.
HERE BEFORE US, THE DELEGATE FOR THE COLONY OF VIRGINIA, MISTER THOMAS JEFFERSON.
IT IS MISTER JEFFERSON'S DESIRE--AND THE FONDEST WISH OF US ALL--THAT HE NOW READ ALOUD A DECLARATION OF INDEPENDENCE THAT WILL SEPARATE THESE UNITED STATES FROM THE TYRANT, GEORGE, AND HIS OPPRESSIVE REGIME.

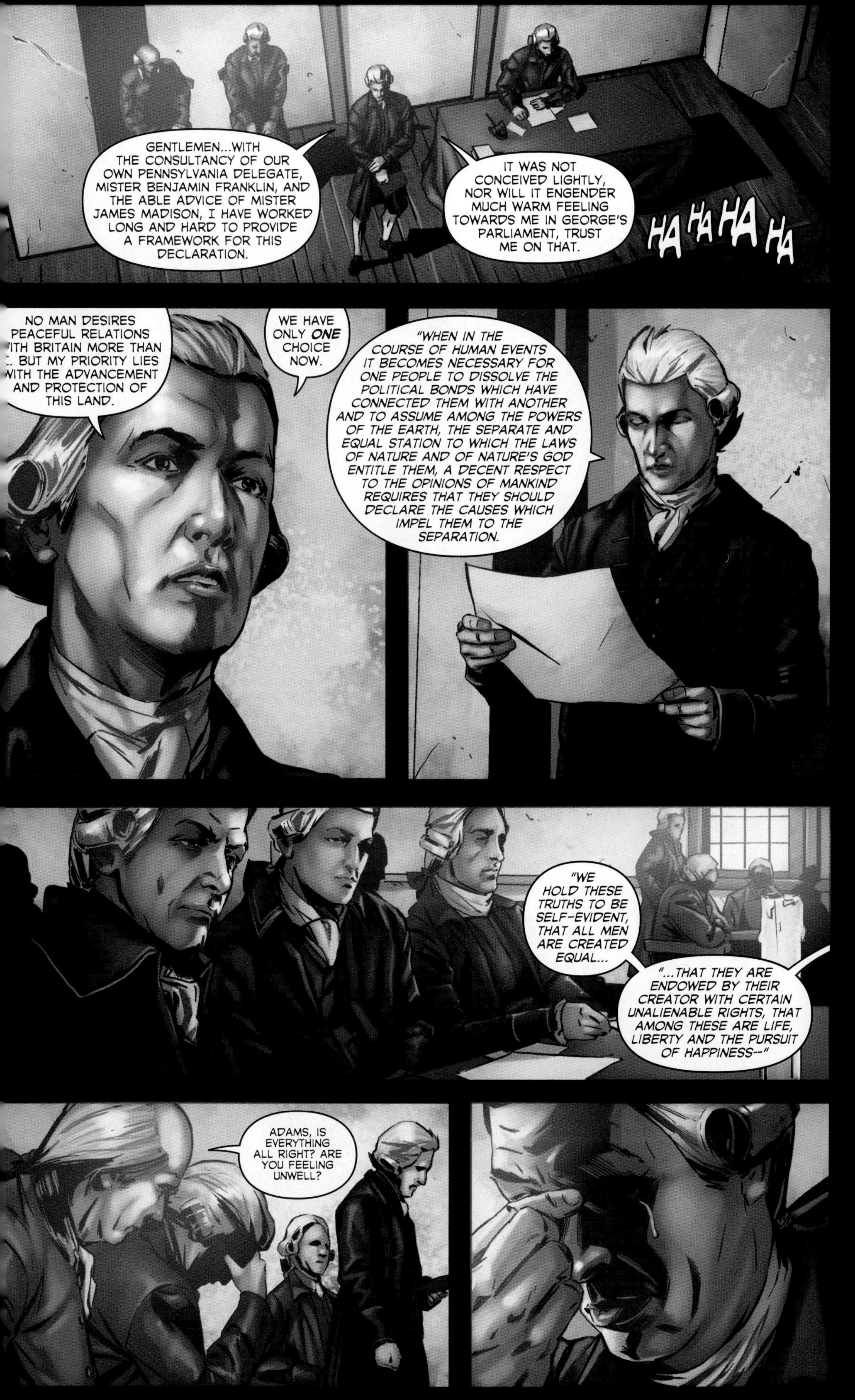

GENTLEMEN...WITH THE CONSULTANCY OF OUR OWN PENNSYLVANIA DELEGATE, MISTER BENJAMIN FRANKLIN, AND THE ABLE ADVICE OF MISTER JAMES MADISON, I HAVE WORKED LONG AND HARD TO PROVIDE A FRAMEWORK FOR THIS DECLARATION.
IT WAS NOT CONCEIVED LIGHTLY, NOR WILL IT ENGENDER MUCH WARM FEELING TOWARDS ME IN GEORGE'S PARLIAMENT, TRUST ME ON THAT.
HA HA HA HA
NO MAN DESIRES PEACEFUL RELATIONS ITH BRITAIN MORE THAN . BUT MY PRIORITY LIES WITH THE ADVANCEMENT AND PROTECTION OF THIS LAND.
WE HAVE ONLY ONE CHOICE NOW.
"WHEN IN THE COURSE OF HUMAN EVENTS IT BECOMES NECESSARY FOR ONE PEOPLE TO DISSOLVE THE POLITICAL BONDS WHICH HAVE CONNECTED THEM WITH ANOTHER AND TO ASSUME AMONG THE POWERS OF THE EARTH, THE SEPARATE AND EQUAL STATION TO WHICH THE LAWS OF NATURE AND OF NATURE'S GOD ENTITLE THEM, A DECENT RESPECT TO THE OPINIONS OF MANKIND REQUIRES THAT THEY SHOULD DECLARE THE CAUSES WHICH IMPEL THEM TO THE SEPARATION.
"WE HOLD THESE TRUTHS TO BE SELF-EVIDENT, THAT ALL MEN ARE CREATED EQUAL...
"...THAT THEY ARE ENDOWED BY THEIR CREATOR WITH CERTAIN UNALIENABLE RIGHTS, THAT AMONG THESE ARE LIFE, LIBERTY AND THE PURSUIT OF HAPPINESS--"
ADAMS, IS EVERYTHING ALL RIGHT? ARE YOU FEELING UNWELL?

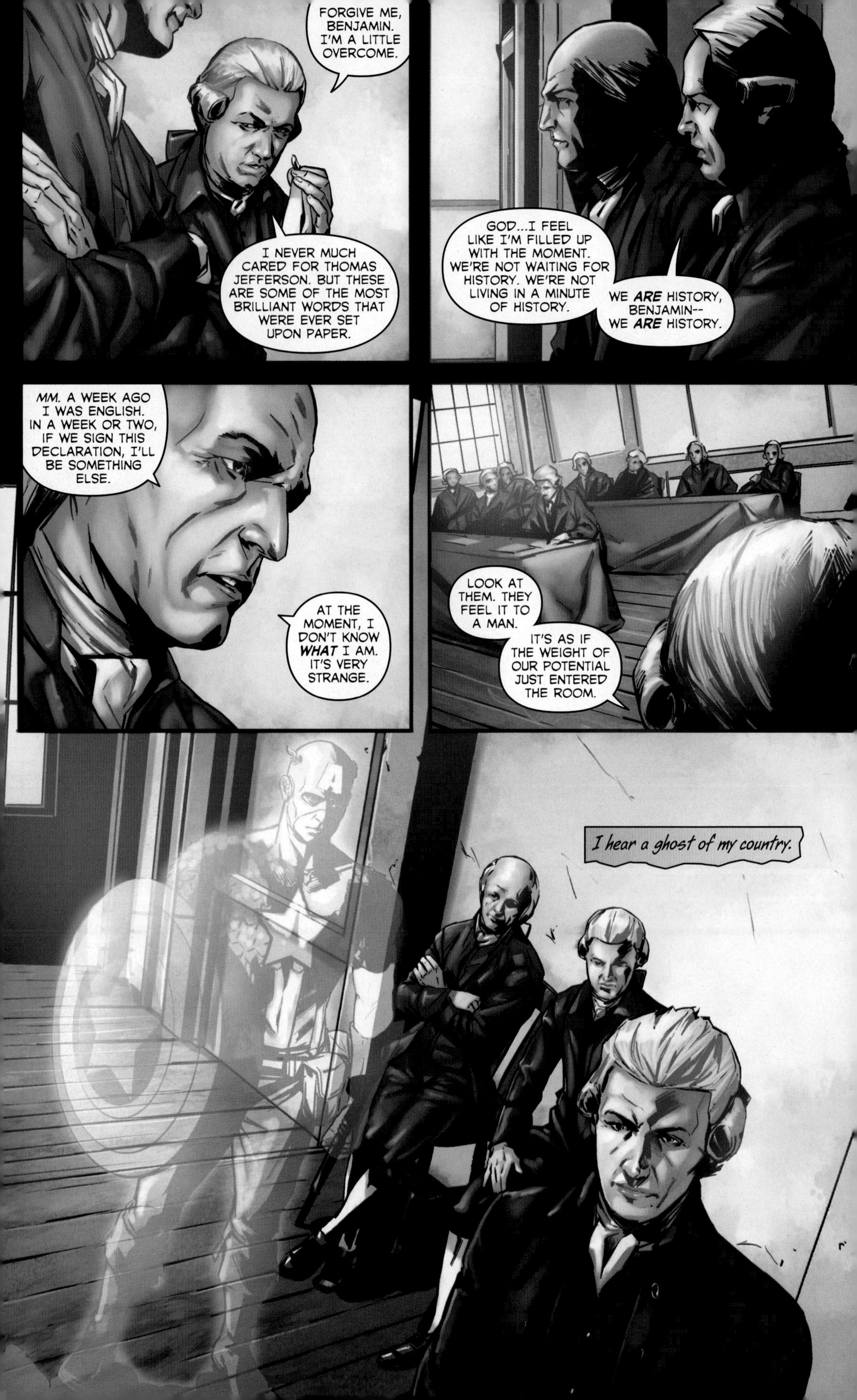
FORGIVE ME, BENJAMIN. I'M A LITTLE OVERCOME.
I NEVER MUCH CARED FOR THOMAS JEFFERSON. BUT THESE ARE SOME OF THE MOST BRILLIANT WORDS THAT WERE EVER SET UPON PAPER.
GOD...I FEEL LIKE I'M FILLED UP WITH THE MOMENT. WE'RE NOT WAITING FOR HISTORY. WE'RE NOT LIVING IN A MINUTE OF HISTORY.
WE ARE HISTORY, BENJAMIN-- WE ARE HISTORY.
MM. A WEEK AGO I WAS ENGLISH. IN A WEEK OR TWO, IF WE SIGN THIS DECLARATION, I'LL BE SOMETHING ELSE.
AT THE MOMENT, I DON'T KNOW WHAT I AM. IT'S VERY STRANGE.
LOOK AT THEM. THEY FEEL IT TO A MAN.
IT'S AS IF THE WEIGHT OF OUR POTENTIAL JUST ENTERED THE ROOM.
I hear a ghost of my country.

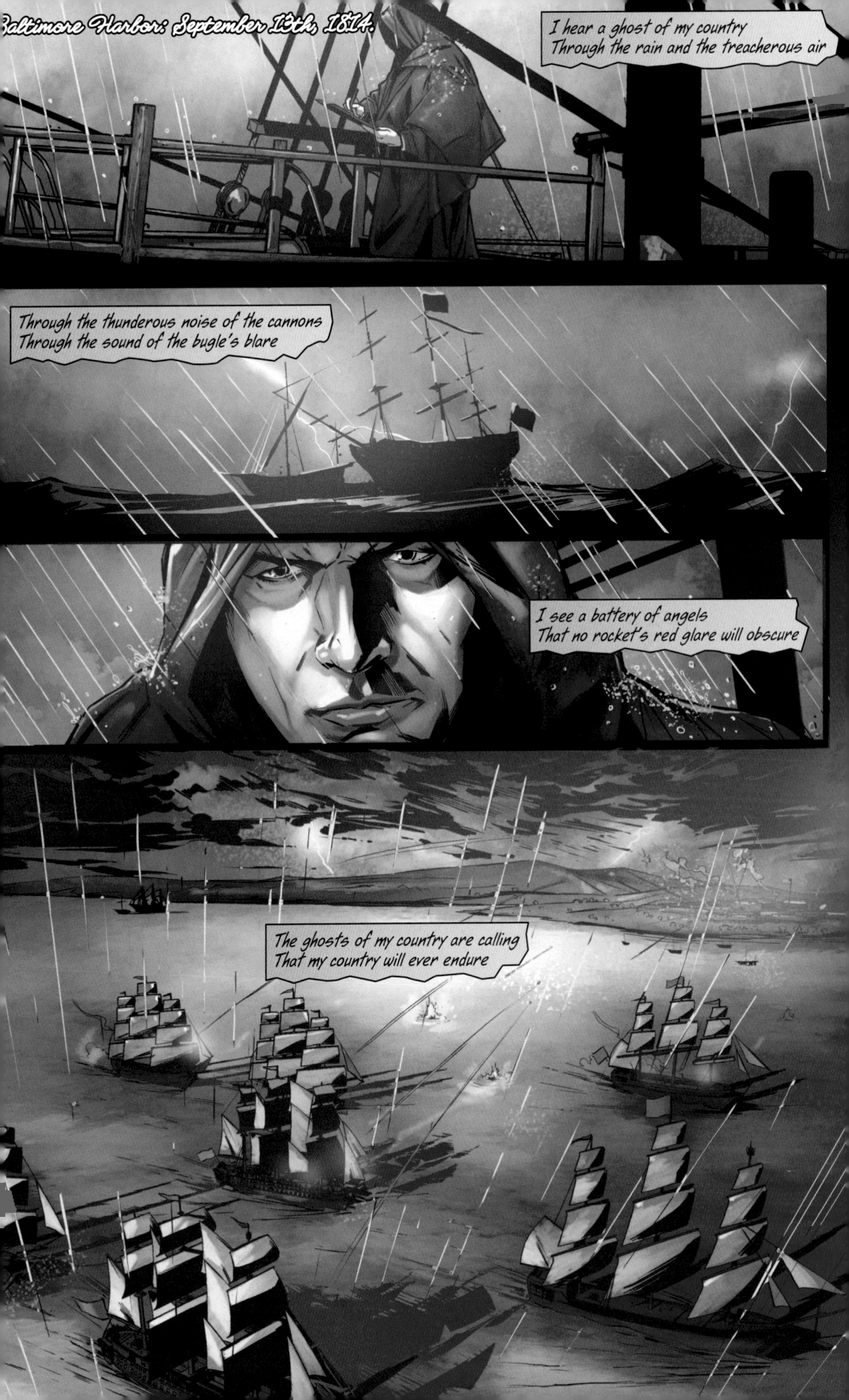
Baltimore Harbor: September 13th, 1814.
I hear a ghost of my country
Through the rain and the treacherous air
Through the thunderous noise of the cannons
Through the sound of the bugle's blare
I see a battery of angels
That no rocket's red glare will obscure
The ghosts of my country are calling
That my country will ever endure

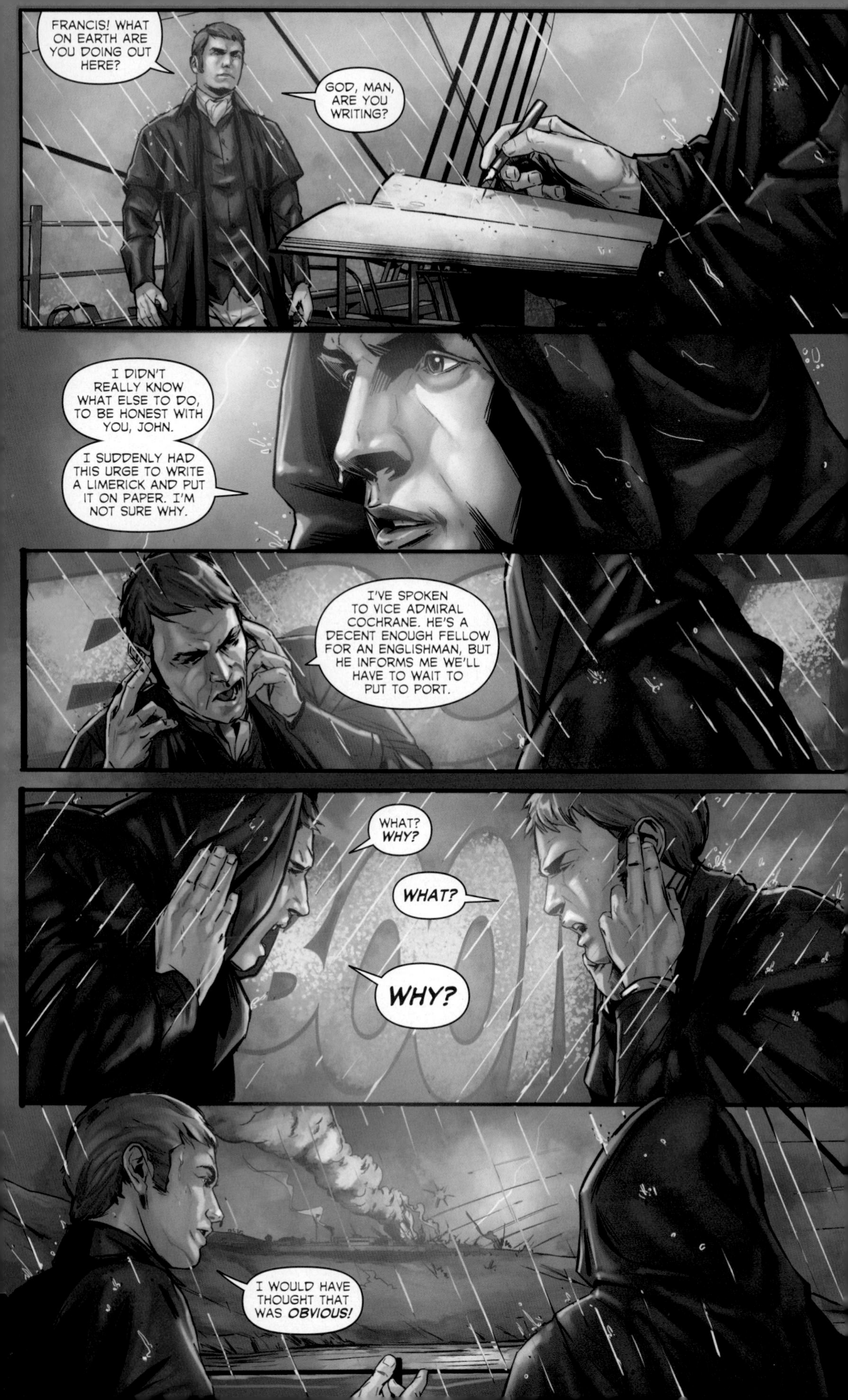
FRANCIS! WHAT ON EARTH ARE YOU DOING OUT HERE?
GOD, MAN, ARE YOU WRITING?
I DIDN'T REALLY KNOW WHAT ELSE TO DO, TO BE HONEST WITH YOU, JOHN.
I SUDDENLY HAD THIS URGE TO WRITE A LIMERICK AND PUT IT ON PAPER. I'M NOT SURE WHY.
I'VE SPOKEN TO VICE ADMIRAL COCHRANE. HE'S A DECENT ENOUGH FELLOW FOR AN ENGLISHMAN, BUT HE INFORMS ME WE'LL HAVE TO WAIT TO PUT TO PORT.
WHAT? *WHY?*
WHAT?
WHY?
I WOULD HAVE THOUGHT THAT WAS *OBVIOUS!*

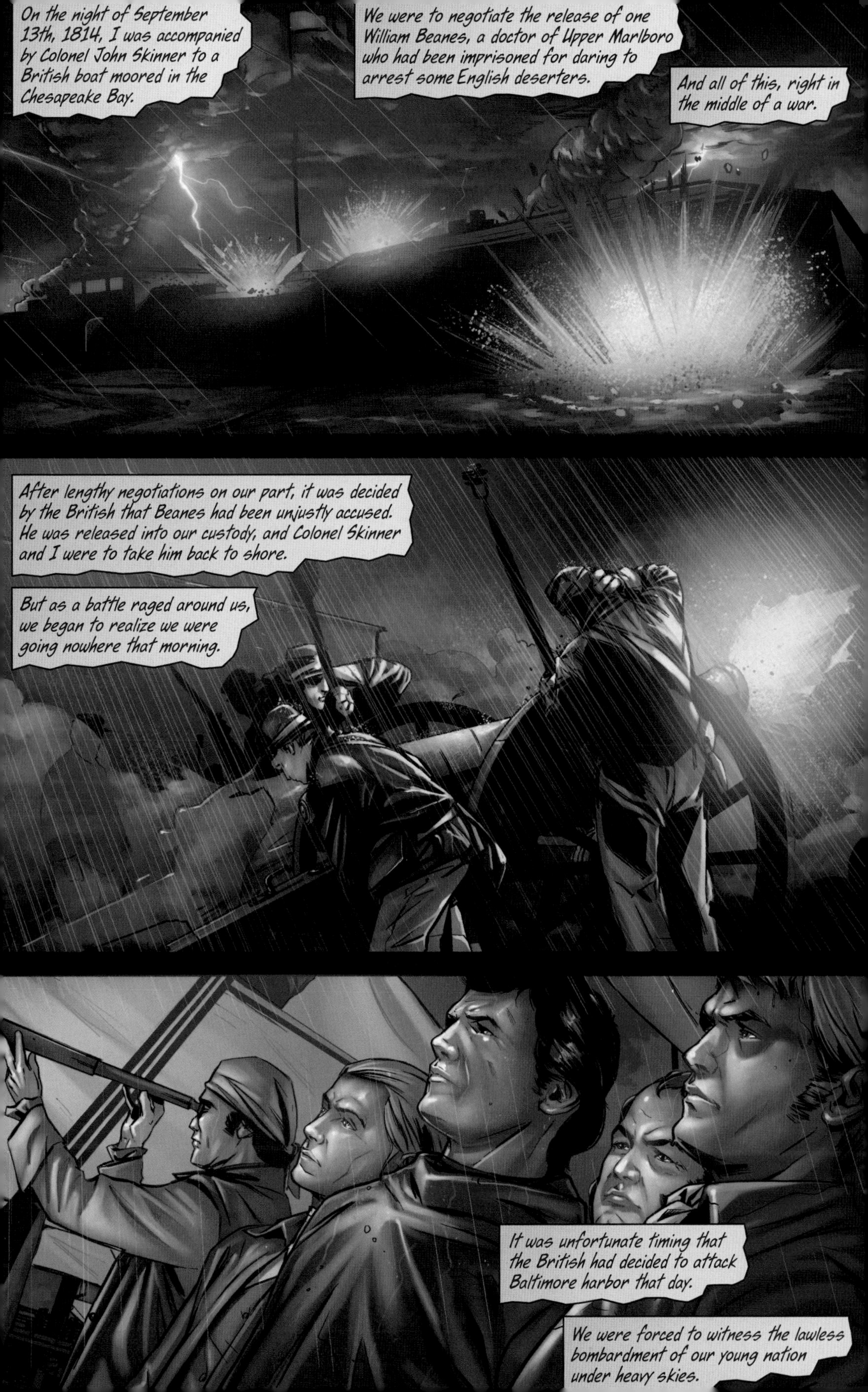
On the night of September 13th, 1814, I was accompanied by Colonel John Skinner to a British boat moored in the Chesapeake Bay.
We were to negotiate the release of one William Beanes, a doctor of Upper Marlboro who had been imprisoned for daring to arrest some English deserters.
And all of this, right in the middle of a war.
After lengthy negotiations on our part, it was decided by the British that Beanes had been unjustly accused. He was released into our custody, and Colonel Skinner and I were to take him back to shore.
But as a battle raged around us, we began to realize we were going nowhere that morning.
It was unfortunate timing that the British had decided to attack Baltimore harbor that day.
We were forced to witness the lawless bombardment of our young nation under heavy skies.

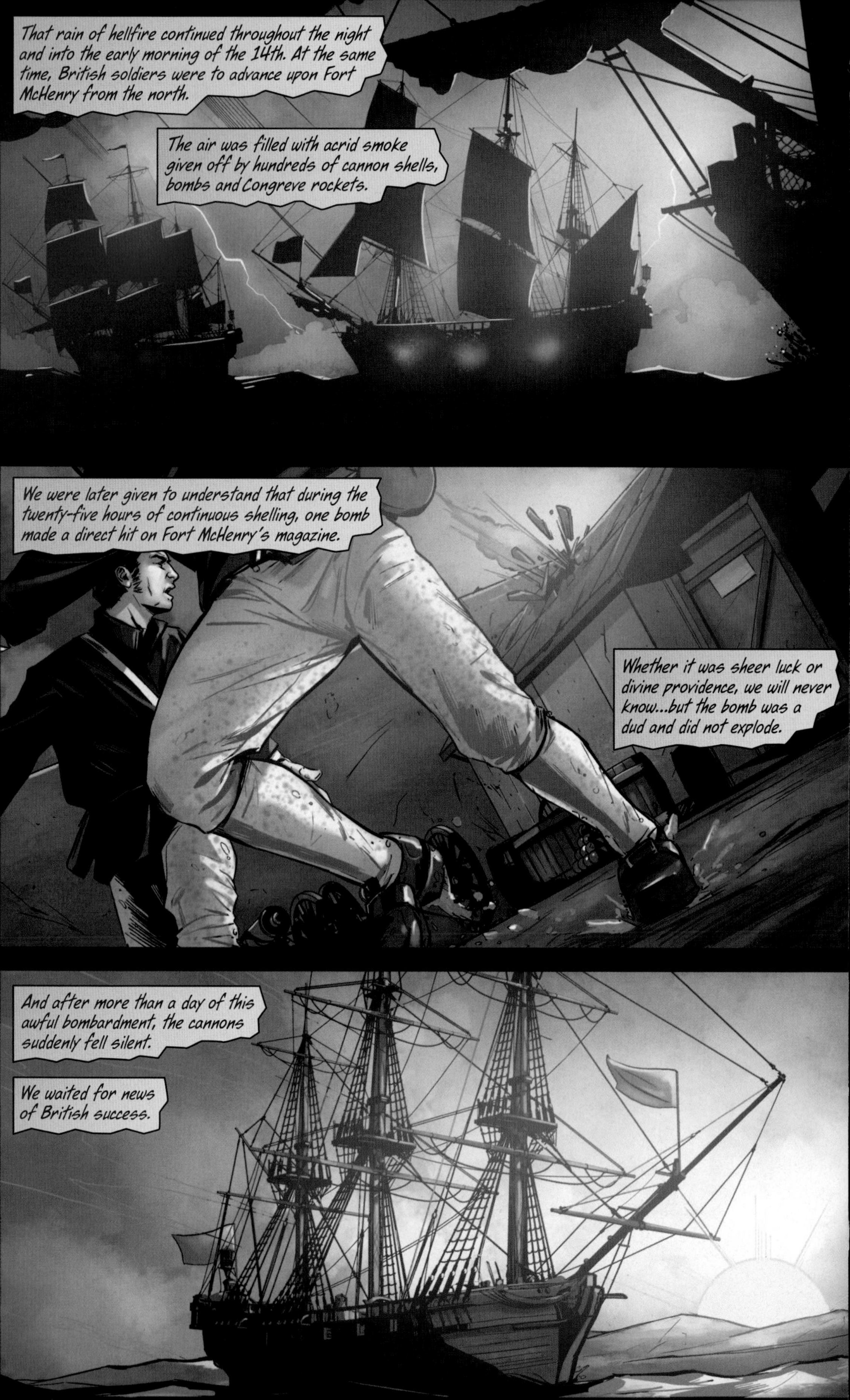
That rain of hellfire continued throughout the night and into the early morning of the 14th. At the same time, British soldiers were to advance upon Fort McHenry from the north.
The air was filled with acrid smoke given off by hundreds of cannon shells, bombs and Congreve rockets.
We were later given to understand that during the twenty-five hours of continuous shelling, one bomb made a direct hit on Fort McHenry's magazine.
Whether it was sheer luck or divine providence, we will never know...but the bomb was a dud and did not explode.
And after more than a day of this awful bombardment, the cannons suddenly fell silent.
We waited for news of British success.

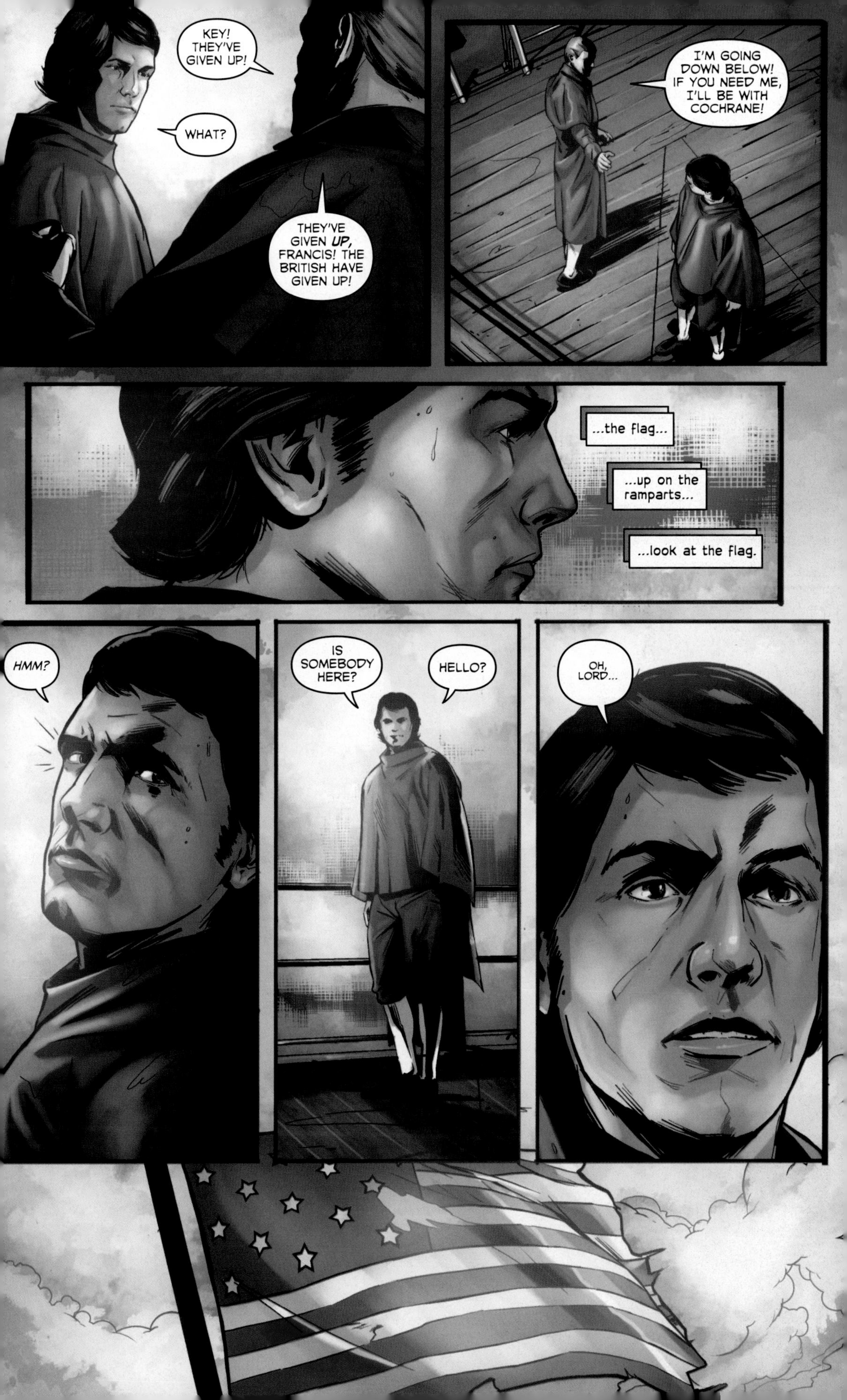
KEY! THEY'VE GIVEN UP!
WHAT?
THEY'VE GIVEN *UP*, FRANCIS! THE BRITISH HAVE GIVEN UP!
I'M GOING DOWN BELOW! IF YOU NEED ME, I'LL BE WITH COCHRANE!
...the flag...
...up on the ramparts...
...look at the flag.
HMM?
IS SOMEBODY HERE?
HELLO?
OH, LORD...

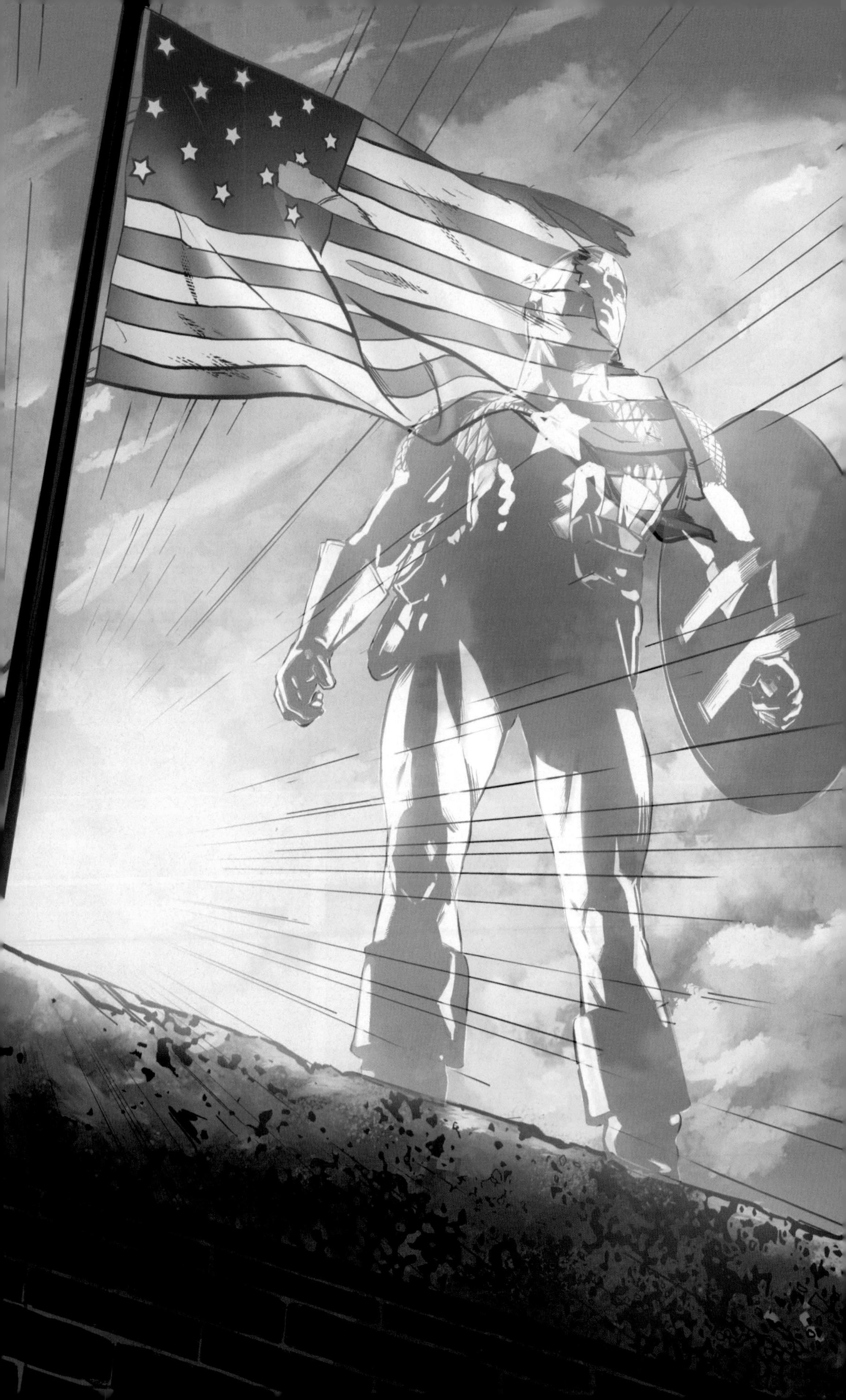

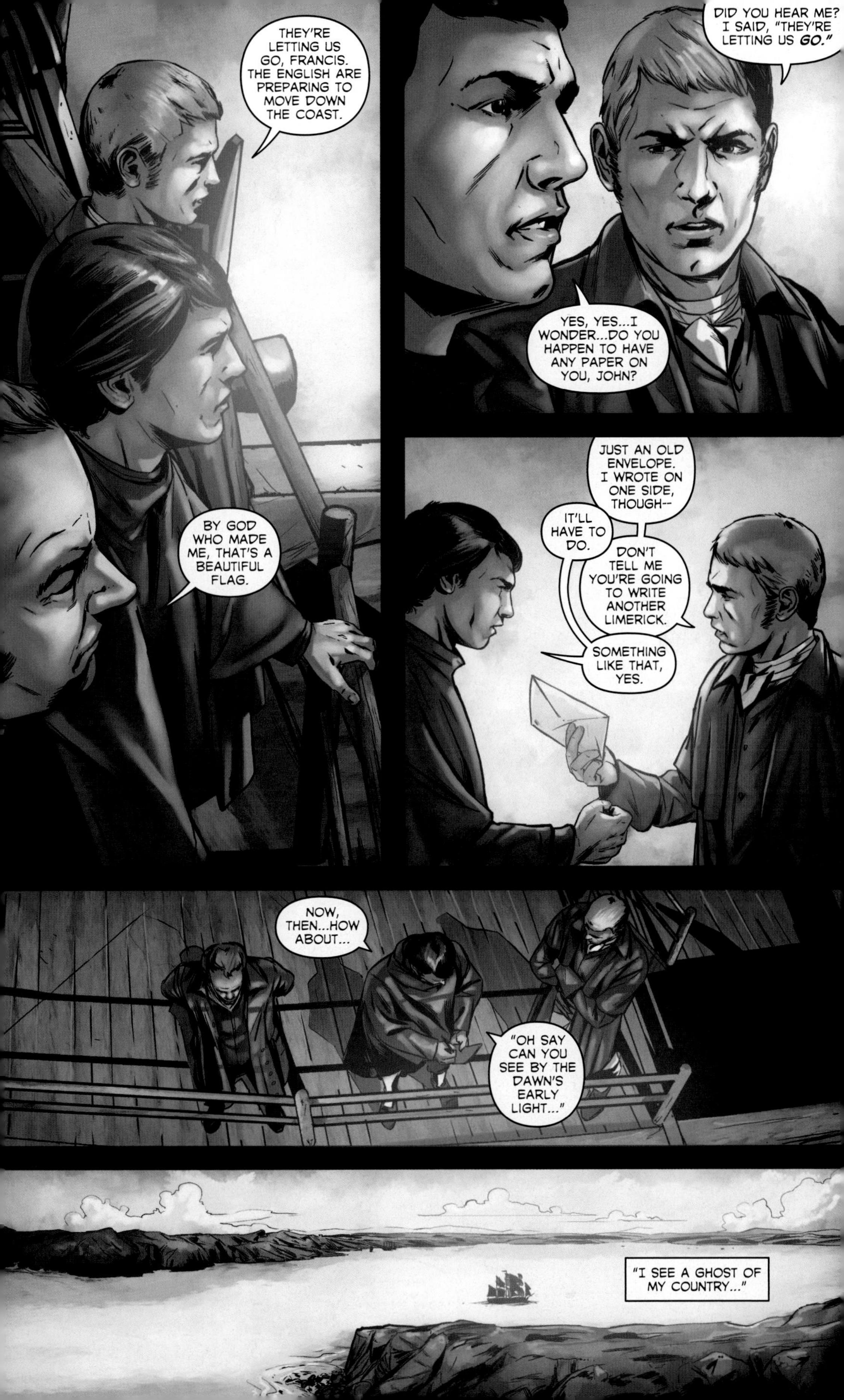
THEY'RE LETTING US GO, FRANCIS. THE ENGLISH ARE PREPARING TO MOVE DOWN THE COAST.
BY GOD WHO MADE ME, THAT'S A BEAUTIFUL FLAG.
DID YOU HEAR ME? I SAID, "THEY'RE LETTING US GO."
YES, YES...I WONDER...DO YOU HAPPEN TO HAVE ANY PAPER ON YOU, JOHN?
JUST AN OLD ENVELOPE. I WROTE ON ONE SIDE, THOUGH--
IT'LL HAVE TO DO.
DON'T TELL ME YOU'RE GOING TO WRITE ANOTHER LIMERICK.
SOMETHING LIKE THAT, YES.
NOW, THEN...HOW ABOUT...
"OH SAY CAN YOU SEE BY THE DAWN'S EARLY LIGHT..."
"I SEE A GHOST OF MY COUNTRY..."

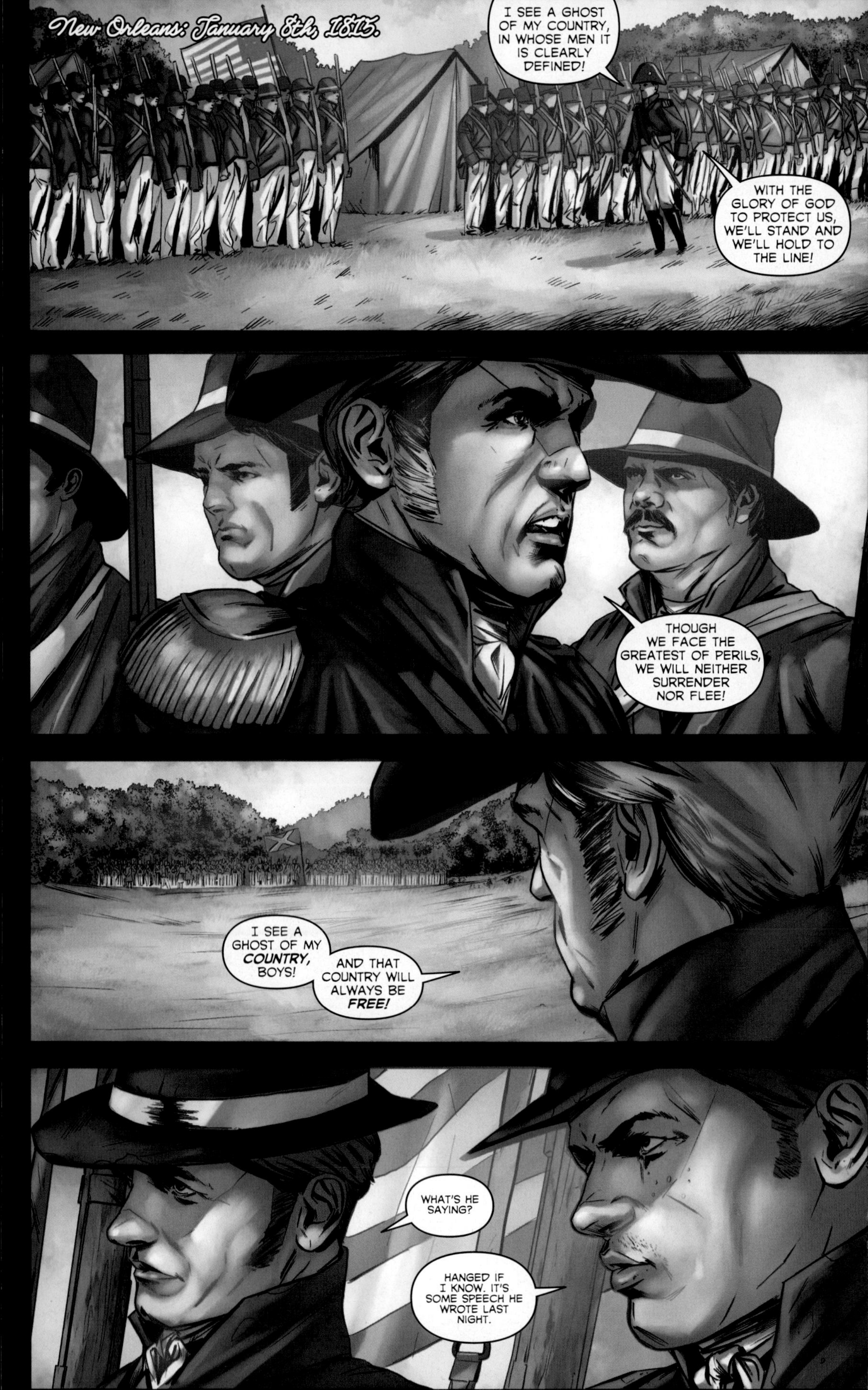
New Orleans: January 8th, 1815.
I SEE A GHOST OF MY COUNTRY, IN WHOSE MEN IT IS CLEARLY DEFINED!
WITH THE GLORY OF GOD TO PROTECT US, WE'LL STAND AND WE'LL HOLD TO THE LINE!
THOUGH WE FACE THE GREATEST OF PERILS, WE WILL NEITHER SURRENDER NOR FLEE!
I SEE A GHOST OF MY COUNTRY, BOYS!
AND THAT COUNTRY WILL ALWAYS BE FREE!
WHAT'S HE SAYING?
HANGED IF I KNOW. IT'S SOME SPEECH HE WROTE LAST NIGHT.

ALMOST THERE, NOW, MY FINE BOYS. TIME TO SHOW THESE BRITISH A THING OR TWO.

YOU-- WHERE ARE YOU FROM, SON?

LEXINGTON, KENTUCKY, GENERAL JACKSON.

THERE ARE THOSE WHO DON'T THINK MUCH OF A KENTUCKY RIFLEMAN!

THEY PROBABLY THINK THAT A MAN FROM KENTUCKY IS SOFT. THAT HE'S DISORGANIZED.

THESE MEN WITH THEIR FINE RED COATS AND THEIR SHINY NEW MUSKETS THINK THEY HAVE THE TAKING OF US.

BUT THEY HAVE SHORT MEMORIES, BOYS! FOR IF I'M NOT MISTAKEN, DIDN'T WE ALREADY SHOW THEIR DADDIES A THING OR TWO ABOUT HOW THE MEN OF THIS LAND CAN FIGHT?

NOW...WHO WANTS TO TEACH THESE BRITISH ANOTHER LESSON ON THE HEART OF A KENTUCKY RIFLEMAN?

AAAAAAAAAAAAAAAAAAAAAGHHH!

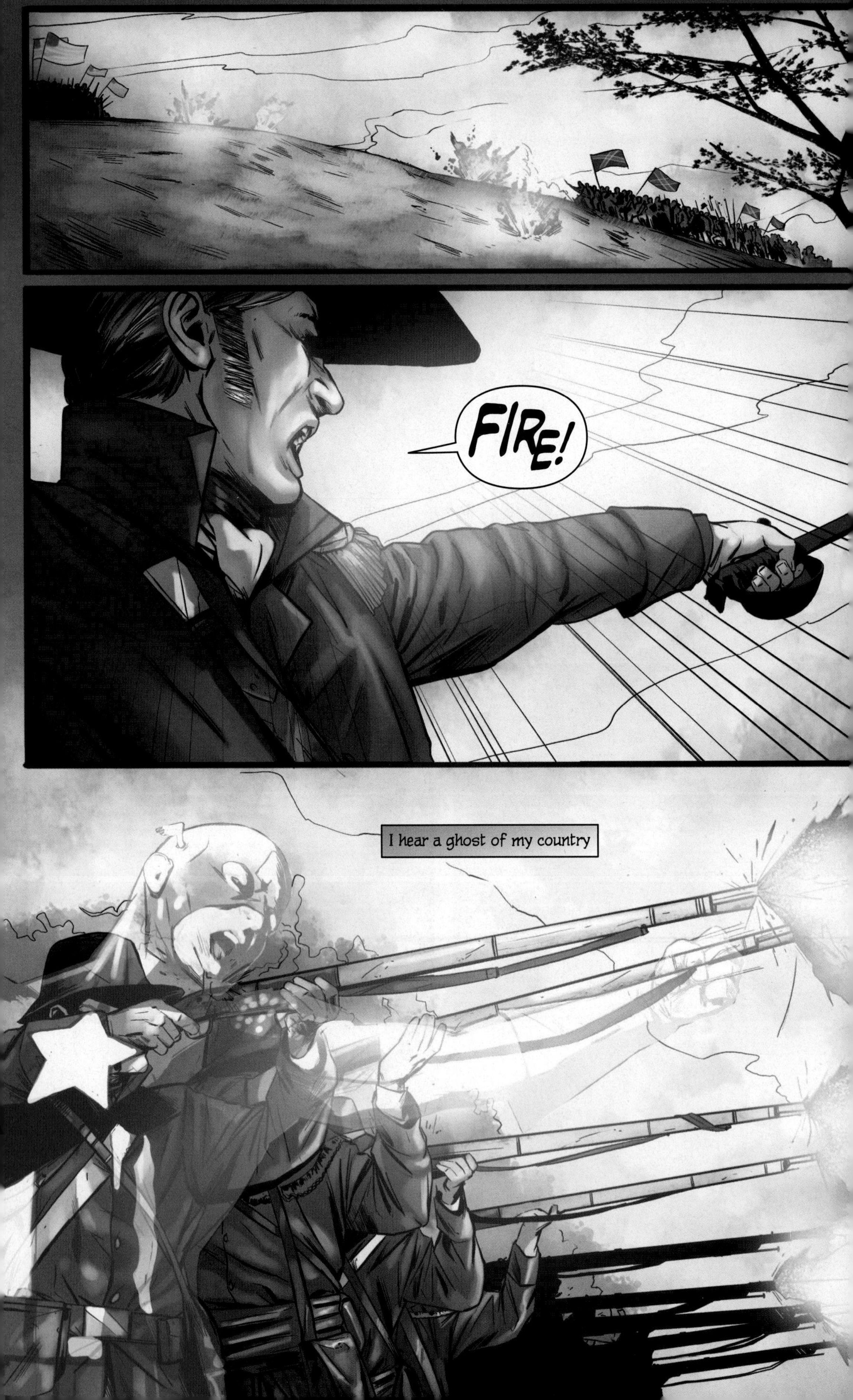
FIRE!
I hear a ghost of my country

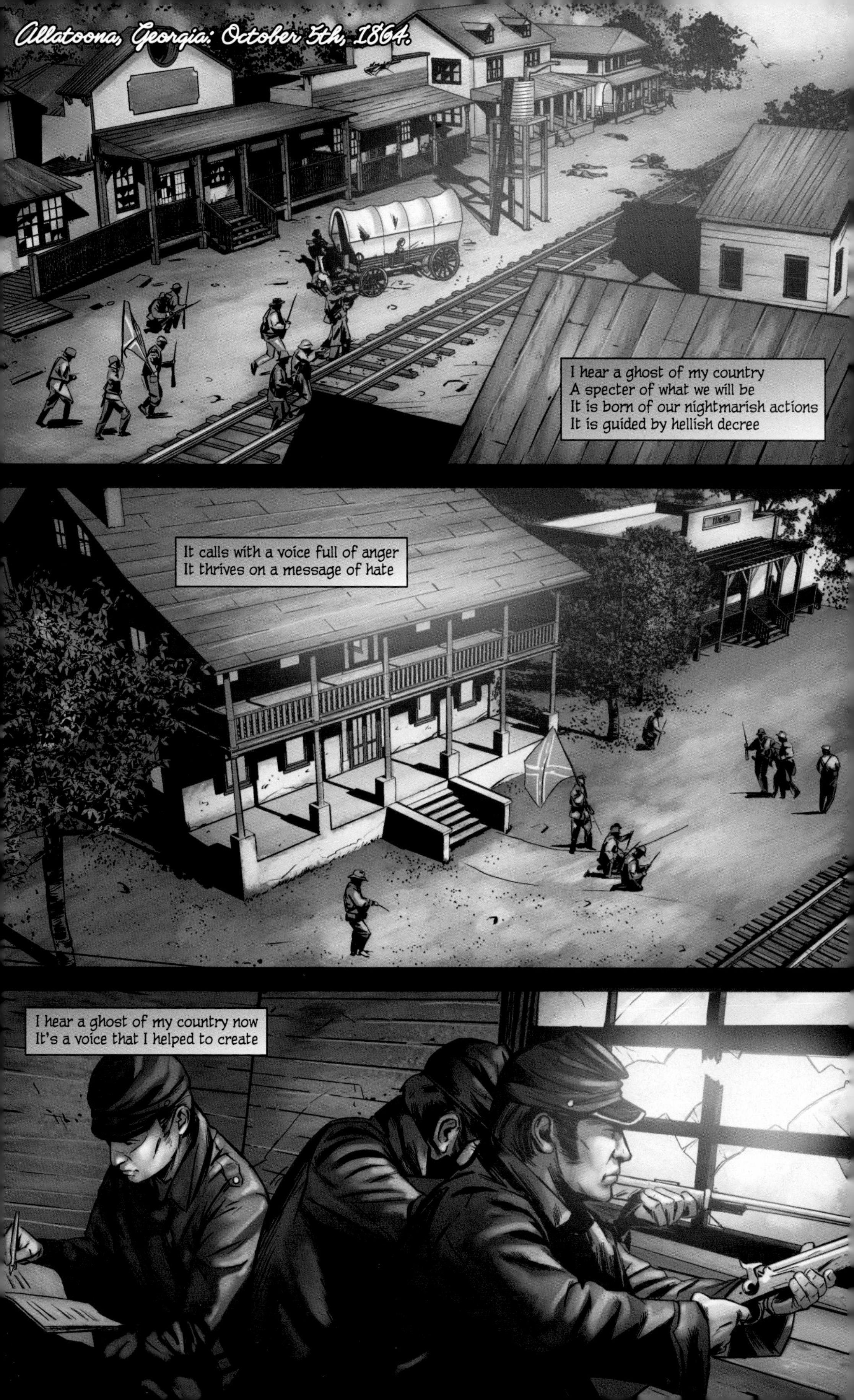

Allatoona, Georgia: October 5th, 1864.
I hear a ghost of my country
A specter of what we will be
It is born of our nightmarish actions
It is guided by hellish decree
It calls with a voice full of anger
It thrives on a message of hate
I hear a ghost of my country now
It's a voice that I helped to create

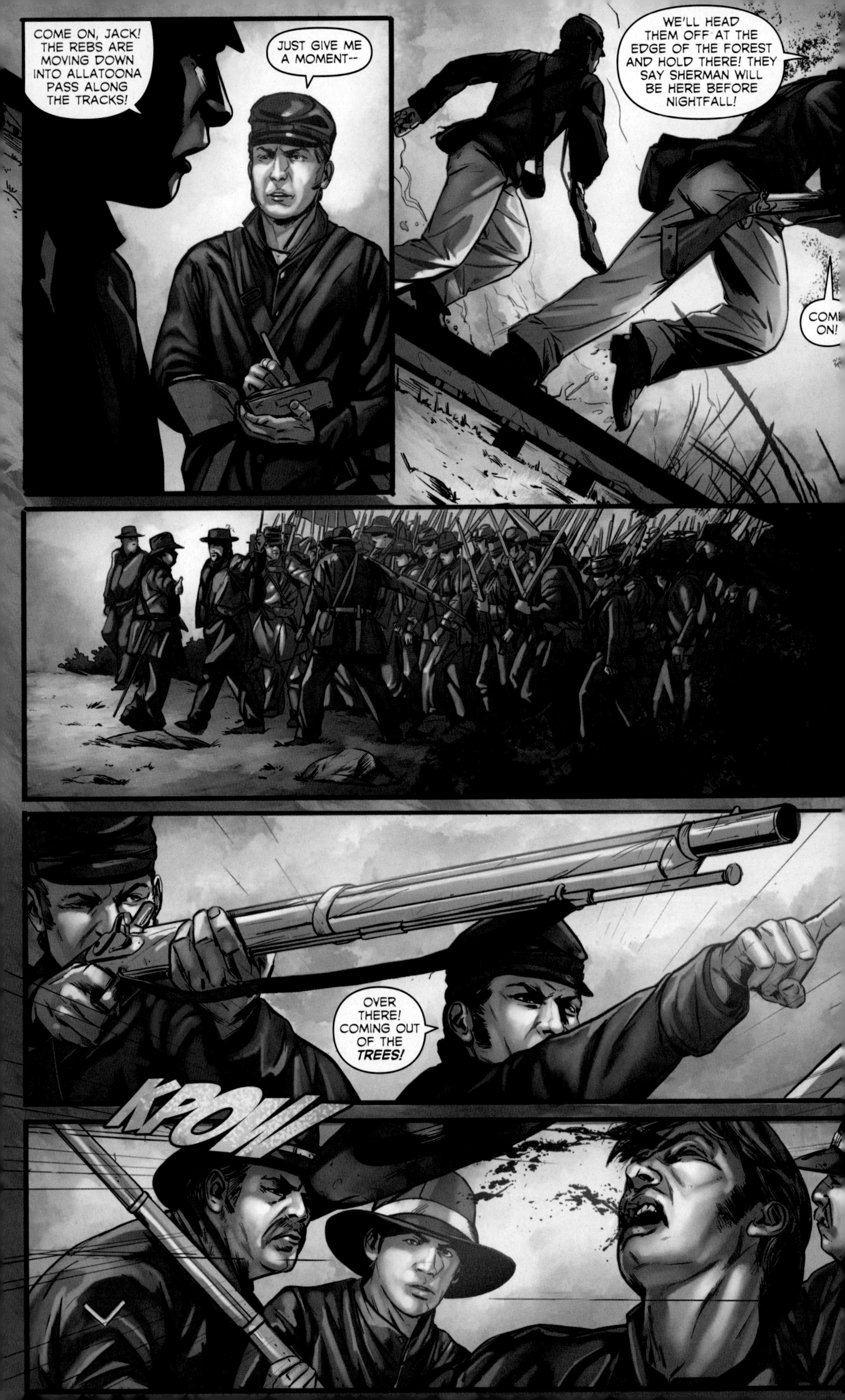
COME ON, JACK! THE REBS ARE MOVING DOWN INTO ALLATOONA PASS ALONG THE TRACKS!
JUST GIVE ME A MOMENT--
WE'LL HEAD THEM OFF AT THE EDGE OF THE FOREST AND HOLD THERE! THEY SAY SHERMAN WILL BE HERE BEFORE NIGHTFALL!
COME ON!
OVER THERE! COMING OUT OF THE *TREES!*
KPOW!

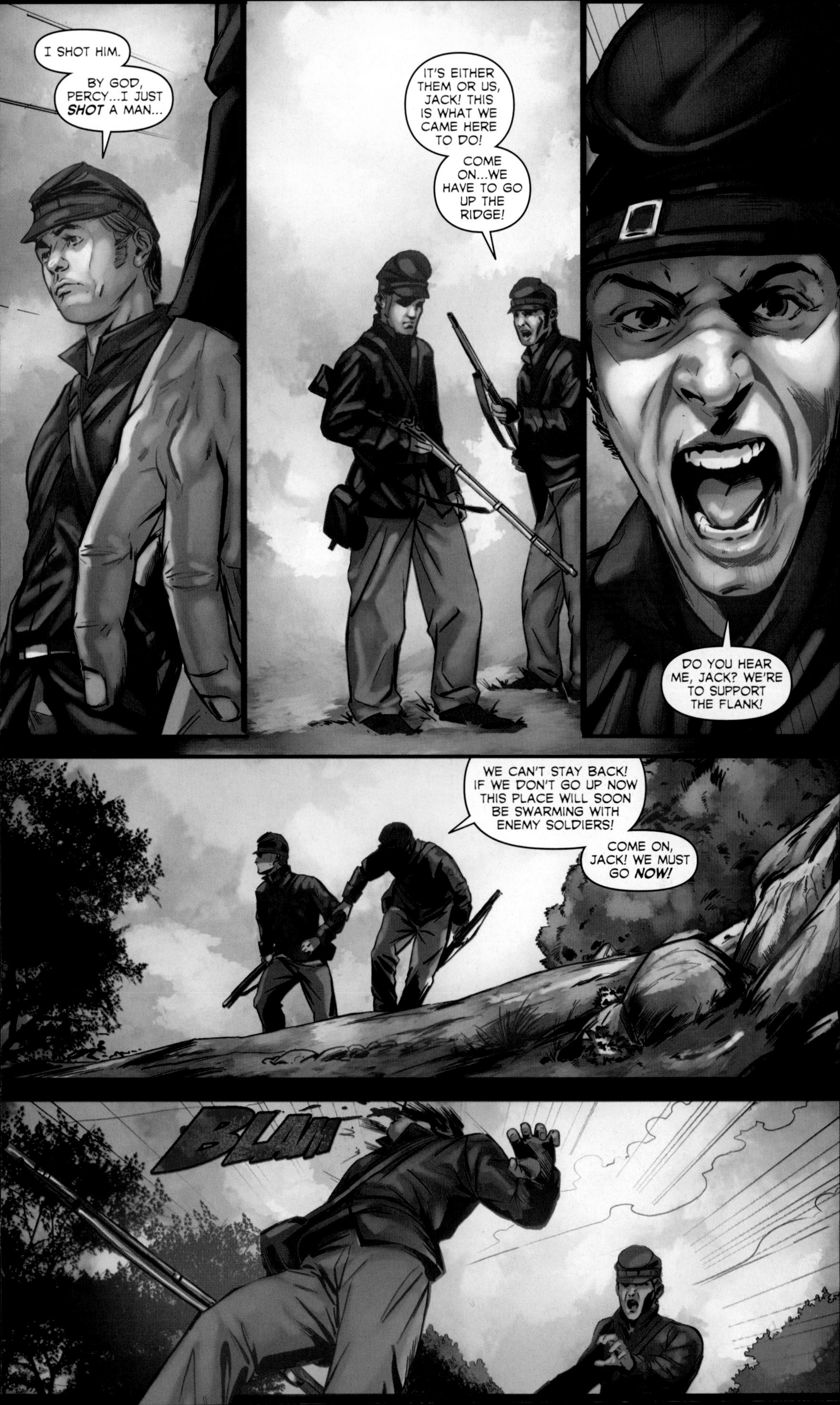

I SHOT HIM.
BY GOD, PERCY...I JUST *SHOT* A MAN...
IT'S EITHER THEM OR US, JACK! THIS IS WHAT WE CAME HERE TO DO!
COME ON...WE HAVE TO GO UP THE RIDGE!
DO YOU HEAR ME, JACK? WE'RE TO SUPPORT THE FLANK!
WE CAN'T STAY BACK! IF WE DON'T GO UP NOW THIS PLACE WILL SOON BE SWARMING WITH ENEMY SOLDIERS!
COME ON, JACK! WE MUST GO *NOW!*
BLAM

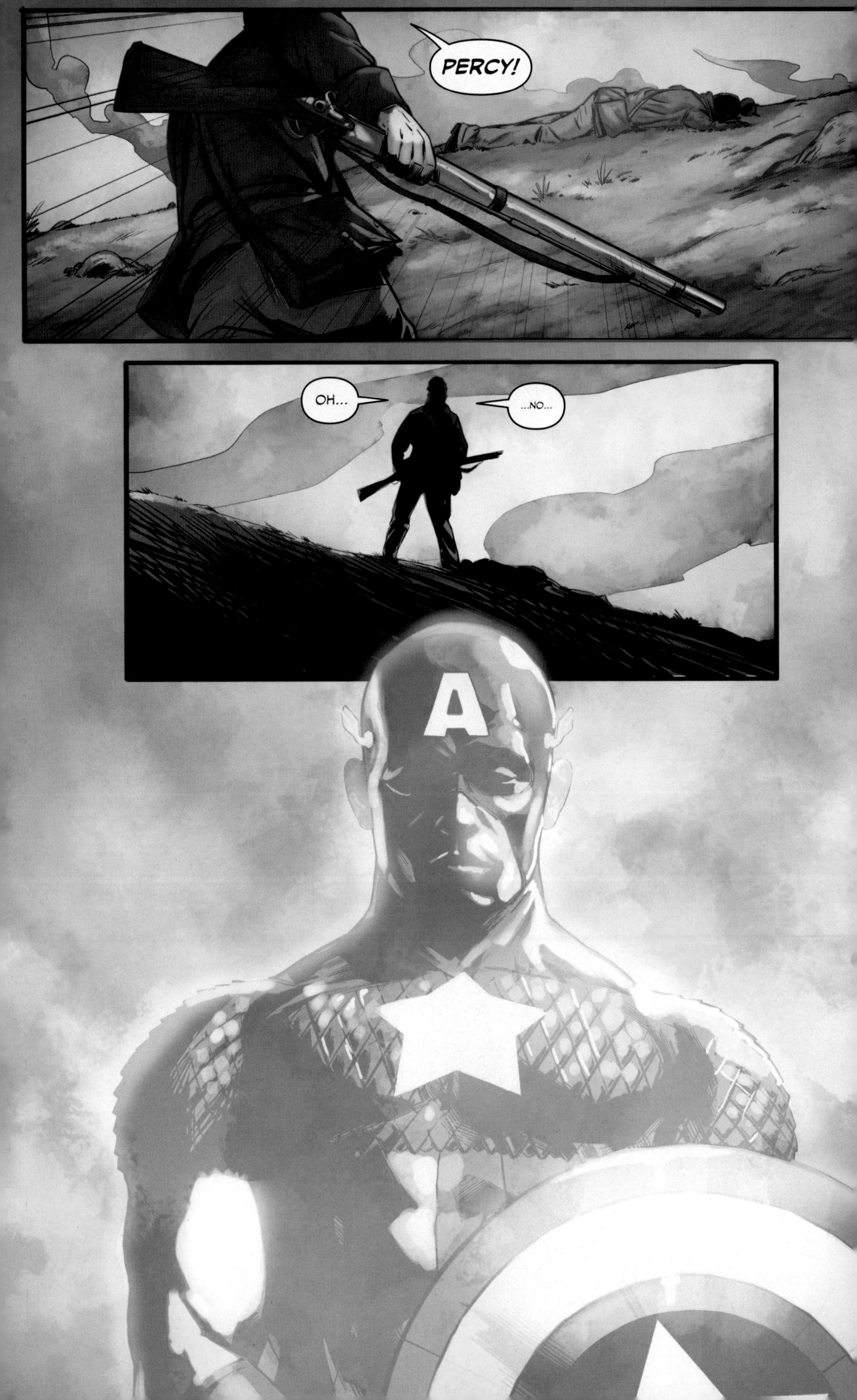
PERCY!
OH...
...NO...

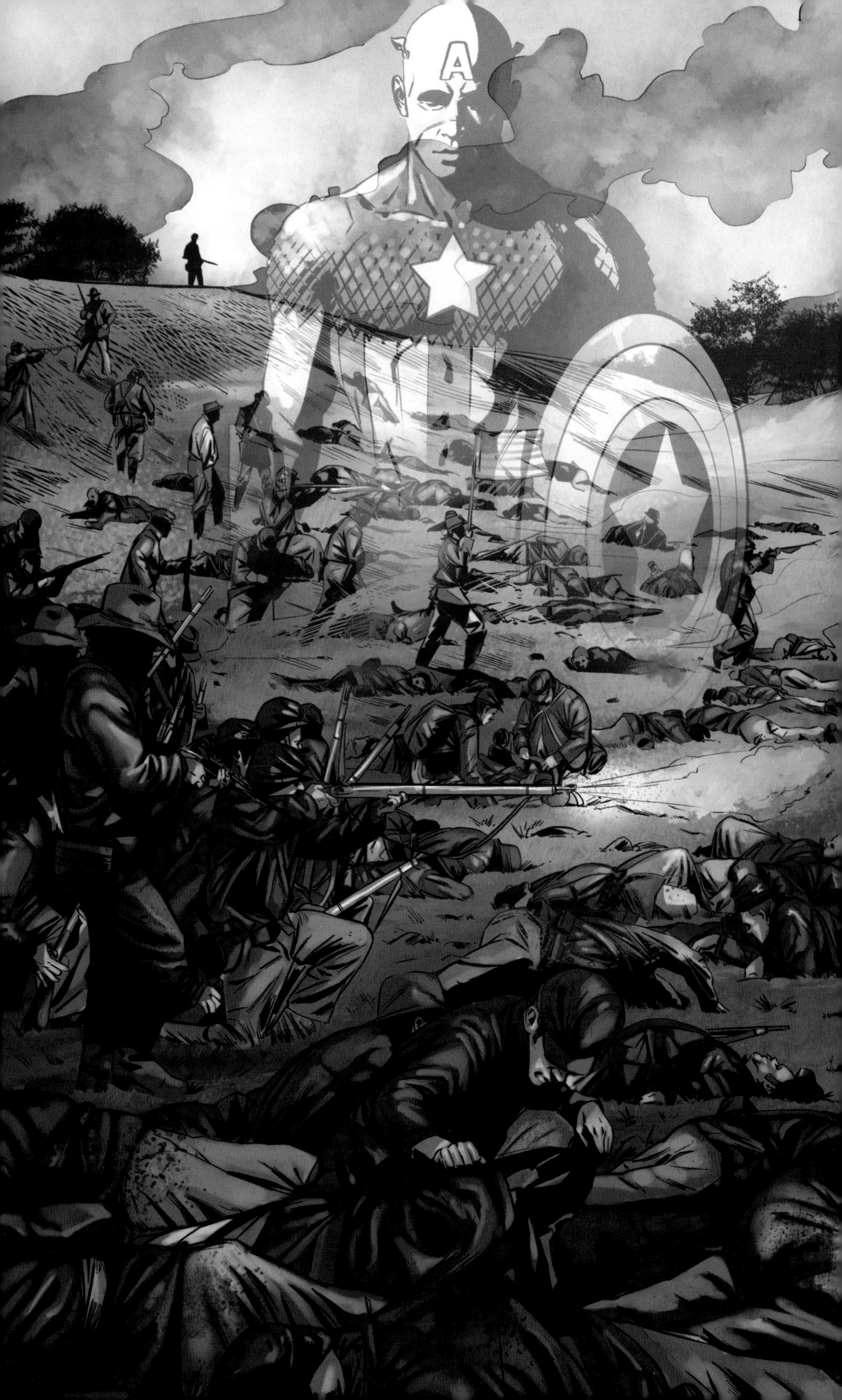

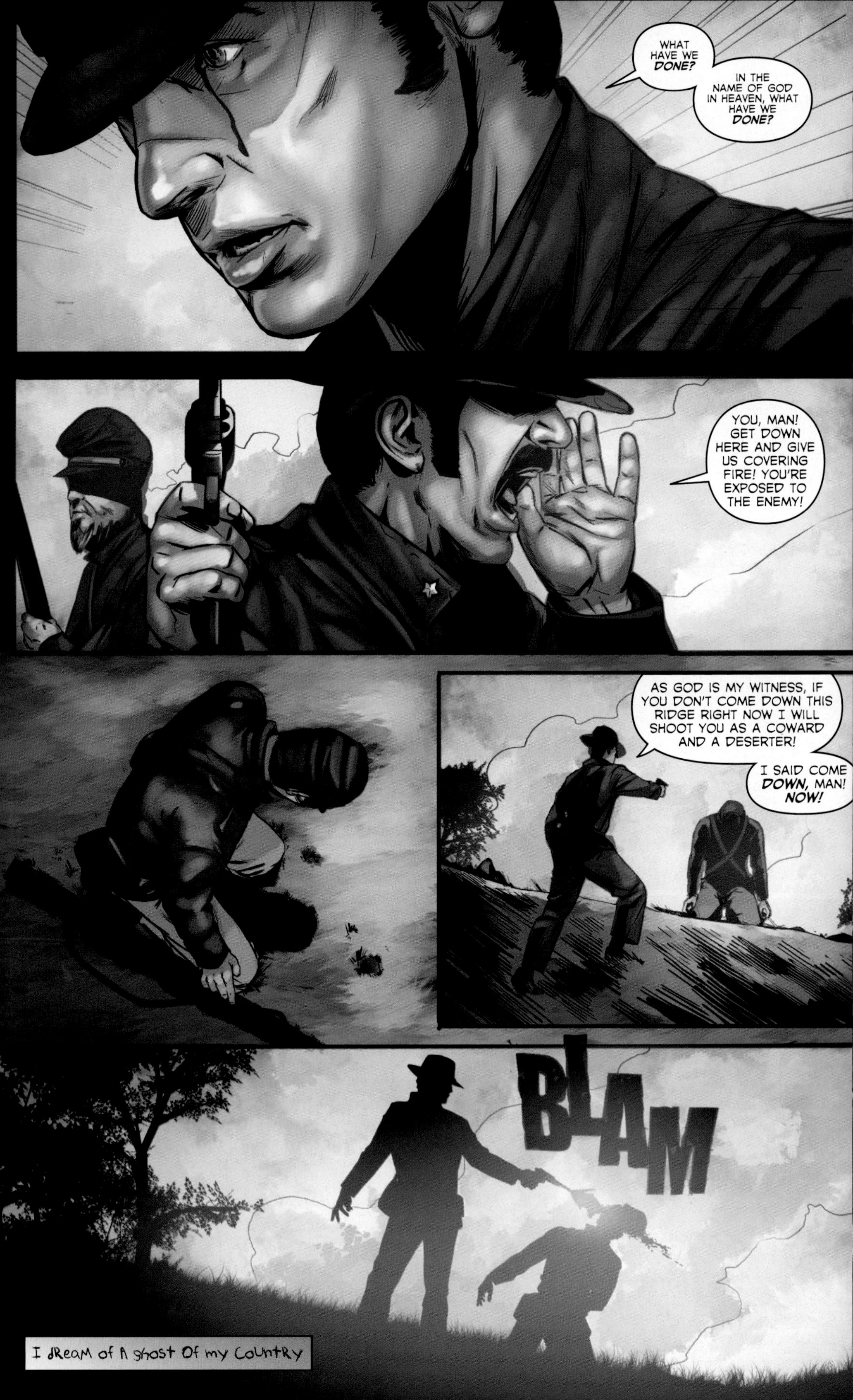
WHAT HAVE WE DONE?
IN THE NAME OF GOD IN HEAVEN, WHAT HAVE WE DONE?
YOU, MAN! GET DOWN HERE AND GIVE US COVERING FIRE! YOU'RE EXPOSED TO THE ENEMY!
AS GOD IS MY WITNESS, IF YOU DON'T COME DOWN THIS RIDGE RIGHT NOW I WILL SHOOT YOU AS A COWARD AND A DESERTER!
I SAID COME DOWN, MAN! NOW!
BLAM
I dReaM of A ghost Of my CountRy

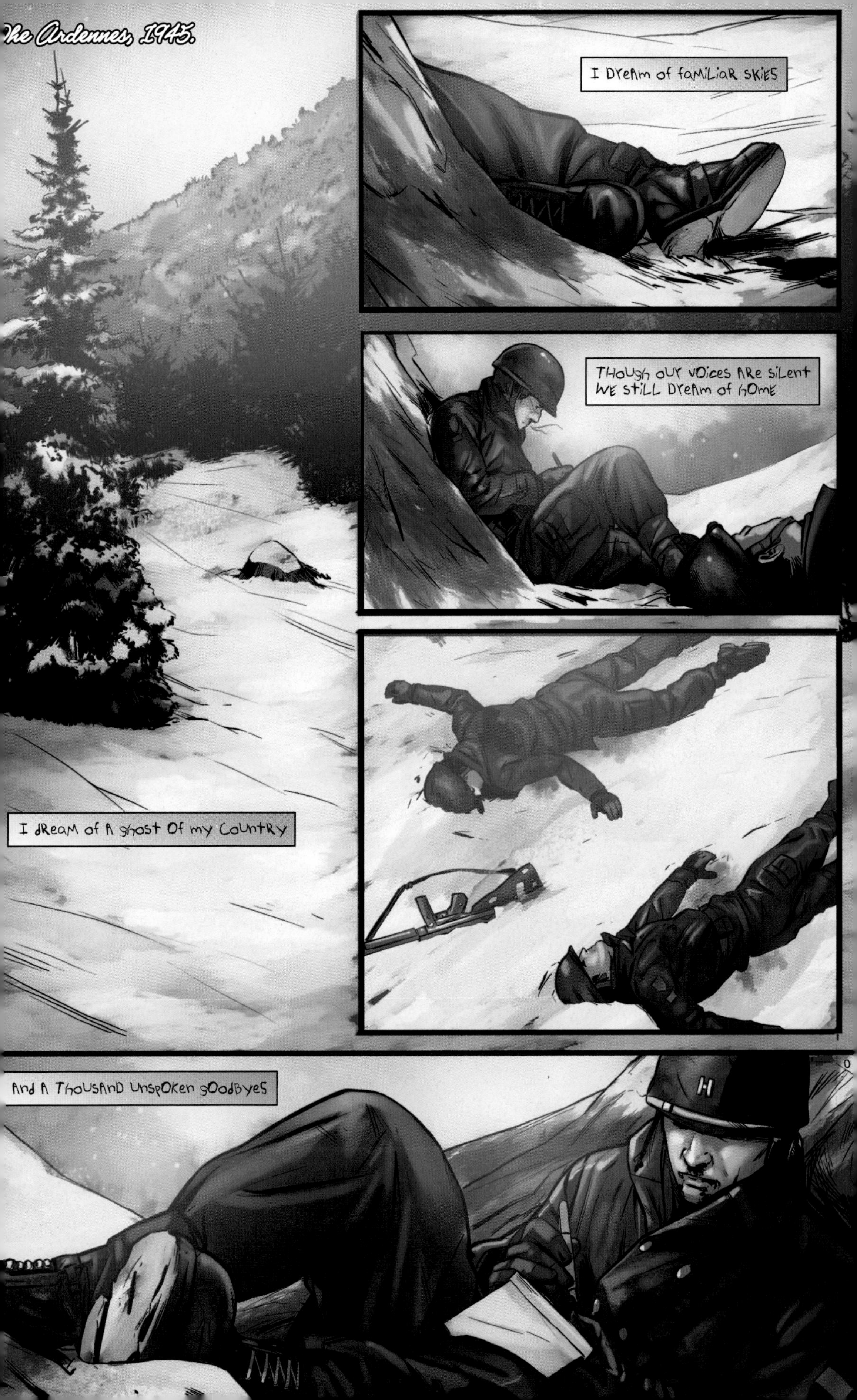
The Ardennes, 1945.
I dream of familiar skies
Though our voices are silent
we still dream of home
I dream of a ghost of my country
And a thousand unspoken goodbyes

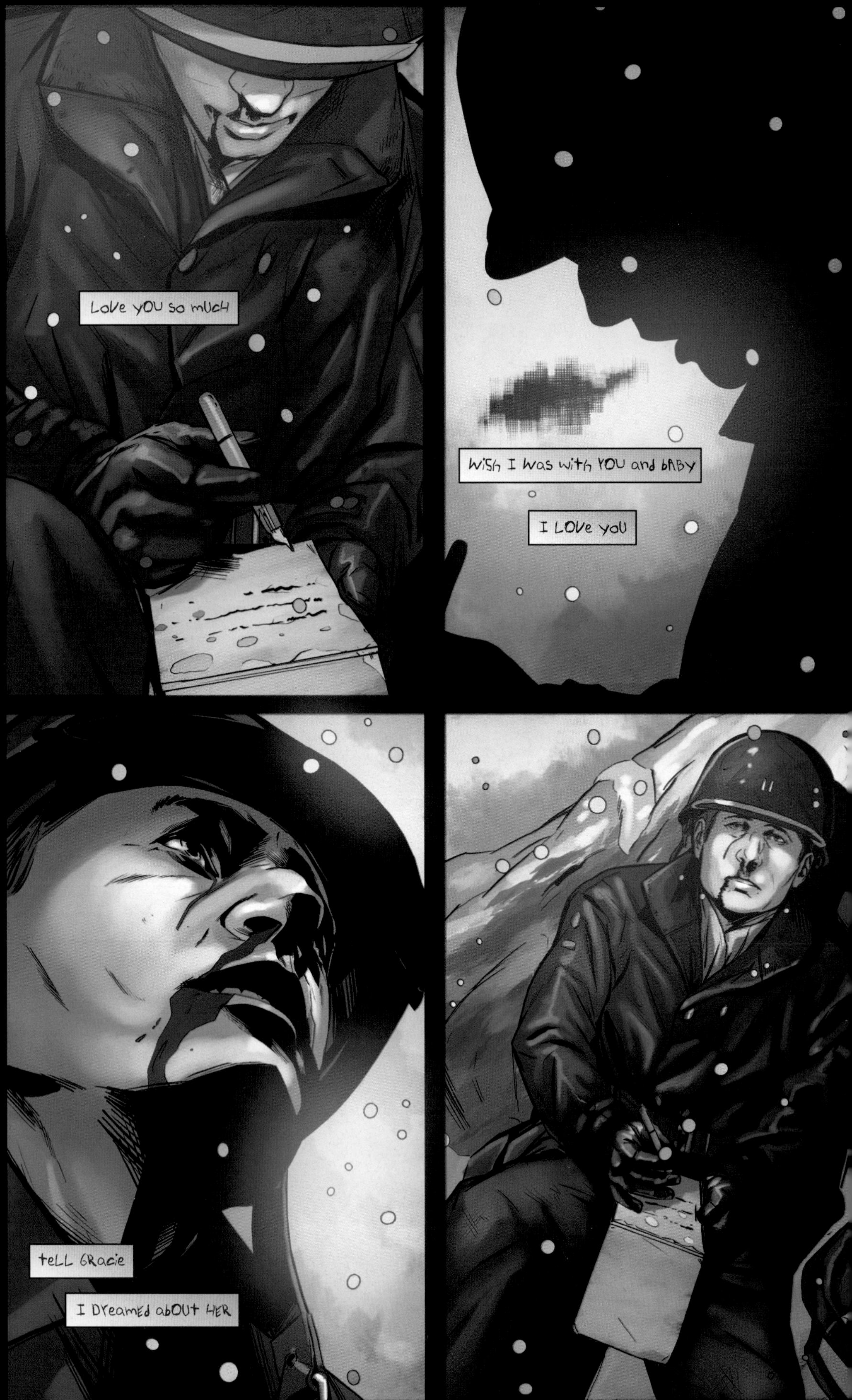
Love YOU so much
Wish I was with YOU and bABY
I LOVe you
teLL GRacie
I DReamed abOUt HER

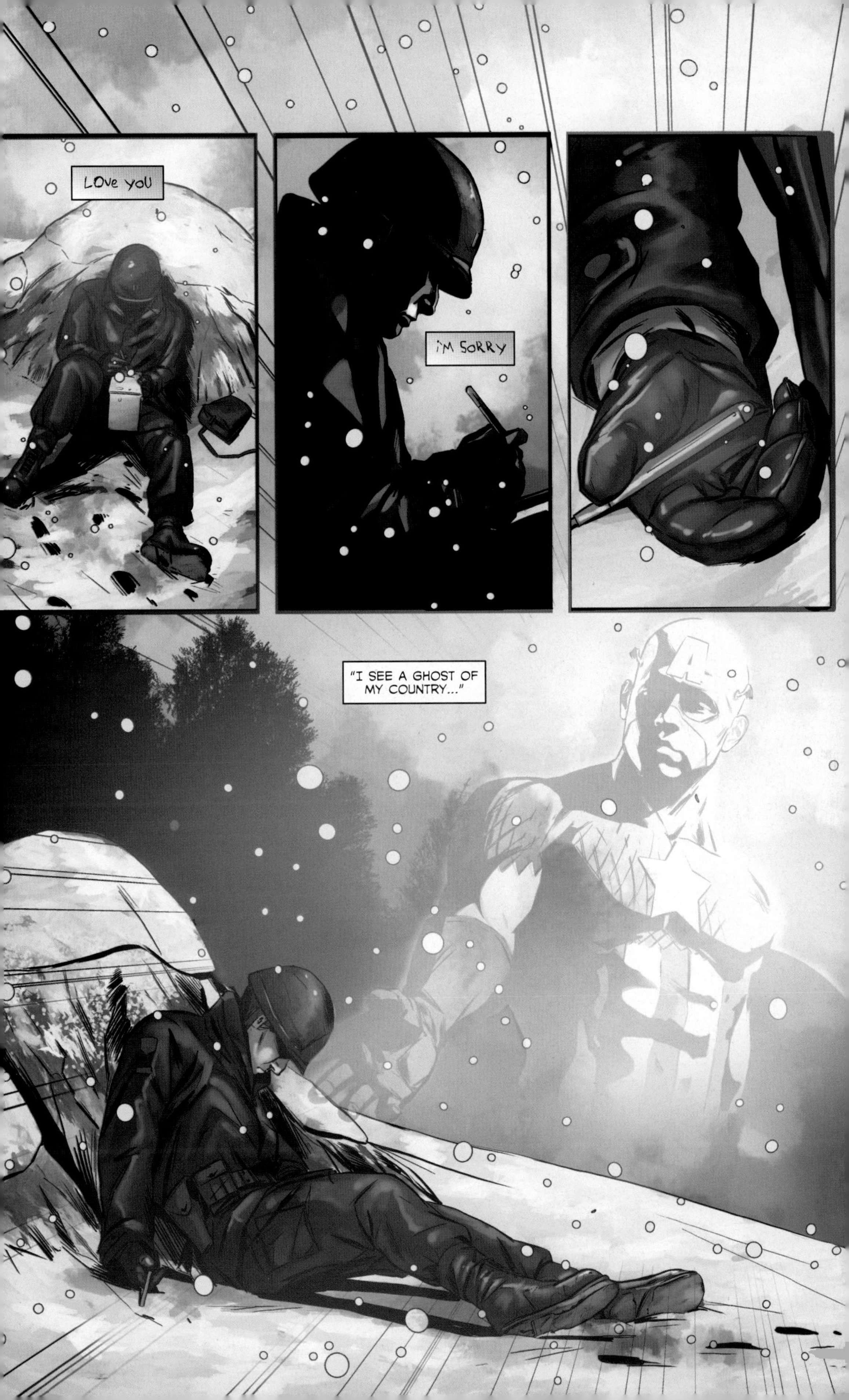
LOVE YOU
I'M SORRY
"I SEE A GHOST OF MY COUNTRY..."

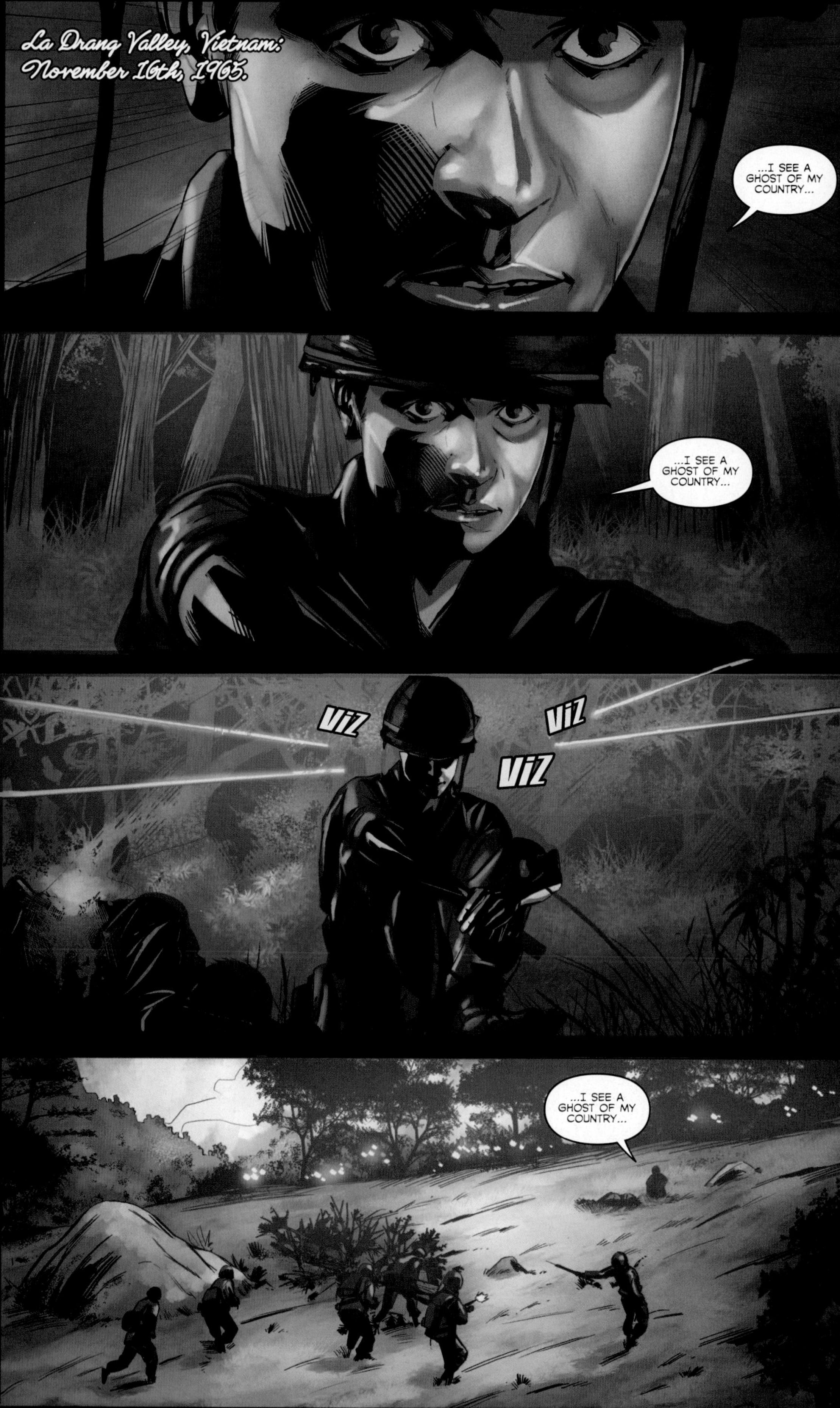
La Drang Valley, Vietnam:
November 16th, 1965.
...I SEE A GHOST OF MY COUNTRY...
...I SEE A GHOST OF MY COUNTRY...
VIZ
VIZ
VIZ
...I SEE A GHOST OF MY COUNTRY...

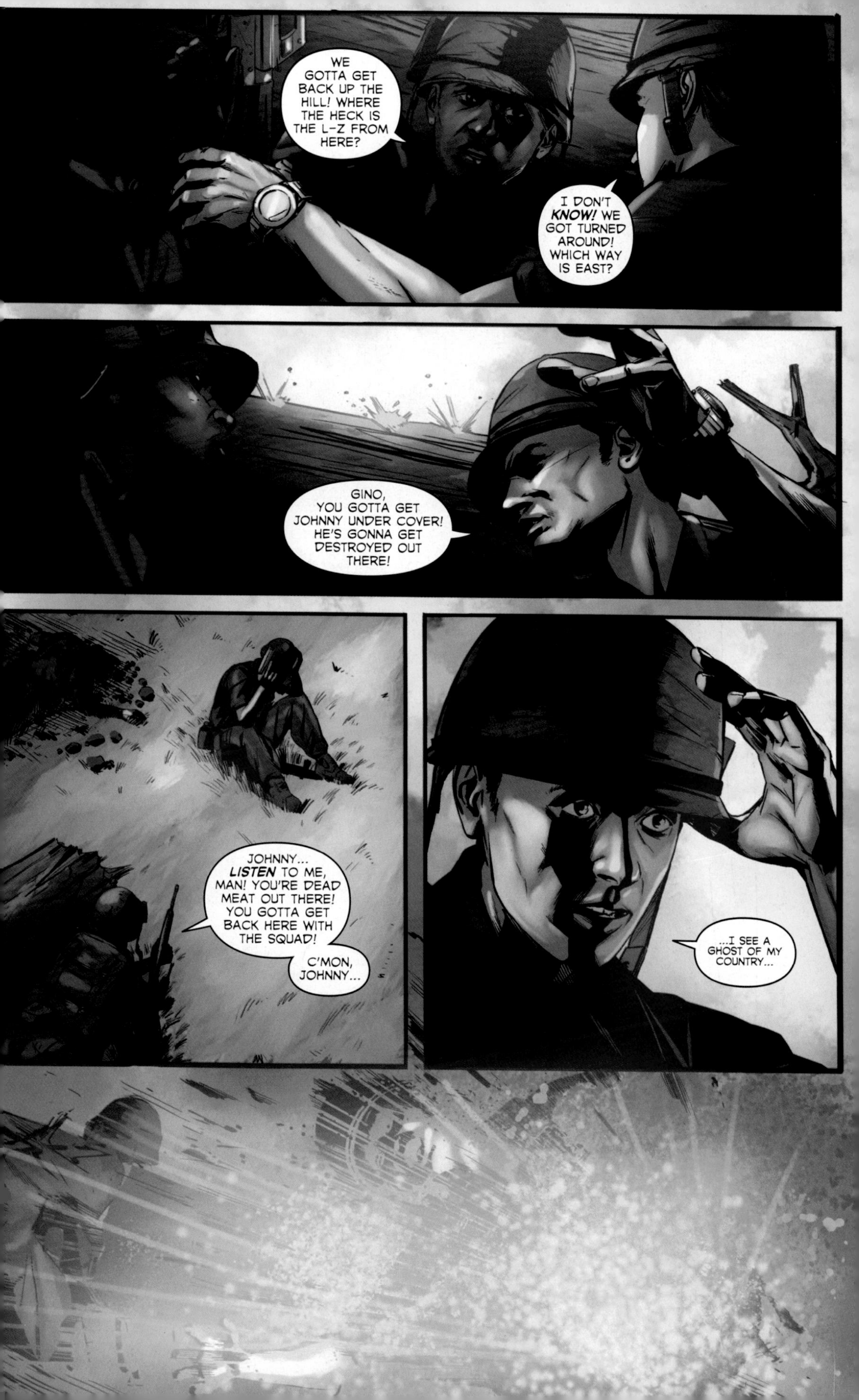
WE GOTTA GET BACK UP THE HILL! WHERE THE HECK IS THE L-Z FROM HERE?
I DON'T KNOW! WE GOT TURNED AROUND! WHICH WAY IS EAST?
GINO, YOU GOTTA GET JOHNNY UNDER COVER! HE'S GONNA GET DESTROYED OUT THERE!
JOHNNY... LISTEN TO ME, MAN! YOU'RE DEAD MEAT OUT THERE! YOU GOTTA GET BACK HERE WITH THE SQUAD!
C'MON, JOHNNY...
...I SEE A GHOST OF MY COUNTRY...

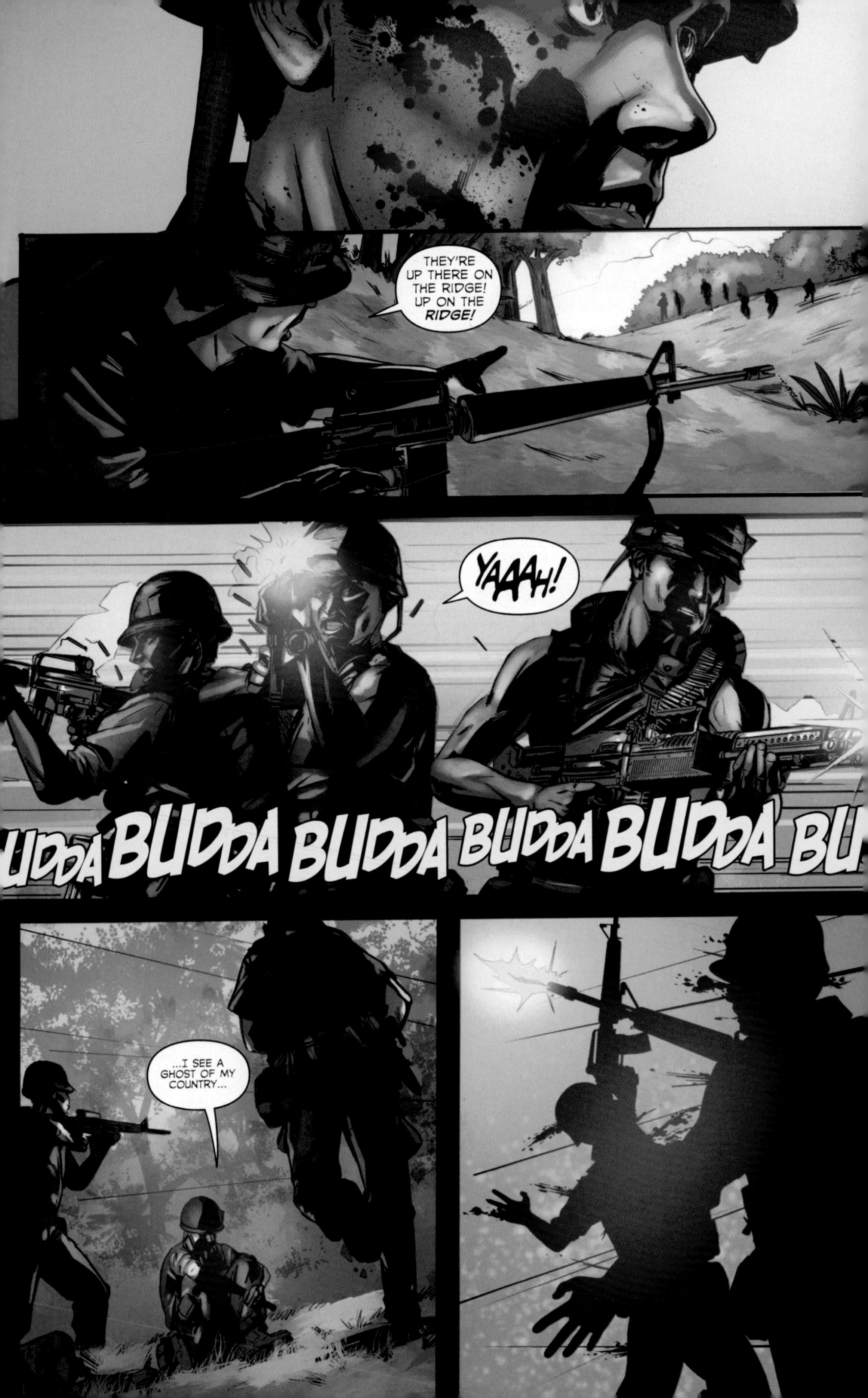
THEY'RE UP THERE ON THE RIDGE! UP ON THE RIDGE!
YAAAH!
UDDA BUDDA BUDDA BUDDA BUDDA BU
...I SEE A GHOST OF MY COUNTRY...

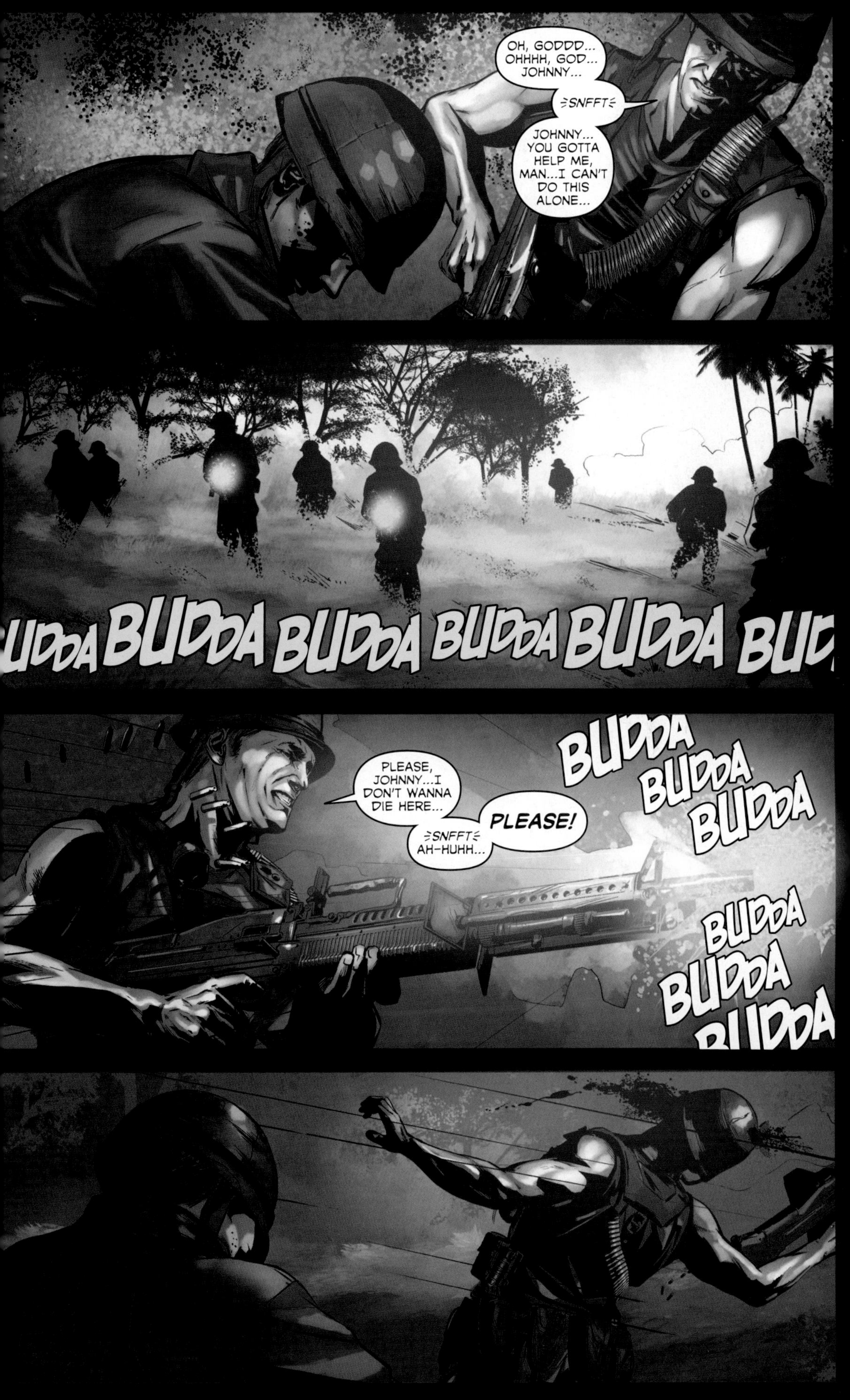
OH, GODDD... OHHHH, GOD... JOHNNY...
≈SNFFT≈
JOHNNY... YOU GOTTA HELP ME, MAN...I CAN'T DO THIS ALONE...
BUDDA BUDDA BUDDA BUDDA BUDDA
BUDDA BUDDA BUDDA
PLEASE, JOHNNY...I DON'T WANNA DIE HERE...
≈SNFFT≈ AH-HUHH...
PLEASE!
BUDDA BUDDA

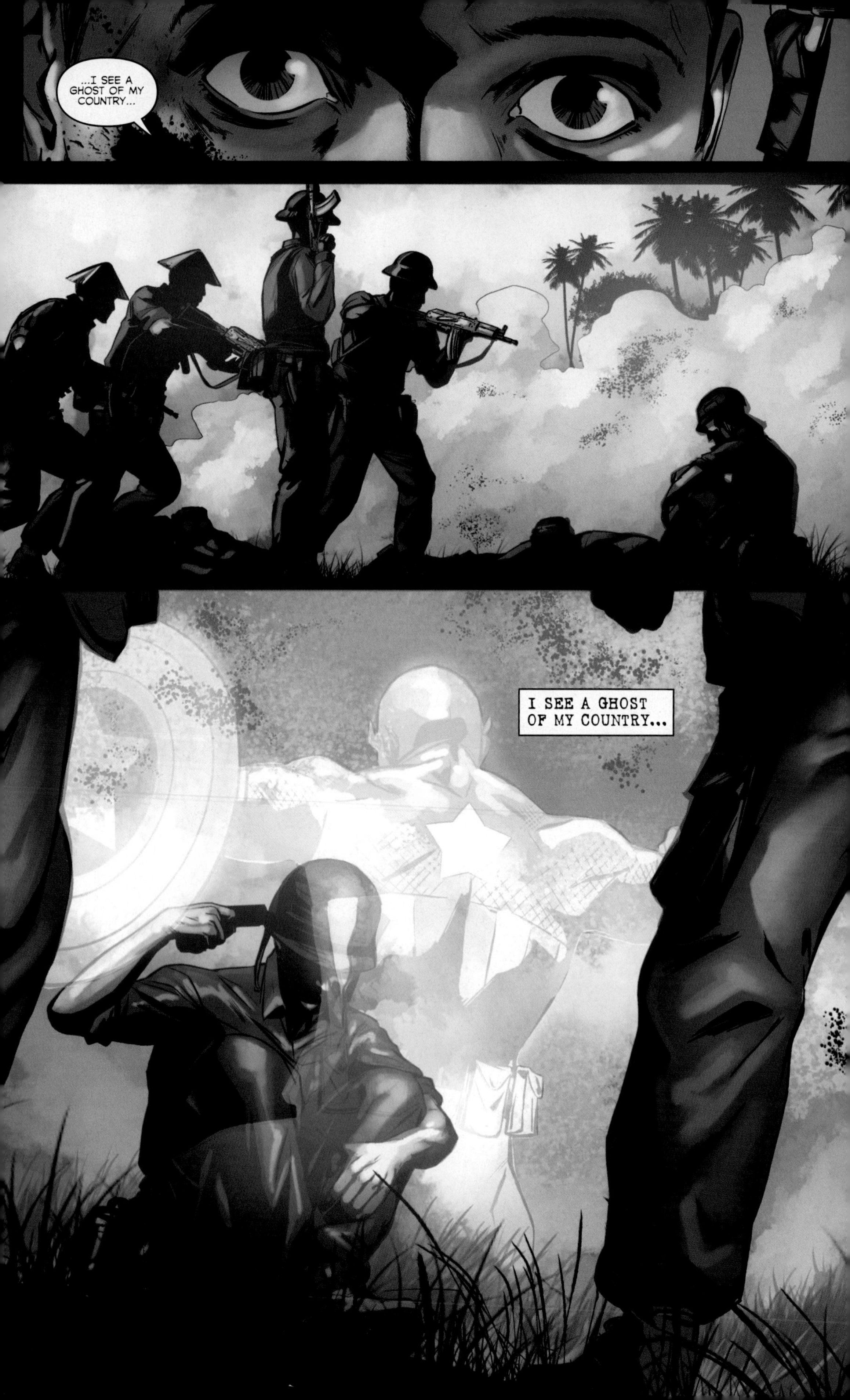
...I SEE A GHOST OF MY COUNTRY...
I SEE A GHOST OF MY COUNTRY...

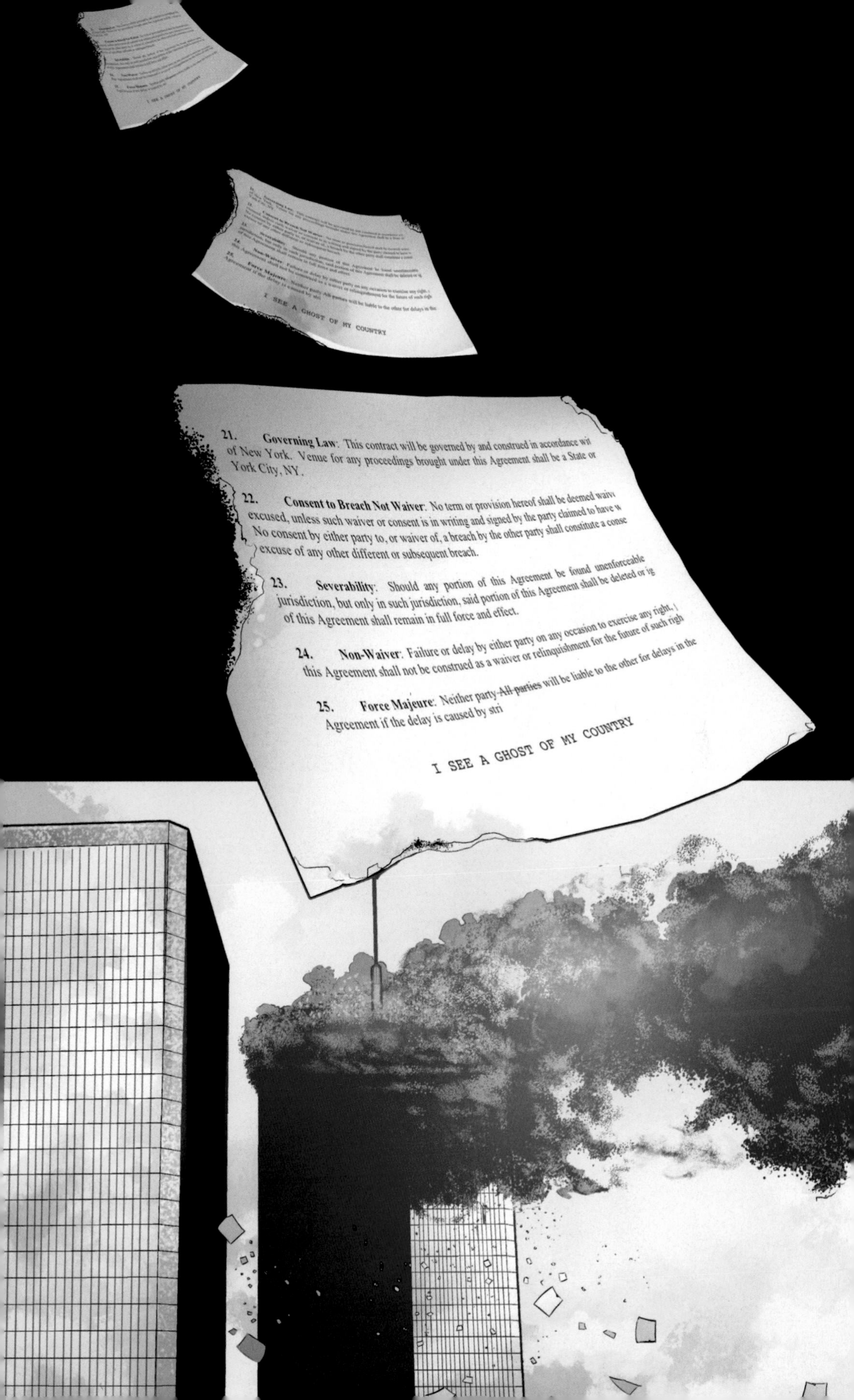
21. Governing Law: This contract will be governed by and construed in accordance wi
of New York. Venue for any proceedings brought under this Agreement shall be a State or
York City, NY.
22. Consent to Breach Not Waiver: No term or provision hereof shall be deemed waiv
excused, unless such waiver or consent is in writing and signed by the party claimed to have w
No consent by either party to, or waiver of, a breach by the other party shall constitute a conse
excuse of any other different or subsequent breach.
23. Severability: Should any portion of this Agreement be found unenforceable
jurisdiction, but only in such jurisdiction, said portion of this Agreement shall be deleted or ig
of this Agreement shall remain in full force and effect.
24. Non-Waiver: Failure or delay by either party on any occasion to exercise any right,
this Agreement shall not be construed as a waiver or relinquishment for the future of such righ
25. Force Majeure: Neither party All parties will be liable to the other for delays in the
Agreement if the delay is caused by stri
I SEE A GHOST OF MY COUNTRY

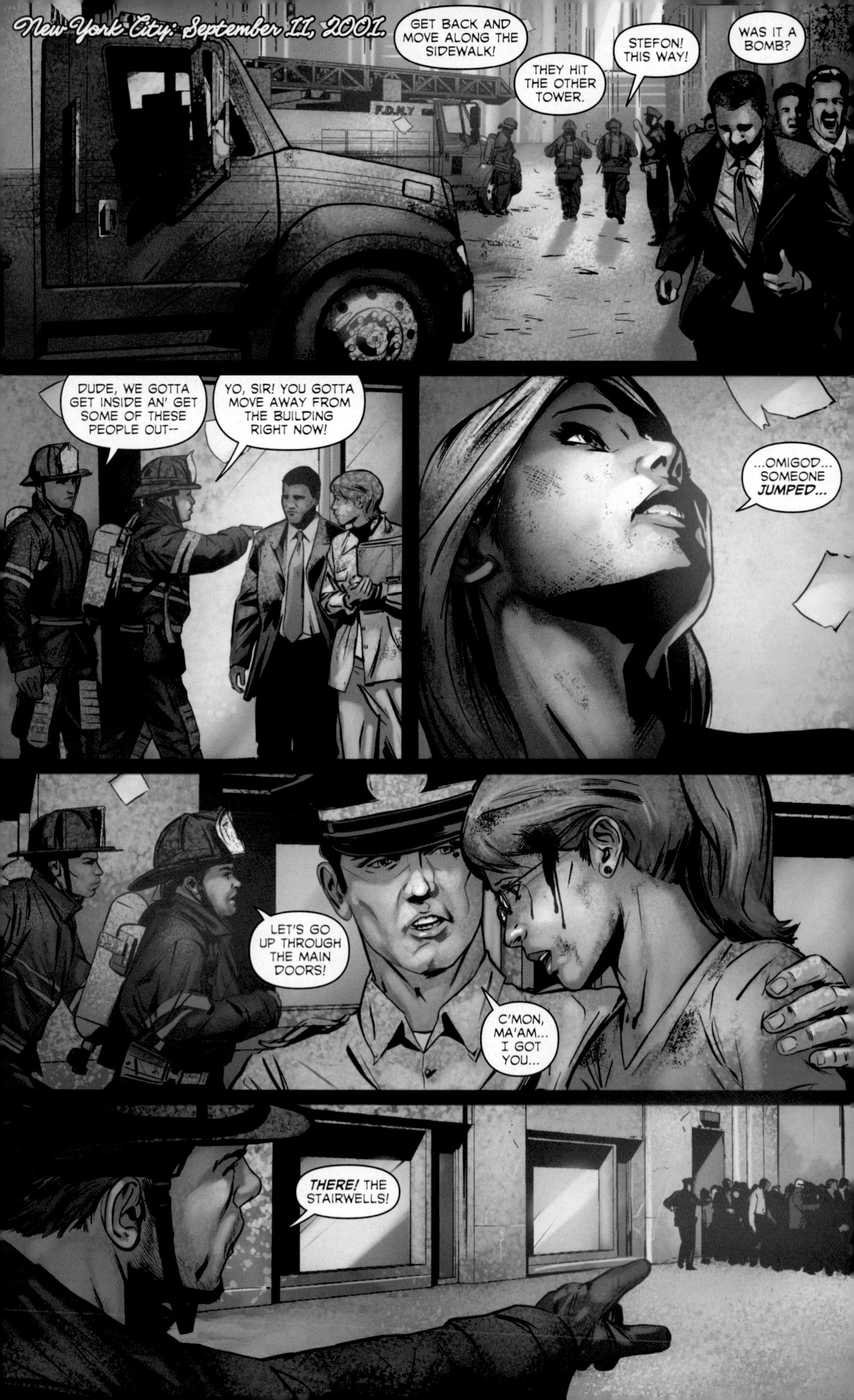
New York City: September 11, 2001.
GET BACK AND MOVE ALONG THE SIDEWALK!
THEY HIT THE OTHER TOWER.
STEFON! THIS WAY!
WAS IT A BOMB?
DUDE, WE GOTTA GET INSIDE AN' GET SOME OF THESE PEOPLE OUT--
YO, SIR! YOU GOTTA MOVE AWAY FROM THE BUILDING RIGHT NOW!
...OMIGOD... SOMEONE JUMPED...
LET'S GO UP THROUGH THE MAIN DOORS!
C'MON, MA'AM... I GOT YOU...
THERE! THE STAIRWELLS!
F.D.N.Y

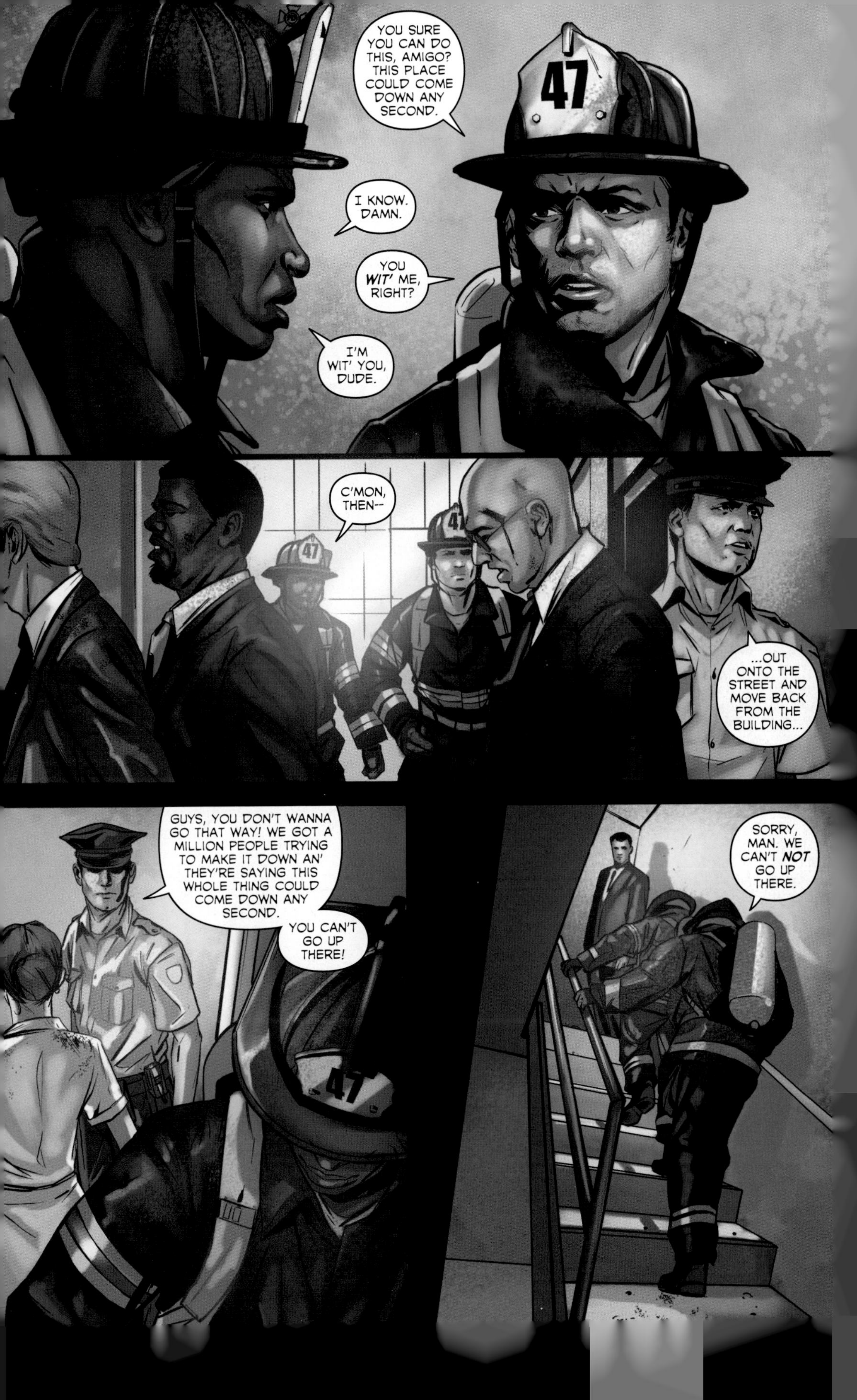
YOU SURE YOU CAN DO THIS, AMIGO? THIS PLACE COULD COME DOWN ANY SECOND.
I KNOW. DAMN.
YOU *WIT'* ME, RIGHT?
I'M WIT' YOU, DUDE.
C'MON, THEN--
...OUT ONTO THE STREET AND MOVE BACK FROM THE BUILDING...
GUYS, YOU DON'T WANNA GO THAT WAY! WE GOT A MILLION PEOPLE TRYING TO MAKE IT DOWN AN' THEY'RE SAYING THIS WHOLE THING COULD COME DOWN ANY SECOND.
YOU CAN'T GO UP THERE!
SORRY, MAN. WE CAN'T *NOT* GO UP THERE.

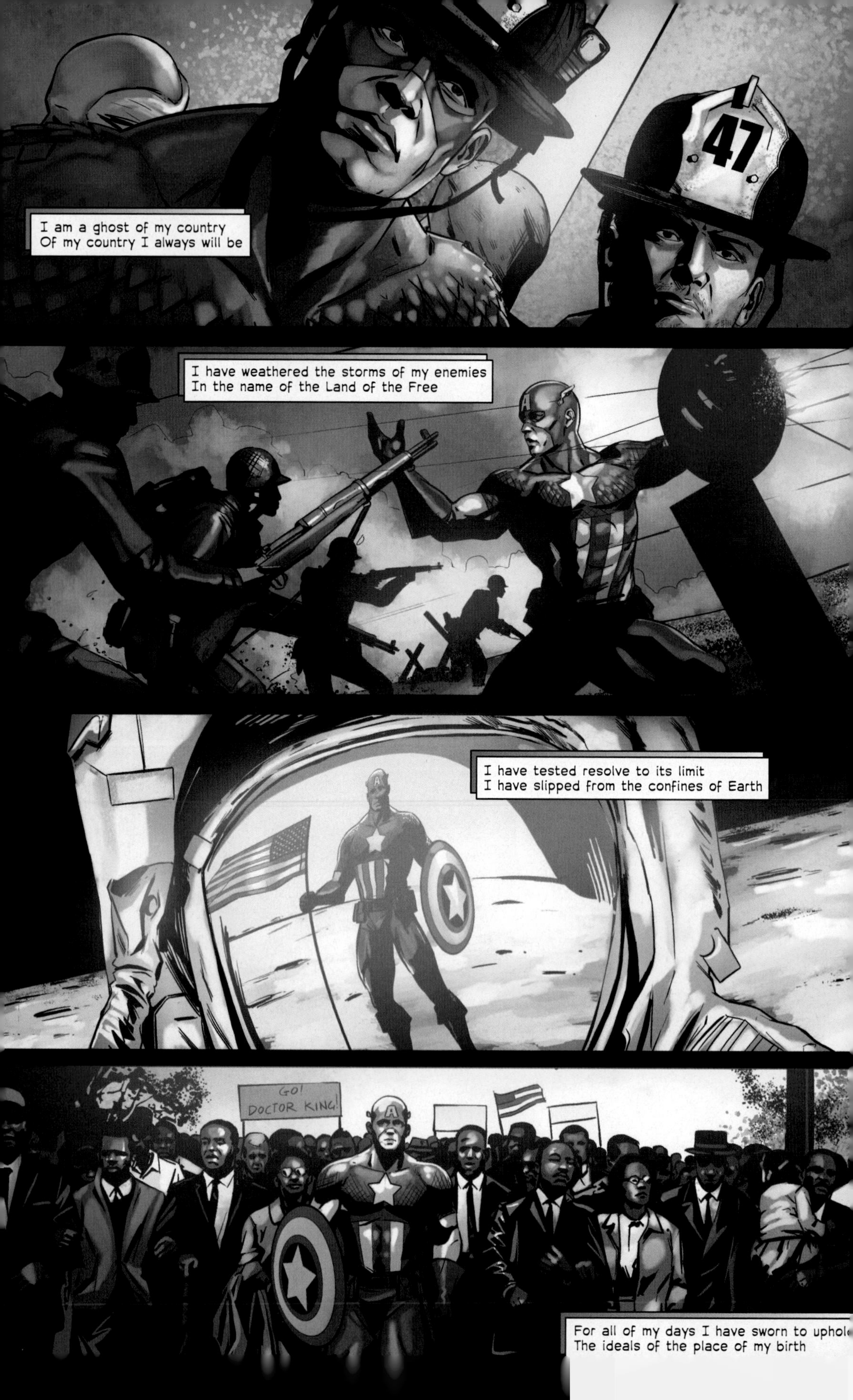
I am a ghost of my country
Of my country I always will be
47
I have weathered the storms of my enemies
In the name of the Land of the Free
I have tested resolve to its limit
I have slipped from the confines of Earth
GO! DOCTOR KING!
For all of my days I have sworn to uphol
The ideals of the place of my birth

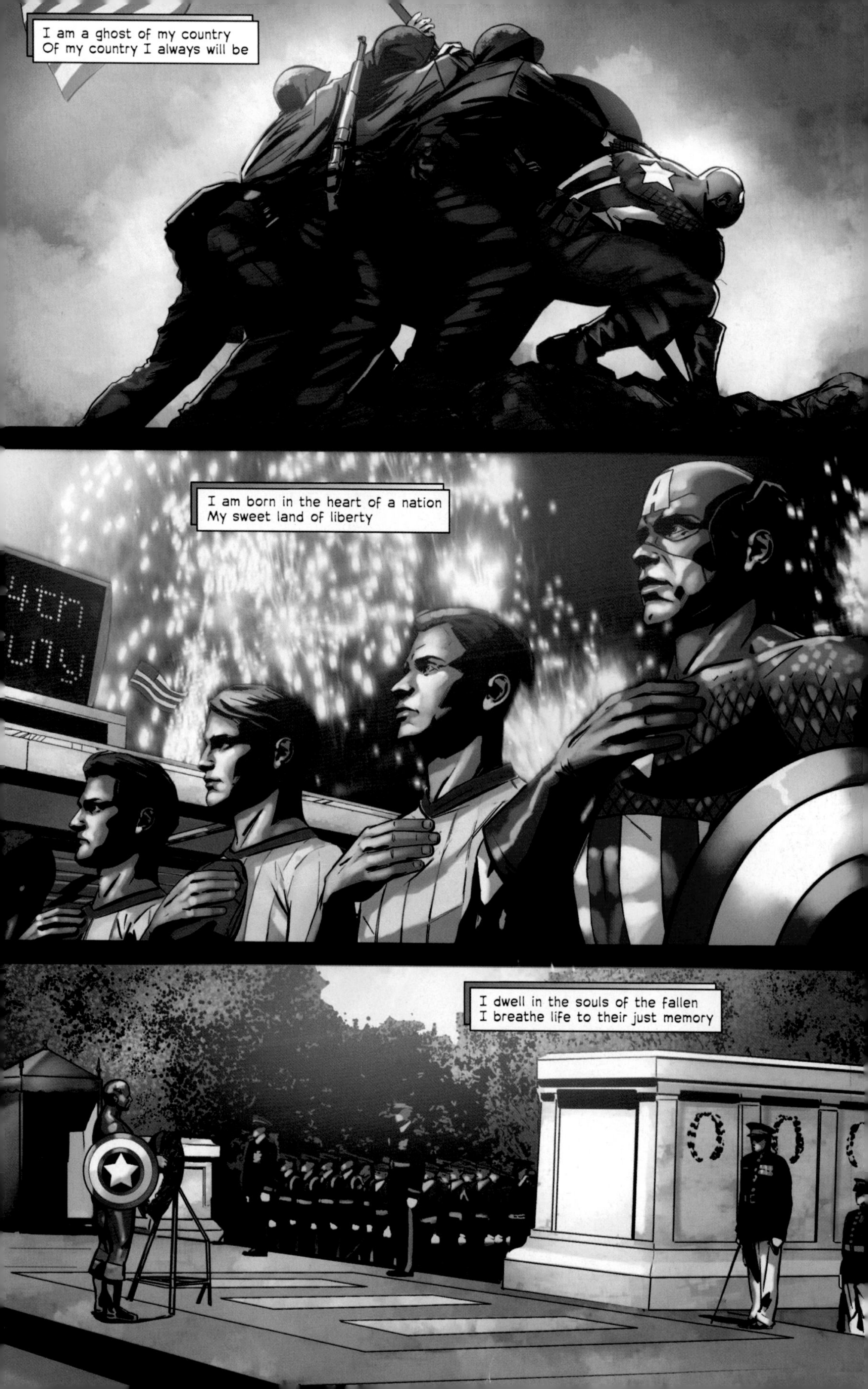
I am a ghost of my country
Of my country I always will be
I am born in the heart of a nation
My sweet land of liberty
I dwell in the souls of the fallen
I breathe life to their just memory

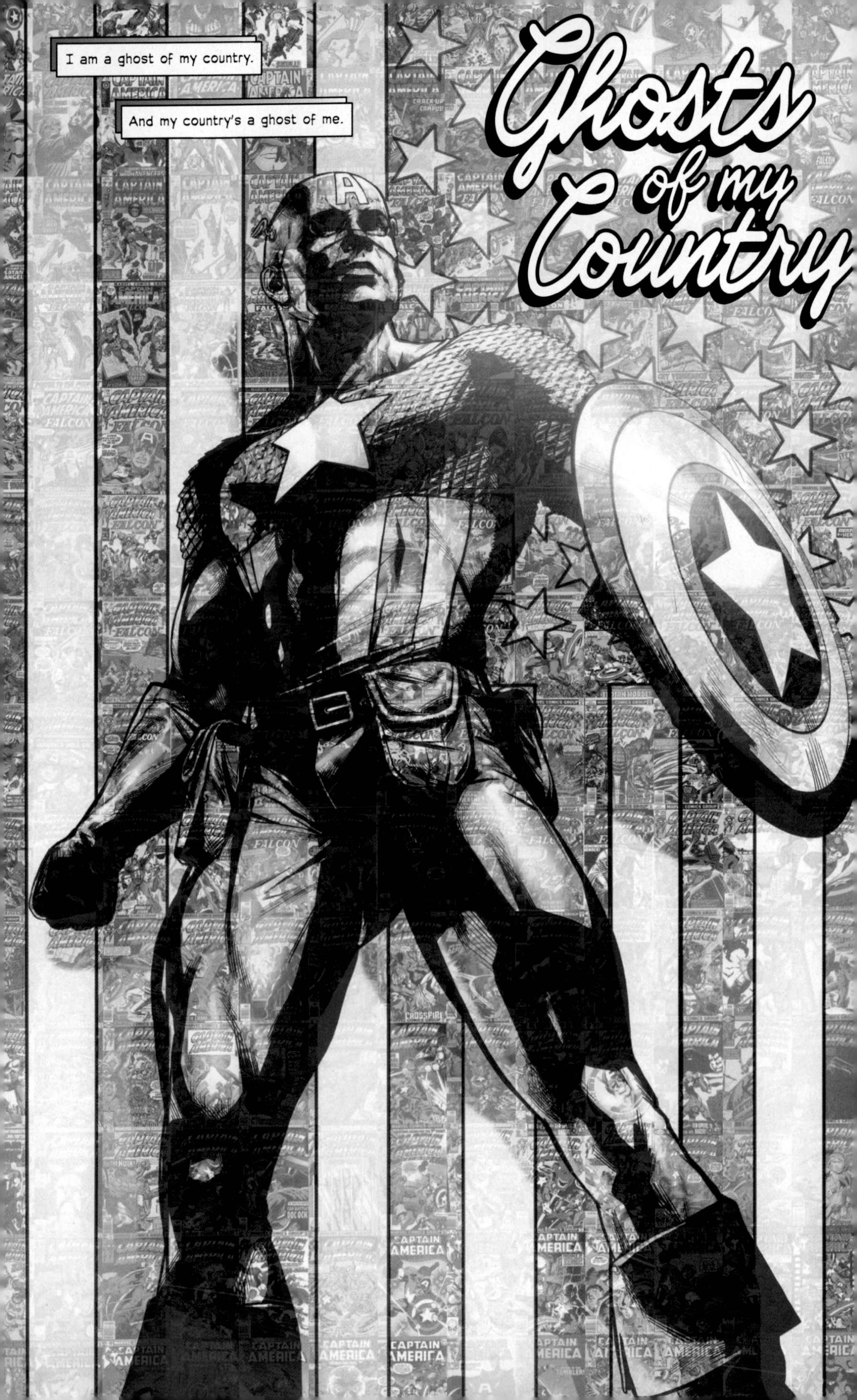
I am a ghost of my country.
And my country's a ghost of me.
Ghosts of my Country

CAPTAIN AMERICA THEATER OF WAR

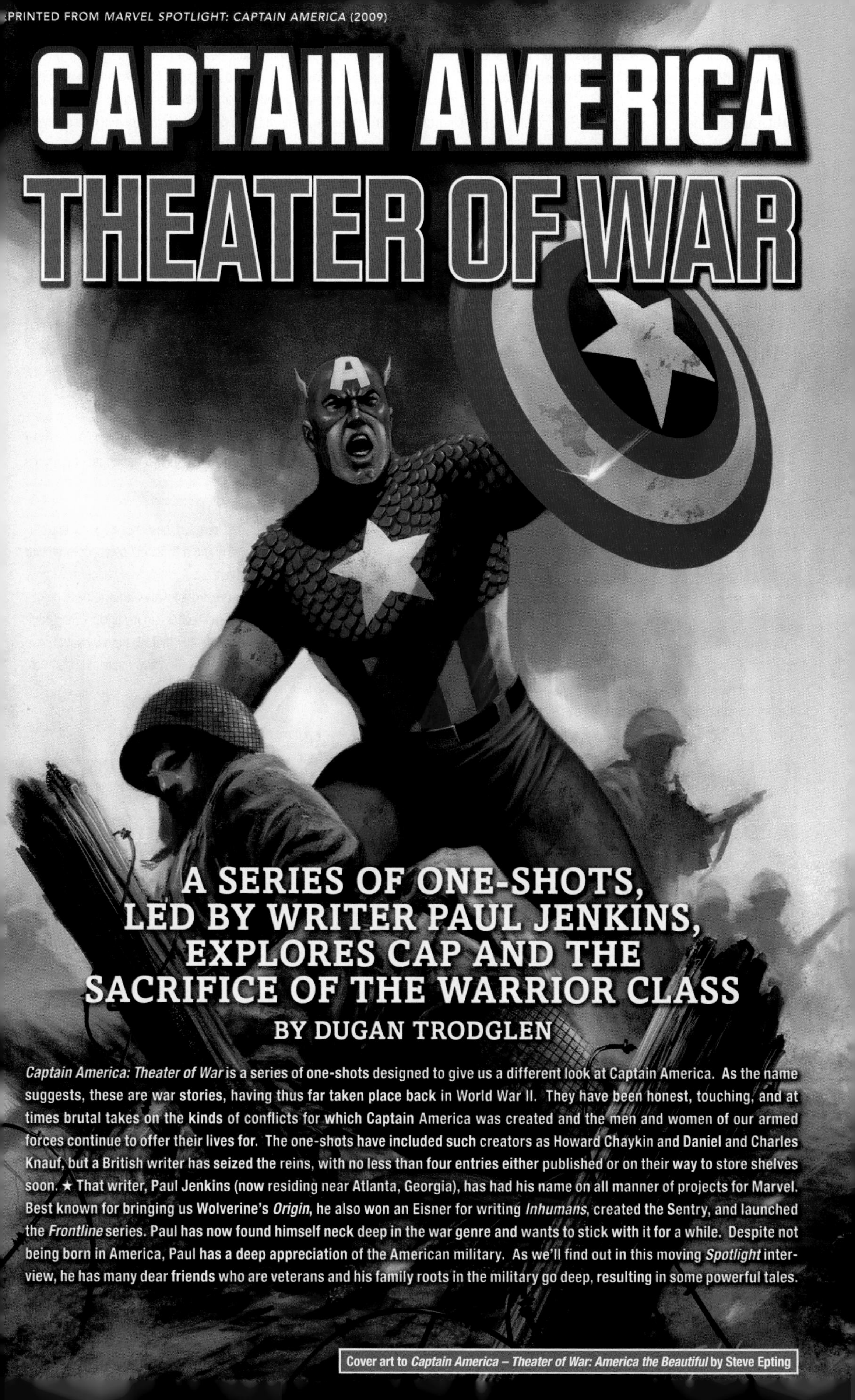

A SERIES OF ONE-SHOTS, LED BY WRITER PAUL JENKINS, EXPLORES CAP AND THE SACRIFICE OF THE WARRIOR CLASS

BY DUGAN TRODGLEN

Captain America: Theater of War is a series of one-shots designed to give us a different look at Captain America. As the name suggests, these are war stories, having thus far taken place back in World War II. They have been honest, touching, and at times brutal takes on the kinds of conflicts for which Captain America was created and the men and women of our armed forces continue to offer their lives for. The one-shots have included such creators as Howard Chaykin and Daniel and Charles Knauf, but a British writer has seized the reins, with no less than four entries either published or on their way to store shelves soon. ★ That writer, Paul Jenkins (now residing near Atlanta, Georgia), has had his name on all manner of projects for Marvel. Best known for bringing us Wolverine's *Origin*, he also won an Eisner for writing *Inhumans*, created the Sentry, and launched the *Frontline* series. Paul has now found himself neck deep in the war genre and wants to stick with it for a while. Despite not being born in America, Paul has a deep appreciation of the American military. As we'll find out in this moving *Spotlight* interview, he has many dear friends who are veterans and his family roots in the military go deep, resulting in some powerful tales.

Cover art to *Captain America – Theater of War: America the Beautiful* by Steve Epting

SPOTLIGHT: Thanks for talking to us, Paul. You've done two *Theater of War* one-shots, with a third coming out...

PAUL: Actually there are going to be four total. It's the kind of material I really like to do so we kept going.

SPOTLIGHT: Originally these series of one-shots were conceived to feature rotating creative teams, but you've sort of taken them over as the writer. Was it your affinity for these war stories that led you to keep doing them?

PAUL: Yeah, it was. I like the material and I certainly have a lot to say on the subject. In the aftermath of me turning in the fourth script, my editor Tom Brevoort and I discussed future work and he said he wanted me to propose more war material. Not necessarily Cap, but war stories in general – we agree upon the fact that this material is clearly working for me right now.

SPOTLIGHT: I understand you have a lot of military history in your family.

PAUL: I lost two great-grandfathers in the Great War – the First World War. My dad in fact just sent me a locket that my great-grandfather took with him all through the war. In it is a photo of my great-grandmother and my grandfather at age 3. I have a son age 3 so this was so powerful to me – to try and see what he must have felt. I just went away to Los Angeles for a week and I was thinking about how I missed my family, but there he was all the way across the world – he died in Palestine a few days before the end of the war – it's just tremendously poignant to me. I also have a watch and chain he carried with him that I keep on a shelf. I've done a little research and learned that another great-grandfather, Bill Eldridge, was killed in 1916 in Flanders. He's buried in a British cemetery in France and I've actually seen his grave and seen his military records. You realize he's just one of those guys – one of millions of guys who have died in war efforts.

Early on in writing about war I realized what heroism is really about. I've always tried – and I think I'm known for this – to make my stories about the characters foremost. Not so much the story elements like time warps and the things that are exploding, but "Why are these characters involved with this stuff?" I've learned that heroism isn't about people that go into battle unafraid; it's about people who go into battle terrified, but do it anyway. If I had to go to war, my fear would not be of dying; it would be of never seeing my wife and kid again. These people lived with it every day. To think about the guys who went up on Omaha Beach on D-Day. So many of them were killed, and you think about the Americans – they were not so much there to protect America directly. They were 3000 miles away trying to help people in another continent. That's incredibly noble to me.

When I wrote *Civil War: Frontline*, I included these four-page backup stories of each issue looking back, giving a historical perspective on war and why people fight, and the last issue was actually about my family – my dad, my grandfather, my great-grandfather. I have these bronze medallions in honor of my great-grandfather and my uncle. I keep them just outside my boy's room as a reminder that we have what we have because members of my family, along with many, many other families, went to war and laid their lives down for that.

As you can see, I have a lot to say on the subject!

Hochspannung
Vorsicht!
Lebensgefahr

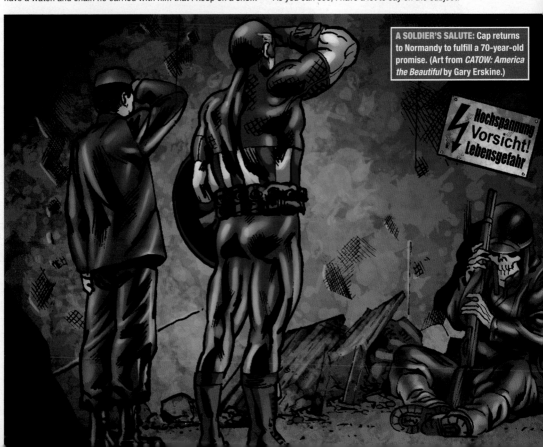

A SOLDIER'S SALUTE: Cap returns to Normandy to fulfill a 70-year-old promise. (Art from *CATOW: America the Beautiful* by Gary Erskine.)

So at the end of that issue, after bringing the body home at last, as he had promised to do 70 years ago, Cap is speaking at a memorial service and says that this man, Bobby Shaw, was the bravest guy he's known because he was the most scared he'd ever known. That's how Cap sees things. And it's the epitome of these soldiers who go shed their blood in a foreign land. Like Rupert Brooke said, "If I should die, think only this of me: That there's some corner of a foreign field/ That is for ever England." That's such a beautiful line to me.

SPOTLIGHT: You dedicated that issue to your friend J. Douglas Huggins and his childhood friend who you named Bobby Shaw after, both veterans. How do you know Mr. Huggins?

PAUL: He's my neighbor. He is one of the most amazingly nice people I've ever met. Doug was at Pearl Harbor, where Bobby Shaw was killed. The picture in the back is Doug and Bobby. Doug was an electrician's mate on the USS St. Louis and Bobby was on the USS Arizona. That picture was taken two days before the attack. There they were smiling in Hawaii with no idea that two days later was the day that shall live in infamy. In comes this attack, and Doug loses his best friend. I went over to Doug's to interview him one time and he brings out this photo. He says, that's my best friend Bobby Shaw, and I thought he was going to tell me an anecdote about him. He said, "Two days after his picture was taken he was killed on the Arizona." My eyes just swelled up.

SPOTLIGHT: I've noticed that the two stories that have come out so far both feature the death of prominent, symbolic characters.

THE LAST GREAT MEASURE: The death of Shaw as a soldier (above) and his immortality as an inspiration to Cap (below, right.) (Art from *CATOW: America the Beautiful* by Gary Erskine.)

"CAP SAYS THAT THIS MAN, BOBBY SHAW, WAS THE BRAVEST GUY HE'S KNOWN BECAUSE HE WAS THE MOST SCARED HE'D EVER KNOWN." — WRITER PAUL JENKINS, DISCUSSING THE FEATURE CHARACTER OF THEATER OF WAR: AMERICA THE BEAUTIFUL.

SPOTLIGHT: Oh, yeah. That's the idea. We have plenty of folks talking about Captain America in this issue of *Spotlight*, and we want to get a different perspective here, just like your *Theater of War* books do.

PAUL: Here's the thing about Captain America. I was given the job by Tom and he asked me if I had anything to say about war and of course I did. The first book ("America the Beautiful") came out and it was about someone who had gone off to a foreign field and had died. The idea was that he was small, afraid and ineffectual. He had a bad leg he claimed was from being shot but in reality he ran over his foot with a lawn mower. His story was bigger than he was, but in the end he did this incredibly heroic thing. At that crunch moment when you think he's going to fail – and he's failed twice in the story already – he kicks a grenade into a side shed and it kills him. His body is left there for 70 years. So many people found things they didn't think they could do like that. You wonder, "How would you react in that situation? What would you really do?"

MOMENTS COME AND THEY GO. DAYS TURN INTO YEARS, AND THEY FADE INTO DUST ALONG WITH OUR MEMORIES OF THEM.

WE MOVE THROUGH OUR BRIEF TIME ON THIS EARTH SEARCHING FOR AN UNDERSTANDING OF WHY WE ARE HERE.

WE ARE HERE BECAUSE OF MEN LIKE BOBBY SHAW. THE MEMORIES OF OUR HEROES MUST ENDURE.

PAUL: That's not necessarily true of the others. (*Laughter.*) Being a European who lives in America, I can really see how massive America really is. America can have a difficult time really seeing and grasping other cultures. It's not selfish or anything. It's just America is so large that it can be hard seeing beyond her borders because there is so much here to be concerned about. In the days before America's involvement in WWII there was a lot of isolationist sentiment: "Why should we? If they can't keep it together why should we go over there?" From the British perspective, we were right in the firing line; we were next. My mother and grandparents lived through the blitz of London. I grew up hearing about this. My mum ate her first banana because an American GI gave it to her.

So in the second issue I did – "A Brother In Arms" – one of the things I really wanted to say was that if you were a German patriot, you were fighting because you were fighting for your country, you're not necessarily a Nazi. So many of them were fighting because they were patriots and that was their job. The soldier in "Brother in Arms" in fact had no love for Hitler.

It talked about the Rules of Engagement. I have a good friend named Chris Dare, a Lt. Colonel in the army and he helped write the army's manual on the protocol of war and rules of engagement so I had an amazing conversation with him where he taught me how to handle this issue. In a way it was not quite accurate because the German soldier would have been ordered not to aid the enemy. But having said that, once his own guys shot at him he was free to choose his own course.

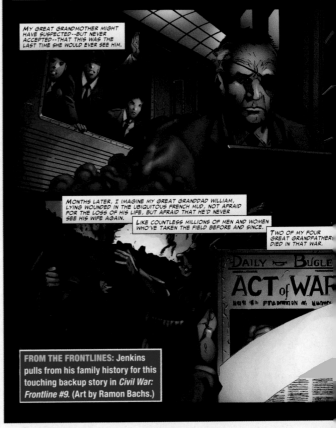

MY GREAT GRANDMOTHER MIGHT HAVE SUSPECTED--BUT NEVER ACCEPTED--THAT THIS WAS THE LAST TIME SHE WOULD EVER SEE HIM.

MONTHS LATER, I IMAGINE MY GREAT GRANDDAD WILLIAM, LYING WOUNDED IN THE UBIQUITOUS FRENCH MUD, NOT AFRAID FOR THE LOSS OF HIS LIFE, BUT AFRAID THAT HE'D NEVER SEE HIS WIFE AGAIN.

LIKE COUNTLESS MILLIONS OF MEN AND WOMEN WHO'VE TAKEN THE FIELD BEFORE AND SINCE.

TWO OF MY FOUR GREAT GRANDFATHERS DIED IN THAT WAR.

DAILY BUGLE
ACT of WAR

FROM THE FRONTLINES: Jenkins pulls from his family history for this touching backup story in *Civil War: Frontline #9*. (Art by Ramon Bachs.)

" IF I HAD TO GO TO WAR, MY FEAR WOULD NOT BE OF DYING; IT WOULD BE OF NEVER SEEING MY WIFE AND KID AGAIN." – JENKINS

SPOTLIGHT: Rules of Engagement and interrogation techniques aren't quite the same thing, but they certainly are both aspects of military ethics. Was the hot button interrogation issue on your mind as you wrote this issue?

PAUL: Very much so. One thing that was strange with *Civil War: Frontline* was that there was a lot of talk of my taking a political side, but no one could agree what side it was. I disassociate from the characters. Some people thought Sally Floyd was my leftwing mouthpiece but others said I was showing her in a bad light, as a fool, because I'm rightwing.

It's the same thing here. It doesn't take a rocket scientist, much less a

PICTURES FROM PEARL HARBOR: Inspirations for Jenkins' *America the Beautiful.*

Democrat or a Republican to see that torturing people – doing to them what they did to us – is the wrong way to go. As John McCain said, he just told them what they wanted to hear to get them to stop torturing him.

I felt that America's greatest strength is its high moral ground, and that strength is rendered ineffectual through things like torture. Looking back at soldiers in WWII, it may be hard to accept at times, but all soldiers are honorable and they must be treated in an honorable fashion.

SPOTLIGHT: It was portrayed well in the story. It made them all human and sympathetic. You could see why the character of Molodec had such a hard time letting the German prisoner of war live after he had killed his friends.

PAUL: It's completely understandable. If you fought next to your best friend and your best friend was killed by that guy over there and then you captured that guy, you wouldn't be in a charitable mood toward that guy. It takes a lot of understanding to work out that that guy was doing his job and once surrendering should be afforded protection. You can hate him but you now have a moral obligation to protect him. I spoke with Chris Dare about that: how does it work; why is there a moral code? We found out what happens without that code in the trenches of the First World War with mustard gas and crap like that.

SPOTLIGHT: So what is coming up in the next one-shot, *Theater of War: To Soldier On?*

PAUL: The third issue is about my good friend Brian Anderson. He and his friends are the three main characters in the book. Brian is a triple amputee. He was in a Humvee and his navigator and gunner were all in the Humvee and got hit by a roadside bomb. Brian lost both legs and one of his arms. He's one of the finest people I know. He's one of the most honest people I know and he said the most incredible thing to me the first time I met him, and I totally understood it. He said that he has a great job now. He's a wheelchair spokesman and he has a lot of people paying attention to him. But Kenny, the gunner, was not injured, and Kenny has a wife and kid. Brian's honest fear was that he felt worried about Kenny. Kenny was likely going back to Iraq. It was so honest of Brian to say that he was more concerned about Kenny than about feeling sorry for himself. He felt like he could move on. Having said that, there are a great many people injured who suffered a lot of emotional damage as well. In many ways, Brian is a success story.

BATTLE ACTION: John McCrea's crisply rendered action artwork showcases the realism of *Theater of War*. (Art from *CATOW: A Brother In Arms*.)

SPOTLIGHT: That is amazing. Do you change the setting of this story to WWII?

PAUL: No, this is set in Iraq, during the first invasion of Baghdad. It's the story of Brian encountering Captain America. Cap ends up representing so many different things. He's a soldier, a commanding officer. He's also in a sense a politician, and also an icon. Brian gets to see him through his own ordeal and sees him in many different ways. At times he completely admires him; after being injured, he resents him. The question at the end of the story is,

A BROTHER IN ARMS: Paul Jenkins sensitively renders the battlefield relationships between opposing forces. (Art from *CATOW: A Brother In Arms* by John McCrea.)

ND ANY
OOD
LDIER--

--NO MATTER YOUR
FRIEND OR ENEMY--

--IS TRULY A
BROTHER IN ARMS.

"Who is Captain America?" I think it has an emotionally satisfying ending. My meter for this is editor Jeanine Schaefer. She calls me up when I send in a script and says, "Okay I cried."(*Laughter.*)

Another good thing is – going back to the "America the Beautiful" story – I told Tom Brevoort about how Captain America brings Bobby Shaw's dog tags home and about how Bobby always wanted a beautiful girl and a swimming hole. So Cap brings the dog tags back and makes this speech at the service. He throws the dog tags into the water and says, "I brought you back to your swimming hole, and your girl is a knockout." We pull back and it's the Statue of Liberty. When I first told Tom that he burst out into an involuntary giggle and I said, "You just did that so you wouldn't get all choked up!" (*Laughter.*) But he knew that fit exactly who Captain America was.

SPOTLIGHT: Anything you can tell us about the fourth book you have coming out?

PAUL: That one to me is by far the most special. It's my love letter to Captain America. Without giving away too much, it's about what Captain America must really be. When we see him and see his shield and his flag-based uniform, he is the sum total of all of the most important and meaningful and meaning*less* and mundane and intense moments throughout the history of the U.S. He is the personification of America. It's called "Ghost of My Country" and we journey across time to see Cap as the ghost of his country. He exists throughout all of the most important moments of American military history. He was there. And he was there because the sum total of everything that was happening made him come alive. It's kind of a strange concept I suppose, but he is alive because of everything these soldiers did. My friend Brian makes him alive; Doug Huggins and Bobby Shaw bring him to life. Every American soldier brings Captain America alive.

Thanks to Paul Jenkins for this stirring interview. Be on the lookout for the **CAPTAIN AMERICA: THEATER OF WAR** *specials already released, including* **AMERICA FIRST!, OPERATION: ZERO POINT, AMERICA THE BEAUTIFUL** *and* **A BROTHER IN ARMS** – *plus* **TO SOLDIER ON**, *scheduled to ship in August!* ■

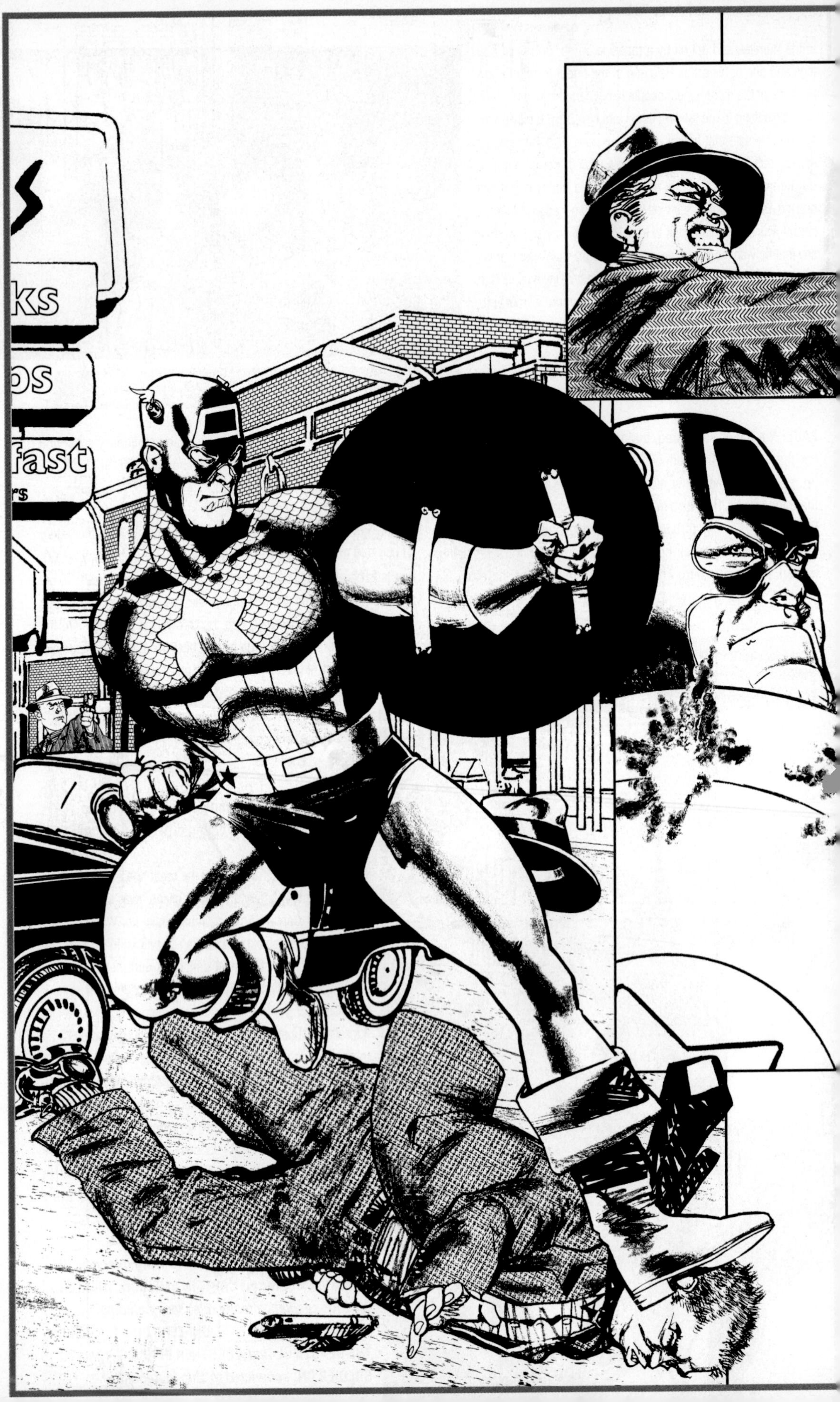
ks
fast

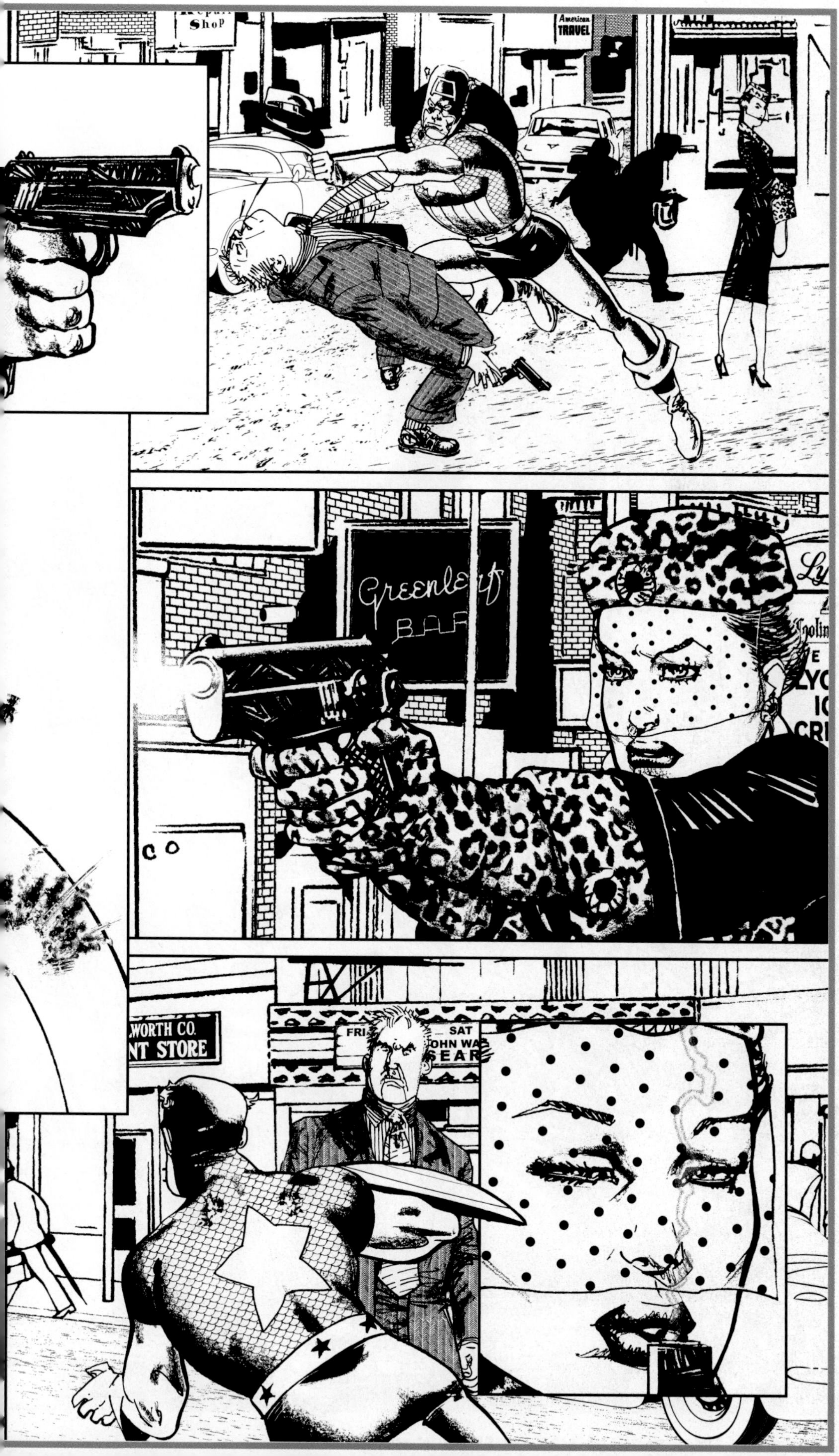

★ AMERICA *FIRST!* PAGES 2-3 ART BY HOWARD CHAYKIN

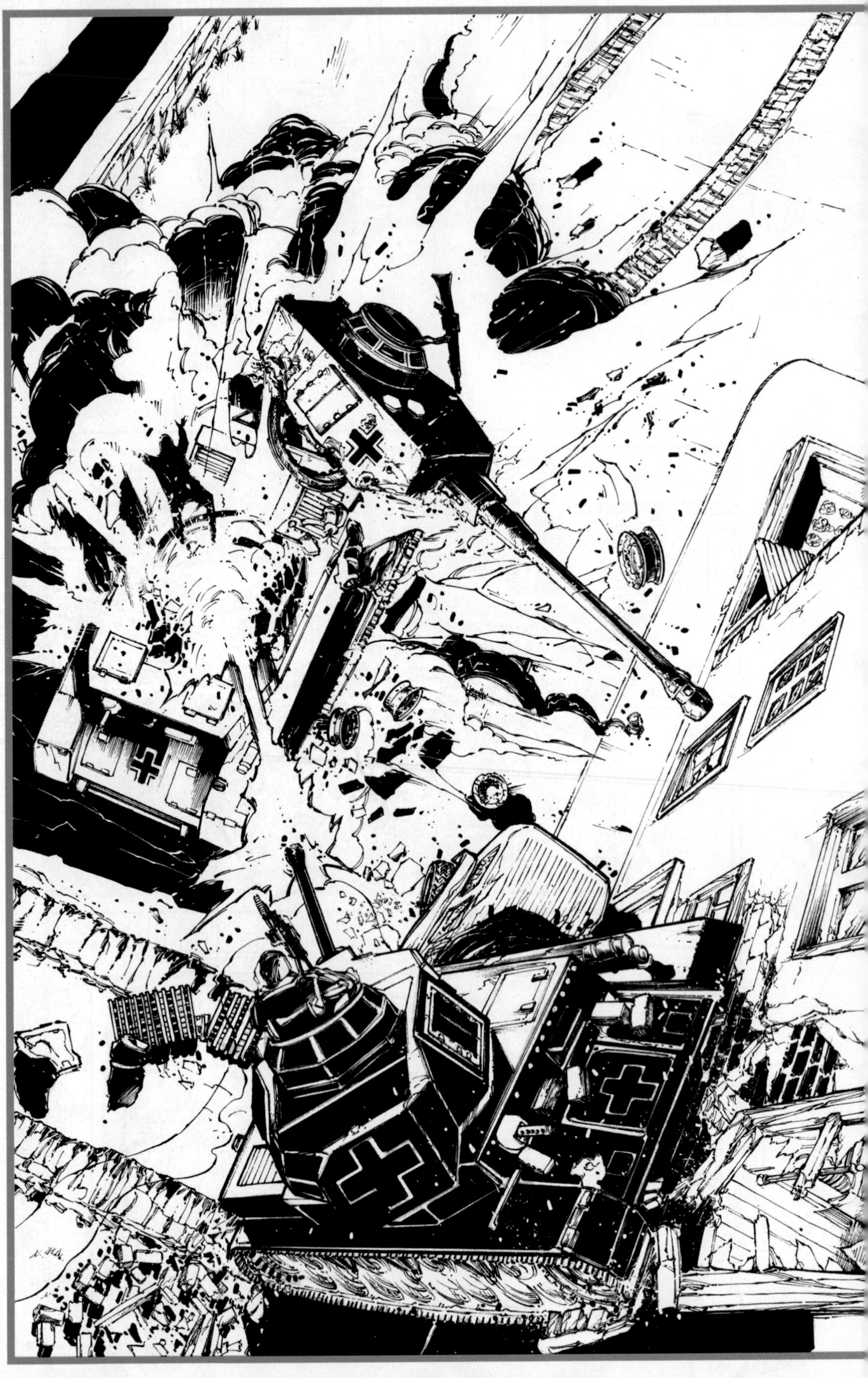

★ *A BROTHER IN ARMS*, PAGES 17 & 35 ART BY JOHN MCCREA

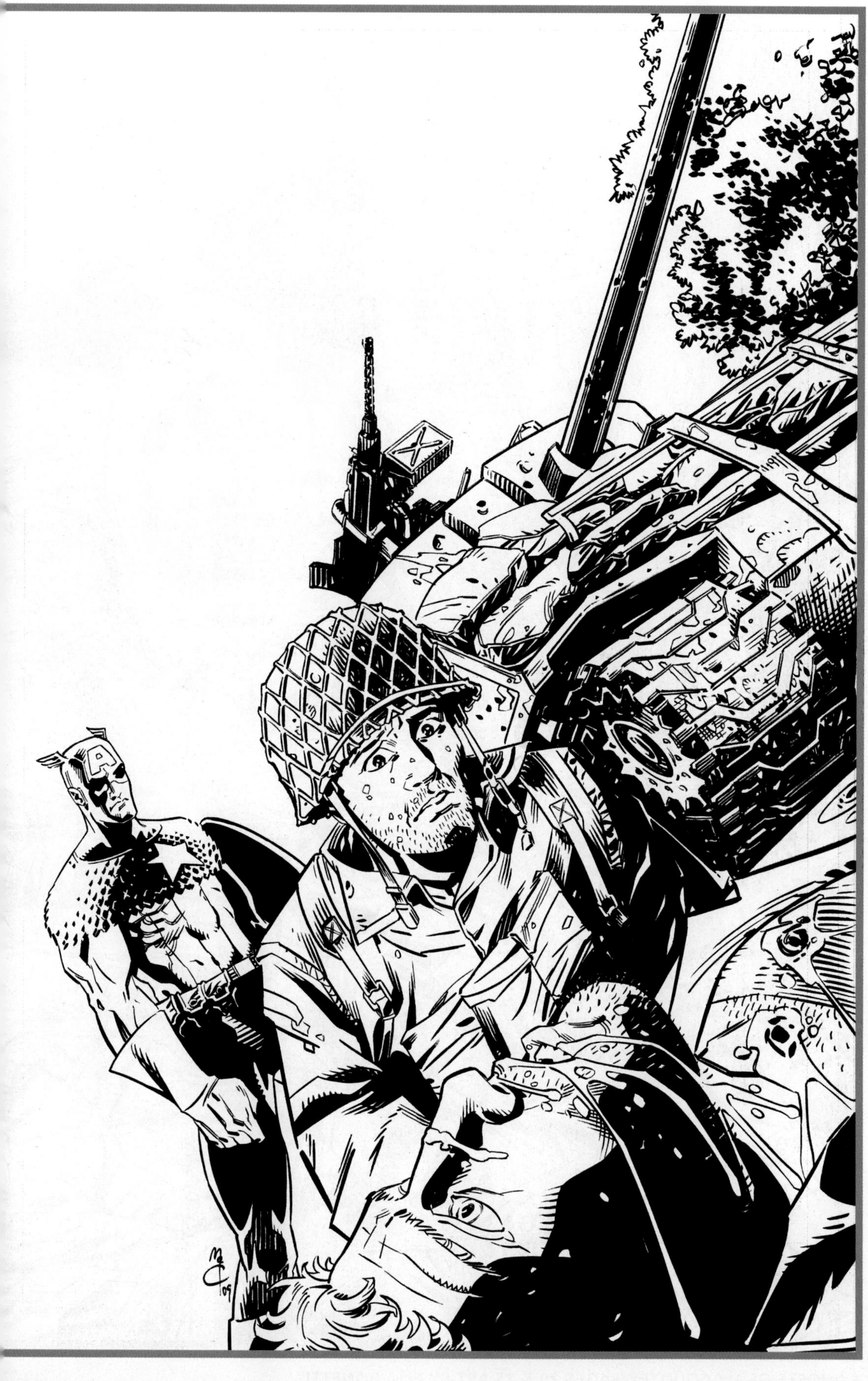

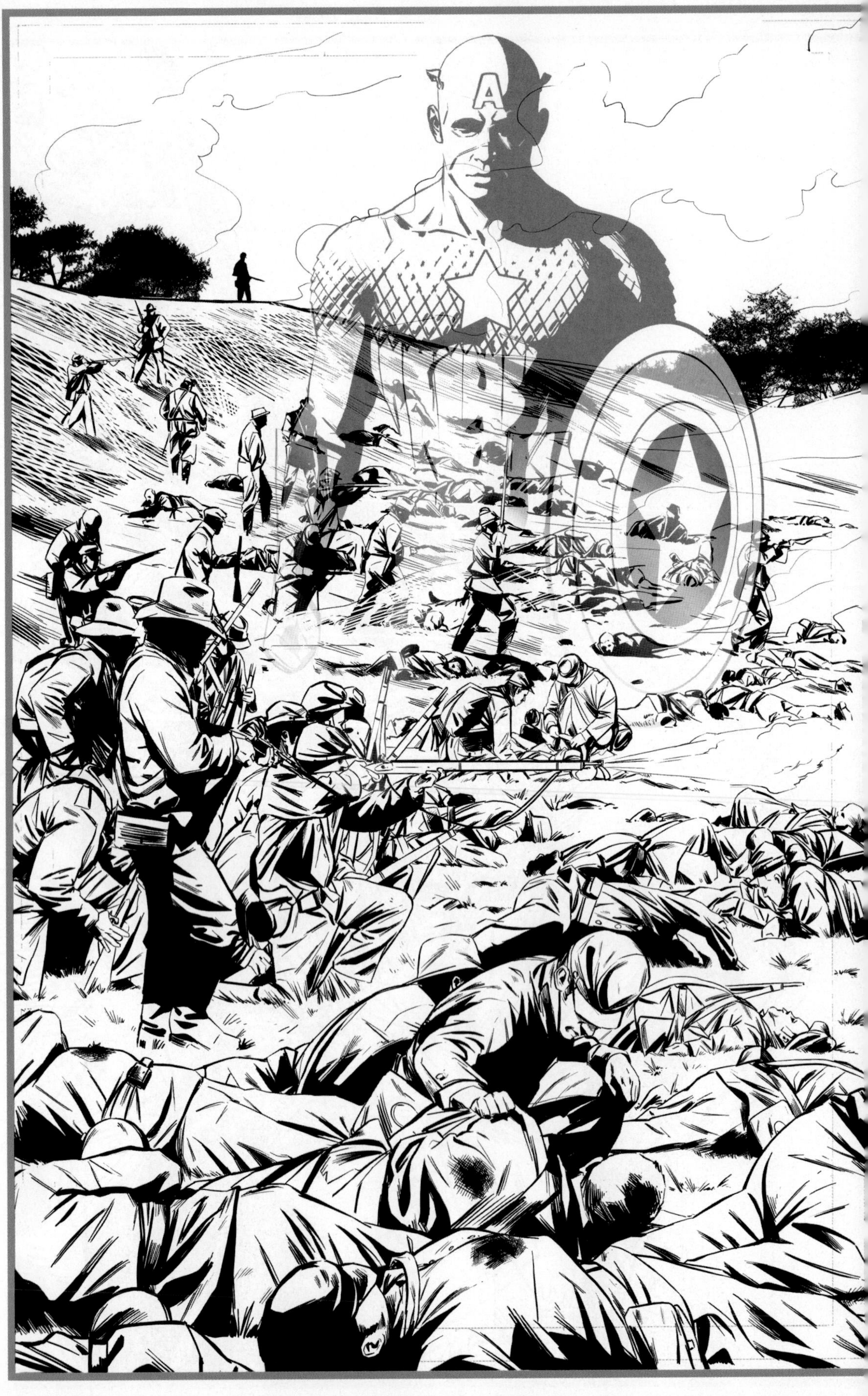

★ *GHOSTS OF MY COUNTRY*, PAGES 20 & 35 ART BY ELIA BONETTI

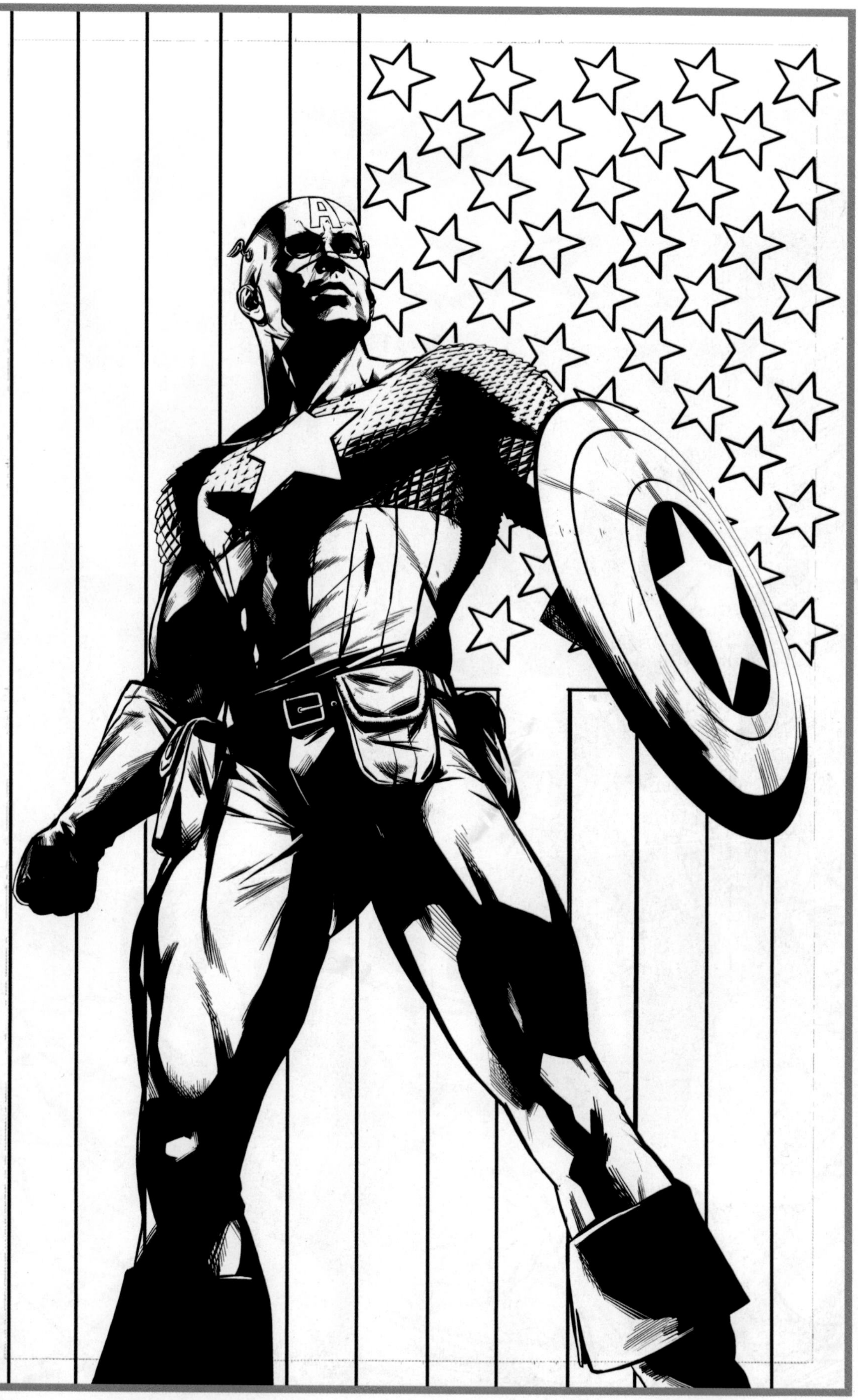

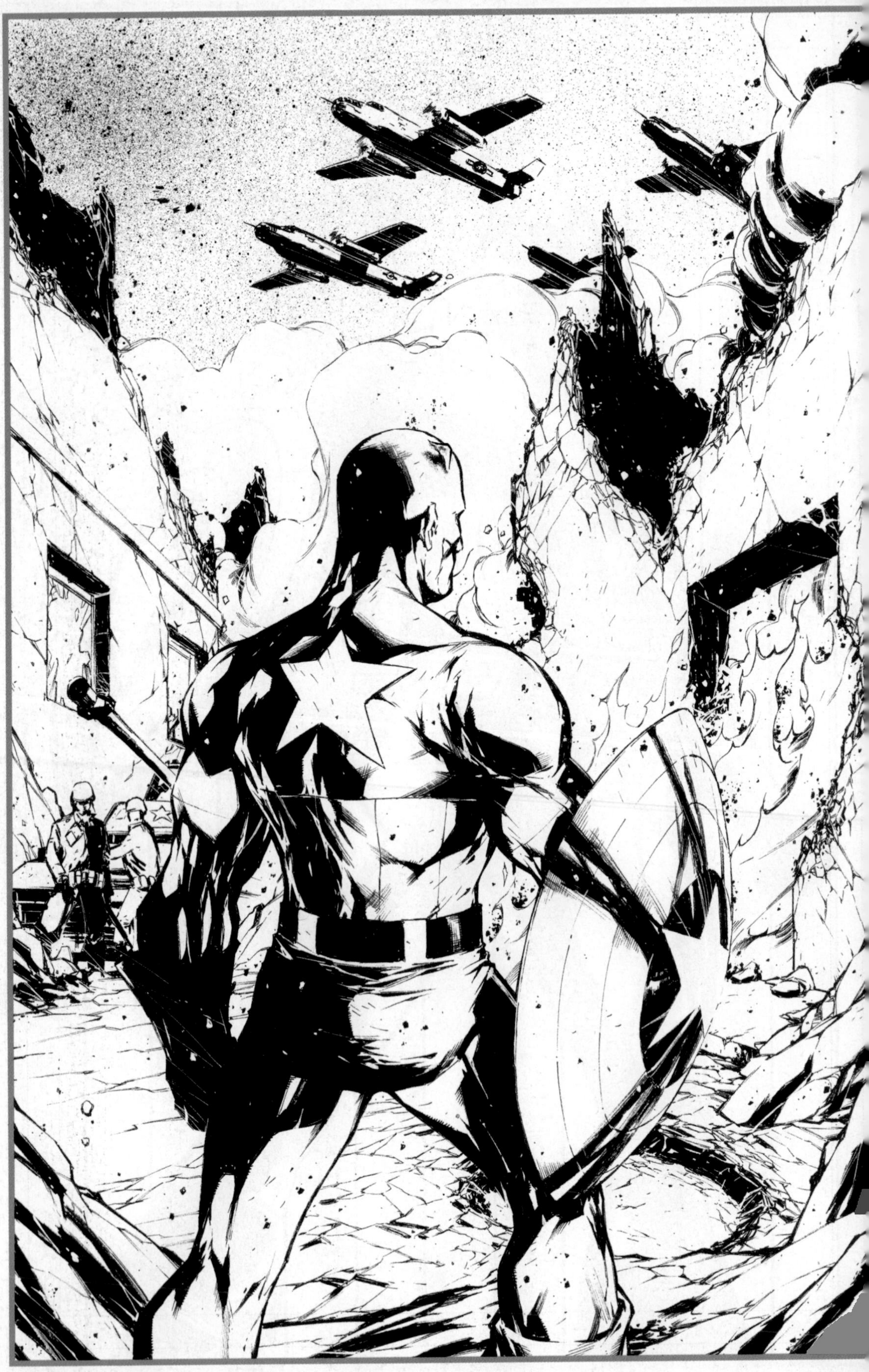

★ *PRISONERS OF DUTY*, PAGE 32 ART BY AGUSTIN PADILLA